GW00372694

PSYCHOLOGY AT THE TURN OF THE MILLENNIUM

(VOLUME 1)

Psychology at the turn of the millennium

Volume 1

Cognitive, biological, and health perspectives

Congress proceedings:
XXVII International Congress of Psychology

Stockholm, 2000

edited by
Lars Bäckman and
Claes von Hofsten

Published in 2002 by Psychology Press Ltd
27 Church Road, Hove, East Sussex, BN3 2FA

www.psypress.co.uk

Simultaneously published in the USA and Canada
by Taylor & Francis Inc
29 West 35th Street, New York, NY 10001

Psychology Press is part of the Taylor & Francis Group

© 2002 by Psychology Press

Chapter 17 is reprinted from the *Journal of Affective
Disorders*, *61*, Lang, Davis, & Öhman (2001). 'Fear
and anxiety: animal models and human cognitive
psychophysiology.' pp. 137–159. Copyright © 2001,
with permission from Elsevier Science.

Chapter 21 is reprinted from EVOLUTIONARY
PSYCHOLOGY AND MOTIVATION, volume 47
of the NEBRASKA SYMPOSIUM ON MOTIVATION
series, by permission of the University of Nebraska Press.
Copyright © 2001 by the University of Nebraska Press.

All rights reserved. No part of this book may be reprinted or
reproduced or utilised in any form or by any electronic,
mechanical, or other means, now known or hereafter invented,
including photocopying and recording, or in any information
storage or retrieval system, without permission in writing from
the publishers.

British Library Cataloguing in Publication Data
A catalogue record for this book is available from the British Library

Library of Congress Cataloging in Publication Data
A catalog record for this book is available from the Library of Congress

ISBN   1-84169-198-4

Cover design by Louise Page
Typeset in the UK by RefineCatch Limited, Bungay, Suffolk
Printed and bound in the UK by
Biddles Ltd, Guildford and King's Lynn

Contents

SECTION FOUR
Interaction between cognitive and emotional processes

SECTION FIVE
Higher cognitive processes

List of contributors

Pavel Balaban, Head of Laboratory of Cellular Neurobiology of Learning, Institute of Higher Nervous Activity and Neurophysiology of the Russian Academy of Sciences, Butlerova 5A, Moscow 117865, Russia

Mireille Besson, Centre de Recherche en Neurosciences Cognitives, CNRS-CRNC, 31 Chemin Joseph Aiguier, 13402 Marseille Cedex 20, France

Debbie Bonetti, School of Psychology, The University at St Andrews, St Andrews, KY16 9JU, Scotland, UK

Claus Bundesen, Professor of Cognitive Psychology, Department of Psychology, University of Copenhagen, Njalsgade 90, DK-2300 Copenhagen S, Denmark

Vicki Bruce, Department of Psychology, University of Stirling, Stirling FK9 4LA, Scotland, UK

Fergus I.M. Craik, Rotman Research Institute, Baycrest Centre, 3560 Bathurst Street, Toronto, Ontario, Canada M6A 2E1

Richard J. Davidson, William James and Vilas Research Professor of Psychology and Psychiatry, Director, W.M. Keck Laboratory for Functional Brain Imaging and Behavior, Wisconsin Center for Affective Science, and Center for Mind-Body Interaction, University of Wisconsin-Madison, 1202 West Johnson Street, Madison, WI 53706, USA

Michael Davis, Department of Psychiatry, School of Medicine, Woodruff Memorial Building, 1639 Pierce Drive, Room 4311, Emory University, Atlanta, GA 30322, USA

Scania de Schonen, Developmental Neurocognition Unit, Laboratory of Cognition and Development, CNRS-Paris 5, 71 Av. Edouard Vaillant, 92774 Boulogne-Billancourt, France

Géry d'Ydewalle, Department of Psychology, University of Leuven, B-3000 Leuven, Belgium

Norman S. Endler, Distinguished Research Professor (Emeritus), Department of Psychology, York University, 4700 Keele Street, Toronto, Ontario, Canada, M3J 1P3

Joseph P. Forgas, Department of Psychology, University of New South Wales, General Office, Level 10, Mathews Building, Gate 11, Botany Street, Randwick, NSW, Australia

Marianne Frankenhaeuser, Department of Psychology, Stockholm University, S-106 91 Stockholm, Sweden

Barrie J. Frost, Department of Psychology, Humphrey Hall, Arch Street, Queen's University, Kingston, Ontario, Canada, K7L 3N6

Gerd Gigerenzer, Centre for Adaptive Behaviour and Cognition, Max Planck Institute for Human Development, Lentzeallee 94, D-14195, Berlin, Germany

Reginald G. Golledge, Department of Geography, 3616 Ellison Hall, University of California at Santa Barbara, Santa Barbara, CA 93106, USA

Kenneth Hugdahl, Department of Biological and Medical Psychology, University of Bergen, Arstadveien 21, N-5009 Bergen, Norway

Marie Johnston, School of Psychology, The University of St Andrews, St Andrews, KY16 9JU, Scotland, UK

Liisa Keltikangas-Järvinen, Department of Psychology, University of Helsinki, Helsinki, Finland

Roberta L. Klatzky, Department of Psychology, Carnegie Mellon University, Pittsburgh, PA 15213–3890, USA

Régine Kolinsky, UNESCOG (C.P. 191), Université Libre de Bruxelles, Av. F.D. Roosevelt 50, B-1050 Brussels, Belgium

Ida Kurcz, Institute of Psychology, Polish Academy of Sciences, Faculty of Psychology, University of Warsaw, ul. Podlesna 61, 01 673 Warszawa, Poland

Peter J. Lang, Center for the Study of Emotion and Attention, PO Box 100165, HSC, University of Florida, Gainesville, FL 32610, USA

Jack M. Loomis, Department of Psychology, 2219 Psychology Building, University of California at Santa Barbara, Santa Barbara, CA 93106, USA

Andrew Mathews, MRC Cognition and Brain Sciences Unit, 15 Chaucer Road, Cambridge, CB2 2EF, UK

José Morais, UNESCOG (C.P. 191), Université Libre de Bruxelles, Av. F.D. Roosevelt 50, B-1050 Brussels, Belgium

Arne Öhman, Institutionen för Klinisk Nervovetenskap, Sektionen för Psykologi, Karolinska Institutet, Stockholm S-17176, Sweden

Beth Pollard, School of Psychology, The University at St Andrews, St Andrews, KY16 9JU, Scotland, UK

Robert Rescorla, Department of Psychology, University of Pennsylvania, 3815 Walnut Street, Philadelphia, PA 19104, USA

Daniele Schön, Centre de Recherche en Neurosciences Cognitives, CNRS-CRNC, 31 Chemin Joseph Aiguier, 13402 Marseille Cedex 20, France

Jaime Vila, Departamento de Personalidad, Evaluación y Tratamientos Psicológicos. Universidad de Granada, Campus de la Cartuja, 18071, Granada, Spain

Christopher D. Wickens, University of Illinois, Institute of Aviation, Willard Airport, mc 394, Savoy, IL 61874, USA

XXVII International Congress of Psychology

Stockholm, Sweden

July 23–28, 2000

Under the sponsorship of
Swedish Psychological Association

Published under the auspices of the
International Union of Psychological Science (IUPsyS)

Congress President
Lars Göran-Nilsson

Executive Committee

Lars-Göran Nilsson (President), Birgit Hansson (Vice-President), Arne Öhman (Vice-President), Gunn Johansson, Ingvar Lundberg, Orjan Salling (Secretary-General), Kurt F. Pawlik (IUPsyS Liaison)

Scientific Committee

Arne Öhman (Chair), Gunn Johansson (Deputy Chair), Lars Bäckman, Margot Bengtsson, Mats Fredrikson, Tommy Gärling, Claes von Hofsten, Olof Rydén, Lars-Göran Nilsson (President), Örjan Salling (Secretary-General)

Organizing Committee

Birgit Hansson (Chair), Ingvar Lundberg (Deputy Chair), Karin Aronsson, Stefan Jern, Outi Lundén, Jarl Risberg, Ann-Charlotte Smedler, Lars-Göran Nilsson (President), Örjan Salling (Secretary-General)

Scientific Advisory Board

Arne Öhman (Chair), Olof Rydén, Bo Ekehammar, Gunn Johansson, Siv Boalt-Boethius, Lars R. Bergman, Trevor Archer, Bengt-Åke Armelius, Karin Aronsson, Mats Fredrikson, Tommy Gärling, Birgit Hansson, Ingvar Lundberg, David Magnusson, Bo Molander, Jarl Risberg, Mariane Hedegaard, Gretty Mirdal, Pirkko Niemelä, Lea Pulkkinen, Francoise D. Alsaker, Astri Heen Wold, Jüri Allik

IUPsyS Executive Committee—1996–2000

Géry van Outryve d'Ydewalle (President), Kurt F. Pawlik (Past-President), Cigdem Kagitçibasi, Jan Strelau (Vice-President), Michel Sabourin (Treasurer), Pierre L.-J. Ritchie (Secretary-General), Merry Bullock (Deputy Secretary-General), John G. Adair, Ruben Ardila, Michel Denis, Hiroshi Imada, Lars-Göran Nilsson, J. Bruce Overmier, Ype H. Poortinga, Juan José Sánchez-Sosa, Houcan Zhang

Preface

Lars Bäckman and Claes von Hofsten

The 27th International Congress of Psychology was held in Stockholm, Sweden, in the last part of July 2000 under the auspices of the International Union of Psychological Science (IUPsyS) and the joint sponsorship of the Swedish Psychological Association. The selection of site for this first international congress in the new millennium was timely, as Stockholm had the honour to host the very first congress in this series in 1952. A total of 5941 scientists from 90 countries representing all continents in the world attended the conference.

Stockholm, built on a large number of islands and surrounded by water, is known for its beautiful summers. However, during the week of the conference the rain poured down. Although this may have been disappointing for many of the participants, it surely contributed to the excellent attendance rates throughout the meeting. Most importantly, sessions were not only crowded; the contributions were characterized by outstanding depth, breadth, and variability.

The scientific programme of the conference entailed a current overview of the multifaceted nature of psychological science at the birth of the new millennium. In the 22 keynote addresses, 45 state-of-the-art lectures, and the IUPsyS presidential address, highly distinguished scientists provided updated accounts of their programmes of research. Representing multiple topics across all major areas in psychology, 204 invited symposia were arranged. In addition, there were 262 thematic oral sessions and 141 interactive poster sessions in which presenters shared their most recent data and ideas. A total of 1009 invited presentations and 3189 submitted contributions were presented at the congress.

A special feature of the programme was the Dag Hammarskjöld Memorial Seminar on Diplomacy and Psychology in which scientists and diplomats discussed pertinent issues related to psychology's role in international conflict prevention. Another highly appreciated general theme of the meeting was health. The health theme spanned all forms of presentations and, thanks to the broad definition of "health" adopted, multiple aspects of both mental and physical health were addressed.

In keeping with the format from preceding world congresses, the two proceedings volumes are based on the keynote addresses and the state-of-the-art lectures. The task of dividing these contributions into two equal-sized volumes has not been an easy one. Indeed, determining whether a specific chapter should be placed in one volume or the other has often been a delicate, if not arbitrary, task. To be sure, this difficulty reflects the multidimensional nature of psychological science, where previous boundaries have become obsolete and subdivisions from the past merge to form new objects of study. Acknowledging these classification problems, the two resulting volumes address cognitive, biological, and health issues (Volume 1), and social, developmental, and clinical perspectives (Volume 2).

Volume 1 is divided into five subsections. The first part is devoted to neural mechanisms underlying psychological processes in both animals and humans. In the opening chapter, Balaban discusses learning and memory functions in animals with simple nervous systems, drawing on both behavioural and neurotransmitter research. Frost then examines how visual and auditory information is processed in the brain at the level of single-cell recordings. Next, De Schonen describes the parallel evolution of the brain and cognitive operations in early childhood, focusing on both normal and abnormal development. This is followed by a chapter by Hugdahl in which he provides new data and theory pertaining to brain asymmetries with special reference to auditory information processing. The section is closed by Schön and Besson who examine recent evidence on the neural underpinnings of how music is perceived and represented.

The second part deals with the core areas in basic experimental psychology, perception, attention, learning, and memory. d'Ydewalle provides a comprehensive account of current work on memory and cognition, highlighting numerous real-life implications of experimental phenomena. Following this, Bundesen outlines a general theory of visual attention that integrates research on attention and short-term memory processes. The way in which human faces are perceived, identified, and remembered is examined by Bruce. Rescorla then provides a new view of the old learning concept of extinction with obvious clinical and neurobiological implications. Next, Klatzky, Loomis, and Golledge discuss perceptual and cognitive functions in the context of spatial information processing in ecological settings. In the last chapter in this section, Craik describes how different memory functions may or may not decline as we grow older.

The third section includes four chapters that examine different aspects of psychological health. It opens with a chapter by Endler that scrutinizes the multiple dimensions of stress, anxiety, and coping. Frankenhaeuser then discusses stress reactions in the workplace and at home from an evolutionary perspective, with a special focus on similarities and differences between women and men. This is followed by a chapter by Johnston, Bonetti, and Pollard that addresses the concepts of disability and impairment from a social-cognitive perspective, highlighting processes such as self-regulation, planning, and perceived control. A chapter by Keltikangas-Järvinen on risk factors for cardiovascular disease, examining, genetic, psychological, and social precursors for circulatory disturbance, closes this part.

The interaction between cognitive and emotional processes is the focus of the fourth part. Drawing on research from the emerging area of emotional neuroscience, Davidson first discusses recent neuroimaging findings on brain correlates of emotional information processing. Next, Lang, Davis, and Öhman examine psychophysiological data and models from animals and humans pertaining to the expression of fear and anxiety. This is followed by a chapter by Vila in which the psychophysiological and clinical implications of emotion and cardiac defence are elaborated on. Mathews then describes automatic and deliberate biases in the processing of emotional information, as exemplified in research on depressed patients. In the final chapter in this section, Forgas discusses how affective processes may affect social-cognitive judgments and behaviours.

The last section is devoted to various types of higher cognitive processes. First, Gigerenzer reviews his ecological approach to decision making in which the simple heuristics proposed are discussed within an evolutionary framework. It is followed by a chapter of Morais and Kolinsky focusing on the role of literacy in the development of different linguistic abilities. In another chapter with a psycholingusitic orientation, Kurcz examines both representational and communicative aspects in language. Finally, Wickens discusses information-processing demands and descion-making operations in the context of aviation and air-traffic control.

Considering that the selection of chapters in these proceedings represents the current status of the accumulated knowledge from psychological research in the last millennium, we felt it was appropriate to give the volumes a common title: "Psychology at the Turn of the Millennium." By the publication of these volumes, we hand over the relay baton to our colleagues in Beijing, China, who are hosting the next International Congress of Psychology in 2004.

Finally, we would like to express our sincere gratitude to Ms. Mildred Larsson, whose skilful secretarial assistance has been instrumental in the production of the two volumes.

SECTION ONE

Neural mechanisms underlying psychological processes

CHAPTER ONE

Declarative and procedural memory in animals with simple nervous systems

Pavel Balaban
Institute of Higher Nervous Activity and Neurophysiology of the Russian Academy of Sciences, Moscow, Russia

INTRODUCTION

It is no longer necessary to praise the usefulness of neurobiological investigations in invertebrates. A number of neuroscientists interested in a cellular analysis of behaviour have exploited the unique properties of invertebrate nervous systems, namely relatively simple and stereotyped behaviour. Investigations of cellular mechanisms of learning and memory in invertebrates have become an important part of contemporary neuroscience.

Learning (as a part of behaviour) is an emergent property of the nervous system. Pinsker (1980) defined an emergent property as the one possessed by an entire system but not by its individual components. We consider the concept of emergence to be the main problem for anyone using reductionist strategy in research. Since an emergent property is not possessed by the individual components, there is only one sequence to follow when analyzing underlying mechanisms. One should begin with characterization of the phenomenon as a whole and then isolate the components for analysis. Molluscs can provide an extremely useful model in this respect because their behaviour is relatively complex, and the nervous net is relatively accessible for analysis. But is their behavioural repertoire relevant for psychological problems? There have, in fact, been a number of demonstrations that associative processes influence behaviour in a variety of invertebrates including *Helix* (Crow & Alkon, 1978; Davis & Jillette, 1978; Maximova & Balaban, 1984; Mpitsos & Collins, 1978; Sahley, Rudy, & Gelperin, 1981; Walters & Byrne, 1983). Not only higher-order conditioning was shown in molluscans by Sahley et al. (1981), but also a possibility for self-stimulation, as shown by Balaban and Chase (1989).

1

It appears that a detailed analysis of behaviour is a necessary prerequisite of neurophysiological studies. The present work is a review containing published and unpublished results concerning the description of two types of memory in terrestrial snails (*Helix* sp.), and an investigation of the role of individual cells and neuromodulatory systems in learning. Analyzing behaviour and memory in snails, it was possible to distinguish declarative memory (which does not require any motor response to certain stimuli, but can influence behavioural performance), and procedural memory, which is manifested in changes in certain motor responses to certain stimuli.

DECLARATIVE MEMORY

Environmental (contextual) conditioning is a form of associative learning in which the contingency between the reinforcing stimulus and environmental properties is set. Memory deriving from such associations can be termed declarative (iconic, sensory) because no specific behavioural response is performed to the presentation of a specific context. Presence of declarative memory is manifested in changes of behavioural responses to a certain stimuli in two different contexts.

Contextual conditioning in snails

In the behaviour of terrestrial snails (*Gastropoda, Pulmonata, Stylommatophora*) one can find all major forms of behaviour characteristic of high vertebrates, including humans, i.e., feeding, escape (avoidance), exploratory, and sexual behaviour. Normally, in the behavioural hierarchy of *Helix* avoidance behaviour suppresses feeding and exploratory locomotion. Adamo and Chase (1991) showed that courtship can suppress feeding and locomotion is suppressed during copulation, but avoidance responses are not suppressed significantly.

To investigate environmental conditioning, responses to noxious stimuli in two different contexts were chosen for comparison.

In the experimental setup, the snail was tethered by its shell in a manner allowing it to crawl on a ball that rotated freely in a 0.01% solution of NaCl (Figure 1a). The ball was laced with bare stainless steel wire to complete an electrical circuit between the animal's foot and a carbon electrode placed in the water. Electric shock was delivered using a 1–10 mA, 0.5 s current through a macroelectrode applied manually to the dorsal surface of the snail's foot. Punctate mechanical stimuli were applied with calibrated von Frey hairs, permitting delivery of pressures ranging from 6 to 68 g/mm².

In the first series of experiments each snail in two groups was exposed for 20 minutes daily to the experimental setup. All animals were tested by applying tactile stimuli in the experimental setup and on the glass lid of the terrarium in which animals were kept between sessions. Only snails from the experimental group received two electrical shocks per day for 5 days. No tactile stimulation was applied during the shock sessions. Three days after completion of sensitizing treatment (animals were fed during 3-day periods of rest), responsiveness to the same tactile stimuli was compared in control and experimental groups of snails. An experimenter blind to the experimental histories of animals applied the tactile stimulus to the skin of the foot, and measured the withdrawal amplitude in percentage of the maximal withdrawal, taken as 100%. Testing was performed in the experimental setup and in the nonreinforced environment: (on the glass lid of terrarium in which animals were kept between sessions). To reduce possible effects of recent handling, the test was administered no sooner than five min after the subjects had been placed in the environment. Only actively locomoting animals were tested. Five tests per day for 2–3 days were scored for each animal. No shocks were delivered during the test sessions. Results are presented in Figure 1b.

Before noxious reinforcement, no significant difference in amplitudes of tentacle withdrawal to the testing tactile stimuli was observed in any groups of snails (using ANOVA). Three days after a 5-day session during which experimental snails received two shocks per day, testing of responsiveness performed in the setup used for sensitizing revealed a significant (Mann-Whitney, $N = 9$ snails, $p < .001$, 2-tailed) increase of the median response amplitude in sensitized animals (Figure 1b). The difference between control groups in different contexts was not significant (Figure 1b). The amplitude of withdrawal was significantly greater in shocked snails in the context previously paired with the shock.

Our next step was to compare responses of control and shocked snails in another environment. Results obtained with the same animals tested on the glass lid of the terrarium in which the animals were maintained continuously between training sessions are shown in Figure 1b. Testing was carried out for 3 days, alternating with testing in the experimental setup. As well as change in the surface texture, the intensity of light was lower, and the snail was not fixed by its shell during testing on the glass. No significant difference in responsiveness was found either between control groups or the experimental groups. In fact, snails displayed a heightened defensive reaction only in the environment that had a history of pairing with shock. This outcome is consistent with the assumption that the snails can differentiate the environment in which shocks were scheduled to occur. The specificity of that enhancement is extremely important because it allows us to rule out the sensitizing effect of the shock as the sole result of sensitization training.

Effect of 5,7-DHT injection

It was shown previously in *Helix* that after 5,7-DHT treatment (ablating the serotonergic neurons), both the sensitization of the withdrawal reaction and associative aversive conditioning are impaired (Balaban, Vehovszky,

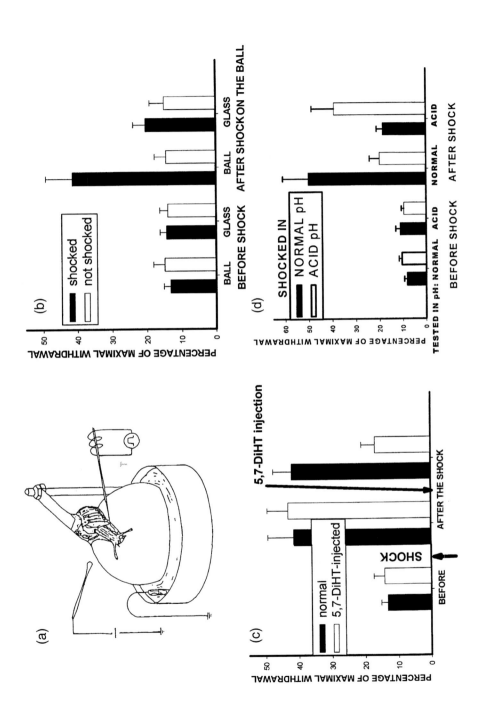

4

Figure 1. Experiments with contextual conditioning:

(a) Setup for behavioural experiments. The animal is fixed by its shell to a holder, but in such a manner that it can move freely on a plastic ball. C = electrode for manual application of current to the skin; T = electrically driven tapper.

(b) Mean amplitude ($\pm$ SEM) of tentacle withdrawal reactions to test tactile stimulation of skin in control (open columns) and sensitized (filled columns) groups of snails in two environments. Responses of the same snails were scored on the ball and the glass lid of terrarium before and 3 days after (right two panels) the shock session.

(c) Mean amplitude of tentacle withdrawal reactions to test tactile stimulation of skin in normal (filled columns) and 5,7-DiHT-injected (open columns) groups of snails before and after the shock. Timing of shock and 5,7-DiHT injections is marked (arrows).

(d) Mean amplitude of tentacle withdrawal reactions to test tactile stimulation of skin in two groups of sensitized snails in same environment (ball) differing only by acidity of water. Responses of the same snails were scored before and after the shock session on the ball in both contexts before and 3 days after (right two panels) the shock session.

Maksimova, & Zakharov, 1987). The feeding behaviour of 5,7-DHT-injected intact animals was visually normal, as were the electrophysiological responses of the investigated neurons to single feeding and noxious stimuli. This is indicative of the fact that the absence of associative learning of this type is not due to changes of responsiveness of the neurons taking part in the feeding and aversive behaviour, respectively.

5,7-DHT treatment after elaboration of aversive conditioning in *Helix* does not impair the conditioned responses (Balaban et al., 1987). This result suggests that 5-HT-containing cells participate in associative learning during the consolidation phase of the conditioned reflex, but are not necessary during its reproduction.

In the present work we tested the possibility of the involvement of 5-HT-containing neurons, which modulate the network underlying avoidance responses (Zakharov & Balaban, 1991) in contextual conditioning. Injection of 5,7-DHT led to disappearance of the effects of training (Figure 1c). Only responses of vehicle-injected sensitized snails differed significantly from responses of snails from other groups in both environments. The difference between vehicle-injected sensitized snails and 5,7-DHT-injected snails was also significant (Mann-Whitney, $p < .001$, 2-tailed). This result suggests that 5-HT-ergic neurons are necessary for reproduction and/or maintenance of contextual conditioning.

Context with one cue different

In the next series of experiments we tested snails in two contexts differing in only one feature. The only difference in the environment in which two groups of snails received sensitizing shocks for 8 days was the acidity of the water in which the ball they walked on was floating (Figure 1a). Acidity of the water in setup A was normal, whereas citric acid was added in setup B. All naive snails sensed this difference, and never tried to make radular rasps (feeding) on the ball in setup B, although such rasps were characteristic for setup A. One group of nine snails was sensitized in setup A with normal water, while another group was sensitized in setup B with acidic water. Testing of each snail was carried out in both contexts before and after 8 days of sensitization training. Each response to tactile stimulation in one context (normal water) was compared to responses of the same animal in another context (water with citric acid). Pooled responses of all snails to testing stimuli before and after sensitization are shown in Figure 1d. The difference in responses between these two groups was not significant before sensitization (Mann-Whitney, $N = 9, 9, p < .2$, 2-tailed), but became highly significant when tested 3–5 days after sensitization training (Mann-Whitney, $N = 8, 8, p < .001$, 2-tailed). Responses of snails shocked in context B increased in this context relative to the responses in context A. Similarly, responses of animals shocked in context A increased in this context. This outcome is consistent with the view that the animals had learned in which context they would receive shocks.

It is essential to note that snails need at least 5–8 days to learn the difference in the two contexts, and this differentiation lasts at least 2 weeks (snails were not tested at longer periods).

These results provides a demonstration in terrestrial snails of the associative nature of a phenomenon known in the invertebrate literature as long-term sensitization. In our experiments we used the "nonassociative" procedure similar to that used in *Aplysia* for elaboration of long-term sensitization (Pinsker, Hening, Carew, & Kandel, 1973). Presented data suggest that the presentation of sensitizing stimuli inevitably elicits the appearance of an associative long-term sensitization, which can be observed only in a certain context. In fact, this associative long-term sensitization is equivalent to contextual (environmental) conditioning.

The long-term changes observed in the withdrawal behaviour of *Helix* after noncontingent application of noxious but nontraumatic stimuli can be due to nonassociative activity-dependent neuromodulation or associative (conditioned) enhancement of responsiveness nonspecific for the testing stimuli, but specific to the environmental cues. We cannot exclude a nonassociative component, which obviously exists, and can be found in isolated preparations from sensitized animals (Kandel & Schwartz, 1982), but will concentrate the discussion on facts proving the participation of associative processes in the long-term enhancement of withdrawal responses.

The starting point of our investigation was a theoretical analysis of what happens during sensitization: what is the behavioural goal (adaptive significance) of an increase of responses to all stimuli? After a noxious stimulus all reactions of the animal to external stimuli are enhanced, and adaptive significance of the enhancement is obvious: to be ready for the next stimulus, which can be more damaging. But what happens in the long run? Is it possible to enhance nonselectively all responses to all potentially dangerous stimuli? If the animal can be nonassociatively sensitized for several weeks (as in the experiments of Pinsker et al., 1973), then the adaptive value of sensitization will be reduced to zero, because the appearance of a new type of noxious stimulus in a different environment would be unnoticed in a sensitized animal. A quite different situation would be if we assume that in the long run (weeks), the animal will develop an association between the sensitizing stimulus and environment. It is essential to note that no association is formed between testing and sensitizing stimuli applied noncontinuously, so one can speak about absence of association between experimentator-applied stimuli, but the long-term behavioural changes are selective and an association is formed between the environment and the sensitizing stimuli. In the present experiments we used nontraumatic sensitizing stimuli and found several properties, which may be due to the associative nature of observed behavioural changes in the terrestrial snail: (1) long-term changes in behaviour appear not after a single strong stimulation, but after several days of stimulation; (2)

responsiveness of the sensitized snails in different environments was maximal in the environment in which the snail was sensitized; (3) changing of only one environmental cue changes the behaviour. We can speculate that each noxious stimulus elicits two parallel chains of events. One is a nonassociative change of responsiveness mediated by neuromodulators, largely dependent on the intensity of the stimulus, and lasting 1–2 days, i.e. the average time of protein turnover. Independent events are triggered in parallel in the network by the same stimuli, and it may be that the same neuromodulators are involved, but these changes are dependent not only on the strength of stimuli, but on the contingency of sensitizing stimuli on the environment; the number of replications of similar situations.

PROCEDURAL MEMORY IN SNAILS

Associative modifications of behaviour in snails

The history of attempts to elaborate a conditioned response to a specific stimulus (conforming to the definition of procedural memory) in snails starts with the experiments of E. Thompson (1917) in the pond snail *Physa gyrina*. He associated tactile stimulation of the foot with food presentation, and after 250 paired trials in 2 days tactile conditioned stimulus (CS) elicited feeding responses in 39.6% of cases compared to 3.3% before conditioning. The changes were maintained for 4 days; no controls with nonpaired presentation or differential conditioning were used. In Russia, experiments in *Physa acuta* were carried out by V. Sokolov (1959), who paired light with water application of noxious 0.2% KCl solution. Conditioned responses (snails moved in dark compartment) were noted after 8 paired presentations and became frequent after 30 trials. However, this reflex was not stable and fast extinction was seen.

The first report on conditioning in terrestrial snails was published in 1976. The pneumostome closure evoked by strong noxious stimuli was used as an unconditioned response in these experiments (Litvinov, Maximova, Babalan, & Masinovsky, 1976). Weak noxious stimuli, which normally do not evoke pneumostome closure, were used as the CS: tactile stimulation, local heating of the foot epithelium, or tapping on the shell. The elaboration was slow and more than 100 trials were necessary for conditioning. However, the CS used was of the same modality as the reinforcement, so the question of nonassociative sensitization as the mechanism of observed changes in behaviour was not elucidated.

Ivan P. Pavlov wrote that in principle, any stimulus initiating any response may serve as the conditioned stimulus (Pavlov, 1951). The only requirement is that this stimulus should not initiate the same reflex which is initiated by the unconditioned stimulus (UCS). In the experiments of O. A. Maksimova (1979), tactile stimulus was used as the CS, and food as the UCS. An animal had to turn to the right when CS was delivered in order to receive a piece of food. Before learning, the CS elicited only withdrawal reactions. After 100–150 paired trials snails began to react to tactile stimulus with feeding behaviour (details are published in a book by Maksimova & Balaban, 1983), turning to the right side where there usually was food. Conditioning with food reinforcement is easy to elaborate, but such reinforcement can not be given as preparation for intracellular investigation. Therefore, another behavioural approach was chosen.

Food-aversion conditioning

The primary purpose of behavioural experiments is to generate rapid and obvious modification in motor responses, reproducible in neurophysiological preparation, and to demonstrate specificity of elaborated behavioural modifications for the pairing of conditioned and unconditioned stimuli. The withdrawal reaction as an unconditioned response meets these criteria, and the underlying neuronal circuitry has already been investigated in *Helix* (Balaban, 1983; Zakharov & Balaban, 1991). Aversive learning appears to be one of the most suitable paradigms for investigation of learning in snails, because it usually concerns two competitive behavioural acts, one of which changes dramatically due to the pairing of two stimuli.

To be suitable for neurophysiological investigation, learning should occur rapidly and, as in a study on the carnivorous mollusc *Pleurobranchaea* (Davis & Jillette, 1978; Mpitsos & Collins, 1978), we reinforced food presentation by strong, electric shock which evoked generalized withdrawal reaction of the snail (Maksimova & Balaban, 1983).

A similar procedure was used in the experiments of Stepanov and Lokhov (1986). Snails chosen for experiments were deprived of food a week prior to conditioning. A day before conditioning snails were tested for their feeding behaviour. Subjects with food refusals were excluded from the experiments. Over 5 days, one session per day was performed, with 10 trials in every session. When a food piece (carrot, cabbage, etc.) is given to an animal at the distance or 4–5 mm from the mouth, the snail begins to search the food (the appetitive phase of feeding behaviour). It lowers its optic tentacles down and tastes the food. Then the animal opens its mouth, captures the food piece, and pulls it away from the needle (consummatory phase). The time interval between the presentation of the food and taking it away from the needle in hungry snails is 20–50 s. This time never exceeds 1 min in active animals. The reinforcement consists of turning on the current when the animal captures the food. The intensity of the current is selected in such a way as to evoke the withdrawal of tentacles and half of the anterior part of the foot. The pneumostome often does not react to this stimulation. It is necessary to use a moderate current intensity to avoid generalized escape reaction. In these conditions every animal begins to avoid the food at the end of the first session. The criterion of the conditioned reaction in a trial was food avoidance for

3 min after food presentation. Food avoidance behaviour manifests itself in different ways. At first a snail ceases to lower its optic tentacles. Then the animal lifts the most anterior part of its foot up to prevent contact of lips with the food. Further, the snail withdraws both pairs of tentacles and the anterior part of its body. And, finally, the animal crawls away from the needle and the food after the first contact with it. In other words, a fully conditioned animal behaves like a sated one. It is important to emphasize that an experimenter can observe and estimate the individual conditioning of every subject. It is enough for this purpose to compute the percentage of conditioned reactions (CR) as a number of food refusals during a session divided by 10 (because 10 trials per session are used) and multiplied by 100%. This percentage increases from the first session to the fifth one.

Properties of conditioning and two-way conditioning

Intensity of reward

In full accordance with Pavlov's (1927) data, intensity of reward in our experiments had great influence on the speed of elaboration of conditioned reflex. In a series of experiments in which we used a weak reinforcement, the dynamics of elaboration were quite different. We consider the reinforcement as weak if it elicits only tentacles and head withdrawal, whereas strong reinforcement, used in some experiments, elicited complete withdrawal of the body in the shell and release of mucus. It was possible to deliver up to 20 trials per day to one snail if a weak reinforcement was used. In all other respects the experiments were similar to experiments with a strong reinforcement. In the cases when the snail did not take food during 150 s, no reinforcement was given, thus encouraging the snail not to respond. Unpaired controls received the same number of food presentations and reinforcements. It appeared that usage of a weak reinforcement requires about 60–100 paired trials to exceed the 60% level of conditioned responses, and only 5–15 trials if a strong reinforcement was used. But in both cases all stimuli should not be given in one session (a day) but no fewer than 3 days should pass from the beginning of experiment. Optimal timing is 5–8 days with 1–2 paired trials for experiments with strong reinforcement, and 10–20 trials for experiments with weak reinforcement. It means that, independently of intensity of reward, some optimal timing exists.

Retention of conditioned reaction

In the major part of learning experiments in snails we tested responsiveness during the first week following the end of the learning session, which lasted 5–10 days. The average percentage of aversive reactions (withdrawal and refusal) during the first week was 85–90%. The measurement of the level of response in trained snails 2, 4, and 6 weeks after training showed that even after 6 weeks the percentage of conditioned responses was about 60% (Maksimova & Balaban, 1983). This result was consistent throughout several independent series of experiments in 28 snails. Therefore, the duration of behavioural changes is long enough to consider it as a long-term modification of behaviour.

Differential conditioning

As well as unpaired controls, which were conventional for all experiments, in some series we used a different door (or type of food), which was presented without the reinforcement. At first presentations of the nonreinforced door a conditioned response can be seen in about 50% of presentations, but very quickly this percentage decreased to 10–15%. Differential conditioned response confirms specificity of elaborated behavioural changes.

Extinction and spontaneous recovery

Active extinction of the conditioned aversion response to food is possible in 1 day. In a series of experiments, five conditioned snails were presented the reinforced type of food with small intervals (3–5 min). After 30 presentations the number of aversive responses decreased to 50%, and continuation of presentation of food led to zero aversive reactions. It should be remembered that the snails are hungry, and feeding motivation is high. Presentation of the same food to the same animals 24 hours after the extinction series revealed spontaneous recovery of the conditioned response, but the rate of extinction was higher. Seventy-two hours after the second extinction series, the level of conditioned responses to the first 10 stimuli was even higher than 24 hours after learning (about 70%), and extinction was rapid. These results conform fully with results obtained in vertebrates (Pavlov, 1927), and allows us to consider the observed modifications of behaviour as classical conditioning.

Two-way conditioning

One of the most interesting paradigms introduced in science by Pavlov's student E. Asratjan (1970) is "two-way conditioning". Operational definition of two-way conditioning is clear and simple: after elaboration of a conditioned feeding response in dogs to light by repeated contingent presentation of light and feeding reinforcement, presentation of food only elicits, before normal feeding, an anticipation of the light stimulus—eye-blinking, turning of the head to the light source. In our opinion, this notion of formation of an associative connection not only between the conditioned stimuli (CS) preceding the unconditioned stimulus (UCS), but in the reverse direction as well, undermines a part of Pavlovian theory which presumes that a connection is formed only when the CS precedes the UCS. Discussion of this point was a taboo in Russian literature until recently, but the phenomenon of two-way conditioning was abundantly described in the literature and is considered as a necessary criterion for the demonstration of associative learning. Therefore, we carried out several series of experiments at a behavioural and cellular level aimed to demonstrate the possibility of the formation of a two-way connection in snails. In fact, all experiments tested what would happen in the animal with developed aversive conditioning if a noxious stimulus (similar to the one used as a reinforcement, but weaker) is applied. It appeared that weak noxious (tactile) stimuli, which before learning evoked no response or withdrawal, after elaboration of aversive conditioning elicited activation of exploratory activity and feeding behaviour. Such behavioural response was never observed before learning. In responses of identified cells involved in feeding, the absence of response to noxious stimuli changed to the activation of a pattern accompanying feeding (Balaban, Maksimova, & Galanina, 1985a). These results suggest that two-way conditioning can be formed in snails.

Results presented in this section confirm the suggestion that *Helix* can associate sensory inputs and adaptively modify its behaviour for a period of time substantially greater than the proteins turnover, thus suggesting involvement of genome.

Serotonin modulation of aversive behaviour and aversive conditioning

There is a growing body of experimental data implicating serotonin (5-hydroxytryptamine, 5-HT) in a wide range of memory processes in molluscs (Carew, Hawkins & Kandel, 1983; Kandel & Schwartz, 1982), as well as in vertebrates (Ogren, Johansson, Johansson, & Archer, 1982). Investigations on a specific role of 5-HT in sensitization (Klein, Camarado, & Kandel, 1982) and on the cellular mechanism of classical conditioning (Hawkins, Abrams, Carew, & Kandel, 1983; Ocorr, Walters, & Byrne, 1985) suggest the role of 5-HT in acquisition of conditioning.

One of the approaches that may be employed to investigate the 5-HT role is the selective ablation of the serotonergic neurons. Both 5,6-DHT and 5,7-DHT (5,7-dihydroxytryptamine) are known to be sequestered selectively within serotonergic neurons by a high affinity uptake system (Baumgarten, Jenner, Bjorklund, Klemm, & Schlossberger, 1982). The toxin is oxidized intracellularly, producing free radicals that ablate serotonergic terminals, both in vertebrates and invertebrates (Elekes, Hiripi, & Nemcsok, 1977; Glover & Kramer, 1982; Vehovszky, Kemenes, & Rozsa, 1989).

In the present section the contribution of 5-HT in aversive learning was studied using 5,7-DHT, the "neurotoxic" analogue of serotonin. The associative changes were compared after training in normal and 5,7-DHT-injected snails, both on the behavioural level of intact animals and on the cellular level using electrophysiological methods in semi-intact preparations.

Effects of 5,7-DHT treatment on feeding behaviour and avoidance reaction

Immediately after injection of 5,7-DHT locomotion abnormalities were observed: the animals had an increased arousal state and they were crawling intensively, frequently changing their direction. No abnormalities were noted in the behaviour of vehicle-injected snails. After several hours, normal behaviour reappeared and no visible differences were notable between control and 5,7-DHT-treated animals.

No significant difference was found between the latency of the consummatory phase of control and 5,7-DHT-injected animals, whereas a significant difference (Mann-Whitney, $N = 50, 80, p < .001$) was noted in the appetitive phase duration. Following 5,7-DHT treatment, changes were observable in the dynamics of the avoidance reaction (pneumostome closure) in the intact snails, as well as in the number of spikes in the neurons responsible for this withdrawal reaction on the semi-intact preparations. During rhythmic tactile stimulation of the skin the increase in amplitude of pneumostome closure and of the neuronal spike discharge could be observed in control animals but this sensitization of responses was absent in 5,7-DHT-injected animals, both at behavioural and cellular level.

In a separate series of experiments using a double-blind procedure the sensitization of pneumostome closure was tested in intact 5,7-DHT-treated and vehicle-injected animals. In all 5,7-DHT-treated snails this sensitization was absent, but the vehicle-injected animals displayed sensitization, like the control noninjected ones.

The modulatory effect of 5-HT on feeding behaviour is well known in gastropods, e.g., as the so-called feeding arousal in *Aplysia* (Kupfermann et al., 1979; Kupfermann & Weiss, 1982). In the *Helix* specimens injected with 5,7-DHT in our experiments the increased time duration of the appetitive phase of feeding behaviour can be explained as a suppression of this generalized excitatory influence. On the contrary, no change in the consummatory phase was observed, suggestive of another transmitter substance being involved. According to Galanina, Zakharov, Maximova, and Balaban (1986), the 5-HT in *Helix lucorum* cannot trigger the consummatory phase of feeding, whereas dopamine evokes the rhythmic movement of buccal mass, as Wieland and Gelperin (1983) demonstrated in other mollusc species.

5-HT might exert its influence not only on central neurons but also directly on muscles (Kobayashi, Muneoka, & Fujiwara, 1982; Kupfermann et al., 1979; Lloyd, 1980). In our experiments, no abnormality in the locomotion of the animals could be observed visually 2–3 hours following the injection. Moreover, the time duration between touch and bite was the same both in control and drug-treated groups, although locomotion is an essential factor in this period of feeding behaviour as well.

Effect of 5,7-DHT treatment on aversive learning of intact animals

The results of all behavioural experiments are shown in Figure 2. In control conditioned animals a highly significant ($p < .001$) decrease of feeding reactions occurred after the learning sessions. The animals refused to touch the food and in some cases a withdrawal reaction was observed after presentation of food. This change in feeding response was specific only for the type of food (carrot) paired with the electric shock.

After unpaired presentation of stimuli most of the animals demonstrated no changes in feeding response. The conditioned 5,7-DHT-injected animals exhibited the same behavioural responses as the unpaired control animals, suggesting that in these cases no aversive learning was acquired (Figure 2).

To answer the question whether 5,7-DHT treatment could change the performance of consolidated aversive conditioned reaction to food, in a series of experiments eight hungry snails were trained to avoid carrot. After six paired presentations of carrot and electric shock the percentage of feeding reactions

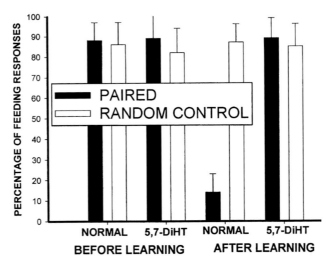

Figure 2.   Mean number of feeding responses (each snail was presented with food 10 times) in unpaired two group (open columns) and two-paired group (filled columns) of snails before and after conditioning. One paired and one control group was injected 3 days prior to the training session with 5,7-DiHT.

decreased from 90 to 15%, as in a control conditioned group. Then four randomly chosen snails were injected with 5,7-DHT, and 2 days later a number of feeding reactions to carrot were scored (blind) in all animals. Both control and treated animals responded with feeding in only 10% of reactions. Thus, 5,7-DHT does not impair the aversive behaviour per se, but exerts its influence only at the stage of consolidation of aversive conditioning. Another suggestion which can be deduced from the presented data is that the 5-HT-containing neurons are not necessary for recall and/or retention of this form of memory.

The absence of sensitization of the withdrawal reaction in 5,7-DHT-injected animals in our experiments suggests that in *Helix* (as in *Aplysia*), serotonin takes part in the withdrawal reaction as a transmitter producing facilitation. In the laboratory of Pavlov (1927) it was shown that after training sessions one of the consequences of reinforcement is an unspecific sensitization, and this effect of reinforcement correlates with the number of trials needed for the elaboration of the conditioned reflex. On the cellular level it was confirmed in *Aplysia* by Hawkins (1984; Hawkins et al., 1983) that the mechanism of classical conditioning may be an elaboration of activity-dependent presynaptic facilitation of synaptic transmission between sensory and motor neurons, resulting in sensitization of the conditioned reaction. Consequently, if the sensitization process is impaired, no associative changes could be elaborated. Our results in *Helix* are in agreement with this theory: after 5,7-DHT treatment (ablating the serotonergic neurons), both the sensitization of the withdrawal reaction and associative aversive conditioning is missing. The feeding behaviour of 5,7-DHT-injected, intact animals was visually normal.

In order to find out whether the injected snails can memorize, in a series of experiments we tried to elaborate in 5,7-DHT-injected hungry snails a feeding conditioned response to weak noxious stimuli (tactile stimulation was used as a CS), using food as a reinforcement. It was found that no difference in the rate of conditioned response existed in vehicle-injected and 5,7-DHT-injected snails. These results suggest that the 5-HT-containing neuronal system is important for elaboration of conditioned reflexes with noxious reinforcement, but not with food reinforcement.

Two synergic components of memory

The results of 5,7-DHT treatment after elaboration of aversive conditioning suggest that 5-HT is necessary for associative learning only during the consolidation phase. Quite different results, demonstrating that 5-HT is necessary for recall and/or retention were obtained in experiments concerning environmental (contextual) conditioning (see earlier), which can be considered as an independent component of memory. Environmental conditioning (declarative memory) is impaired by suppression of the serotonergic system in learned animals, thus suggesting that serotonin-containing cells are involved in reproduction and maintenance of this acquired behaviour. Independence of the cellular mechanisms involved suggests that during learning the animal acquires information about the context in which it receives the reinforcement, and *independently* stores information about certain specific stimuli which are contingent on reinforcement. The adaptive value of the independence of these two components is evident: the animal can perceive the same conditioned stimulus in another context as a novel one, and in the known context is prepared to respond to noxious stimuli.

NEURAL MECHANISMS OF DECLARATIVE AND PROCEDURAL MEMORY

Here we should admit that there is not enough knowledge concerning the changes in neural networks during learning to propose any mechanism of learning and memory. The outcome of the preceding sections can be formulated as follows: acquisition and maintenance of declarative memory requires activity of modulatory cells, while these cells are only involved in acquisition of procedural memory, but are not necessary for its maintenance. It suggests the existence of at least two loci of plasticity in the nervous system. One locus is connected with plasticity of modulatory cells, and another locus with plasticity of premotor interneurons (Figure 3). Right now we are not able to investigate the plasticity of modulatory cells, mostly because their synaptic responses to noxious stimuli are biphasic, and changes are distributed in time: a short-term (0, 1 s) tactile stimulation elicits changes for several minutes (unpublished data). Responses of premotor neurons to stimuli are much easier to interpret, mostly because their spike output correlates with the amplitude of withdrawal responses (Balaban, 1983). In order to have the ability to investigate cellular mechanisms of memory in a simplified situation we investigated the possibility of reducing the reinforcing stimuli to the stimulation of only one identified neuromodulatory cell while recording changes in premotor neurons.

Changes in behaviour that correspond to the activity of a single invertebrate nerve cell were described in literature quite early (Nolen & Hoy, 1984; Wiersma, 1938; Willows, 1967). Well-known examples are lateral giant neurons in crayfish (Wiersma & Ikeda, 1964), Mauthner cells in fish (Eaton, 1984), and neurons controlling withdrawal in molluscs (Balaban, 1979). These cells are called command neurons and constitute a class of premotor interneurons, whose intracellular activation elicits a goal-directed behavioural response similar to the responses evoked by adequate sensory stimuli (Wiersma & Ikeda, 1964). Nine giant premotor neurons (Balaban, 1979, 1983) located in the parietal and pleural ganglia of the snail *Helix* satisfy three criteria for command neurons introduced by Kupfermann and

Weiss (1978). First, they respond to the presentation of a noxious tactile stimulus by a discharge which precedes the behavioural response ("participation" criterion). Second, intracellular activation of one neuron releases a part of the withdrawal response ("sufficiency" criterion). The last, "necessity" criterion is fulfilled for a component of the withdrawal behaviour elicited by intracellular stimulation—this component disappears from the withdrawal response when the putative command cell is hyperpolarized. Thus, withdrawal responses in the snail are mediated by nine putative command neurons of pleural and parietal ganglia triggering head withdrawal, body withdrawal, pneumostome closure, and receiving common polymodal synaptic input (Balaban, 1979, 1983; Zakharov & Balaban, 1987; Balaban & Zakharov, 1992).

In addition to putative command neurons for withdrawal behaviour in *Helix*, a group of serotonin-containing cells modulating the network underlying the snail withdrawal behaviour (Zakharov, Ierusalimsky, & Balaban, 1995) was described. Firing in these neurons did not elicit any forms of behaviour, but changed the behavioural responses evoked by noxious stimuli: such properties conform to a definition of modulatory cells. Extracellular stimulation of these serotonergic cells led to a short-term facilitation of synaptic and action potential responses in the putative withdrawal command neurons induced by noxious stimuli. Individual serotonergic cells responded with a stronger discharge to ipsilateral than contralateral stimulation, and

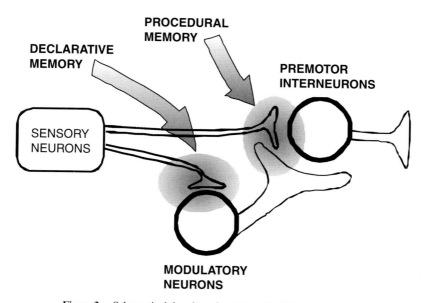

Figure 3. Schematical drawing of putative plasticity loci. Details in text.

exhibited differences in receptive fields (Zakharov et al., 1995). Immuno-chemical investigation showed presence of serotonergic terminals in the neuropile and somata layer surrounding putative command neurons of the parietal ganglia for withdrawal (Vehovszky, Hernadi, Elekes, & Balaban, 1993), suggesting a direct interaction between serotonergic neurons and these command neurons.

It was shown previously in *Helix* that after treatment with the neurotoxin 5,7-dihydroxytriptamine (5,7-DiHT) selectively impairing the serotonergic neurons, contextual conditioning (declarative memory), and associative food-aversion conditioning (procedural memory) were impaired (Balaban & Bravarenko, 1993; Balaban et al., 1987; Zakharov & Balaban, 1991). This suggests that the serotonergic modulatory neurons can be involved in the reinforcement process underlying the development of conditioning.

In the present section, we describe possible participation of the whole group and of individual serotonergic modulatory neurons in mediating the reinforcement. In a model situation the synaptic inputs to premotor interneurons for withdrawal were paired or explicitly unpaired with the activation of modulatory cells.

Contingent extracellular activation of the pedal serotonergic cells can serve as a reinforcement

Previously published results showed the necessity of serotonergic cells for long-term behavioural sensitization and elaboration of context conditioning and food aversion (Balaban & Bravarenko, 1993; Balaban et al., 1987; Zakharov & Balaban, 1991; Zakharov et al., 1995). The presence of serotonergic fibres surrounding the soma of withdrawal premotor interneurons with a dense network without synaptic specializations, suggesting a modulatory influence was clearly demonstrated immunochemically (Vehovzsky et al., 1993). Therefore, we tested the assumption that serotonergic cells can mediate reinforcement. We performed experiments in which the EPSPs induced by nerve stimulation in the withdrawal interneurons were paired with local extracellular stimulation of serotonergic neurons located in the rostral part of the ipsilateral pedal ganglion. It should be noted that in 12 pilot experiments no significant short- or long-term effects on the amplitude of complex EPSPs in withdrawal interneurons were found when we extracellularly stimulated serotonergic cells located on the border of visceral and right parietal ganglia.

In our experiments the test stimuli to the intestinal nerve were applied with a 20-min intertrial interval. A 20-min interval between test stimuli was selected in order to diminish habituation of complex EPSPs in premotor interneurons. During 5 hours of experimentation the EPSPs amplitude usually decreased to the 85–90% level of the initial amplitude with a 20-min intertrial interval (Maksimova, unpublished data). First three test stimuli (pre-testing) were followed by paired or explicitly unpaired procedures, then five post-test stimuli were applied. The beginning of extracellular stimulation (5 s training duration, regular 3 ms pulses with 5 Hz frequency) of serotonergic cells during the paired procedure coincided with the beginning of the test stimuli, while during the explicitly unpaired procedure (in other preparations) a similar extracellular stimulation was given in the middle of the intertrial interval (10 min apart from the test stimuli). The averaged data from 38 experiments showed a significant difference ($p < .01$, 100 min after the last reinforcing stimulus, Mann-Whitney rank sum test) between the amplitudes of EPSPs to test stimuli in premotor withdrawal neurons of paired and unpaired groups 60–100 min after the start of reinforcing extracellular stimulation. These results suggested that pedal serotonergic neurons were capable of contingently increasing the amplitude of the withdrawal neuron responses to nerve stimulation. At a behavioural level this increase would result in facilitation of withdrawal responses similar to the one observed in our earlier experiments during context conditioning (Balaban & Bravarenko, 1993) and associative learning (Balaban et al., 1987).

One modulatory cell can mediate the reinforcement

The experiments using extracellular stimulation described in the previous section can not identify the individual neurons involved in neuromodulation or provide important information about cellular mechanisms. Therefore, we used intracellular stimulation of individual cells in the rostral region of the pedal ganglia. The training procedure was changed in order to shorten the training session. Test stimuli were delivered with a 5 min interval before and after the pairing session. Increase of test stimulation frequency normally increases the habituation rate (Balaban & Zakharov, 1992). At a frequency of 1 every 5 min, the response in parietal giant cells to test stimulation via the intestinal nerve usually habituates to 65–75% of the initial value (Bravarenko, Gusev, Balaban, & Voronin, 1995; Malyshev, Bravarenko, & Balaban, 1997). A pairing session (Figure 4a) consisted of five test stimuli with 2-min intervals, and five "reinforcing" intracellular training sessions to the pedal neurons (Figure 4b), which were given simultaneously with the test stimuli (paired procedure) or between test stimuli in a pairing session (explicitly unpaired group, Figure 4a). The EPSP amplitude was not analyzed during the testing session (the gap on Figure 4c) because the artefacts of tetanization in the paired procedure masked the form of the EPSPs. The "reinforcing" intracellular tetanization consisted of one 10 s duration training section of 25–33 ms depolarizing pulses at 15–20 Hz. The current strength (5–10 nA) was suprathreshold. Giant parietal withdrawal interneurons (mainly LPa3 and RPa3) and one of the pedal serotonergic cells were penetrated with one or two glass microelectrodes. The second electrode in the pedal cell was used for intracellular tetanization and injection of biocytin (Figure 4b). In most experiments, the training procedure was repeated twice: one paired and one unpaired session. In total 27 animals were used for experiments. Twelve of them were the snails with serotonergic cells previously vitally labelled by 5,7-dihydroxytryptamine (Balaban, Zakharov, & Matz, 1985b). Brown pigmentation characteristic for 5,7-DiHT-labelled cells allowed us to be sure that a serotonergic cell was impaled in these preparations. In most experiments, pedal cells were filled with biocytin after the experiment to verify the morphology of the recorded cell.

To our surprise, we never observed any modulatory or pairing-specific effects in the experiments, in which we tetanized an unidentified small serotonergic pedal neuron or serotonergic cell Pd2. The difference between responses in paired and unpaired situations was close to zero in 17 snails, and never exceeded the standard error of the mean on averaging. Only when intracellular tetanization of cell Pd4 was used as a reinforcement did we observe an increase in EPSP amplitude during the paired procedure ($N = 10$ snails; Figure 4c) relative to the experiments with unpaired stimulation of Pd4 cells ($N = 6$, same snails; Figure 4c). A significant difference was observed immediately after the last tetanization ($p < .05$, Mann-Whitney rank sum test, corresponding values were compared in experiments with paired and unpaired procedures). Thirty minutes after the pairing session the difference was even more significant ($p < .01$), and up to the 50th minute the difference between paired and explicitly unpaired situations was significant (Figure 4c). In general, results were similar to those obtained in the experiments with extracellular stimulation of serotonergic neurons. Thus, intracellular stimulation of only one Pd4 cell can mediate a pairing-specific increase of the amplitudes of the EPSPs in the parietal giant neurons controlling withdrawal behaviour.

The role of serotonin in withdrawal behaviour

Numerous studies in several gastropod species have indicated that the neurotransmitter serotonin (5-HT) has a modulatory role in feeding behaviour (Gelperin, 1981; Kupfermann & Weiss, 1982) as well as withdrawal behaviour. Serotonin also plays an essential role in modulation of withdrawal reactions in molluscs (Balaban et al., 1987; Glanzman et al., 1989; Kandel & Schwartz, 1982).

Serotonin-containing cells are described in the pedal ganglia of practically all gastropod species (see Croll, 1988, for discussion). Unlike the giant cerebral serotonergic cells whose involvement in the control of feeding behaviour was described in many species (Gelperin, 1981; Gillette & Davis, 1977; Granzow & Kater, 1977; Weiss & Kupfermann, 1976) including *Helix*

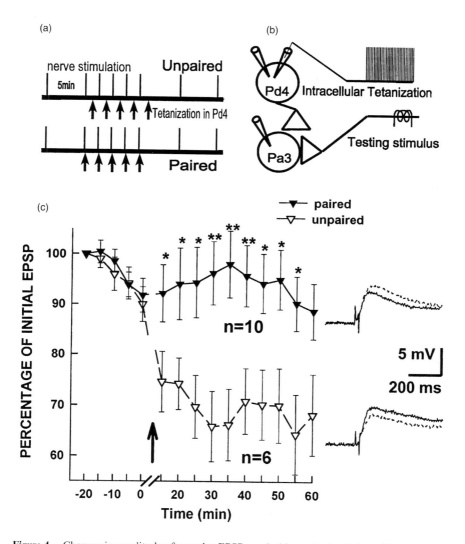

Figure 4. Changes in amplitude of complex EPSPs evoked in parietal withdrawal interneurons by stimulation of the intestinal nerve paired and explicitly unpaired with intracellular activation of cell Pd4:

(a) diagram of experiment;

(b) scheme of recording and experimental setup;

(c) averaged results (mean ± SEM), *$p < .05$, **$p < .01$, Mann-Whitney rank sum test. Initial response was taken in all experiments as 100%. The training session is marked by breaks in axes and an arrow. On the right examples of EPSPs before (solid line) and 30 min after training session (dotted line) from the same experiment are shown.

(Galanina et al., 1986; Weiss & Kupfermann, 1976), the behavioural role of pedal serotonergic neurons has not been extensively investigated.

There are three groups of serotonergic neurons described in *Helix* (Sedden, Walker, & Kerkut, 1968; Zakharov & Balaban, 1987, 1991). The cerebral group of serotonergic cells modulates feeding behaviour (Balaban, 1991). A group of serotonergic cells located on the border of the left parietal and visceral ganglion may be involved in the control of the heart and intestinal tract activities (Balaban, unpublished), although their precise function is still unknown. Pedal serotonergic cells are involved in the modulation of withdrawal behaviour (Zakharov et al., 1995) and possible control of locomotion (suggested by their branching pattern).

The role of serotonin in the withdrawal behaviour of terrestrial snails was investigated by manipulating 5-HT levels either (1) directly, by increasing the concentration of 5-HT in the medium bathing the CNS, or (2) indirectly, by selectively destroying serotonergic nerve terminals using 5,7-DiHT injections into intact animals (Balaban et al., 1987; Vehovszky et al., 1989). An increase of 5-HT concentration up to 5×10^{-5} M elicited, in semi-intact preparations, sensitization of behavioural responses to noxious stimuli with a corresponding increase of synaptic responses in the withdrawal interneurons (Zakharov & Balaban, 1991), and changes in the duration of action potentials in sensory neurons responding to noxious stimuli (Balaban, 1987). These data suggested that serotonin is a facilitating modulatory transmitter for withdrawal behaviour.

Injection of a selective neurotoxin 5,7-DiHT resulted in changes in the dynamics of the withdrawal reactions in intact snails, and corresponding changes in the number of spikes in the withdrawal command neurons. An increase in the amplitude of pneumostome closure and corresponding increase of the action potential discharge in the withdrawal interneurons during rhythmic tactile stimulation of the skin were always observed in the control animals (Balaban, 1983, 1991). However, this sensitization was absent in 5,7-DiHT-injected snails both at behavioural and cellular levels. (Balaban, 1983; Balaban & Bravarenko, 1993; Balaban et al., 1987). These data confirm the suggested modulatory role for serotonin in withdrawal behaviour.

Pedal serotonergic cells constitute a functional neuromodulatory group

Each group of serotonergic cells has its target areas where most processes of the cells are branching. With the exception of the well-studied giant metacerebral serotonergic cell (Osborne, 1984), cerebral and parieto visceral serotonergic cells have not been investigated in detail. The morphology of the pedal serotonergic cells described in the present paper suggests that they represent several heterogeneous populations. Some cells send a single process to the peripheral nerves (V. Ierusalimsky, unpublished observations), whereas others send processes and branches to the neuropile of the pleural ganglia. Only the Pd4 cell from this group sends processes to the neuropile of parietal ganglia. Noxious tactile stimuli elicit an increase in the background spiking frequency in the serotonergic modulatory neurons and a corresponding increase in the stimulus-evoked action potential responses of the withdrawal interneurons. Although the entire group of serotonergic cells responds to noxious stimuli, most individual cells respond with a stronger discharge to ipsilateral than contralateral stimulation, and exhibit differences in receptive fields. Sensory inputs to putative modulatory cells and their characteristic background firing are worth special attention. In order to facilitate withdrawal reactions, a putative modulatory neuron should receive information concerning each noxious stimulus, that is delivered to the animal. In addition, changes elicited by such a stimulus must last for tens of seconds because behavioural facilitation usually lasts that long. It appears that responses of the investigated pedal serotonergic cells to noxious tactile stimulation are compliant with these conditions. These cells can be activated by stimulation of any part of the animal's skin, but only by a strong noxious stimulus that also evokes a behavioural sensitization. Only some cells respond to adequate stimulation of a given area, whereas intrinsic interconnections within the group recruit other members in the case of a strong noxious stimulus. Weakness of electrical coupling between serotonergic cells (Zakharov et al., 1995) prevents recruitment of all cells in the group into responses to relatively weak stimuli, which are not dangerous for the snail. The tonic feature of their response to external stimuli is consistent with their role in the facilitation of the withdrawal response. Extracellular stimulation of the investigated serotonergic cells led to facilitation of action potential responses to noxious stimuli in the putative command neurons for withdrawal behaviour, suggesting their reinforcing role in this behaviour.

Thus, pedal serotonergic cells apparently function as modulatory system for withdrawal behaviour, which facilitates synaptic responses in the underlying network.

A single cell can be responsible for modulation of behaviour

Contingent activation of only one pedal serotonergic cell (Figure 4) produces facilitation of the synaptic inputs to the withdrawal interneurons, which is similar to the facilitation induced by exogenous serotonin (Balaban et al., 1987; Balaban, Zakharov, & Chistyakova, 1991; Zakharov et al., 1995). It is also similar to the facilitation elicited by the contingent extracellular activation of the group of pedal serotonergic neurons. These results suggest that the activation of individual pedal serotonergic modulatory neuron Pd4 can mediate the reinforcement. We cannot exclude the possibility that this activation of a single cell activates other serotonergic cells as well. No synaptic potentials were recorded in parietal cells during the activation of serotonergic neurons. This may be due to the remoteness of synaptic connections or non-synaptic release of a transmitter from varicosities that are characteristic of the serotonergic cells in *Helix* (Osborne, 1984). Immunochemical characterization of serotonergic fibres surrounding soma of premotor giant parietal cells and lack of synaptic specializations suggest modulatory function of the serotonergic input (Vehovzsky et al., 1993). We cannot completely exclude the existence of intermediate neurons. However, it seems unlikely, because the effect of direct contingent application of serotonin on synaptic transmission was shown in cultured identified neurons (Bao, Kandel, & Hawkins, 1998), and serotonin was shown to be necessary for long-term facilitation in molluscs (Glanzman et al., 1989). Overlapping of neurites of the Pd4 cell and giant parietal cells suggests that serotonin released from the Pd4 cell can affect presynaptic activation to the withdrawal interneuron sensory neurons, or synapses between sensory neurons and withdrawal interneurons shown to be present in the same neuropile (Arakelov, Marakjueva, & Palikhova, 1991).

Participation of individual modulatory cells in modifications of behaviour was shown in different invertebrates. Intracellular stimulation of identified cerebral *Aplysia* neurons CB1 produced facilitation of the EPSPs from siphon-sensory neurons to motor neurons, suggesting participation of these individual serotonergic cells in the mediation of presynaptic facilitation (Mackey, Kandel, & Hawkins, 1989). There are several published examples of identified neuromodulatory interneurons, which serve the reinforcing function during associative learning. The octopaminergic VUMmx1 neuron, which mediates the reinforcing function of rewards in honeybees during olfactory conditioning, innervates most principal brain neuropiles with axo-dendritic arborizations. This neuron responds to sucrose (reward) with long-lasting excitation, and its depolarization substitutes for the reward in single-trial conditioning (Hammer & Menzel, 1995). It was clearly shown in cultured *Aplysia* neurons that temporal pairing of presynaptic activity and serotonin application enhances facilitation at sensory-motor neuron synapses (Bao et al., 1998 Eliot, Hawkins, Kandel, & Schacher, 1994). Activation of an identified modulatory cell (slow oscillator) in *Lymnaea stagnalis* elicited associative enhancement of the fictive feeding response (Kemenes, Staras, & Benjamin, 1997).

The neuromodulatory serotonergic cell Pd4 in *Helix* innervates neuropiles of pedal, pleural, parietal, and visceral ganglia. It responds with long-lasting excitation to short noxious stimuli, which serve as a reinforcement in aversive conditioning (Balaban et al., 1987; Zakharov et al., 1995). Intracellular depolarization of this cell changed the effectiveness of synaptic input in withdrawal interneurons, while the hyperpolarization of the Pd4 cell decreased the rate of spontaneous activity in interneurons. Conditional depolarization of the Pd4 cell elicits a pairing-specific increase in the amplitude of synaptic inputs to premotor withdrawal interneurons, suggesting an increase in behavioural response. We suggest here that a single Pd4 cell can trigger the aversive reinforcement in the snail. This cell can be viewed as a "delegate" neuron, representing activity in a large group of modulatory serotonergic cells receiving sensory inputs from all parts of the body, but which do not send processes to the target (parietal) neuropile.

Observed differences in paired versus unpaired treatments may be attributed to activity-dependent increase of presynaptic release due to the fact that serotonin application alone is effective in isolated nervous system and in cultured neurons of molluscs (Bao et al., 1998; Eliot et al., 1994). Still, a prolonged depolarization in a postsynaptic neuron also may contribute to the potentiation of response due to coincidence of activity in presynaptic and postsynaptic neurons in a Hebbian way. Additional experiments are necessary to distinguish these possibilities.

ACKNOWLEDGEMENTS

The author is indebted to his collaborators Drs O.A. Maksimova, I.S. Zakharov, and N.I. Bravarenko for their participation and help. The work was partly supported by grants from Russian Foundation for Basic Research, INTAS grant 99–1481, and Howard Hughes Medical Institute grant #75195–544301.

REFERENCES

Adamo, S.A., & Chase, R. (1988). Courtship and copulation in the terrestrial snail *Helix aspersa*, *Canadian Journal of Zoology*, *66*, 1446–1453.

Adamo, S.A., & Chase, R. (1991). "Central arousal" and sexual responsiveness in the snail, *Helix aspersa*. *Behavioural and Neural Biology*, *55*, 194–213.

Arakelov, G.G., Marakjueva, I.V., & Palikhova, T.A. (1991). Structural and functional analysis of monosynaptic connections between identified neurons of *Helix lucorum*. In D.A. Sakharov & W. Winlow (Eds.), *Simpler nervous systems* (pp. 258–269). Manchester: Manchester University Press.

Asratjan, E.A. (1970). *Essays on physiology of conditioned reflexes*. Moscow: Nauka.

Balaban, P.M. (1979). A system of command neurons in snail's escape behavior. *Acta Neuurobiologica Experimentalis*, *39*, 97–107.

Balaban, P.M. (1983). Postsynaptic mechanism of withdrawal reflex sensitization in the snail, *Journal of Neurobiology*, *14*, 365–375.

Balaban, P.M. (1987). Serotonin-induced changes of the action potential duration in functionally different neurons of the snail. *Neurophysiologia*, *19*, 316–322.

Balaban, P.M. (1991). Command neurons and decision making. In D.A. Sakharov & W. Winlow (Eds.), *Simpler nervous systems* (pp. 360–374), Manchester: Manchester University Press.

Balaban, P., & Bravarenko, N. (1993). Long-term sensitization and environmental conditioning in terrestrial snails. *Experimental Brain Research*, *96*, 487–493.

Balaban, P.M., & Chase, R. (1989). Selfstimulation in snails. *Neuroscience Research and Communication*, *4*, 139–146.

Balaban, P.M., Maksimova, O.A., & Galanina, G.N. (1985a). Cellular responses during elaboration of two-way conditioned reaction in snail. *Zhurnal vysshej nervnoj dejatelnosti I.P.Pavlov*, *35*, 497–503.

Balaban, P.M., Vehovszky, A., Maksimova, O.A., & Zakharov, I.S. (1987). Effect of 5,7-dihydroxytryptamine on the food-aversive conditioning in the snail Helix *lucorum* L. *Brain Research*, *404*, 201–210.

Balaban, P.M., & Zakharov, I.S. (1992). *Learning and development: Common basis of two phenomena* (in Russian). Moscow: Nauka.

Balaban, P., Zakharov, I.S., & Chistyakova, M. (1991). Integrative role of serotonin in avoidance and feeding behavior in the terrestrial snail. In W. Winlow, O.S. Vinogradova, & D.A. Sakharov (Eds.), *Signal molecules and behavior* (pp. 77–100), Manchester: Manchester University Press.

Balaban, P.M., Zakharov, I.C., & Matz, V.N. (1985b). Method of vital selective staining of serotonergic nerve cells by 5,7-dihydroxytryptamine. *Dokladi Akademii Nauk USSR*, *283*, 735–738.

Bao, J.-X., Kandel, E.R., & Hawkins, R.D. (1998). Involvement of presynaptic and postsynaptic mechanisms in a cellular analogue of classical conditioning at Aplysia sensory-motor neuron synapses in isolated cell culture. *Journal of Neuroscience*, *18*, 458–466.

Baumgarten, H.G., Jenner, S., Bjorklund, A., Klemm, H.P., & Schlossberger, H.G. (1982). Serotonin neurotoxin. In N.N. Osborne (Ed.), *Biology of serotonergic transmission* (pp. 249–277). New York: John Wiley.

Bravarenko, N.I., Gusev, P.V., Balaban, P.M., & Voronin, L.L. (1995). Postsynaptic induction of long-term synaptic facilitation in snail central neurons. *Neuroreport*, *6*, 1182–1186.

Carew, T.J. (1989). Developmental assembly of learning in *Aplysia*. *TINS*, *12*, 389–394.

Carew, T.J., Hawkins, R.D., & Kandel, E.R. (1983). Differential classical conditioning of a defensive withdrawal reflex in Aplysia californica, *Science*, *219*, 397–400.

Croll, R.P. (1998). Distribution of monoamines within the central nervous system of the juvenile pulmonate snail, *Achatina fulica*. *Brain Research*, *460*, 29–49.

Crow, T., & Alkon, D.L. (1978). Retention of associative behavioural change in Hermissends. *Science*, *201*, 1239–1241.

Davis, W.J., & Jillette, R. (1978). Neural correlates of behavioral plasticity in command neurons of *Pleurobranchaea*. *Science*, *199*, 801–804.

Eaton, R.C. (1984). *Neural mechanisms of startle behaviour*. New York: Plenum Press.

Elekes, K., Hiripi, L., & Nemcsok, J. (1977). Ultrastructural effects of 6-hydroxydopamine and 5,6-dihydroxytryptamine on the central nervous system of freshwater mussel *Anodonta cygnea* L. *Acta Biologica Academy of Science Hungary*, *28*, 259–272.

Eliot, L.S., Hawkins, R.D., Kandel, E.R., & Schacher, S. (1994). Pairing-specific, activity-dependent presynaptic facilitation at *Aplysia* sensory-motor neuron synapses in isolated cell culture. *Journal of Neuroscience*, *14*, 368–383.

Galanina, G.N., Zakharov, I.S., Maximova, O.A., & Balaban, P.M. (1986). Role of giant serotonergic cell of the snail cerebral ganglia in feeding behavior. *Zhurnal vysshej nervnoj dejatelnosti I.P.Pavlov*, *36*, 110–116.

Gelperin, A. (1981). Synaptic modulation by identified serotonin neurons. In B. L. Jacobs, A. Gelperin (Eds.), *Serotonin nerotransmission and behaviour* (pp. 288–307), Cambridge, MA: MIT Press.

Gillette, R., & Davis, W.J. (1977). The role of the metacerebral giant neuron in the feeding behavior of Pleurobranchaea. *Journal of Comparative Physiology*, *116*, 125–159.

Glanzman, D.L., Mackey S.L., Hawkins, R.D., Dyke, A.M., Lloyd, P.E., & Kandel, E.R. (1989). Depletion of serotonin in the nervous system of *Aplysia* reduces the behavioural enhancement of gill withdrawal as well as the heterosynaptic facilitation produced by tail shock. *Journal of Neuroscience*, *9*, 4200–4013.

Glover, J.C., & Kramer, A.P. (1982). Serotonin analog selectively ablates identified neurons in the leech embryo. *Science*, *216*, 317–319.

Granzow, B., & Kater, S.B. (1977). Identified higher-order neurons controlling the feeding motor program of *Helisoma. Neuroscience, 2,* 1049–1063.

Hammer, M., & Menzel, R. (1995). Learning and memory in the honeybee. *Journal of Neuroscience, 15,* 1617–1630.

Hawkins, R.D. (1984). A cellular mechanism of classical conditioning in Aplysia, *Journal of Experimental Biology, 112,* 113–128.

Hawkins, R.D., Abrams, T.W., Carew, T.J., & Kandel, E.R. (1983). A cellular mechanism of classical conditioning in Aplysia: Activity-dependent amplification of presynaptic facilitation, *Science, 219,* 400–405.

Kandel, E.R., & Schwartz, J.H. (1982). Molecular biology of learning: Modulation of transmitter release, *Science, 218,* 433–443.

Kemenes, G., Staras, K., & Benjamin, P.R. (1997). In vitro appetitive classical conditioning of the feeding response in the pond snail *Lymnaea stagnalis. Journal of Neurophysiology, 78,* 2351–2362.

Klein, M., Camardo, J., & Kandel, E.R. (1982). Serotonin modulates a specific potassium current in the sensory neurons that show presynaptic facilitation, *Proceedings of the National Academy of Sciences USA, 79,* 5713–5717.

Kobayashi, M., Muneoka, Y., & Fujiwara, M. (1980). The modulatory actions of the possible neurotransmitter in the molluscan radular muscles. In K.S. Rozsa (Ed.), 22, *Advanced Physiological Science. Neurotransmitters in invertebrates* (pp. 319–337). Budapest: Akademiai Kiado.

Kupfermann, I., Cohen, J., Mandelbaum, D.E., Schonberg, M., Susswein, A.J., & Weiss, K.R. (1979). Functional role of serotonergic neuromodulation in Aplysia. *Proceedings of the Federation of American Societies for Experimental Biology, 38,* 2095–2106.

Kupfermann, I., & Weiss, K. (1978). The command neuron concept. *Behavioural Brain Science, 1,* 3-15.

Kupfermann, I., & Weiss, K.R. (1982). Activity of an identified serotonergic neuron in free moving Aplysia correlates with behavior arousal, *Brain Research, 241,* 334–337.

Litvinov, E.G., Maximova, O.A., Balaban, P.M., & Masinovsky, B.P. (1976). Defensive conditioned reaction in a snail Helix lucorum. *Zhurnal vysshej nervnoj dejatelnosti, 26,* 203–206.

Lloyd, Ph. E. (1980). Mechanism of action of 5-hydroxytryptamine and endogenous peptide on neuromuscular preparation in the snail *Helix aspersa, Journal of Comparative Physiology, 139,* 341–347.

Mackey, S.L., Kandel, E.R., & Hawkins, R.D. (1989). Identified serotonergic neurons LCB1 and RCB1 in the cerebral ganglia of Aplysia produce presynaptic facilitation of siphon sensory neurons. *Journal of Neuroscience, 9,* 4227–4235.

Maksimova, O.A. (1979). Elaboration in the snail of an instrumental food-searching conditioned reflex with a two-way connection. *Zhurnal vysshej nervnoj dejatelnosti, 29,* 793–800.

Maksimova, O.A., & Balaban, P.M. (1983). *Neural mechanisms of behavioral plasticity* (in Russian). Moscow: Nauka.

Malyshev, A., Bravarenko, N., & Balaban, P. (1997). Dependence of synaptic facilitation post-synaptically induced in snail neurons on season and serotonin level. *Neuroreport, 8,* 1179–1182.

Maximova, O.A., & Balaban, P.M. (1984). Neuronal correlates of aversive learning in command neurons for avoidance behaviour of *Helix lucorum* L. *Brain Research, 292,* 139–149.

Mpitsos, G.J., & Collins, S.D. (1978). Learning: A model system for physiological studies. *Brain Research, 199,* 497–506.

Nolen, T.G., & Hoy, R.R. (1984). Initiation of behaviour by single neurons: The role of behavioural context. *Science, 226,* 992–994.

Ocorr, K.A., Walters, E.T., & Byrne, J.H. (1985). Associative conditioning analogue selectively increases cAMP levels of tail sensory neurons in Aplysia. *Proceedings of the National Academy of Sciences USA, 82,* 2548–2552.

Ogren, S.O., Johansson, C., Johansson, G., & Archer, T. (1982). Serotonin neurons and aversive conditioning in the rat. *Scandinavian Journal of Physiology* (Suppl. 1), 7–15.

Osborne, N.N. (1984). Putative neurotransmitters and their coexistence in gastropod molluscs. In V. Chan-Palay & S.L. Palay (Eds.), *Coexistence of neuroactive substances in neurons* (pp. 395–410). New York: John Wiley.

Pavlov, I.P. (1927). *Conditioned reflexes, and investigation of the physiological activity of the cerebral cortex.* Oxford: Oxford University Press.

Pavlov, I.P. (1951). Twenty years experience of investigation of higher nervous activity (behaviour) in animals. *I.P. Pavlov's Proceedings, Vol. 5.* Moscow: Akademy of Sciences Press.

Pinsker, H. (1980). Neuroethological analysis of information processing during behaviour. In H.M. Pinsker & W.D. Willis Jr (Eds.), *Information processing in the nervous system.* New York: Raven Press.

Pinsker, H.M., Hening, W.A., Carew, T.J., & Kandel, E.R. (1973). Long-term sensitization of a defensive withdrawal reflex in Aplysia. *Science, 182,* 1039–1042.

Sahley, C., Rudy, J.W., & Gelperin, A. (1981). An analysis of associative learning in a terrestrial mollusc. I. Higher-order conditioning, blocking and transient US pre-exposure effect, *Journal of Comparative Physiology, 144,* 1–8.

Sedden, C.B., Walker, R.J., & Kerkut, G.A. (1968). The localization of dopamine and 5-hydroxytryptamine in neurons of *Helix aspersa. Symposia of the Zoological Society of London, 22,* 19–32.

Sokolov, V.A. (1959). A conditioned reflex in gastropod mollusc, Physa acuta. *Vestnik Leningradskogo Universiteta, N9, Serija Biologicheskaij, 2,* 82–86.

Stepanov, I.I., & Lokhov, M.I. (1986). Dynamics of elaboration of conditioned reflex and differentiation in snail. *Zhurnal vysshej nervnoj dejatelnosti, 36,* 698–706.

Thompson, E.L. (1917). An analysis of the learning process in the snail *Physa gyrina Say. Behaviour Monogrophs, 3,* 89–110.

Vehovzsky, A., Hernadi, L., Elekes, K., & Balaban, P. (1993). Serotonergic input on identified command neurons in *Helix. Acta Biol. Hung., 44,* 97–101.

Vehovzsky, A., Kemenes, G., & Rozsa, K. (1989). Monosynaptic connections between serotonin-containing neurones labelled by 5,6-dihydroxytryptamine-induced pigmentation in the snail *Helix pomatia L. Brain Research, 484,* 404–407.

Walters, E.T., & Byrne, J.H. (1983). Associative conditioning of single sensory neurons suggests a cellular mechanism for learning. *Science, 219,* 405–408.

Weiss, K.R., & Kupfermann, I. (1976). Homology of the giant serotonergic neurons (metacerebral cells) in *Aplysia* and pulmonate molluscs. *Brain Research, 117,* 33–49.

Wieland, S.J., & Gelperin, A. (1983). Dopamine elicits feeding motor program in Limax maximus. *Journal of Neuroscience, 2,* 1735–1745.

Wiersma, C.A.G. (1938). Function of the giant fibers of the central nervous system of the crayfish. *Proceedings of the Society of Experimental Biological Medicine, 38,* 661–662.

Wiersma, C.A.G., & Ikeda, K. (1964). Interneurons commanding swimmeret movements in the crayfish, *Procambarus clarkii (Girard). Comparative Biochemistry and Physiology, 12,* 509–525.

Willows, A.O.D. (1967). Behavioral acts elicited by stimulation of single identifiable brain cells. *Science, 157,* 570–574.

Zakharov, I.S., & Balaban, P.M. (1987). Neural mechanisms of age-dependent changes in avoidance behavior of the snail *Helix lucorum. Neuroscience, 23,* 721–729.

Zakharov, I.S., & Balaban, P.M. (1991). Serotonergic modulation of avoidance behavior in *Helix.* In D.A. Sakharov & W. Winlow (Eds.), *Simpler nervous systems* (pp. 316–329). Manchester: Manchester University Press.

Zakharov, I.S., Ierusalimsky, V.N., & Balaban, P.M. (1995). Pedal serotonergic neurons modulate the synaptic input of withdrawal interneurons in Helix. *Invertebrate Neuroscience, 1,* 41–51.

CHAPTER TWO

Neural processing of visual and auditory information

Barrie J. Frost
Queen's University, Kingston, Ontario, Canada

INTRODUCTION

Over the past decade there has been considerable progress in understanding how the brains of many species process visual and auditory information relevant to their ecological niche. However, it is perhaps the last three decades that have witnessed the truly remarkable advance in our knowledge in these domains, and this has happened because of the enormous volume of dedicated work undertaken by a very large number of neuroscientists around the world. Perhaps the best indication of this blossoming of our knowledge in the field of visual and auditory information processing can be seen by inspecting the huge volume of research targeting these areas that occurs in the *Society of Neuroscience Abstracts* every year.

In the case of vision research the neural structures that have been investigated range from the retina itself, right through to the frontal eye-fields in the cortex. This enormous amount of neuroanatomical territory encompasses at least three major anatomical pathways, over 30 distinct cortical areas, and roughly an equal number of subcortical structures. Moreover, there is a dense pattern of interconnections between many of these areas which poses real problems for understanding all the subsystems and feedback loops that occur, and tracing how "top-down" information flow interacts with "bottom-up" afferent flow. Needless to say, there has also been an incredible number of different techniques brought to bear on many of these problems and they range from immunocytochemistry for pinpointing early gene expression in plasticity, through to the use of functional magnetic resonance imaging (fMRI) to study visual and auditory processing in humans. Given this wealth of information, it goes without saying that the 50-minute talk on which this paper was based, and this paper itself, must be highly selective. For a more detailed review of many of the topics reported here the reader will, wherever possible, be referred to review papers that cover this material in much greater depth in specific subfields. In the talk many more figures were used than can possibly be included in this paper and the reader is referred to the website http://tuatara.psyc.queensu.ca/~sdavid/icp2000.html where these are still available for inspection, and where their origin is referenced (Frost, 2000).

A general point that should be emphasized is that many studies have used particular animals to provide "model systems" in order to reveal important underlying mechanisms of sensory processing. For example, the elegant work of Knudsen and his colleagues (Knudsen & Brainard, 1995) on the Barn Owl have provided us with great insights about how sound localization is accomplished, since this bird not only has exquisite sensitivity to sound position, but has hypertrophied brain structures that allow the underlying neuroanatomy and neurophysiology to be described. Likewise, Suga and his colleagues' work (Riquimaroux, Gaioni, & Suga, 1991; Suga, 1994) on ultrasonic perception in bats has shown how the cortex can decompose the complex signals into salient features and process each of them independently. The processing of song information in songbird brains, the discovery of cells computing time to collision in pigeons and desert locusts, and the analysis of self-produced visual flow fields through locomotion in flies (Krapp & Hengstenberg, 1996), honeybees (Srinivasen, Poteser, & Kral, 1999), and a variety of vertebrates (Frost & Wylie, 2000) have similarly demonstrated the importance of the judicious choice of an experimental animal model to discover the underlying principles employed to solve common information-processing problems.

One of the reasons that various comparative animal models are useful is the fact that the fundamental plans of the visual and auditory systems have been highly conserved through evolution. Even in the case of invertebrate systems we often find that the same or similar algorithms are used for solving similar problems, and that here convergent evolution has forged a similar optimal form of processing. Since I will later give an example of specificity of single cell processing from our work on the pigeon visual system I will also use this animal to illustrate this point.

Figure 1 shows a highly simplified black diagram of the pigeon visual system. It should be noted that the fundamental plan of all vertebrate visual systems can be seen in this diagram. First the pathway shown on a white background, at the top of the figure, is essentially the retina-lateral geniculate nucleus (LGN)-cortical pathway described so extensively in basic textbooks. The middle pathway shown in gray is perhaps more prominent in fish, amphibians, reptiles, and birds, but is still conserved in mammals as well, and likewise converges into telencephalic or cortical structures. Finally, the accessory

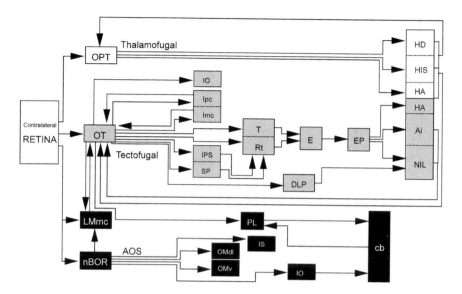

Figure 1.   A schematic diagram of the three major visual pathways in birds. The pathway illustrated at the top is the equivalent pathway to the retino-geniculo-striate pathway in mammals, while the pathway in the middle is the tectofugal pathway (superior colliculus), which also projects to the telencephalon (cortex). The pathway at the bottom is the accessory optic system (AOS), which is also highly conserved and present in mammals. After Frost and Wylie (2000). Copyright © 2000 Academic Press. Reprinted with permission. See Frost and Wylie (2000) for a full description of all structures.

optic system, which has been firmly implicated in the processing of optic flow information, is shown in black at the bottom. This pathway is again highly conserved in all vertebrates and has been shown to process information in the service of the control of posture, locomotion, and possibly navigation.

SINGLE NEURON SPECIFICITY

One of the continuing revelations from many decades of single neuron recording studies of both the visual and auditory systems is the remarkable specificity for certain environmentally relevant attributes that can be found in the brains of many animals. The example I will give here comes from our own work, where we have found that neurons in the dorsal zone of the nucleus rotundus of pigeons (which is putatively homologous to the pulvinar of mammals) compute time to collision of approaching objects. Throughout the animal kingdom the sight of a rapidly approaching object on a direct collision course almost universally signals danger and elicits an escape or avoidance response. When confronted with such a looming stimulus, the visual system must determine precisely the 3D flight path, and compute the time-to-contact of the object, to provide the information necessary for eliciting and controlling the appropriate evasive action (Fishman & Tallarico, 1961; Schiff, Caviness, & Gibson, 1962; Schiff, 1965; Hayes & Saiff, 1967; Tronick, 1967; Bower, Broughton, & Moore, 1970; Ball & Tronick, 1971; Dill, 1974; Yonas et al., 1977; Ingle & Shook, 1983). In a similar vein, it has been shown that large expanding flow fields, such as those produced by locomotion of the animal itself, may provide information that is critical for triggering and timing manoeuvres such as turning, stopping, and landing (Borst & Bahde, 1988a, b; Coggshall, 1972). From behavioural observations in these situations it has been determined that it is the relative retinal expansion velocity, or tau as it is usually designated, which specifies time to contact with the approaching object and provides the best fit to the behavioral data (Lee & Reddish, 1981; Wagner, 1982).

In the nucleus rotundus of pigeons we have recently found cells that are extremely specific in their response tuning. First we studied *only* those cells that responded to an object *approaching on a direct collision course toward the bird*. Usually visual physiologists confine their stimuli to 2D motion patterns presented on a screen and moving in the fronto-parallel plane. Here we used high-level graphics computers to simulate an object (a soccer ball pattern consisting of black and white panels so that the overall luminance was controlled) that could move in any direction in simulated 3D space. Figure 2 shows the fine-grained tuning of a couple of these cells to show just how narrowly tuned they were. This means that if the direct collision path was slightly rotated so that the ball would narrowly miss the pigeon's head these cells' responses dropped off precipitously.

However, the important specificity of these cells was not revealed until we conducted even more detailed tests to reveal which optical parameter of an expanding image these cells were responding to. Figure 3 shows several of the possible parameters the cells might have been responding to, and by varying the size and velocity of the approaching stimuli we were able to show that these cells, which only responded to a directly approaching stimuli, fell neatly into three nonoverlapping classes. Most of the cells were computing the variable tau,

$$\tau = \left(\frac{\theta_t}{\frac{d\theta_t}{dt}} \right),$$

which previous work had shown was advantageous for determining time to collision. Interesting other cells were computing rho,

$$\rho = \left(\frac{d\theta_t}{dt} \right),$$

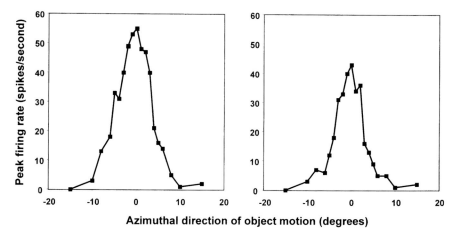

Figure 2.   Fine tuning of two cells located in the pigeon dorsal nucleus rotundus. First these cells were presented with a soccer ball stimulus that moved in 26 directions 45 degrees apart in 3D space, and they only responded to the direct collision course direction. The graphs shown here are the fine-grained tuning curves and show that when the soccer ball, which travelled along a simulated path of 15 metres, was rotated by small amounts each time passing through the centre of the path, the cells reduced their firing substantially. The few degrees of rotation of the path indicate that now the soccer ball would travel in a "near miss" and not collide with the bird.

which is the denominator required for the computation of tau. And finally, another group were calculating eta,

$$\eta = \left(C \times \frac{d\theta_t}{dt} \times e^{a\theta_t} \right),$$

a variable that others had shown was computed by desert locusts, and which was also putatively involved in time to collision decisions. Moreover, all cells that responded selectively to the direct collision course direction fell neatly into one of these three classes, indicating that there were no intermediate levels of tuning and no cells unaccounted for that might otherwise end up in some "junk category". All of this is simply to show that single cell recording studies continue to reveal very important aspects of visual sensory processing, and from a theoretical point of view, this particular finding seems to be a vindication of J.J. Gibson's (1979) assertion that optical expansion can inform us of an approaching object, although Gibson would not have been much interested in the underlying neural mechanism that accomplished such a task. One can only hope that in future more studies will specifically test many of Gibson's other assertions by devising more ecologically valid stimulus patterns.

Timing of the response

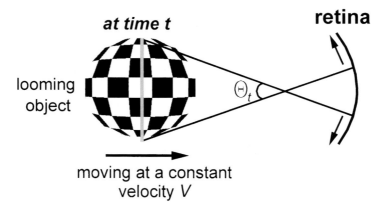

- ## ROE neurons encode

$$\rho = \frac{d\Theta_t}{dt}$$

- ## TAU neurons encode

$$\tau = \frac{\Theta_t}{\dfrac{d\Theta_t}{dt}}$$

- ## ETA neurons encode

$$\eta = C \times \frac{d\Theta_t}{dt} \times e^{\alpha \Theta_t}$$

Figure 3. Shows some of the various optical parameters of expansion that the soccer ball stimulus would undergo if the ball moved at constant velocity toward the pigeon. Data from individual neurons, examples of which can be seen on the website, indicate these looming specific neurons fell neatly into three classes, one group computing tau, and the others either rho or eta. See Sun and Frost (1998), for a full description. This illustrates the remarkable specificity that can be found in some cells in the visual system.

PROCESSING IN THE PRIMATE
GENICULO-STRIATE PATHWAY

In spite of the fact that there have been insights like this gained from the study of subcortical structures and through work on lower vertebrate and invertebrate species, much of visual neuroscience has been focused on the geniculo-striate visual pathway in primates. Figure 4 shows a modified version of Van Essen's diagram of this particular visual pathway (Van Essen, Anderson, & Felleman, 1992). What this figure shows, especially in the cortical flat-mount version, is how much cortical territory is devoted to visual processing, and the large number of separate maps and areas there are in the cortex. Also illustrated in this figure are some of the columnar and slab micro maps that occur within each of the larger retinotopic maps.

One of the questions that has been researched extensively in recent years is the organization of the geniculo-cortical pathway into a dorsal and ventral

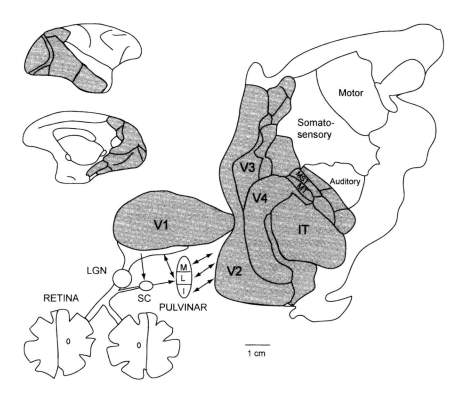

Figure 4. This figure illustrates the organization of the geniculo-striate visual system of primates and the associated cortical areas receiving projections from it (based on a figure from Van Essen, 1985). Note that a very large portion of the entire cortex shown in the flat mount is concerned with visual processing.

stream. This distinction was first elaborated by Ungerleider and Mishkin (1982) and was based on their lesion work that showed deficits in object perception and recognition after lesions to the inferotemporal regions of the cortex, and deficits in spatial location behaviour, with lesions of the parietal cortex. Recently, Milner and Goodale (1995) have suggested that the dorsal stream can best be characterized as processing visual information required for action, whereas the ventral stream is processing information for perception. Much of this work is based on brain damage to human patients, specifically patients with damage to the posterior parietal cortex who seem unable to use information about the size, shape orientation, and location of objects to control reaching and grasping movements (Goodale, Milner, Jacobson, & Carey, 1991; Jakobson, Archibald, Carey, & Goodale, 1991; Perenin & Vighetto, 1988), yet can usually identify and perceive the same objects they cannot grasp. These authors have also described another patient with lesions, where the ventrolateral regions of the occipital lobe are particularly compromised, and who has the opposite dissociation. This patient can produce accurate reaching and grasping movements, but cannot identify or discriminate objects. Figure 5 shows a simplified diagram of these two streams of visual information processing. Milner and Goodale (1995) concluded that spatial information, especially that required for the guidance of visual action (and of which we may be quite unaware), is processed in the dorsal stream, and the representation of objects that may be more closely related to conscious perception is processed in the ventral stream.

VENTRAL STREAM PROCESSING

Using single unit recording studies in awake behaving monkeys, Logothetis and his colleagues explored the specificity of some of the inferior temporal (IT) regions in detail, including the superior temporal polysensory area. It should be remembered, however, that the IT is interconnected with both the prestriate cortex, the temporopolar and prefrontal cortex, and also with the limbic system. Not only are many IT neurons sensitive to various three-dimensional objects (Tanaka, 1997), but this region also possesses many neurons that respond to human and monkey faces, hands, and other body parts (Gross, 1994). Some IT neurons show very clear selectivity for specific views of objects as though they were coding the object in one of several canonical views. Figure 6 shows the responses of some of these IT neurons to complex objects, in this case artificial wire-frame objects (Logothetis, 1998). Some neurons appear to be responding to a simple or moderately complex element in the total figure as shown in Figure 6(a) and (b), whereas other cells are responding to the whole gestalt shape, where even the removal of a single element dramatically reduces their response (see Figure 6c and d).

Perhaps as interesting as the specificity itself is the observation that Leopold and Logothetis (1996) have made of a steady progression of cells

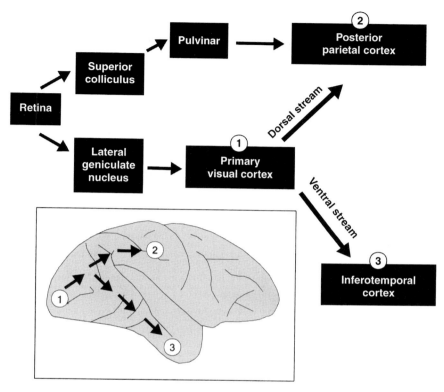

Figure 5.   The dorsal and ventral streams in the primate cortex. Reprinted from *Current Biology*, *8*, Goodale, 1998, 'Visuomotor control: Where does vision end and action begin?' R489–R491. Copyright (1998), with permission from Elsevier Science.

that correlate with perception as one moves from area V1 through V4 to IT and the superior temporal sulcus (STS). Using a binocular rivalry paradigm they found that only a very small proportion of cells in the striate cortex changed their activity during perceptual alternations. In V4, however, 38% of cells were modulated with the monkey's report of alternation, one third of which were more active during the nonreported stimulus, and two thirds more active to the perceived stimulus. They hypothesized that those neurons more active when the stimulus was not reported may indeed have been responsible for the inhibitory mechanisms thought to suppress one of the rival stimuli. In the inferior temporal cortex, however, 90% of cells responded contingent on the perceptual dominance of the effective stimulus and none were responsive to the suppressed stimulus.

Making similar use of the binocular rivalry phenomenon used in conjunction with fMRI, Tong, Nakayama, Vaughan, and Kanwisher (1998) were able to show that similar processing appears to occur in the human ventral stream.

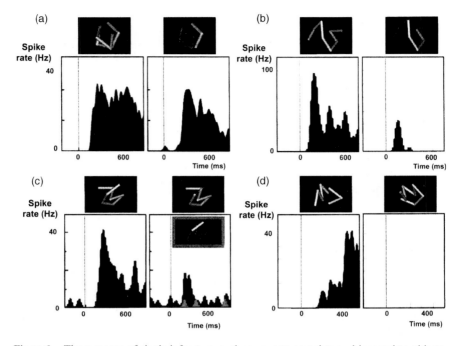

Figure 6.   The response of single inferotemporal neurons to complete and incomplete objects. (a) and (b) show recordings from cells that respond to simple (a), or moderately complex (b) features. (c) and (d) show that these cells require the complete or near-complete figure to fire optimally. Note that removing even a single line element in (c) can almost abolish the firing of this neuron. Reprinted from *Current Opinion in Neurobiology*, *8*, Logothetis, 1998, 'Object vision and visual awareness.' 536–544. Copyright (1998), with permission from Elsevier Science.

They presented images of a human face to one eye of their subjects and a house to the other eye. In localizer scans where the same house image was externally alternated with the face image, differential activation was seen respectively in the fusiform face area (FFA) associated with presentation of the face, and the parahippocampal place area (PPA) for presentation of the house stimulus. When rivalry switches "from face to house" percepts and from "house to face" percepts where analyzed separately, there was increased activity in the appropriate cortical area; FFA for perceptual switches from "house to face" and PPA for switches "from face to house" percepts. This study illustrates very nicely the synergy that appears to be occurring between some of the higher-order visual physiology performed on monkeys and the studies that are now possible with the fMRI technique, a trend we will undoubtedly see more of in the first part of this century. Some typical results from this study are shown on the website.

PROCESSING IN THE DORSAL STREAM

An example of how different perceptual effects in conjunction with fMRI can show visual processing activity in the dorsal cortical stream has recently been demonstrated by Goebel, Khorram-Sefat, Muckli, Hacker, and Singer (1998) using various motion phenomena. In this study they used static stimuli, objective motion, apparent motion employing subjective contours, and controls for flicker and subjective contours themselves. Four of these conditions are shown in Figure 7a. The fMRI responses in Figure 7b show that in area V1 all stimuli produce a substantial increase in activation, whereas in area MT/MST only the motion and flickering stimuli produce a substantial response and the static control produces very little activity at all. Again this study indicates how the combined use of fairly well-established perceptual studies in conjunction with the new imaging studies can confirm that processing studied in detail in animal models is present in humans as well.

Recent advances in fMRI have also allowed investigators to produce accurate maps of the retinotopic projections and functional organization of the human cortex. With sophisticated image-processing techniques the raw fMRI scans can be unfolded to produce the equivalent to cortical flat-mounts obtained on animals through histological means. When this is done the separate cortical areas can be localized accurately on the inflated brain and compared between individuals and other primate species. Space does not permit the reproduction of these patterns here but the reader is referred to the website containing the slides used in my talk presented at the International Congress of Psychology in Stockholm (Frost, 2000). Tootell, Hadjikhani, Mendola, Marrett, and Dale (1998), using fairly simple sine wave grating patterns of different spatial frequencies, and perimetry stimuli, have been able to provide us with fairly good maps of V1, V2, VP, V3A, V4, LOC and LOP, but the many associated areas around MT have yet to be differentiated. Several studies have taken localization even further by attempting to define those areas of cortex involved when human participants imagine stimuli (Kosslyn, Thompson, Kim, & Alpert, 1995). Although there are still many open questions in this regard, some studies have indeed found that even V1 may be activated in retinotopic co-ordinates when humans are imagining stimuli. With all the massive feedforward and feedback connections that are known to exist between various visual processing regions, and especially the cortex itself, this is hardly surprising.

As mentioned earlier, one of the more recent ideas to have emerged concerning processing in the retino-geniculo-striate system is that the dorsal and ventral streams, rather than mediating the "What" and "Where" as originally proposed by Ungerleider and Mishkin (1982), are processing visual information for "perception" and "action". Milner and Goodale (1995) propose that the dorsal stream is processing visual information required for action (such as

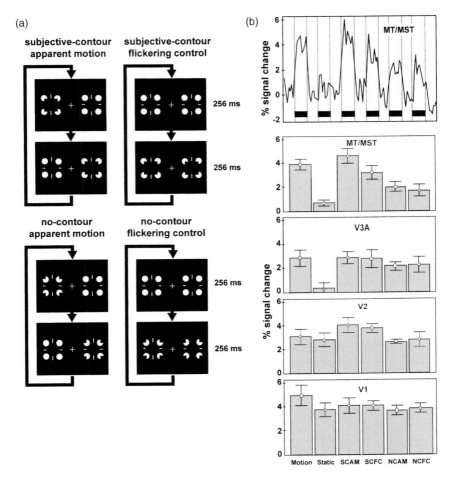

Figure 7. The effect of different motion stimuli on the fMRI measured activation in various cortical brain sites in the dorsal stream pathway. Panel (a) shows some of the stimulus conditions including the use of cognitive contours, while (b) shows changes in MT/MST to the various classes of motion stimuli. It can be seen that most stimuli produce a response in V1, whereas only motion and flicker stimuli produce significant amounts of activation in MT. From Goebel, Khorram-Sefat, Muckli, & Singer (1998), 'The constructive nature of vision: Direct evidence from functional magnetic resonance imaging studies of apparent motion and motion imagery.' *European Journal of Neuroscience, 10,* with permission from Blackwell Science.

reaching, grasping, fixating, etc.) while the ventral stream is involved in processing for perception. In a study designed to mediate this debate Aglioti, DeSouza, and Goodale (1995) measured subjects' grip aperture while they were picking up stimuli perceptually modified by Tichner's illusion. In this case, viewing two identical circles or discs while one is surrounded by a set of smaller circles and the other is surrounded by a set of larger circles, produces a striking illusion that the two physically identical inner circles are quite unequal in size, the one surrounded by small circles appearing much larger than the other. So the question Aglioti et al. (1995) asked was "is grip aperture, which is known to scale beautifully to the size of objects to be picked up, affected by the illusion or not?" Using a 3D version of the Tichner's illusion they first performed a psychophysical task to determine the size where real discs looked perceptually identical (even though they weren't, due to the illusory effect of the surrounding context). Then they measured grip aperture while the participants picked up discs which either appeared perceptually identical, but were physically different, in size, or discs which appeared perceptually different, but were really physically identical. Figure 8 shows that subjects' grip aperture was very little affected by the illusory perceptions and instead was determined basically by the true size of the disc. Thus on trials where the two discs were perceived as being the same size they nevertheless opened their grip wider for the larger disc than the smaller one. Remarkably, this grip aperture effect held whether or not the two discs were judged to be the same size, or when they were judged to be different (Figure 8b). Aglioti et al. conclude that these results are best understood if one assumes that the dorsal stream is processing visual information for action where real size is important for the execution of appropriate motor acts, and that it is the ventral stream where the contextual perceptual (illusory) effects are likely to be taking place. However, recent evidence by Franz, Gegenfurtner, Bülthoff and Fahle (2000) is at variance with this finding.

CORTICAL MICROSTIMULATION

Often advances in our understanding occur as the result of the development of new techniques, and this is especially true of the cortical microstimulation techniques developed by Newsome and his colleagues at Stanford. For the past four decades there has been considerable debate about the significance of the specificity one sees in single cell recording studies for the determination of perceptual experience. Obviously, any simple stimulus will stimulate many neurons in multiple parts of the visual system and it is often assumed that the population response is what will determine the perceptual experience. But the question remains: How big is the population of neurons that is involved? Is it small or incredibly large? This debate has occurred in many forms over the years and is often jokingly referred to when discussing the combinatorial improbability of finding neurons such as "grandmother" cells or "yellow Volkswagen" detectors. For an excellent recent review of this problem the reader is referred to Lennie (1998). What Newsome and his colleagues did was to carefully record from cells in cortical area MT of monkeys to determine that they were in a column, and then at the same time determine the psychophysical threshold of the monkey to see movement in the particular direction coded by those cells, using stimuli centred over the receptive field area. They did this by systematically changing the proportion of dots moving

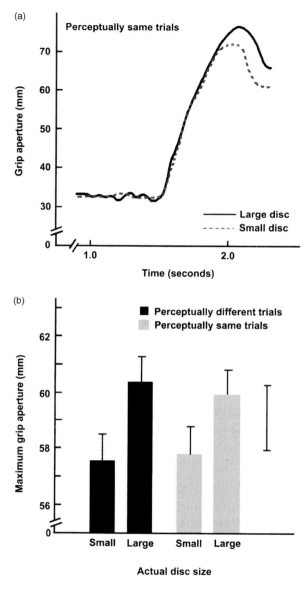

Figure 8. (a) Shows representative grip aperture of a subject picking up a large disc and small disc he had judged to be identical in size (even though they were physically different). (b) Mean maximum grip aperture of 14 subjects. The grey bars indicate aperture where the two discs were judged to be perceptually the same, and the white bars where they were judged to be perceptually different. Note that the grip setting, putatively processed by the dorsal stream, is not "fooled" by the illusion. Reprinted from *Current Biology*, 5, Anglioti, DeSouza, & Goodale, 1995, 'Size-contrast illusions deceive the eye but not the hand.' 679–685, Copyright (1995), with permission from Elsevier Science.

in the preferred direction while the remaining dots moved in random directions, until the monkey reliably reported motion direction. Then, while the monkey repeated the psychophysical experiment, they applied microstimulation of a few microamps to the column where the electrode was located. By this method they were able to shift the psychophysical threshold substantially. In another experiment DeAngelis, Cumming, and Newsome (1998) used a very similar approach, but this time they applied microstimulation to modify the depth perception in alert monkeys. Using random dot stereograms covering the monkey's receptive field they manipulated the number of dots having the same disparity (as cells in the cortical column) among many other dots having random disparities, as illustrated in Figure 9. The monkey's eye movements to different fixation targets were used as responses to signal whether he saw the stimulus as "near" or "far", and thus a psychophysical function was obtained by varying the number of dots with the common disparity amongst the random disparity dots. When microstimulation was applied to a column where far disparities were aggregated, the psychophysical function was shifted so that fewer actual "far" disparity points were required for the monkey to "see" the stimulus as "far". Thus like the movement paradigm it can be seen that the monkey's perception is changed when real disparity stimuli additively interact with activity produced by the microstimulation. This produces a systematic shift in the whole psychophysical function of perceived depth, as shown in Figure 9. The important point here is that the microstimulation is very small (about 20 microamps at 200 HZ) and can therefore, according to most estimates, affect only a small number of cells.

THE "BINDING" OR INTEGRATION PROBLEM

One problem that arises from the fact that there are multiple visual pathways, and multiple sites within each pathway where different features may be extracted or attributes processed, is how the unique constellation of features that define an object are tagged and associated together. Hence the "binding problem", which has, indeed, been at the centre of perception ever since the Gestaltists formally brought it to our attention. As many people have pointed out, this problem is not simply one that occurs in the field of perception, but also in memory, and indeed in motor acts themselves. Here the problem is how the individual actions of muscle fibres get composed into the rich repertoire of actions that all animals make so effortlessly. This problem also is related to the combinatorial explosion, which makes it impossible for there to be specificity at the level of every object or pattern we may possibly perceive in a lifetime. Therefore it has long been recognized that the same set of elementary feature analyzers must be used to construct the many different perceptions and relations we perceive. Some form of assembly code is needed and then the complex objects and relations of the world can be signalled by

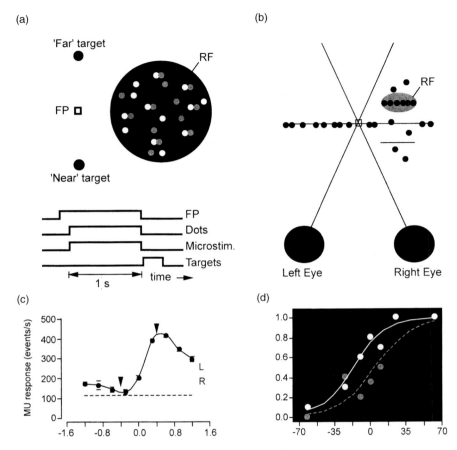

Figure 9. (a) Shows the stimulus set up and the temporal pattern of fixation stimuli, random dot displays, microstimulation, and response targets. (b) Shows the top view to explain the monkey's view of the stimuli. (c) Shows the disparity tuning curve at the site of stimulation. (d) Shows the two psychophysical functions obtained, "with" (filled circles), and "without" (open circles) concurrent microstimulation. Note how the microstimulation and real disparities combine in an additive fashion to influence the monkey's depth perception. Reprinted by permission from *Nature* (DeAngelis, Cumming, & Newsome, 1998) copyright (1998) Macmillan Magazines Ltd.

the coordinated activity in an ensemble of neurons. As Singer et al. (1997) point out, the requirements for the generation of an integrating assembly are that; (a) feature selective neurons with the sort of specificities we have seen revealed in so many experiments can be associated into numerous different assemblies (much like subroutines can be used extensively in many different programs); (b) this group is constructed in a context-dependent way using gestalt principles so that particular objects always excite the same assembly; and (c) then the joint responses of neurons constituting an assembly need to be labelled so that they themselves can be used at subsequent stages of processing. How these assemblies are formed has been the question of much theorizing and debate, but recent advances in the field of vision have suggested that assemblies may be tagged by the synchronization of the firing rate of feature specific neurons. This idea arose from direct demonstration that many neurons do not fire continuously but in repetitive bursts, and that synchronization occurs over a considerable cortical distance, and even between hemispheres. From the time when lateral cortical connections, often of a hypercolumn spacing (Rockland & Lund, 1982, 1983), were suggested as a possible mechanism for sewing together continuous features, such as an extended line, it has been a distinct possibility that these would also induce a pacemaker-like synchronization, where both spatial and temporal summation could conjunctively lead to mutual facilitation (say, from both ends of a line). Moreover it has been pointed out by Singer et al. (1997) that this form of interactivity can reduce the possibility of false conjunctions, enhance processing speed, and thus encode relations rapidly.

Singer et al. (1997) illustrate these principles well in Figure 10, which is taken from their review. Figure 10a shows an array of cells that respond specifically to oriented line segments where neurons with similar orientations are likely to be grouped if they are colinear. Figure 10b shows how colinear receptive fields should become synchronized, as has been reported in the literature. Thus cells 1 and 2, 3 and 4, and 5 and 6 become synchronized. If, for example, the line segments move coherently, which we know is perhaps the strongest perceptual force for binding, cells in area MT that prefer the same direction of motion would also become synchronized. This is illustrated in Figure 10d, where cells I, II, III, and IV would be synchronized and others would not. This would indeed mean that the stimulus pattern "Z" as shown in 10e would be the pattern that would lead to synchronization in all elements and result in the unambiguous percept. Many other examples are to be found in the Singer et al. (1997) review and additional figures of interest used in my talk appear on the website (Frost, 2000).

AUDITORY PROCESSING

Just as multiple areas for visual processing have been described in the visual system of animals, so also have auditory physiologists and anatomists identified multiple tonotopic areas in the monkey cortex. Following early work by Merzenich and Brugge (1973) who described several separate tonotopic cortical maps, these areas have been confirmed by subsequent histochemical analyses and consist of two–three core areas and several surrounding belt areas and para belt areas. Recent work by Rauschecker (1998) and his colleagues has suggested that, like the visual system, the auditory system appears to be organized both in series and in parallel. These in turn may be arranged into a dorsal stream that seems to be concerned with processing auditory

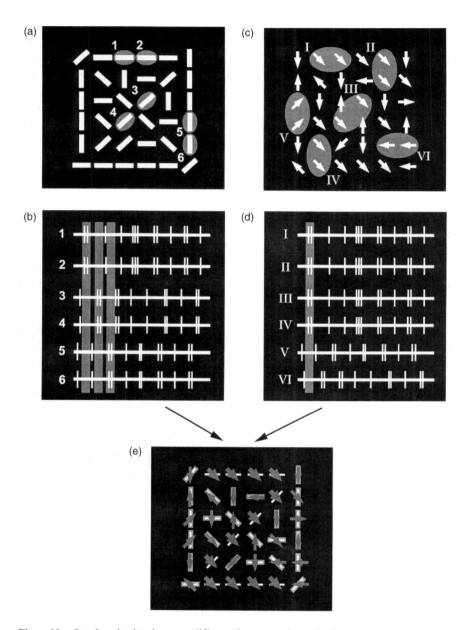

Figure 10. Synchronization between different feature analyzers indicates how they might be bound together into assemblies representing specific objects. See text for details. Reprinted from *Trends in Cognitive Science*, *1*, Singer et al., 1997, 'Neuronal assemblies: Necessity, signature and detectability.' 252–261. Copyright (1997), with permission from Elsevier Science.

spatial information, and a ventral stream that is specialized for processing auditory patterns, including communication sounds and speech. Just as visual cortical neurons were hard to drive with discrete light spots, cells in A1 are hard to drive with pure tone stimuli. By broadening the bandwidth of frequency-centred sound bursts many more cells can be driven. This is like the size (spatial frequency) specificity seen in visual cortical neurons, and the frequency-modulated specificity found by Whitfield and Evans (1965) is somewhat akin to orientation or directional specificity. In terms of the micro-maps seen in the visual cortex it appears that bandwidth is organized orthogonally to the tonotopic organization. It should be noted that both band-passed noise bursts and FM sweeps are ubiquitous elements in sound communication signals across a broad spectrum of animal species. Indeed, in the lateral belt of the auditory cortex many cells respond to either component of monkey calls or to specific call patterns. In many cases these cells responded outside the frequency tuning range of the cell when it was combined with frequencies inside the tuning range. In other cases the temporal order was extremely important, as others have found in bird-song. Furthermore, temporal summation occurs over relatively long time intervals of the order of hundreds of milliseconds, indicating that long time-course patterns are the critical features driving the response. One might be allowed a speculation here, that maybe the feature binding synchronization seen in many visual neurons is also the mechanism that is involved in the integration of the separate features that constitute a complex vocal signal.

Sound localization also requires the processing of spectrally complex information and sounds utilizing the spatial cues of interaural time, interaural intensity, and spectral cues played over headphones have produced heavy signs of positron emission tomography (PET) activation of parietal areas, where previously it was considered only visual information was processed. Either the same or adjacent areas also appear to be processing sounds moving in space (Weeks, Tian, Wessinger, Cohen, Hallett, & Rauschecker, 1997). These studies also suggest that the dorsal stream might be involved in processing auditory spatial information, as Rauschecker has suggested. A summary diagram of these pathways and their arrangement is presented on the website (Frost, 2000).

ANALYSIS OF TEMPORAL STRUCTURE IN THE AUDITORY SYSTEM

In the study of visual processing the invention of stimulus patterns that help elucidate underlying mechanisms of analysis has been critical for further understanding. One of these has been Julesz's random dot stereograms, which allowed the presentation of retinal disparities isolated from other figural or surface features of objects (Julesz, 1971). In a similar vein random dot kinematograms allowed the isolation of pure motion stimuli in the absence of other visual features (Frost, Cavanagh, & Morgan, 1988). For a very long time auditory psychophysicists and physiologists have explained pitch perception by the spectral analysis carried out in the cochlea, where frequency components produce activity in different places in relation to their frequencies, and that is why pure tone stimuli have been used so extensively. However, if one uses more "natural" sounds, such as a musical note that is rich in harmonics, and then filters out many of the low-frequency components, the same pitch is perceived. Such effects have resulted in the development of temporal models that associate pitch with the dominant time interval in the neural activity pattern (Patterson, Handel, Yost, & Datta, 1996; Yost, Patterson, & Sheft, 1996). As a consequence these modellers have developed a stimulus in which noise is delayed and added to itself continuously. This is perceived as a tone whose pitch is determined by the frequency of repetitions, mixed in with a background windy noise. Figure 11 shows the neural activity patterns that would be produced for a 62.5 Hz musical note in (a) and a "delay and add" noise stimulus in (b), where noise is replicated every 16 ms to produce a note of the same perceived pitch. Like the regular note, the perceived pitch of the delayed noise stimulus is preserved when it is high-pass filtered.

Temporal models of pitch perception assume that pitch is extracted by an autocorrelation process where a neural pattern is correlated with a delayed version of itself similar to that shown in Figure 12, where it can be seen that there is a dominant concentration of time intervals of 16 ms in both the conventional and noise stimuli.

Recently Griffith, Büchel, Frackowiak, and Patterson (1998) used the delayed noise paradigm and positron emission tomography (PET) to study where temporal regularity might be processed. The "delay-and-add" noise stimuli allowed them to create stimulus patterns that had the same total energy and the same auditory spectra, but different amounts of temporal regularity. The fundamental argument here was that these stimuli should produce equal levels of activity in brain sites prior to temporal integration and very different amounts of activity after temporal integration. First they used delayed noise to produce the perception of a series of notes, which were compared with activity where the temporal regularity was absent but total spectral energy was the same. Results showed that there was increased activation in both primary auditory left and right cortices.

Again using this delay-and-add noise stimulus paradigm these authors produced melodies made up of notes constructed by delay-and-add noise. The control condition had the same spectral energy over time and indeed the same notes, but in this case not arranged into the melody. Such a design aimed to identify the areas of the human listeners that were processing the longer-term time structure, and produced distinct patterns of activation

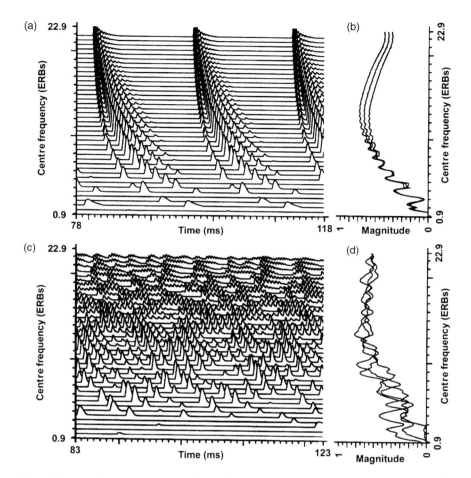

Figure 11. Spectral representations of complex sounds both that have the same pitch and with a frequency of 62.5 Hz. (a) Shows a hypothetical activity pattern in the auditory nerve in response to a musical note and (b) the auditory nerve pattern produced to a delay-and-add noise pattern of the same perceived pitch. See text for explanation. Reprinted from Griffiths et al. (1998), *Nature Neuroscience*, *1*, with permission from Nature Publishing Group.

revealed by the PET in two areas located in the anterior and posterior regions of the temporal lobe distinct from the primary auditory cortex. Figures illustrating these findings are available on the website (Frost, 2000). Griffith et al. (1998) suggest that these areas are most likely analyzing the longer-term time structure in an auditory stream at the level of seconds, but in a manner that is not yet specific to music or speech. This view is quite consistent with human lesion studies where these same areas have been implicated in processing of melody and prosody.

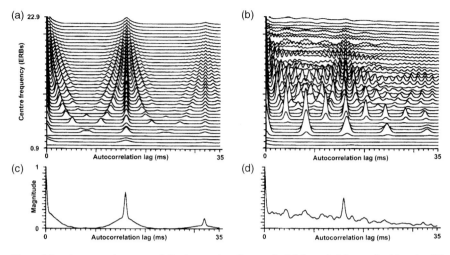

Figure 12. Autocorrelograms of the two notes, the musical (a), and delay-and-add noise (b) shown in Figure 11. (c) and (d) represent the summary autocorrelograms for the two stimuli. Reprinted from Griffiths et al. (1998), *Nature Neuroscience, 1,* with permission from Nature Publishing Group.

SUMMARY AND CONCLUSIONS

There have been an incredible number of papers appearing over the past several years that are related to the area of visual and auditory neuroscience, the topic of this brief review, and space and time constraints have not allowed most of this fine work to be reported here. Rather, studies have been included that illustrate trends in the field. Single unit analysis has continued to reveal very specific levels of processing that in particular are related to the ecological demands of the animals used as model systems. Thus neuroethological studies continue to reveal very specific patterns of selectivity in populations of single cells, for stimuli and events that are critical for the continued survival of an individual species.

A very large body of work has used monkey animal models and coupled these with concurrent behavioural analyses to relate neural activity to both visual and auditory perception and cognition. Both the auditory and visual systems seems best characterized by a complex set of parallel pathways in which there are distinct levels of hierarchical processing. In many cases the description of what is actually processed at any level in these many structures is determined both by what was known previously to have been accomplished in that pathway, and the ingenuity of researchers and their knowledge of the total set of problems to be solved by that system. In this respect we still have a long way to go to identify the site(s) where many of the perceptual constancies are processed, where multiple depth cues are integrated, or where ambiguous interpretations are resolved.

The development of techniques such as fMRI and PET, which permit brain activity to be sampled, albeit somewhat crudely at present, while concurrently monitoring human observers' and listeners' experience and/or psychophysical responses, will surely advance our progress, although many of the studies performed to date are rather confirmatory of what has been deduced from extremely well-controlled animal experiments.

One of the really interesting developments in the field is that the "big questions", such as "how are attributes integrated or bound together?" or "how is experience modified by activity in specific areas of the brain?", are being addressed. A considerable amount of work has also been directed at the whole question of neural plasticity and how genetic expression of the wiring and processing in various brain areas is modified by experience. As we move into the 21st century there is every reason to feel optimistic about our hope to understand the brain, and visual and auditory perception and processing in particular. There are no completely "terra incognito" regions of the brain left, but we should all be humbled in the realization the human brain is arguably the most complex structure in the universe, and presents us with an incredible array of challenges for scientific understanding for the future.

ACKNOWLEDGEMENTS

The author thanks Ms Sharon David for her expert technical assistance in the preparation of this manuscript and the figures, and for preparing the PowerPoint figures for the lecture. These are available on the website at http://tuatara.psyc.queensu.ca/~sdavid/icp2000.html. Thanks are also due to Drs Ken Nakayama, Dave Crewther, Sheila Crewther, Mel Goodale, and Dennis Phillips for helpful discussions about possible material to include in this talk and paper.

REFERENCES

Aglioti, S., DeSouza, J.F.X., & Goodale, M.A. (1995). Size-contrast illusions deceive the eye but not the hand. *Current Biology, 5*, 679–685.

Ball, W., & Tronick, E. (1971). Infant responses to impending collision. *Science, 171*, 818–820.

Borst, A., & Bahde, S. (1988a). Visual information processing in the fly's landing system. *Journal of Comparative Physiology, A, 163*, 167–173.

Borst, A., & Bahde, S. (1988b). Spatio-temporal integration of motion. *Naturwissenschaften, 75*, 265–267.

Bower, T.G.R., Broughton, J.M., & Moore, M.K. (1970). Infant responses to approaching objects: An indicator of response to distal variables. *Perception and Psychophysics, 9*, 193–196.

Coggshall, J.C. (1972). The landing response and visual processing in the milkweed bug, Oncopeltus fasciatus. *Journal of Experimental Biology, 57*, 401–413.

DeAngelis, G.C. (2000). Seeing in three dimensions: The neurophysiology of stereopsis. *Trends in Cognitive Sciences, 4*, 80–90.

DeAngelis, G.C., Cumming, B.G., & Newsome, W.T. (1998). Cortical area MT and the perception of stereoscopic depth. *Nature, 394*, 677–680.

Dill, L.M. (1974). The escape response of the zebra danio (*Brachydanio rerio*). I. The stimulus for escape. *Animal Behaviour, 22*, 771–722.

Fishman, R., & Tallarico, R.B. (1961). Studies of visual depth perception: II. Avoidance reaction as an indicator response in chicks. *Perceptual and Motor Skills, 12*, 251–257.

Franz, V.H., Gegenfurtner, K.R., Bülthoff, H.H., & Fahle, M. (2000). Grasping visual illusions: No evidence for a dissociation between perception and action. *Psychological Science, 11*, 20–25.

Frost, B.J. (2000). *Neural processing of visual and auditory information.* [On-line]. Available: http://tuatara.psyc.queensu.ca/~sdavid/icp2000.html

Frost, B.J., Cavanagh, P., & Morgan, B. (1988). Deep tectal cells in pigeons respond to kinematograms. *Journal of Comparative Physiology, 162*, 639–647.

Frost, B.J., & Wylie, D.W. (2000). A common frame of reference for the analysis of optic flow and vestibular information. In M. Lappe (Ed.), *Neuronal processing of optic flow* (pp. 121–140). London: Academic Press.

Gibson, J.J. (1979). *The ecological approach to visual perception.* Boston: Houghton Mifflin.

Goebel, R., Khorram-Sefat, D., Muckli, L., Hacker, H., & Singer, W. (1998). The constructive nature of vision: Direct evidence from functional magnetic resonance imaging studies of apparent motion and motion imagery. *European Journal of Neuroscience, 10*, 1563–1573.

Goodale, M.A. (1998). Visuomotor control: Where does vision end and action begin? *Current Biology, 8*, R489–R491.

Goodale, M.A., Milner, A.D., Jacobson, L.S., & Carey, D.P. (1991). A neurological dissociation between perceiving objects and grasping them. *Nature, 349*, 154–156.

Griffiths, T.D., Büchel, C., Frackowiak, R.S.J., & Patterson, R.D. (1998). Analysis of temporal structure in sound by the human brain. *Nature Neuroscience, 1*, 422–427.

Gross, C.G. (1994). How inferior temporal cortex became a visual area. *Cerebral Cortex, 4*, 455–469.

Hayes, W.N., & Saiff, E.I. (1967). Visual alarm reactions in turtles. *Animal Behaviour, 15*, 102–108.

Ingle, D.J., & Shook, B.L. (1983). Action-oriented approaches to visuospatial brain functions. In D. Ingle, M. Jeannerod & D. Lee (Eds.), *Brain mechanisms of spatial vision* (pp. 229–258). Dordrecht, The Netherlands: Martinus Nijhoft.

Jakobson, L.S., Archibald, Y.M., Carey, D.P., & Goodale, M.A. (1991). *Neuropsychologia, 29*, 803–809.

Julesz, B. (1971). *Foundation of cyclopean perception.* Chicago: University of Chicago Press.

Knudsen, E.I., & Brainard, M.S. (1995). Creating a unified representation of visual and auditory space in the brain. *Annual Review of Neuroscience, 18*, 19–43.

Kosslyn, S.M., Thompson, W.L., Kim, I.J., & Alpert, N.M. (1995). Topographical representations of mental images in primary visual cortex. *Nature, 378*, 496–498.

Krapp, H.G., & Hengstenberg, R. (1996). Estimation of self-motion by optic flow processing in single visual interneurons. *Nature, 384*, 463–466.

Lee, D.N., & Reddish, P.E. (1981). Plummeting gannets: A paradigm of ecological optics. *Nature, 293*, 293–294.

Lennie, P. (1998). Single units and visual cortical organization. *Perception, 27*, 889–935.

Leopold, D.A., & Logothetis, N.K. (1996). Activity changes in early visual cortex reflect monkey's percepts during binocular rivalry. *Nature, 379*, 549–553.

Logothetis, N. (1998). Object vision and visual awareness. *Current Opinion in Neurobiology, 8*, 536–544.

Merzenich, M.M., & Brugge, J.F. (1973). Representation of the cochlear partition on the superior temporal plane of the macaque monkey. *Brain Research, 50*, 275–296.

Milner, A.D., & Goodale, M.A. (1995). *The visual brain in action.* Oxford: Oxford University Press.

Patterson, R.D., Handel, S., Yost, W.A., & Datta, A.J. (1996). The relative strength of the tone and the noise components in iterated rippled noise. *Journal of the Acoustical Society of America, 100*, 3286–3294.

Perenin, M.T., & Vighetto, A. (1988). Optic ataxia: A specific disruption in visuomotor mechanisms. I. Different aspects of the deficit in reaching for objects. *Brain, 111,* 643–674.

Rauschecker, J.P. (1998). Cortical processing of complex sounds. *Current Opinion in Neurobiology, 8,* 516–521.

Riquimaroux, H., Gaioni, S.J., & Suga, N. (1991). Cortical computational maps control auditory perception. *Science, 251,* 565–568.

Rockland, K.S., & Lund, J.S. (1982). Widespread periodic intrinsic connections in the tree shrew visual cortex. *Science, 214,* 1532–1534.

Rockland, K.S., & Lund, J.S. (1983). Intrinsic laminar lattice connections in primate visual cortex. *Journal of Comparative Neurology, 216,* 303–318.

Schiff, W. (1965). Perception of impending collision: A study of visually directed avoidant behaviour. *Psychological Monographs, 79,* 1–26.

Schiff, W., Caviness, J.A., & Gibson, J.J. (1962). Persistent fear responses in rhesus monkeys to the optical stimulus of "looming". *Science, 136,* 982–983.

Singer, W., Engel, A.K., Kreiter, A.K., Munk, M.H.J., Neuenschwander, S., & Roelfsema, P.R. (1997). Neuronal assemblies: Necessity, signature and detectability. *Trends in Cognitive Sciences, 1,* 252–261.

Srinivasen, M.V., Poteser, M., & Kral, K. (1999). Motion detection in insect orientation and navigation. *Vision Research, 39,* 2749–2766.

Suga, N. (1994). Multi-function theory for cortical processing of auditory information: Implications of single-unit and lesion data for future research. *Journal of Comparative Physiology. A: Sensory, Neural and Behavioral Physiology, 175,* 135–144.

Sun, H.J., & Frost, B.J. (1998). Computation of different optical variables of looming objects in pigeon nucleus rotundus neurons. *Nature Neuroscience, 1,* 296–303.

Tanaka, K. (1997). Mechanisms of visual object recognition: Monkey and human studies. *Current Opinion in Neurobiology, 7,* 523–529.

Tong, F., Nakayama, K., Vaughan, J.T., & Kanwisher, N. (1998). Binocular rivalry and visual awareness in human extrastriate cortex. *Neuron, 21,* 753–759.

Tootell, R.B.H., Hadjikhani, N.K., Mendola, J.D., Marrett, S., & Dale, A.M. (1998). From retinotopy to recognition: fMRI in human visual cortex. *Trends in Cognitive Neurosciences, 2,* 174–183.

Tronick, E. (1967). Approach response of domestic chicks to an optical display. *Journal of Comparative and Physiological Psychology, 64,* 529–531.

Ungerleider, L.G., & Mishkin, M. (1982). Two cortical visual systems. In D. Ingle, M. Goodale, & R. Mansfield (Eds.), *Analysis of visual behaviour.* Cambridge, MA: MIT Press.

Van Essen, D. (1985). Functional organization of primate visual cortex. *Cerebral Cortex, 3,* 259–329.

Van Essen, D.C., Anderson, C.H., & Felleman, D.J. (1992). Information processing in the primate visual system: an integrated systems perspective. *Science, 255,* 419–423.

Wagner, H. (1982). Flow-field variables trigger landing in flies. *Nature, 297,* 147–148.

Weeks, R.A., Tian, B., Wessinger, M., Cohen, L.G., Hallett, M., & Rauschecker, J.P. (1997). Identification of the inferior parietal lobule as the site of auditory space perception in humans. *Neurology, 48,* S30.

Whitfield, I.C., & Evans, E.F. (1965). Responses of auditory cortical neurons to stimuli of changing frequency. *Journal of Neurophysiology, 28,* 655–672.

Yonas, A., Bechtold, A.G., Frankel, D., Gordon, F.R., McRoberts, G., Norcia, A., & Sternfels, S. (1977). Development of sensitivity to information for impending collision. *Perception and Psychophysics, 21,* 97–104.

Yost, W.A., Patterson, R., & Sheft, S. (1996). A time domain description for the pitch strength of iterated rippled noise. *Journal of the Acoustical Society of America, 99,* 1066–1078.

CHAPTER THREE

Epigenesis of the cognitive brain: A task for the 21st century

Scania de Schonen
LCD-CNRS-Paris 5 and INSERM 9935, Hopital Robert Debré, Paris, France

We have presently no definite idea on how information is coded in neural networks, and we have only a poor knowledge of how the various neuro-transmitters and neuromodulators as well as glial cells shape the activity patterns of neural networks. Nevertheless, we can agree, as prudently sum-marized by Kolb in the beginning of his book on *Brain plasticity and behavior* (1995), that structural properties of the brain are important in understanding its functions, that behavioural and mental states correspond to brain states, that mental activity, perception, and action arise from the activity pattern of populations of neurones, and that plasticity is a property of the synapse. The pattern of activity of a neuronal network has a "meaning" for other neuronal networks. Presently it is only possible to interpret the activity of a neurone in terms of meaningful aspects of the environment of the brain (that is in terms of stimuli coming from the environment). But it is becoming possible to interpret the activity of a cortical neurone in terms of "meaningful" aspects of its neuronal environment (see, for instance, Oram, Földiak, Perrett, & Sengpiel, 1998; Singer, 1995).

Even after having agreed on these points, there remains strong disagree-ment, however, about how much of the adult brain organization is due to its postnatal physical-socio-emotional-cognitive environment during develop-ment and how much is due to developmental, purely endogenous, constraints. One of the most well-known disagreements concerns language development. It is claimed that the structure of language cannot be extracted by the brain from the environmental events unless this structure is inscribed in one way or another in the cortex. This is why many studies have investigated whether language is localized early in some cortical regions, before any interaction with the postnatal environment (see, for instance, Bertoncini et al., 1990; Molfese & Molfese, 1979; Witelson, 1995). But it was discovered that the issue of early brain localization of language is not a simple issue. Indeed, children with early left-hemisphere damage can develop language; also peri-natal right-hemisphere damage can have specific consequences on language development (Bates et al., 1997; Vargha-Khadem, & Polkey, 1992; Witelson, 1995). Therefore, it has been concluded too prematurely that the cortex learns language from the environment without any cortical preorganized device. Some points of this polemic are somehow a nonsense. Not because con-nectionist work on neural network models have shown that the same artificial network can learn a piece of language as well as a visual pattern, suggesting that potentially any piece of the human cortex can develop language provided it receives the relevant inputs and sends the relevant outputs. Rather, because early cortical localization might not be the relevant sign of cortical preor-ganization. The possibility of human language might not be inscribed early in a particular region of the cortex, but in a particular sequence of interactions between pre- and postnatal environment and the brain, resulting in successive reorganizations through converging mechanisms. Successive competencies and successive state of functioning of the brain allow the brain to pick up specific information in the environment that in turn transforms the cortical organization into another new tool to interact with other aspects of the environment, and so on. It is this snowball story that constitutes the preor-ganized aspects of language development. In this snowball story, there might be variations within the most frequent trajectory, variations within the most frequent sequence of brain/environment interactions, that can lead to the development of approximately the same competencies.

From Piaget, this description retains three aspects: the snowball metaphor, the assumption that interactions with the environment have an effect on the cortical organization (but it is not easy to discover which aspect of the environment is relevant), and the assumption that endogenous constraints contribute strongly to selecting the successive aspects of the environment with which to interact. Many other claims by Piaget have not resisted empir-ical research. From Changeux's proposal (Changeux & Danchin, 1976; Changeux & Dehaene, 1989; Changeux, Heidmann, & Patte, 1984) our description retains the claim that interactions with the environment select, within a general envelope of possible outcomes, several possible connectivity organizations. Trajectories of cognitive competencies development are partly fully constrained, partly optional.

One of the main purposes of developmental cognitive (or mental) neuro-science is to produce a coherent description of cognitive development and cognitive changes with age (in the wide sense of cognition, that is, including emotional and affective competencies and behaviours) that covers all levels of neurobiology from molecular biology to cognitive behaviour. The concept of epigenesis, of gene expression, the ideas of "strong" and "weak canalization", of "proximate and ultimate causal sequences", have now become meaningful to developmental psychologists (see, for instance, Brauth, Hall, & Dooling, 1991; Elman et al., 1996; Johnson, 2000). There are no genetic constraints without environmental constraints, not vice versa. It is meaningless to fight about a competence being innate or not. Genes are proteins and there are cascades of mechanisms between proteins and mental states and thoughts. Even when the genetic origin of a set of behaviours is known, which is the case, for instance, with Williams syndrome, we have no idea how the particular cognitive profiles observed in children with Williams syndrome emerge from this genetic abnormality (Bellugi, Lichtenberger, Mills, Galaburda, & Korenberg, 1999; Tassabehji et al., 1999).

Another example of the kind of problems that developmental neuroscience has to solve is provided by literacy. Everybody can agree on the fact that reading and writing, which are an invention in human history, can be said to be somewhat learned from the environment and somewhat innate as far as these competencies rely on anatomical pathways, connectivity, and synaptic transmission times that make possible the transformation of various segmentations of sounds into arbitrary signs, various segmentation of the visual array into phonological units, and so on. The reason why reading and writing are so exciting to study is not only because it is useful to rescue children doing poorly at school, but also because here we have a good example of a behaviour that is recent in human history but which has cortical prerequisites, as shown by the presence of developmental cortical abnormalities in dyslexic brains (Galaburda, Sherman, & Rosen, 1985; Geschwind & Galaburda, 1985). Moreover, some aspects of behaviour observed in individuals with phonological dyslexia can be found in murin models (Frenkel, Sherman, Bashan, Galaburda, & LoTurco, 2000).

The crucial issue is "what are the mechanisms of cognitive development?": which genes interact with which other genes and molecules, which neurobiological events interact with which others, which neural networks interact with which environmental events at which time and resulting in which outcome? Which aspects of this mechanism or this neurobiological structure is anticipating the environment with which it will interact and which will be modified by this interaction? The issue has to be addressed at all levels—the molecular, cellular, neuronal networks, neuronal structures, the whole brain, the individual and some aspects of his/her personal story, and all the various environments at these several levels. Not only the issue has to be addressed at all levels from molecular to behavioural level, but it should also be seen as a set of continuous transformations, a series of snowball stories that constitute the cognitive epigenesis. Neuroscientists have shown that signals from the environment have an effect on the organization of neural networks (see "experience-dependent changes" in neurone size, density, dendrite branching, spine density, number of synapses per neurone, and so on; for a review see Kolb, 1995). Therefore it is clear that brain maturation cannot be seen as the primary cause of cognitive development. However, agreeing on bidirectional interactions between brain organization and functioning does not mean that any kind of functioning is made possible by any effects from the environment: developmental trajectory depends on what happens in the previous phases, so cognitive trajectories can be more or less constrained or rigid (Bresson & de Schonen, 1979). Also, the maturation timetable contributes to brain organization to the extent that it makes neural networks sensitive to a given class of signals before other neural networks, with a different possible architecture, become sensitive (de Schonen, Deruelle, Mancini, & Pascalis, 1993; de Schonen & Mathivet, 1989; Turkewitz, 1989, 1993).

Many aspects of brain organization that will play a critical role in cognitive functions are set before any interactions with a social, cognitive, or emotional world take place. Many aspects of cortical organization, for instance, result from an interaction between endogenous mechanisms. For instance, guidance of thalamic projections to cortical cells is partly under the control of a programme intrinsic to cortical cells. Donoghue and Rakic (1999), for instance, demonstrate the existence of molecular distinctions among cells of the embryonic primate neocortex, revealing compartmentalization early in corticogenesis that might anticipate functional cortical specialization. Therefore the formation of appropriate thalamic connections might be influenced by these early functional biases harboured by cortical cells. Transplants of foetal frontal cortex grafted into the occipital cortex of newborn rats receive a substantial thalamic input from nuclei normally projecting to the frontal cortex (Frappe, Roger, & Gaillard, 1999). Now, examples of guidance and constraints from the environment onto the cortical regions can also be given. Differentiation and precise delineation of cytoarchitectonic cortical areas might also depend on the interaction of target regions with thalamic inputs (O'Leary, 1993).

At a later phase of brain development (postnatal), all studies concerned with the fate of cortical activity in the visual or in the auditory cortices in animals partly or fully deprived of vision or audition from birth show that structural organization and functional specialization of the cortex are also dependent on environmental input. Several phenomena of competitions are well known (see, for a review, Turkewitz & Kenny, 1982). But the underlying mechanism of competition itself is not simple and has to be taken into account (for instance, see the normal developmental outcome of vision in infant rats deprived of vision and injected with growth factor; Faggiolini, Pizzorusso, Porciatti, Cenni, & Maffei, 1997).

QUESTIONS

What kind of mechanisms guide the infant brain to pick up a particular aspect of the environmental event rather than others, faces and voices rather leaves or sounds of the tyres on the road in the rain, to bind this piece of information with this other one (why do Italian infants, like British ones, relate lip movements to spoken sounds despite the fact that in the Italian talking environment speech sounds cohere with hand movements almost as much as with lip movements?). Why is perceptual object categorization helped by naming very early in development (see, for instance, Nazzi & Gopnik, in press; Waxman & Hall, 1993; Waxman & Markow, 1995)? How is an infant brain constrained to segment an array into precisely these pieces and not other pieces, to represent an environmental event as it does. Studies like those by Jusczyk's group (Jusczyk, 1999a, b) have discovered, using behavioural techniques, some of the cues on which speech is segmented by infants; studies by Molfese (Molfese, 1990; Molfese, Wetzel, & Gill, 1993) and by Neville's lab (Mills, Coffey, & Neville, 1998; Mills, Coffey-Corina, & Neville, 1997) have shown electrophysiological brain correlates of meaningful versus nonmeaningful speech segments. We are far, however, from being able to follow the neural transformations corresponding to the development of segmentation and to understand what makes it possible or impossible.

If mental imaging involves activity of the primary cortex (Kosslyn, Thompson, Kim, & Alpert, 1995; Mellet et al., 2000), what kind of mechanism constrains the brain to discriminate an event occurring in the surrounding world from an event that occurs in the brain but not outside, and why does this discrimination sometimes fail? Do infants discriminate these mental states from birth? What are the constraints that make talking so late in development? Why do infants become able to do this and this before that and that? Are there different developmental trajectories that end up with exactly similar competencies? From whence do individual differences come? What should the environment provide in order for the brain to unfold its best potentialities? These questions cannot be answered without collaboration between cognitive psychologists and neuroscientists. This is because, as put by Johnson and Morton (1991), the brain does not interact only with molecules but at some point in its development it also interacts with objects, beliefs, concepts, and so on. Presently there is no way to define a concept in terms of neural mechanisms. How does the neural activity representing a perceptual category differ from a neural activity representing a concept? To understand the mechanisms and how they develop, we need to enter the brain with cognitive questions as well as questions on cellular or molecular or network activity patterns. It is with these studies that we will become able to answer general developmental issues such as how far the development of a given competence depends on the development of another one, and how far they are independent one from the other.

DEPENDENCE BETWEEN COGNITIVE DOMAINS DURING DEVELOPMENT

Once upon a time it was possible to propose "logical" assumption without empirical data. For instance, aspects of physical knowledge in infancy were said to derive from the properties of sensorimotor actions (see Piaget). In some way this was a "logical" point of view. It has been challenged by studies showing independence between the knowledge guiding various actions and the knowledge guiding perception (de Schonen & Bresson, 1981; Spelke, Breinlinger, Macomber, & Jacobson, 1992; Spelke, Vishton, & Von Hofsten, 1995). Nevertheless, development of the neural patterns underlying sensorimotor actions might have some effect on mechanisms of cognitive development.

Another instance of independence between two domains that should have been related "logically" and a priori was provided by Bellugi's studies on children with Williams syndrome. These authors showed that in children with Williams syndrome, face processing can develop independently from other visuospatial processing abilities. This strongly supports the assumption that face processing is a functional module independent in its development from other visuospatial competencies (Bellugi, Bihrle, Neville, Jernigan, & Doherty, 1991; Singer Harris, Bellugi, Bates, Jones, & Rossen, 1997). However, as we shall see later in this particular case, it seems that face processing in children with Williams syndrome is not identical to normal face processing and might develop along a trajectory different from normal. With the increase in the number of studies on specific domain deficit, development appears to consist neither of a development of several functionally independent modules, nor of a differentiation process from a single unitary machine. We shall show some examples later on.

DEPENDENCE BETWEEN TWO SUCCESSIVE ANALOGOUS BEHAVIOURS DURING DEVELOPMENT

Another important issue is that concerning the identification of the ancestor of a competence: is an early competence the "ancestor" or not of another later competence? Is there some continuity between different forms or states of knowledge, or not? How far does early experience have a consequence on later competence? We have to be cautious about the similarity between two behaviours that emerge successively. How do we know that a behaviour is the "ancestor" in development of another behaviour? How do we know that practice of a behaviour has an effect on another one that emerges later on?

Recently Thelen has examined an aspect of this issue from a different point of view, when she looked at how movement organization changes with practice during development (Thelen & Smith, 1994). Here we lack information on the neural transformation correlated with movement reorganization.

What developmentalists are finding and will discover in the future will have consequences not only on fundamental research but in the medical domain—paediatric neurology and psychiatry—and in educational and social domains. Moreover, these studies will probably enrich technological advances as they might provide ideas on how to build intelligent robots that are able to adapt to "unpredictable environments".

THE EXAMPLE OF FACE PROCESSING DEVELOPMENT

During its development, the brain builds successive tools by means of which it will interact with aspects of its environment with which it could not interact in an earlier state of its maturation. I would like to turn to a small piece of development as an example of the complexity and the surprises revealed by the developmental studies: the development of face processing. Of course the development of face processing cannot represent the development of all cognitive competencies. It is in some way an environment-driven competence, as are many aspects of perception (contrary to aspects of arithmetic, for instance). Nevertheless, if one compares the ease with which adults recognize faces with the obstacles met by people attempting to build a machine that recognizes faces, despite the important progress made by pattern recognition machines, it can be concluded that the adult brain has developed processing tools particularly adapted to that kind of object. Also, visual processing starts at birth, so we can follow the interactions between brain maturation and the effect of experience with faces.

Face recognition in adults

We know many neuropsychological aspects of this competence in adults. Years ago, Henry Hecaen suggested the existence of some specific system for processing faces (Hecaen & Angelergues, 1962). Later on, Fodor (1983) proposed face processing as a good candidate for modularity. Indeed, several data support the existence in adults of a dedicated face-processing system. Several arguments converge to show that face processing is dissociated from other object processing; it is based on different visual information processing than objects and involves neural networks that are localized in the right fusiform gyrus. Correlates of face processing are found in the middle right fusiform gyrus in the so-called "Face area" (Kanwisher, McDermott, & Chun, 1996; McCarthy, Puce, Gore, & Allison, 1997; Sergent, Ohta, &

MacDonald, 1992). Behavioural experiments have shown that face recognition relies in many cases on configural information rather than local information (Tanaka & Farah, 1993; Young, Hellawell, & Hay, 1987); that the adult's right hemisphere selects configural information (Hillger & Koenig, 1991; for review see Hellige, 1993). It was recently shown that the right middle fusiform gyrus is activated more when matching whole faces than face parts. A reversed pattern is observed in the left middle fusiform gyrus. These lateralized differences are observed for faces but not for other objects (houses) (Rossion et al., 2000).

Other arguments coming from studies of patients with brain damage support the assumption of a dedicated system for face processing dissociated from the processing of other objects and crucially involving cortical regions of the right rather than the left hemisphere. In prosopagnosic patients, deficit in recognizing facial identity can be independent from other face-processing abilities such as recognizing facial expressions or lip-reading (Campbell, Landis, & Regard, 1986; Young, Newcombe, de Haan, Small, & Hay, 1993). Prosopagnosia can be related to unilateral right damage (De Renzi, 1986; De Renzi, Prabi, Carlesimo, Siveri, & Fazio, 1994). Recently the case of a patient with agnosia of objects and high performances with faces was described (Moscovitch, Winocur, & Behrmann, 1997), confirming that face processing is independent of object processing (see also a review by Cabeza and Nyberg, 1997). It seems that it is not the difference between the categories "face" versus "object" that is relevant but the difference between great and poor expertise with systematic variations within a category of objects. Once expertise is acquired with a category of objects, an activation is observed in the "face area" under presentations of these objects (Gauthier, Tarr, Anderson, Skudlarski, & Gore, 1999). This suggests that the way in which the exemplars of an object category are cortically represented changes with the number of exemplars, the kind of inter-object differences, and the expertise acquired with them. This also shows that the cortical region is not exclusively involved in face processing but can become committed to the processing of other categories of objects.

How does the adult brain get there?

Face recognition in neonates

Visual preference for faces during the first three days of life: What is processed?

Is there a specific system at birth that automatically selects faces in the environment and acquires representations of faces with more and more details around a common structure as vision becomes finer and expertise increases? Is there a specific system selectively sensitive to voice or/and milk or/and somaesthetic contact and warmth with which faces are always co-present and which makes them attractive? Or is there just nothing truly face-specific to guide the infant's visual behaviour and learning toward faces except the conjunction of a set of mechanisms, none of which is face-specific?

A few-minutes-old neonate (after a normal delivery) visually follows with eyes and head the motion of a face-like schema on a longer path than when a symmetric but non-face-like schema is presented (Goren, Sarty, & Wu, 1975). Kleiner and Banks (1987; Kleiner, 1993) showed that when presented with a static schematic face, until the age of 2 months infants are more sensitive to the amplitude of the signal than to its structure (see, for an earlier review, Maurer, 1985). Johnson, Dziurawiec, Ellis, and Morton (1991) replicated Goren et al.'s results. Johnson and Morton (1991) suggested that the reason why neonates seem not to be sensitive to the structure of the face stems mainly from the fact that visual preference for face-like stimuli is due to a subcortical system, which does not control visual fixation in the same way as the cortex will control fixation later on (see, for details of the arguments, Johnson & Morton, 1991). The subcortical system orients visual attention towards a face-like pattern. This is the Conspec system. Around the 6th postnatal week, preferences change (Mondloch et al., 1999) and Conspec does not work any more. Johnson and Morton assumed that this change corresponds to the onset of cortical control on visual fixation and the beginning of learning about faces. Simion and her group gave experimental arguments supporting the concept that visual orientation towards the face-like schema in neonates might be controlled by a subcortical system (Simion, Valenza, & Umiltà, 1998a; Simion, Valenza, Umiltà, & Dalla Barba, 1998b; Valenza, Simion, Cassia, & Umiltà, 1996).

However, besides the subcortical detection system, a number of cortical networks involved in vision might be functional a few hours after birth and might contribute to preference for faces. Three-day-old infants discriminate between differently oriented static grating patterns, suggesting that some signal is processed by the visual cortex (Atkinson, 1998; Atkinson & Braddick, 1989; Slater et al., 1998). Preference for a schematic face over its inverted orientation in 3-day-olds is observed in orientation behaviour but also in duration of fixation, which suggests cortical activity. Moreover, 3-day-olds can learn about schematic faces: when an infant is familiarized with a schematic face with square eyes, he/she will look longer (novelty preference) at a new face with circular eyes (Farroni, Macchi Cassia, Turati, & Simion, 2000a). The plasticity demonstrated by learning is a characteristic of the cortex rather than of a subcortical structure. Some visual cortical networks are probably functional much before the 6th week. The subcortical Conspec might orient visual attention towards face-like patterns while the cortex learns about the pattern to which the gaze has been oriented by a subcortical system, as it would learn about any other pattern. However it seems that additional constraints coming from the visual cortex contribute to preference for faces. Indeed, Simion's group (Simion, Valenza, Macchi Cassia, Turati, & Umiltà, 2000a, b) has shown that 3-day-olds look longer at horizontal gratings than at vertical gratings and longer at patterns in which there is more contrast in the upper part than in the lower part of the field (for instance, neonates look longer at a T than at an inverted-T, at an inverted-U than at a U). In the face-like schema the contrast is greater in the upper part than in the lower part and the eyes constitute a well-contrasted horizontal stimulus. It looks as if cortical cells sensitive to horizontal contrast and to signals from the upper field were functioning before other cells. Therefore preference for the face schema would be the consequence of a temporary neural state of functioning due to partial immaturity of the visual cortex. The timetable of maturation of neural networks might be responsible for visual preference for faces. The consequence of the cortical maturational timetable would be the same as if there were a subcortical mechanisms guiding visual attention towards faces: infants would also look more to face-like objects than to objects of different structure. It might also be that two systems are at work simultaneously, one subcortical system (Conspec) that orients attention towards face patterns and one cortical system which is but a temporary state of maturation of the cortex, which maintains fixation. This might or might not have consequences on learning about faces: so far it has not been demonstrated that this early experience plays any role in face-processing development.

What is the cortex learning about faces at this time? Does Conspec act as a filter, helping the cortex to select and organize information about the inner pattern of the face? Or does preference for the horizontal and upper part of the field result in learning about eyes and hairline?

If this were the case, the infant should be more familiar with the mother's face than with that of a stranger. This is indeed what happens. Three-day-old neonates can recognize the mother's face-head (they look longer at the mother's than at a stranger's face-head) (Bushnell, Sai, & Mullin, 1989; Field, Cohen, Garcia, & Greenberg, 1984; Pascalis, de Schonen, Morton, Deruelle, & Fabre-Grenet, 1995; Walton, Bower, & Bower, 1992). Moreover, 3-day-olds show a visual preference for a novel head-face after having been familiarized with another head-face. They show novelty preference even after a 2-minute delay filled with interference between the familiarization and a visual preference test (Pascalis & de Schonen, 1995).

If the infant were sensitive to aspects of faces useful for discriminating between two individual faces, then he/she should be sensitive to the inner face pattern of his/her mother's face compared to the inner pattern of a stranger's face. However, 3-day-olds recognize their mother only if the outer contour of the mother's head and hairline are not masked with a scarf attached behind the head (Pascalis et al., 1995). This suggests that the visual representation of the mother face-head acquired during the first 3 days of life is a pattern that includes the outer contour of the whole head-face as a critical cue. Clearly characteristics of the inner structure of the mother's face are not sufficient for discriminating her from another woman's face or for recognizing her. This fits well with a preference for horizontal and greater contrast in the upper field: the eyes and the hair/forehead line constitute horizontal contrasts in the upper field of the neonate, the characteristics of which might be learned.

However, 3-day-olds do process some aspects of internal face configuration. Work on imitation of facial gesture in neonates (Meltzoff & Moore, 1989) shows that infants attend to events occurring within the face configuration. Here, however, movement might help to segment some aspects of the face.

Visual preference for attractive over nonattractive upright faces and lack of preference when these same faces are inverted shows that 3-day-olds are sensitive to some general aspect of the inner facial pattern (Slater et al., 1998). Moreover, infants maintain their preference for the attractive face over the unattractive one even if the hair is the same for both faces (Slater et al., 2000). This demonstrates that 3-day-old infants process some aspects of the internal face configuration. However, when they learn about a particular head-face, the pattern they learn includes the outer contour of the face and head as a crucial element.

Neonates rely on the whole head-face of an individual for discriminating between two face-heads. Presentation of the inner pattern with a different outer contour of the head precludes recognition of the individual face but not sensitivity to "attractiveness". Neonates are sensitive to some information present within the face pattern, information that broadly discriminates between two general classes of faces (attractive vs. nonattractive faces) rather than between two individual faces. This preference might result from the rapid building up of a general prototype for faces. The characteristics of this prototype might be elicited by the interaction with faces during the first few days but should rely heavily on endogenous perceptual organization rules (Symmetry? Localization of contrast? Value of the signal energy?) rather than exclusively on experienced exemplars. It seems that during the first weeks of life at least, there is no learning about possible variations among the internal configurations of individual faces. It is only by about the 6th–8th week of life after birth (at term) that infants show signs of recognition of the mother's face even when the outer contour of her hair is masked by a scarf (Bartrip, Morton, & de Schonen, 2001). One can say the reason for this is the limitation of visual acuity and contrast sensitivity during the first days. This is probably not the case, however. Of course, confusions between faces are certainly more frequent with very low pass vision and low contrast sensitivity, but many discriminations can be successful. Moreover, acuity and contrast sensitivity should be sufficient for differentiating between different shapes of the area of the eyes (the contrast of this area with the skin is high).

Rather, we believe that before the age of 6–8 weeks, infants learn the whole head-face pattern from the exemplars and rely heavily on the outer contour for recognizing and discriminating individual faces. The variations of the inner configuration are not yet processed or not processed separately. As well as this learning, infants might also build a general face prototype from their experience with faces and under the guidance of perceptual gestalt rules. If this prototype were used to compare the exemplars of faces of the environment then infants should be more sensitive to the inner pattern of their mother's face than they are. Moreover, at the age of 3—but not 2—months infants are able to form a face prototype based on exemplars (Johnson, unpublished work).

In summary, during the first days of life, visual attention towards faces might be guided by a subcortical system. The specific Conspec system would attract visual attention of the neonates on face-like patterns but does not directly help to select the relevant information that characterizes an individual face pattern and discriminate it from another one. Simultaneously, visual attention to faces might also be maintained by temporary selective preferences for horizontal and upper contrast of some cortical visual cells; meanwhile it is possible that selective preferences of visual cortical cells contribute to the building of a general prototype of facedness through neural projections towards the temporal cortex. Finally, the learning performances observed in neonates demonstrate that at any time of cortical maturation, experience-dependent activity leaves some traces. These traces might or might not have long-term effects on the organization of the cortex. We shall see some aspects of this issue later.

A cortical tool: Prototyping

Even at the age of 2 months, face processing is crude. For instance recognizing an individual face under a pose that has not yet been experienced seems to become possible at the age 3–4 months not before (Pascalis, de Haan, Nelson, & de Schonen, 1998). Among the various constraints that constitute the preorganization imposed by the cortex onto input from the environment, one might be particularly interesting: it is related to how the cortex represents and compares objects or faces through prototyping (see for face prototype in adults, Valentine & Endo, 1992). We mentioned earlier the building of prototypes from exemplars by 3-month-old infants (Johnson, unpublished work). It seems that the infant brain, like the adult brain, simultaneously builds two kinds of representation from an exemplar: one, composed with other exemplars, to form a prototype and one that will be used to recognize an individual and which is linked with specific contextual information.

Kuhl (1992; see also Iverson & Kuhl, 2000) describes prototypes as building bricks for the representation of speech sounds in the cortex at about the age of 6–8 months. Werker (Werker & Polka, 1993) has shown that discrimination between speech sounds that are not represented in the mother tongue tend to be poorly discriminated at about 10 months of age. In the domain of face processing a similar but later effect seems to exist. The "other race effect" which relies on experiencing more faces belonging to one ethnical morphology than to another one, seems to emerge only at about 27 months of age (Sangrigoli & de Schonen, 2000). Moreover, when it emerges, it does not seem to rely on exactly the same characteristics as in adults until age 5 years. These data show a very protracted development of face processing and prototype building compared to speech sounds, despite the fact that as for speech sound, face processing starts very early in life. It seems that prototyping does not develop simultaneously in the different basic cognitive domains.

Why the right hemisphere? Why configural processing?

Nevertheless, several aspects of face processing in infants, at least from the age of 4 months, look like adult abilities. Infants recognize their mother's face faster with their right than with their left hemisphere (de Schonen, Gil de Diaz, & Mathivet, 1986), and they discriminate better between two faces with their right than with their left hemisphere with duration of presentation as short as 300 to 350 ms (de Schonen & Mathivet, 1990). ERPs data confirm that the amplitude of the Nc wave in 6-month-old infants differs for the mother's face and a stranger's face under the right but not the left temporal electrodes (de Haan & Nelson 1997, 1999).

The right-hemisphere advantage is not related to a possible left-hemisphere failure to recognize what is a face and what is not: both hemi-spheres are able to give a categorial response discriminating between face-like patterns and non-face-like patterns in infants aged from 12 to 26 weeks (de Schonen & Bry, 1987). Neither is the right-hemisphere advantage due to a general advantage in pattern processing over the left (Deruelle & de Schonen, 1991, 1995); rather, it seems to be due to the two hemispheres pro-cessing different visual information (Deruelle & de Schonen, 1995, 1998). As in adults, the infant right hemisphere is sensitive to visual information on relative location, distances, and configuration whereas the left hemisphere is more sensitive to visual information on local shape. This is true with geo-metrical patterns as well as with faces. From identical offers, the two hemi-spheres do not build identical representations. This suggests that besides the contribution of subcortical and/or cortical mechanisms contributing to guide the cortex towards learning about faces, there exist other general constraints in the cortical organization which differ between the two hemispheres and which contribute to shape face processing.

In summary, data show that during their first days of life infants look more at face-like patterns and learn about some aspects of the face-head, but the process at work might be the result of several converging mechanisms rather than the result of a mechanism specifically committed to face detection and learning. From the fourth month of postnatal life (possibly before) a difference in visual information processing between the two hemispheres is present, which looks like the difference observed in adults. This difference concerns geometrical patterns as well as faces.

The hemispheric differences in pattern and face processing might be built in to the organization of the right and left cortex. However, it might come over through interaction during information processing by neural networks. Some years ago we suggested that some neural networks in the temporal cortex might become specialized for face processing because of the convergence of at least two factors (de Schonen & Mathivet, 1989): (1) The associative cortical regions (those located in the temporal cortex) which integrate several kinds of visual information might become functional at an earlier age in the right hemisphere than in the left (for a discussion see de Schonen et al., 1993; de Schonen & Mathivet, 1989; Turkewitz, 1989, 1993). (2) When functional networks become sufficiently large or numerous or organized in this region (between birth and the age of 9 weeks), they receive visual information that is conveyed mainly by the low spatial frequency channels (Atkinson & Braddick, 1989; Banks & Dannemiller, 1987; Banks, Stephens, & Hartmann, 1985; Slater, 1993). As a result, what can be recognized (hence stabilized) from one presentation of a pattern to the next presentation of the same pattern is the configural representation of the pattern rather than a representation of local aspects that might be compatible with too many other different patterns. In addition, it is also plausible that the neural architecture of the right temporal cortex has some specific organization that makes coding of configuration during infancy more frequent than coding of local information. In particular, rapid growth of the dendritic arborizations might result in connectivity architecture that differ from the connectivity resulting from slower dendritic growth. (3) Networks receiving sufficient visual signals in order to represent faces (without being "specialized" in this task) and related to other kinds of processing, such as voice processing, may therefore first start functioning in the right hemisphere, mainly on the basis of low spatial visual frequency information. (4) The advantage of this early processing system over the left-hemisphere networks is not only related to the fact that the right temporal cortex matures earlier than the left. It is also related to the advantage of configural encoding of faces. The advantage of configural encoding might stem from the fact that it is more resistant to transformations of a face by changes in light or in points of view, therefore increasing the probability of a pattern of neural activity to remain invariant on different occasions. The fact that the right hemisphere retains and keeps a face-processing advantage might be due not so much to the development of a specific face-processing system at an early stage of development, as to the information processed by the right hemisphere being particularly suitable for representing and recognizing patterns and objects with properties as complex as those of individual human faces. The information processed by the left hemisphere may perhaps be invariant throughout a smaller number of transformations than the right hemisphere, or possibly ones of a different kind, but may more efficiently show up small local changes in patterns, such as the changes in the shape of the mouth that occur during speech (Campbell et al., 1986), or possibly small differences in a smile that make the difference between a polite smile and genuine smile.

As long as nothing interferes to change the stabilizing process, there is no reason for the right-hemisphere advantage to change and, at some point in development, the process will become specific to the right hemisphere.

Presently we do not know how far this scenario is correct. What must be underscored is that neural networks might become specialized during development, not because they are precisely preorganized for a given object category before their interactions with specific signals, but because several factors contribute at a given time to provide them with given interactions rather than with others (see Acerra, Burnod, & de Schonen, 2002).

HEMISPHERIC SPECIALIZATION AND INTERHEMISPHERIC COMMUNICATION

Interhemispheric interaction plays a crucial role in several adult cognitive competencies (see review, Hoptman & Davidson, 1994). Commissurotomized patients, for instance can hardly if ever (1) make same/different judgements on letters or shapes presented each to a single hemisphere and (2) attend to the left and right fields simultaneously and coordinate them (Corballis, 1994; Gazzaniga, 1987; Johnson, 1984; Sergent, 1983, 1987, 1991; Seymour, Reuter-Lorenz, & Gazzaniga, 1994). These deficits show that one of the roles of the callosal fibres is to enable the cooperation between the processing carried out by the left and right hemispheres. This cooperation might be especially crucial in the coordination of asymmetrically controlled competencies. The coordination between the two hemispheres also increases the computing capacities relatively to a unilateral computation, as shown by the so-called "bilateral advantage" (Liederman & Meehan, 1986; Ludwig, Jeeves, Norman, & DeWitt, 1993; Norman, Jeeves, Milne, & Ludwig, 1992).

Knowing when in development such interhemispheric coordination becomes functional is crucial for our understanding of normal cognitive development as well as for our understanding of post-lesional plasticity. Thus it is all the more interesting that some functional hemispheric asymmetries are known to exist in infancy, as mentioned earlier. The existence of these early functional asymmetries raises the issue of how and when in development can processing in one hemisphere be coordinated with processing in the other. Coactivations mentioned earlier might be one of the first steps for this interhemispheric coordination to find its way. If two networks are coactivated simultaneously through subcortical inputs, the callosal fibres might "recognize" which networks have to be coordinated.

It has been shown that transfer of visual learning is not possible at the age of 7–11 months (Deruelle & de Schonen, 1991); the simultaneous visual attention to two stimuli, one in each visual field, and same/different responses do not emerge before the age of 24 months of age (Liegeois, Bentejac, & de Schonen, 2000; Liegeois & de Schonen, 1997). However, a categorial task based on face versus nonface discrimination can transfer from one hemisphere to the other from the age of 19 weeks, but not before (de Schonen & Bry, 1987). This shows that subcortical interhemispheric connections can possibly coactivate in the two hemispheres' cortical networks that represent perceptual categories built very early. This is not to say that interhemispheric categorial transfer in general develops before transfer of more specific information. In the present case, however, it seems to be so. In any case, the temporary lack of adult-like functional interhemispheric communications (callosal communications) might contribute to specialize the two hemispheres and therefore to make more specific the various cognitive processing that develops in each hemisphere, while permitting coordination between categorial representations of objects and faces.

CORTICAL LOCALIZATION AND FUNCTIONAL SPECIALIZATION IN EARLY INFANCY

On the one hand we have seen that development of face processing is protracted; on the other we have suggested that the right temporal cortex advantage in face processing might be due to its earlier maturation compared to that of the left cortex. What can be expected concerning cortical localization in infancy? Are cortical neuronal networks involved in face processing localized in the same region in infants and in adults? Or is the processing and storage of signals widespread and then progressively restrained to the right fusifom gyrus? In general, questions of this kind are answered on the basis of data collected on the long-term effects of neonatal brain lesions. The question concerning where in the cortex are the neural networks crucially involved in the development of a given competence also has to be answered by brain-imaging studies and not only by the study of long-term effects of brain damage. Here we have some information on the cortical localization of face processing in young infants.

It has been possible to identify a wave by ERP recording upon presentation of faces to 6-month-old infants (de Haan & Nelson, 1997; de Haan, Pascalis, & Johnson, in press; Johnson et al., in press). This wave is less specifically elicited by human faces than it is in adults and more widespread under the skull electrodes. Johnson interpreted these results as showing that lots of neural networks are involved in the development of face processing, with a progressive restriction to a subset later in development. Data from another method of brain imaging, however, show a somewhat different picture.

We had the opportunity to carry out a positron emission tomography (PET scan) study using H2 015 as marker on 2-month-old infants born at risk, with a view to developing a system of diagnosis and prognosis which would make it possible to apply suitable aid and rehabilitation procedures at an early age, before the onset of the behavioural deficit (Tzourio-Mazoyer et al., 1999, 2002). These infants were no longer under medication at the time of the study, the neurological signs were mild, and MRI was normal at that time. The regional patterns of brain activation were compared in two situations. In the first, control, situation, a visual stimulus was presented, consisting of a small circular set of red and green LEDs that lit up alternately at a variable speed. The speed was varied every 4 seconds. In the second situation, colour slides of women's faces, photographed frontally under the same lighting conditions, with a neutral expression and wearing a scarf, were presented for 4 seconds each.

Before giving the location of the neural activations observed under the two situations, lets us look at what we know about the state of maturation of the cortex in 2-month-olds. At the age of 2 months, the density of the synapses in the human cortex is increasing but is still low (Huttenlocher, 1979, 1990, 1994; Huttenlocher & de Courten, 1987; Huttenlocher, de Courten, Garey, & Van der Loos, 1982), dendritic arborizations in the cortex are still poorly developed (Scheibel, 1993), and cortical metabolic activity is much lower than a few months later (Chugani, Phelps, & Mazziotta, 1987). Therefore the presentation of a double ring of diodes and that of human faces might seem unlikely to give rise to any regional differences in the metabolic activity occurring in the associative cortex, nor might a visual stimulus such as a face seem likely to trigger anything other than a diffuse increase in the overall synaptic activity. Indeed, the results showed that the overall cortical activity was relatively poor whereas the activity in the subcortical structures was high. Nevertheless, the subtraction of the pattern of activity associated with the circle stimuli from the one associated with the face stimuli revealed a significant increase of activation in the right fusiform gyrus, as in adults. Other cortical regions were also activated, which are not all activated by faces in adults.

In other words, when infants are just starting to process and represent individual faces and their differences, and still show poor face recognition competence, the right fusiform gyrus is activated by the presentation of faces. Now given that we do not know which neural networks would be activated by complex nonface stimuli, we of course cannot conclude that there exists a specific cortical system in 2-month-olds that process faces. The activation of the right fusiform gyrus might not be specific to faces at 2 months of age, but its activators includes faces and exclude circles of diodes. It might be that all complex patterns could activate the right fusiform gyrus. What is important to note is that some constraints on maturation of the anatomical functional cortical organization are already present at the age of 2 months which can explain that face processing is allotted to some particular region of the cortex and will develop there.

Some cortical regional activations were observed in infants that are not observed with face stimuli in adults (in the parietal cortex and in the speech area). First, a methodological remark should be made. In adults, most of the data come from the comparisons of two very close experimental situations (faces minus objects, or faces among objects vs. objects only); our two situations were quite distant one from the other (diodes patterns vs. faces). As a consequence, more activations were present under face stimulations than under the control situation. Second, it might also be that in infants some regions are coactivated (by construction and/or by learning). The auditory cortex might be activated under face presentation because it is coactivated daily by voice and face. Coactivation implies the existence either of connections between the two coactivated regions or that the auditory regions receive visual input and visual regions receive auditory inputs. Bavelier et al. (2001) have described a very similar picture in deaf people. She proposed that in congenitally deaf people, visual projection to the auditory cortex remains from infancy on. Later on in development, either the "surnumerary" projections die or in other cases, automaticity of coactivations present in infancy becomes inhibited. How this kind of inhibiting process can develop might be one of the critical questions for the future. Presently research on this point is rare or conducted within different domains (see, for instance, Houde, 2000; Houde et al., 2000).

Unless they are a suspicious coincidence between localization of activation in infants and adults (an assumption that cannot be totally excluded), these data strongly suggest that some neural networks of the ventral pathway mature very early in life. This is not to say that the cortex is maturing according to ready-made specialized networks. We do not believe that neural networks pre-specified for face processing are developing in the right fusiform gyrus between birth and the age of 2 months. We should remember that ERP studies show that at the age of 6 months specificity of the electrical correlate is less than in adults: monkey and human faces stimuli share the same electrophysiological correlates in infants despite the fact that 6-month-old infants can respond categorically to human versus monkey and other nonprimate faces (de Schonen & Bry, unpublished data). The right fusiform gyrus activity might therefore be far less specific in 2-month-old infants than in adults. Rather we believe that future research will discover the constraints that can act so as to bias the development of a given competence in a given set of associative regions (for a model, see Acerra et al., 2002).

In summary, at an age when the processing of information about faces is undergoing changes in infants, while the cortex is still very immature, local patterns of activity occur involving the same associative cortical areas that will be involved in adults. This suggests that the cortical maturation process does not encompass one cortical region after another, but rather groups of networks across primary, secondary, and associative areas, according to a scheme where the emphasis is a more functional one, as if cortical maturation proceeds by successive waves in the whole cortex guided by unknown factors and by interactions between brain and environment in the postnatal period.

LONG-TERM EFFECT OF EARLY BRAIN LESIONS AND PLASTICITY

Many arguments on how the functional specialization of the cortex develops rely on considerations of the long-term effect of brain lesions. In adults, vascular accidents that locally damage neural tissue can result in very specific cognitive deficits (see earlier, for instance, agnosia without prosopagnosia or prosopagnisia without agnosia, prosopagnosia without agnosia of facial expressions, blindness for visual movement, etc. . . .). The problem of post-lesional plasticity and reorganization is not the same as in infancy given that the neural networks that have been destroyed by a lesion in the adult cortex were connected to other specialized networks that have not been destroyed. The activity of the later networks might constitute, if the lesion is not too large, a constraint that might guide the reorganization of the connections. In early infancy, destruction of neurons occurs in a neural environment that might not be very functionally specialized. Moreover, the molecular response to damage of the neural tissue is different in adult and infants. Neural plasticity in these circumstances might be a benefit or, on the contrary, harmful and disorganizing as far as new connections might be functionally irrelevant. Depending on the state of functional maturation of the neural environment as well as its state of sensitivity to neuroprotective factors, the outcome of a lesion can be very different according to the age of onset (also the presence or absence of epilepsy is globally a negative factor). It has been repeatedly claimed that early brain lesions have a better outcome than lesions occurring later in development (this claim is known as the Kennard doctrine, 1942).

For language development after an early brain lesion, all possible results have been observed, from no rescuing behaviour to normal albeit delayed development whatever the age of the lesion, from the perinatal period to several years of age (Bates et al., 1997; Vargha-Khadem & Polkey, 1992; Witelson, 1995). Moreover, it has been underscored that not only left but also right perinatal hemisphere damage can result in a slowing down of language development (Bates et al., 1997). As mentioned earlier, this observation is seen as supporting the assumption that language develops equally well in both hemispheres and not in specific parts of the cortex. However, a damage in one hemisphere might affect the contralateral hemisphere by inducing some neural reorganization which, depending on the state of maturation, might or might not be functional. The fact that right-hemisphere damage in infancy can induce difficulties in language development can be interpreted as showing that a right lesion has consequences on the neural organization of the left cortex. Additionally the right neural network might play a role during acquisition of language. Once language is developed and can function without referencing continuously to, for instance, some spatial or contextual representation, i.e., when it has become self-sufficient, it no longer requires activation of the right neural networks. Hence, observing difficulties in the development of language in infants with a right lesion might mean that the right hemisphere contributes to language acquisition, not because language is not localized but because language acquisition relies on connections between several processes that are no longer necessary in adults. We are not saying that language development relies heavily on object and spatial vision and experience, nor that there is no relative independence between language development and other cognitive competencies. We are saying something slightly different: that the left networks might require the right networks for reasons that have to be explained in the future.

The fact that language can develop after an early left cortical damage shows that the constraints guiding normal language development do not come exclusively from characteristics of the cortex normally allotted to language. Is this also the case for a completely different kind of competence? How does face processing develop after either an early brain lesion or an abnormal input, and what does this tell us about functional specialization?

POST-LESIONAL FUNCTIONAL PLASTICITY FOR FACE PROCESSING

We mentioned earlier that the right fusiform gyrus is activated by faces in 2-month-old infants. We also mentioned a right-hemisphere advantage in face processing during the first year of life. The two hemispheres do not each extract the same information from the environment, or rather they do not aggregate the lower-level pieces of information extracted from the environment in the same way. These early hemispheric characteristics are obviously not taught to the hemispheres by the environment, even if they probably result from different kinds of earlier interactions. We also mentioned the lack of interhemispheric communication for visual information. What happens in case of posterior unilateral perinatal damage? Will right-hemisphere damage preclude normal development of face processing or whether functional plasticity is the rule? Can face processing develop in the left hemisphere alone and if this is the case, does it develop on the basis of local or configural information?

The results of the first two studies we have conducted on children who had perinatal unilateral brain damage are as follows. Patients were tested between 6 and 17 years of age. Thus they had plenty of time and opportunity to learn about faces after the damage. A huge deficit (relative to their matched control) in some of the face competencies studied was observed in patients with posterior unilateral damage, not in patients with anterior damage. The patients did not have a deficit in all the face tasks, showing that some tasks involved a kind of processing that was preserved or that was rescued by processing of a different kind. Also, the level of face-processing competency was independent of IQ level and all patients had learnt to read. In other words, daily exposure and experience for years with faces is not sufficient to help the infant develop normal face-processing competencies. The surprising result was that right-hemisphere as well as left-hemisphere damage can result in a face-processing deficit.

Stiles and her colleagues showed that post-lesional plasticity seems to be poorer in the domain of visuospatial competence than in the domain of language (Bates et al., 1997; Stiles & Nass, 1991; Stiles-Davis, 1988; Stiles-Davis, Janowski, Engel, & Nass, 1988). Young and Ellis (1989) described a case of prosopagnosia in an 11-year-old child who sustained cerebral injury (meningitis) at the age of 14 months with subsequent infectious problems. After 10 years of everyday experience with faces, this child did not recover individual face recognition. By contrast, she could "classify a visual input as a face", was "able to perceive and imitate facial expression", to match faces "to an extent limited by her use of a feature by feature matching strategies", and had learnt to read. The deficit of this child was more severe than the deficit we observed in our patients. This might be due either to a lesion of a greater extent or to the fact that the lesion occurred late in development, at the age of 14 months.

In one of the sample of patients, we investigated whether those children who exhibit a deficit in face processing also have a deficit in other-object processing and a deficit in configural processing. From our previous findings on hemispheric asymmetries in visual processing during the first year of life (see earlier), we expected that a right-hemisphere lesion would result in a deficit in configural and global processing whereas a left-hemisphere lesion would result in a deficit in local processing. Patients with unilateral ischaemic damage undergone around birth (six patients with left-hemisphere damage, five with right-hemisphere damage) were divided into two groups: those who had a performance level significantly lower than their matched control in one of four face-processing tasks and those who did not differ from their matched controls in any face-processing task. A task was designed to investigate whether each patient and matched control was using a configural or a local processing mode in the recognition of a geometrical pattern. Other tasks evaluated the ability to recognize "objects" (shoes, dogs, houses).

Only posterior but not anterior damage to the brain was associated with a face-processing deficit. We confirmed, moreover, the fact that right-hemisphere as well as left-hemisphere damage can be associated with a long-term deficit in face processing despite the fact that in the first year of life the right hemisphere has an advantage in face processing over the left hemisphere. Second, it was observed that patients who had a deficit in face processing also had a deficit in other-object processing (no deficit specific to face processing was observed), some patients had no deficit in face processing but a deficit in object processing. More significant was the finding concerning configural processing. Children who had a face-processing deficit were more inclined to use local processing to recognize geometrical patterns than their matched control, whereas patients without face processing deficit did not differ from their matched control. This association between a deficit in face processing and a deficit in configural processing is an argument in favour of the assumption that a deficit in configural processing can generate a deficit in face processing and that the face competencies developed by these patients rely more on local processing whether they had a left or a right lesion. So far, then, children can develop face processing using local processing; however, as a result their level of performance in some of the tasks is not as high as that of normal children because they do not process exactly the same information.

In summary, despite the early cortical localization of the neural networks involved in face processing, a certain level of competence can develop in other cortical regions, although based on information of a different kind from that normally used. Now it should be noted that in Young and Ellis's child patient (see earlier) feature-by-feature analysis for comparing two faces was preserved, but the child could not develop individual face recognition on the basis of local processing only. Therefore preservation of some local-processing abilities is not sufficient per se if this processing is not used very early in the acquisition of knowledge about faces—before the end of the first year, as was probably the case with our unilateral brain-damaged patients. Even if we are right in saying that the adult characteristics of face processing results from the characteristics of early visual processing rather than from characteristics of a preorganized specific face processor, it remains that if visual information provided by faces is not acquired in the early state of visual processing, be it configural or local, processing face identity will not develop. One possible interpretation is that some of the perceptive or mental tools that develop and adapt to process information have to be developed in a given state of maturation of the networks (with a given neural architecture, or with a given kind of neurotransmitter). If this precise state of the cortex is not maintained, these tools will not develop, but other tools will. If the relevant information is not provided at the relevant period of time by the environment, the tools will not develop either, or they will be somewhat different. In other words, the organization of the cortex changes spontaneously and continuously: rapidly in infancy and childhood, and slower thereafter. The environment provides patterns of signals, some of which are processed in a particular way, and more or less stabilized (for instance prototypes); they modify the spontaneous changes of the cortex. But not all signals offered by the environment can be processed in the same way at any time. Face processors can develop during a certain period only because the state of the networks at that time makes this possible. There are probably at least two successive chances to develop face processing, one of which results in configural processing, the other in more local processing. After that period, all depends on what has been damaged and what has already developed: the neural architecture is no longer adequate, but can be adequate for different processing.

Given the very early right-hemisphere involvement observed in our PET study and in ERPs studies (see earlier), it is surprising that left-hemisphere damage can result in face processing and configural processing. First, the existence of a right-hemisphere advantage does not rule out the possibility that processing by both hemispheres is necessary to develop a normal level of competence, even though only preservation of the right hemisphere is necessary for face processing in adults. We have seen that in 2-month-olds, some cortical regions that are not activated by faces in adults are activated in infancy: as we suggested earlier, it might be that during development the relationships between the activity of several regions is necessary for one or another competence to develop and to communicate later on one with the other according to the requirements of the task. Progressive inhibition of these communications might be one of the mechanisms of development.

As already suggested, the second possible explanation is that early left-hemisphere damage has consequences on right cortical development. The corpus callosum is not yet able to coordinate visual episodes, but callosal neurones most probably already coordinate other kinds of neural activity: insult to callosal neurons can result in some contralateral disorganization or reorganization that might not always be functional. This reorganization would result in a deficit in some perceptual competencies depending on the region. Presently we do not see arguments supporting one of these two explanations more than the other.

Both interpretation underscore that there is more dependence between cortical networks in infancy than in adulthood. However we should be careful not to translate this dependence into another, i.e. that "there is more dependence between cognitive competencies during infancy and childhood than in adults". This last point is much more questionable.

We have shown that in children with perinatal unilateral brain injury, face processing can develop on the basis of local information rather than on

configural information. We have another example of a developmental trajectory different from the normal one. It has been said that in children with
Williams syndrome, face processing is preserved despite a very important
deficit in visuoconfigural processing (Bellugi et al., 1991, 1999; Singer Harris
et al., 1997). However, it was found that children with Williams syndrome are
not very good at face processing and that they tend to use more local processing than configural processing (Deruelle, Mancini, Livet, Cassé-Perrot,
& de Schonen, 1999; Donnai & Karmiloff-Smith, 2000; Karmiloff-Smith,
Brown, Grice, & Paterson, in press).

FUNCTIONAL PLASTICITY AFTER
EARLY DEPRIVATION

Another way to investigate how far cortical localization and characteristics of
face processing depends on the interaction between a given state of organization of the cortex and early visual experience, is to study the effect of early
visual deprivation. Maurer and her collaborators have developed a set of
studies with patients deprived of patterned input during early infancy by
bilateral congenital opaque cataracts. These patients were treated after
deprivation lasting 2 to 22 months by surgical removal of cataracts and fitting
the eyes with contact lenses. In one of the studies (Geldart et al., in press;
Mondloch et al., 2000), patients were tested after age 10 and compared with
6- and 10-year-old normal children and with adults. There were several tasks
involving face processing. When compared to normal controls, patients made
more errors than their controls on tasks involving identity despite changes in
head orientation, but they performed normally on other tasks (matching
identity despite change in expression, matching expression, lip-reading, gaze
direction). The results of the tasks which investigated whether the patients
were using either local, global (outer contour), or configural information
suggest that patients, independently of the duration of deprivation, are
poorly sensitive to configural information LeGrand et al., 2001. It might be
possible that recognition of a face through different orientations requires
more configural information than recognizing faces through different expressions, or recognizing different expressions. Anyway, as predicted by our own
scenario (de Schonen & Mathivet, 1989), the results show that visual deprivation from patterned light during the first 2 years of life or less does modify
the characteristics of face processing without damaging it severely.

It would be unwise to conclude very general claims on functional plasticity
from this data. Several main pieces of the story are lacking, in particular
pieces coming from two kinds of studies. On the one hand we need more
functional brain-imagery data during development. On the other hand
studies of a different scale of observations are necessary. For instance it
was assumed by the Maffei group (Faggiolini et al., 1997) that visual experience drives the maturation of functional properties of the visual cortex by

regulating cortical levels of neurotrophins. If this were correct they should have observed that the exogenous supply of neurotrophins during dark-rearing of rats from birth should prevent the effects of a lack of visual experience. This is exactly what they observed. Single-cell responses, visual-evoked potentials, and behavioural measures were in the range of normal adult values in treated dark-reared rats after 1 month of visual experience whereas they were abnormal in non-treated dark-reared rats. Neurotrophins have not "replaced" all the effects of visual experience but only a few of them, those that maintain plasticity during a period of time. This dissociation between the factor of plasticity and the factor of specialization is just one of several examples of why we feel far from understanding functional specialization.

In summary we shall underscore several points. First, early cortical maturation proceeds in waves, with different networks maturing before others. Functional specialization is progressive. Second, early cortical functional localization of a competence related to an adult competence does not mean that the early activated region contains a reduced model of the adult competence. The existence of a very early localized cortical set of neural networks involved in face processing is contemporary with a very poor face-processing competence that does not have all the characteristics of adult face processing. Some change in the processing and in the structure of the neural networks has to occur before face processing becomes as it is in adults. The relevant changes might occur through the effect of the environmental offer (stimulation and learning), but some neural changes that are independent of the details of environmental stimulations might also be involved.

Early localized cortical activity does not imply that only one region has the required general characteristics to perform a given kind of computation. The development of the functional specificity of a region probably results from constraints other than localization alone. Therefore functional localization does not exclude the possibility of another developmental trajectory in case some constraints are not present at the proper time (in the case of early deprivation as well as in the case of early brain lesion, some constraints normally present are lacking). On the other hand, the existence of other possible developmental trajectories and functional plasticity do not exclude the existence of constraints on cortical localization and functional specialization. The development of a competence probably results from the activity of several networks in several regions (see the fact that several cortical regions are activated under face presentations in 2-month-old infants in the PET study whereas these regions are not all activated in adults). If one region is damaged the functioning of the other networks will differ from normal, but the preservation of these networks will probably constrain and bias the functioning of other preserved networks so that a competence not totally similar to the normal one will develop. This would result in what is called functional plasticity: children who had an early unilateral posterior damage have a deficit in face processing but are not prosopagnosic. On the other hand, we also have seen that the rescuing systems do not seem to perform exactly the same kind of processing as the normal (most common) one: children with an early unilateral posterior damage develop a face-processing competency which is based more on local processing than it is in normal children. As predicted by the scenario, timing of the input seems also to be crucial: children deprived of vision for a relatively short period after birth develop some face processing but they use more local processing than normal children.

All this suggests that there exists more than one efficient developmental pathway and, in case some constraints normally present are lacking at the proper time, some variations around the normal pathway can preserve the general capacity (recognizing faces, expressions and so on) as far as a different kind of information processing can be used (for instance, local instead of configural information). However, if the preserved constraints are not strong enough, the outcome might be a severe deficit. The deficit might be very important if a neural reorganization takes place that has no way to be functional.

ACKNOWLEDGEMENTS

This chapter was partly supported by European Grant, BMH4 CT97 2032.

REFERENCES

Acerra, F., Burnod, Y., & de Schonen, S. (2002). A model of face recognition development in infants. *Developmental Science*, *5*(1), 132–151.

Atkinson, J. (1998). The visual system in early development. In F. Simion & G. Butterworth (Eds.), *The development of sensory, motor and cognitive capacities in early infancy: From perception to cognition* (pp. 1–24). Hove, UK: Psychology Press.

Atkinson, J., & Braddick, O. (1989). Development of basic visual functions. In A. Slater & G. Bremner (Eds.), *Infant development*. Hove, UK: Lawrence Erlbaum Associates Ltd.

Banks, M.S., & Dannemiller, J.L. (1987). Infant visual psychophysics. In P. Salapatek & L. Cohen (Eds.), *Handbook of infant perception, Vol. 1* (pp. 115–184). Orlando, FL: Academic Press.

Banks, M.S., Stephens, B.R., & Hartmann, E.E. (1985). The development of basic mechanisms of pattern vision. Spatial frequency channels. *Journal of Experimental Child Psychology*, *40*, 501–527.

Bartrip, J., Morton, J., & de Schonen, S. (2001). Responses to mother's face in 3-week to 5-month-old infants. *British Journal of Developmental Psychology*, *19*, 219–232.

Bates, E., Thal, D., & Janowsky, J. (1992). Early language development and its neural correlates. In I. Rapin & S. Segalowitz (Eds.), *Handbook of neuropsychology: Vol 7. Child neuropsychology* (pp. 69–110). Amsterdam: Elsevier.

Bates, E., Thal, D., Trauner, D., Fenson, J., Aram, D., Eisele, J., & Nass, R. (1997). From first words to grammar in children with focal brain injury. *Developmental Neuropsychology*, *13*, 275–344.

Bavelier, D., Brozinsky, C., Tomann, A., Mitchell, T., Neville, H., & Liu, G. (2001). Impact of early deafness and early exposure to sign language on the cerebral organization for motion processing. *Journal of Neuroscience, 15;21*(22), 8931–8942.

Bellugi, U., Bihrle, A., Neville, H., Jernigan, T., & Doherty, S. (1991). Language, cognition and brain organization in a neurodevelopmental disorder. In W. Gunnar & C. Nelson (Eds.), *Developmental behavioral neuroscience*. Hillsdale, NJ: Lawrence Erlbaum Associates Inc.

Bellugi, U., Lichtenberger, L., Mills, D., Galaburda, A., & Korenberg, J.R. (1999). Bridging cognition, the brain and molecular genetics: Evidence from Williams syndrome. *TINS, 22*, 197–207.

Bertoncini, J., Morais, J., Bijeljac-Babic, R., McAdams, S., Peretz, I., & Mehler, J. (1990). Dichotic perception and laterality in neonates. *Brain and Language, 37*, 591–605.

Brauth, S.E., Hall, W.S., & Dooling, R.J. (1991). *Plasticity of development*. Cambridge, MA: MIT Press.

Bresson, F., & de Schonen, S. (1979). Le développement cognitif. Les problèmes que pose aujourd'hui son étude. *Revue de Psychologie Appliquée, 29*, 119–127.

Bushnell, I.W.R., Sai, F., & Mullin, J.T. (1989). Neonatal recognition of the mother's face. *British Journal of Developmental Psychology, 7*, 3–15.

Cabeza, R., & Nyberg, L. (1997). Imaging cognition: An empirical review of PET studies with normal subjects. *Journal of Cognitive Neuroscience, 9*(1), 1–26.

Campbell, R., Landis, T., & Regard, M. (1986). Face recognition and lipreading: A neurological dissociation. *Brain, 109*, 509–521.

Changeux, J.P., & Danchin, A. (1976). Selective stabilization of developing synapses as a mechanism for the specification of neuronal networks. *Nature, 264*, 705–721.

Changeux, J.P., & Dehaene, S. (1989). Neuronal models of cognitive functions, *Cognition, 33*, 63–110.

Changeux, J.P., Heidmann, T., & Patte, P. (1984). Learning by selection. in P. Marler & H. Terrace (Eds.), *The biology of learning*. Berlin: Springer-Verlag.

Chugani, H.T., Phelps, M.E., & Mazziotta, J.C. (1987). Positron emission tomography study of human brain functional development. *Annals of Neurology, 22*, 487–497.

Corballis, M.C. 1994. Can commissurotomized subjects compare digits between the visual fields? *Neuropsychologia, 32*, 1475–1486.

de Haan, M., Johnson, M., Hatzakis, H.A., & Pacalis, O. (1999). *Does face specificity develop? A high-density ERP study* (p. 344). IX European Conference on Developmental Psychology, Spetses, Greece, September 1–5.

de Haan, M. & Nelson, C. (1997). Recognition of the mother's face by six-month-old infants: A neurobiological study. *Child Development, 68*, 187–210.

de Haan, M., & Nelson, C. (1999). Brain activity differentiates face and object processing in 6-month-old infants. *Developmental Psychology, 35*, 1113–1121.

de Haan, M., Pascalis, O., & Johnson, M.H. (in press). Electrophysiological correlates of face processing by adults and 6-month-old infants. *Journal of Cognitive Neuroscience*.

De Renzi, E. (1986). Current issues in prosopagnosia. In H.D. Ellis, M.A. Jeeves, F. Newcombe & A. Young (Eds.), Aspects of face processing (pp. 199–210). Dordrecht, The Netherlands: Martinus Nijhoff.

De Renzi, E., Prabi, D., Carlesimo, G.A., Siveri, M.C., & Fazio, F. (1994). Prosopagnosia can be associated with damage confined to the right hemisphere—an MRI and PET study and a review of the literature. *Neuropsychologia, 32*, 893–902.

Deruelle, C., & de Schonen, S. 1991. Hemispheric asymmetries in visual pattern processing in infancy. *Brain and Cognition, 16*, 151–179.

Deruelle, C., & de Schonen, S. (1995). Pattern processing in infancy: Hemispheric differences in the processing of shape and location of visual components. *Infant Behavior and Development, 18*, 123–132.

Deruelle, C., & de Schonen, S. (1998). Do the right and left hemispheres attend to the same visuospatial information within a face in infancy? *Developmental Neuropsychology, 14,* 535–554.

Deruelle, C., Mancini, J., Livet, M.O., Cassé-Perrot, C., & de Schonen, S. (1999). Configural and local processing of faces in children with Williams syndrome. *Brain and Cognition, 41,* 276–298.

de Schonen, S. (1989). Some reflections on brain specialization in facedness and physiognomy processing. In A. Young & H.D. Ellis (Eds.), *Handbook of research on face processing* (pp. 379–389). Amsterdam: North-Holland.

de Schonen, S., & Bresson, F. (1981). Données et perspectives nouvelles sur les débuts du développement. In S. de Schonen (Ed.), *Le développement dans la première année* (pp. 13–23). Paris: PUF.

de Schonen, S., & Bry, I. (1987). Interhemispheric communication of visual learning: A developmental study in 3–6-month-old infants. *Neuropsychologia, 25,* 601–612.

de Schonen, S., Deruelle, C., Mancini, J., & Pascalis, O. (1993). Hemispheric differences in face processing and brain maturation. In B. de Boysson-Bardies, S. de Schonen, P. Jusczyk, P. MacNeilage, & J. Morton (Eds.), *Developmental neurocognition: Speech and face processing in the first year of life* (pp. 149–163). Dordrecht, The Netherlands: Kluwer.

de Schonen, S., Gil de Diaz, M., & Mathivet, E. (1986). Hemispheric asymmetry in face processing in infancy. In H.D. Ellis, M.A. Jeeves, F. Newcombe & A. Young (Eds.), Aspects of face processing (pp. 199–210). Dordrecht, The Netherlands: Martinus Nijhoff.

de Schonen, S., & Mathivet, E. 1989. First come first serve: A scenario about the development of hemispheric specialization in face processing in infancy. *European Bulletin of Cognitive Psychology (CPC), 9,* 3–44.

de Schonen, S., & Mathivet, E. (1990). Hemispheric asymmetry in a face discrimination task in infants. *Child Development, 61,* 1192–1205.

de Schonen, S., Mathivet, E., & Deruelle, C. (1989). A timing puzzle. *European Bulletin of Cognitive Psychology (CPC), 9,* 147–159.

Donnai, D., & Karmiloff-Smith, A. (2000). Williams syndrome: From genotype through to the cognitive phenotype. *American Journal of Medical Genetics: Seminars in Medical Genetics, 97,* 164–171.

Donoghue, M.J., & Rakic, P. (1999). Molecular gradients and compartments in the embryonic primate cerebral cortex. *Cerebral Cortex, 9,* 586–600.

Elman, J.L., Bates, E.A., Johnson, M.H., Karmiloff-Smith, A., Parisi, D., & Plunkett, K. (1996). *Rethinking innateness.* Cambridge, MA: MIT Press.

Faggiolini, M., Pizzorusso, T., Porciatti, V., Cenni, M.C., & Maffei, L. (1997). Transplant of Schwann cells allows normal development of the visual cortex of dark-reared rats. *European Journal of Neuroscience, 9,* 102–112.

Farah, M.J., Tanaka, J.W., & Drain, H.M. (1995). What causes the face inversion effect. *Journal of Experimental Psychology: Human Perception and Performance, 21,* 628–634.

Farroni, T., Macchi Cassia, V., Turati, C., & Simion, F. (2000a). *Face discrimination in newborns.* XIIth Biennial International Conference on Infant Studies (ICIS). Brighton, UK, July 16–19.

Farroni, T., Valenza, E., Simion, F., & Umilta, C. (2000b). Configural processing at birth: Evidence for perceptual organization. *Perception, 29,* 355–372.

Field, T., Cohen, D., Garcia, R., & Greenberg, R. (1984). Mother-stranger face discrimination by the newborn. *Infant Behaviour and Development, 7,* 19–26.

Fodor, J.A. (1983). *The modularity of mind.* Cambridge, MA: MIT Press.

Frappe, I., Roger, M., & Gaillard A. (1999). Transplants of fetal frontal cortex grafted into the occipital cortex of newborn rats receive a substantial thalamic input from nuclei normally projecting to the frontal cortex. *Neuroscience. 89,* 409–421.

Frenkel, M., Sherman, G,F., Bashan, K.A., Galaburda, A.M., & LoTurco, J.J. (2000). Neocortical ectopias are associated with attenuated neurophysiological responses to rapidly changing auditory stimuli. *Neuroreport, 11,* 575–579.

Galaburda, A.M., Sherman, G., & Rosen, G. (1985). Four consecutive patients with cortical anomalies. *Annals of Neurology, 18,* 222–233.

Gauthier, I., Tarr, M.J., Anderson, A.W., Skudlarski, P., & Gore, J.C. (1999). Activation of the middle fusiform "face area" increases with expertise in recognizing novel objects. *Nature Neuroscience, 6,* 568–573.

Gauthier, I., Skudlarski, P., Gore, J.C., & Anderson, A.W. (2000a). Expertise for cars and birds recruits brain areas involved in face recognition. *Nature. Neuroscience, 3,* 191–197.

Gauthier, I., Tarr, M.J., Moylan, J., Skudlarski, P., Gore, J.C., & Anderson, A.W. (2000b). The fusiform "face area" is part of a network that processes faces at the individual level. *Journal of Cognitive Neuroscience, 12,* 495–504.

Gazzaniga, M.S. (1987). Perceptual and attentional processes following callosal section in humans. *Neuropsychologia, 25,* 119–133.

Geldart, S., Mondloch, C., Maurer, D., de Schonen, S., & Lewis, T. (in press). The effect of early visual deprivation on the development of face processing. *Developmental Science.*

Geschwind, N., & Galaburda, A. (1985). Cerebral lateralization: Biological mechanisms, associations and pathology. *Archives of Neurology, 42,* 428–459.

Goren, C.C., Sarty, M., & Wu, P.Y.K. (1975). Visual following and pattern discrimination of face-like stimuli by newborn infants. *Pediatrics, 56,* 544–549.

Hecaen, H.T. & Angelergues, R. (1962). Agnosia for faces (prosopagnosia). *Archives of Neurology, 7,* 92–100.

Hellige, J.B. (1993). *Hemispheric asymmetry. What's right and what's left.* Cambridge, MA: Harvard University Press.

Hillger, L.A., & Koenig, O. (1991). Separable mechanisms in face processing: Evidence from hemispheric specialization. *Journal of Cognitive Neuroscience, 3,* 42–58.

Hoptman, M.J., & Davidson, R.J. (1994). How and why do the two cerebral hemispheres interact? *Psychological Bulletin, 116,* 195–219.

Houde, O. (2000). Inhibition and cognitive development: Objects, number, categorization and reasoning. *Cognitive Development, 15,* 63–73.

Houde, O., Zago, L., Mellet, E., Moutier, S., Pineau, A., Mazoyer, B., & Tzourio-Mazoyer, N. (2000). Shifting from the perceptual brain to the logical brain: the neural impact of cognitive inhibition training. *Journal of Cognitive Neurosciences, 12,* 721–728.

Huttenlocher, P.R. (1979). Synaptic density in human frontal cortex—developmental changes and effects of aging. *Brain Research, 163,* 195–205.

Huttenlocher, P.R. (1990). Morphometric study of human cerebral cortex development. *Neuropsychologia, 28,* 517–527.

Huttenlocher, P.R. (1994). Synaptogenesis, synapse elimination and neural plasticity in human cerebral cortex. In C.A. Nelson (Ed.), Threats to optimal development: Integrating biological, psychological, and social risk factors. *Minnesota Symposium on Child Psychology, 27,* 35–54. Hillsdale, NJ: Lawrence Erlbaum Associates Inc.

Huttenlocher, P.R., & de Courten, C. (1987). The development of synapses in striate cortex of man. *Human Neurobiology, 6,* 1–19.

Huttenlocher, P.R. & de Courten, C., Garey, L., & Van der Loos, H. (1982). Synaptogenesis in human visual cortex: Evidence for synapse elimination during normal development. *Neuroscience Letters, 33,* 247–252.

Iverson, P., & Kuhl, PK. (2000). Perceptual magnet and phoneme boundary effects in speech perception: Do they arise from a common mechanism? *Perception and Psychophysics, 62,* 874–886.

Johnson, L.E. (1984). Bilateral visual cross-integration by human forebrain commissurotomy subjects. *Neuropsychologia, 22*, 167–175.

Johnson, M.H. (2000). Functional brain development in infants: Elements of an interactive specialization framework. *Child Development, 71*, 75–81.

Johnson, M.H., de Haan, M., Oliver, A., Smith, W., Hatzakis, H., Tucker, L.A., & Csibra, G. (in press). Recording and analyzing high density ERPs with infants using the Geodesic Sensor Net. *Developmental Neuropsychology*.

Johnson, M.H., Dziurawiec, S., Ellis, H.D., & Morton, J. (1991). Newborns' preferential tracking of face-like stimuli and its subsequent decline. *Cognition, 40*, 1–19.

Johnson, M.H., & Morton, J. (1991). *Biology and cognitive development: The case of face recognition*. Oxford: Blackwell.

Jusczyk, P.W. (1999a). Narrowing the distance to language: One step at a time. *Journal of Communication Disorders, 32*, 207–222.

Jusczyk, P.W. (1999b). How infants begin to extract words from speech. *Trends in Cognitive Sciences, 3*, 323–328.

Kanwisher, N., McDermott, J., & Chun, M.M. (1996). A module for the visual representation of faces? *Neuroimage, 3*, S361.

Karmiloff-Smith, A., Brown, J.H., Grice, S., & Paterson, S. (in press). Dethroning the myth: Cognitive dissociations and innate modularity in Williams syndrome. *Developmental Neuropsychology*.

Kennard, M. (1942). Cortical reorganization of motor function. Studies on series of monkeys of various ages from infancy to maturity, *Archives of Neurology and Psychiatry, 48*, 227–240.

Kleiner, K.A. (1993). Specific versus nonspecific face recognition device? In B. de Boysson-Bardies, S. de Schonen, P. Jusczyk, P. MacNeilage, & J. Morton (Eds.), Developmental neurocognition: Speech and face processing in the first year of life (pp. 125–134). Dordrecht, The Netherlands: Kluwer.

Kleiner, K.A., & Banks, M. (1987). Stimulus energy does not account for two-month-old infants face preferences. *Journal of Experimental Psychology: Human Perception and Performance, 13*, 594–600.

Kolb, B. (1995). *Brain plasticity and behavior*. Mahwah, NJ: Lawrence Erlbaum Associates Inc.

Kosslyn, S.M., Thompson, W.L., Kim, I.J., & Alpert, N.M. (1995). Topographical representations of mental images in primary visual cortex. *Nature, 30*, 496–498.

Kuhl, P.K. (1992). Speech prototypes: Studies on nature, function, ontogeny and phylogeny of the "centers" of speech categories. In Y. Tokhura, E. Vatikiotis-Bateson, & Y. Sagisaka (Eds.), Speech perception, production and linguistic structure (pp. 239–264). Ohmsha: Tokyo.

Le Grand, R., Mondloch, C.J., Maurer, D., & Brent, B.P. (2001). Neuroperception. Early visual experience and face processing. *Nature, 410*(6831), 890.

Liederman, J., & Meehan, P. (1986). When is between hemisphere division of labour advantageous? *Neuropsychologia, 24*, 863–874.

Liegeois, F., Bentejac, L., & de Schonen, S. (2000). When does interhemispheric integration of visual events emerge in infancy? A developmental study on 19- to 28-month-old infants. *Neuropsychologia, 38*, 1382–1389.

Liegeois, F., & de Schonen, S. (1997). Simultaneous attention in the two visual hemifields and interhemispheric integration: A developmental study on 20- to 26-month-old infants. *Neuropsychologia, 35*, 381–385.

Ludwig, T.E., Jeeves, M.A., Norman, W.A., & DeWitt, R. (1993). The BFA in a letter matching task. *Cortex, 29*, 69–713.

Mancini, J., Casse-Perrot, C., Giusiano, B., Girard, N., Camps, R., Deruelle, C., & de Schonen, S. (2001). *Face processing development after a perinatal unilateral brain lesion*. Manuscript submitted for publication.

Mancini, J., de Schonen, S., Deruelle, C., & Massoulier, A. (1994). Face recognition in children with early right or left brain damage. *Developmental Medicine and Child Neurology, 36,* 156–166.

Maurer, D. (1985). Infants' perception of facedness. In T.M. Field & N.A. Fox (Eds.), *Social perception in infants* (pp. 73–100). Norwood, NJ: Ablex.

McCarthy, G., Puce, A., Gore, J.C., & Allison, T. (1997). Face specific processing in the human fusiform gyrus. *Journal of Cognitive Neuroscience, 9,* 605–610.

Mellet, E., Tzourio-Mazoyer, N., Bricogne, S., Mazoyer, B., Kosslyn, S.M., Denis, M. (2000). Functional anatomy of high-resolution visual mental imagery, *Journal of Cognitive Neuroscience, 12,* 98–109.

Meltzoff, A. & Moore, M.K. (1989). Imitation in newborn infants: Exploring the range of gestures imitated and underlying mechanisms. *Developmental Psychology, 25,* 954–962.

Mills, D.C., Coffey, S., & Neville, H. (1993). Language acquisition and cerebral specialization in 20-month-old children. *Journal of Cognitive Neuroscience, 5,* 317–334.

Mills, D.C., Coffrey-Corina, S., & Neville, H. (1997). Language comprehension and cerebral specialization from 13 to 20 months. *Developmental Neuropsychology, 13,* 397–447.

Molfese, D. (1990). Auditory evoked responses recorded from 16-month-old human infants to words they did and did not know. *Brain and Language, 38,* 345–363.

Molfese, D.L., & Molfese, V.J. (1979). Hemispheric and stimulus differences as reflected in the cortical responses of newborn infants to speech stimuli. *Developmental Psychology, 15,* 505–512.

Molfese, D.L., Wetzel, W.F., & Gill, L.A. (1993). Known versus unknown word discriminations in 12-month-old infants: Electrophysiological correlates. *Developmental Neuropsychology, 9,* 241–258.

Mondloch, C., Lewis, T.L., Budreau, D.R., Maurer, D., Dannemiller, J.L., Stephens, B.R., & Kleiner, K.A. (1999). Face perception during early infancy. *Psychological Science, 10,* 419–422.

Mondloch, C., Maurer, D., LeGrand, R., Geldart, S., de Schonen, S., Lewis, L., Brent, H.P., & Levin, A.V. (2000). *The effects of early visual deprivation on the development of cortical specialization for face perception.* Paper at the ICIS 2000, Brighton, 16–19 July.

Morton, J., & Johnson, M.H. (1991). Conspec and conlern: A two-process theory of infant face recognition. *Psychological Review, 98,* 164–181.

Moscovitch, M., Winocur, G., & Behrmann, M. (1997). What is special about face recognition? Nineteen experiments on a person with visual object agnosia and dyslexia but normal face recognition. *Journal of Cognitive Neuroscience, 9,* 555–604.

Nazzi, T., & Gopnik, A. (in press). Linguistic and cognitive abilities in infancy: When does language become a tool for categorization? *Cognition.*

Nelson, C.A., & Ludemann, P.M. (1989). Past, current, and future trends in infant face perception research. *Canadian Journal of Psychology, 43,* 183–198.

Norman, W.D., Jeeves, M.A., Milne, A., & Ludwig, T. (1992). Hemispheric interactions: The BFA and task difficulty. *Cortex, 28,* 623–642.

O'Leary, D.D. (1993). Do cortical areas emerge from a protocortex. In M. Johnson (Ed.), *Brain development and cognition: A reader* (pp. 323–337). Oxford: Blackwell Publishers.

Oram, M.W., Földiak, P., Perrett, D.I., & Sengpiel, F. (1998). The "ideal homunculus": Decoding neural population signals. *TINS, 21,* 259–265.

Pascalis, O., de Haan, M., Nelson, C., & de Schonen, S. (1998). Long-term recognition memory for faces assessed by visual paired comparison in 3- and 6-month-old infants. *Journal of Experimental Psychology: Learning, Memory and Cognition, 24,* 249–260.

Pascalis, O., & de Schonen, S. (1995). Recognition memory in 3–4-day-old human infants. *NeuroReport, 5,* 1721–1724.

Pascalis, O., de Schonen, S., Morton, J., Deruelle, C., & Fabre-Grenet, M. (1995). Mother's face recognition by neonates: a replication and an extension. *Infant Behavior and Development, 18,* 79–85.

Patterson, K.S., & Bradshaw, J.L. (1975). Differential hemispheric mediation of nonverbal visual stimuli. *Journal of Experimental Psychology: Human Perception and Performance, 1,* 246–252.

Rentschler, I., Treutwain, B., & Landis, T. (1994). Dissociation of local and global processing in visual agnosia. *Vision Research, 34,* 963–971.

Robertson, L.C., & Lamb, M.R. (1991). Neuropsychological contributions to theories of part/ whole organization. *Cognitive Psychology, 23,* 299–330.

Rossion, B., Dricot, L., Devolder, A., Bodart, J.M., Crommelinck, M., De Gelder, B., & Zoontjes, R. (2000). Hemispheric asymmetries for whole-based and part-based face processing in the human fusiform gyrus. *Journal of Cognitive Neuroscience, 12,* 793–802.

Rossion, B., Gauthier, I., Tarr, M.J., Pierenne, D., Debatisse, D., & Despland, P.A. (1999). *The N170 occipito-temporal component is delayed to inverted faces but not to inverted objects: Electrophysiological evidence of face-specific processes in the human brain.* Poster No. 864 (abstract), 5th International Conference on Functional Mapping of the Human Brain, June, Dusseldorf.

Sangrigoli, S., & de Schonen, S. (2000). Effect of early experience on face processing: the "other race effect" and the inversion effect in children aged between 11 and 33 months [Abstract]. *Conference of the Cognitive Sciences in Paris.*

Scheibel, A. (1993). Dendritic structure and language development. In B. de Boysson-Bardies, S. de Schonen, P. Jusczyk, P. MacNeilage, & J. Morton (Eds.), *Developmental neurocognition: Speech and face processing in the first year of life* (pp. 51–62). Dordrecht, The Netherlands: Kluwer.

Sergent, J. (1983). Unified response to bilateral hemispheric stimulation by a split-brain patient. *Nature, 305,* 801–802.

Sergent, J. (1987). A new look at the human split-brain. *Brain, 110,* 1375–1392.

Sergent, J. (1991). Processing of spatial relations within and between the disconnected hemispheres. *Brain, 114,* 1025–1043.

Sergent, J., Ohta, S., & MacDonald, B. (1992). Functional neuroanatomy of face and object processing. A positon emission tomography study. *Brain, 115,* 15–36.

Seymour, S.E., Reuter-Lorenz, P.A. & Gazzaniga, M.S. (1994). The disconnection syndrome: Basic findings reaffirmed. *Brain, 117,* 105–115.

Simion, F., Valenza, E., Macchi Cassia, V., Turati, C., & Umiltà, C. (2000a). *Are faces special for newborns?* Presentation at the XIIth Biennial International Conference on Infant Studies, Brighton, UK, July 16–19.

Simion, F., Valenza, E., Macchi Cassia, V., Turati, C., & Umiltà, C. (2000b). *Newborns' preference for structural properties.* Euresco Conference on "Brain Development and Cognition in Human Infants—II". La Londe-Les Maures, France, September 15–20.

Simion, F., Valenza, E., & Umiltà, C. (1998a). Mechanisms underlying face preference. In F. Simion & G. Butterworth (Eds.), *The development of sensory, motor and cognitive capacities in early infancy: From perception to cognition* (pp. 87–101). Hove, UK: Psychology Press.

Simion, F., Valenza, E., Umilta, C., Dalla Barba, B. (1998b). Preferential orienting to faces in newborns: A temporal-nasal asymmetry. *Journal of Experimental Psychology: Human Perception and Performance, 24,* 1399–1405.

Singer, W. 1995. Time as coding space in neocortical processing: A hypothesis. In M.S. Gazzaniga (Ed.), *The cognitive neurosciences* (pp. 91–104). Cambridge, MA: MIT Press.

Singer Harris, N.G., Bellugi, U., Bates, E., Jones, W., & Rossen, M. (1997). Contrasting profiles of language development in children with Williams and Down syndromes. *Developmental Neuropsychology, 13,* 345–370.

Slater, A.M. (1993). Visual perceptual abilities at birth: Implications for face perception. In B. de Boysson-Bardies, S. de Schonen, P. Jusczyk, P. MacNeilage, & J. Morton (Eds.), *Develop-*

mental neurocognition: Speech and face processing in the first year of life (pp. 125–134). Dordrecht, The Netherlands: Kluwer.

Slater, A.M. Bremner, G., Johnson, S.P., Sherwood, P., Hayes, R., & Brown, E. (2000). Newborn infants' preference for attractive faces: The role of internal and external facial features. *Infancy, 1*, 265–274.

Slater, A.M., Van der Schulenburg, C., Brown, E., Badenoch, M., Butterworth, G., Parsons, S., & Samuels, C. (1998). Newborn infants prefer attractive faces. *Infant Behavior and Development, 21*, 345–354.

Spelke, E.S., Breinlinger, K., Macomber, J., & Jacobson, K. (1992). Origins of knowledge. *Psychological Review, 99*, 605–632.

Spelke, E., Vishton, P. & Von Hofsten, C. (1995). Object perception, object-directed action, and physical knowledge in infancy. In M.S. Gazzaniga (Ed.), *The cognitive neurosciences* (pp. 165–180). Cambridge, MA: MIT Press.

Stiles, J., & Nass, R. (1991). Spatial grouping ability in young children with congenital right or left hemisphere injury. *Brain and Cognition, 15*, 201–222.

Stiles, J., & Thal, T. (1993). Linguistic and spatial cognitive development following early focal brain injury: Patterns of deficit and recovery. In M. Johnson (Ed.), *Brain development and cognition: A reader* (pp. 643–664). Oxford: Blackwell.

Stiles-Davis, J. (1988). Developmental change in young children's spatial grouping activity. *Developmental Psychology, 24*, 522–531.

Stiles-Davis, J., Janowski, J. Engel, M., & Nass, R. (1988). Drawing ability in four young children with congenital unilateral brain lesions. *Neuropsychologia, 26*, 359–371.

Tanaka, J.W., & Farah, M.J. (1993). Parts and wholes in face recognition. *Quarterly Journal of Experimental Psychology, 46A*, 225–245.

Tassabehji, M., Metcalfe, K., Karmiloff-Smith, A., Carette M.J., Grant, J., Dennis, N., Reardon, W., Splitt, M., Read, A.P., & Donnai, D. (1999). Williams syndrome: Use of chromosonal microdeletions as a tool to dissect cognitive and physical phenotypes. *American Journal of Human Genetics, 64*, 118–125.

Thelen, E., & Smith, L.B. (1994). *A dynamic systems approach to the development of cognition and action.* Cambridge, MA: MIT Press.

Turkewitz, G. (1989). Face processing as a fundamental feature of development. In A. Young & H.D. Ellis (Eds.), *Handbook of research on face processing* (pp. 401–404). Amsterdam: North-Holland.

Turkewitz, G. (1993). The origin of differential hemispheric strategies for information processing in the relationships between voice and face perception. In B. de Boysson-Bardies, S. de Schonen, P. Jusczyk, P. MacNeilage, & J. Morton (Eds.), *Developmental neurocognition: Speech and face processing in the first year of life* (pp. 165–170). Dordrecht, The Netherlands: Kluwer.

Turkewitz, G., & Kenny, P.A. (1982). Limitations on input as a basis for neural organization and perceptual development: A preliminary theoretical statement. *Developmental Psychobiology, 15*, 357.

Tzourio-Mazoyer, N., de Schonen, S., Quinton, O., Crivello, F., Reutter, B., & Mazoyer, B. (1999). The right fusiform face area is functional in two-month-old infants, Dusseldorf, 5th International Conference on Functional Mapping of the Human Brain. *NeuroImage, 9*, 6.

Tzourio-Mazoyer, N., de Schonen, S., Quinton, O., Crivello, F., Reutter, B., Aujard, Y., & Mazoyer, B. (in press). Neural correlates of face processing by two-month old infants. *Neuroimage.*

Valentine, T., & Endo, M. (1992). Towards an exemplar model of face processing: The effects of race and distinctiveness. *Quarterly Journal of Experimental Psychology A, 44*, 671–703.

Valenza, E., Simion, F., Cassia, V.M., & Umiltà, C. (1996). Face preference at birth. *Journal of Experimental Psychology: Human Perception Performance, 22*, 892–903.

Vargha-Khadem, F., & Polkey, C.E. (1992). A review of cognitive outcome after hemidecortica-tion in humans. In F.D. Rose & M.H. Johnson (Eds.), *Recovery from brain damage. Reflections and directions* (pp. 137–148). London: Plenum Press.

Walton, G.E., Bower, N.J.A., & Bower, T.G.R. (1992). Recognition of familiar faces by newborns. *Infant Behavior and Development, 15*, 265–269.

Waxman, S.R., & Hall, D.G. (1993). The development of a linkage between count nouns and object categories: Evidence from 15- to 21-month-old infants. *Child Development, 64*, 1224–1241.

Waxman, S.R., & Markow, D.B. (1995). Words as invitations to form categories: Evidence from 12- to 13-month-old infants. *Cognitive Psychology, 29*, 257–302.

Werker, J., & Polka, L. (1993). The ontogeny and developmental significance of language-specific phonetic perception. In B. de Boysson-Bardies, S. de Schonen, P. Jusczyk, P. MacNeilage, & J. Morton (Eds.), *Developmental neurocognition: Speech and face processing in the first year of life* (pp. 273–288). Dordrecht, The Netherlands: Kluwer.

Witelson, S.F. (1995). Neuroanatomical bases of hemispheric functional specialization in the human brain: Possible developmental factors. In F. L. Kitterle (Ed.), Hemispheric communication: Mechanisms and models (pp. 61–84). Hillsdale, NJ: Lawrence Erlbaum Associates Inc.

Young, A.W., & Ellis, H.D. (1989). Childhood prosopagnosia. *Brain and Cognition, 9*, 16–29.

Young, A.W., Hellawell D.J., & Hay, D.C. (1987). Configural information in face perception. *Perception, 16*, 747–759.

Young, A.W., Newcombe, F., de Haan, E.H.F., Small, M., & Hay, D.C. (1993). Face perception after brain injury: Selective impairments affecting identity and expression. *Brain, 116*, 941–959.

CHAPTER FOUR

Brain asymmetry and cognition

Kenneth Hugdahl
University of Bergen, Norway

The present chapter is a review of research in our laboratory over the last 20 years on the lateralization of cognitive functions in the human brain. For related articles see Hugdahl (1995, 1996; Hugdahl & Carlsson, 2001; Hugdahl et al., 1999a, b).

In the foreword to the 1995 volume on brain asymmetry, the editors Richard Davidson and Kenneth Hugdahl (Davidson & Hugdahl, 1995) wrote that "because of the extraordinary diverse range of phenomena studied within the context of brain asymmetry, the extant literature is spread across a number of different disciplines including psychology, cognitive neuroscience, neurology, and the neurosciences" (p. xii). To this list one could also add psychiatry, education disciplines, anatomy, and biology. Probably no other phenomenon has attracted the interest of researchers, teachers, and clinicians from such wide-ranging areas as brain asymmetry, including the Nobel prize in medicine or physiology which was awarded to Roger Sperry in 1981.

HEMISPHERIC ASYMMETRY: A SIMPLE DICHOTOMY?

Figure 1 shows the two cerebral hemispheres, seen from the anterior/ventral, dorsal, and lateral view. Starting with the dorsal view, the most conspicuous anatomical feature of the human brain is the longitudinal fissure which liter-ally divides the brain into two halves, or hemispheres. The longitudinal fissure

(a)   **(b)**   **(c)**

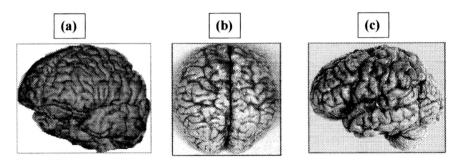

Figure 1. Basic anatomy of the two cerebral hemispheres, seen from the anterior/ventral, dorsal, and lateral view.

indents the brain all the way down to the corpus callosum, which connects the two hemispheres through a massive bundle of nerve fibers. A brief glimpse at the two hemispheres would reveal that they apparently seem to be similar in shape and size, the main difference being the mirror-reversed orientation of the two in relation to each other. A major question in the present paper is therefore to what extent the two cerebral hemispheres are similar in a structural way, and to what extent they differ. A second major question is to what extent the two hemispheres differ in function despite being structurally similar or dissimilar. It is a fact after more than a hundred years of research on the differences in function between the two hemispheres, we still have a limited knowledge of anatomical, or structural, asymmetry, and in particular those areas with a correspondence between structural and functional asymmetry. In the present paper I will review data from our laboratory that addresses the issue of correspondence between structural and functional hemispheric asymmetry.

A typical statement in "folk psychology" as well as in standard psychological and medical textbooks is that the "left hemisphere is specialized, or dominant, for language while the right hemisphere is specialized, or dominant, for visuospatial functions, sometimes also called room orientation." If we consider for a moment the implications of statements like this it is obvious that there is something wrong with them. First of all they imply that the brain is basically specialized for only two functions, language and the ability to orient in the environment. No matter how important these two functions have been in the evolution of modern man, the brain is far more complex in its specialization than language and room orientation. Second, it is implied that half the brain only does language and the other half only does visual processing. This is obviously also wrong. However, very few theories of hemispheric asymmetry consider sensory modalities other than the visual modality (see Kimura, 1967, for an exception), although perhaps the best example of structural-functional asymmetry correspondence is for asymmetry of the planum temporale area in the upper posterior part of the temporal lobe, and auditory-phonetic processing (Hugdahl et al., 1999b; Jäncke, Schlaug, Huang, & Steinmetz, 1994; Steinmetz & Galaburda, 1991; Tervaniemi et al., 2000). Equally wrong is the notion that "language" can be treated in some way as a unified concept. Language consists of many different modules, or subprocesses, phonetics, morphology, semantics, syntax, and prosody or intonation, all of which may be uniquely lateralized to one or both hemispheres. For example, if by language is meant only the expressive speech function, it may be correct to state that the left hemisphere performs "language-functions" (cf. Sperry, 1974). However, if by language we also include prosody, the right hemisphere plays an important role, perhaps being even more "specialized" than the left hemisphere (Zaidel & Seibert, 1997).

In the present review the concept of hemispheric asymmetry, or brain lateralization (I will not make a distinction between the two) needs to be broken down into much more specific subprocesses, both with regard to exactly what brain areas or structures we are talking about, and with regard to exactly what aspect(s) of language that we are studying. I will therefore focus on the planum temporale area in the upper plane of the superior temporal gyrus in the temporal lobe, and the importance of a structural asymmetry in the planum temporale area for functional asymmetry of speech perception, or language phonology (cf. Heiervan et al., in press; Hugdahl et al., 1999b).

Thus, a first conclusion is that traditional views of asymmetry, as only reflecting differences between the hemispheres in the processing of language and visuospatial stimuli, are replaced today by a much more elaborated concept, where brain asymmetry is associated with such constructs as low versus high spatial frequencies (Christman, 1989; Hellige, 1995; Sergent, 1987) and processing of categorical versus coordinate stimulus elements (Brown & Kosslyn, 1995; Kosslyn, 1987), to give a few examples. Spatial frequency refers to the number of black and white alternations in a visual display. A general finding is that the higher the spatial frequency, the more details the display will contain. The left hemisphere has been found to be specialized for higher spatial frequencies, while the right hemisphere is specialized for lower frequencies. Similarly, the concept of categorical versus coordinate spatial relations relates to the view that the left hemisphere is specialized for categorical relations ("is the object above or below the line"), while the right hemisphere is specialized for coordinate relations ("how many mm above or below the line is the object") (Kosslyn, 1987). Both of these models emphasizes the distinction between an upper, dorsal, and lower, ventral, stream in the visual processing pathways, within a hemisphere. Another central concept that will be covered in the present paper is the notion of bottom-up versus top-down asymmetry (see Hugdahl, 1996; Hugdahl &

Carlsson, 2001) for further aspects of conceptual approaches to brain asymmetry.

BOTTOM-UP VERSUS TOP-DOWN ASYMMETRY

With bottom-up processing is meant that the flow of information is analyzed from the level of sensory registration ("the bottom") upward to the higher, cognitive levels ("the top"). Bottom-up processing means beginning with the sensory data, which is transformed and combined to concepts of perception, attention, and memory. Bottom-up processing may be compared with inductive reasoning. Top-down processing, or concept-driven processing, focus on an individual's concepts on shaping registration and "lower" level processing. Within this view, existing concepts and memories modulate incoming sensory registrations that combine two new concepts and models. Top-down processing may be compared with hypothetic-deductive reasoning (see Hugdahl, 1995, for further details). Within the context of brain asymmetry, bottom-up processing could be equated with stimulus-driven asymmetry, whereas top-down processing could be equated with instruction-driven asymmetry. Stimulus-driven asymmetry means that certain stimuli or stimulus arrangements will produce a laterality bias. An example is the right ear advantage in dichotic listening to phonological stimuli, when listening to consonant-vowel syllables (Bryden, 1988; Hugdahl, 1995). An example of instruction-driven asymmetry is the modulation of the right ear advantage by instructing the subject to pay attention only to the right or left ear stimulus element in the dichotic stimulus complex (Asbjørnsen & Hugdahl, 1995; Hugdahl & Andersson, 1986; Bryden, Munhall, & Allard, 1983; Hiscock & Beckie, 1993).

Examples from dichotic listening

Dichotic listening means that two different auditory stimuli are presented at the same time, one in each ear (see left panel in Figure 2). The subject is free to report the stimuli heard, although often instructed to report only the item heard first or best (other procedures also exist in the dichotic listening literature). The stimuli used in the studies reviewed here consist of presentations of pairwise combinations of consonant-vowel (CV) syllables that are made up of the six stop-consonants /b/, /d/, /g/, /p/, /t/, /k/ and the vowel /a/. Thus, examples of dichotic listening stimulus-pairs are /ba/ – /pa/; /ga/ – /pa/, etc. The result is typically better recall from the right ear (when controlling for hearing differences between the ears), which is taken as an indication of left temporal lobe processing superiority for phonological stimuli (see right panel in Figure 2). The right ear advantage (REA) in dichotic listening is a robust empirical phenomenon in asymmetry research (see Hugdahl, 1995) and is

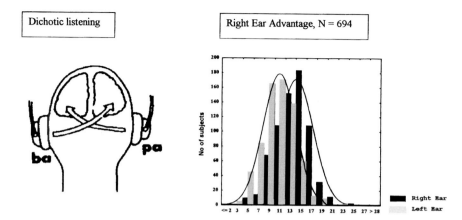

Figure 2. Schematic overview of the principles of dichotic listening (left panel) and illustration of the right ear advantage from 694 healthy individuals (right panel).

considered to be the result of several interacting factors (Kimura, 1967). The REA is believed to be caused by the fact that although auditory input is transmitted to both auditory cortices in the temporal lobes, the contralateral projections are stronger and more preponderant, interfering with the ipsilateral projections. This is shown in the left panel in Figure 2. The advantage for the contralateral auditory projections means that the language (phonology)-dominant left hemisphere receives a stronger signal from the right ear. The contralateral signal from the left ear to the right hemisphere must first pass the corpus callosum in order to be processed in the left hemisphere. Following the same logic, a left ear advantage (LEA) indicates the right hemisphere to be dominant for phonological processing, and a no-ear advantage (NEA) indicates a bilateral phonological dominance pattern.

Figure 3 shows results from a validation study where dichotic listening performance was validated against the Wada-test (Hugdahl, Carlsson, Uvebrant, & Lundervold, 1997). The Wada-test (Wada, 1949) involves the administration of a sedative drug (e.g., sodium amytal or amobarbital) into the left or right hemisphere through a catheter that is threaded into the carotid artery from the femoral artery. The release of the drug sedates the hemisphere for about 5–10 minutes, during which time the examiner may test for side localization of speech language comprehension functions. The data in Figure 3 are from 13 children/adolescents who were tested before they underwent surgical treatment for epilepsy. The subjects were first tested with the Wada-test, and then with the dichotic listening test (knowing the side of speech dominance in advance of the dichotic listening

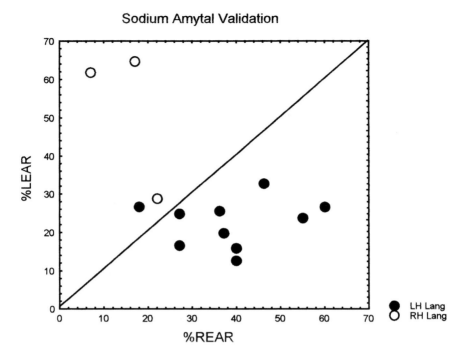

Figure 3. Results from Sodium-Amytal validation of the dichotic listening technique. LH = subjects with left-hemisphere language according to the Wada-test. RH = subjects with right-hemisphere language according to the Wada-test. Each "dot" in the scatter-plot represents a single individual. From Hugdahl et al., 1997, reprinted with permission from the publisher.

test). The Wada-test results revealed that 10 subjects had left-hemisphere language, while three subjects had right-hemisphere language. Eight of the 10 subjects with language in the left hemisphere showed a right ear advantage on the dichotic listening test. All three right-hemisphere language subjects showed a left ear advantage on the dichotic listening test. The data are plotted as scatter-plots of the individual scores from the right and left ear, respectively.

Another kind of validation is shown in Figure 4, which contains PET brain imaging data from 12 adults who were scanned while performing a dichotic monitoring task contrasted against listening to simple tones (from Hugdahl et al., 1999b). The results showed increased activations in the temporal lobe on both sides of the brain. However, the activation was significantly more intense and widespread on the left side, indicating a left temporal lobe asymmetry dominance for listening to phonologically relevant sounds (CV-syllables). In a different condition, the subjects listened to short musical

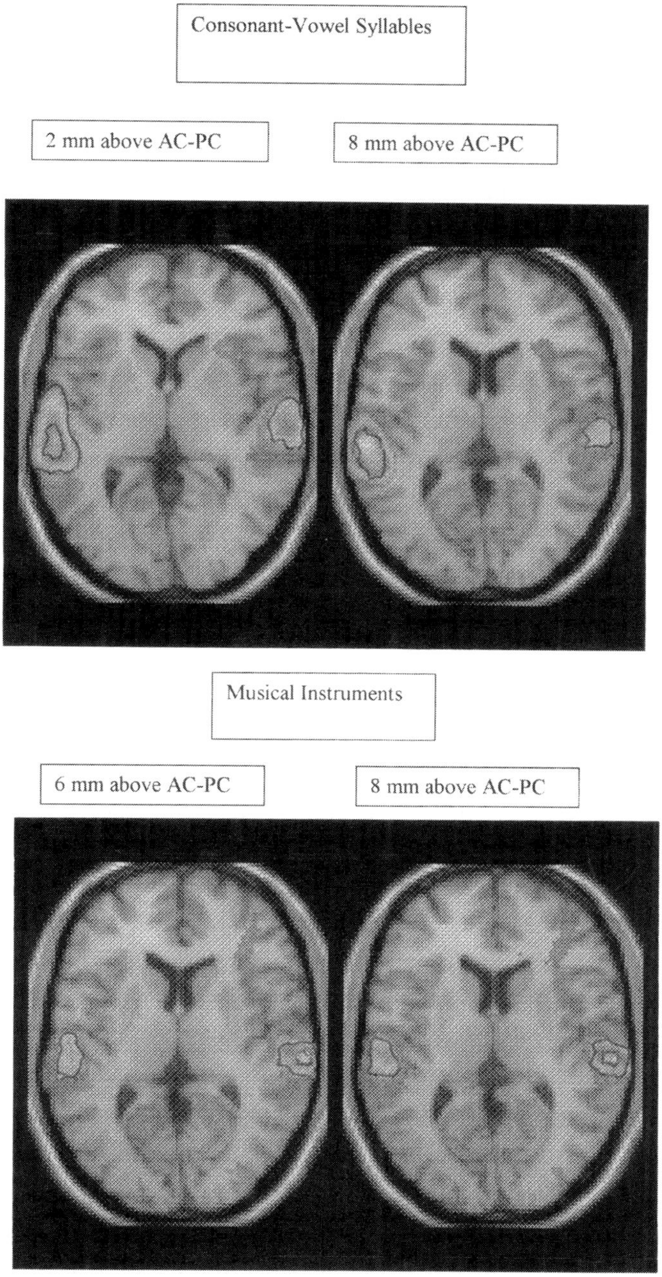

Figure 4. ¹⁵O-PET activation data when subjects listened to dichotic presentations of consonant–vowel syllables or musical instruments. From Hugdahl et al., 1999a. Reprinted with permission from the publisher.

| Phonemes | Musical chords |

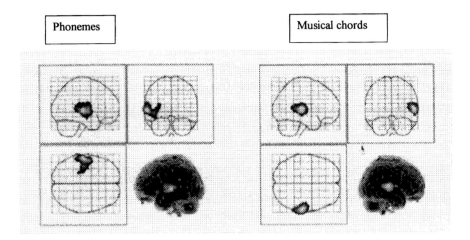

Figure 5. PET activation data in the left and right temporal lobes to presentations of phoneme sounds and musical chords. From Tervaniemi et al., 2000, reprinted with permission from the publisher.

chords from different instruments. The results to these nonphonological stimuli showed a rightward neuronal activation asymmetry. These findings were essentially replicated in an even more recent study by Tervaniemi et al. (2000)—see Figure 5.

Using an oddball paradigm with infrequent and frequent presentations of different sounds, Tervaniemi et al. (2000) found a significant lateralization to the left hemisphere when subjects listened to phonetic sequences, and a significant lateralization to the right hemisphere when subjects listened to musical chords that were matched in spectral complexity with the phonemes.

TOP-DOWN MODULATION: THE EFFECTS OF ATTENTION

Paying attention to the right ear will increase the right ear advantage, while paying attention to the left ear will decrease or shift the right ear advantage to a left ear advantage (LEA) (see Hugdahl & Andersson, 1986). It should be kept in mind that the stimuli remain the same CV-syllables during all three attentional conditions, whether noninstructed (NF), forced-right attention (FR), or forced-left attention (FL). Thus, the modulation of the ear advantage as an effect of attentional instructions shows the dynamic aspect of brain asymmetry, the ability to shift an asymmetry pattern from one hemisphere to another through endogenous cognitive efforts, despite the same external stimulus. The attentional effect in dichotic listening is illustrated in

APPLICATIONS TO SCHIZOPHRENIA

A final example of the inability to modulate the ear advantage in dichotic listening as a consequence of shifting attention to either ear is a study from our laboratory on cognitive flexibility in schizophrenia (Løberg, Hugdahl, & Green, 1999). Schizophrenic patients are impaired on several cognition functions, particularly executive functions that put heavy demands on cognitive flexibility (Green, 1998). In addition, several authors have suggested that the neurocognitive impairments seen in schizophrenia may go back to failure of speech laterality involving the temporal lobe (Crow, 1997). Such a view was supported in a previous study (Green, Hugdahl, & Mitchell, 1994), where we found that schizophrenic patients were impaired on the dichotic listening test (cf. Green, 1998). This was particularly evident for a subgroup of hallucinating patients, who failed to show the expected right ear advantage in the hallucinatory state. Thus, the schizophrenic patients seemed to lack aspects of the normal left-hemisphere language lateralization, particularly in a hallucinatory state (cf. Bruder, 1988; Crow, 1997; Wale & Carr, 1988; Wexler & Heninger, 1979).

The subjects in the study shown in Figure 10 were 33 schizophrenic in-patients, and an age, gender, and handedness matched healthy control group. The schizophrenic patients were drawn from a population of treatment-resistant inpatients at the UCLA Clinical Research Unit at the Camarillo State Hospital, CA, USA, as a part of a larger clinical study (for a more detailed description of inclusion criteria, see Green et al., 1997). Patients were excluded if they had a history of substance abuse (as defined by DSM-III-R, *Diagnostic and statistical manual of mental disorders*; American Psychiatric Association, 1987) within the last 6 months, identifiable neurological disorders (including head injury), physical, cognitive, or language impairment (including hearing deficits), or a period of good functioning in the past 5 years (defined as a score on the DSM-II-R Global Assessment of Functioning Scale above 70).

All subjects were tested with the consonant-vowel syllables dichotic listening paradigm. The subjects were tested under the three different attentional conditions; nonforced attention, with no specific instructions about deployment of attention; forced-right attention, focusing attention to the right ear stimulus; forced-left attention, focusing attention to the left ear stimulus. The main findings were an absence of the expected right ear advantage in the schizophrenic group during the nonforced attention condition, and a failure to modify dichotic listening performance through shifting of attention to either the right or left ear. The control group showed a right ear advantage during the nonforced and forced-right attention conditions (increased ear advantage during the forced-right condition), and a left ear advantage during the forced-left attention condition. Løberg et al. (1999) concluded that the

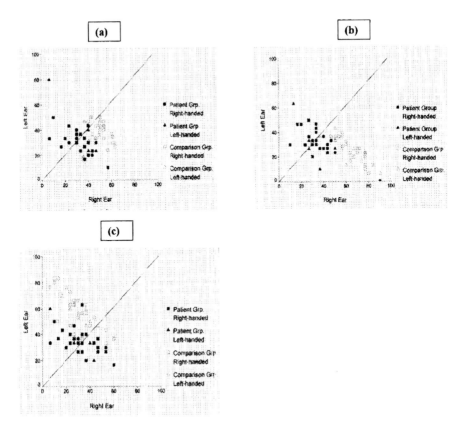

Figure 10. Effects of attention in the dichotic listening paradigm in schizophrenic (black dots) and control (open dots) subjects, under nonforced (a), forced-right (b), and forced-left (c) attentional conditions. Data from Løberg et al., 1999, reprinted with permission from the publisher.

schizophrenic subjects failed to reveal an expected right ear advantage during the nonforced attention condition.

Second, shifting attention to the right ear did not help in advancing the right ear reports, which is almost always found in normal subjects. This may indicate a "dual deficit" involving both "automatic", or bottom-up, and "controlled", or top-down processing deficits. The data in Figure 10 are presented as scatter-plots of the number of schizophrenic subjects and control subjects that showed a REA, LEA, or no ear advantage (NEA) as a function of attentional instruction. The 45-degree line indicates the "symmetry-line", with subjects positioned below the line having a REA and subjects positioned above the line having a LEA. Looking at Figure 10 reveals a static positioning of the schizophrenic cluster across the three attentional conditions, with very little evidence for cognitive flexibility with regard to the specific instruction given. The control subjects cluster, on the other hand, clearly shifted position within the response-space area as a result of shifting attention to the right or left ear, with all subjects, except one, shifted to the right during the FR condition. Similarly, all control subjects, except for three, were shifted to the left during the FL condition. The schizophrenic subjects, however, remained relatively unchanged during all three conditions, indicating an impairment in top-down modulation of a stimulus-driven laterality.

STRUCTURAL VERSUS FUNCTIONAL ASYMMETRY

Despite the research efforts put into the study of functional asymmetry over the last three to four decades, there are few overlapping findings where a functional symmetry corresponds with a structural, or anatomical, asymmetry. Anatomical differences between the hemispheres in cortical organization and connectivity are scarcely reported in the literature. Galaburda and his colleagues (see Galaburda, 1995) have been interested in this aspect of brain asymmetry for more than 20 years. Despite considerable methodological sophistication, they have not found any fundamental differences in architectonic organization or chemical characteristics between the two hemispheres. In a summary of this work, Galaburda (1995) wrote that: ". . . by and large . . . we have only found side differences in the amount of brain substrate devoted to a particular architectonic area or a particular gross anatomical landmark. In other words, despite the fact that the left hemisphere is significantly different in function from the right, there appears to be no structure or chemical constituent that is present in one hemisphere but not in the other . . . There are gyri with the same names and general structure on both sides. All architectonic areas are present in both hemispheres. There are no cell types found in one hemisphere but not in the other. There is no known pattern of connections that appears to be specific to the dominant hemisphere. And as far as has been determined, there are no physiologic properties in neurons of one hemisphere that are not present in the other, this leaves quantitative differences as the only difference between areas present in both hemispheres" (pp. 51–52).

The main argument put forward by Galaburda is therefore that when looking for anatomical differences between the hemispheres, the researcher has to look for quantitative differences, in the hope that such differences may lead to qualitative differences through a leap in thresholding when a quantitative difference becomes large enough. Quantitative differences between the hemispheres have been reported for several structures and areas. For example, in 1985 Sandra Witelson reported that the corpus callosum, which connects the two hemispheres, was larger by about 10–12% in left-handed subjects compared with right-handers. Witelson interpreted this finding as a result of greater connectivity between the hemispheres in left-handers, which would fit other data showing that left-handers, in general, are less lateralized than right-handers on a variety of lateralized tasks.

Asymmetry of other anatomical landmarks have been reported in the literature, from the early findings by Cunningham (1892) that the left Sylvian fissure was longer than the right. This finding has later been related to the larger planum temporale area on the left side which extends the Sylvian fissure on this side (cf. Ide et al., 1999). That is, the Sylvian fissure continues further in the horizontal plane on the left side, before it bends upward (Rubens, Mahowold, & Hutton, 1976). Moreover, the total cortical folding is somewhat greater on the left side, while the right hemisphere is overall heavier and tends to involve more tissue. The left occipital pole is wider and pro-trudes more than the right, while the right frontal pole and the prefrontal cortex is larger on the right side (see Bradshaw & Nettleton, 1983, for an overview of anatomical differences).

THE PLANUM TEMPORALE

However, although anatomical differences do exist between the hemispheres, it is not always obvious what the functional significance may be of a reported difference in structure or appearance. Therefore, it is possible that a given anatomical difference is the result of random factors in the evolution of man, rather than a correlate to a specific functional difference. There is, however, one exception to this, and that concerns the asymmetry of the planum tempo-rale in the upper posterior surface of the temporal lobe. In a now classic paper, Geschwind and Levitsky (1968) found that the left planum temporale was longer in a majority of the brains they investigated. Geschwind and Levitsky investigated 100 brains postmortem, and found that the left planum was larger in 65 of the measured brains. Eleven brains showed a reverse pattern, with longer planum in the right hemisphere, while 24 brains did not show any difference between the left and right side. Although Geschwind and Levitsky were not the first to report anatomical differences between the hemi-spheres, their paper got widespread recognition and boosted interest in hemi-spheric asymmetry research (see historical account by Springer & Deutsch, 1989). The interest in the asymmetry of the planum temporale was not only because of its apparent asymmetry, but also because of the location of the planum in the axial plane in the upper portion of the superior temporal gyrus (see Figure 11).

The upper posterior surface of the temporal lobe is functionally overlap-ping with Wernicke's area (Brodmann areas 41/42), which is considered the primary cortical area for speech perception and language comprehension. The planum temporale is also located just behind the posterior wall of

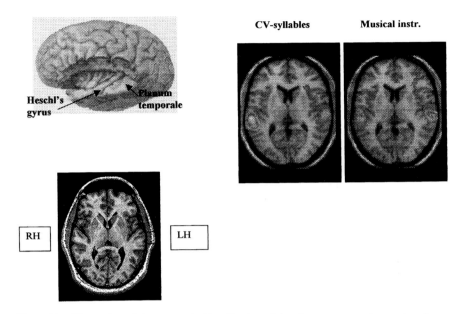

Figure 11. Illustration of the anatomical localization of the planum temporale area in a drawing (upper left; from Heimer, 1994), and MRI (lower left) image. The panels to the right show corresponding neuronal activation (measured with PET) to CV-syllables at the + 8 mm level above the AC-PC midline according to the Talairach and Tournoux (1988) coordinate system. PET data from Hugdahl et al., 1999a, reprinted with permission from the publisher.

Heschl's gyrus, which makes up the primary auditory cortex in man. Thus, a larger left planum temporale could therefore be a structural correlate to the functional specialization of the left hemisphere for language, especially for language comprehension and speech perception, overlapping with the major auditory areas in the brain.

Applications to dyslexia

If the planum temporale asymmetry is critical for adequate understanding of speech and phonological decoding of both auditory and written input, it would not be far to hypothesize that individuals who are impaired in aspects of phonological processing, like individuals with dyslexia, would also show a reduction in the planum temporale asymmetry. This has been the subject of intense research over the last 10–12 years, using magnetic resonance imaging (MRI) as the major tool for visualizing the planum (cf. Dalby, Elbro, & Stødkilde-Jørgensen, 1998; Duara et al., 1991; Galaburda, 1993; Hynd, Semrud-Clikeman, Lorys, Novey, & Eliopulos, 1990; Kushch et al., 1993; Larsen, Høien, Lundberg, & Ødegaard, 1990; Leonard et al., 1993; Rumsey et al., 1997; Schultz et al., 1994). The literature with regard to reduced planum temporale asymmetry in dyslexia is inconsistent, with some authors reporting reduced or reversed asymmetry (e.g., Larsen et al., 1990), while others have failed to find any differences between dyslexic and control subjects (e.g. Leonard et al., 1993). Part of the explanation for these inconsistencies in the literature may be due to the specific method used to measure the planum area, and the problems inherent in the definition of its borders, particularly the posterior border at the end of the Sylvian fissure. Ide et al. (1999) have suggested that the observed planum temporale asymmetry may not be a consequence of differences in size between the left and right planum, but rather a difference in the positioning of the two plana (see also Jäncke et al., 1994; Leonard et al., 1993; Witelson & Kigar, 1992).

Planum temporale and functional brain imaging

The functional correlate to planum temporale asymmetry was studied by Hugdahl et al. (1999a) using the ^{15}O-PET technique. As described previously, the subjects listened to presentations of CV-syllables or different musical chords contrasted against the presentation of simple tones. Figure 12 shows brain activations to the two types of stimuli in axial slices when going vertically "slice-by-slice" through the planum temporale area. Each slice in Figure 12 had a thickness of 2 mm. Activation data are shown from 12 mm below the AC-PC midline to 200 mm above the midline (according to coordinates from the Talairach & Tournoux, 1988, brain atlas).

Although it is difficult to delineate exactly the upper and lower borders of the planum temporale in axial slices, the main portion of the planum temporale would be within a region defined by + 6/8 mm to + 18/20 mm above the AC-PC midline. For the musical instrument stimuli, reliable activations in the planum temporale area were observed from −2 mm to + 20 mm, with essentially greater activations on the right side. Interestingly, the musical instrument stimuli also activated a small area in the upper part of the cerebellum. The speech-related CV-syllable sounds, on the other hand, showed greater activations in the left planum temporale area, particularly from + 4 mm to + 18 mm. The CV-syllables also activated areas below the planum temporale, in the inferior and medial temporal gyri (−10 mm to 0 mm). The left-sided asymmetry was also much more marked for the CV-syllables than the right-sided asymmetry for the musical instrument stimuli. The activation in the more ventral areas of the temporal lobe to the CV-syllable stimuli fit with recent data published by Binder and his colleagues (see Binder et al., 1996, 2000), who suggested that the planum temporale may not be unique for the processing of speech stimuli, and that more ventral areas in the medial and inferior temporal gyri may be critical for phonological processing, while the planum temporale may be more tuned to processing of the acoustical features

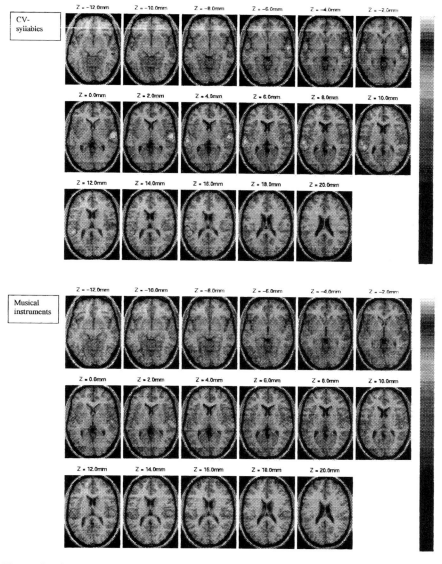

Figure 12. Same data as in Figure 11 (right hand panels), but plotted in 2 mm axial slices from −12 mm below to 20 mm above the AC-PC midline, to both CV-syllables and musical instruments stimuli.

of the speech signal. Although supporting Binder's findings in general, our data also point to a more complex activation pattern for different kinds of acoustic stimuli. A final comment regarding the data presented in Figure 12 is that the CV-syllables caused greater overall activation compared to the musical instrument stimuli.

Qualitative versus quantitative differences

Thus, although both the left and right planum temporale was activated to both kinds of stimuli, there was a quantitative difference in functional asymmetry favoring the left hemisphere for the speech stimuli and the right hemisphere for the musical instrument stimuli. This may be an important observation regarding the current controversy in the literature about the exact role of the planum temporale in speech perception. As discussed in the previous section, Binder has suggested that the planum temporale may be specialized only for analyzing the acoustical aspects of speech, while more ventral areas in the temporal lobe are responsible for the phonological analysis. This suggestion is partly based on the fact that *both* plana are activated during phonological and nonphonological stimuli. However, as seen in the data in Figure 12, the critical issue is not whether there should be a qualitative difference, with for example absence of activation on the right side to phonological stimuli, but rather whether there are quantitative asymmetry differences to different kinds of stimuli that fit a general theory of hemispheric asymmetry and speech perception.

Methodological issues

Another explanation for current controversies regarding the role played by the planum temporale in research on brain asymmetry may be differences in the way the data are analyzed. One frequently used method has been the use of an asymmetry index, based on the difference between the left and right side. A typical index measure is to divide the (left − right) difference with the total area (left + right), expressing the function as a percentage difference. There are two problems with such index measures. First of all, a difference in asymmetry index between a pathological group and a control group may be caused by either the left side being smaller, the right side being larger, or both the left being smaller and the right side being larger in the pathological group. The asymmetry index will not distinguish between these alternatives. The other problem concerns the role played by the right planum temporale. A conservative approach would claim that there is no theory predicting a specific role for the right planum for the understanding of speech or language, neither from experimental nor lesion studies. Thus, it does not make sense to use an asymmetry index when comparing different groups, which does not distinguish between the unique contributions from the left and right side. An alternative explanation has been provided by Galaburda, Corsiglia, Rosen, and Sherman (1987), who suggested that the reduced planum temporale asymmetry observed in dyslexic individuals is also due to a larger than normal right-side planum, caused by pathology of neuronal migration and cell pruning in the embryonic stage of development. This is a plausible explanation considering that neuronal pruning is a major characteristic of the developing brain.

Figure 13 show data from a recent study in our laboratory (Heiervang et al., in press) on the size of the left and right planum temporale in 20 dyslexic and control children measured with MRI and subjected to morphometry analysis according to the technique developed by Helmuth Steinmetz (Steinmetz & Galaburda, 1991; Steinmetz et al., 1989). The subjects in the Heiervang et al. study were screened from a population of 950 children between the ages 11 and 12 years. As the first stage of the screening consisted of a spelling test with 40 normal single words (Johnsen, 1984). In the second stage of the screening, children with scores below the 10th percentile on the spelling test were subsequently given five single-word reading tests, the KOAS test (Høien & Lundberg, 1989). The KOAS test is a computerized test-battery that taps orthographic as well as phonologic decoding strategies in reading, and is standardized for a Norwegian sample. A reading score of at least 2 *SD* below the age mean was required to be classified as reading disabled. In addition, the children should have an IQ of at least 85. This was assessed by an estimation from four verbal subscales, and four performance subscales on the WISC-R (Wechsler, 1981). Handedness was determined according to Annett's 12-items inventory (Annett, 1967).

The results (see Figure 13) showed that both the dyslexics and control subjects had a leftward asymmetry. Thus, dyslexic children also show a larger left than right planum temporale. There were, furthermore, no significant differences when the analysis was based on the asymmetry index. However, as also seen in Figure 12, the left planum temporale area was markedly reduced in the dyslexic group compared with the control subjects, while the right planum area was almost identical in the two groups. The results also showed that there was a positive correlation between a leftward planum temporale asymmetry and spelling and reading in the control group, with an association between planum temporale asymmetry and reading in normal reading individuals. Rumsey et al. (1997) also reported significant correlations in their control group between leftward planum temporale asymmetry and Verbal IQ, reading skills, and phonological competence. The lack of correlation between planum temporale size and reading in the present dyslexia group suggest that reading in this group may also be influenced by other factors than planum temporale size or asymmetry.

The mechanisms which determine planum temporale size or asymmetry

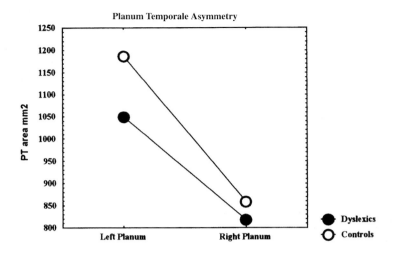

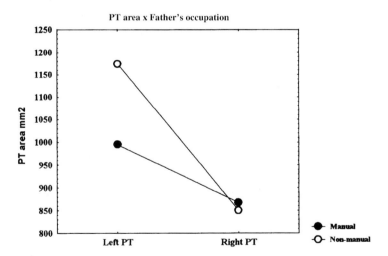

Figure 13. Planum temporale area size measured from MRI sagittal images acquired from 20 dyslexic and 20 control subjects (upper panel). The lower panel shows PT area size from the same 40 subjects, arranged by the father's occupation (manual/non-manual). Data from Heiervang et al. (in press), reprinted with permission from the publisher.

are largely unknown. Brain size has recently been shown to be largely under genetic control (Bartley et al., 1997), and brain asymmetry has also been suggested to be due to genetic predisposition (Galaburda, 1993). However, environmental factors may also be involved in regional brain growth and brain asymmetry (Amunts et al., 1997; Steinmetz, Hertzog, Schlaug, Huang, & Jäncke, 1995). Age and brain volume have been found to interact with planum temporale size or asymmetry (Preis, Jäncke, Schittler, Huang, & Steinmetz, 1998; Schultz et al., 1994). Total (right and left) planum temporale size showed a significant positive correlation with age in the present control group, but no group differences for age or total planum temporale size was observed. Differences in birthweight and Verbal IQ did not interact with planum temporale asymmetry.

The lower panel in Figure 13 shows a significant interaction between planum temporale area in the children (across both groups) and the occupation of the father of the children, dichotomized as "manual" or "nonmanual" from the background data for the project. Note the apparent reduction in area size for the left planum in children whose fathers had manual occupation, with no difference at all for the right planum. Although the three-way interaction involving the subject groups was not significant, post hoc analyses showed that the two-way interaction was primarily driven by the fathers of the dyslexic children. This may be a spurious, accidental effect without theoretical significance, or it may point to a possible genetical link in dyslexia.

HEMISPHERIC INTEGRATION: THE ROLE OF THE CORPUS CALLOSUM

In a recent review of research on commissurotomized patients—or "split-brain" patients because they have the hemispheres surgically disconnected—Gazzaniga (2000) suggested that the corpus callosum, which connects the two cerebral hemispheres, functions as "the great communication link" between the left and right hemisphere (see Figure 14).

Gazzaniga suggested that the development of the corpus callosum made the specialization of functions in one hemisphere possible by linking the two together, like a communication network. Thus, when a specialized cognitive function emerged in one hemisphere at the expense of a pre-existing bilateral perceptual system, the old system could be preserved in the non-specialized hemisphere. The communication between the hemispheres through the corpus callosum may be critical for the subjective experience of an integrated and unified "self", as if we had only one single hemisphere. An important observation with the split-brain patient, from the perspective of the present paper, is that the right hemisphere seems to lack the ability for phonological processing. The disconnected right hemisphere lacks

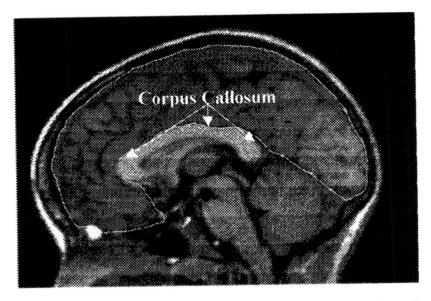

Figure 14. Midline sagittal MRI image showing the positioning of the corpus callosum. From Von Plessen et al. (2001). Reprinted with the permission of the publisher.

many of the specific features that characterizes the perception of speech sounds, like for example categorical perception (Sidtis, Volpe, Holtzman, Wilson, & Gazzaniga, 1981) and the recognition of rhyming words from a text (Zaidel & Peters, 1981). The right hemisphere may perceive speech units as whole words and not as phonemes. Thus, the right hemisphere may process speech sounds quite differently from the left hemisphere, with the corpus callosum transferring phonological information between the hemispheres.

If the right and left hemispheres have different resolutions when decoding phonological input, with the right hemisphere operating with whole words as the smallest unit, while the left hemisphere operates at the phoneme level, it could be hypothesized that individuals with impaired phonological decoding may have reduced callosal transfer between the hemispheres. This would slow down trafficking between the hemispheres and the speed at which phono-logical input is processed. The core problem in dyslexia has been suggested to be impairment of phonological decoding when reading (Olson, Gillis, Rack, DeFries, & Fulker, 1991). That is, the dyslexic child is impaired in finding the corresponding phoneme structure of the written input when reading. Using high-resolution magnetic resonance imaging (MRI), with 1.2 mm thick sagittal slices, we investigated the size and shape of the corpus callosum in dyslexic and control children (Von Plessen et al., 2001). Several studies have looked for structural abnormalities in the corpus callosum in dyslexic individuals. The findings have, however, been mixed, with some studies reporting smaller overall size in dyslexic children, others failing to find any differences when compared with normal controls (see Beaton, 1997, for review). A closer look at these studies, however, indicates wide variations in the subjects' age, sex, handedness, and with respect to study setting. A majority of the studies have only reported size differences in the corpus callosum of dyslexic and control children (e.g., Larsen, Høien, & Ødegaard, 1992). A few other studies have investigated both size and explicit shape differences between dyslexics and controls in various regions of the corpus callosum (e.g., Robichon & Habib, 1998). We investigated both shape and size with a new method by manually tracing the corpus callosum perimeter on the aligned midsagittal MR slice and comparing total callosal area as subdivisions between the groups. A shape analysis and subsequent classification by shape characteristics was then performed. The results showed no significant differences between the groups with respect to overall corpus callosum area, or for the subregions. However, the shape-analysis revealed a shortening of the midbody-isthmus region in the dyslexic group. The isthmus region in the posterior one-third of the corpus callosum is the area where the nerve fibers from the superior temporal gyrus cross between the hemispheres (Pandya & Seltzer, 1986). Thus, the isthmus region connects the fibers from the planum temporale and Wernicke's area, areas that play a critical role in speech perception and language comprehension. It is therefore possible that part of the problem in dyslexia lies within a deficient transfer function between the hemispheres for phonological stimulus units.

SUMMARY AND CONCLUSIONS

In the present paper I have reviewed experimental and clinical studies in our laboratory over the last 20 years with regard to lateralization of cognitive functions in the brain. Two emerging concepts are discussed in some detail: top-down modulation of stimulus-driven, low-level asymmetry patterns, and the relation between functional and structural asymmetry. Using the dichotic listening technique with speech sounds and musical chords, we have found that a stimulus-specific asymmetry pattern can be shifted to the other hemisphere in the intact brain by focusing attention to either side in auditory space. Shifting attention to the right or left side also changes blood flow distribution in the left and right hemisphere, although lateralized stimulus presentations remain constant across testing conditions. Using magnetic resonance morphometry we have investigated the planum temporale area in the posterior upper part of the temporal lobe in dyslexic and control children. The planum temporale is one of the few areas in the brain with a structural asymmetry that corresponds to functional asymmetry for phonological processing. Dyslexic children have reduced overall size of the left planum temporale, which may be a correlate to their impaired phonological decoding ability.

ACKNOWLEDGEMENTS

The present research was financially supported by grants from the Norwegian Medical Research Council, Haukeland University Hospital, and from the School of Psychology, University of Bergen.

The contribution of Alf Inge Smievoll, Arve Asbjørnsen, Roger Barndon, Lars Ersland, Arvid Lundervold, Britta Andersson, Einar Heiervang, Gunilla Walldebo, Gunnar Rosen, Helmuth Steinmetz, Ian Law, Kerstin von Plessen, and Richard Davidson is greatly acknowledged. Special thanks to Ian Law at the National Hospital in Copenhagen, Denmark for providing the data analysis for Figure 12, and Helmuth Steinmetz, University of Frankfurt, Germany for analyzing the MR image data presented in Figure 13.

REFERENCES

American Psychiatric Association. (1987). Diagnostic and statistical manual of mental disorders, (3rd ed., revised), DSM-III. Washington, DC: APA.

Amunts, K., Schlaug, G., Jäncke, L., Steinmetz, H., Schleicher, A., Dabringhaus, A., & Zilles, K. (1997). Motor cortex and motor skill: structural compliance in the human brain. *Human Brain Mapping, 5*, 206–215.

Annett, M. (1967). The bimodal distribution of right, mixed and left handedness. *Quarterly Journal of Experimental Psychology, 19*, 327–333.

Asbjørnsen, A., & Hugdahl, K. (1995). Attentional effects in dichotic listening. *Brain and Language, 49*, 189–201.

Bartley, A.J., Jones, D.W., & Weinberger, D.R. (1997). Genetic variability of human brain size and cortical gyral patterns. *Brain, 120*, 257–269.

Beaton, A.A. (1997). The relation of planum temporale asymmetry and morphology of the corpus callosum to handedness, gender, and dyslexia: A review of the evidence. *Brain and Language, 60*, 255–322.

Beaton, A., Hugdahl, K., & Ray, P. (2000). Lateral asymmetries in aging: A review and some data. In M. Mandal, M.B. Bulman-Fleming, & G. Tiwari (Eds.), *Side-bias: A neuropsychological perspective*. Dordrecht, Netherlands: Kluwer Academic Publishers.

Binder, J.R., Frost, J.A., Hammeke, T.A., Bellgowan, P.S.F., Springer, J.A., Kaufman, J.N., & Possing, E.T. (2000). Human temporal lobe activation by speech and non-speech sounds. *Cerebral Cortex, 10*, 512–528.

Binder, J.R., Frost, J.A., Hammeke T.A., Rao, S.M., & Cox, R.W. (1996). Function of the left planum temporale in auditory and linguistic processing. *Brain, 119*, 1239–1247.

Bradshaw, J.L. & Nettleton, N.C. (1983). *Human cerebral asymmetry*. Englewoods Cliffs, NJ.: Prentice Hall Publishers.

Brown, H.D., & Kosslyn, S.M. (1995). Hemispheric differences in visual objects processing: Structural versus allocation theories. In R.J. Davidson & K. Hugdahl (Eds.), *Brain asymmetry* (pp. 77–98). Cambridge, MA: MIT Press.

Bruder, G.E. (1988). Dichotic listening in psychiatric patients. In K. Hugdahl (Ed.), *Handbook of dichotic listening: Theory, methods, and research* (pp. 527–564). Chichester, UK: Wiley & Sons.

Bryden, M.P. (1988). An overview of the dichotic listening procedure and its relation to cerebral organization. In K. Hugdahl (Ed.), *Handbook of dichotic listening: Theory, methods, and research* (pp. 1–44). Chichester, UK: Wiley & Sons.

Bryden, M.P., Munhall, K., & Allard, F. (1983). Attentional biases and the right-ear effect in dichotic listening. *Brain and Language, 18,* 236–248.

Christman, S. (1989). Perceptual characteristics in visual laterality research. *Brain and Cognition, 11,* 238–257.

Crow, T.J. (1997). Schizophrenia as a failure of the hemispheric dominance for language. *Trends in Neurosciences, 20,* 339–343.

Cunningham, D.J. (1892). *Contribution to the surface anatomy of the cerebral hemispheres.* Dublin: Royal Irish Society.

Dalby, M.A., Elbro, C., & Stødkilde-Jørgensen, H. (1998). Temporal lobe asymmetry and dyslexia: An in vivo study using MRI. *Brain and Language, 62,* 51–69.

Davidson, R.J., & Hugdahl, K. (Eds.) (1995). *Brain asymmetry.* Cambridge, MA: MIT Press.

Duara, R., Kushch, A., Gross-Glenn, K., Barker, W.W., Jallad, B., Pascal, S., Loewenstein, D.A., Sheldon, J., Rabin, M., Levin, B.E., & Lubs, H. (1991). Neuroanatomic differences between dyslexic and normal readers magnetic resonance imaging scans. *Archives of Neurology, 48,* 410–416.

Galaburda, A. (1993). The planum temporale (editorial). *Archives of Neurology, 50,* 457.

Galaburda, A.M. (1995). Anatomical basis of cerebral dominance. In R.J. Davidson & K. Hugdahl (Eds.), *Brain asymmetry* (pp. 31–50). Cambridge, MA: MIT Press.

Galaburda, A., Corsiglia, J., Rosen, G.D., & Sherman, G.F. (1987). Planum temporale asymmetry, reappraisal since Geschwind and Levitsky. *Neuropsychologia, 25,* 853–868.

Gazzaniga, M.S. (2000). Cerebral specialization and interhemispheric communication—Does the corpus callosum enable the human condition? *Brain, 123,* 1293–1326.

Geschwind, N., & Levitsky, W. (1968). Left-right asymmetries in temporal speech region. *Science, 161,* 186–187.

Green, M.F. (1998). *Schizophrenia from a neurocognitive perspective.* Boston, MA: Allyn & Bacon.

Green, M.F., Hugdahl, K., & Mitchell, S. (1994). Dichotic listening during auditory hallucinations in schizophrenia. *American Journal of Psychiatry, 151,* 357–362.

Green, M.F., Marshall, B.D. Jr, Wirshing, W.C., Ames, D., Marder, S.R., McGurk, S., Kern, R.S., & Mintz, J. (1997). Does Risperidone improve verbal working memory in treatment-resistant schizophrenia? *American Journal of Psychiatry, 154,* 799–804.

Heiervang, E., Hugdahl, K., Steinmetz, H., Smievoll, A.I., Stevenson, J., Ersland, L., Lund, A., & Lundervold, A. (in press). Planum temporale, planum parietale and dichotic listening in dyslexia. *Neuropsychologia.*

Heimer, L. (1994). *The human brain and spinal cord* (p. 79). New York: Springer Verlag.

Hellige, J.B. (1995). Hemispheric asymmetry for components of visual information processing. In R.J. Davidson & K. Hugdahl (Eds.), *Brain asymmetry* (pp. 199–122). Cambridge, MA: MIT Press.

Hiscock, M., & Beckie, J.L. (1993). Overcoming the right-ear advantage: A study of focused attention in children. *Journal of Clinical and Experimental Neuropsychology, 15,* 754–772.

Høien, T., & Lundberg, I. (1989). A strategy for assessing problems in word recognition among dyslexics. *Scandinavian Journal of Educational Research, 33,* 185–201.

Hugdahl, K. (1995). Dichotic listening: Probing temporal lobe functional integrity. In R.J. Davidson & K. Hugdahl (Eds.), *Brain asymmetry* (pp. 123–156). Cambridge MA: MIT Press.

Hugdahl, K. (1996). Brain laterality: Beyond the basics. *European Psychologist, 1,* 206–220.

Hugdahl, K., & Andersson, L. (1986). The "forced-attention paradigm" in dichotic listening to CV-syllables: A comparison between adults and children. *Cortex, 22,* 417–432.

Hugdahl, K., Brønnick, K., Kyllingsbæk, S., Law, I., Gade, A., & Paulson, O.B. (1999a). Brain activation during dichotic presentations of consonant-vowel and musical instruments stimuli: A ^{15}O-PET study. *Neuropsychologia, 37*, 431–440.

Hugdahl, K., & Carlsson, G. (2001). Age effects in dichotic listening to consonant-vowel syllables: Interactions with attention. *Developmental Psychology, 20*, 449–461.

Hugdahl, K., Carlsson, G., Uvebrant, P., & Lundervold, A.J. (1997). Dichotic listening performance and intracarotid amobarbital injections in children/adolescent: Comparisons pre- and post-operatively. *Archives of Neurology, 54*, 1494–1500.

Hugdahl, K., Heiervang, E., Nordby, H., Smievoll, A.I., Steinmetz, H., Stevenson, J., & Lund, A. (1999b). Central auditory processing and brain laterality: Applications to dyslexia. *Scandinavian Journal of Audiology, 27*, Suppl 49, 26–34.

Hugdahl, K., Law, I., Kyllingsbæk, S., Brønnick, K., Gade, A., & Paulson, O.B. (2000). Effects of attention on dichotic listening: An ^{15}O-PET study. *Human Brain Mapping, 10*, 87–97.

Hynd, G.W., Semrud-Clikeman, M., Lorys, A.R., Novey, E.S., & Eliopulos, D. (1990). Brain morphology in developmental dyslexia and attention deficits disorder/hyperactivity. *Archives of Neurology, 47*, 919–926.

Ide, A., Dolezal, C., Fernandez, M., Labbé, E., Mandujano, R., Montes, S., Segura, P., Verschae, G., Yarmuch, P., & Aboitiz, F. (1999). Hemispheric differences in variability of fissural patterns in parasylvian and cingulate regions of human brains. *The Journal of Comparative Neurology, 410*, 235–242.

Jäncke, L., Schlaug, G., Huang, Y., & Steinmetz, H. (1994). Asymmetry of the planum parietale. *NeuroReport, 5*, 1161–1163.

Johnsen, K. (Ed.) (1984). *Ord-diktater 1.-6. klasse.* Oslo: Universitetsforlaget.

Kimura, D. (1967). Functional asymmetry of the brain in dichotic listening. *Cortex, 3*, 163–168.

Kosslyn, S.M. (1987). Seeing and imagining in the cerebral hemispheres. A computational approach. *Psychological Review, 94*, 148–175.

Kushch, A., Gross-Glenn, K., Jallad, B., Lubs, H., Rabin, M., Feldman, E., & Duara, R. (1993). Temporal lobe surface area measurements on MRI in normal and dyslexic readers. *Neuropsychologia, 31*, 811–821.

Larsen, J.P., Høien, T., & Ødegaard, H. (1992). Magnetic resonance imaging of the corpus callosum in developmental dyslexia. *Cognitive Neuropsychology, 9*, 123–134.

Larsen, J.P., Høien, T., Lundberg, I., & Ødegaard, H. (1990). MRI evaluation of the size and symmetry of the planum temporale in adolescents with developmental dyslexia. *Brain and Language, 39*, 255–288.

Leonard, C.M., Voeller, K.K.S., Lombardino, L.J., Morris, M.K., Hynd, G.W., Alexander, A.W., Andersen, H.G., Garofalakis, M., Honeyman, J.C., Mao, J., Agee, O.F., & Staab, E.V. (1993). Anomalous cerebral structure in dyslexia revealed with magnetic resonance imaging. *Archives of Neurology, 50*, 461–469.

Løberg, E.M., Hugdahl, K., & Green, M.F. (1999). Hemispheric asymmetry in schizophrenia: A "dual deficits" model. *Biological Psychiatry, 45*, 76–81.

Olson, R.K., Gillis, J.J., Rack, J.P., DeFries, J.C., & Fulker, D.W. (1991). Confirmatory factor analysis of word recognition and process measures in the Colorado Reading Project. *Reading and Writing, 3*, 235–248.

Pandya, D.N., & Seltzer, B. (1986). The topography of commissural fibers. In F. Lepore, M. Ptito, & H.H. Jasper (Eds.), *Two hemispheres-one brain: Functions of the corpus callosum* (pp. 47–73). New York: Alan R. Liss.

Posner, M.I., & Riachle, M.E. (1994). *Images of mind.* New York: Scientific American Library.

Preis, S., Jäncke, L., Schittler, P., Huang, Y., & Steinmetz, H. (1998). Normal intrasylvian anatomical asymmetry in children with developmental language disorder. *Neuropsychologia, 36*, 849–855.

Robichon, F., & Habib, M. (1998). Abnormal callosal morphology in male adult dyslexics: Relationship to handedness and phonological abilities. *Brain and Language*, 62, 127–146.

Rubens, A.B., Mahowold, M.W., & Hutton, J.T. (1976). Asymmetry of the lateral (Sylvian) fissures in man. *Neurology*, 26, 620–624.

Rumsey, J.M., Donohue, B.C., Brady, D.R., Nace, K., Giedd, J.N., & Andreason, P. (1997). A magnetic resonance imaging study of planum temporale asymmetry in men with developmental dyslexia. *Archives of Neurology*, 54, 1481–1489.

Schultz, R.T., Cho, N.K., Staib, L.H., Kier, L.E., Fletcher, J.M., Shaywitz, S.E., Shankweiler, D.P., Katz, L., Gore, J.C., Duncan, J.S., & Shaywitz, B.A. (1994). Brain morphology in normal and dyslexic children: The influence of sex and age. *Annals of neurology*, 35, 732–742.

Sergent, J. (1987). Failures to confirm the spatial-frequency hypothesis: Fatal blow or healthy complication? *Canadian Journal of Psychology*, 41, 412–428.

Sidtis, J.J., Volpe, B.T., Holtzman, J.D., Wilson, D.H., & Gazzaniga, M.S. (1981). Cognitive interaction after staged callosal section: Evidence for transfer of semantic activation. *Science*, 212, 344–346.

Sperry, R.W. (1974). Lateral specialization in the surgically separated hemispheres. In *The Neuroscience: Third Study Program* (pp. 5–19). Cambridge, MA: MIT Press.

Springer, S.P., & Deutsch, G. (1989). *Left brain, right brain (3rd edn.)*. San Francisco: W.H. Freeman & Co.

Steinmetz, H., & Galaburda, A.M. (1991). Planum temporale asymmetry: In-vivo morphometry affords a new perspective for neuro-behavioral research. *Reading and Writing*, 3, 331–343.

Steinmetz, H., Hertzog, A., Schlaug, G, Huang, Y., & Jäncke, L. (1995). Brain (a)symmetry in monozygotic twins. *Cerebral Cortex*, 5, 296–300.

Steinmetz, H., Rademacher, J., Huang, Y., Hefter, H., Zilles, K., Thron, A., & Freund, H.J. (1989). Cerebral asymmetry: MR planimetry of the human planum temporale. *Journal of Computer Assisted Tomography*, 13, 996–1005.

Talairach, J., & Tournoux, P. (Eds.) (1988). *Co-planar stereotaxic atlas of the human brain. 3-D propotional system: An approach to cerebral imaging.* Stuttgart & New York: Georg Thieme Verlag.

Tervaniemi, M., Medvedev, S.V., Alho, K., Pakhomov, S.V., Roudas, M.S., Van Zuijen, T.L., & Näätänen, R. (2000). Lateralized automatic auditory processing of phonetic versus musical information: A PET study. *Human Brain Mapping*, 10, 74–80.

Von Plessen, K., Lundervold, A., Duta, N., Heiervang, E., Klauschen, F., Ersland, L., Smievoll, A.I., &, Hugdahl, K. (2001). *Size and shape of the corpus callosum in dyslexic boys—a structural MRI study.* Manuscript submitted for publication.

Wada, J. (1949). A new method for the determination of the side of cerebral speech dominance. A preliminary report on the intracarotid injection of sodium amytal in a man. *Medical Biology*, 14, 221–222.

Wale, J., & Carr, V. (1988). Dichotic listening asymmetries and psychotic symptoms in schizophrenia: A preliminary report. *Psychiatry Reseach*, 25, 31–39.

Wechsler, D. (Ed.) (1981). *Examiner's manual: Wechsler intelligence scale for children—revised.* New York: Psychological Corporation.

Wexler, B.E., & Heninger, G.R. (1979). Alterations in cerebral laterality during acute psychotic illness. *Archives of General Psychiatry*, 36, 278–284.

Witelson, S.F. (1985). The brain connection: The corpus callosum is larger in left-handers. *Science*, 229, 665–668.

Witelson, S.F., & Kigar, D.L. (1992). Sylvian fissure morphology and asymmetry in men and women: Bilateral differences in relation handedness in men. *Journal of Comparative Neurology*, 323, 326–340.

Zaidel, E., & Peters, A.M. (1981). Phonological encoding and ideographic reading by the disconnected right hemisphere: Two case studies. *Brain and Language, 14*, 205–234.

Zaidel, E., & Seibert, L. (1997). Speech in the disconnected right hemisphere. *Brain and Language, 60*, 188–192.

CHAPTER FIVE

Musica, maestro!

Daniele Schön and Mireille Besson
Center for Research in Cognitive Neuroscience, CNRS-Marseille, France

If you can walk you can dance. If you can talk you can sing.

Zimbabwe proverb

INTRODUCTION

The series of experiments that we describe in this chapter are centered on the question of the specificity of the computations involved in language processing. In order to address this question, language is compared with another well-organized cognitive function, that, although very different in many respects, nevertheless presents interesting similarities to language: music. Language and music differ by the nature of their respective constitutive elements, phonemes, morphemes, words in spoken language and notes and chords in music, and their structural organization. Whereas language is organized horizontally, a succession of sounds in time, music offers both a horizontal organization, the melody formed by the pitch relationship between successive sounds, and a vertical organization, the simultaneous production of two or more sounds such as in chords. Furthermore, language and music differ by their social function. Whereas most authors will agree that the basic function of language is to express thoughts in order to communicate with other individuals, the function of music is a subject of controversy, maybe because music is more culturally bound than language. In Western cultures, music has evolved in such a way as to become more and more isolated from other expressive forms. By contrast, in other cultures, in which the magical thought is still alive, the bond between music, song, dance, poetry, and rite has not been lost (Blacking, 1973; Schön & Schön, 1999). Ethnomusicological studies have often emphasized that music translates emotional experiences into artistic forms, and allows communication with the unknown, as can be seen from the religious rituals in primal tribes (e.g., Nadel, 1930; Von Hornbostel, 1928). Moreover, Kubik (1969) has pointed out that, in African cultures, music is the acoustic result of an action and action is an intrinsic part of musical performance. Motor patterns are themselves sources of aesthetic pleasure, independently from the sound they are associated with. This strong intertwining between music and action is even reflected in language, the same word being used in several African languages to refer to music and dance. This concept stands in marked contrast with the passive perceptive status of music within the Western tradition. Thus, for instance, most of the studies in the psychology of music are centered on music perception (and our studies are, unfortunately, of no exception), and music performance has received much less attention (but see Sloboda, 2000).

Aside from these differences, language and music have both been developed by all human cultures and seem specific to humans; they both ensure the cohesion of the social group and, as such, play a powerful social function in all human societies (Arom & Khalfa, 1999; Boucourechliev, 1993; Levman, 1992; Nadel, 1930). Blacking (1973), for instance, maintained that members of a culture share a common way of structuring musical experience. He defines music as "sound that is organized into socially accepted patterns". Moreover, he argues that every piece of music has its own inherent logic, as the creation of an individual reared in a particular cultural background. However, his claim that patterns of sounds reflect patterns of social organization seems somewhat coarse, and in need of further elaboration. Still, in much the same way that a context-sensitive grammar is a more powerful analytical tool than a context-free grammar, the cognitive systems underlying different styles of music shall be better understood if music is considered in context. Different musical styles should thus not be considered as "sonic objects" but as humanly organized sound, whose patterns are related to the social and cognitive processes of a particular society and culture. Finally, both language and music rely on a sequential organization of sounds that unfold in time. These sound are in both cases characterized by their pitch, duration, intensity and timbre. They are structured into separate units by variations in voice intonation, prosody, that tend to go down at the end of sentences, and by the cadence at the end of musical phrases (i.e., the classic succession of tonic, dominant, sub-dominant and tonic chords at the end of musical phrases). Most importantly, both language and music rely on different levels of processing. In the first part of this chapter, we will lay the cognitive basis to compare language and music by describing the different levels of processing at play within the musical and linguistic systems. We will then quickly review some of the theoretical and experimental arguments in favor or against the question of the specificity of the computations involved in language processing. We will finally report some experiments conducted in the fields of neuropsychology and cognitive neurosciences, using brain imaging methods, and aimed at specifying the brain mechanisms and the cerebral structures involved in some aspects of language and music processing, before summarizing the results of our own research.

MUSIC AND LANGUAGE STRUCTURE

From a cognitive perspective, music and language cannot be considered as single entities. In order to be analyzed and compared they need to be reduced to their constitutive elements. Within music, one can classically differentiate the temporal (meter and rhythm), melodic (contour, pitch, and interval), and harmonic (chords, voices) aspects. Each aspect most likely involves different types of processing, so that the processes called into play to process rhythm may differ from those involved in the processing of pitch and melodic intervals. Similarly, within language, at least four different levels of processing have been taken into consideration. The phonetic-phonological level, which comprises both segmental (phonemes) and suprasegmental (prosody); the morpho-syntactic level, which encompasses the combination of phonemes into morphemes and of morphemes into words; the syntactic level, which governs the relations between words, and the lexico-semantic level, with access to the meaning of words and sentences. Finally, although often ignored in psycholinguistic and neurolinguistic experiments, the pragmatic level, which comprises discourse organization and contextual influences, represents an essential aspect of language organization. Although it is of great interest to compare these different levels of processing in language and music, one should keep in mind that this comparison might highlight either their similarities or their differences depending upon the grain chosen for the analysis. Thus, similarities at one level of processing may be interpreted as differences at another level.

Phonetic/phonological level

At a phonetic level two interesting phenomena have been demonstrated in music as well as in language: categorical perception and phonemic restoration (Aiello, 1994). The categorical perception phenomenon occurs when discrimination within the same category is poor, but discrimination between different categories is good. The segmentation of the sound continuum into discrete units (pitches or phonemes) is found in all music and languages. In

Western music, sounds are categorized according to tonal parameters, thus into the intervals of a scale. Luckily for the violin player, although small errors are often detected by musicians, they are not heard by naïve, nonmusician listeners, who show a large range of acceptability (Locke & Kellar, 1973). This is similar in a way to an English speaker going to Nepal, and trying to detect the differences between some phonemes of the Nepali alphabet like /ka/, /kha/ and /khha/. Moreover, as speakers of different languages have a categorical perception of the phonemes of their own language, musicians of different musical cultures are sensitive to different pitch changes, depending upon the musical system with which they are familiar. Finally, in playing music as well as in speaking language, categorical perception seems to favor both a better and easier recognition and comprehension, regardless of individual differences.

However, when comparing phonemes and intervals of a musical scale, several differences must also be taken into consideration. Although the variability of the number of pitches by octave across musical cultures is relatively small, the number of phonemes differ greatly between languages (from 11, in Polynesian, to 141 in the language of the Bushmen, Pinker, 1994; with 44 phonemes in English and 36 in French). Moreover, some of the perceptual properties of the basic elements in music have no equivalent in language, as for instance the fact that octaves are perceived as equivalent in almost all cultures. This effect is linked with the fact that two notes separated by an octave are related by a simple frequency ratios of 2:1. Generally speaking, the relationships between different pitches in a musical piece are much simpler than the relationships between different phonemes in a linguistic sentence.

The second phenomenon is that of phonemic restoration, occurring in both music and language. It occurs when a noise, replacing a pitch in music or a phoneme in language, is not perceived by the listener, who believe they heard an intact auditory signal. In this case, lexical knowledge and lexico-semantic expectations in one case, and musical knowledge and expectancies in the other case, take over low-level processing analysis, filling in the missing information.

Syntactic level

All languages are organized according to a syntactic structure that some authors consider to be universal (Chomsky, 1988, 1991). Thus, verbs and nouns are always present. However, the order in which those elements are presented vary between languages (Subject–Verb–Object (French, English, . . .); Subject–Object–Verb (German; Japanese, . . .); Verb–Object–Subject (Malgache, . . .) (François, 1998). Even if it is common to refer to a musical syntax or a musical grammar, the extent to which this analogy goes beyond a simple metaphor remains to be determined. Music perception shares universal laws of auditory perception that have a strong influence on music syntactic structure. For instance, the perception of a musical phrase is automatically influenced by factors such as the grouping of discrete notes into meaningful sequences. Halpern and Bower (1982) showed that musical patterns are memorized by musicians as single chunks, while the recall of random or less frequently used patterns is more likely to rely on unspecific strategies, similar to those used by nonmusicians. Different groups or chunk of notes constitute a musical phrase, with precise boundaries, just like in language. Several studies, conducted on music reading, have demonstrated the extent to which musicians rely on significant structures, ignore superfluous material, and fail to notice printing errors (Sloboda, 1985). Moreover, the feeling of closure elicited by a cadence at the end of a musical phrase is similar to the Gestalt principle of closure in visual perception. Some musical phenomena such as grouping are universally shared, and others, just as in verbal language, are culturally shared. However, even if there is such a thing as a musical grammar, the rules seem more flexible and ambiguous than the syntactic rules used in language. If the communicative function of language favors syntactical stability, ambiguity is a key element of the grammar and aesthetics of music (Aiello, 1994). There are always several ways to perceive and enjoy a musical piece. Finally, musical elements are most often played simultaneously and each element may have its own "syntax." As noted previously, this vertical dimension of musical structure, commonly referred to as harmony, is not present in language. Whereas different words sung at the same time may melt in a sublime combination of rhythm, melody, and harmony (as in the polyphonic compositions of Gesualdo da Venosa, 1560–1613), different words produced at the same time by different speakers will only create an unpleasant cacophony, like in a political debate!

Meaning, expectancy, and affect

Even if the similarities and differences between music and language depend upon the level of details considered for the analysis, one fundamental difference nevertheless remains. Although the meaning of words is understood in relation to an extralinguistic designated space, music is considered to be mostly self-referential (Boucourechliev, 1993; Jakobson, 1973; Kivy, 1991; Meyer, 1956). This does not mean that music is asymbolic. Simply that, However, whereas the meaning of words is defined by an arbitrary convention relating sounds to meaning, notes or chords have no extra-musical space in which they would acquire meaning. The internal sense of music may be conceived as something that goes beyond any objective reference structure and the possibilities of verbal language (Piana, 1991). Like Wittgenstein (1953), who asked: "Describe the coffee aroma!," music is the kingdom of the ineffable. As stated by Leonard Meyer in his wonderful book *Emotion and meaning in music* (1956): "Music means itself. That is, one musical event (be it a tone, a phrase or a whole section) has meaning because it points to and makes us expect another musical event" (p. 35). Interestingly, this statement not only highlights one of the most important differences between language and music, that is the unsolved question of musical (a)semantics, but also emphasizes one of their strongest similarities: In their own way, both systems generate strong expectancies. Just as a specific word is expected within a specific linguistic context, specific notes or chords are expected at a given moment within a musical phrase. Either these expectations are fulfilled, giving rise to a resolution or satisfaction, or they are not fulfilled, giving rise to o a tension or surprise.

An important consequence of the "expectation-realization theory" proposed by Meyer (1956.) is its relation to musical affect. However, one problem with a theory of musical affect based upon the intuitive notion of expectation is that when listening to a well-known piece, one can anticipate how the music will continue. As a consequence, the affect evoked by the piece should diminish proportionally to the degree of familiarity. This is not the case and Jackendoff (1991) suggests a potential explanation. First, he argues that we should not believe that expectation may "bear the entire burden of deriving affect". Other factors such as tempo, intensity, and nonmechanical interpretation of music also influence musical emotions. are weel known by experienced musicians. Still, the structure of music has intrinsic points of instability that tend to resolve, and the tension/resolution phenomenon induces affects. Moreover, tensions are perceived at different levels depending upon the analysis performed. In analogy to language, thus tension might be within and between levels of analysis. he author (Jackendoff, 1991) points out that a modular and informationally encapsulated parser might be at work, independently from conscious memory. This independence from memory may explain why we keep enjoying a piece on repeated hearings: An autonomous parser will keep analyzing and recreating whatever structure is retrieved from memory. Then "surprise will still occur within the parser" (Jackendoff, 1991).

Do these considerations really lead to a better insight on the frequently asked question "what is the meaning of music?". We may suggest that, rather than asking this question, a more fruitful approach is to reflect on "what can I do with sounds?" We may then discover that music is first of all a set of choices and the flow of these choices might possibly become visible as a musical thought. Behind all this, the image of children playing appears. When the child plays with small wood blocks we could say that the game is a way of answering the question: "what can I do with my small wood blocks?" From the pleasure of playing we get directly into the aesthetical pleasure. Then we could possibly describe music as a game: The musician plays an instrument, the composer plays with sounds and the listener plays with his perception and emotions (Leipp, 1977). As every game, music obeys a set of rules, even if they may vary depending upon the period, the history, and the culture.

Concluding this quick and necessarily incomplete excursus, and before turning to language specificity, it is important to keep in mind that musical meaning is the sum of analytic approaches (musical parser), individual and/ or cultural associations to the external/internal world (during some periods in the last centuries "music was conceived as conveying precise emotional and conceptual meanings, established by codes, or at least, *repertoires*"; Eco, 1979, p. 11), and aesthetic reaction. The importance of the aesthetic component of music becomes evident in considering that "the form of a work of art gains its aesthetic validity precisely in proportion to the number of different perspectives from which it can be viewed and understood" (Eco, 1989, p. 3).

SPECIFICITY OF THE COMPUTATIONS INVOLVED IN LANGUAGE PROCESSING?

The generative grammar theory

Language is necessary for the expression of rational thought and the organization of human societies. It may well have evolved from the need for social bonding between individuals belonging to the same group (Nadel, 1930). Language also permits projections in the past and in the future and is necessary for the transmission of knowledge (Leroi-Gourhan, 1988). Whereas these characteristics, among others, make language specific to *Homo sapiens*, they also seem to contribute to the splendid isolation of the linguistic function among the other human cognitive activities. Largely because of the enormous impact in cognitive sciences of the Generative Grammar theory, developed by Chomsky (1957), language is often considered as relying on specific cognitive principles. Bickerton (2000), for instance, argues that the principles that govern language "seem to be specifically adapted for language and have little in common with general principles of thought or other apparatuses that might be attributable to the human mind" (p. 158). Thus, one of the most important claims of the Generative Grammar (GG) theory is that language is autonomous from the other cognitive functions (Chomsky, 1957, 1991; Jackendoff, 1997; Pinker, 1994; Pollock, 1997). Language is considered as a computational module that entails its own functional and neural architecture (Molino, 2000). Moreover, the linguistic module comprises different submodules, each responsible for different levels of language processing, as reviewed earlier: phonology, morphology, syntax, semantics, and pragmatics. Each submodule is encapsulated (Fodor, 1983) such that the processing of information taking place within a module is performed independently of the processing of information in the other submodules. Phonological processing, for instance, is realized without being influenced by the morphological, syntactic, semantic, or pragmatic aspects of language processing. Thus, the computations required to process language are specific to language, and the computations within one module are performed independently from those in the other modules.

Another basic claim of the GG theory is that languages are defined by their deep syntactic structure: syntax plays a dominant role in the structural organization of language. Moreover, from a functional perspective, syntax is first (Frazier, 1987). Logico-mathematic computations are first performed on symbols that have no intrinsic meaning; they only acquire meaning in a second step. Therefore, the chain of computations necessary to process language is considered as serially and hierarchically organized.

Other linguistic theories

It should be noted, however, that other linguistic theories have been developed in the last 20–30 years that advocate very different views of the structural and functional organization of language (François, 1998; Victorri, 1999). Although it is beyond the scope of this chapter to go into the details of these different linguistic theories, which differ from each other in many respects (functional grammar: Dik, 1997; Van Valin & La Polla, 1997; cognitive grammar: Lakoff, 1987; Langacker, 1987; Talmy, 1988; linguistic functional typology; Croft, 1995; Givón, 1995; Greenberg, 1995), the important point is that these theories call into question the two basic claims of the GG theory summarized earlier. First, they reject the idea that language is an autonomous function relying on its own structural and functional architecture. In contrast, they consider that language is an emergent property, relying on general cognitive principles, linked with perceptual and sensory-motor experiences (Fuchs, 1997; Robert, 1997). Second, they reject the syntactico-centrism of the GG and the idea of the autonomy of syntax relative to phonology, morphology, semantics, and pragmatics (François, 1998). Following Langacker (1987), for instance, semantics, morphology, and syntax form a continuum with specific meaning associated to lexico-semantic units and schematic meaning associated to grammatical units. Thus, in contrast with the GG view that grammatical units are semantically empty, all grammatical elements have meaning. Moreover, linguistic units are not static but constructed through a dynamic process influenced by the context of enunciation (Culioli, 1999) and the interactions between individuals in a situation of communication (Fauconnier, 1997). Therefore, language should not be studied in isolation but rather in relation to other cognitive functions, specifically attention and short-term and episodic memory (Givón, 1995).

Success of generative grammar in cognitive neurosciences

Several reasons may explain the success of the GG theory both in linguistic and cognitive sciences, but two are of particular interest. First, the cognitive stakes of the GG theory have been clearly explained. It has therefore been possible to make predictions and design experiments to test these predictions (Chomsky, 1991; Robert, 1997). Second, the modular organization of the functional aspects of language processing is clearly neuro-compatible. The conception following which language is organized in submodules, each responsible for one specific processing stage, find strong support in the localizationist views of cerebral organization. The recent development of brain imaging methods, together with older data from the neuropsychological literature, largely contribute to the idea that specific functions are implemented in specific brain structures. However, a quick review of the literature will show that whereas this conception is probably correct regarding the mapping of basic sensory functions into the organization of primary, sensory brain areas, the story certainly becomes more complicated when trying to localize such higher-order cognitive abilities as language or music.

NEUROPSYCHOLOGY AND BRAIN IMAGING

Insofar as one agrees with the conception following which music and language cannot be considered as wholes but need to be subdivided into their component operations, it becomes unrealistic, for instance, to view the musical function as localized in the right hemisphere and language in the left. Rather, it may be that some aspects of music processing preferentially involve right cerebral structures, whereas others require structures on the left. The same remark also applies to language. With this view in mind, the task of the cognitive neuroscientist is to delineate the different computations performed within one level of processing, to understand the mechanisms that underlie these computations, and to localize where in the brain these mechanisms are implemented. Of course, this task is bound with both philosophical and methodological problems (Pacherie, 1999), but science is advancing rapidly and new methods are available to track these issues. We will now review some findings issued from studies in neuropsychology and in cognitive neurosciences relevant for our understanding of the functional and structural organization of music and language.

Some aspects of the neuropsychology of music

As the neuropsychology of music is a very recent field of research, the aim of most studies has often been very general. Thus, results appear still unsatisfying and fragmentary when compared to results obtained within other domains, such as language. At least four nonexclusive factors may account for the specific difficulties encountered in this field. First, complex musical functions can only be studied in professional musicians, as complex linguistic functions can only be studied in humans. Unfortunately, music education in most countries is very poor, when compared to linguistic education. Thus, the study of impairment in music abilities has been limited by the scarcity of suitable patients. In saying this we are not arguing that the study of music deficits in nonmusicians is uninteresting, but rather that it is limited to certain implicit musical abilities. Most importantly, when dealing with nonmusicians, it is often difficult to know how musical the patient was premorbidly. Second, most of the available case descriptions of amusia, although sometimes admirably detailed, lack a theoretical frame (Schön, Semenza, & Denes, 2001). Third, Basso (1999) clearly underlines the fact that "the encounter between a neuropsychologist and a brain-damaged musician has generally caused the study of the patient's musical ability, independently of the researcher's interest for music" (pp. 410). Thus, a brain-damaged musician rarely comes across a musically competent neuropsychologist. Fourth, no standardised test battery for music exists to our knowledge (exception made for the Seashore test, 1960, originally created to test musical talent, possibly available on long-playing 78 rev/min!), whereas different standardised national and international neuropsychological tests exist within other domains (e.g. WAIS, Raven Progressive Matrices). Thus, it is unlikely that a hospitalized patient will be submitted even a general music test. In the lucky case that he is, it would remain difficult to compare those results with results of other studies using completely different tests.

Keeping these remarks in mind, there are nevertheless interesting studies of amusic patients reported in the neuropsychological literature. The first neuropsychological studies of music contrasted global musical abilities and other abilities such as language. Several studies reported musical disturbances in the absence of language deficits (Dorgeuille, cited in Peretz, Belleville, & Fontaine, 1997; Basso, 1999; Marin, 1982) and vice versa (Assal & Buttet, 1983; Basso & Capitani, 1985; Luria, Tsvekova, & Futer, 1965; Signoret, Van Eeckhout, Poncet, & Castaigne, 1987). This kind of double dissociation suggests both a functional independence and a structural independence, in the sense of underlying neural networks, of these two faculties. However, what is dissociated and what is independent from what, remains to be determined. As noted earlier, neither music nor language can be considered as single entities but both rather need to be decomposed into their component operations. For instance, recent results have demonstrated that, within the musical domain, specific subcomponents can be selectively damaged. Peretz and Kolinsky (1993), based on results obtained from a patient showing amelodia without arhythmia, argued for partial separability between melody and rhythm. In another study, Peretz (1990) advocated the idea that the left hemisphere is better equipped for dealing with local features of melody (intervals) and the right hemisphere for arriving at global melody representations (contour).

Other results have shown that patients with right temporal lobe lesions exhibited a significant deficit in musical timbre perception, in comparison to patients with left temporal lobe lesions and normal control subjects (Samson & Zatorre, 1994). Moreover, Peretz (1996) described a patient markedly impaired at naming a tune, judging its familiarity, and memorizing new musical materials. The author suggested the existence of a perceptual memory, specialized for music, that can be selectively damaged, therefore producing deficits in recognition ability. Results of a different patient showed that tonal interpretation of melodic sequences was impaired, while the ability to process temporal information, melodic contour and to some extent interval size was preserved (Peretz, 1993). The author interprets her findings as evidence for a modular organization of tonal knowledge, and argues that tonal encoding "possesses several properties of a module in Fodor's sense."

Interestingly, there seems to be some confusion regarding the Fodorian concept of modularity. It is often considered that, to be a module, a cognitive system has to possess all the features proposed by Fodor. However, Fodor (1983) did not offer a definition of modularity ("I am not, in any strict sense, in the business of defining my terms," p. 37); nor was he proposing any criteria. Rather, as Coltheart (1999) points out, Fodor only suggested a number of properties that are typical of modular systems. Thus, an interpretation in terms of strong and complete modularity is misleading. Fodor himself speaks of degrees of modularity and refers to a modular cognitive system as meaning "to some interesting extent."

As mentioned previously, the modularity of language processing is based on the idea that the computations necessary for analyzing linguistic information differ from those required within other cognitive domains. Indeed, within the information-processing chain leading to meaning from a series of acoustic or visual signals, some computations are probably language specific. However, others are probably common to other non linguistic auditory and visual signals, organized according to precise structural and functional rules. Nevertheless, the specificity of the processes involved within one domain is hardly ever tested in comparison with those involved in other domains. For example, studies on language impairments are rarely concerned with music impairments and vice versa, and this holds for other researches as well. Therefore, this brings to the conclusion that, taking into account the current organization of research, if interactions between domains were to exist, they would be difficult to find.

Importantly, however, a few studies have aimed to compare music and language directly. Although an exhaustive review is beyond the point we would like to make here, it is of interest to illustrate how such comparisons can be performed at different cognitive levels. To explore the relationship between the processing of melodic and rhythmic patterns in speech and music, Patel, Peretz, Tramo, and Labreque (1998b) tested the prosodic and musical discrimination abilities of two "amusic" patients. Prosody is an important aspect of spoken language, which encompass as the melodic variations of the voice (intonation), the accents and accentuations, as well as the rhythm and pauses within sentences (see Cutler, Dahan, & Van Donselaar, 1997; Hirst & Di Cristo, 1998, for reviews). This aspect has, however, long been neglected mainly due to the technical and methodological difficulties encountered in the analysis and manipulation of the speech signal. Prosodic discrimination was assessed using sentence pairs where members of a pair differed by intonation or rhythm. Musical discrimination was tested using musical-phrase pairs derived from the prosody of the sentence pairs. This materials was used in order to make task demands as comparable as possible across domains. Results showed that the level of performance was similar across domains, good on both linguistic and musical discrimination tasks for one patient, and poor for the other. These results suggest shared neural resources for prosody and music. One potential problem with this interpretation is linked with the lack of musicality of the musical phrases derived from the prosody of the sentence pairs. Such "musical phrases" thus lack some musical structure. Moreover, rather than keeping the two domains separate in two different tasks, it could be more appropriate to design a task with both dimensions included. In doing so their interaction could then be tested. But this is by no mean an easy task!

A very good example of how this can be achieved is found in Peretz et al. (1997). Studying an amusic patient, the authors designed an experiment to compare language and music directly. They chose the song form, as words and music are tightly bound in this musical form. In a song, the linguistic and musical structures go together, at least from a metric point of view. Moreover, even though the words used in a song have already been heard in a nonmusical context, lyrics and tunes have a comparable degree of familiarity, since they are mostly sung together. The authors argue that, since lyrics and tunes are necessarily associated in a song, it should be possible to find priming effects. Finding a priming effect only for words in the amusic patient, who could no longer recognize familiar music, would argue for the independence of language and music processing in songs. In contrast, the finding of a priming effect on both dimensions, even if smaller than for control subjects, would claim for an integrated representation of lyrics and tunes. Unfortunately, probably due to the fact that working with patients implies strong time constraints, they tested word priming on word targets and music priming on music targets, but they did not cross the two dimensions. Moreover, another problem arises when considering that music recognition is not as well determined in time as word recognition. Even though this design still presents some problems, this task is a very good example of how music and language can be combined together to yield important information on how they are processed by the brain.

Some evidence from brain imaging

Brain imaging methods are aimed at understanding the functional activity of the brain either directly through the measures of the electric activity of single neurons (intra-cellular recordings) or of neuronal populations (electro-encephalography, EEG, and magnetoencephalography, MEG, through the analysis of the magnetic activity that is coupled with the electrical activity), or indirectly, through the measures of the brain metabolic activity (Positron Emission Tomography, PET, and functional Magnetic Resonance Imaging, fMRI). Overall, direct methods have an excellent temporal resolution and a relatively poor spatial resolution, and the reverse is true for indirect methods. Very elegant works have been conducted using these different methods demonstrating, for instance, the retinotopic organization of the visual cortex using fMRI (Tootell et al., 1998) and the tonotopic organization of the auditory cortex using intra-cellular recordings, MEG (Pantev et al., 1989), or fMRI (Strainer et al., 1997). Thus, there is a strict mapping between the organization of the receptor fields at the periphery, either in the retina or in the cochlea, and the functional organization of the primary visual and auditory cortex. Aside from extending to humans previous discoveries in animals, these findings validate the use of such complex methods as fMRI to study human perception and cognition.

Semantic, melody and harmony

A starting point in the study of the neurophysiological basis of language processing has been the discovery of the N400 component by Kutas and Hillyard (1980). This negative component of the ERPs, peaking around 400 ms after word onset, is elicited by words that are semantically unexpected or incongruous within a linguistic context (e.g., "The pizza was too hot to cry", see Figure 1). Further results have shown that N400 amplitude is modulated by semantic priming, so that an unexpected word related to the best sentence completion (e.g., "drink" when the expected word is "eat", see Figure 1) elicit a smaller N400 than a completely unexpected word (e.g., "cry"; Kutas & Hillyard, 1984). These results, together with those issued from a large number of experiments, have lead to the concensus that the N400 is a good index of the integration process of a word within its linguistic context.

The first experiments that we designed were aimed at finding out whether an N400 component would also be elicited when melodically and harmonically unexpected notes are presented within a melodic context (Besson & Faita, 1995; Besson, Faita & Requin, 1994; Besson & Macar, 1987). We

LANGUAGE

THE PIZZA WAS TOO HOT TO....

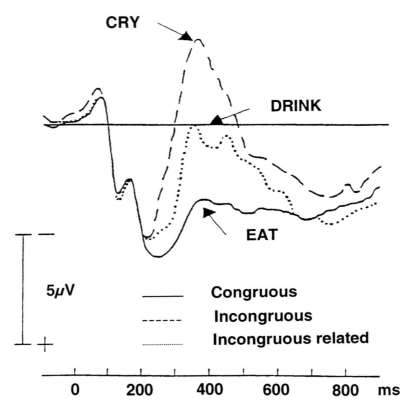

Figure 1. ERPs elicited by sentence-final words at the central recording site (Cz) for congruous and incongruous words and for incongruous words that are semantically related to the best sentence completion. The amplitude of the negative component, peaking at 400 ms post-final word onset (N400) is largest for incongruous words, intermediate for incongruous words related to the best sentence completion, and smallest for congruous words. In this and subsequent figures, amplitude (μV) is represented on the ordinate, with negative voltage up, and time (ms) on the abscissa (adapted from Kutas & Hillyard, 1984).

132

presented both familiar and unfamiliar monodic musical phrases to musicians and nonmusicians. The familiar melodies were chosen from the classical repertoire of Western occidental music from the 18th and 19th centuries, and the unfamiliar musical phrases were composed by a musician following the rules of tonal harmony (see Figure 2). These melodies were ended by the congruous or most expected note, by a note out of the tonality of the musical phrase (nondiatonic incongruities perceived as wrong notes), or by a note within the tonality but not the most expected ending (melodic or diatonic incongruities). Thus, we created a degree of musical incongruity from diatonic to nondiatonic.

Results clearly showed that both types of unexpected notes elicited the occurrence of late positive components, peaking around 600 ms (P600). As demonstrated for the N400 component, P600 amplitude was shown to depend upon the degree of musical incongruity: It was larger for the most unexpected, nondiatonic wrong notes than for the less unexpected, diatonic incongruities. Moreover, the amplitude of the P600 was larger for familiar than unfamiliar musical phrases and for musicians than for nonmusicians (see Figure 3). These findings clearly demonstrate not only that specific notes are expected within a musical phrase, but that such expectations depend upon the familiarity of the musical excerpts and the expertise of the listener. Thus, one of the interesting similarities between language and music mentioned earlier, the ability to generate strong expectancies, is supported by empirical evidence. However, our results also show that the processes that govern semantic expectancy, and reflected by a negative component, peaking around 400 ms, the N400, are qualitatively different from those involved in musical

Familiar Melody

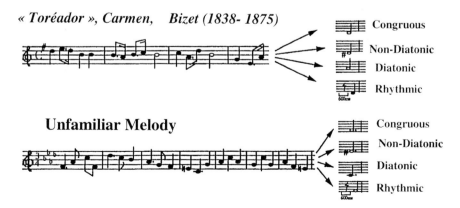

Figure 2.   Examples of the stimuli used in the experiment (adapted from Besson & Faita, 1995).

expectancies, and reflected by a positive component peaking around P600 ms, the P600. Although, to our knowledge, the functional significance of positive versus negative polarities in the ERPs is not clearly established, our results, by demonstrating qualitative differences between language and music processing, nevertheless strongly argue for the specificity of the processes involved in computing the semantic aspects of language. Thus, one of the most important differences between language and music outlined in the Introduction, the fact that, in contrast to language, music has no intrinsic meaning and is a self-referential system, seems to find some support in these experimental findings.

Semantic and harmony in opera

Opera is perhaps the most complete art form as it calls upon music, language, drama, and choreography. It originated in Italy at the end of the 16th century with the *Euridice* of the Florentine composer Jacopo Corsi (1561–1602), played as a wedding gift to Maria de Medici and Henri IV (1600). Opera, as a new art form, then spread to other Italian courts with the better known *Orfeo* of Monteverdi (1604). Since this time, a question that has interested both music analysts and composers has been to determine which of the words or the music plays the most important role in opera. In his *Life of Rossini*, Stendhal (1783–1842) argued that music is most important: "its function is to animate the words." Later, ethnomusicologists such as Levman (1992) have pointed out that the lyrics are subordinate to the music in tribal songs and rituals. In contrast, Richard Wagner (1813–1883) considered that both aspects are intrinsically linked: "Words give rise to the music and music develops and reinforces the language," an opinion shared by Boulez (1966): "The text is the center and the absence of the musical piece." Richard Strauss (1864–1949) once even composed an opera *Capriccio* (1940) to illustrate the complementarity of words and music.

To try to determine, based on scientific grounds, whether the words or the music play the most important role when we listen to opera, we selected 200 excerpts from French operas from the 19th and 20th centuries (Besson et al. 1998). Each excerpt lasted between 8 and 20 seconds and was sung a capella by a woman in each of four experimental conditions: the final word of the excerpt was semantically congruous and sung in tune, semantically incongruous and sung in tune, semantically congruous and sung out of tune, and both semantically incongruous and sung out of tune (see Figure 4).

Based on previous results (Kutas & Hillyard, 1980), it was of interest to determine whether semantically incongruous words will also elicit an N400 component when they are sung. Similarly, it was of interest to determine whether congruous words sung out of tune will also elicit a P600 component (Besson & Faita, 1995). Of most interest was the double incongruity condition: Will semantically incongruous words sung out of key elicit both an

Familiar   # Unfamiliar

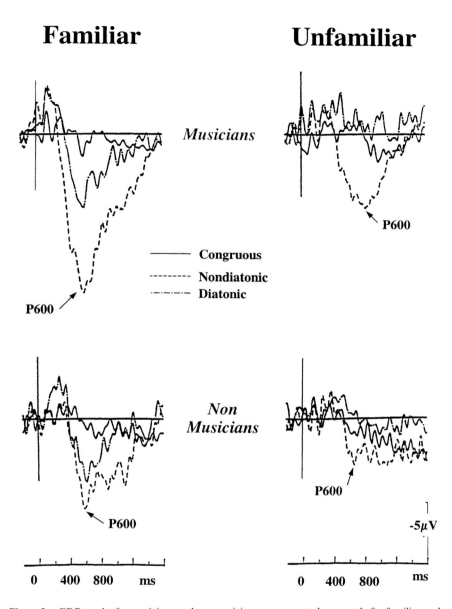

Musicians

─────── **Congruous**
- - - - - **Nondiatonic**
-·─·─·─ **Diatonic**

P600

P600

Non Musicians

P600

P600

-5μV

0   400   800   ms

0   400   800   ms

Figure 3. ERP results for musicians and nonmusicians are presented separately for familiar and unfamiliar musical phrases. The vertical lines mark the onset of the final note. Results are from one typical recording site, the parietal location (Pz). The amplitude of the positive component, P600, is larger for nondiatonic than for diatonic incongruity, for musicians than for nonmusicians, and for familiar than for unfamiliar musical phrases (adapted from Besson & Faïta, 1995).

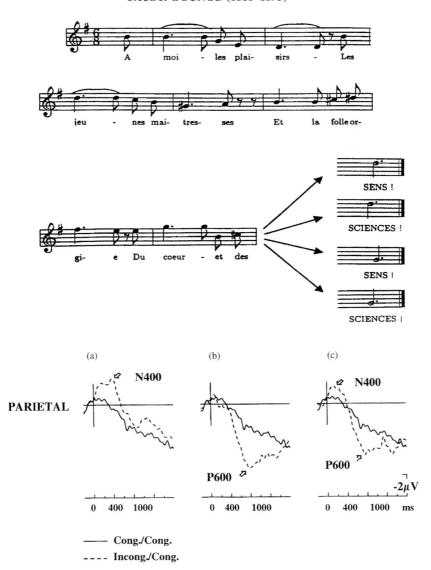

Figure 4. Top: Example of the opera's excerpts used in the experiment. Approximate translation of the excerpts, from "Faust" (Gounod): "For me the pleasures and young mistresses, the crazy orgy of the heart and the senses." Note that, in French, the final incongruous word "sciences" rhymes with the expected completion "sens." The final note of the excerpt is in or out of tune (adapted from Besson et al., 1998).

136

N400 and a P600 component? If language plays the most important role when we listen to opera, then results may show an N400 but no P600. Conversely, if music is the cornerstone of opera, then results may show a P600 without N400. But maybe both effects will be elicited; they may then be additive (i.e., equal to the sum of the effect associated with each type of incongruity alone) or interactive. To answer these questions, we recorded the ERPs associated with the final words of each excerpt, from 16 professional musicians from the opera in Marseille.

To summarize, results demonstrated that sung incongruous words did elicit an N400 component, thus extending to songs results previously reported for written and spoken language (Kutas & Hillyard, 1980; MacCallum, Farmer & Pocock, 1984); see Figure 4a. Moreover, words sung out of tune did elicit a P600 component, thus extending to songs results previously reported for out-of-tune notes (Besson & Faita, 1995; Paller, McCarthy, & Wood, 1992; Regnault, Bigand, & Besson, 2001); see Figure 4b. Most interesting are the results in the double incongruity condition. They show that incongruous words sung out of tune elicit both a N400 and a P600 component (see Figure 4c). Interestingly, the N400 occurred earlier than the P600, which is taken as evidence that the words were processed faster than the music. Finally, effects in the double incongruity condition were not significantly different from the sum of the effects observed in each condition of simple incongruity (see Figure 5). This finding provides a strong argument in favor of the independence (i.e., the additivity) of the computations involved in processing the semantic aspects of language and the harmonic aspects of music. Therefore, when we listen to opera, we process both the lyrics and the tunes in an independent fashion, and language seems to be processed before music.

The influence of attention

We tracked these results further by conducting another series of experiments aimed at studying the effect of attention, again testing some professional musicians from the opera in Marseille. We hypothesized that if lyrics and tunes are processed independently, listeners should be able to focus their

---

Bottom (opposite): ERP results averaged across 16 professional musicians and recorded from the parietal electrode (Pz). Terminal congruous words sung in key (Cong./Cong.) are compared to (a) semantically incongruous words sung in tune (Incong./Cong.), (b) semantically congruous words sung out of tune (Cong./Incong.), and (c) semantically incongruous words sung out of tune (Incong./Incong.). The vertical lines mark the onset of the final word of the excerpts. A large N400 component develops in the 50–600 ms that follow the presentation of semantically incongruous words (a). In marked contrast, a P600 develops in the 400–1200 ms that follow the presentation of words sung out of tune (b). Most importantly, both an N400 and a P600 develop in response to the double incongruity (C) (Adapted from Besson et al., 1998).

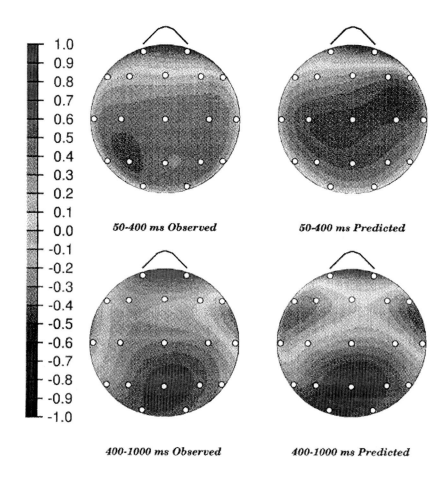

1.0
0.9
0.8
0.7
0.6
0.5
0.4
0.3
0.2
0.1
0.0
-0.1
-0.2
-0.3
-0.4
-0.5
-0.6
-0.7
-0.8
-0.9
-1.0

50-400 ms Observed

50-400 ms Predicted

400-1000 ms Observed

400-1000 ms Predicted

- Center for Research in Cognitive Neuroscience -

Figure 5. Topographical maps of the effects observed (left) and predicted (right) by an additive model of semantic and harmonic processing within two latency bands of interest: the N400 latency band (50–400 ms) and the P600 latency band (400–1000 ms). Results of statistical analysis show that the observed and predicted data are not significantly different.

attention only on the lyrics or only on the tunes depending upon the instructions. Without going into the details of the results, an N400 component was elicited to sung incongruous words and a P600 was associated with congruous words sung out of tune, thus replicating our previous findings (Besson et al., 1998). Most interestingly, the N400 to incongruous words completely vanished when participants focused their attention on the music (see Figure 6). Thus, musicians were able not to process the meaning of words; they did

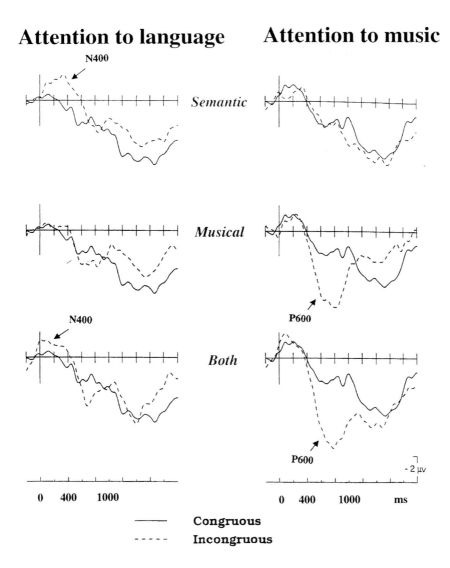

Attention to language **Attention to music**

Semantic

Musical

Both

Congruous
Incongruous

Figure 6. Overlapped are the ERPs to congruent and incongruent endings, recorded at the central recording site (Cz), when participants paid attention only to the language (left column) or only to the music (right column) of the opera's excerpts. A large N400 effect is generated when participants focus their attention on language. This effect completely vanishes when attention is focused on music (top row). Similarly, the P600 effect is much larger when participants paid attention to music than when they paid attention to language (medium row). Finally, when words are both semantically incongruous and sung out of tune, the N400 effect is larger when participants paid attention to the language and the P600 effect is larger when they paid attention to the music (bottom row; from Regnault, Bigand, & Besson, 2001).

not notice whether or not the terminal word made sense within the linguistic context when they only listened to the music. Conversely, P600 amplitude was significantly reduced when musicians focused attention on language, so that they did not hear that the final word was sung out of tune. Taken together, these results again provide strong arguments in favor of the independence of lyrics and tunes. There is some limit to such processing independence, however. Results in the double incongruity condition showed that the presence of one type of incongruity influenced the processing of the other type of incongruity. When words were both semantically incongruous and sung out of tune, musicians could not help but hear the musical incongruity even if they were asked to focus their attention on language.

Syntax and harmony

The rules of harmony and counterpoint are often described as the grammar of tonal music. As syntax is used to extract the fundamental structure of an utterance by assigning different functions to different words, the rules of harmony allow the specification of the different elements, notes, and chords that fulfill a specific harmonic function. Results of experiments manipulating the harmonic function of target chords have shown that violations of harmonic expectancies are associated with P600 components (Janata, 1995; Regnault et al., 2001). Interestingly, research on syntax using ERPs has also shown that different types of syntactic violations, such as violations of gender, word order, or noun–verb agreement, elicit a positive component, peaking around 600 ms (Friederici 1998; Hagoort, Brown & Groothusen, 1993; Osterhout and Holcomb, 1992). Moreover, both components show a similar parietal distribution over the scalp, which, together with their similar polarity and latency, seems to indicate that they reflect qualitatively similar processes.

In order to test this hypothesis further, Patel and collaborators (Patel et al., 1998a) conducted an experiment directly aimed at comparing the P600 components elicited by harmonic and syntactic (phrase structure) violations. ERPs associated to a word within a grammatically simple, complex, or incorrect sentence were compared to those associated with the presentation of a chord that belonged to the same, a nearby, or a distant tonality than the one induced by the chords sequence (see Figure 7). Results showed that, aside from early morphological differences in the ERPs to words and chords, due to the differences in the acoustic characteristics of these two types of auditory signals, the effects associated with the violation of syntactic and harmonic expectancies were not significantly different (see Figure 7). Therefore, these results raise the interesting possibility that a general cognitive process is called into play when participants are asked to process the structural aspects of an organized sequence of sounds, be it language or music. Finally, an early right anterior negativity was found around 300–400

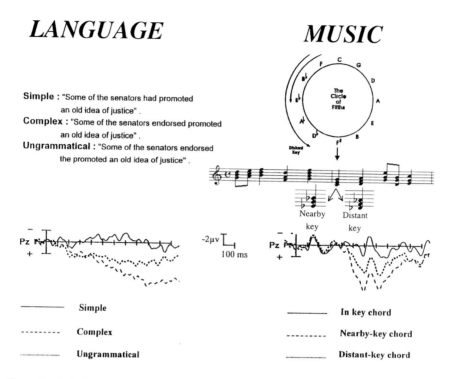

Figure 7. Left side: Examples of the sentences presented in the auditory language experiment. Results showed an increased positivity from the simple to the ungrammatical sentences. Right side: Representation of the circle of fifths. Examples of the stimuli used in the experiment. The target chord, shown by the downward-pointing vertical arrow, is the congruous chord. The two arrows below the musical notation point to moderately incongruous (nearby key) and highly incongruous (distant key) target chords. Results also showed an increased positivity from the in-key chords to the distant-key chords (adapted from Patel et al., 1998a).

ms in response to a chord belonging to a distant tonality. These results parallelled those obtained in language experiments showing that an early left anterior negativity is also associated with some syntactic violations (Friederici, Pfeifer, & Hahne, 1993). Although these two negative components showed a different distribution over the scalp, with a left predominance for language and a right predominance for music, they may reflect functionally similar processes.

Temporal structure

Spoken language, as music, is composed of acoustic events that unfold in time. Because of the temporal structure inherent to both language and music, specific events are expected at specific times. The main question addressed in the next series of experiments was to determine whether the processes involved in analyzing temporal structures rely on general cognitive mechanisms, or rather differ as a function of the specific characteristics of the materials to be processed. We used both the ERP and the MEG methods to analyze the time course of the effects of temporal structure violations in language and music, and fMRI to localize the cerebral structures activated by these violations. We hypothesized that, if a general mechanism is responsible for processing of the temporal structures in language and music, qualitatively similar effects should be revealed in the ERP and MEG recordings, and similar brain areas should be shown to be activated, by temporal violations. In contrast, if processing temporal information in both systems rely on different mechanisms, qualitatively different effects and different brain areas should be found in language and music.

In previous experiments (Besson & Faita, 1995) we introduced an unexpected silence between the next to the last and the last note of a musical phrase (see Figure 2). Results showed that a large biphasic, negative then positive potential, the emitted potential (Sutton, Braren, Zubin, & John, 1967), was elicited when the final note should have been presented but was not since it was delayed by 600 ms. The amplitude of this effect was similar for musicians and nonmusicians, but was larger for familiar than unfamiliar melodies (see Figure 8). These findings clearly indicate that both musicians

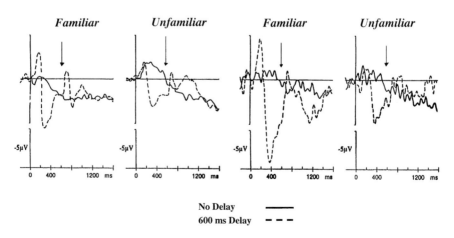

Figure 8. Overlapped are the ERPs to congruous notes and to the rhythmic incongruities ending familiar and unfamiliar musical phrases for musicians and nonmusicians. Recordings are from the parietal electrode (Pz). Large emitted potentials are elicited when the final note should have been presented (vertical bar) but was delayed by 600 ms. The arrow points to the moment in time when the final note was presented (adapted from Besson & Faita, 1995).

and nonmusicians were able to anticipate the precise moment when the final note was to be presented, and were surprised when it was not. Moreover, knowing the melodies allowed participants to generate more precise expectancies than when melodies were unfamiliar. Therefore, these results indicate that the occurrence of an emitted potential can serve as a good index of temporal expectancy.

It was then of interest to determine whether similar results would be found for spoken language (Besson, Faita, Czernasty, & Kutas, 1997). To this aim, we presented both familiar (e.g., proverbs) and unfamiliar auditory sentences to participants. In half the sentences, final words occurred at their normal position, while in the other half they were delayed by 600 ms. Results showed that an emitted potential, very similar to the one described for temporal ruptures in music, developed when the final word should have been presented (see Figure 9). Therefore, these ERP results indicate that qualitatively similar processes seem to be responsible for temporal processing in language and music.

In order to strengthen this interpretation, it was important to determine whether the same brain structures are activated by the processing of temporal ruptures in language and music. As mentioned earlier, fMRI allows the

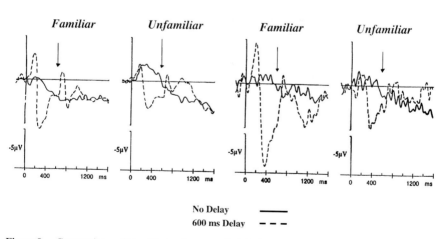

Figure 9. Comparison of the effects of temporal violations in language and music. Recordings are from the parietal electrode (Pz). Left side: Overlapped are the ERPs to congruous words and to the temporal disruptions ending familiar and unfamiliar sentences. In both language and music, large emitted potentials are elicited when the final event should have been presented (vertical bar) but was delayed by 600 ms. Note that the amplitude of the emitted potential is larger in music than in language, but that in both cases, its amplitude is larger for familiar than unfamiliar materials (adapted from Besson et al., 1997; Besson & Faita, 1995).

localization of brain activation with an excellent spatial resolution. Moreover, the MEG permits to localize the generators of the effects observed on the scalp more precisely than the ERP method, while also offering an excellent temporal resolution. Therefore, in collaboration with Professor H. Heinze and his research team, we conducted three experiments, in which we presented both auditory sentences and musical phrases (Weyert et al., 2001). These experiments used a blocked design in which only sentences or musical phrases without temporal ruptures were presented within a block of trials, and only sentences or musical phrases with temporal ruptures at unpredictable positions were presented within another block of trials. The ERP method was used in the first experiment to replicate, within subjects, the results found previously with two different groups of subjects (Besson & Faïta, 1995; Besson et al., 1997), and the fMRI and the MEG methods were used respectively in the other two experiments, trying to localize the effects of interest.

Overall, the ERP results replicated, within subjects, those previously found in music and language separately (i.e., an emitted potential). However, the comparison of the conditions with and without temporal violations revealed a somewhat different pattern of activation using the MEG and fMRI methods. Source localization based on the MEG data revealed that the underlying generators of the biphasic potential recorded on the scalp were most likely located in the primary auditory cortex of both hemispheres. In contrast, fMRI results showed activation of the associative auditory cortex in both hemispheres, as well as some parietal activation. Several factors may account for these differences, but the main point is that similar brain areas were activated by temporal violations in both language and music. Therefore, taken together our results suggest that processing temporal information in both language and music rely on general cognitive mechanisms.

CONCLUSION

In this chapter we have addressed one of the central question of human cognition, the specificity of language processing. Is language an autonomous system, independent from other human cognitive abilities, or does language rely on general cognitive principles? To address this question, we have conducted several experiments aimed at comparing some aspects of language processing with some aspects of music processing. We mainly used the event-related potentials method, which offers an excellent temporal resolution, and therefore permits the study of the time course of information processing, and the determination of whether the processes involved in language and music are qualitatively similar or different.

Taken together, results have shown that the semantic computations required to access the meaning of words, and their integration within a linguistic context, seem to be specific to language. Indeed, whereas unexpected words within a sentence context are associated with the occurrence of an N400 component, unexpected notes or chords within musical phrases elicit a P600 component. In contrast, words that are unexpected on the basis of the syntactic structure of the sentence, and chords that are unexpected as a function of the harmonic structure of the musical sequence, elicit similar effects in both cases, namely a P600 component. Early negative effects, the Left Anterior Negativity and the Right Anterior Negativity, which developed between 200–300 ms, have also been reported in experiments manipulating syntax and harmony, respectively. Although their different scalp distribution seems to indicate that they reflect the involvement of different brain structures, more research is needed to further track their functional significance. Finally, violations of temporal structure within language and music also elicit similar effects, a biphasic negative-positive complex, the emitted potential. The occurrence of the emitted potential shows that, in both language and music, words and notes or chords are expected at specific moments in time. Therefore, when we listen to language and music we do not only expect words or chords, with specific meaning and function, but we also expect them to be presented on time!

The question of the specificity of language processing has broad implications for our understanding of the human cognitive architecture, and even more generally, for the fundamental problem of the relationship between structures (the different brain regions) and functions (language, music, . . .). Although researches reported here shed some light on some aspects of language processing and highlight some of the similarities and differences with music processing, more research clearly needs to be conducted within this fascinating research domain. It is of most interest to combine brain imaging methods that offer an excellent temporal resolution, as the ERPs method used in the experiments described earlier, and TEP and fMRI which offer and excellent spatial resolution, in order to pinpoint the spatio-temporal dynamics of the networks of cerebral structures involved when we are engaged in two of the most human cognitive abilities: language and music.

Some experiments have already been designed to directly compare language and music using fMRI and PET. Binder et al. (1996) compared tones, and word processing in an fMRI study. Results showed that several brain structures, including the left superior temporal sulcus, the middle temporal gyrus, the angular gyrus, and the lateral frontal lobe showed stronger activation for words than tones. However, both types of stimuli activated the Heschl gyrus and the superior temporal plane, including the planum temporale (PT). The authors concluded that whereas the PT is similarly involved in the auditory processing of words and tones, other broadly distributed areas are specifically involved in word processing. Gandour et al. (Gandour, Wong,

& Hutchins, 1998) conducted a PET study in which both Thai and English participants were required to discriminate pitch patterns and Thai lexical tones derived from accurately filtered Thai words. Results of the tone minus pitch subtraction indicated that only native Thai speakers showed activation in the left frontal operculum (BA44/45). This finding was taken as evidence that Thai lexical tones are meaningful for native Thai speakers, but not for English speakers. However, for our purposes, it is also interesting to note that for both Thai and English speakers, several structures—the left anterior cingulated gyrus (BA32), the left and right superior temporal gyrus (BA 22), and the right cerebellum—were activated in both the pitch and the tone tasks.

More generally, results have shown that primary auditory regions (BA 41 & 42) respond in similar ways to speech and music (Zatorre et al., 1992). Secondary auditory regions (BA22) are activated by hearing and understanding words (Falk, 2000) as well as by listening to scales (Sergent, Zuck, Terriah et al., 1992), auditory imagery for sounds (Zatorre, Halpern, Perry et al., 1996), and access to melodic representations (Platel, Price, Wise et al, 1997). The supramarginal gyrus (BA 40) seems to be involved in understanding the symbolism of language (Falk, 2000) and the reading of musical scores (Sergent et al., 1992). Broca's area is known to be involved in motor activity related to language, and was also shown to be active when playing music (Sergent et al., 1992) and when musicians were engaged in a rhythmic task (Platel et al., 1997). The supplementary motor areas (BA 6) and the right cerebellum are also active when playing and imaging playing music (Chen, Kato, Zhu et al., 1996; Sergent et al., 1992). Although this list is far from exhaustive, it nevertheless suffices to show that some of the most important language areas are clearly involved in music processing as well. Of course, some brain structures also seem to be specifically or preferentially involved in language processing (Grabowski & Damasio, 2000) and the converse is true for music (Zatorre & Binder, 2000).

In order to have a better understanding of the specific brain structures involved in language processing, one would need a meta-analysis of the results obtained across the many experiments aimed at localizing the different aspects of language processing. One would then need to do the same for music, or for any other cognitive function of interest, and then compare the results of these meta-analyses. Although such meta-analyses are starting to be performed for some aspects of language processing, such as language production (Indefrey & Levelt, 2000) or prelexical and lexical processes in language comprehension (Norris & Wise, 2000), the data in the neuroimaging of music are still too scarce for such an enterprise. Moreover, assuming that such meta-analyses are performed for music as well, it will still remain extremely difficult to compare the results of experiments that were not directly designed to compare language and music processing. Indeed, even leaving aside the theoretical problem of which level of processing in language is best compared with which level of processing in music, the choice of the task to be performed on the stimuli, its difficulty, as well as experimental factors such as the mode (blocked versus mixed) and rate of stimulus presentation, stimulus repetition, and data analysis (subtraction method, correlative analyses, etc.), have been shown to exert a predominant influence on the results obtained. As progress in neuroimaging is extremely rapid, one can hope that these difficulties will be overcome in the very near future.

REFERENCES

Aiello, R. (1994). Music and language: Parallels and contrasts. In R. Aiello & J. Sloboda (Eds.), *Musical perceptions*: (pp. 40–63). New York: Oxford University Press.

Arom, S., & Khalfa, J. (1999). Descartes en Afrique. In V. Gomez Pin (Ed.), *Descartes lo racional y lo real*. Barcelona: Univesitat Autonoma de Barcalona.

Assal, G., & Buttet, J. (1983). Agraphie et conservation de l'écriture musicale chez un professeur de piano bilingue. *Revue Neurologique, 139*, 569–574.

Basso, A. (1999). The neuropsychology of music. In G. Denes & L Pizzamiglio (Eds.), *Handbook of neuropsychology*. Hove, UK: Psychology Press.

Basso, A., & Capitani, E. (1985). Spared musical abilities in a conductor with global aphasia and ideomotor apraxia. *Journal of Neurology, Neurosurgery, and Psychiatry, 48*, 407–412.

Besson, M., & Faita, F. (1995). An event-related potential (ERP) study of musical expectancy: Comparison of musicians with non-musicians. *Journal of Experimental Psychology: Human Perception and Performance, 21*, 1278–1296.

Besson, M., Faita, F., Czernasty, C., & Kutas, M. (1997). What's in a pause: Event-related potential analysis of temporal disruptions in written and spoken sentences. *Biological Psychology, 46*, 3–23.

Besson, M., Faita, F., Peretz, I., Bonnel, A.M., & Requin, J. (1998). Singing in the brain: Independence of lyrics and tunes. *Psychological Science, 9*, 494–498.

Besson, M., Faita, F., & Requin, J. (1994). Brain waves associated with musical incongruity differ for musicians and nonmusicians. *Neuroscience Letters, 168*, 101–105.

Besson, M., & Macar, F. (1987). An event-related potential analysis of incongruity in music and other non-linguistic contexts. *Psychophysiology, 24*, 14–25.

Bickerton, D. (2000). Can biomusicology learn from language evolution studies? In N.L. Wallin, B. Merker & S. Brown (Eds.), *The origins of music* (pp.153–164). Cambridge, MA: MIT Press.

Binder, J.R, Frost, J.A., Hammeke, T.A., Rao, S.M., & Cox, R.W. (1996). Function of the left planum temporale in auditory and linguistic processing. *Brain, 119*, 1239–1247.

Blacking, J. (1973). *How musical is man?* Seattle, WA: University of Washington Press.

Boucourechliev, A. (1993). *Le langage musical. Collections les chemins de la musique*. Paris: Fayard.

Boulez, P. (1966). *Relevés d'apprenti*. Paris: Editions du Seuil.

Chen, W., Kato, T., Zhu, X.H., et al. (1996). Functional mapping of human brain during music imagery processing. *NeuroImage, 3*, S205.

Chomsky, N. (1957). *Syntactic structures*. The Hague: Mouton & Co.

Chomsky, N. (1988). *Language and problems of knowledge. The Managua lectures*. Cambridge, MA. MIT Press.

Chomsky, N. (1991). Linguistics and cognitive science: Problems and mysteries. In A. Kasher (Ed.), *The Chomskyan turn* (26–53). Cambridge, MA: Basil Blackwell.

Coltheart, M. (1999). Modularity and cognition. *Trends in Cognitive Neuroscience, 3*, 115–120.

Croft, W. (1995). Autonomy and functionalist linguistics. *Language, 71*, 490–532.

Culioli, A. (1999). *Pour une linguistique de l'énonciation.* Paris: Ophrys.

Cutler, A., Dahan, D., & Van Donselaar, W. (1997). Prosody in the comprehension of spoken language: A literature review. *Language and Speech, 40,* 141–201 .

Darwin, C. (1871). *The descent of man, and selection in relation to sex.* London: Murray.

Dik, S. (1997). *The theory of functional grammar.* Berlin: Mouton De Gruyter.

Eco, U. (1979). *Trattato di semiotica generale.* Milano: Bompiani.

Eco, U. (1989). *The open work.* Cambridge, MA: Harvard University Press.

Falk, D. (2000). Hominid brain evolution and the origin of music. In N.L. Wallin, B. Merker, & S. Brown (Eds.), *The origins of music* (pp. 197–216). Cambridge, MA: MIT Press.

Fauconnier, G. (1997). *Mappings in thought and language.* Cambridge: Cambridge University Press.

Fodor, J. (1983). *Modularity of mind.* Cambridge, MA: MIT Press,

François, J. (1998). Grammaire fonctionnelle et dynamique des langues—de nouveaux modèles d'inspiration cognitive et biologique. *Verbum XX, 3,* 233–256.

Frazier, L. (1987). Sentence processing: A tutorial review. In M. Coltheart (Ed.), *Attention and performance XII* (pp. 559–586). Hove, UK: Lawrence Erlbaum Associates Ltd.

Friederici, A.D. (1998). The neurobiology of language comprehension. In A.D. Friederici (Ed.), *Language comprehension: A biological approach* (pp. 263–301). New York: Springer

Friederici, A.D., Pfeifer E., & Hahne, A. (1993). Event-related brain potentials during natural speech processing: Effects of semantic, morphological and syntactic violations. *Cognitive Brain Research, 1,* 182–192.

Fuchs, C. (1997). Diversité des représentations linguistiques: Quels enjeux pour la cognition? In C. Fuchs & S. Robert (Eds.), *Diversité des langues et représentations cognitives* (pp. 5–24). Paris: Ophrys.

Gandour, J., Wong, D., & Hutchins, G. (1998). Pitch processing in the human brain is influenced by language experience. *Neuroreport, 9,* 2215–2119.

Givón, T. (1995). *Functionalism and grammar.* Amsterdam: Benjamins.

Grabowski, T.J., & Damasio, A.R. (2000). Investigating language with functional neuroimaging. In A. W. Toga & J. C. Mazziotta (Eds.), *Brain mapping: The systems* (pp. 425–458). London: Academic Press.

Greenberg, J. (1995). The diachronic typological approach to language. In M. Shibatani & T. Bynon, (Eds.), *Approaches to language typology* (pp. 145–166). Oxford: Clarendon Press.

Hagoort, P., Brown, C., & Groothusen, J. (1993). The syntactic positive shift as an ERP-measure of syntactic processing. *Language and Cognition Processes, 8,* 439–483.

Halpern, A.R., & Bower, G.H. (1982). Musical expertise and melodic structure in memory for musical notation. *American Journal of Psychology, 95,* 31–50.

Hirst, D.J., & Di Cristo, A. (1998). A survey of intonation systems. In D.J. Hirst & A. Di Cristo (Eds.), *Intonation systems: A survey of twenty languages* (pp. 1–44). Cambridge: Cambridge University Press.

Indefrey, P., & Levelt, W.J.M. (2000). The neural correlates of language production. In M.S. Gazzaniga (Ed.) *The new cognitive neurosciences* (pp. 845–865). Cambridge, MA: MIT Press.

Jackendoff, R. (1997). *The architecture of the language faculty.* Cambridge, MA: MIT Press.

Jackendoff, R. (1991). Musical parsing and musical affect. *Music Perception, 9,* 199–230.

Jakobson, R. (1973). *Essais de linguistique générale. II. Rapports internes et externes du langage.* Paris: Editions de Minuit, Arguments.

Janata, P. (1995). ERP measures assay the degree of expectancy violation of harmonic contexts in music. *Journal of Cognitive Neuroscience, 7,* 153–164.

Kivy, P. (1991). *Music alone. Philosophical reflection on the purely musical experience.* New York: Cornell University Press.

Kubik, G. (1969). Composition techniques in Kiganda xylophone music. *The African Music Journal, 4,* 3.

Kutas, M., & Hillyard, S.A. (1980). Reading sensless sentences: Brain potentials reflect semantic incongruity. *Science, 207,* 203–205.

Kutas, M., & Hillyard, S.A. (1984). Event-related brain potentials (ERPs) elicited by novel stimuli during sentence processing. *Annals of the New York Academy of Sciences, 425,* 236–241.

Lakoff, G. (1987). *Women, fire and dangerous things.* Chicago: University of Chicago Press.

Langacker, R.W. (1987). *Foundations of cognitive grammar. Vol. I: Theoretical prerequisites.* Stanford, CA: Stanford University Press.

Leipp, E. (1977). *La machine à écouter: Essais de psychoacoustique.* Paris: Masson.

Leroi-Gourhan, A. (1988). *Le geste et la parole. Vol. I: La mémoire et les rythmes. Sciences d'aujourd'hui.* Paris: Albin-Michel.

Levman, B.G. (1992). The genesis of music and language. *Ethnomusicology, 36,* 147–170.

Locke, S., & Kellar, L. (1973). Categorical perception in a nonlinguistic mode. *Cortex, 9,* 355–369.

Luria, A., Tsvekova, L., & Futer, J. (1965). Aphasia in a composer. *Journal of Neurological Science, 2,* 288–292.

MacCallum, W.C., Farmer, S.F., & Pocock, P.V. (1984). The effects of physical and semantic incongruities on auditory event-related potentials. *Electroencephalography and Clinical Neurophysiology, 59,* 477–488.

Marin, O. (1982). Neurological aspects of music perception and performance. In D. Deutsch (Ed.), *The psychology of music.* New York: Academic Press.

Meyer, L. (1956). *Emotion and meaning in music.* Chicago: University of Chicago Press.

Molino, J. (2000). Toward an evolutionary theory of music and language. In N.L. Wallin, B. Merker, & S. Brown (Eds.) *The origins of music* (pp. 165–176). Cambridge, MA: MIT Press.

Nadel, S. (1930). The origin of music. *Musical Quarterly, 16,* 531–546.

Norris, D., & Wise, R. (2000). The study of prelexical and lexical processes in comprehension: Psycholinguistics and functional neuroimaging. In M.S. Gazzaniga, (Ed.), *The new cognitive Neurosciences.* (pp. 867–880). Cambridge, MA: MIT Press.

Osterhout, L., & Holcomb, P.J. (1992). Event-related brain potentials elicited by syntactic anomaly. *Journal of Memory and Language, 31,* 785–804.

Pacherie, E. (1999). Philosophie et sciences cognitives. In J.F. Mattéi (Ed.), *Encyclopédie philosophique universelle,* Paris: PUF.

Paller, K.A., McCarthy, G., & Wood, C.C. (1992). Event-related potentials elicited by deviant endings to melodies. *Psychophysiology, 29,* 202–206.

Pantev, C., Hoke, M., Luetkenhoener, B., & Lehnertz, K. (1989). Tonotopic organization of the auditory cortex: Pitch versus frequency representation. *Science, 246,* 486–488.

Patel, A., Gibson, E., & Ratner, J., Besson, M., & Holcomb, P. (1998a). Processing syntactic relations in language and music: An event-related potential study. *Journal of Cognitive Neuroscience, 10,* 717–733.

Patel, A., Peretz, I., Tramo, M., & Labreque, R. (1998b). Processing prosodic and musical patterns: A neuropsychological investigation. *Brain and Language, 61,* 123–144.

Peretz, I. (1990). Processing of local and global musical information by unilateral brain-damaged patients. *Brain, 113,* 1185–1205.

Peretz, I. (1993). Auditory agnosia: A functional analysis. In S. McAdams & E. Bigand (Eds.), *Thinking in sound: The cognitive psychology of human audition* (pp. 199–230). Oxford: Oxford University Press.

Peretz, I. (1996). Can we lose memory for music? A case of music agnosia in a nonmusician. *Journal of Cognitive Neuroscience, 8,* 481–496.

Peretz, I., Belleville, S., & Fontaine, S. (1997). Dissociations entre la musique et le langage après atteinte cérébrale: un nouveau cas d'amusie sans aphasie. *Revue Canadienne de psychologie expérimentale, 51,* 354–367.

Peretz, I., & Kolinsky, R. (1993). Boundaries of separability between melody and rhythm in music discrimination: A neuropsychological perspective. *The Quarterly Journal of Experimental Psychology*, *46A*, 301–325.

Peretz, I., & Morais, J. (1989). Music and modularity. *Contemporary Music Review*, *4*, 279–293.

Piana, G. (1991). *Filosofia della musica*. Milano: Guerini e associati.

Pinker, S. (1994). *The language instinct: How the mind creates language*. New York: Harper Perennial.

Platel, H., Price, C., Baron, J.C., Wise, R., Lambert, J., Frackowiak, R.S.J., Lechevalier, B., & Eustache, F. (1997). The structural components of music perception. *Brain*, *120*, 229–243.

Pollock, J.Y. (1997). *Langage et cognition. Introduction au programme minimaliste de la grammaire générative*. Paris: PUF.

Regnault, P., Bigand, E., & Besson, M. (2001). Different brain mechanisms mediate sensitivity to sensory consonance and harmonic context: Evidence from auditory event related brain potentials. *Journal of Cognitive Neuroscience*, *13*, 241–255.

Robert, S. (1997). Variation des représentations linguistiques: des unités à l'énoncé. In C. Fuchs & S. Robert (Eds.), *Diversité des langues et représentations cognitives* (pp. 25–39). Paris: Ophrys.

Samson, S., & Zatorre, R.J. (1994). Contribution of the right temporal lobe to musical timbre discrimination. *Neuropsychologia*, *32*, 231–240.

Schön, A., & Schön, D. (1999). Il potere del suono e della musica. Fuga a più voci. *Psiche*, (*1–2*), 159–165.

Schön, D., Semenza, C., & Denes, G. (2001). Naming of musical notes: A selective deficit in one musical clef. *Cortex*, *37*, 407–421.

Sergent, J., Zuck, E., Terriah, S., & McDonald, B. (1992). Distributed neural network underlying musical sight-reading and keyboard performance. *Science*, *257*, 106–109.

Signoret, J.L., Van Eeckhout, P., Poncet, M., & Castaigne, P. (1987). Aphasie sans amusie chez un organiste aveugle. *Revue Neurologique*, *143*, 172–181.

Sloboda, J.A. (1985). *Musical mind. The cognitive psychology of music*. Oxford: Oxford University Press.

Sloboda, J.A. (2000). Individual differences in music performance. *Trends in Cognitive Sciences*, *4*, 397–403.

Spencer, H. (1857). The origin and function of music. *Fraser's Magazine*, *56*, 396–408.

Strainer, J.C., Ulmer, J.L., Yetkin, F.Z., Haughton, V.M., Daniels, D.L., & Millen, S.J. (1997). Functional magnetic resonance imaging of the primary auditory cortex: Analysis of pure tone activation and tione discrimination. *American Journal of Neuroradiology*, *18*, 601–610.

Sutton, S., Braren, M., Zubin, J., & John, E.R. (1967). Evoked potential correlates of stimulus uncertainty. *Science*, *150*, 1187–1188.

Talmy, L. (1988). The relation of grammar to cognition. In B. Rudzka-Ostyn (Ed.), *Topics in cognitive linguistics*. Amsterdam: Benjamins.

Tootell, R.B.H., Hadjikhani, N.K., Mendola, J.D., Marrett, S., & Dale, A.M. (1998). From retinotopy to recognition: fMRI in human visual cortex. *Trends in Cognitive Sciences*, *2*, 174–183.

Van Valin, R.D., & LaPolla, R.J. (1997). *Syntax structure, meaning and function*. Cambridge: Cambridge University Press.

Victorri, B. (1999). Le sens grammatical. *Languages*, *136*, 85–105.

Von Hornbostel, E.M. (1928). African negro music. *Africa*, *1*, 30–62.

Weyert, H., Besson, M., Tempelmann, C., Scholz, M., et al. (2001). *An analysis of temporal structure in language and music using ERPs, MEG and fMRI techniques*. Manuscript in preparation.

Wittgenstein, L. (1953). *Philosophical investigations* (Trans. by G.E.M. Anscombe). Oxford: Basil Blackwell.

Zatorre, R.J., & Binder, J.R. (2000). Functional and structural imaging of the human auditory system. In A.W. Toga & J.C. Mazziotta (Eds.), *Brain mapping: The systems* (pp. 365–402). London: Academic Press.

Zatorre, R.J., Evans, C., Meyer, E., & Gjedde, A. (1992). Lateralization of phonetic pitch discrimination in speech processing. *Science, 256,* 846–849.

Zatorre, R.J., Halpern, A., Perry, D.W., et al. (1996). Hearing in the mind's ear: A PET investigation of musical imagery and perception. *Journal of Cognitive Neuroscience, 8,* 29–46.

SECTION TWO

Experimental psychology: Perception, attention, learning and memory

CHAPTER SIX

The mind at the crossroad of multiple ongoing activities: A challenge to cognitive psychology

Géry d'Ydewalle
University of Leuven, Belgium

INTRODUCTION

At any time, our mental system is involved in many activities which up to a certain extent are carried out in parallel. The density of the ongoing processes has been neglected for a long time as our science has been a victim of conceiving the mind as a linear sequence of successive processing. Already at the time of Wundt, the founder of our science, it was implicitly agreed that the simultaneous processing of several sensory inputs is next to impossible; one needs to switch attention from one sensory input to another and there are processing costs in switching attention. In *Die Geschwindigkeit des Gedankens*, Wundt (1862) noticed that it takes time to switch attention from the auditory input to the visual one. On the response side, the phenomenon of the Psychological Refractory Period (PRP) has been investigated under the same assumption: Telford (1931) found that if a relatively short interval (0.5 s or less) separates the stimulus (e.g., auditory tone) for one response (e.g., a key press) from the next stimulus for a subsequent response, then the reaction time of the subsequent response increases relative to those with a longer interval (1 s or more) between stimuli. The increase in reaction time implied that there may be a psychological refractory period that is analogous to the refractory period between successive neural impulses.

Of course, the most prominent case of linear, successive mental steps was introduced by Broadbent (1958). He proposed that stimuli first enter a sensory buffer in parallel, where their physical features are analyzed and made available to an attentional filter. The filter was assumed to select particular stimuli for transmission through a limited-capacity channel that identifies them, determines the meanings, and performs other operations at a fixed maximum rate. In Atkinson and Shiffrin (1968), information first enters a sensory register before being transferred to a short-term store, and thereafter to a long-term store. Control processes define the amount and form of the information that is being transferred from one store (or register) to the next.

Slightly more elasticity in the mental system was apparent in the unitary-resource theories (e.g., Kahneman, 1973), in which a mental commodity was assumed to mediate multiple-task performance. However, the approach focused mainly on the performance decrements that occur when concurrent tasks compete for access to the same structures, yielding structural interference. Although a flexible graded allocation of limited processing capacity to various competing processes is brought forward, the empirical work in that tradition paid particular attention to see how one performance is at the expense of another, underestimating the circumstances where multiple simultaneous activities are possible.

Fortunately, major empirical and theoretical progress has gradually cracked down the conceptual emphasis on a linear sequence of mental activities. The filter hypothesis of Broadbent has quickly been questioned by studies showing that under some conditions, observers notice semantic information in putatively unattended auditory messages (e.g., Moray, 1959; Treisman, 1960, 1964). Schneider and Shiffrin (1977; Shiffrin & Schneider, 1977), based on an extended set of visual-search experiments, kept the original distinction of short-term and long-term stores. However, the emphasis of successive information transfer from one store to the next disappears, partly by assuming parallel processing (next to controlled sequential processing) and partly by equating the short-term store as temporary activation of passive, inactive nodes in the long-term store.

Numerous empirical results that did not mesh well with Kahneman's unitary-resource theory led to the development of multiple-resource theories (e.g., Navon & Gopher, 1979), where various sets of processing resources are used, simultaneously and in combination, for performing multiple tasks. In Meyer and Kieras (1997a, b), computational models are presented to explain the Psychological Refractory Period, with the assumption that people can apply distinct sets of production rules simultaneously for executing the procedures of multiple tasks.

More recently, there has been interest in building neuron-like models in which mental functioning is expressed in terms of activities in neuron-like units. Such connectionist models had some apparent advantages. They appeared, at least in principle, more biologically plausible. Particularly important for the present chapter, they provided a relatively easy way to think about a number of parallel computations going on in our mind. Such PDP

(Parallel Distributed Processing) models were particularly powerful when applied to pattern and object classification. For a good introduction to connectionism, see Quinlan (1991). Despite some initial (and convincing) successes in modeling psychological processes, connectionism is already almost out of the field of psychology. Growing now are the ties of psychology with research in neurosciences.

Partly due to the recent theoretical advances, almost everyone will no longer question the flexibility of the human mind in performing multiple tasks. Notwithstanding this acknowledgement, a full appraisal of its implication to our understanding of the nature of human activities in various tasks has not been achieved. In the next two sections, we describe two tracks of our research, including a few illustrative empirical works, which demonstrate how humans deal either with multiple sources of information (research on the processing of subtitled television programs) or with multiple task requirements (a prospective-memory task embedded in another ongoing, concurrent task). We close the chapter with some general considerations on how to conceive the mind and how such considerations can appropriately take into account the density of the numerous mental activities going on at any time.

WATCHING SUBTITLED MOVIES

Smaller countries import a large number of television programs from abroad. The imported programs are generally either dubbed or subtitled in the local language. The debate between dubbing and subtitling has been settled by considerations of speed and cost; most countries with a smaller language community typically apply subtitling due to its lower cost and easy translation. In most countries in the world where subtitling is applied, the same rules of thumb are used for timing the subtitles. Two lines of text, each with a maximum of 32 characters and spaces, can be used at a time. If there are two lines of 32 characters and spaces each, the subtitle is displayed for 6 s. Shorter subtitles are time-scheduled proportionally according to this 6-s rule. Nobody seems to know how this 6-s rule was arrived at.

With subtitled movies, there are at least three different input channels (see Figure 1): the visual image, the soundtrack (including the foreign voices) and the subtitles (a translation of the voices). The text lines of the subtitles should, ideally, be completely overlapping with the translated information of the soundtrack. Most imported programs in Belgium are in English, a language which is fairly well known by the adult Belgian participants; anecdotal evidence further suggests that translation errors in the subtitles are noticed almost immediately.

The visual image (not including the subtitle) and the sequence of events in the movie typically provide abundant information which sometimes makes either understanding the spoken language or reading the subtitle superfluous.

Figure 1.   The processing of subtitled TV programs.

Moreover, it has been claimed that people unconsciously lipread to a certain extent.

The discussion in the earlier part of this chapter raises important issues for research in audiovisual broadcasts. For example, implications from the earlier studies of Broadbent are straightforward: At any given time, only one among the sensory inputs is fully analyzed. Moreover, it should take time to switch the inputs. If some parallel processing or multiple-resource allocations are accepted, more flexibility within the human system is likely to occur. As most film and television research does not address attention and processing issues, the purpose of our studies was to look at the dynamics of attention.

As the main question is how a person is able to divide and shift his or her attention in such a complex situation, the eye-movement patterns between image and subtitles were measured. d'Ydewalle, Van Rensbergen, and Pollet (1987) showed that Dutch-speaking subjects were able to switch effortlessly between the visual image and the subtitle. Moreover, the time spent in processing the subtitle did not change when reading the subtitle was made either more important for understanding the program (by switching off the soundtrack) or less compelling (when the subject knows the foreign language very well). Therefore, it was concluded that reading the subtitle at its onset presentation is more or less obligatory; it is unaffected by major contextual factors such as the availability of the soundtrack and important episodic characteristics of actions in the movie.

In order to explain the findings, two hypotheses were formulated. First, reading a subtitle is more efficient than listening. Second, Dutch-speaking subjects are very familiar with subtitles before they ever master the foreign language. The experience may still later lead them to read the subtitle even when they know the foreign language very well.

The main evidence in favor of the first hypothesis came from d'Ydewalle, Praet, Verfaillie, and Van Rensbergen (1991). In Experiment 1, American subjects watched an American movie with English soundtrack and subtitles. Despite their lack of familiarity with subtitles, they spent considerable time in the subtitled area. Accordingly, subtitle reading cannot be due to habit formation from long-term experience. In Experiment 2, a movie in Dutch with Dutch subtitles was shown to Dutch-speaking subjects. They also looked extensively at the subtitles, suggesting that reading the subtitles is preferred because of efficiency in following and understanding the movie.

In d'Ydewalle and Van Rensbergen (1989), some evidence was gathered for the second hypothesis by recording eye movements of young children. Although the attention pattern of fourth- and sixth-grade children did not differ from the pattern of adults, the pattern of second-grade children depended largely on the movie shown. For example, second-grade children watched a subtitled "Garfield" (a heavily verbally loaded cartoon) exactly as adults did, but they did not read the subtitles in "Popeye" (an action-oriented cartoon). This suggests that reading subtitles is not yet completely compulsory for young children, although they are well able to read them (as evidenced by their behavior when watching "Garfield").

The preceding studies all used segments from film or a television series. As summarized in d'Ydewalle and Gielen (1992), we also used news broadcasts. News broadcasts differ in several respects from film. First, one is not used to watching a news broadcast with subtitles whereas 90% of the films shown on Belgian television networks are foreign and subtitled in Dutch (or French). Second, film represents entertainment, deals with only one story with a beginning and an end, and features a number of reappearing characters. The images are often more attractive than the dialogue, and the pace is, in general, rather slow. A news broadcast, on the other hand, is meant to inform the viewers of what is going on in the world at large. The text is often far more important than are the images. A news broadcast provides a great deal of concrete information in a short period of time. Moreover, the different news items within a news broadcast do not relate to one another. The Dutch-speaking subjects were divided into four conditions: a Dutch film, a German film, a Dutch news broadcast, and a German news broadcast, all provided with Dutch subtitles. The results can be summarized as follows. With the news broadcast, subjects had a greater need for subtitles as they started to look at the subtitles at a faster pace and read them for longer periods, even when the spoken news broadcast was in their own language.

In a survey research, Tonla Briquet (1979) reported that elderly people complain more about subtitles than other age groups. d'Ydewalle, Warlop, and Van Rensbergen (1989), again using eye-movement recordings, found that with longer subtitles, younger people looked longer at the subtitle than the older people. As younger people read faster than older people and therefore finish reading earlier, younger people start re-reading the subtitles and therefore, linger longer in the subtitles. The age-related difference does not occur with shorter subtitles because in that case nobody has extra time available due to their shorter presentations. Watching subtitled programs requires the continuous integration of the information from the image, subtitles, and sound, and older subjects are considerably slower to integrate; therefore, older subjects return to the image as quickly as possible after a first reading of the subtitles. A number of detailed analyses of the data as well as the screening of the video recordings confirmed this explanation.

Verfaillie and d'Ydewalle (1987) investigated subjects who were deaf from birth. Three different sources of information were presented: subtitles, sign language, and information from lip movements. The eye movements of the subjects were measured while they were watching a spoken television story. All subjects were shown stories in four different modalities: (1) speaker, sign interpreter, and subtitles at the same time; (2) subtitles and sign interpreter; (3) subtitles and speaker; and (4) speaker and sign interpreter. The results overwhelmingly showed a preference for the subtitles. When enough time was left after reading the subtitles, the subjects looked at other parts of the screen, preferring signs to lip reading.

Although so far it is clear that reading of subtitles does occur, and switching attention from the visual image to reading subtitles happens to be effortless and almost automatic, the next question is whether the soundtrack is also processed simultaneously to a certain extent. Most of the subtitled films that are shown on the Dutch-speaking television networks are spoken in English or French, two languages that most Dutch-speaking adults are at least familiar with. As such, it is perfectly possible that part of the soundtrack is processed as well. This is already suggested incidentally, by spontaneous reports from the subjects that the translation in the subtitle did not fully agree with the spoken dialogue, in cases where such a mismatch had occurred. In several experiments (d'Ydewalle & Van de Poel, 2000; Sohl, 1989; Vanachter, De Bruycker, & d'Ydewalle, 2000), we used a double-task technique. Apart from watching a television program, the subjects had to react to flashing lights (+ a sound beep) as quickly as possible. The reaction time to the flashing lights was taken as a measurement for the amount of processing done with the first task, which was the viewing of a television program. The flashing lights were given at specific moments: subtitle and speaker(s) present, no subtitle, and neither subtitle nor speaker(s) present. From Figure 2 it appears that the presence of subtitles consumes resources and, independently, the presence of

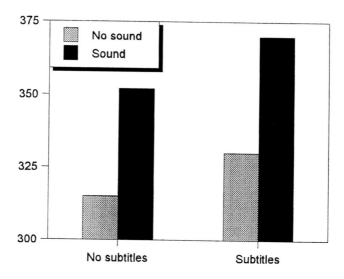

Figure 2.   Reaction times (ms) to flash+beep.

voice also slows down the reaction times. The slowest reaction times were obtained whenever both a speaker and a subtitle were present, which suggests that the subjects do make an effort to follow the speech.

Another set of studies demonstrated that the soundtrack is indeed being processed. Simply enjoying a subtitled foreign movie leads to the acquisition of the foreign language. Such language acquisition is an implicit, unconscious process, and has to be distinguished from language learning, which is conscious and occurs in more formal situations where a foreign language is systematically taught (Krashen, 1981). In our experiments, the language in the soundtrack and in the subtitles was manipulated: either the foreign language or the mother language in the soundtrack, or no soundtrack; likewise, either the foreign language or mother language in the subtitle, or no subtitles, leading to a 3 x 3 design. The standard condition, is of course, when the foreign language is in the soundtrack and the mother language in the subtitle; reversed subtitling refers to the condition where the mother language is in the soundtrack and the subtitles are in the foreign language.

In one particularly large-scale experiment (d'Ydewalle & Pavakanun, 1997), a third independent variable was included into the basic 3 x 3 design. The incidental acquisition of foreign language could perhaps be facilitated when the foreign language shows more similarities with the mother language. To put it simply, watching a Chinese movie with subtitles in the Dutch mother-language will not lead to much acquisition as compared with a German movie for Dutch-speaking students, German being rather similar to Dutch. In d'Ydewalle and Pavakanun, the effect of the similarity between the foreign and mother languages upon language acquisition was investigated by using nine different foreign languages which varied in their similarity to Dutch (South African, German, Spanish, Italian, Russian, Hungarian, Japanese, Chinese, and Thai).

Immediately following the 12-minute movie, acquisition of the foreign vocabulary and syntax was assessed. After watching the movie, there were four different types of tests. Each test had two subtests: auditory and printed subtests. In the Identification Test, subjects had to pick out the correct sound or printed word of the foreign language. In the Simple Structural Test, 15 simple sentences (involving only noun and verb) from the soundtrack or the subtitles, which were presented at least five times in the movie, were used. Some sentences were literally the same as in the movie (a correct sentence), while the word order was changed in other sentences. Subjects had to choose the correct one. The Vocabulary Test involved words from the native language which were presented at least five times in the subtitles or in the sound track. Each of the selected words were followed by five words in the foreign language, and subjects had to choose the correct translation. In the Sentence Construction Test (involving compound sentences, namely a noun phrase with a clause phrase), sentences from the sound track or the subtitles were intermixed with three distractor sentences which differed from each other only in the order of the words in the sentence.

The findings established without any doubts that there is considerable incidental language acquisition simply by watching a short subtitled movie. Surprisingly, there was not necessarily less foreign language acquisition when the foreign and mother languages were vastly different. In fact, there was not much support for distinguishing the language families as a function of their acquisition (see also d'Ydewalle & Pavakanun, 1997). In agreement with other studies (d'Ydewalle & Pavakanun, 1995; Holobow, Lambert, & Sayegh, 1984; Lambert, Boehler, & Sidoti, 1981; Lambert & Holobow, 1984; Pavakanun & d'Ydewalle, 1992), reversed subtitling enhanced language acquisition even more than standard subtitling. Children also acquire foreign languages simply by watching subtitled movies but, contrary to the sensitive-period hypothesis (Lenneberg, 1967), their acquisition is not superior to that of adults (d'Ydewalle & Van de Poel, 1999).

In conclusion, there is clear evidence that subtitles are being read and the soundtrack is being processed. Accordingly, we need to accept that with subtitled movies, observers are simultaneously processing the visual image and the voice in the soundtrack; they also simultaneously process the subtitles and the soundtrack. With the three information channels (voice, subtitles, and visual image), the only limitation in parallel activities is the simultaneous processing of the visual images on the screen and the subtitles, which is impossible due to the foveal constraints in capturing visual information.

PROSPECTIVE MEMORY

Prospective memory and age

Recently, there has been a growing interest in the study of prospective memory (Brandimonte, Einstein, & McDaniel, 1996). Formerly, research on memory involved the influence of past events on current activities (either implicitly, as in priming studies for example, or explicitly, when the task requires the retrieval of those events), and this is now called retrospective memory. Prospective memory refers to the memory required to carry out planned actions in the future. Following Einstein and McDaniel (1990), a distinction needs to be made between event-based and time-based prospective memory. In event-based prospective memory, the planned actions are triggered by some type of external event or cue (e.g., meeting a friend reminds one to request something from him or her); it is assumed that event-based prospective memory requires less self-initiated processing or mental effort than time-based prospective memory. Time-based prospective memory (e.g., to remember a faculty meeting tomorrow at 3 o'clock in the afternoon) is more effortful as it requires more self-initiated activities at a specific time in the absence of triggering cues.

Age deficits in retrospective memory have now been well documented (for a review, see Light, 1991); older people are particularly deficient in memory tasks involving self-generated activities (e.g., Craik, 1986; Craik & McDowd, 1987). In prospective memory, the age effect seems to depend on whether the participants are tested in a constraining laboratory setting or in a less-controlled environment (Maylor, 1990).

In field studies (e.g., when the participants are requested to call the experimenter on a few consecutive days), older participants typically perform better than the younger ones (Devolder et al., 1990; d'Ydewalle & Brunfaut, 1996; Martin, 1986; Moscovitch, 1982; Patton & Meit, 1993). Findings from laboratory studies are more inconclusive. For example, Einstein and McDaniel (1990) and Einstein, McDaniel, Richardson, Guynn, and Cunfer (1995) failed to find age differences in an event-based prospective-memory task whereas others have found age decrements (Dobbs & Rule, 1987; Einstein, Holland, McDaniel, & Guynn, 1992; Mäntylä, 1993; Maylor, 1993, 1996). In time-based prospective memory, a series of experiments by Einstein et al. (1995) showed substantial disadvantage of the older participants. The disadvantage is explained by the amount of self-initiated processing, which is more necessary in time-based prospective-memory tasks, and older people are less prone to initiate such processing.

If the amount of self-generated activity is critical to account for the age differences in event-based and time-based prospective-memory tasks, it is then important to compare the performance of older and younger participants in the two tasks using, as far as possible, the same setting, except for the self-initiated activities. In Einstein et al. (1995, Experiment 3), the participants had to answer general-knowledge and problem-solving questions. Additionally, participants were asked to press a key every 5 min in the time-based task, whereas in the event-based task, participants were asked to press a key whenever they were presented with a question about US Presidents. A direct comparison of event-based to time-based prospective memory resulted in an Age × Memory Type interaction because of the clearly inferior performance of the older participants on the time-based but not on the event-based task. In the following experiment, we also hypothesized that older people would show particularly inferior performance in the time-based task due to a deficit in self-initiated activities.

Groups of younger and older participants were tested twice individually. In the first session, each participant was randomly assigned to one of the two prospective-memory conditions. When the participant in the first session performed the event-based prospective-memory task, the time-based prospective-memory task was then given in the second session (which immediately followed the first session); or vice versa.

Each session involved the presentation of a series of slides, showing each time the face of a well-known person. The main aim of the experiment was said to be research on memory for famous faces; we called this task the identification task. Participants were then given time to read the instructions carefully, the experimenter stressing that the most important points would be repeated orally afterwards. Participants had to write down on a card the name of the person projected on the screen. Afterwards, they were told, they would have to recall as many faces as possible.

The prospective-memory task was introduced as a way of hindering the use of using memory strategies in the identification task. In the event-based task, the participants had to give an additional response when there was a particular critical feature on the slide (e.g., a face with a beard, hat, bow tie, etc.). In the time-based prospective-memory condition, a clock was available to help the participants to monitor the time. The clock was about 1.5 m away over their left shoulder, and quite readable. The position of the clock required participants to turn their heads to monitor it, and this allowed the experimenter to record the number of times the participant checked or monitored the clock. The participants had different actions to perform when the clock read either 00:02 (2 min), 00:03 (3 min), 00:05 (5 min), or 00:06 (6 min), respectively.

In the second session, the procedure was exactly the same except for the prospective-memory task: If the prospective task in the first session was time-based, then the second session it would be event-based, or vice versa.

Older participants identified the faces ($M = 75\%$) more successfully than the younger participants ($M = 65\%$; see Figure 3a). However, in the prospective-memory task, the younger participants performed better ($M = 92\%$) than the older participants ($M = 72\%$). It is noteworthy that the interaction between age and the two prospective-memory tasks was not significant. In fact, both age groups performed slightly better on the time-based than on the event-based prospective-memory task (see Figure 3b). This was not in agreement with our initial hypothesis.

As the better performance of the older participants in the face-identification task was rather unexpected, we carried out additional analyses as a function of the nature of the faces on the slides. The overall better performance of the older participants in the face-identification task was due to a much larger number of slides with political figures, and on those slides, older participants were particularly good at identifying the faces.

Older participants identified more faces but showed inferior prospective-memory performance than the younger participants, suggesting a negative correlation between the performance in the face-identification and prospective-memory tasks. For both prospective-memory tasks, the correlation was indeed negative. In the event-based prospective-memory task, one also can look at the prospective-memory performance on the critical target slides affecting the identification of those slides (or vice versa). Younger and older participants both identified more faces when the prospective task was not done than when the prospective task was done (.75 and .54 proportion face identification for the younger participants; .44 and .36 for the older participants), confirming the negative correlation between the face-identification and event-based prospective-memory performances at the level of the individual items.

The age-related difference in the face-identification task accounted for the age-related deficit in the prospective-memory task. The contribution from age in the multiple regressions on the prospective-memory performance was no longer significant when the face-identification performance was included in the equations for the event- and time-based prospective-memory performance separately.

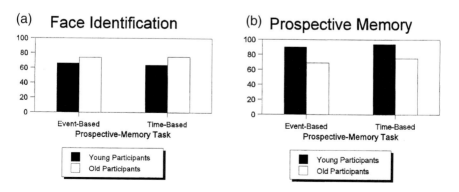

Figure 3.   (a) Face Identification (b) Prospective Memory.

The next experiment was designed to confirm the negative tradeoff and to clarify its nature in explaining prospective-memory performance of the young and older participants. Half of the two groups of participants received slides containing only political figures; the other half received slides with only television and show-business people.

This time, younger participants identified the faces more successfully ($M = .77$) than did the older participants ($M = .59$). However, there was a significant interaction between the age groups and the nature of the slides (see Figure 4a): Younger participants identified slightly more slides with television and show-business people ($M = .82$) than with political figures ($M = .71$); the opposite was true for the older participants (political figures: $M = .74$; television and show-business people: $M = .45$). This pattern confirmed the findings on face identification from the preceding experiment.

In the analysis of prospective memory performance, again the younger participants performed better ($M = .95$) than the older participants ($M = .74$). Although both age groups performed slightly better in the time-based than in the event-based prospective-memory task in the preceding experiment, the same difference was much larger in the present experiment. Younger participants showed perfect performance in the time-based task, and .90 in the event-based task; the difference was particularly large ($Ms = .88$ and .60, respectively in the time- and event-based tasks) in the older participants.

Although both groups of participants performed less well in the prospective-memory task when political figures were presented on the slides, this poor performance was quite salient with the older participants (television and show-business figures: $Ms = 1.00$ and .85 for the young and old participants respectively; political figures: $Ms = .90$ and .62 for the young and old participants respectively, see Figure 4b).

We again correlated the performance on the prospective-memory task

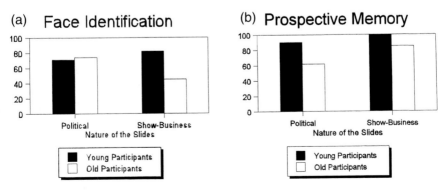

Figure 4.   (a) Face Identification (b) Prospective Memory.

with the performance on the face-identification task, and all correlations were again consistently negative (the correlation among young participants with the time-based task could not be correlated due to the perfect performance on the prospective-memory task). In the event-based prospective-memory task, there was again a (negative) tradeoff between the face-identification and prospective-memory performance at the level of the critical target slides. When the prospective task was carried out, the proportion of slides where the faces were correctly identified was smaller than the proportion of correctly identified slides when the prospective task was not carried out (.65 and 1.00 for younger participants; .48 and .62 for older participants).

The age effect on prospective-memory performance did not disappear when the face identification and the nature of the slides were entered in the multiple-regression equation, neither for the event-based nor the time-based tasks. However, if the regression equation involved not the overall performance of the identification task but only the identification performance on the critical target slides, then the age effect in the event-based task disappeared completely; due to the procedure, such an analysis was not possible in the time-based task.

As in Einstein et al. (1995), we started with the hypothesis that the time-based prospective-memory performance should be worse than the performance in the event-based prospective-memory task, particularly among the elderly. This followed from the assertion that the time-based task requires more self-generating activities, that is, the participants have to take the initiative to turn their head in order to check the clock; in the event-based task, the critical feature is directly available on the presented slide. Whereas Einstein et al. (1995) were able to confirm the hypothesis, we failed to provide further evidence. In fact, there was a slightly better performance in the time-based task than in the event-based task in the first experiment; in the second experiment, this better performance was significant. Given some consensus that time-based prospective-memory tasks are harder than event-based prospective-memory tasks, finding better performance with the time-based task is noteworthy, especially in older groups.

There are, of course, a number of procedural differences between Experiment 3 of Einstein et al. (1995) and the present two experiments, and it is hard to speculate what difference has been critical. In Einstein et al., the participants had to answer general-knowledge and problem-solving questions whereas we used a face-identification task; however, d'Ydewalle, Luwel, and Brunfaut (1999) showed that this task difference does not matter. Relative to Einstein et al. (1995; Experiment 3), the time periods in the present two experiments were shorter and, in most conditions, the target events occurred at a denser rate. Such a procedure could have created an experimental situation that involved more vigilance than the paradigm of Einstein et al. (1995; Experiment 3). With participation in both sessions and with target events occurring in a short time period, participants in the present experiments may have been ever-vigilant for the prospective-memory target events. There may be indeed an important difference between short- and long-term prospective memory tasks. This denser rate could also make the prospective task "primary" rather than "secondary".

How do we explain the worse performance of the elderly in both prospective-memory tasks? Our several analyses suggest that the worse performance is related to a tradeoff between the performance in the ongoing concurrent task and the prospective-memory task. In the first experiment, older participants performed better in the face-identification task and worse in the prospective-memory task than the younger participants, and the performance in the two tasks correlated negatively. The age effect on prospective memory disappeared when the regression analysis took into account the performance in the face-identification task. In the second experiment, with slides involving political leaders, the same tradeoff between the two tasks emerged in the event-based task; unfortunately, the procedure and ceiling effects prohibited further analyses in the time-based tasks to see whether the age effect on prospective memory disappears when one takes into account the nature of the slides and the performance level in the identification task.

The negative effect of loading the ongoing task on prospective memory has already been observed in event-based tasks. In McDaniel, Shaw, Einstein, and Smith (1996), increasing the attentional demands of the ongoing task exacerbated age differences on prospective memory in an event-based task. Park, Hertzog, Kidder, Morrell, and Mayhorn (1997; see also Kidder, Park, Hertzog, & Morrell, 1997) showed that the event-based prospective-memory performance is more sensitive to the loading by the concurrent activity than the time-based prospective-memory performance. However, Maylor (1996) did relate performance of the ongoing task and the event-based prospective-memory task, and the age effect did not disappear.

The nature of the slides had a critical influence on the pattern of findings in our two experiments. Although all presented faces were chosen among famous people, there still could be a difference as a function of the age groups: television and show-business people being more familiar to the young participants, and political figures being more familiar to the older people. Einstein et al. (1992) and McDaniel and Einstein (1993) have shown that unfamiliar target events benefit event-based prospective-memory performance. The face-identification task in our first experiment rather confirms this finding: Older participants identified more political figures, who presumably are more familiar to them, while the younger participants identified more television and show-business people. As the majority of the slides contained political figures, who are less familiar to the younger participants, they accordingly showed better prospective-memory performance than the older participants. Following McDaniel and Einstein (1993), more familiar events may have more pre-existing associations; therefore those events will probably cue information other than that needed for the requested prospective-memory response; less familiar events have fewer pre-existing associations, thereby making it more likely that information cued by those events will be relevant to the prospective task.

However, the explanation in terms of interfering activities with familiar slides faces a number of problems in the present set of experiments. First, one should expect a more important influence of the interfering responses on familiar slides in the event-based than in the time-based prospective-memory task: In the event-based task, the prospective response was to be given directly to the critical slides. However, we did not obtain an interaction effect between the nature of the slides and the two prospective-memory tasks in our second experiment. Second, we assume that the face-identification data reflect the familiarity of the slides. In the second experiment, the political figures were equally well identified by the younger and older participants; nevertheless, the older participants showed a considerable prospective-memory deterioration in the condition with the slides containing the political figures. We rather suggest that the nature of the slides affects how many resources will be used to comply with the instructions for the several tasks that have to be carried out simultaneously.

The present set of findings leads to two major conclusions. First, prospective-memory performance heavily depends on the nature of the con-current ongoing activity. Second, contrary to the conclusion of Einstein et al. (1995), time-based prospective-memory of the elderly is not necessarily worse than event-based prospective-memory; in fact, time-based prospective-memory is even significantly better than event-based prospective-memory in our second experiment.

Prospective memory and Korsakoff patients

Research on the underlying brain structures suggests that prospective func-tioning relies more on the frontal lobes than retrospective memory (Bisiacchi, 1996; Fuster, 1985; Ingvar, 1985; Shallice & Burgess, 1991). The decision about what action needs to be performed, and the creation of the intent to carry it out fall within the traditional domain of the executive function (Bur-gess & Shallice, 1997). The frontal lobes are responsible for formulating plans, initiating actions, monitoring ongoing behavior, and evaluating out-comes, and therefore probably also for prospective remembering (Glisky, 1996). When cognitive deficits appear in frontal lobe dementias, they typically involve disorders of planning and organization (Sungaila & Crockett, 1993).

Korsakoff patients are known to have serious difficulties with retrospective memory. They suffer from severe anterograde and retrograde amnesia (But-ters, 1985; Butters & Cermak, 1980; Butters & Delis, 1995; Lezak, 1983). Far less is known about their prospective-memory functioning. While the precise anatomical localization of the Korsakoff syndrome remains a problem, it is assumed that there is damage in the medial thalamus, and possibly in the mammillary bodies of the hypothalamus as well as a generalized cerebral atrophy, especially in the frontal lobe (Joyce & Robbins, 1991; Kolb & Whishaw, 1990; Squire, 1982a, b). A prospective-memory task always implies retrospective- and prospective-memory components. The amnesic nature of the Korsakoff patients will greatly affect the retrospective component. Their frontal lobe atrophy will additionally influence the prospective component. They do show impairment in the planning of behavior and the formation of judgment (Freedman & Oscar-Berman, 1986; Squire, 1982b). Therefore, we predict that Korsakoff patients will show a considerably impaired prospective memory.

In Brunfaut, Vanoverbergh, and d'Ydewalle (2000), there were 24 male and 3 female Korsakoff patients and 24 (20 male and 4 female) alcoholics. All participants had abstained from alcohol for at least 1 month. The 27 Korsakoff patients were residents in a psychiatric institution. The average age of the group was 50.6 years (range 37–64 years). All patients showed severe antero-grade and retrograde amnesia. Their general cognitive functioning, however, was not affected. The chronic alcoholics were hospitalized in a detoxication ward of a psychiatric institution. The average age was 41.8 years (range 35–59 years). Among the alcoholics, there were no signs of any memory problems.

All participants were tested twice individually. In the two sessions, half of the participants received a perceptual prospective-memory task (to push the red button whenever the presented word contained five letters), while the other participants received a semantic prospective-memory task (to push the red button of the keyboard whenever a word belonged to the category of animal). In Session 1, half of the participants received the instruction to count the letters of the presented words and to enter this number on the keyboard in front of them (perceptual ongoing task). The other participants received the instruction to explain briefly the meaning of the words (semantic ongoing task) and then to push the yellow button of the keyboard to get the next word. In Session 2, which followed Session 1 after a 1-min break, the participant received the instructions for the other ongoing task. This results in 2 (Korsakoff patient vs. alcoholic) × 2 (perceptual vs. semantic prospective-memory task) × 2 (first perceptual then semantic ongoing task vs. first semantic then perceptual ongoing task) between-subjects variables.

After Session 1, participants who were first given the instruction to count the letters of words in Session 1 (perceptual ongoing task) now received the instruction to give the meaning of the words (semantic ongoing task), or vice versa. Both groups were again given the instruction to push the red button whenever a word belonged to the category of animal or contained five letters (depending on the prospective-memory condition).

The proportion of correctly counted letters was larger when the prospective-memory task was perceptual ($M = .964$) than when it was semantic ($M = .89$). On explaining the words correctly, almost all participants displayed perfect performance ($M = .97$ and 1.00 for the Korsakoff patients and alcoholics, respectively).

On the prospective-memory task, both groups of participants performed better when the prospective-memory task was embedded in a semantic ongoing task ($M = .77$) than when it was embedded in a perceptual ongoing task ($M = .64$), and the alcoholics ($M = .88$) performed better than the Korsakoff patients ($M = .53$). Critically important was the interaction between the nature of the prospective-memory tasks and the nature of the ongoing-tasks (see Figure 5). Best performance in both groups was obtained when the prospective-memory task and the ongoing task were both either perceptual or semantic; particularly striking was the worst performance, when the prospective-memory task was semantic and the ongoing task was perceptual.

The nature of the prospective-memory and ongoing tasks was manipulated in order to have an ongoing task sharing the same processes as the prospective-memory task in some conditions; in other words, the processing requirements of the ongoing task could provide the participants with an internal reminder of the prospective-memory task. Indeed, prospective-memory performance was better when the ongoing task was more similar to the prospective-memory task.

Critical in the present study was again the nature of the prospective-memory task and its relationship to the processes in the ongoing task. Our studies on prospective memory and age obtained a negative performance tradeoff between the ongoing and prospective-memory tasks; in fact, age differences in prospective memory disappeared when the analysis took into account the performance level in the ongoing task. A number of studies were designed where the attentional demands of the ongoing activities were

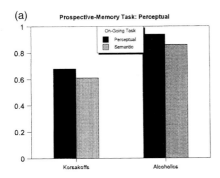
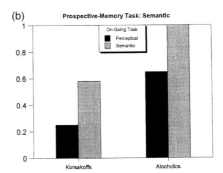

Figure 5. (a) Prospective-Memory Task: Perceptual (b) Prospective-Memory Task: Semantic (Adapted from Brunfaut et al., 2000).

manipulated more directly; they provided a mixed pattern of results. In Einstein et al. (1995; Experiment 3) and Otani et al. (1997), increasing the attentional demands of the ongoing task did not affect prospective memory. In other studies (Kidder et al., 1997; McDaniel, Robinson-Riegler, & Einstein, 1998), however, a major influence of the ongoing load on prospective memory was observed.

Fortunately, Marsh and Hicks (1998) clarified the mixed pattern of findings by referring to the working memory model of Baddeley (1986, 1992). No negative impact of the ongoing tasks on prospective memory was expected and was observed as long as the ongoing tasks predominantly involved the slave systems (i.e., the phonological loop or the visuospatial sketchpad). However, if the ongoing tasks implied central executive functioning, they competed with the prospective-memory task in using the same executive resources; in such cases, they obtained a negative effect on prospective memory. In d'Ydewalle, Bouckaert, and Brunfaut (2001), the performance in the ongoing task involved considerable central executive functioning (solving arithmetic tasks); in agreement with Marsh and Hicks (1998), time-based prospective memory among the elderly literally collapsed when the complexity of the ongoing task was increased.

We may even go one step further: Within the central executive, the different processes need not necessarily compete against each other; they may facilitate each other. Maylor (1996) already proposed that compatibility of processing for both the prospective and the ongoing tasks is critical. She suggested that whenever different processes are required for the prospective and ongoing tasks, constantly shifting from one level of processing to the other may impair prospective-memory performance. When there is considerable overlap between the two processing activities necessary to perform each task, no such impairment is predicted. Maylor reported age differences on a prospective event-based task when semantic processing was required on the ongoing task and when perceptual processing was required on the prospective task. Mäntylä (1994) reported a similar finding for a prospective and ongoing task with different processing requirements.

Maylor's task-appropriate processing explanation should in fact predict a better performance when the two tasks share the same level of processing. Our study with the Korsakoff patients nicely illustrates such a facilitation: Particularly striking was the much better prospective memory in the semantic prospective-memory task when the ongoing task required a semantic analysis than when it required perceptual processing. Describing the meaning of the word (the semantic ongoing task) prompted the semantic prospective-memory response of pushing a particular button when the name of an animal appeared; in such a prospective-memory task, counting the number of letters in the word did not help.

We also obtained a better prospective memory score in the perceptual prospective-memory task when the ongoing task required a perceptual analysis than when it required semantic processing. However, the difference was much smaller. The absence of a larger effect among the alcoholics could perhaps be due to a ceiling effect, but this explanation doesn't hold for the Korsakoff patients. In fact, the prospective memory of the Korsakoff patients was surprisingly good in the perceptual prospective-memory task. It should be noted that all participants in the perceptual prospective-memory task (and not in the semantic prospective-memory task) were requested to repeat the instructions of the experimenter loudly before starting the experiment, and this could explain the better performance of the Korsakoff patients in the perceptual prospective-memory task.

As an alternative to the task-appropriate processing explanation, the present findings could also be explained by the instance theory of automaticity (Logan, 1988, 1990; Logan & Etherton, 1994). The attention hypothesis (Logan, Taylor, & Etherton, 1996), which is derived from the instance theory, claims that learning is a side effect of attending: People will learn about things they attend to and they will not learn much about the things they do not attend to. As applied to the present experiment, the requested prospective-memory response is a cue-action association that needs to be automatized. Such an automatization of the association will be facilitated when the ongoing task directs the attention to what is to be learned for the prospective-memory task. When the two tasks are totally different, the ongoing task will not direct the attention to the cue that is relevant for the prospective-memory response.

The task-appropriate processing explanation and the attention hypothesis from the instance theory of automaticity predict the same critical interaction between the nature of the ongoing and prospective-memory tasks. The attention hypothesis additionally predicts a gradual strengthening of the prospective association. However, no such improvement was observed in the present study. We therefore slightly favor the task-appropriate processing explanation.

In the introduction to the experiment, we focused on the frontal requirements of the prospective component in prospective-memory tasks, and chose Korsakoff patients because of their frontal lobe deficits. As Korsakoff patients are also amnesic as a result of diencephalic pathology, the retrospective component in the prospective-memory task will also be affected. We therefore predicted a collapse of their prospective-memory functioning. However, contrary to the prediction and the frontal lobe hypothesis in general, their performance can be surprisingly good. In Session 2, their prospective memory was no worse than the prospective memory of the alcoholics. Even in Session 1, they showed reasonably good performance levels when the prospective-memory and ongoing tasks involved the same processing level; in those conditions, their performance also did not differ significantly from that of the alcoholics. The present study, however, does not answer whether the remaining performance difference between the Korsakoff patients and the alcoholics reflects frontal or diencephalic deficits, and whether the difference is due to the retrospective or prospective components of the prospective-memory task.

We emphasized the importance of detailed analyses of the processing interactions between the prospective-memory and ongoing tasks in order to explain prospective memory; by its nature, a prospective-memory task is always embedded in another task. Our studies (see also d'Ydewalle, 1995; d'Ydewalle et al., 1999, 2001; d'Ydewalle, Utsi, & Brunfaut, 1996) focused upon the typically negative tradeoff (particularly among older people) between the performance in the ongoing task and the prospective-memory task, suggesting that attention to one task is at the expense of performance in the other task. While such a tradeoff could not be examined empirically in the present experiment (due to ceiling effects in the ongoing tasks), it shows that the nature of the ongoing task can also positively affect prospective remembering.

CONCLUSION

Our studies on subtitling amply demonstrated the density and variety of ongoing processing: While pictorial information is captured, the voice stream is analyzed, and while the subtitles are being read, there are no problems in attending simultaneously to the spoken foreign voice. Almost by definition, a prospective-memory task is embedded in another task, which needs to be interrupted or processed simultaneously. Age differences in prospective memory vanish when the performance on the other task is taken into account. Korsakoff patients typically perform very poorly on a variety of memory tasks. However, when the ongoing and prospective-memory tasks involve similar processing requirements, Korsakoff patients are able to show a much better prospective memory. All presented studies in this chapter high-light the importance of scrutinizing in detail the several activities of the subjects in their task(s). At any time, the subjects are engaged in a variety of processing.

In our research endeavors, we may start to be more sensitive to the density and variety of ongoing processing if we always acknowledge the importance of a few critical features in our subject matter, the psychology of the mind, and its activities.

First, our activities are almost always goal-directed. People are active par-ticipants in the world with purposes and goals they want to attain. Many, if not most, of our responses to the environment in the form of judgments, decisions, and behavior are determined not solely by the information avail-able in that environment but rather by how it relates to whatever goal(s) we are currently pursuing. However, this goal-directedness is not an easy issue in psychology. The same goal can be reached through different activities, and the same activity, as a function of the context, may refer to different goals. Worse, a particular activity may be referring to various goals at the same time. Going out for dinner tonight may satisfy my biological need for food but may at the same time be directed to enjoy the good company of close friends. Goals are also to a large extent implicit; they are largely unconscious, and may be activated by situational features (Bargh & Chartrand, 1999). Goals do not require an act of will to operate and guide information processing and behavior. They can be activated instead by external, environmental information and events. Once they are put in motion, they operate just as if they had been consciously intended.

Second, acknowledging the multiplicity of ongoing processes also needs to be extended to very simple behavior. The speed of our reaction times to a simple stimulus (e.g., a flashing light) is already heavily affected by a number of intervening activities. We typically need 250 ms to react to a flashing light, and this is indeed awfully slow. An expert typist needs only 40 ms between two strokes on the keyboard!

Third, the many processes need to be integrated by a central executive as a function of our goals. As some of our goals are consciously experienced, we do have the (illusory?) feeling that the activities are indeed emanating from a conscious "self". Often the reference to a central executive is an easy scientific scapegoat, considering our limited knowledge about its role and components. There is here a real danger to see a kind of "homunculus" appearing. Neisser's (1967) seminal book *Cognitive psychology* describes the problem of the executive in which the flexible choice and selection processes are described as a homunculus or "little person in the head" that does not constitute a scientific explanation. However, we do agree with Baddeley (1996, p. 26) that ". . . the homunculus can be useful, given two provisos: (1) the continued recognition that it constitutes a way of labelling the problem, not an adequate explanation; (2) a continued attempt to understand the component processes that are necessary for executive control, gradually stripping away the various functions we previously attributed to our homunculus, until eventually it can be declared redundant. Whether we will then be left with a single coordinated system that serves multiple functions, a true executive, or a cluster of largely autonomous control processes—an executive committee—remains to be seen".

Finally, our activities and mental processes are obviously rooted in neural activities in the brain. A better knowledge of the neuroscience will help us to acknowledge the constraints in the cognitive activities and the modular organization of the cognitive system. Recent advances in positron emission tomography (PET) and functional magnetic resonance imaging (fMRI), now routinely applied to the mapping of cognitive systems in the brain, have generated an explosion of activity in numerous research centers around the world. The potential of this new method for assessing brain activation in relation to cognitive tasks has great interest and appeal. There is the hope and the widely held expectation that these major developments will ultimately add important insights on brain-behavior relationships that may not be accomplished using other techniques. For cognitive scientists, such insights concern the nature of the functional architecture mediating our behavioral and mental activities. From this perspective, the recent neuroscience approach is bypassing the many solutions (e.g., dualism, psychophysical parallelism, or materialism/monism) which in the past have been developed to conceive the brain-behavior relationship.

REFERENCES

Atkinson, R.C., & Shiffrin, R.M. (1968). Human memory: A proposed system and its control processes. In K.W. Spence & J.T. Spence (Eds.), *The psychology of learning and motivation: Advances in research and theory, Vol. 2* (pp. 89–195). New York: Academic Press.

Baddeley, A.D. (1986). *Working memory*. Oxford: Oxford University Press.

Baddeley, A.D. (1992). Is working memory working? The fifteenth Bartlett Lecture. *Quarterly Journal of Experimental Psychology, 44A*, 1–31.

Baddeley, A. (1996). Exploring the central executive. *Quarterly Journal of Experimental Psychology, 49A*, 5–28.

Bargh, J.A., & Chartrand, T.L. (1999). The unbearable automaticity of being. *American Psychologist, 54*, 462–479.

Bisiacchi, P.S. (1996). The neuropsychological approach in the study of prospective memory. In M. Brandimonte, G.O. Einstein, & M.A. McDaniel (Eds.), *Prospective memory: Theory and applications* (pp. 297–317). Hillsdale, NJ: Lawrence Erlbaum Associates Inc.

Brandimonte, M., Einstein, G.O., & McDaniel, M.A. (Eds.). (1996). *Prospective memory: Theory and applications*. Mahwah, NJ: Lawrence Erlbaum Associates Inc.

Broadbent, D.E. (1958). *Perception and communication*. London: Pergamon.

Brunfaut, E., Vanoverbergh, V., & d'Ydewalle, G. (2000). Prospective remembering of Korsakoffs and alcoholics as a function of the prospective-memory and on-going tasks. *Neuropsychologia, 38*, 975–984.

Burgess, P.W., & Shallice, T. (1997). The relationship between prospective and retrospective memory: Neuropsychological evidence. In M.A. Conway (Ed.), *Cognitive models of memory: Studies in cognition* (pp. 247–272). Cambridge, MA: MIT Press.

Butters, N. (1985). Alcoholic Korsakoff's syndrome: Some unresolved issues concerning aetiology, neuropathology and cognitive deficits. *Journal of Clinical and Experimental Neuropsychology, 7*, 181–210.

Butters, N., & Cermak, L.S. (1980). *Alcoholic Korsakoff syndrome: An information processing approach to amnesia*. New York: Academic Press.

Butters, N., & Delis, D.C. (1995). Clinical assessment of memory disorders in amnesia and dementia. *Annual Review of Psychology, 46*, 493–523.

Craik, F.I.M. (1986). A functional account of age differences in memory. In F. Klix & H. Hagendorf (Eds.), *Human memory and cognitive capabilities: Mechanisms and performances, Part A* (pp. 409–422). Amsterdam: North-Holland.

Craik, F.I.M., & McDowd, J.M. (1987). Age differences in recall and recognition. *Journal of Experimental Psychology: Learning, Memory, and Cognition, 13*, 474–479.

Devolder, P.A., Brigham, M.C., & Pressley, M. (1990). Memory performance awareness in younger and older adults. *Psychology and Aging, 5*, 291–303.

Dobbs, A.R., & Rule, B.G. (1987). Prospective memory and self-reports of memory abilities in older adults. *Canadian Journal of Psychology, 41*, 209–222.

d'Ydewalle, G. (1995). Age-related interference of intervening activities on a prospective memory task. *Psychologica Belgica, 35*, 189–203.

d'Ydewalle, G., Bouckaert, D., & Brunfaut, E. (2001). Age-related differences and complexity of ongoing activities in time- and event-based prospective memory. *American Journal of Psychology, 114*, 411–423.

d'Ydewalle, G., & Brunfaut, E. (1996). Are older subjects necessarily worse in prospective memory tasks? In J. Georgas, M. Manthouli, E. Besevegis, & A. Kokkevi (Eds.), *Contemporary psychology in Europe: Theory, research, and applications* (pp. 161–172). Göttingen, Germany: Hogrefe & Huber.

d'Ydewalle, G., & Gielen, I. (1992). Attention allocation with overlapping sound, image, and text. In K. Rayner (Ed.), *Eye movements and visual cognition: Scene perception and reading* (pp. 415–427). New York: Springer-Verlag.

d'Ydewalle, G., Luwel, K., & Brunfaut, E. (1999). The importance of on-going concurrent activities as a function of age in time- and event-based prospective memory. *European Journal of Cognitive Psychology, 11*, 219–237.

d'Ydewalle, G., & Pavakanun, U. (1995). Acquisition of a second/foreign language by viewing a television program. In P. Winterhoff-Spurk (Ed.), *Psychology of media in Europe: The state of the art—perspectives for the future* (pp. 51–64). Opladen, Germany: Westdeutscher Verlag.

d'Ydewalle, G., & Pavakanun, U. (1997). Could enjoying a movie lead to language acquisition? In P. Winterhoff-Spurk & T. van der Voort (Eds.), *New horizons in media psychology* (pp. 145–155). Opladen, Germany: Westdeutscher Verlag.

d'Ydewalle, G., Praet, C., Verfaillie, K., & Van Rensbergen, J. (1991). Watching subtitled television: Automatic reading behavior. *Communication Research, 18*, 650–666.

d'Ydewalle, G., Utsi, S., & Brunfaut, E. (1996). *Time- and event-based prospective memory as a function of age: The importance of on-going concurrent activities.* (Psych. Rep. No. 201). Leuven, Belgium: Katholieke Universiteit Leuven, Laboratory of Experimental Psychology.

d'Ydewalle, G., & Van de Poel, M. (1999). Incidental foreign-language acquisition by children watching subtitled television programs. *Journal of Psycholinguistic Research, 28*, 227–244.

d'Ydewalle, G., & Van de Poel, M. (2000). *Do children listen to the spoken foreign language while watching subtitled television programs?* Unpublished manuscript.

d'Ydewalle, G., & Van Rensbergen, J. (1989). Developmental studies of text-picture interactions in the perception of animated cartoons with text. In H. Mandl & J.R. Levin (Eds.), *Knowledge acquisition from text and pictures* (pp. 233–248). Amsterdam: Elsevier Science Publishers (North-Holland).

d'Ydewalle, G., Van Rensbergen, J., & Pollet, J. (1987). Reading a message when the same message is available auditorily in another language: The case of subtitling. In J.K. O'Regan & A. Lévy-Schoen (Eds.), *Eye movements: From physiology to cognition* (pp. 313–321). Amsterdam: Elsevier Science Publishers (North-Holland).

d'Ydewalle, G., Warlop, L., & Van Rensbergen, J. (1989). Television and attention: Differences between young and older adults in the division of attention over different sources of TV information. *Medienpsychologie: Zeitschrift für Individual- und Massenkommunikation, 1*, 42–57.

Einstein, G.O., Holland, L.J., McDaniel, M.A., & Guynn, M.J. (1992). Age-related deficits in prospective memory: The influence of task complexity. *Psychology and Aging, 7*, 471–478.

Einstein, G.O., & McDaniel, M.A. (1990). Normal aging and prospective memory. *Journal of Experimental Psychology: Learning, Memory, and Cognition, 16*, 717–726.

Einstein, G.O., McDaniel, M.A., Richardson, S.L., Guynn, M.J., & Cunfer, A.R. (1995). Aging and prospective memory: Examining the influences of self-initiated retrieval processes. *Journal of Experimental Psychology: Learning, Memory, and Cognition, 21*, 996–1007.

Freedman, M., & Oscar-Berman, M. (1986). Bilateral frontal lobe disease and selective delayed response deficits in humans. *Behavioral Neuroscience, 100*, 337–342.

Fuster, J.M. (1985). The prefrontal cortex, mediator of cross-temporal contingencies. *Human Neurobiology, 4*, 169–179.

Glisky, E.L. (1996). Prospective memory and the frontal lobes. In M. Brandimonte, G.O. Einstein, & M.A. McDaniel (Eds.), *Prospective memory: Theory and applications* (pp. 249–266). Hillsdale, NJ: Lawrence Erlbaum Associates Inc.

Holobow, N.E., Lambert, W. E., & Sayegh, L. (1984). Pairing script and dialogue: Combinations that show promise for second or foreign language learning. *Language Learning, 34*, 59–76.

Ingvar, D.H. (1985). "Memory for future": An essay on the temporal organization of conscious awareness. *Human Neurobiology, 4*, 127–136.

Joyce, E.M., & Robbins, T.W. (1991). Frontal lobe function in Korsakoff and non-Korsakoff alcoholics: Planning and spatial working memory. *Neuropsychologia, 29*, 709–723.

Kahneman, D. (1973). *Attention and effort*. Englewood Cliffs, NJ: Prentice-Hall.

Kidder, D.P., Park, D.C., Hertzog, C., & Morrell, R.W. (1997). Prospective memory and aging: The effects of working memory and prospective memory task load. *Aging, Neuropsychology, and Cognition, 4*, 93–112.

Kolb, B,. & Whishaw, I.Q. (1990). *Fundamentals of human neuropsychology*. New York: Freeman.

Krashen, S.D. (1981). *Second language acquisition and second language learning*. Oxford: Pergamon.

Lambert, W.E., Boehler, I., & Sidoti, N. (1981). Choosing the languages of subtitles and spoken dialogues for media presentations: Implications for second language acquisition. *Applied Psycholinguistics, 2*, 133–148.

Lambert, W.E., & Holobow, N.E. (1984). Combinations of printed script and spoken dialogue that show promise for students of a foreign language. *Canadian Journal of Behavioural Science, 16*, 1–11.

Lenneberg, E.H. (1967). *Biological foundations of language*. New York: Wiley.

Lezak, M.D. (1983). *Neuropsychological assessment*. Oxford: Oxford University Press.

Light, L.L. (1991). Memory and aging: Four hypotheses in search of data. *Annual Review of Psychology, 42*, 333–376.

Logan, G.D. (1988). Toward an instance theory of automatization. *Psychological Review, 95*, 492–527.

Logan, G.D. (1990). Repetition priming and automaticity: Common underlying mechanisms? *Cognitive Psychology, 22*, 1–35.

Logan, G.D., & Etherton, J.L. (1994). What is learned during automatization? The role of attention in constructing an instance. *Journal of Experimental Psychology: Learning, Memory, and Cognition, 20*, 1022–1050.

Logan, G.D., Taylor, S.E., & Etherton, J.L. (1996). Attention in the acquisition and expression of automaticity. *Journal of Experimental Psychology: Learning, Memory, and Cognition, 22*, 620–638.

Mäntylä, T. (1993). Priming effects in prospective memory. *Memory, 1*, 203–218.

Mäntylä, T. (1994). Remembering to remember: Adult age differences in prospective memory. *Journal of Gerontology: Psychological Sciences, 49*, 276–282.

Marsh, R.L., & Hicks, J.L. (1998). Event-based prospective memory and executive control of working memory. *Journal of Experimental Psychology: Learning, Memory, and Cognition, 24*, 336–349.

Martin, M. (1986). Ageing and patterns of change in everyday memory and cognition. *Human Learning, 5*, 63–74.

Maylor, E. (1990). Age and prospective memory. *Quarterly Journal of Experimental Psychology, 42A,* 471–493.

Maylor, E. (1993). Minimized prospective memory loss in old age. In J. Cerella, J.M. Rybash, W. Hoyer, & M.L. Commons (Eds.), *Adult information processing: Limits on loss* (pp. 529–551). San Diego, CA: Academic Press.

Maylor, E.A. (1996). Age-related impairment in an event-based prospective-memory task. *Psychology and Aging, 11,* 74–78.

McDaniel, M.A., & Einstein, G.O. (1993). The importance of cue familiarity and cue distinctiveness in prospective memory. *Memory, 1,* 23–41.

McDaniel, M.A., Robinson-Riegler, B., & Einstein, G.O. (1998). Prospective remembering: Perceptually driven or conceptually driven processes? *Memory and Cognition, 26,* 121–134.

McDaniel, M., Shaw, P., Einstein, G., & Smith, R. (1996). *Selective effects of attentional demands in prospective remembering.* Paper presented at the International Conference on Memory, Padua, Italy, July.

Meyer, D.E., & Kieras, D.E. (1997a). A computational theory of executive cognitive processes and multiple-task performance: Part 1. Basic mechanisms. *Psychological Review, 104,* 3–65.

Meyer, D.E., & Kieras, D.E. (1997b). A computational theory of executive cognitive processes and multiple-task performance: Part 2. Accounts of Psychological Refractory-Period phenomena. *Psychological Review, 104,* 749–791.

Moray, N. (1959). Attention in dichotic listening: Affective cues and the influence of instructions. *Quarterly Journal of Experimental Psychology, 11,* 56–60.

Moscovitch, M. (1982). A neuropsychological approach to memory and perception in normal and pathological aging. In F.I.M. Craik & S. Trehub (Eds.), *Aging and cognitive processes* (pp. 55–78). New York: Plenum Press.

Navon, D., & Gopher, D. (1979). On the economy of the human-processing system. *Psychological Review, 86,* 214–255.

Neisser, U. (1967). *Cognitive psychology.* Englewood Cliffs, NJ: Prentice-Hall.

Otani, H., Landau, J.D., Libkuman, T.M., St. Louis, J.P., Kazen, J. K., & Throne, G.W. (1997). Prospective memory and divided attention. *Memory, 5,* 343–360.

Park, D., Hertzog, C., Kidder, D.P., Morrell, R.W., & Mayhorn, C.B. (1997). Effect of age on event-based and time-based prospective memory. *Psychology and Aging, 12,* 314–327.

Patton, G.W.R., & Meit, M. (1993). Effect of aging on prospective and incidental memory. *Experimental Aging Research, 19,* 165–176.

Pavakanun, G., & d'Ydewalle, G. (1992). Watching foreign television programs and language learning. In F.L. Engel, D.G. Bouwhuis, & G. d'Ydewalle (Eds.), *Cognitive modelling and interactive environments in language learning* (pp. 193–198). Berlin: Springer-Verlag.

Quinlan, P. (1991). *Connectionism and psychology: A psychological perspective on new connectionist research.* New York: Harvester Wheatsheaf.

Schneider, W., & Shiffrin, R.M. (1977). Controlled and automatic human information processing: I. Detection, search, and attention. *Psychological Review, 84,* 1–66.

Shallice, T., & Burgess, P.W. (1991). Deficits in strategy application following frontal lobe damage in man. *Brain, 114,* 727–741.

Shiffrin, R.M., & Schneider, W. (1977). Controlled and automatic human information processing: II. Perceptual learning, automatic attending, and a general theory. *Psychological Review, 84,* 127–190.

Sohl, G. (1989). *Het verwerken van de vreemdtalige gesproken tekst in een ondertiteld TV-programma [Processing foreign spoken text in a subtitled television program].* Unpublished licence thesis, University of Leuven, Belgium.

Squire, L.R. (1982a). The neuropsychology of human memory. *Annual Review of Neuroscience, 5,* 241–273.

Squire, L.R. (1982b). Comparisons between forms of amnesia: Some deficits are unique to

Korsakoff's syndrome. *Journal of Experimental Psychology: Learning, Memory and Cognition, 8,* 560–571.

Sungaila, P., & Crockett, D.J. (1993). Dementia and the frontal lobes. In R.W. Parks, R.F. Zec, & R.S. Wilson (Eds.), *Neuropsychology of Alzheimer's disease and other dementias* (pp. 235–264). Oxford: Oxford University Press.

Telford, C.W. (1931). The refractory phase of voluntary and associative response. *Journal of Experimental Psychology, 14,* 1–35.

Tonla Briquet, G. (1979). *Investigation into the subtitling of film and TV.* Unpublished thesis, Higher Governments Institute for Translators and Interpreters, Brussels.

Treisman, A.M. (1960). Contextual cues in selective listening. *Quarterly Journal of Experimental Psychology, 12,* 242–248.

Treisman, A.M. (1964). Verbal cues: Language and meaning in selective attention. *American Journal of Psychology, 77,* 206–219.

Vanachter, I., De Bruycker, W., & d'Ydewalle, G. (2000). *Attention allocation while watching subtitled television programs.* Manuscript in preparation.

Verfaillie, K., & d'Ydewalle, G. (1987). *Modality preference and message comprehension in deaf youngsters watching TV* (Psych. Rep. No. 70). Leuven, Belgium: Katholieke Universiteit Leuven, Laboratory of Experimental Psychology.

Wundt, W. (1862). *Die Geschwindigkeit des Gedankens.* Berlin: Breitkopf.

CHAPTER SEVEN

A general theory of visual attention

Claus Bundesen
University of Copenhagen, Denmark

This chapter presents a computational theory of selective attention in vision. The theory was originally published under the title *A Theory of Visual Attention* (Bundesen, 1990), and it is now called TVA. The theory originated from earlier models of visual selection—in particular experimental tasks. To put the theory in perspective, I describe its development. First I present a *choice model* for visual selection from displays with multiple elements. Building on work by Luce (1959), Sperling (1967), and others, my collaborators and I developed the choice model in the early 1980s (Bundesen, Pedersen, & Larsen, 1984). The choice model provides a rule for calculation of selection probabilities, and it is easy to apply.

Second, I describe a *race model* for selection from multi-element displays (Bundesen, 1987; Shibuya & Bundesen, 1988). Because the choice model can be derived from the race model, the race model explains all that the choice model explains. In addition to this, the race model accounts for the temporal course of processing. The choice model is only a descriptive model, but the race model is a process model.

Third, I outline the general theory called TVA. Because the earlier race model can be derived from TVA, TVA explains all that the race model explains. In addition to this, TVA accounts for the mechanisms by which selection is assumed to be done. The race model is only a process model, but TVA is a computational theory of visual attention. Besides the basic theory, I describe some applications of TVA, including recent use of TVA as an instrument for systematic analysis of deficits in visual attention (Duncan et al., 1999).

Finally, I sketch two other lines of current work: work toward a neural interpretation of TVA (Bundesen, 1991a, 2000) and work toward a more comprehensive theory of visual cognition (Logan, 1996, in press; Logan & Gordon, 2001).

CHOICE MODEL

The choice model for visual selection was developed to describe performance in a series of partial-report experiments conducted in our laboratory (Bundesen et al., 1984; Bundesen, Shibuya, & Larsen, 1985). In a typical experiment, the participants were presented with brief visual displays showing a number of different elements. The participants' task was to report as many as possible of those elements that satisfied a particular selection criterion (the targets) and ignore any other elements (the distractors). For example, in one experiment on selection by color, the display showed a mixture of red and black letters, and the task was to name as many as possible of the red letters and ignore the black ones. The exposure duration was kept constant at a value of 100 ms, and the field was dark both before and after the presentation of a stimulus display. We investigated how the number of correctly reported targets depended on the selection criterion and the numbers of targets and distractors in the display. The results could be described by a simple model: the choice model.

In the choice model for partial report, a subject can report a given display element if, and only if, the element has been encoded into visual short-term memory (VSTM). The capacity of VSTM is limited to K elements, and K is one of two basic parameters in the model.

Encoding into VSTM is regarded as selective sampling of elements from the stimulus display. Each element in the display has a certain attentional weight. Until VSTM has been filled up with elements, the probability that any not-yet-encoded element is the next one to be encoded equals the weight of that element divided by the sum of the weights of all those elements that have not yet been encoded. Thus, selection occurs in accordance with a Luce (1959) choice rule.

In our partial-report experiments, the elements were alphanumeric characters, and it seemed plausible to assume that targets had higher attentional weights than distractors, but any target had the same attentional weight as any other target, and any distractor had the same attentional weight as any other distractor. Without loss of generality, then, the weight of a target could be set to 1 and the weight of a distractor to a. Parameter a is the second of the two basic parameters in the model.

Parameter a measures the efficiency of selection. If $a = 0$, the probability that a distractor is encoded into VSTM also equals 0. In this case selection is perfect; only targets are encoded. If $a = 1$, the probability that an element is encoded into VSTM is independent of whether the element is a target or a distractor. In that case encoding is nonselective.

Figure 1 shows a maximum likelihood fit of the choice model to results from a representative individual subject in an experiment on partial report based on a clear difference in color (blue vs. green; Bundesen et al., 1985). The figure displays the mean number of correctly reported targets as a function of the number of distractors in the display with the number of targets in

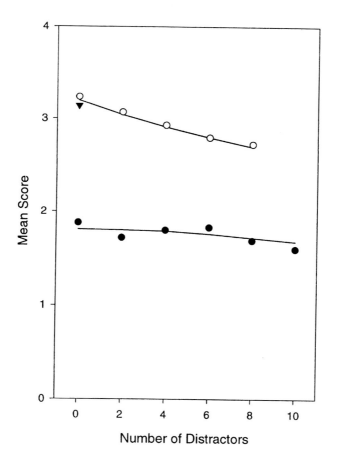

Figure 1. Number of correctly reported targets (Mean Score) as a function of the number of distractors with the number of targets as a parameter in partial report by color. Data are shown for Subject HS. The number of targets was 2 (solid circles), 4 (open circles), or 12 (triangle). Unmarked points connected by straight lines represent a theoretical fit to the data by the choice model. Adapted from *Attention and performance XI* (pp. 631–649) by M.I. Posner and O.S.M. Marin (Eds.), 1985, Hillsdale, NJ: Lawrence Erlbaum Associates Inc. Copyright 1985 by The International Association for the Study of Attention and Performance.

the display as the parameter. The curves show predictions from the choice model with VSTM capacity K at a value of 3.5 elements and parameter a at 0.06. Figure 2 shows a similar maximum likelihood fit to results from an experiment on partial report by alphanumeric class (letters vs. digits) with the same subject. This fit was obtained with parameter K at 3.5 elements and parameter a at 0.42. In general, estimates for K were the same for selection by alphanumeric class as for selection by color, but estimates for a were much

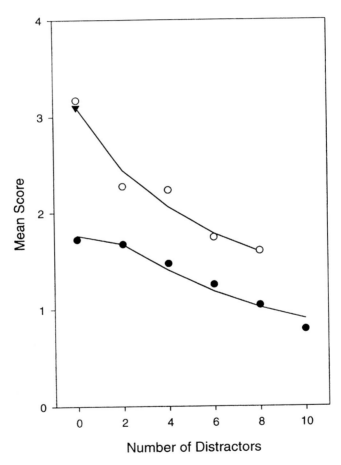

Figure 2. Number of correctly reported targets (Mean Score) as a function of the number of distractors with the number of targets as a parameter in partial report by alphanumeric class. Data are shown for Subject HS. The number of targets was 2 (solid circles), 4 (open circles), or 12 (triangle). Unmarked points connected by straight lines represent a theoretical fit to the data by the choice model. Adapted from *Attention and performance XI* (pp. 631–649) by M.I. Posner and O.S.M. Marin (Eds.), 1985, Hillsdale, NJ: Lawrence Erlbaum Associates Inc. Copyright 1985 by The International Association for the Study of Attention and Performance.

higher for selection by alphanumeric class than for selection by color. Thus the effect of the selection criterion was completely accounted for by variation in parameter a.

RACE MODEL

The choice model for selection from multi-element displays has yielded a precise description of many experimental results, but the model lacks depth. It gives a rule for calculation of selection probabilities, but no explanation for that rule. However, the choice model can be derived from a simple race model of the underlying processes (Bundesen, 1987, 1993b; Bundesen et al., 1985).

Choice by race

"Every one knows what attention is" (James, 1890, p. 403), and most people seem to agree that attention is related to processing capacity so that the processing of an item is speeded up when more attention is devoted to the item. Race models of selection from multi-element displays are based on the assumptions that (a) elements are processed in parallel and (b) the processing of an element is speeded up when more attention (processing capacity) is devoted to the element (Bundesen, 1987; also see Bundesen, 1996). The assumptions imply that selection of targets rather than distractors may be done by first allocating more attention (processing capacity) to the targets and then selecting those elements that first finish processing (the winners of the race).

FIRM

Shibuya and Bundesen (1988) developed a *Fixed-capacity Independent Race Model* (FIRM), which describes the processing of a stimulus display as a two-stage process. At the first stage of processing, an attentional weight is computed for each element in the display. The attentional weight is a measure of the strength of the sensory evidence that the element is a target.

At the second stage of processing, the race between the elements takes place. The total processing capacity at this stage of the system is assumed to be a constant, C elements per second, which is a basic parameter in the model. The processing capacity is distributed across the elements in proportion to their weights. Thus, every element in the display is allocated a certain fraction of the total processing capacity; the fraction equals the attentional weight of the element divided by the sum of the attentional weights across all of the elements in the display.

The amount of processing capacity that is allocated to an element determines how fast the element can be encoded into VSTM. Specifically, the time taken to encode an element is assumed to be exponentially distributed with a rate parameter equal to the amount of processing capacity that is allocated to the element. Encoding times for different elements are stochastically independent, and the elements actually selected are those elements whose encoding processes complete before the stimulus presentation terminates and before VSTM has been filled up.

The choice model for partial report can be derived from FIRM, so FIRM explains all that the choice model explains (see Bundesen, 1987, 1993b; Bundesen et al., 1985). FIRM also predicts effects of variations in the exposure duration of the stimuli. We tested such predictions in a comprehensive study of partial report of digits from mixtures of letters and digits. Exposure durations ranged from 10 ms up to 200 ms, and each display was terminated by a pattern mask.

Figure 3 shows the probability distribution of the number of correctly reported targets as a function of the exposure duration, the number of targets (T), and the number of distractors (D) in the display for one representative subject. Each panel shows the results for a particular combination of T and D. The top curve in the panel shows the probability of reporting at least one element correct as a function of exposure duration, the second curve from the top shows the probability of reporting at least two elements correct, etc. The fit shown by the smooth curves was obtained with VSTM capacity K at a value of 3.7 elements, total processing capacity C at 49 elements per second, parameter a (the weight ratio of a distractor to a target) at 0.40, and minimum effective exposure duration t_0 at 19 ms. As can be seen, the fit was strikingly close.

EVIDENCE ON INDEPENDENCE
BETWEEN CATEGORIZATIONS

FIRM describes the selection process as a race between the elements in the visual field. In our computational theory of visual attention, TVA, the selection process is described as a race among categorizations of elements in the visual field. The change in emphasis from elements to categorizations was due to evidence of substantial independence between different types of visual categorizations of the same elements. For example, in partial report of a colored shape that was cued by its location (poststimulus cueing), Nissen (1985) and Isenberg, Nissen, and Marchak (1990) found evidence of stochastic independence between processing of color and processing of shape: The probability of reporting both features of the cued element correctly was approximately the same as the product of the probability of reporting the color correctly and the probability of reporting the shape correctly. Later studies of performance in Nissen's paradigm have cast doubt on the original

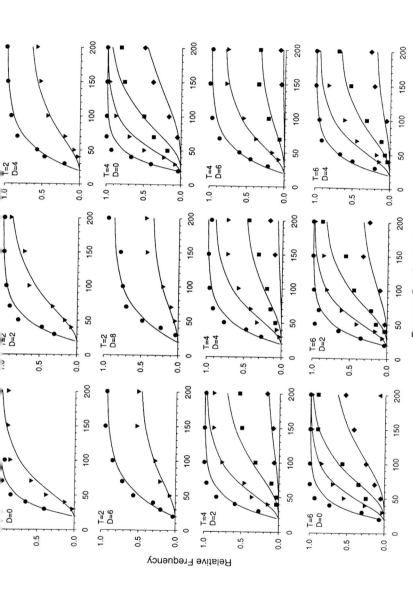

Figure 3. Relative frequency of scores of j or more (correctly reported targets) as a function of exposure duration with j, number of targets T, and number of distractors D as parameters in partial report by alphanumeric class. Data are shown for Subject MP. Parameter j varies within panels; j is 1 (circles), 2 (downwards-pointing triangles), 3 (squares), 4 (diamonds), or 5 (upwards-pointing triangle). T and D vary among panels. Smooth curves represent a theoretical fit to the data by the race model. For clarity, observed frequencies less than .02 were omitted from the figure. Adapted with permission from H. Shibuya and C. Bundesen, 1988, *Journal of Experimental Psychology: Human Perception and Performance, 14*, 591–600. Copyright © 1988 by the American Psychological Association.

conclusions (Johnston, Ruthruff, & Monheit, 1997; Monheit & Johnston, 1994; Van der Velde & Van der Heijden, 1997; see also Bundesen, 1991b). However, recent findings obtained with a new paradigm I have explored with Søren Kyllingsbæk and Axel Larsen provide stronger evidence of independence.

In one of our experiments, each stimulus display showed a pair of colored letters, one to the left and one to the right of fixation. The exposure was brief (29 ms), and the letter pair was followed by a mask. The observer was asked to pay equal attention to the two letters and try to report the color and the shape of each letter, but refrain from pure guessing. Order of report was free, but the observer should indicate whether a report of a feature referred to the letter on the left or the letter on the right.

The 16 possible combinations of correctly and not correctly reported features are listed in Table 1. On the strong assumption that reports of the four individual features (the left shape, the left color, the right shape, and the right color) were mutually independent, the probabilities of each of the 16 possible combinations of correctly and not correctly reported features should be predictable from the probabilities of report of the four individual features. Some of the eight observers showed systematic deviations between the observed and predicted probabilities, but the majority of the observers showed close

TABLE 7.1
Possible types of report[a]

Type	Left		Right	
	Shape	Colour	Shape	Colour
1	0	0	0	0
2	1	0	0	0
3	0	1	0	0
4	0	0	1	0
5	0	0	0	1
6	1	1	0	0
7	0	0	1	1
8	1	0	1	0
9	0	1	0	1
10	1	0	0	1
11	0	1	1	0
12	1	1	1	0
13	1	1	0	1
14	1	0	1	1
15	0	1	1	1
16	1	1	1	1

[a] 1 = correctly reported; 0 = not correctly reported.

fits (see Figure 4). For three of the eight observers (including the observers whose data are depicted in Panels a and b of Figure 4), the agreement between observed and predicted probabilities was virtually perfect, with correlations exceeding .99. For these observers, the likelihood that one of the features (color or shape) of a given letter was correctly reported seemed completely independent of whether the other feature was correctly reported and independent of whether features of the other letter were correctly reported.

COMPUTATIONAL THEORY

The computational Theory of Visual Attention, TVA, is a generalization of FIRM. It integrates findings on single-stimulus recognition, whole report, partial report, detection, and search in a race model framework.

Basic theory

In TVA, both visual identification and selection of elements in the visual field consist of making visual categorizations. A visual categorization has the form "element x has feature i," or equivalently, "element x belongs to category i." Here element x is an object (a perceptual unit) in the visual field, feature i is a visual feature (e.g., a certain color, shape, movement, or spatial position), and category i is a visual category (the class of all elements that have feature i).

That a visual categorization is made means that the categorization is encoded into VSTM. If and when one makes the visual categorization that x belongs to i (i.e., if and when the categorization is encoded into VSTM), element x is said both to be selected and to be identified as a member of category i. Thus, an element is said to be selected if, and only if, it is identified as a member of one or another category. Similarly, an element is said to be represented in VSTM if, and only if, some categorization of the element is represented in VSTM.

Once a visual categorization of an element completes processing, the categorization enters VSTM, provided that memory space for the categorization is available in VSTM. The capacity of VSTM is limited to K different elements. Space is available for a new categorization of element x if element x is already represented in the store (with one or another categorization) or if less than K elements are represented in the store (cf. Luck & Vogel, 1997). There is no room for a categorization of element x if VSTM has been filled up with other elements.

Consider the event that a particular visual categorization, "x belongs to i," completes processing at time t. The hazard function of this event (i.e., the probability density that the event occurs at time t, given that it has not occurred before time t) has a certain value, which is called the v value of the visual categorization. Thus the v value is a measure of the speed at which the

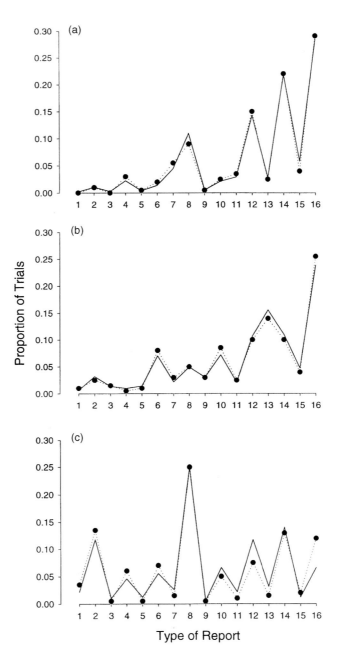

Figure 4. Observed and predicted probability distributions of reports of pairs of colored shapes across 16 types of report. (a) Data for Observer S1. Observed probabilities are shown by solid circles connected with dotted lines. Predicted probabilities are indicated by unmarked points connected with unbroken lines. The predictions were derived from observed probabilities of correct identification of the left shape, the left color, the right shape, and the right color, respectively, by assuming mutual independence between reports of the four features. The 16 types of report are defined in Table 1. (b), (c) Similar data for Observers S3 and S5, respectively.

visual categorization is processed. In TVA, the v value is determined by two basic equations. By Equation 1,

$$v(x, i) = \eta(x, i)\beta_i \frac{w_x}{\sum_{z \in S} w_z},$$

(1)

where $\eta(x, i)$ is the instantaneous strength of the sensory evidence that element x belongs to category i, β_i is a perceptual decision bias associated with category i, and $w_x/\sum_{z \in S} w_z$ is the relative attentional weight of element x (i.e., the weight of element x, w_x, divided by the sum of weights across all elements in the visual field, S).

The attentional weights are derived from priority (pertinence) values. Every visual category is supposed to have a certain priority. The priority of a category is a measure of the current importance of attending to elements that belong to the category. The weight of an element x in the visual field is given by Equation 2,

$$w_x = \sum_{j \in R} \eta(x, j)\pi_j,$$

(2)

where R is the set of all visual categories, $\eta(x, j)$ is the instantaneous strength of the sensory evidence that element x belongs to category j, and π_j is the priority value of category j. By Equation 2, the attentional weight of an element is a weighted sum of priority values. The priority of a given category enters the sum with a weight equal to the strength of the sensory evidence that the element belongs to the category.

Mechanisms of selection

Equations 1 and 2 describe two mechanisms of selection: a mechanism for selection of elements (filtering) and a mechanism for selection of categories (pigeonholing). The *filtering* mechanism is represented by priority values and attentional weights. As an example, if selection of red elements is wanted, the priority of *red* should be high. Equation 2 implies that when *red* has a high priority, red elements get high attentional weights. Accordingly, by Equation 1, processing of red elements is fast, so red elements are likely to win the processing race and be encoded into VSTM.

The *pigeonholing* mechanism is represented by perceptual decision bias parameters. Priority values determine which elements are selected, but perceptual decision bias parameters determine how the elements are categorized. If particular types of categorizations are desired, decision bias parameters of the relevant categories should be high. By Equation 1, then, the desired types of categorizations are likely to be made.

Consider how filtering and pigeonholing can be combined. For example, consider partial report of red digits from a mixture of red and black digits. A sufficient strategy for performing the task is as follows. In order to select the red elements, the priority value of the visual category *red* is set high, but other priority values are kept low. The effect is to speed up the processing of red elements with respect to all types of categorizations. In order to perceive the identity of the red digits rather than any other attributes of the elements, 10 perceptual decision bias parameters, 1 for each type of digit, are set high, but other perceptual decision bias parameters are kept low. The effect is to speed up the processing of categorizations with respect to digit types. The combined effect of the adjustments of priority and decision bias parameters is to speed up the processing of categorizations of red elements with respect to digit types in relation to any other categorizations.

This example demonstrates the power of the mechanisms of selection contained in TVA. When the selection system is coupled to a sensory system that supplies appropriate η values, and when priority and decision bias parameters have been set, both filtering and pigeonholing are accomplished by a race between visual categorization processes whose rate parameters are determined through the simple algebraic operations of Equations 1 and 2. Thus the theory yields a computational account of selective attention in vision.

Applications

TVA has been applied to findings from a broad range of paradigms concerned with single-stimulus recognition and selection from multi-element displays.

Single-stimulus recognition

For single-stimulus recognition, TVA provides a simple derivation of a classical model of effects of visual discriminability and bias: the biased-choice model of Luce (1963) (see Bundesen, 1990). This is noteworthy because the biased-choice model has been successful in explaining many experimental findings on effects of visual discriminability and bias in single-stimulus identification (see, e.g., Townsend & Ashby, 1982).

Selection from multi-element displays

Bundesen (1990) applied TVA to many findings on selection from multi-element displays. The findings included effects of object integrality in selective report (e.g., Duncan, 1984), number and spatial position of targets in studies of divided attention (Posner, Nissen, & Ogden, 1978; Sperling, 1960, 1967; Van der Heijden, La Heij, & Boer, 1983), selection criterion and number of distractors in studies of focused attention (Bundesen & Pedersen,

1983; Estes & Taylor, 1964; Treisman & Gelade, 1980; Treisman & Gormican, 1988), joint effects of numbers of targets and distractors in partial report (Bundesen et al., 1984, 1985; Shibuya & Bundesen, 1988), and consistent practice in search (Schneider & Fisk, 1982). Some of the applications were based on the fact that the fixed-capacity independent race model of Shibuya and Bundesen (1988), model FIRM, can be derived as a special case of TVA.

FIRM describes the selection process as a race between the elements in the visual field. TVA describes the selection process as a race between categorizations of elements in the visual field. The correspondence between FIRM and TVA is established by identifying the encoding of an element in VSTM with the encoding of a visual categorization of the element. The K parameter of FIRM corresponds to the K parameter of TVA, and the attentional weights of FIRM correspond to the attentional weights of TVA, the w parameters.

Consider the C parameter of FIRM and the associated assumption that the total capacity of the processing system is constant. In TVA, the total processing capacity C can be defined as the sum of v values across all categorizations of all elements in the visual field,

$$C = \sum_{x \in S} \sum_{i \in R} v(x, i). \tag{3}$$

In certain conditions, C is approximately constant. Suppose there is a constant k such that

$$\sum_{i \in R} \eta(x, i)\beta_i = k, \tag{4}$$

for every display element x. The left-hand side of Equation 4 equals the overall rate of processing of element x when x is presented alone (i.e., in a single-element display), so Equation 4 implies that the stimulus material is homogeneous with respect to detectability. By Equations 1, 3, and 4,

$$C = \sum_{x \in S} \sum_{i \in R} \eta(x, i)\beta_i w_x / \sum_{z \in S} w_z = k, \tag{5}$$

that is, the total processing capacity C is a constant.

Analysis of attentional impairments

A variety of impairments in visual attention can follow damage to the brain. In collaboration with John Duncan, Glyn Humphreys, and their associates, Hitomi Shibuya and I have begun using TVA as an instrument for systematic analysis of attentional deficits in brain-damaged patients. We recently reported an analysis of a group of nine patients with lesions affecting the right inferior parietal lobule and variable spatial neglect (Duncan et al.,

1999). In whole-report conditions, the patients reported letters from vertical arrays presented briefly in either the left or the right visual field. Compared with an age-matched group of normal control subjects, the patients showed substantial impairments in processing capacity. The impairments were largely bilateral, which implies a major nonlateralized aspect to neglect. The result is illustrated in Figure 5, which shows the distributions of both the processing capacity in the left visual field, C_L elements per second, and the processing capacity in the right visual field, C_R elements per second, for controls and patients. The figure makes clear the overall loss of processing capacity in the patients; the loss was stronger on the left but very clear on both sides.

In partial-report conditions, the patients were presented with arrays containing one or two letters, each of which could be red or green. The task was to report those letters that had a prespecified target color (red or green). We expected that the patients would show a lateral bias consisting of lower attentional weights for elements in the left as compared with the right visual field. To measure the lateral bias, we computed the ratio $w_L/(w_L + w_R)$, where w_L is

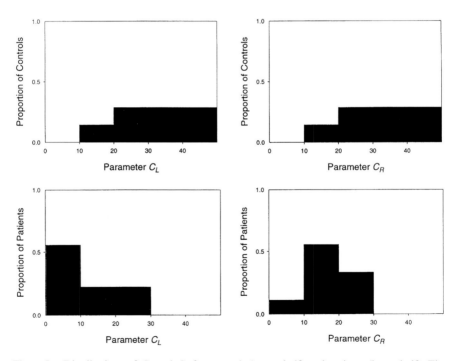

Figure 5.   Distributions of C_L and C_R for controls (upper half) and patients (lower half). The upper bin in each panel represents all values above 40. Adapted by permission from J. Duncan, C. Bundesen, A. Olson, G. Humphreys, S. Chavda, and H. Shibuya, 1999, *Journal of Experimental Psychology: General, 128*, 450–478. Copyright © 1999 by the American Psychological Association.

the mean attentional weight for elements in the left field and w_R is the mean weight for elements in the right field. Figure 6 shows the distribution of this ratio for controls and for patients. As expected, the controls showed a distribution peaked around 0.5. For all patients but one, the index was below 0.5, showing greater attentional weights on the right. The one exception instead showed a strong bias to the left. Thus, compared with the controls, lateral bias was much more extreme among the patients, in eight cases to the right and in one case to the left.

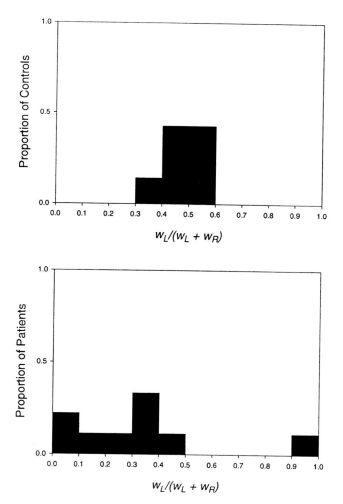

Figure 6. Distributions of $w_L/(w_L + w_R)$ for controls (upper half) and patients (lower half). Adapted by permission from J. Duncan, C. Bundesen, A. Olson, G. Humphreys, S. Chavda, and H. Shibuya, 1999, *Journal of Experimental Psychology: General, 128*, 450–478. Copyright © 1999 by the American Psychological Association.

In addition to the expected lateral bias, the patients showed striking bilateral preservation of top-down control in the form of attentional selectivity for targets rather than distractors as measured by parameter a (the weight ratio of a distractor to a target). Parameter a varied between subjects, but the distribution of the parameter was essentially the same for patients as for controls and essentially the same in the neglected hemifield of the patients as in the nonneglected hemifield.

Not all of the results found for the patients could have been predicted, but they all made sense. Apparently, in combination with methods of partial and whole report, use of TVA opens the way to clear measurement and systematic analysis of deficits in visual attention.

FURTHER DEVELOPMENTS

Two further lines of development of TVA shall be mentioned. The first line aims at a neural interpretation of TVA. The second line aims at a unified account of visual cognition.

Toward a neural theory of visual attention

I briefly outline a tentative neural interpretation of Equation 1 of TVA (Bundesen, 1991a, 2000). In this interpretation, $v(x, i)$ is the expected value of the total rate of firing of the population of neurons that represent the categorization that "element x has feature i" at the level of processing where elements compete for entrance into VSTM. At this level of processing, the classical receptive fields (RFs) of neurons are so large that each RF covers the entire visual field. However, at any point in time, the *effective* RF of a neuron is assumed to be contracted so that the neuron represents the properties of only one of the elements in the visual field. Each element x has an attentional weight w_x such that the probability that the neuron represents element x (i.e., the probability that the RF of the neuron is contracted around x) equals $w_x / \sum_{z \varepsilon S} w_z$.

Each neuron is specialized with respect to the feature it represents. Formally, if the neuron represents the categorization "x has feature i" at one time and the categorization "y has feature j" at another time, then x may differ from y, but i must equal j. That is, a neuron can represent different elements at different times, but it always represents the same feature i.

Let the feature-i neurons (i.e., the neurons representing feature i) be numbered 1, 2, ... , N, and let $\eta_k(x, i)$ be the firing rate of the kth ($1 \leq k \leq N$) feature-i neuron when the neuron represents element x (i.e., the RF is contracted around x) and the perceptual decision bias in favor of feature i is maximal. In the same terminology, $\eta_l(y, i)$ is the firing rate of the lth ($1 \leq l \leq N$) feature-i neuron when the neuron represents element y and the featural bias in favor of i is maximal. If the featural bias in favor of i is less than maximal, the firing rates of the two neurons are assumed to be reduced by multiplication with the same factor β_i ($0 \leq \beta_i \leq 1$). Thus, β_i is a measure of the strength of the featural bias in favor of i. Given that the featural bias in favor of i equals β_i, the firing rate of the kth feature-i neuron equals $\eta_k(x, i)\beta_i$ when the neuron represents element x.

The total firing rate of the population of neurons that represent the categorization that "element x has feature i" equals the sum of the firing rates of those feature-i neurons that represent element x. The contribution to this sum from the kth feature-i neuron equals $\eta_k(x, i)\beta_i$ if the neuron represents element x, but 0 if the neuron represents any other element. As the probability that the neuron represents element x is $w_x/\sum_{z \in S} w_z$, the expected contribution to the sum from the kth feature-i neuron equals $\eta_k(x, i)\beta_i w_x/\sum_{z \in S} w_z$. Hence, the expected value of the sum, $v(x, i)$, is given by

$$v(x, i) = \sum_{k=1}^{N} \eta_k(x, i)\beta_i \frac{w_x}{\sum_{z \in S} w_z}. \tag{6}$$

By defining

$$\eta(x, i) = \sum_{k=1}^{N} \eta_k(x, i), \tag{7}$$

Equation 6 reduces to Equation 1 of TVA.

By Equation 7, $\eta(x, i)$ equals the total rate of firing in the set of all feature-i neurons when every feature-i neuron represents element x (say, x is the only element in the visual field) and the featural bias in favor of i is maximal (i.e., $\beta_i = 1$). Thus, the value of $\eta(x, i)$ depends on (a) the number and responsiveness of feature-i neurons and (b) the extent to which stimulus x has the features "preferred" by the feature-i neurons (in particular, feature i).

In the neural interpretation I have sketched, the *filtering* mechanism of selection affects the number of neurons in which an element x is represented (the number of neurons allocated to the element) at the level of processing where elements compete for entrance into VSTM. By dynamic remapping of receptive fields, the number of neurons in which element x is represented becomes proportional to the relative attentional weight of element x. (Bundesen, 1991a, sketched a possible neural mechanism for remapping receptive fields in accordance with this assumption.) The interpretation was suggested by electrophysiological findings from single-cell studies in monkeys (Moran & Desimone, 1985).

Moran and Desimone found that, when a target and a distractor were both within the RF of a cell in visual areas V4 or IT (inferotemporal cortex), the rate of firing in the cell showed little effect of the distractor. For example,

Moran and Desimone recorded the response of a cell to a pair of stimuli consisting of (a) a stimulus that elicited a high rate of firing in the cell when the stimulus was presented alone (an effective sensory stimulus) and (b) a stimulus that had little or no effect on the rate of firing in the cell when the stimulus was presented alone (an ineffective sensory stimulus). On trials in which the effective sensory stimulus was the target and the ineffective sensory stimulus was a distractor, the cell showed a high rate of firing, but on trials in which the ineffective sensory stimulus was the target and the effective sensory stimulus was a distractor, the cell showed a low rate of firing. In each case, the typical cell responded "as if its RF had contracted around ... [the] ... attended stimulus" (Desimone & Ungerleider, 1989, p. 293). The effect depended on both the target and the distractor being located within the recorded neuron's RF, but in IT cortex the RFs were so large that they covered most of the visual field.

Reynolds, Chelazzi, and Desimone (1999) corroborated and extended the findings of Moran and Desimone (1985). Recording from neurons in monkey areas V2 and V4, they found that the mean firing rate of a cell to a pair of stimuli in its RF approximated a weighted average of the firing rates of the cell to each of the stimuli in the pair when they were presented alone. When the monkey's attention was directed to one of the stimuli in the pair, this increased the weight on the target stimulus so that the mean response of the neuron was driven (up or down) toward the response elicited when the target stimulus was presented alone. The results fit in with the dual conjectures that (a) at any time, a cell was driven by only one of the stimuli in its RF, and (b) the probability that the cell was driven by any given stimulus (the probability that the cell represented the stimulus) was proportional to the attentional weight of the stimulus.

Whereas the filtering mechanism of selection affects the number of neurons in which an element x is represented, the *pigeonholing* mechanism of selection affects the way in which the element is represented in each of those neurons that are allocated to the element. The rate of firing in a neuron representing the categorization that element x has feature i should be proportional to the multiplicative bias, β_i, which is applied to all members of the set of feature-i neurons (neurons preferring stimuli with feature i). Recent recordings from single cells in the visual system of monkeys have provided evidence of such a mechanism of selection: a *feature-based* mechanism of attention (Treue & Trujillo, 1999) that selects groups of neurons with similar stimulus preferences for a multiplicative enhancement in response strength (cf. McAdams & Maunsell, 1999a, b).

Toward a unified account of visual cognition

TVA accounts for much empirical data on human performance in visual recognition and attention tasks (see Bundesen, 1990, 1998a, b), but TVA has been criticized of neglecting spatial effects in visual attention (see Van der Heijden, 1993; Van der Velde & Van der Heijden, 1993; but also see Bundesen, 1991b, 1993a). In 1996, Logan proposed an extension of TVA, the CODE theory of Visual Attention (CTVA), which combines TVA with the COntour DEtector theory of perceptual grouping by proximity (Van Oeffelen & Vos, 1982, 1983). CTVA explains a wide range of spatial effects in visual attention (see Logan, 1996; Logan & Bundesen, 1996; also see Alvarado, Santella, & Santisteban, 1999; Bundesen, 1998a).

More recently, Logan and Gordon (2001) have extended CTVA into a theory of executive control in dual-task situations that accounts for crosstalk, set-switching cost, and concurrence costs as well as dual-task interference. The theory, ECTVA, assumes that executive processes control subordinate processes by manipulating their parameters. TVA is used as the theory of subordinate processes, so a task set is defined as a set of TVA parameters that is sufficient to configure TVA to perform a task. Set switching is viewed as a change in one or more of these parameters, and the time taken to change a task set is assumed to depend on the number of parameters to be changed.

Most recently, Logan (in press) has proposed an Instance Theory of Attention and Memory (ITAM) that combines ECTVA with the *exemplar-based random walk model* of categorization (Nosofsky & Palmeri, 1997). The exemplar-based random walk model itself is a combination of Nosofsky's (1986) *generalized context model* of categorization and Logan's (1988) *instance theory of automaticity*. By integrating theories of attention, categorization, and memory, the development of ITAM seems to be an important step toward a unified account of visual cognition.

REFERENCES

Alvarado, J.M., Santalla, Z., & Santisteban, C. (1999). An evaluation of the CODE theory of visual attention extended to two dimensions. *Acta Psychologica, 103*, 239–255.

Bundesen, C. (1987). Visual attention: Race models for selection from multielement displays. *Psychological Research, 49*, 113–121.

Bundesen, C. (1990). A theory of visual attention. *Psychological Review, 97*, 523–547.

Bundesen, C. (1991a). *Towards a neural network implementation of TVA*. Paper presented at The First Meeting of the HFSP Research Group on Brain Mechanisms of Visual Selection, School of Psychology, University of Birmingham, UK, October.

Bundesen, C. (1991b). Visual selection of features and objects: Is location special? A reinterpretation of Nissen's (1985) findings. *Perception and Psychophysics, 50*, 87–89.

Bundesen, C. (1993a). The notion of elements in the visual field in a theory of visual attention: A reply to Van der Velde and Van der Heijden (1993). *Perception and Psychophysics, 53*, 350–352.

Bundesen, C. (1993b). The relationship between independent race models and Luce's choice axiom. *Journal of Mathematical Psychology, 37*, 446–471.

Bundesen, C. (1996). Formal models of visual attention: A tutorial review. In A.F. Kramer, M.G.H. Coles, & G.D. Logan (Eds.), *Converging operations in the study of visual selective attention* (pp. 1–43). Washington, DC: American Psychological Association.

Bundesen, C. (1998a). A computational theory of visual attention. *Philosophical Transactions of the Royal Society of London, Series B, 353*, 1271–1281.

Bundesen, C. (1998b). Visual selective attention: Outlines of a choice model, a race model, and a computational theory. *Visual Cognition, 5*, 287–309.

Bundesen, C. (2000). *A neuropsychological theory of visual attention and short-term memory.* Manuscript in preparation.

Bundesen, C., & Pedersen, L.F. (1983). Color segregation and visual search. *Perception and Psychophysics, 33*, 487–493.

Bundesen, C., Pedersen, L.F., & Larsen, A. (1984). Measuring efficiency of selection from briefly exposed visual displays: A model for partial report. *Journal of Experimental Psychology: Human Perception and Performance, 10*, 329–339.

Bundesen, C., Shibuya, H., & Larsen, A. (1985). Visual selection from multielement displays: A model for partial report. In M.I. Posner & O.S.M. Marin (Eds.), *Attention and performance XI* (pp. 631–649). Hillsdale, NJ: Lawrence Erlbaum Associates Inc.

Desimone, R., & Ungerleider, L.G. (1989). Neural mechanisms of visual processing in monkeys. In E. Boller & J. Grafman (Eds.), *Handbook of neuropsychology*, Vol. 2 (pp. 267–299). Amsterdam: Elsevier.

Duncan, J. (1984). Selective attention and the organization of visual information. *Journal of Experimental Psychology: General, 113*, 501–517.

Duncan, J., Bundesen, C., Olson, A., Humphreys, G., Chavda, S., & Shibuya, H. (1999). Systematic analysis of deficits in visual attention. *Journal of Experimental Psychology: General, 128*, 450–478.

Estes, W.K., & Taylor, H.A. (1964). A detection method and probabilistic models for assessing information processing from brief visual displays. *Proceedings of the National Academy of Sciences, USA, 52*, 446–454.

Isenberg, L., Nissen, M.J., & Marchak, L.C. (1990). Attentional processing and the independence of color and orientation. *Journal of Experimental Psychology: Human Perception and Performance, 16*, 869–878.

James, W. (1890). *The principles of psychology. Vol. 1.* New York: Holt.

Johnston, J.C., Ruthruff, E., & Monheit, M. (1997). Dependence by any other name smells just as sweet: Reply to Van der Velde and Van der Heijden (1997). *Journal of Experimental Psychology: Human Perception and Performance, 23*, 1813–1818.

Logan, G.D. (1988). Toward an instance theory of automatization. *Psychological Review, 95*, 492–527.

Logan, G.D. (1996). The CODE theory of visual attention: An integration of space-based and object-based attention. *Psychological Review, 103*, 603–649.

Logan, G.D. (in press). An instance theory of attention and memory. *Psychological Review.*

Logan, G.D., & Bundesen, C. (1996). Spatial effects in the partial report paradigm: A challenge for theories of visual spatial attention. In D.L. Medin (Ed.), *The psychology of learning and motivation, Vol. 35* (pp. 243–282). San Diego, CA: Academic Press.

Logan, G.D., & Gordon, R.D. (2001). Executive control of visual attention in dual-task situations. *Psychological Review, 108*, 393–434.

Luce, R.D. (1959). *Individual choice behavior.* New York: Wiley.

Luce, R.D. (1963). Detection and recognition. In R.D. Luce, R.R. Bush, & E. Galanter (Eds.), *Handbook of mathematical psychology, Vol. 1* (pp. 103–189). New York: Wiley.

Luck, S.J., & Vogel, E.K. (1997). The capacity of visual working memory for features and conjunctions. *Nature, 390,* 279–281.

McAdams, C.J., & Maunsell, J.H.R. (1999a). Effects of attention on orientation-tuning functions of single neurons in macaque cortical area V4. *Journal of Neuroscience, 19,* 431–441.

McAdams, C.J., & Maunsell, J.H.R. (1999b). Effects of attention on the reliability of individual neurons in monkey visual cortex. *Neuron, 23,* 765–773.

Monheit, M.A., & Johnston, J.C. (1994). Spatial attention to arrays of multidimensional objects. *Journal of Experimental Psychology: Human Perception and Performance, 20,* 691–708.

Moran, J., & Desimone, R. (1985). Selective attention gates visual processing in the extrastriate cortex. *Science, 229,* 782–784.

Nissen, M.J. (1985). Accessing features and objects: Is location special? In M.I. Posner & O.S.M. Marin (Eds.), *Attention and performance XI* (pp. 205–219). Hillsdale, NJ: Lawrence Erlbaum Associates Inc.

Nosofsky, R.M. (1986). Attention, similarity, and the identification-categorization relationship. *Journal of Experimental Psychology: General, 115,* 39–57.

Nosofsky, R.M., & Palmeri, T. (1997). An exemplar-based random walk model of speeded classification. *Psychological Review, 104,* 266–300.

Posner, M.I., Nissen, M.J., & Ogden, W.C. (1978). Attended and unattended processing modes: The role of set for spatial location. In H.L. Pick & E. Saltzman (Eds.), *Modes of perceiving and processing information* (pp. 137–157). Hillsdale, NJ: Lawrence Erlbaum Associates Inc.

Reynolds, J.H., Chelazzi, L., & Desimone, R. (1999). Competitive mechanisms subserve attention in macaque areas V2 and V4. *Journal of Neuroscience, 19,* 1736–1753.

Schneider, W., & Fisk, A.D. (1982). Degree of consistent training: Improvements in search performance and automatic process development. *Perception and Psychophysics, 31,* 160–168.

Shibuya, H., & Bundesen, C. (1988). Visual selection from multielement displays: Measuring and modeling effects of exposure duration. *Journal of Experimental Psychology: Human Perception and Performance, 14,* 591–600.

Sperling, G. (1960). The information available in brief visual presentations. *Psychological Monographs, 74* (11, Whole No. 498).

Sperling, G. (1967). Successive approximations to a model for short-term memory. *Acta Psychologica, 27,* 285–292.

Townsend, J.T., & Ashby, F.G. (1982). Experimental test of contemporary mathematical models of visual letter recognition. *Journal of Experimental Psychology: Human Perception and Performance, 8,* 834–864.

Treisman, A.M., & Gelade, G. (1980). A feature-integration theory of attention. *Cognitive Psychology, 12,* 97–136.

Treisman, A.M., & Gormican, S. (1988). Feature analysis in early vision: Evidence from search asymmetries. *Psychological Review, 95,* 15–48.

Treue, S., & Trujillo, J.C.M. (1999). Feature-based attention influences motion processing gain in macaque visual cortex. *Nature, 399,* 575–579.

Van der Heijden, A.H.C. (1993). The role of position in object selection in vision. *Psychological Research, 56,* 44–58.

Van der Heijden, A.H.C., La Heij, W., & Boer, J.P.A. (1983). Parallel processing of redundant targets in simple visual search tasks. *Psychological Research, 45,* 235–254.

Van der Velde, F., & Van der Heijden, A.H.C. (1993). An element in the visual field is just a conjunction of attributes: A critique of Bundesen (1991). *Perception and Psychophysics, 53,* 345–349.

Van der Velde, F., & Van der Heijden, A.H.C. (1997). On the statistical independence of color and shape in object identification. *Journal of Experimental Psychology: Human Perception and Performance, 23,* 1798–1812.

Van Oeffelen, M.P., & Vos, P.G. (1982). Configurational effects on the enumeration of dots: Counting by groups. *Memory and Cognition, 10*, 396–404.

Van Oeffelen, M.P., & Vos, P.G. (1983). An algorithm for pattern description on the level of relative proximity. *Pattern Recognition, 16*, 341–348.

CHAPTER EIGHT

Face perception

Vicki Bruce
University of Stirling, Scotland, UK

INTRODUCTION

In the 25 years or so that I have been studying aspects of face perception, the face has moved from being an idiosyncratic and marginal topic of investigation for the perceptual psychologist interested in pattern processing, to something of central importance for a range of psychologists interested in perception, cognition, cognitive neurosciences, and cognitive science[1]. The total number of articles which matched the search keys "face" and "perception" in the SCI/SSCI indexes for the 3-year period 1982 through 1984 was just four; for the 3-year period to the end of 1999 it was 403[2]. In this review I will highlight some of the important developments in face perception over this period of time.

The face supplies a rich variety of information that is important in social interaction. Faces are the most reliable key to individual identity when a person is familiar to the observer. But even unfamiliar faces reveal a great deal about the social group to which the bearer belongs—we can, with various degrees of accuracy and precision, tell sex, age, and race from the face alone. We may also make use of information in facial accessories to derive information about the personal preferences of the bearer—e.g., facial

---

[1] To be fair, it was always central for social psychologists.

[2] Other topics that I investigated also grew over the same period, but while the number of articles on face perception increased a hundred-fold, those on, for example, the topics of visual imagery and music perception—which have also boomed—increased only about ten-fold.

"piercing" in young Europeans, designer spectacles, hairstyle and colouration are all indicative of lifestyle preferences.

Such facial adornment is also one of the things that people deliberately vary in order to appear more (or sometimes less) attractive—and facial attractiveness is another important judgement made by observers from faces alone, which may affect how or whether they choose to get to know someone better.

Identity, social group, and attractiveness are aspects of a face that remain relatively constant—certainly across periods of days or months. In contrast, there are a number of further important but time-varying signals from the face, which signal changes in mood, through facial expression, help us to decipher speech through lip and other facial movements, and signal direction of attention.

The field of face perception encompasses research on all these many processes, and it is a field within which there are strong contributions from cognitive neuroscientists and computer scientists as well as psychologists. Moreover, understanding face recognition and perception has important applications, with implications for many other professional groups such as police and lawyers (eye-witness testimony), doctors and surgeons (cosmetic surgery), and film makers and artists (animation, morphing, caricature). What follows must necessarily be a selective review of just some topics within this field, and I will focus mainly on research conducted by perceptual and cognitive psychologists, neglecting many of the interdisciplinary and applied perspectives. For broader recent perspectives, see Bruce and Young (1998) for an introductory-level interdisciplinary survey of a broad range of material, Young (1998) for an edited collection of key articles with a strong neuro-psychological and theoretical focus, a recent special issue of the journal *Cognitive Neuropsychology* (Kanwisher & Moscovitch, 2000) for up-to-date work on brain mechanisms using imaging and single-case studies, and Wechsler, Phillips, Bruce, Soulie, and Huang (1998) for a collection of work on computer recognition and image processing of faces.

THEORETICAL FRAMEWORKS

How are the different meanings and messages conveyed by the face deciphered by the human perceptual system? Bruce and Young (1986) used neuropsychological and experimental evidence to elaborate a framework for understanding information processing of the face (drawing together and developing earlier suggestions by Bruce, 1979; Ellis, 1986; Hay & Young, 1982; Rhodes, 1985; Young, Hay, & Ellis, 1985a). There are two important features of this framework. First, that the retrieval of personal identity of a familiar face is a sequential process involving perceptual, semantic, and name retrieval stages. And second, that this identification sequence proceeds independently of the derivation of other kinds of meaning from the face—such as expressions and facial speech—which each involve independent information-processing pathways.

In the 15 years since the publication of this framework, there have been important refinements and developments of it. The workings of the identification route have been specified in more detail and implemented in a connectionist model based upon an interactive activation and competition architecture (Burton, Bruce, & Hancock, 1999a; Burton, Bruce, & Johnston, 1990). This allowed apparently tricky neuropsychological observations of covert recognition of faces by prosopagnosic patients to be explained (Burton, Young, Bruce, Johnston, & Ellis, 1991).

Moreover, the suggestion that there are independent processing routes deriving different kinds of meaning from the face has received some challenges in recent years. Schweinberger and Soukup (1998) used a Garner (1976) interference paradigm to test the independence between face identification and facial speech processing, and face identification and expression analysis. Consistent with the Bruce and Young framework, they observed that responses based upon facial identities were unaffected by variation in expressions, or by facial speech; however, responses based upon facial expressions and facial speech were affected by variations in identity, suggesting that the identity of a face can influence the analysis conducted within these other routes. This asymmetric interference of identities onto expressions, but not expressions onto identities, was replicated by Schweinberger, Burton, and Kelly (1999). Moreover, Walker, Bruce, and O'Malley (1995) also observed an effect of facial identity on facial speech processing. They showed that when faces and voices were familiar to observers, these would be much less likely to perceive McGurk "blends" (cf. McGurk & Macdonald, 1976) of visual and acoustic information if the presented faces and voices were drawn from different people. When the identities were unfamiliar, however, McGurk blends were perceived just as strongly for mis-matched identities of face and voice as for matching ones.

These recent findings suggest that there may be some moderation of the facial expression routes and the facial speech analysis routes on the basis of facial identity (see also Baudouin, Sansone, & Tiberghien, 2000). Do such findings invalidate the parallel routes model? At the present time my tentative conclusion is that the model may require some moderation, but in detail rather than at a more fundamental level, since in recent years there has been considerable further support for the differentiation of different processing routes deriving from evidence from cognitive neuroscience.

For example, Young, Newcombe, de Haan, Small, and Hay (1993) studied a large number of patients with localized brain injuries and showed a clear double dissociation between the inability to recognize faces and to process their expressions. Moreover, Sergent, Ohta, MacDonald, and Zuck (1994) examined PET and MRI images as participants performed tasks involving the recognition of faces or their emotions, and found some segregation of the brain areas engaged by identity compared with expressive tasks. Recent studies implicating the amygdala in the processing of fear stimuli, and the anterior insula in disgust (Phillips et al., 1997; Sprengelmeyer et al., 1999) suggest further differentiation of the emotion-processing systems themselves, but in no way challenge the independence of facial expression processing from identification.

However, as a recent special issue of *Cognitive Neuropsychology* (see Kanwisher and Moskovitch, 2000) makes clear, the functional specialisation of cortical and subcortical structures revealed by techniques such as ERP and fMRI is revealing considerably more rather than less complexity. It is possible that there may be functional separation and also complex interactions between different systems.

It is also clear that while there is on the one hand logical independence of—say—expression and identity, on the other hand, their separate analyses must be recombined *at some point* for social interaction—if your teacher looks pleased this has different implications for you than if your greatest rival looks pleased. The challenge for the next generation of theory will be to spell out the nature and locus of the interactions between these routes.

The recent special issue of *Cognitive Neuropsychology* also reveals that there is increasing scope for mapping elements of the functional models of face perception onto neurological structures and pathways. Unfortunately, however, not all the neuroscience research is guided by clear functional theory, which can make interpretation of some findings difficult. Nonetheless, progress using the newer imaging techniques is exciting.

THE POWER OF COMPUTERS

The study of face perception has been transformed over the past 15 years by developments in computer graphics, which allow faces to be manipulated or morphed in novel yet realistic ways. Whereas all psychological research has to some degree been transformed by computer-based stimulus presentation and data analysis, face research has probably been more profoundly affected than many other fields, since we are able to manipulate faces in digital ways that were simply not possible photographically. Here I provide several examples of topics given new life by graphics developments.

Spatial scales and face processing

An early example of the application of computer graphics to face processing was work by Harmon (1973), who investigated the effects of pixellation on face recognition. An initial image of a face—represented as the brightness of each of a large number of pixels—can be compressed by averaging together the brightness in a number of adjacent pixels and displaying the average brightness over larger blocks that encompass the original pixels. Harmon's example of Abraham Lincoln is particularly well known, and formed the basis of a novel art-science liaison in Salvador Dali's 1976 work *Gala looking at the Mediterranean*. (See Bruce & Young, 1998, for illustrations, and further explorations of how art and science can liaise in the topic of face perception.) Pixellation has the effect of filtering the original face image so that only the relatively low spatial frequencies are preserved—the smaller the number of pixel squares used to depict the image, the lower is the cutoff of the spatial frequency spectrum preserved in the transformed image. The pixellation process itself introduces further high-frequency information at the pixel edges, which is why it becomes easier to recognise the pixellated faces if the eyes are squinted to defocus these sharp edges.

A number of researchers have shown that faces can be well recognized from quite coarse-scale pixellated images, as long as these preserve something in the order of 16 to 20 pixels along each dimension of the face (Bachmann, 1971; Harmon, 1973). Such demonstrations have been used to suggest that the representations which are important for face perception are based upon a relatively low spatial frequency band.

Recently, there have been some important qualifications of this conclusion. First, it has been appreciated since seminal work by Sergent (1986) that the spatial frequency range critical for face perception depends very much on the task being conducted. Schyns and Oliva (1999) have recently illustrated this rather elegantly using "hybrid" faces, in which the low spatial scale information for one individual face was superimposed on the high spatial frequency information derived from a second face. Figure 1 shows an example of this kind of hybrid.

In Schyns and Oliva's experiments, the two faces differed in expression and gender—for example, a high pass male angry face could be superimposed on a low pass female neutral face. Participants who were asked to categorize the gender of the face showed no particular bias towards high or low spatial frequencies. When participants were asked if the face shown was expressive or not, responses were dominated by the high spatial frequency information, whereas when they were asked to categorise the specific expression shown, the lower spatial frequencies dominated. Thus different frequency bands within the same stimulus determined different kinds of response. Schyns and Oliva suggest that decisions about whether or not a face shows an expression can be made by examining fine-scale detail at specific features (e.g., is there crinkling of the eyes), whereas deciding which expression is shown demands examination of the more global configuration of the face.

Second, a number of researchers have suggested that where there is an optimal band for face recognition; this tends to be a range of middle rather

© Philippe G. Schyns & Aude Oliva, 1997.

Figure 1. This image appears to resemble the British Prime Minister Tony Blair when viewed close, but Margaret Thatcher from a distance. The hybrid image was constructed by Philippe Schyns and Aude Oliva from the low spatial frequency information from Thatcher's face and the high spatial frequency information from Blair's face. After Bruce and Young (1998). Reprinted with the permission of the publisher.

than low or high spatial frequencies (e.g., Costen, Parker, & Craw, 1996). One possible reason for this is that a middle range of frequencies is more likely to overlap with frequencies present in the original face. Liu, Collin, Rainville, and Chaudhuri (2000) have shown that spatial frequency overlap appears to be more important than absolute range, at least in determining abilities to match between images of the same face.

Configurations vs. local features

But what is it that is processed from within these spatial patterns? Psychologists studying face perception have for many years suggested—to varying degrees and with different emphases—that upright (but not inverted) faces are processed in a way that emphasises the spatial relationships within the face, and/or the holistic pattern of the face, more than isolated "features".

Relatively low spatial frequencies convey this overall configuration, while relatively high spatial frequencies add detail of local features. Computer software packages such as Adobe Photoshop allow images to be altered in subtle ways in order to examine the effects of manipulations on local and relational aspects. For example, Leder and Bruce (1998) used photo-manipulated images like those shown in Figure 2. Some faces had local features altered (e.g., eyebrows made bushier) and others had subtle changes to feature positions. Both types of manipulation rendered the faces more distinctive when upright, as assessed by ratings and by memory performance. When the faces were inverted, however, only those with local feature manipulations retained their distinctiveness (see also related studies by Bartlett & Searcy, 1993; Farah, Tanaka, & Drain, 1995; Leder & Bruce, 2000; Searcy & Bartlett, 1996; Tanaka & Farah, 1993; and a review of these and many further studies by Rakover, in press).

A number of companies have produced software packages to be used by the police to allow faces to be created from witness descriptions, and these packages allow even more scope for use in experiments with faces, since they allow specific features to be altered or relocated rather than relying on artistic skills within a package such as Photoshop. Such packages have been used to good effect to investigate local and holistic feature processing. For example, Tanaka and Farah (1993) used the line-drawn composite package Mac-a-Mug to examine how well people could remember individual face features from different contexts. They showed that memory for a particular feature,

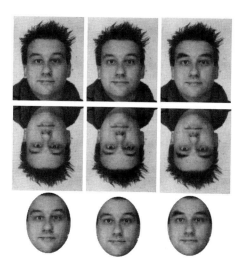

Figure 2. The original face shown in the centre of the top row has been made more distinctive by changing the spacing of features (top left) or altering a local feature (top right). Only the local changes maintain their distinctiveness when the faces are inverted. After Leder and Bruce (1998). Reprinted with the permission of the Experimental Psychology Society.

such as the nose, was much more accurate when shown in the context of a whole face than in isolation or in a jumbled face, which they used to suggest that face representations were holistic. The idea is that the face is not decomposed into features such as eyes, nose, mouth, and so probing with these features in isolation is problematic. Leder and Bruce (2000) provided further tests of the holistic processing idea using Mac-a-Mug faces, with the addition of colour and shading. They showed that naming of learned faces was disrupted by inversion only when the faces differed in terms of the spatial arrangement of their features, but not when the faces were distinguished in terms of unique combinations of colour or brightness of local features, a result that does not support the most extreme version of "holistic" processing of face images.

Much more realistic computer-based composite systems are now available, and can be used to generate excellent likenesses of individual faces. Such systems allow the possibility of developing systematic variations of the shape and placement of individual face features, which will allow further good experiments on face processing to be conducted in the future.

Caricatures and morphs

As well as manipulating specific images of faces, graphics techniques have been developed to allow the morphing and merging of photographic-quality faces. In 1985, Susan Brennan described an algorithm to create caricatures automatically by distorting the locations of facial features in proportion to their deviation from the norm, or "average". To do this, a set of key points (such as tip of nose, corner of eye) was located on a large set of faces and their locations averaged to produce the key points of an average face. To caricature any individual face, the location of its individual points was compared with the average, and their difference multiplied by a constant—so large differences were exaggerated more than small ones. The resulting locations could then be used to redraw the new "caricature". Rhodes, Brennan, and Carey (1987) were able to demonstrate that moderate degrees of caricature created more recognizable images than the originals. This "superportrait" effect has been found in other studies using line-drawn faces (e.g., Rhodes & Tremewan, 1994).

When the caricature algorithm is run on line drawings this outcome is perhaps not surprising; the caricature exaggerates distinctive features, potentially compensating for the loss of grey-scale information on which face perception is so dependent. However, during the 1990s, Phil Benson, Dave Perrett, and colleagues at the University of St Andrews extended this work by using the same principles to create caricatures and other kinds of "morph" of full-colour images of faces (Benson & Perrett, 1991a, b). They were able to show that small amounts of caricature applied to a high-quality photograph could sometimes yield an image judged as a better likeness of the individual than their veridical photograph! This is potentially a challenging observation, and there are a number of different possible accounts of such an effect. One possible explanation suggests that through familiarization, stored visual representations of faces themselves become caricatured. Another account suggests that it is access to these visual representations that is facilitated by caricatures—for example, a caricature accesses a more sparsely populated region of face space than the original, reducing the possibility of false matches with other faces. This offsets any disadvantage coming from the nonveridical shape of the caricature itself. An account which is in some respects a blend of these two is Tanaka and Simon's (1997) connectionist model, which demonstrates that during learning, distinctive features of a pattern will be more closely associated with a target identity than will less distinctive features—they are more discriminating. So, a caricatured probe that enhances distinctive as compared with less distinctive features can benefit recognition. It would be interesting to repeat such simulation studies with real rather than hypothetical face patterns.

However, it should be noted that clear examples of superportrait effects with caricatured photographs are difficult to find (see Rhodes, 1996). One such example comes from Calder et al. (1996b), who showed an advantage for caricatured images in an experiment where the measure was how much benefit an immediately prior photograph of a person gave to recognition of a name (self-priming). Experiment 3 used +50% caricatures, original images and −50% caricatures as primes, and showed a significant advantage for the +50% caricatures compared with the other two conditions. A number of other experiments show similar, though slight, trends, suggesting that when high-quality veridical information about a face is present, there is little or no benefit of caricaturing. Nonetheless, the fact that the caricature distortion never appears to harm face recognition suggests that the exaggeration of distinctive information is able to at least compensate for the distortion to the appearance that it creates.

Caricaturing is only one of the techniques that contemporary morph packages allow. The process of comparing and averaging faces via a set of key points allows any two faces to be combined in different proportions, so that the effects of morphing between different types of face can be explored. Morphed images have been used to investigate categorical perception of facial expressions (Etcoff & Magee, 1992; Calder, Young, Perrett, Etcoff, & Rowland, 1996a) and of facial identities (Beale & Keil, 1995), and to refine experimental explorations of the relationships between expression and identity processing (Schweinberger et al., 1999).

Moreover, caricaturing by increasing distinctive aspects can be applied to categories other than individual identity. Masculinity or femininity of faces can be enhanced by increasing the difference between an individual face and an average of both sexes, or faces can be artificially aged by moving them in the direction of the average face of an older age group (Burt & Perrett, 1995). Dave Perrett and colleagues (Perrett, et al., 1998; Perrett, May, & Yoshikawa, 1994) have investigated the relationship between the exaggeration of sex-linked face features and ratings of attractiveness. As expected, feminized female faces were rated as more attractive than original or masculinized versions. But unexpectedly, feminized male faces were also preferred—a result replicated more recently by Rhodes, Hickford, and Jeffery (2000). Perrett and colleagues explain their findings by suggesting that feminine personality characteristics were more valued in prospective mates than male ones. Enhancing masculinity of male faces increased perceived dominance and some negative attributions, such as coldness or dishonesty, which might make such individuals less attractive as prospective partners. However, in some circumstances the more masculine, testosterone-related features may be preferred. For example, Penton-Voak and Perrett (2000) showed that women who were ovulating were more likely to prefer masculinized male faces than at other phases of their cycle, though the magazine-based study they used requires replication under more controlled conditions.

3D faces

All the work cited is based upon two-dimensional face patterns. But faces are three-dimensional objects whose appearance changes considerably in different viewpoints. Range finders allow the shape of the face surface to be measured and displayed in 3D, and such surface images have been used productively in experiments exploring how face recognition is affected by viewpoint (Hill, Schyns, & Akamatsu, 1997) and lighting (Hill & Bruce, 1996). Some recent work has examined how face perception is influenced by changes to 3D shape, or by changing 3D shape independently of surface texture features. This research has been facilitated by the use of range-finders, which can measure 3D shapes of faces and simultaneously record information about the surface texture (colour) of the face. Hill, Bruce, and Akamatsu (1995), for example, made use of a Cyberware scanner, which separately records 3D shape and surface colour from each point in a face, and then recombines these shapes and colours in novel ways. They explored how judgements of sex and race (Japanese or European) were influenced by 3D as opposed to texture/colour, by producing composite images in which the shape from one category (e.g., Japanese male shape) was combined with the texture of another (Japanese female colour/texture) and the composite presented for a categorization task (male-female, in this example). They found that texture information dominated 3D shape in full-face images, but when the faces were presented in angled views the 3D shape information played a greater role, particularly for judgements of race. O'Toole and her colleagues (O'Toole,

Vetter, Troje, & Bulthoff, 1997a) have also made use of 3D shapes of faces alongside grey-level image (GLI) information in Principal Components-based Analyses, and they have shown that 3D shape plays a relatively greater role than GLI in such judgements. The same group has also conducted interesting preliminary experiments on caricaturing 3D shapes (O'Toole, Vetter, Volz, & Salter, 1997b).

What have we learned about face representations using these techniques? The visual representations of faces used for their recognition appear not to comprise a list of simple features of the kind that we can label from the face (eyes, nose, mouth, etc.). Relationships between features are as important as local features themselves. Moreover, the relative importance of relatively low spatial frequencies, and the impediments to face processing created by changes in lighting or more dramatic effects of negation, suggest that the representations used preserve much information about relatively low-level "image" features.

Such observations have influenced the way in which psychologists think about the kind of image/feature analyses which lead into later stages of person identification. For example, our own model of person identification has been interfaced with a simple pattern analysis "front end" based on Principal Components Analysis (PCA) of facial images (cf. O'Toole et al., 1997b; Turk & Pentland, 1991) to provide a "complete" model of person identification (Burton et al., 1999a). In a PCA scheme, faces are described in terms of a set of "holistic" features—"eigenfaces"—which describe the major dimensions along which samples of faces vary. PCA is only one of a family of low-level image coding schemes that seem to capture something about the way that humans see faces, and more sophisticated variants are needed to mirror more precisely the way the human visual system analyses faces (e.g., see Hancock, Bruce, & Burton, 1998; Biederman & Kalocsai, 1997). Nonetheless, the general approach is promising.

So, advances in computer-based manipulations of faces have fed through to influence the further development of theoretical models of face processing in humans. In the final section, I outline three recent topics that are likely to influence developments in the future, but which for now are not readily accommodated within our theoretical frameworks.

HOT TOPICS IN FACE PERCEPTION

The following are topics that appear to be particularly exciting at the moment, and where I anticipate rapid progress in the future. They also each, in different ways, pose challenges for the current generation of models of face processing.

Gaze

The use of gaze to signal direction of attention was a strange omission from the Bruce and Young (1986) framework for face processing. In the past few years, gaze processing has become a hot topic for perceptual and cognitive psychologists (see Langton, Watt, & Bruce, 2000, for a review). Simon Baron-Cohen (e.g., Baron-Cohen & Cross, 1992; Baron-Cohen & Ring, 1994) suggested that gaze processing was at the heart of human understanding of other mental states; while Perrett, Hietanen, Oram, and Benson (1992) demonstrated that some of the apparent viewpoint specificity of face-specific cells in primate brains actually arose from specific responses to direction of attention. (For example, a cell that responded optimally to a full-face view would also respond to an angled view with eye gaze directed head-on, and would not respond to a full-face view where gaze was averted.) Gaze signals appear to be difficult or impossible to ignore; a series of studies from different labs (Driver et al., 1999; Friesen & Kingstone, 1998; Langton & Bruce, 1999) have shown that gaze cues from a centrally fixated head provide attentional cueing which facilitates detection of targets at peripheral locations (cf. Posner, 1980). Langton and Bruce (1999) observed that the pattern of cueing, in which effects were observed at short but not at longer SOAs and were independent of cue diagnosticity, resembled that of exogenous cueing.

Most of the studies on perception of social attention have looked at information derived from eye gaze and head direction. But attention is also signalled by body posture and by gestures such as pointing, and a number of studies have shown that different cues from face and body are combined in the computation of direction of attention (Langton & Bruce, 2000; Perrett et al., 1992). Such observations raise the question of how social attention perception—which takes inputs from signals beyond the face—fits in with the face perception system, for which there appears to be such a degree of specialisation both functionally and cortically. Clearly this is a further area where interactions between different subsystems merit further analysis and exploration.

Dynamics

Virtually all the research described in this article has used static images of faces to probe face processing. Dynamic cues have been thought important for expression perception (see Kamachi et al., 2000) and probably for speech (Rosenblum & Saldana, 1996), but nevertheless have been generally neglected in these areas of face processing, and ignored completely in others. However, recent research suggests that representations for recognition may in some way incorporate dynamic characteristics. Knight and Johnston (1997) showed that recognition of famous faces shown in photographic negative images was increased if animated clips rather than single images were shown. Here in Stirling, Karen Lander has replicated and extended this finding to show that recognition of faces from any difficult-to-recognise format is aided by motion (e.g., see Lander, Bruce & Hill, 2001). Lander, Christie, and Bruce (1999) and Lander and Bruce (2001) have shown that the beneficial effect does not arise just because of the additional static viewpoint information in an image sequence (though this additional information does contribute). Image sequences that are shown in their original tempo are recognized more accurately than those that are slowed down, speeded up, altered in terms of their timing, or reversed. These results suggest that our representations of faces include, or are able to access, some information about how the faces normally move, and this information can provide useful supplementary information when recognition is made difficult. To accommodate such findings, models of face processing will need to consider how information about dynamic characteristics may be integrated within, or accessed via, the face recognition system.

Familiar vs. unfamiliar faces

These observations of the enhancement of recognition through motion apply to familiar faces, but it is much more difficult to demonstrate that movement helps the recognition of relatively unfamiliar faces (Christie & Bruce, 1998; but see Pike, Kemp, Towell, & Phillips, 1997). There are a number of further differences between the processing of familiar and unfamiliar faces (e.g., Ellis, Shepherd, & Davies, 1979; Young, Hay, McWeeny, Flude, & Ellis, 1985b), and these have been emphasized recently in our own work on the identification of faces from CCTV (security video) images. We have found that familiar faces are recognized extremely well, even from images of such poor quality that they yield near-chance recognition of unfamiliar ones (Bruce, Henderson, Newman, & Burton, 2000; Burton, Wilson, Cowan, & Bruce, 1999b). Unfamiliar faces, in contrast, pose difficulties even when image quality is extremely high—performance at matching identities across slightly different images of the same person can yield remarkably high error rates (Bruce et al., 1999; Henderson, Bruce, & Burton, 2001). An important question posed by this research is how familiar a face must be to overcome the image-bound performance that characterises unfamiliar face perception. Our own current work will be investigating the processes by which faces become familiar.

There are both simple and more subtle reasons for needing to understand the differences and transitions between processing of unfamiliar and familiar faces. At the simplest level, some theories of face recognition more easily describe processes of recognizing familiar faces than unfamiliar ones (e.g.,

Bruce & Young, 1986). At a more subtle level, image-specific coding schemes such as PCA seem to provide a better account of our perception and memory for unfamiliar faces than familiar ones (Hancock et al., 1998), so clearly using PCA to drive the model of familiar face recognition (Burton et al., 1999a) can be only a preliminary step in the model's development. Moreover, although Burton (1994) described how the IAC architecture can be developed to accommodate learning of new faces, this has yet to be implemented for actual face patterns, and it will be the development of an account of learning from varying facial images which will be needed to further advance our understanding of how human face perception furnishes representations suitable for recognizing the faces of friends and family.

REFERENCES

Bachmann, T. (1991). Identification of spatially quantised tachistoscopic images of faces: How many pixels does it take to carry identity? *European Journal of Cognitive Psychology, 3*, 87–104.

Baron-Cohen, S., & Cross, P. (1992). Reading the eyes: Evidence for the role of perception in the development of a theory of mind. *Mind and Language, 7*, 182–186.

Baron-Cohen, S., & Ring, H. (1994). A model of the mindreading system: Neuropsychological and neurobiological perspectives. In C. Lewis & P. Mitchell (Eds.), *Children's early understanding of mind: Origins and development* (pp. 183–207). Hove, UK: Lawrence Erlbaum Associates Ltd.

Bartlett, J.C., & Searcy, J. (1993). Inversion and configuration of faces. *Cognitive Psychology, 25*, 281–316.

Baudouin, J.Y., Sansone, S., & Tiberghien, G. (2000). Recognising expression from familiar and unfamiliar faces. *Pragmatics and Cognition, 8*, 123–146.

Beale, J.M., & Keil, F.C. (1995). Categorical effects in the perception of faces. *Cognition, 57*, 217–239.

Benson, P.J., & Perrett, D.I. (1991a). Synthesising continuous-tone caricatures. *Image and Vision Computing, 9*, 123–129.

Benson, P.J., & Perrett, D.I. (1991b). Perception and recognition of photographic quality facial caricatures: Implications for the recognition of natural images. *European Journal of Cognitive Psychology, 3*, 105–135.

Biederman, I., & Kalocsai, P. (1997). Neurocomputational bases of object and face recognition. *Philosophical Transactions of the Royal Society, B352*, 1203–1219.

Brennan, S.E. (1985). The caricature generator. *Leonardo, 18*, 170–178.

Bruce, V. (1979). Searching for politicians: An information-processing approach to face recognition. *Quarterly Journal of Experimental Psychology, 31*, 373–395.

Bruce, V., Henderson, Z., Greenwood, K., Hancock, P., Burton, A.M., & Miller, P. (1999). Verification of face identities from images captured on video. *Journal of Experimental Psychology: Applied, 5*, 339–360.

Bruce, V., Henderson, Z., Newman, C., & Burton, A.M. (2000). *Matching identities of familiar and unfamiliar faces caught on CCTV images*. Manuscript submitted for publication.

Bruce, V., & Young, A. (1986). Understanding face recognition. *British Journal of Psychology, 77*, 305–327.

Bruce, V., & Young, A. (1998). *In the eye of the beholder: The science of face perception*. Oxford: Oxford University Press.

Burt, D.M., & Perrett, D.I. (1995). Perception of age in adult Caucasian male faces: Computer graphic manipulation of shape and colour information. *Proceedings of the Royal Society of London, B259*, 137–143.

Burton, A.M. (1994). Learning new faces in an Interactive Activation and Competition Model. *Visual Cognition, 1*, 313–348.

Burton, A.M., Bruce,V., & Hancock, P.J.B. (1999a). From pixels to people: A model of familiar face recognition. *Cognitive Science, 23*, 1–31

Burton, A.M., Bruce, V., & Johnston, R.A. (1990). Understanding face recognition with an interactive activation model. *British Journal of Psychology, 81*, 361–380.

Burton, A.M., Wilson, S., Cowan, M., & Bruce, V. (1999b). Face recognition in poor-quality video: Evidence from security surveillance. *Psychological Science, 10*, 243–248.

Burton, A.M., Young, A.W., Bruce, V., Johnston, R.A., & Ellis, A.W. (1991). Understanding covert recognition. *Cognition, 39*, 129–166.

Calder, A.J., Young, A.W., Perrett, D.I., Etcoff, N.L., & Rowland, D. (1996a). Categorical perception of morphed facial expressions. *Visual Cognition, 3*, 81–117.

Calder, A.J., Young, A.W., Rowland, D., Perrett, D.I., Hodges, J.R., & Etcoff, N.L. (1996b). Facial emotion recognition after bilateral amygdala damage: Differentially severe impairment of fear. *Cognitive Neuropsychology, 13*, 699–745.

Christie, F., & Bruce, V. (1998). The role of movement in the recognition of unfamiliar faces. *Memory and Cognition, 26*, 780–790.

Costen, N.P., Parker, D.M., & Craw, I. (1996). Effects of high-pass and low-pass spatial filtering on face identification. *Perception and Psychophysics, 58*, 602–612.

Driver, J., Davis, G., Ricciardelli, P., Kidd, P., Maxwell, E., & Baron-Cohen, S. (1999). Gaze perception triggers reflexive visuospatial orienting. *Visual Cognition, 6*, 509–540.

Ellis, H.D. (1986). Processes underlying face recognition. In R. Bruyer (Ed.), *The neuropsychology of face perception and facial expression*. Hillsdale, NJ: Lawrence Erlbaum Associates Inc.

Ellis, H.D., Shepherd, J.W., & Davies, G.M. (1979). Identification of familiar and unfamiliar faces from internal and external features: Some implications for theories of face recognition. *Perception, 8*, 431–439.

Etcoff, N.L., & Magee, J.J. (1992). Categorical perception of facial expressions. *Cognition, 44*, 227–240.

Farah, M.J., Tanaka, J.W., & Drain, H.M. (1995). What causes the face inversion effect. *Journal of Experimental Psychology: Human Perception and Performance, 21*, 628–634.

Friesen, C.K., & Kingstone, A. (1998). The eyes have it! Reflexive orienting is triggered by nonpredictive gaze. *Psychonomic Bulletin and Review, 5*, 490–495.

Garner, W.R. (1976). Interaction of stimulus dimensions in concept and choice processes. *Cognitive Psychology, 8*, 98–123.

Hancock, P.J.B., Bruce, V., & Burton, A.M. (1998). Comparing two computer systems and human perceptions of faces. *Vision Research, 38*, 2277–2288.

Harmon, L.D. (1973). The recognition of faces. *Scientific American, 227 (Nov)*, 71–82.

Hay, D.C., & Young, A.W. (1982). The human face. In A.W. Ellis (Ed.), *Normality and pathology in cognitive functions* (pp. 173–202). London: Academic Press.

Henderson, Z., Bruce, V., & Burton, A.M. (2001). Matching the faces of robbers captured on video. *Applied Cognitive Psychology, 15*, 445–464.

Hill, H., & Bruce, V. (1996). Effects of lighting on matching facial surfaces. *Journal of Experimental Psychology: Human Perception and Performance, 22*, 986–1004.

Hill, H., Bruce, V., & Akamatsu, S. (1995). Perceiving the sex and race of faces: The role of shape and colour. *Proceedings of the Royal Society of London, B261*, 367–373.

Hill, H., Schyns, P.G., & Akamatsu, S. (1997). Information and viewpoint dependence in face recognition. *Cognition, 62*, 201–222.

Kamachi, M., Bruce, V., Mukaida, S., Gyoba, J., Yoshikawa, S., & Akamatsu, S. (2000).

Dynamic properties influence the perception of facial expressions. Manuscript submitted for publication.

Kanwisher, N., & Moscovitch, M. (2000). The cognitive neuroscience of face processing: An introduction. *Cognitive Neuropsychology, 17*, 1–11.

Knight, B., & Johnston, A. (1997). The role of movement in face recognition. *Visual Cognition, 4*, 265–273.

Lander, K., & Bruce, V. (2000). Dynamic information and famous face recognition. Exploring the beneficial effect of movement. *Ecological Psychology, 12*, 259–272.

Lander, K., Bruce, V., & Hill, H. (2001). Evaluating the effectiveness of pixelation and blurring on masking the identity of familiar faces. *Applied Cognitive Psychology, 15*, 101–116.

Lander, K., Christie, F., & Bruce, V. (1999). The role of movement in the recognition of famous faces. *Memory & Cognition, 27*, 974–985.

Langton, S., & Bruce, V. (1999). Reflexive orienting to social attention signals. *Visual Cognition, 6*, 541–567.

Langton, S., & Bruce, V. (2000). You *must* see the point: Automatic processing of cues to the direction of social attention. *Journal of Experimental Psychology: Human Perception and Performance, 26*, 747–757.

Langton, S., Watt, R.J., & Bruce, V. (2000). Do the eyes have it? Cues to the direction of social attention. *Trends in Cognitive Science, 4*, 50–59.

Leder, H., & Bruce, V. (1998). Local and relational aspects of facial distinctiveness. *Quarterly Journal of Experimental Psychology, 51A*, 449–473.

Leder, H., & Bruce, V. (2000). When inverted faces are recognised: The role of configural information in face recognition. *Quarterly Journal of Experimental Psychology, 53A*, 513–536.

Liu, C.H., Collin, C.A., Rainville, S.J.M., & Chaudhuri, A. (2000). The effects of spatial frequency overlap on face recognition. *Journal of Experimental Psychology: Human Perception and Performance, 26*, 956–979.

McGurk, H., & MacDonald, J. (1976). Hearing lips and seeing voices. *Nature, 264*, 746–748.

O'Toole, A.J., Abdi, H., Deffenbacher, K.A., & Valentin, D. (1993). Low dimensional representation of faces in higher dimensions of the face space. *Journal of the Optical Society of America A, 10*, 405–411.

O'Toole, A.J., Vetter, T., Troje, N.F., & Bulthoff, H.H. (1997a). Sex classification is better with three-dimensional head structure than with image intensity information. *Perception, 26*, 75–84.

O'Toole, A.J., Vetter, T., Volz, H., Salter, E.M. (1997b). Three-dimensional caricatures of human heads: Distinctiveness and the perception of facial age. *Perception, 26*, 719–732.

Penton-Voak, I.S., & Perrett, D.I. (2000). Female preference for male faces changes cyclically: Further evidence. *Evolution and Human Behaviour, 21*, 39–48.

Perrett, D.I., Hietanen, J.K., Oram, M.W., & Benson, P.J. (1992). Organisation and functions of cells responsive to faces in the temporal cortex. *Philosophical Transactions of the Royal Society of London, 335*, 23–30.

Perrett, D.I., Lee, K.J., Penton-Voak, I., Rowland, D., Yoshikawa, S., Burt, D.M., Henzi, S.P., Castles, D.L., & Akamatsu, S. (1998). Effects of sexual dimorphism on facial attractiveness. *Nature, 394*, 884–887.

Perrett, D.I., May, K.A., & Yoshikawa, S. (1994). Facial shape and judgements of female attractiveness. *Nature, 368*, 239–242.

Phillips, M.L., Young, A.W., Senior, C., Brammer, M., Andrew, C., Calder, A.J., Bullmore, E.T., Perrett, D.I., Rowland, D., Williams, S.C.R., Gray, J.A., & David, A.S. (1997). A specific neural substrate for perceiving facial expressions of disgust. *Nature, 389*, 495–498.

Pike, G.E., Kemp, R.I., Towell, N.A., & Phillips, K.C. (1997). Recognizing moving faces: The relative contribution of motion and perspective view information. *Visual Cognition, 4*, 409–437.

Posner, M.I. (1980). Orienting of attention. *Quarterly Journal of Experimental Psychology*, *32*, 3–25.

Rakover, S. (in press). Featural and configurational information in faces: A conceptual and empirical analysis. *British Journal of Psychology*.

Rhodes, G. (1985). Lateralised processes in face recognition. *British Journal of Psychology*, *76*, 249–271.

Rhodes, G. (1996). *Superportraits: Caricature and recognition*. Hove, UK: Psychology Press.

Rhodes, G., Brennan, S., & Carey, S. (1987). Identification and ratings of caricatures: Implications for mental representations of faces. *Cognitive Psychology*, *19*, 473–497.

Rhodes, G., Hickford, C., & Jeffery, L. (2000). Sex-typicality and attractiveness: Are supermale and superfemale faces super-attractive. *British Journal of Psychology*, *91*, 125–140.

Rhodes, G., & Tremewan, T. (1994). Understanding face recognition: Caricature effects, inversion and the homogeneity problem. *Visual Cognition*, *1*, 275–311.

Rosenblum, L.D., & Saldana, H.M. (1996). An audiovisual test of kinematic primitives for visual speech perception. *Journal of Experimental Psychology: Human Perception and Performance*, *22*, 318–331.

Schweinberger, S.R., Burton, A.M., & Kelly, S.W. (1999). Asymmetric dependencies in perceiving identity and emotion: Experiments with morphed faces. *Perception and Psychophysics*, *61*, 1102–1115.

Schweinberger, S.R., & Soukup, G.R. (1998). Asymmetric relationships among perceptions of facial identity, emotion, and facial speech. *Journal of Experimental Psychology: Human Perception and Performance*, *24*, 1748–1765.

Schyns, P.G., & Oliva, A. (1999). Dr. Angry and Mr. Smile: When categorisation flexibly modifies the perception of faces in rapid visual presentations. *Cognition*, *69*, 243–265.

Searcy, J.H., & Bartlett, J.C. (1996). Inversion and processing of component and spatial-relational information in faces. *Journal of Experimental Psychology: Human Perception and Performance*, *22*, 904–915.

Sergent, J. (1986). Microgenesis of face perception. In H.D. Ellis, M.A. Jeeves, F. Newcombe, & A. Young (Eds.), *Aspects of face processing*. Dordrecht, The Netherlands: Martinus Nijhoff.

Sergent, J., Ohta, S., Macdonald, B., & Zuck, E. (1994). Segregated processing of facial identity and emotion in the human brain: A PET study. *Visual Cognition*, *1*, 349–370.

Sprengelmeyer, R., Young, A.W., Schroeder, U., Grossenbacher, P.G., Federlein, J., Buttner, T., & Przuntek, H. (1999). Knowing no fear. *Proceedings of the Royal Society of London, B 266*, 2451–2456

Tanaka, J.W., & Farah, M.J. (1993). Parts and wholes in face recognition. *Quarterly Journal of Experimental Psychology*, *46A*, 225–245.

Tanaka, J.W., & Simon, V.B. (1997). Caricature recognition in a neural network. *Visual Cognition*, *3*, 305–324.

Turk, M., & Pentland, A. (1991). Eigenfaces for recognition. *Journal of Cognitive Neuroscience*, *3*, 71–86.

Walker, S., Bruce, V., & O'Malley, C. (1995). Facial identity and facial speech processing: Familiar faces and voices in the McGurk effect. *Perception and Psychophysics*, *57*, 1124–1133.

Wechsler, H., Phillips, P.J., Bruce, V., Soulie, F.F., & Huang, T.S. (Eds.) (1998). *Face recognition: From theory to applications*. New York: Springer-Verlag.

Young, A.W. (1998). *Face and mind*. Oxford: Oxford University Press.

Young, A.W., Hay, D.C., & Ellis, A.W. (1985a). The faces that launched a thousand slips: Everyday difficulties and errors in recognising people. *British Journal of Psychology*, *76*, 495–523.

Young, A.W., Hay, D.C., McWeeny, K.H., Flude, B.M., & Ellis, A.W. (1985b). Matching familiar and unfamiliar faces on internal and external features. *Perception*, *14*, 737–746.

Young, A.W., Newcombe, F., de Haan, E.H.F., Small, M., & Hay, D.C. (1993). Face perception after brain injury: Selective impairments affecting identity and expression. *Brain*, *116*, 941–959.

CHAPTER NINE

Extinction

Robert A. Rescorla
University of Pennsylvania, Philadelphia, USA

INTRODUCTION

Perhaps the two most fundamental findings of associative learning are that
behavior changes when a relation is arranged between two entities and that
this behavior returns toward its prior state when this relation is rescinded.
This is true both in Pavlovian conditioning, in which one arranges for some
stimulus to signal some outcome, and in instrumental learning, in which an
organism's response produces an outcome. Over the years, our understanding
of the nature of the associative changes that occur when such relations are
arranged has become very detailed and our theories extremely sophisticated.
What is surprising is that our understanding of the loss of behavior when
these relations are removed is much more primitive. Even more surprising is
the fact that the study of the phenomenon of extinction has decreased, rather
than increased, over the years. Whereas learning textbooks used to devote
whole chapters to it in the 50s, 60s, and 70s, contemporary texts often give it
only a few pages of discussion, sometimes confined exclusively to the partial
reinforcement extinction effect. Nevertheless, if we are to understand learning processes, it is obvious that we must understand the nature of extinction.

Figure 1 shows a concrete example of changes that occur during acquisition and extinction, taken from a recent experiment in my laboratory. These
data come from a commonly used Pavlovian procedure, conditioned magazine approach situation with rats. The procedure is extremely simple: rats are
placed in a barren chamber that permits the presentation of a variety of

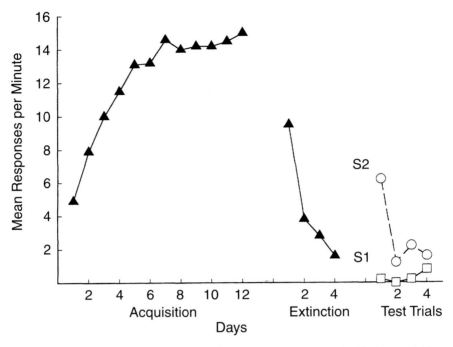

Figure 1. Typical acquisition, extinction, and spontaneous recovery results. During acquisition, rat subjects received pairings of a noise with pellets, resulting in increased rate of magazine approach. When the pellets were removed in extinction responding declined, but recovered when tested after a 1-week delay (S2), compared with immediate testing (S1).

auditory and visual stimuli which can serve as signals, as well as several positive events (e.g., dry pellets and liquid sucrose) which can serve as outcomes. The latter are delivered in a small hole in one wall of the chamber, the magazine, typically after being signaled by one of the auditory or visual stimuli. The animal retrieves the outcome when it is delivered; but as it learns the meaning of the signal it approaches and places its head into the magazine in anticipation of the food, a response that we measure by a photobeam placed just inside the magazine opening. The data in Figure 1 come from an experiment in which a 30-s stimulus signaled the delivery of a pellet at its termination. This arrangement clearly produced a marked growth of anticipatory magazine approach over the eight daily trials. Then the pellets ceased to follow the stimulus, resulting in the loss of that approach response. The question we are interested in answering is why the response deteriorates.

It is important to be clear at the outset that there are likely to be many contributors to the deterioration one observes with extinction. Many things have to be in place for a stimulus to generate responding and the disruption of any one of them could lead to disruption of the response. Some of these are likely to involve performance mechanisms. For instance, if one changes aspects of the situation from training to extinction one would naturally expect to observe stimulus generalization decrement. Indeed, the simple removal of the food itself represents a change that might have such an effect. The effects of such changes are well documented. They are frequently used in the explanation of such intriguing phenomena as the PRE (e.g., Amsel, 1967; Capaldi, 1967).

However, our interest has focused not on deterioration of performance during nonreinforcement per se but rather on the possible changes in knowledge that might take place in extinction. In particular, we have been interested in the changes in the associative learning of the animal that occurs when nonreinforcement is instituted. As a result, many of the experiments described here will involve test presentations of stimuli after they have or have not been subjected to extinction, rather than focusing on the deterioration of behavior during the course of nonreinforcement.

The obvious explanation for the loss of behavior during extinction is that just as the establishment of the contingency led to the development of an association, so the removal of that contingency led to the destruction of that association. But we have known since Pavlov's (1927) original experiments that extinction does not act simply by removing the association established during acquisition. The classic result suggesting that extinction has left some of the original association is spontaneous recovery, an example of which is shown on the far right in Figure 1. That shows responding to the extinguished stimulus when it was tested either immediately after extinction (S1) or after a 1-week delay (S2). As you can see, the stimulus tested immediately after extinction (S1) showed little evidence of responding; but the stimulus tested after a week (S2) showed substantial restoration of the behavior. That recovery occurred "spontaneously", without any further training, leading Pavlov to argue (and others to concur) that not all of original training was destroyed by extinction. Instead he suggested that the effects of training persisted but were masked by some contrary process.

Two comments need to be made about this finding. First, we need to be clear on just what inference one can draw from spontaneous recovery. It shows that extinction did not entirely wipe out the effects of acquisition; but it does not show that those effects remain fully intact. Two features of the result make this apparent. First, notice that recovery, although substantial, is well below the final level at the end of acquisition. This is partly a matter of our impatience. Had we waited a month there would have been more recovery; but no matter how long we wait, we have never seen complete recovery. More to the point, notice that the recovery is primarily confined to the initial test trial; there is rapid re-extinction. Both of these suggest that there may in fact have been some loss of the original learning, as well as partial preservation. But the difficulty is that we do not understand spontaneous recovery well enough to know whether such observations reflect partial loss of the original learning or an incompleteness of operation in the mechanism that allows us to observe the recovery.

The second comment is that spontaneous recovery is only one of a variety of procedures which seem to unmask underlying evidence of the original learning after extinction. Another classic example is disinhibition (the restoration of responding caused by the presentation of a novel stimulus). My own view is that this phenomenon can be safely ignored. There are very few good demonstrations and we have repeatedly been unable to find it in our laboratory. I think it is an example of a phenomenon gaining value by association with another: Textbooks always describe it in the same paragraph as spontaneous recovery. The false impression is thereby given that disinhibition is just as robust and large as spontaneous recovery. Two other unmasking techniques, both of which have received extensive and elegant analysis by Bouton (e.g., 1993), are context change and reinstatement. The first involves testing an extinguished stimulus in a novel context, which can lead to recovery of the response; the second involves simple re-exposure to the reinforcer, unpaired with the stimulus, which again can lead to recovery of responding to the stimulus. All of these procedures involve post-extinction manipulations that lead to some restoration of responding, they all do so only partially, and they all have the same limitations as spontaneous recovery of not allowing us to estimate the degree to which the original learning remains intact.

PROCEDURES FOR MEASURING ASSOCIATIVE STRENGTH

In order to assess more carefully the state of the association after extinction, my laboratory has recently been applying two techniques we began using some years ago for the general study of associations, the outcome-devaluation and the selective-transfer technique. These have proven to be very powerful for studying the presence and strength of associations in other contexts. Consequently, they seemed promising for conducting an analysis of the associations in extinction.

We first exploited the outcome-devaluation procedure for the study of associations in the acquisition of instrumental learning (Colwill & Rescorla, 1985). I will here describe a Pavlovian application focusing on extinction. The idea of the devaluation technique is to identify the strength of an association between a stimulus and an outcome by manipulating the state of that outcome after conditioning has taken place. If the observed behavior to a stimulus is dependent on its association with a valued outcome, then manipulations which change that value should also change the response to the stimulus. That turns out to be a highly useful analytic tool.

Figure 2 shows an example of a rather complicated application intended

Phase 1	Ext	Phase 2	Devaluation	Test
S1--O1	S1--	S1--O3		S1
S2--O2	S2--	S2--O3		S2
			O1--LiCl	
S3--O1		S3--O3		S3
S4--O2		S4--O3		S4

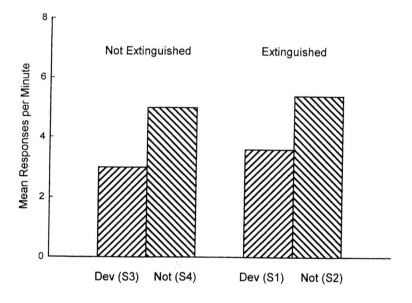

Figure 2. Design and results of a typical devaluation study. Initially four stimuli (S1-S4) were conditioned using two different outcomes (O1 and O2). Then one pair of stimuli was extinguished and all four stimuli paired with a third outcome. Prior to testing, one outcome was devalued by pairing with lithium chloride (LiCl). Devaluation of an outcome reduced responding to stimuli paired with it whether or not the stimulus had been extinguished. (After Rescorla, 1996. Reprinted by permission of The Experimental Psychology Society.)

to use that tool to investigate extinction (Rescorla, 1996). The experiment began with Pavlovian magazine conditioning of four stimuli (S1-S4, two visual and two auditory), using two different outcomes (O1 and O2, counterbalanced as solid pellets and liquid sucrose). The animals naturally came to respond with increased activity in the food magazine during all four stimuli. The intention was eventually to change the value of one of those outcomes by pairing it with the toxin, LiCl. We knew that a few such pairings make O1 lose all of its attraction for the animal. More importantly, we knew that stimuli such as S1 and S3, which had been conditioned by such an outcome, show marked deterioration in their ability to evoke a response, compared with stimuli such as S2 and S4, whose outcome has not been devalued. But the question of this experiment was whether this effect of outcome-devaluation would also apply to stimuli that have received extinction. Consequently, prior to devaluation, one pair of stimuli (S1 and S2) received extinction whereas the other pair (S3 and S4) did not.

Our goal was to compare the size of the difference in responding to the extinguished S1 and S2 with that in responding to the nonextinguished S3 and S4. However, the extinction will, of course, lead to virtually complete loss in responding to S1 and S2. That would make it impossible to look for a reduction in behavior to S1 as a function of its outcome being devalued. Consequently, in this experiment we artificially raised the level of responding without retraining with the original outcomes. We simply paired all stimuli, extinguished or not, with a third outcome (O3, polycose), in order to bring behavior to a common level prior to devaluation. We knew from other experiments (examples of which are described later) that such a procedure does not by itself destroy the original associations. But it does give us a good level of performance from which to compare extinguished and nonextinguished stimuli.

After all of this, we tested the four stimuli. The results for the nonextinguished S3 and S4 are shown to the left in Figure 2. Those results confirm the prior observation that O1 devaluation selectively depressed responding to the S3 with which it had been paired. To the right in Figure 2 are the data from the extinguished stimuli, S1 and S2. In that case too, we see selective depression of responding to S1, the stimulus which had been paired with O1. Indeed, neither the eye nor statistical procedures can discern any difference between the results of the two sets of bars.

These results from the devaluation procedure thus have two implications. First, they suggest that we may have a detection technique that we can apply to both extinguished and nonextinguished stimuli so as to measure the strength of their outcome-based associations. Second, the present application of that technique suggests a strong answer to the question of what is left of the original learning after extinction: everything. The analogous experiment performed on four instrumental responses has yielded the same answer (Rescorla, 1993).

The second technique that we have found useful in much the same way is a selective-transfer technique. If one uses an outcome to condition a stimulus, either as a Pavlovian CS or as an instrumental discriminative stimulus, then that stimulus takes on the ability to transfer its control over responding to new responses—but only insofar as those new responses have themselves been rewarded by the same outcome as that used with the stimulus (e.g., Colwill & Rescorla, 1988; Kruse, Overmier, Konz, & Rokke, 1983). In experiments with multiple stimuli, responses, and outcomes, such selective transfer implies the presence of the associations with the shared outcome. One can then use that transfer to measure the learned associations with and without the intrusion of an extinction operation.

Figure 3 illustrates the logic and results from an instrumental learning experiment recently conducted in my laboratory. In this experiment, rats were first trained to make two instrumental responses, R1 and R2 (counterbal-anced as lever press and chain pull), each earning a particular outcome, O1 or O2 (counterbalanced as a pellet and liquid sucrose). Then they received dis-criminative training with two different stimuli, S1 and S2, a light and a noise. A third response, R0 (nosepoking) was present during this latter training. Nosepoking was never rewarded in the absence of a stimulus; but when the light come on nosepoking led to O1 and when the noise came on it led to O2. Eventually the animals were given a transfer test in which the light and the noise were presented when the animals also had available to them the transfer responses, R1 and R2. We knew that in such a test we could expect S1 to transfer successfully to R1 and S2 to do the same to R2, based on their shared outcomes. However, prior to the transfer test, we extinguished one of the stimuli, S1. The question of interest was whether this extinction would dimin-ish the ability of S1 to transfer selectively to R1, thereby indicating that some diminution of the S1-O1 association had occurred in extinction.

The bottom portion of Figure 3 shows the results of that transfer test. Shown to the left are the results for the original response, nosepoking, which was also available during the transfer test. These data show that our extinc-tion had been very successful—responding was much greater during the nonextinguished S2 than during the extinguished S1. To the right are shown the results for the transfer responses. The leftmost set of three bars shows responding prior to the presentation of the nonextinguished S2 and then on the response that had previously earned the same outcome as S2 (i.e., R2) and on the response that had previously earned a different outcome from S2 (i.e., R1). It is clear that for the nonextinguished S2, the same-outcome response occurred more frequently than the different-outcome response. This verifies what we knew from other experiments—that the S-O associations support transfer. It provides a measure of the strength of the S-O association in the absence of extinction. The rightmost set of bars show the comparable data for the extinguished stimulus, S1. Again the stimulus selectively promoted the response with which it shared an outcome. In fact the pattern looks remark-ably like that for the nonextinguished stimulus. In this, and in many other such experiments, we continue to find just as good transfer after extinction as

R train	Cond	Ext	Test
R1--O1	S1: Ro--O1	S1: Ro-	S1: Ro, **R1**, R2
R2--O2	S2: Ro--O2		S2: Ro, R1, **R2**

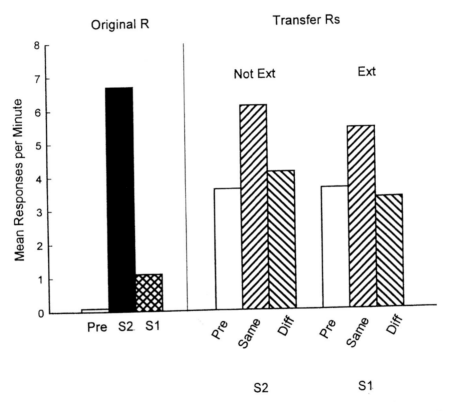

Figure 3. Design and results of a transfer study. Initially rats received instrumental training of two responses (R1 and R2) with two different outcomes (O1 and O2). Then they received discriminated instrumental training in which two different stimuli (S1 and S2) signaled that a third R (R0) would produce those different outcomes. Following extinction with one stimulus, both stimuli were presented at a time when the animal might make either the original response or either of the transfer responses or the original response. Results showed that, although S1 was markedly reduced in producing its original response, it continued to transfer to other responses with which it shared an outcome. (From Rescorla, 2001 with permission from Lawrence Erlbaum Associates, Inc.)

we find with no extinction. Indeed, again, it looks as though extinction had no impact on the associations with the outcomes.

Like the devaluation results, these transfer results have both methodological and theoretical implications. First, they leave us with another excellent tool for assessing the state of associations. Neither devaluation nor transfer depends on unmasking operations and so they can be applied to both extinguished and nonextinguished behavior—in such a way that allows us to compare the state of the associations in a relatively quantitative way. Second, they suggest that extinction may leave all of the original learning intact.

Results such as these suggest that we look elsewhere than changes in the S-O association for any associative changes that might be occurring in extinction. Despite the repeated finding that behavior deteriorates with extinction, these tests suggest that the outcome-based associations remain very strong.

WHAT LEARNING OCCURS IN EXTINCTION?

This, then, leaves two important questions: First, what is the nature of the learning that occurs in extinction? If there is new learning that is preventing exhibition of the old learning, what is its character? Second, what is the nature of the interaction between the original learning and that which occurs during extinction? Why does the latter prevent exhibition of the former? The remainder of this chapter addresses each of these in turn, beginning first with the issue of what is learned in extinction. Then it points to some implications of the resulting analysis for associative learning in general.

Response involvement in extinction

We can gain some insight into what is being learned in extinction by looking at the events that actually occur. In a typical extinction experiment, a stimulus comes on, the animal makes its conditioned response, and then the US fails to occur. It is the last that has led some to suggest that during extinction the animal develops an association with the "no-US". It is, of course, true that no US occurs, but using the term "no-US" sounds suspiciously as if we are trying to pretend that some stimulus did in fact occur, one that forms associations in the same manner as a real stimulus. What this suggestion fails to mention is that despite the absence of a US, there is not an absence of a response. In addition to the occurrence of the conditioned response itself, the failure of the US to occur at a time when it is expected normally leads to a substantial emotional response on the part of the animal. So the salient events that occur in extinction really consist of a stimulus the experimenter presents and then two responses on the part of the animal—the conditioned responses and a post-trial emotional response triggered by the absence of the

US. That is, one might expect responses rather than stimulus events to be major players in extinction.

Recent experiments in our laboratory have been exploring various implications of the thought that responses might be intimately involved in the learning underlying extinction. Two implications seem especially straightforward: Extinction should show some response-specificity and the amount of extinction should be a function of the amount of responding during nonreinforcement. Recent data in our laboratory provide evidence for both of these propositions.

Consider first the implication that extinction ought to be relatively specific to the responses which occur during extinction. Some hint of support for that implication arose in an experiment described previously, Figure 3. In that transfer experiment, the animal was trained to nosepoke in presence of two stimuli and then received extinction with one. As a result of that extinction, the stimulus lost the ability to elicit that nosepoke response; however, it retained its ability to transfer to other responses. Extinction was carried out when only the nosepoke was possible and, of the responses which the stimulus could control, only it was depressed. Delamater (1996) saw a similar pattern in a comparable experiment with Pavlovian magazine approach behavior. He found that a stimulus paired with food in a Pavlovian fashion not only evoked magazine approach but also transferred its control to other responses associated with that outcome. He also found that extinction of the Pavlovian CS diminished the likelihood of the magazine response that is allowed to occur during extinction, but did not diminish transfer to other responses that were absent during extinction. That is, he observed response-specificity of the action of extinction.

In some recent experiments, we have attempted to pursue this idea by deliberately manipulating which of several equally possible responses actually occurs during the extinction of a stimulus. Figure 4 shows the design and results of one such experiment. The idea was to take advantage of the transfer procedure to guarantee that one, rather than another, of two responses that a stimulus might possibly evoke in extinction was actually made. The experiment began by training the animal to make two different instrumental responses, lever press and chain pull, to earn pellets. Then Pavlovian conditioning was carried out with two different stimuli, S1 and S2 (light and noise), each signaling the occurrence of response-independent pellets. We knew from the sort of transfer experiments described above that if we presented the S1 or S2 while either the lever or chain was available, then it would augment the occurrence of that response. So the idea of this experiment was to extinguish both S1 and S2, but to arrange for one of the response possibilities to be available during one stimulus and the other response to be available during the other stimulus. The question was whether the impact on extinction of S1 and S2 would be relatively specific to the response that

Trans R	Cond	Ext	Test
R1--P	S1--P		S1: R1, R2
		S1: R1-, S2: R2-	
R2--P	S2--P		S2: R1, R2

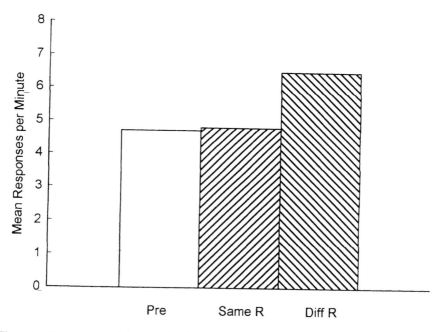

Figure 4. Response specificity of extinction. Rats first received instrumental training in which two different responses (R1 and R2) both earned pellets (P). Then they received Pavlovian conditioning in which two different stimuli (S1 and S2) signaled pellets. Extinction of S1 and S2 was then conducted with one response available. A test of both responses in both stimuli showed that each stimulus failed to augment the response which had been present during its extinction (same R) but continued to augment the other response (Diff R).

occurred in its presence. To assess that, after extinction we tested the animal with each stimulus when each response was available. Notice that with such a design both stimuli have been nonreinforced and both responses have been nonreinforced in the presence of one of the stimuli. So the question was whether the impact of extinction with a stimulus would be specific to the response that occurred during that extinction.

The bottom portion of Figure 4 shows the results of that experiment. That figure displays the responding on the test during the pre-CS period, when neither stimulus was presented, and then the responding when the stimulus extinguished with that response was presented, and finally the responding when the stimulus that had been extinguished with the other response was presented. It is clear that, although a stimulus had lost the power to evoke the response that was present during its extinction, it retained the ability to evoke the other response. That is, there was some degree of response specificity to the extinction. This is consistent with the possibility that extinction at least partly involves learning not to make a particular response to a stimulus. Supporting results have been obtained in a variety of more complicated procedures (e.g., Rescorla, 1997a).

A second implication of the thought that responses are involved in extinction is that manipulations which increase the frequency of responding during extinction should increase the amount of learning that takes place. This is actually quite an old idea. One example of its statement is inherent in Skinner's (1938) notion of reflex reserve. Indeed, one may argue that one of the most successful generalizations that we have about extinction is that the greater the responding that occurs during extinction the greater the learning that it produces. Two examples of manipulations that affect responding during extinction and which have consequences for the amount of learning occurring are shown in Figure 5. That figure displays some quite old results collected by Holland and Rescorla (1975) using a general activity measure. They come from two Pavlovian conditioning experiments in which a stimulus signaled the delivery of food and the anticipatory general body activity was measured. After initial training in which a tone signaled a pellet, all animals received extinction. However, for half the animals in each figure, the pellet outcome was temporarily devalued during the extinction, either by satiation (top panel) or pairing with an illness inducing high-speed rotation (bottom panel). Notice that both of these ways of devaluing the outcome produced a depression in the likelihood of responding during the stimulus. Then in both cases the outcome had its value restored, either by redeprivation or by extinction of the aversive conditioning, and the stimuli were again tested. It is clear that when extinction was carried out under circumstances that temporarily depressed responding, it was much less successful—more responding in extinction produced more permanent change as measured in a subsequent test.

Figure 5 (opposite). Effect of different levels of responding during extinction. Rats initially received pairings of a tone with food, resulting in increased general activity. The tone was then extinguished at a time when the animal was sated or not (top panel) or the food had been devalued or not (bottom panel). Both manipulations reduced responding during extinction. After the animal was redeprived or the devaluation extinguished, testing of the tone showed less responding for the animals which made more responses during extinction. (After Holland & Rescorla, 1975. Copyright © 1975 by the American Psychological Association. Reprinted with permission.)

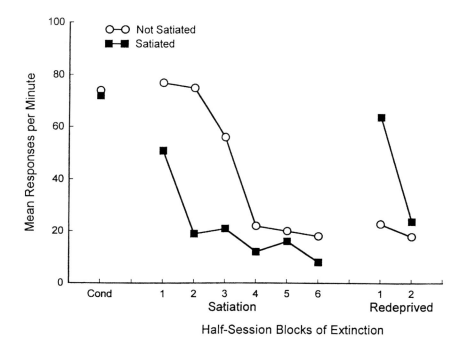

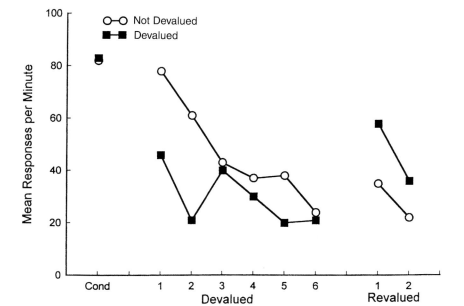

231

Recently, we have investigated the importance of level of responding during extinction using an associative means to augment responding during a stimulus. It is well known that many conditioning preparations show evidence of summation: The concurrent presentation of two stimuli, both of which have been paired with a US, results in an augmentation of responding compared with that which either stimulus will evoke alone (e.g., Pavlov, 1927; Rescorla, 1999). One question of interest is whether such augmented responding, induced by the presence of another excitor, will produce especially large decrements in a target stimulus undergoing extinction.

Figure 6 shows an example of one magazine approach experiment using this procedure during extinction of a noise stimulus (Rescorla, 2000a). Each of four groups of rats received Pavlovian conditioning of the form A +, B −, X +, where A and B were two visual stimuli and X was white noise. Then all animals were subjected to extinction. For three of the groups, X was repeatedly nonreinforced; but this was done either with X alone, X in the presence of the excitatory A, or X in the presence of the nonexcitatory B. The fourth, control group received no stimulus presentations during this phase of the experiment. Then, all animals received separate test presentations of X in order to see how much depression X had undergone as a result of its nonreinforcement in these various contexts.

The far left-hand points of the figure show that the level of responding to X at the end of conditioning was comparable across the groups. The next three points show the level of responding to X during extinction. Not surprisingly, there was no responding in the group receiving no stimulus. Only moderately more surprising was the fact that the concurrent presence of A augmented responding during X, relative to that seen when X was presented alone or in compound with a relatively neutral B. Of course, behavior declined during nonreinforcement.

The results of most interest, from the test of X alone, are shown in the far right in Figure 6. In that test, responding to X alone was the mirror image of the responding observed in extinction. The group with no extinction showed the most test responding, the group which had received extinction of X in the presence of A the least responding, and the other two groups were intermediate. Of particular interest, of course, is the observation that nonreinforcing X in the presence of the excitatory A led to greater loss in responding to X than did simply nonreinforcing X on its own. These data confirm the claim that responding is an important component of extinction, consistent with the idea that learning not to respond is involved.

Consequently, one answer to the question of what associative changes occur in extinction is that the animal learns about the particular response that it makes. Apparently, at least some of the learning involves not making a particular response.

Acq	Ext	Test
A+, B-, X+	AX-	X?
A+, B-, X+	BX-	X?
A+, B-, X+	X-	X?
A+, B-, X+	0	X?

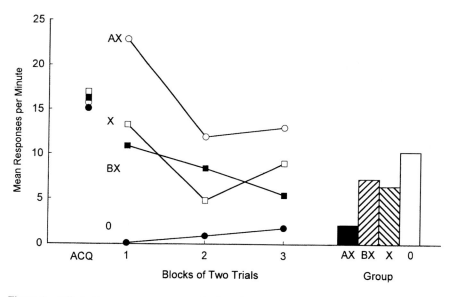

Figure 6. Effect of concurrent presence of other stimuli on extinction. Rats received magazine approach conditioning with three stimuli (A, B, and X) and then were extinguished by presenting X with the excitatory A, the neutral B, alone, or not at all. Then all animals were tested for responding to X. Responding is shown in terms of the increase in responding (CS-pre CS rate) at the end of acquisition (ACQ), during extinction, and during the test. A augmented responding during extinction, resulting in less final responding to X in the test. (After Rescorla, 2000a. Copyright © 2000 by the American Psychological Association. Reprinted with permisssion.)

Interaction of associations acquired in acquisition and extinction

A second issue is raised by the observation that extinction seems to leave the original learning intact and superimpose a new learning: What is the nature of the interaction between the two kinds of learning? If the animal preserves its outcome-based associations and superimposes on them some response-based learning, how do the two interact?

One attractive possibility is that when the animal learns successive, and perhaps contrary, bits of information about a stimulus, then it retains both but selectively retrieves one or the other depending on the circumstances of the test. In the case of training followed by extinction, it has been thought plausible that the animal exits from the extinction phase retrieving the most recent experience and so does not respond. In effect, extinction leads to the animal's putting the information acquired on the back burner and preferentially using the more recent extinction information. This idea is consistent with a number of results in human memory and animal conditioning.

However, there is a perhaps simpler possibility that also deserves exploration: that the animal continues to use all the information that it has learned about a stimulus on each of its occurrences, but that the performance generated is a product of the total learning. This differs from the first account in imagining that following extinction the original learning continues to make its full contribution to performance. It is not put on the back burner for later possible retrieval but rather continues to have its full force in all cases of current performance.

Again the transfer results shown in Figure 3 provide a hint that this is not an entirely silly possibility. In that experiment a stimulus which had been trained to control nosepoking, and then extinguished on that response, was tested for transfer to other responses following that extinction. The relevant result is that in the same session during which the stimulus failed to evoke nosepoking it also transferred successfully to new target responses; indeed that transfer was as substantial as was the transfer from a nonextinguished stimulus. That is, in the same session (indeed on the same trials) in which the stimulus showed evidence of substantial decrement in controlling the original response, it showed evidence that it fully used the original learning in transferring to new responses. This certainly encourages the thought that extinction does not require the selective nonretrieval of the original learning.

Recently we have been doing experiments intended to comment more explicitly on this possibility. Two examples will be described here. The first is from simple extinction in a Pavlovian preparation and the second is from what one might think of as a counterconditioning procedure in instrumental training.

The idea of the extinction experiment was to assess responding to a CS which has two associations—one which has been trained and extinguished and one which has been simply trained. The question we wanted to answer was whether the S-O association subjected to extinction continues to contribute as much to performance as does the S-O association not subjected to extinction. The top portion of Figure 7 shows the way in which this was addressed. Responding was examined to a compound consisting of two stimuli, S1 and S2, which had a history of pairing with different outcomes.

Experimental Treatment

Cond	Ext	Test
S1--O1	**S1-**	**S1S2**
S2--O2		

Assumed Associative Structure

S1--O1	S1--|R	S1--O1
S2--O2		S2--O2
		S1--|R

Figure 7. Design and associative structures presumed to result in an experiment assessing the continued contribution of S-O associations after extinction. Initially two different stimuli (S1 and S2) were paired with different outcomes (O1 and O2). Then S1 was extinguished and the S1S2 compound was tested. If the animal accumulates its total knowledge, the final test of the compound engages three associations, the originally trained S1-O1 and S2-O2 associations plus some outcome-independent, response-specific association with S1.

Prior to the compound test, one of those stimuli had been extinguished and one had not been extinguished. We knew both that these stimuli would summate to produce responding to the compound and that extinction of S1 would reduce that summation. The question is whether that reduction in summation really represents a reduction in the degree to which the extinguished stimulus brings its S-O association or represents the fact that it continues to bring that S-O association but also brings its response-based decremental process. The idea was to find whether the S1-O1 association contributed less than the S2-O2 association by asking whether devaluing the two outcomes had a differential effect. Presumably, if the S1-O1 association is being poorly retrieved, devaluing O1 would have less impact than devaluing O2.

That result would not be expected on the basis of a second possibility. According to that possibility, both associations continue to contribute but responding to the compound is reduced because of a response-based depressive process controlled by S1. One rendering of that view is shown at the bottom of Figure 7. The S1-O1 and S2-O2 associations established in conditioning persist through extinction, during which a response-based depressive process is conditioned to S1. In the compound test, both of the original associations contribute equally; consequently, one would expect equivalent impacts of their devaluation.

Figure 8 shows the results of this experiment. The two sets of bars to the

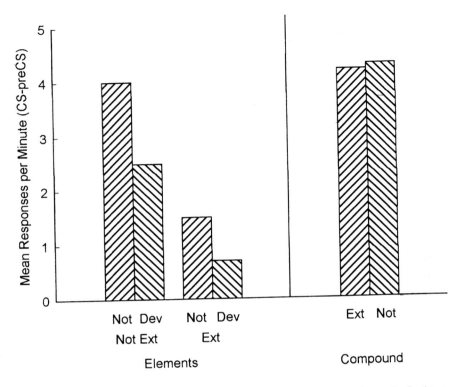

Figure 8.   Results of the experiment whose design is shown in Figure 7. Prior to the final test, one of the outcomes, either that paired with the extinguished or the nonextinguished stimulus, was devalued. Testing of elements showed reduced responding in the stimulus being extinguished and in the stimulus whose outcome had been devalued. But responding to the compound was the same whichever outcome had been devalued.

left show responding to the individual stimuli after conditioning and devaluation. It is clear that both extinction and devaluation depressed performance. The nonextinguished S2 showed more responding than the extinguished S1 whether or not their outcomes had been devalued. But the question of most interest is the level of responding to the compounds, one of which received devaluation of the outcome associated with its extinguished stimulus and one of which received devaluation of the outcome associated with its nonextinguished stimulus. Those results are shown in the right-hand set of bars in Figure 8. It is clear that it made little difference which outcome had been devalued. That suggests that devaluation had a similar impact on the two—the result one would expect if the extinguished stimulus continued to make its full contribution to performance.

A similar observation can be made for decremental procedures other than extinction. Indeed, the argument may be more transparent in such cases.

One other decremental procedure we have been investigating involves the substitution of one outcome for another equally valued outcome. For instance, one can train an animal that a response first produces O1 and then that the same response instead produces a different outcome, O2. In fact, one can think of such a procedure as successively doing training and extinction of the response with O1, but also superimposing O2 during the extinction phase. It is then of interest to ask about the relative contributions of the R-O1 and R-O2 associations to performance. Is the first-learned association put on the back burner, with the second being currently retrieved, or are they both fully operative?

Figure 9 shows the results from one experiment that supports the latter interpretation (Rescorla, 1995). These are data from a devaluation experiment in which responses were sequentially trained with two outcomes after which they received devaluation of either the first-earned, the second-earned, or neither outcome. It is clear that devaluation depressed responding, whichever outcome had been devalued. Moreover, with equivalent training, the effect of devaluation was equivalent. The same sort of result occurs with two

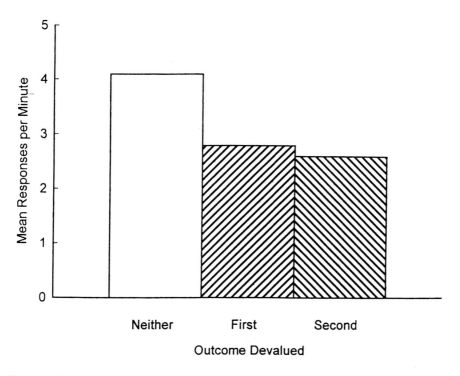

Figure 9.   Results of instrumental responding when the response had first earned one outcome and then another and then either the first-earned, the second-earned, or neither outcome was devalued. (After Rescorla, 1995. Reprinted by permission of The Experimental Psychology Society.)

Pavlovian stimuli presented in sequence with different outcomes. These results encourage the view that as the animal acquires new information, it does not discard or even temporarily devalue old information, but rather accumulates all of that information and continues to allow it to govern current performance.

These results suggest that extinction involves learning about responses and that that learning is superimposed on the original outcome-based associations in such a way as to allow those associations to continue to contribute fully to current performance.

MORE GENERAL IMPLICATIONS

This analysis of the associative changes in extinction has a variety of implications for other conditioning preparations. Two will be mentioned here, both of which can be thought of as paradoxical: that one should be able to obtain stable Pavlovian associations between S and O even in the absence of a relation between them and that one should be able to obtain spontaneous recovery even in the absence of the decrement which normally occurs in extinction.

Stable Pavlovian conditioning without a relation

Some years ago I suggested a control procedure for conditioning called the "truly random control" (Rescorla, 1967). The idea behind that control was that if one wanted to assess the degree to which arranging a relation between a CS and US was essential to obtaining conditioning, then one needs to make a comparison with a procedure in which no relation is arranged between the two. This has commonly been implemented by arranging for complete randomness in the presentation of the US, regardless of whether or not the CS is present.

Over the years this suggested control has come in for its share of criticism, some of it leveled by me. One disconcerting observation is that sometimes this procedure can produce substantial changes in the ability to the CS to evoke a response, especially early in its application. Figure 10 shows an example taken from a recent magazine approach experiment we did. That figure displays the degree to which a noise stimulus presented in a random relation to pellets produces an increase in the magazine approach response (relative to that of the baseline) as a function of number of days of application of the procedure. It is clear that there is an initial increase in responding during the stimulus, followed by a gradual return to its having no effect. Some authors have suggested that this initial increase means that the so-called control procedure in fact produces conditioning. Of course that inference is by no means forced, since the change in behavior could well be nonassociative in character. Indeed, it is just that possibility which necessitates the use of a control

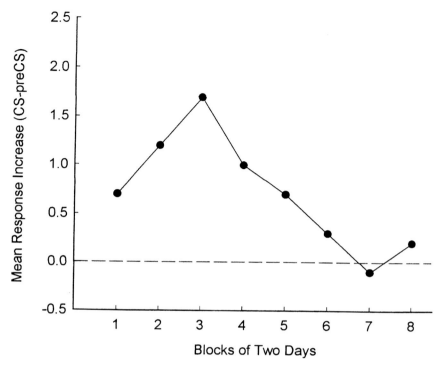

Figure 10. Magazine responding to a stimulus which bore a random relation to a pellet outcome, over the course of exposure to the treatment. The stimulus first increased responding and then lost the ability to do so. (After Rescorla, 2000b. Reprinted by permission of The Experimental Psychology Society.)

procedure to begin with. If we could take all changes in behavior as indicating conditioning, we would need no controls. But even if this early performance does indicate some initial conditioning, one could take solace in the observation that the responding goes away with more extensive exposure, perhaps suggesting that the procedure is especially useful with extensive application. Indeed, just this interpretation of results like these has been made by many contemporary contiguity theories, such as the Rescorla-Wagner (Rescorla & Wagner, 1972) model. Those theories view the early joint occurrences of CS and US that happen "accidentally" as producing initial excitatory conditioning. But that conditioning is then lost as a result of the conditioning that is also occurring to the background, which allows the animal to detect that this CS is not in fact informative. In effect, those theories have said that any initial conditioning would be removed by continued application of a random procedure. Since such theories have argued that the random procedure could well be used as an extinction procedure after deliberate excitatory conditioning, they have been comfortable with the assertion that the same thing is happening here. Any excitatory conditioning that occurs early would be removed by its functioning as an extinction procedure with additional experience.

However, the analysis of extinction given here suggests that any solace we obtain from this reasoning is in fact misplaced. The prior results suggest that when we remove a relation we do not destroy the original learning but merely prevent its showing in behavior. That argument has been made explicitly for extinction and replacement of one outcome by another, but it also applies to arranging a random relation. Indeed, Delamater (1996) has shown that exposure of an excitatory CS to a random relation leaves the excitation in place, in the same way as does extinction. If that is right, then this loss that is seen in the random procedure does not in fact represent loss of the excitation but rather a failure of it to appear in that particular response measure. That is, one could use the detection procedures described earlier to show that even after extensive exposure the random procedure generates an association.

Figure 11 shows some recent data which encourage that thought

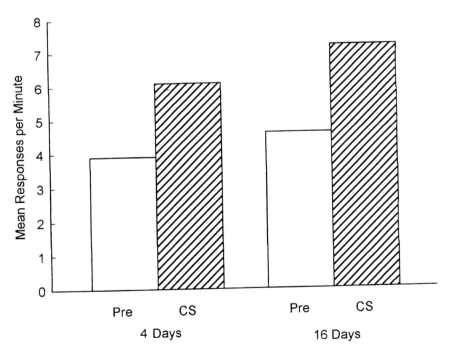

Figure 11. Transfer test results for a stimulus given a random relation to food. Testing occurred after 4 and 16 days of exposure to the schedule. Despite the loss of magazine-approach responding (displayed in Figure 10), the stimulus continued to transfer to a response which had earned the pellet. (From Rescorla, 2000b. Reprinted with the permission of the Experimental Psychology Society.)

(Rescorla, 2000b). These data are from a test of transfer of the noise stimulus whose acquisition performance was shown in Figure 10. The left-hand set of bars shows the results of transferring the noise to a lever which had earned pellets after 4 days of noise conditioning (when the magazine responding was high). The successful transfer agrees with the magazine results in suggesting the presence of an association. Although not shown here, it turns out that the transfer is selective, occurring only to responses which have earned that particular US. Such data are among the first to really force the interpretation that the increase in responding is associative in character. Even more interesting are the results shown in the right-hand set of bars, from animals tested after 16 days of exposure to the random treatment (by which time the noise no longer increased magazine approach). Those data show that transfer based on a shared outcome continued to be just as strong after extensive training. That is, the association remained in place despite the loss of the original response. This clearly disagrees with the comforting interpretation that contemporary theories have made of this procedure and will force us to be even more skeptical of this control procedure.

The second paradoxical prediction involves a return to the topic with which this chapter began: spontaneous recovery. The preceding argument is that as the organism goes through a sequence of consequences for a stimulus, it retains what it learns at each stage and adds on what it learns in the next stage. Consider, then, the situation in which a stimulus is followed first by one outcome and then by another. As noted previously, one way to look at the pairing with the second outcome is that it constitutes two treatments: a reinforcement with the new outcome and an extinction on the old outcome. If that is the case, one might well expect what one observes, that by using equivalent outcomes there is no change in the overall level of performance. However, one might also expect that underlying the equivalence of performance reflects a complex associative structure, consisting of both the S-O1 and S-O2 associations as well as the kind of decremental process that one observes in conventional extinction. On one account that would be the addition of an inhibitory process involving the response. If that is the case, then one should also observe the same kind of recovery from that inhibitory process that one observes in extinction. That is, one should observe spontaneous recovery of responding after successively training with two outcomes—even though one sees no decrement from which to recover.

Figure 12 provides some relevant evidence (Rescorla, 1997b). That figure shows the results for two stimuli, both of which were originally paired with one outcome and then another outcome. But for one of those stimuli (S1) that second pairing came well before the test (allowing for recovery), whereas for the other (S2) it came immediately before the test. Responding to the two stimuli was similar at the end of training with both the first and the second outcome. However, in the test, there was much greater responding during the

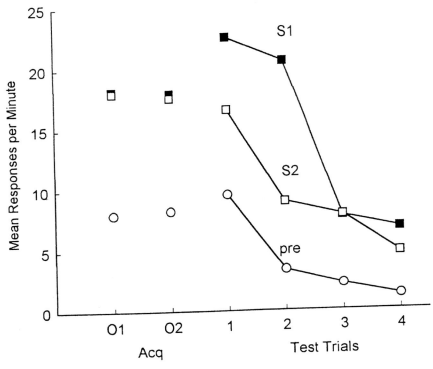

Figure 12. Spontaneous recovery of a stimulus paired first with one outcome (O1) and then with another (O2). Magazine approach responding is shown at the end of each training phase and then for a stimulus tested immediately (S2) or after a 1-week delay (S1). (After Rescorla, 1997b.)

stimulus with the opportunity to show recovery—just as one might expect. This is consistent with the possibility that response-based decremental processes can occur even in procedures that do not result in observable loss of responding.

CONCLUSION

So what is the upshot of all this? It seems to me that these results suggest a number of important conclusions: First, they confirm in a highly detailed way the suspicion which many of us have had for a long time, that extinction does not wipe out original learning. Indeed, the use of the transfer and devaluation techniques allows us to document the full preservation of that learning despite extensive extinction. Notice that this conclusion could not be reached on the basis of more conventional results, such as spontaneous recovery. Second, they suggest that the decrement is achieved by the superimposition of a response-based depressive process that is independent of the identity of the original outcomes. This conclusion comes both from the response-specificity of extinction and from the observation that the amount of learning that occurs during extinction depends on the amount of responding. Consequently, extinction involves new and different processes, other than those seen in acquisition. Third, these results suggest that the original learning not only persists unscathed but that it continues to govern current performance to the same degree as it would had no extinction been given. That is, the original and depressive process appear to be engaging in an ongoing competitive process that does not involve differential biasing of retrieval. Fourth, the analysis presented here has a variety of general implications. Some of those involve phenomena close to the heart of an associationist, the results of random treatments and spontaneous recovery. But, as usual with learning experiments, there are also implications for other fields. For instance, these results suggest that clinical applications involving attempts to remove behavior by extinction are unlikely to remove the underlying initial learning. The best that can be hoped for is to suppress responding. Similarly, our findings have important implications for the neurobiological study of learning. They suggest that new and different processes will be involved in extinction. Any neurobiological understanding that does not include extinction will be seriously deficient.

Finally, these results suggest that extinction clearly has interesting properties with important implications. There remains much to be learned about it. I hope that the research reported here will help encourage others to refocus attention on the phenomenon.

ACKNOWLEDGEMENTS

The research reported in this chapter was made possible by a series of generous grants from the National Science Foundation and the National Institute of Health.

REFERENCES

Amsel, A. (1967). Partial reinforcement effects on vigor and persistence. In K.W. Spence & J.T. Spence (Eds.), *The psychology of learning and motivation, Vol. 1* (pp. 1–65). New York: Academic Press.

Bouton, M.E. (1993). Context, time, and memory retrieval in the interference paradigms of Pavlovian learning. *Psychological Bulletin, 114*, 8–99.

Capaldi, E.J. (1967). A sequential hypothesis of instrumental learning. In K.W. Spence & J.T. Spence (Eds.), *Psychology of learning and motivation, Vol 1* (pp. 67–156). New York: Academic Press.

Colwill, R.M., & Rescorla, R.A. (1985). Post-conditioning devaluation of a reinforcer affects instrumental responding. *Journal of Experimental Psychology: Animal Behavior Processes, 11*, 120–132.

Colwill, R.M., & Rescorla, R.A. (1988). The role of response-reinforcer associations in creases throughout extended instrumental training. *Animal Learning and Behavior, 16*, 105–111.

Delamater, A.R. (1996). Effects of several extinction treatments upon the integrity of Pavlovian stimulus-outcome associations. *Animal Learning and Behavior*, *24*, 437–449.

Holland, P.C., & Rescorla, R.A. (1975) Second-order conditioning with food unconditioned stimulus. *Journal of Comparative and Physiological Psychology*, *88*, 459–467.

Kruse, J.M., Overmier, J.B., Konz, W.A, & Rokke, E. (1983). Pavlovian conditioned stimulus effects upon instrumental choice behavior are reinforcer specific. *Learning and Motivation*, *14*, 165–181.

Pavlov, I.P. (1927). *Conditioned reflexes*. Oxford: Oxford University Press.

Rescorla, R.A. (1967). Pavlovian conditioning and its proper control procedures. *Psychological Review*, *74*, 71–80.

Rescorla, R.A. (1993). Preservation of response-outcome associations through extinction. *Animal Learning and Behavior*, *21*, 238–245.

Rescorla, R.A. (1995). Full preservation of a response-outcome association through training with a second outcome. *Quarterly Journal of Experimental Psychology*, *48B*, 252–261.

Rescorla, R.A. (1996). Preservation of Pavlovian associations through extinction. *Quarterly Journal of Experimental Psychology*, *49B*, 245–258.

Rescorla, R.A. (1997a). Response-inhibition in extinction. *Quarterly Journal of Experimental Psychology*, *50B*, 238–252.

Rescorla, R.A. (1997b). Spontaneous recovery after Pavlovian conditioning with multiple outcomes. *Animal Learning and Behavior*, *25*, 99–107.

Rescorla, R.A. (1999). Summation and overexpectation with qualitatively different outcomes. *Animal Learning and Behavior*, *27*, 50–62.

Rescorla, R.A. (2000a). Extinction can be enhanced by a concurrent excitor. *Journal of Experimental Psychology: Animal Behavior Processes*, *26*, 251–260

Rescorla, R.A. (2000b). Associative changes with a random CS-US relationship. *Quarterly Journal of Experimental Psychology*, *53B*, 325–340

Rescorla, R.A. (2001). Experimental extinction. In R.R. Mowrer & S. Klein (Eds.), *Handbook of contemporary learning theories* (pp. 119–154). Hillsdale, N.J: Lawrence Erlbaum Associates Inc.

Rescorla, R.A., & Wagner, A.R. (1972). A theory of Pavlovian conditioning: Variations in the effectiveness of reinforcement and nonreinforcement. In A. Black, & W.F. Prosy (Eds.), *Classical conditioning II* (pp. 64–99). New York: Appleton-Century-Croft.

Skinner, B.F. (1938). *The behavior of organisms*. New York: Appleton-Century-Croft.

CHAPTER TEN

Nonvisual navigation based on information about self-motion

Roberta L. Klatzky
Carnegie Mellon University, Pittsburgh, PA, USA

Jack M. Loomis and Reginald G. Golledge
University of California at Santa Barbara, USA

NAVIGATION BASED ON LANDMARKS AND SELF-MOTION

Vision, hearing, and, to some extent, olfaction provide information about a traveler's current position and orientation even when the traveler has no prior estimate, such as might be gained from self-movement. If the traveler has an external or internal map of the environment, visual, auditory, and olfactory information from known locations (landmarks) within the map can be used to determine current position and orientation, using triangulation (based on bearings), trilateration (based on distances), a combination of the two, and other techniques (Gallistel, 1990).

Lacking direct cues to location and orientation in space, a navigator can alternatively use knowledge about self-motion. There are two types of information about self-motion. Allothetic information involves sensing of the environment whereas idiothetic information does not, arising solely within the traveler's body. Allothetic information includes optical flow, acoustic flow, light and heat information about the sun's direction, and directional information from wind. Idiothetic information (sometimes called proprioception) derives from muscles, tendons, joints, and the vestibular sense, along with efference copy of commands sent to the musculature. This paper is concerned with the mechanisms by which people make their way in space using idiothetic cues to self-motion.

Why, one might ask, should we consider how people might navigate in such restricted circumstances? Nonvisual navigation occurs more often than one might think (although the additional exclusion of information from sound, wind, and sun is perhaps extreme, and such information is excluded here largely for experimental and conceptual control). Here are some of the situations in which nonvisual navigation might occur.

- A person who has low vision or is blind must find his or her way in space.
- A traveler has normal vision, but the visual field is obscured, for example, by fog or smoke, which preclude its use.
- Vision is occupied by sources irrelevant to navigation, for example, reading a display screen or a book.
- A person navigates within an imagined or remembered environment.

PATH INTEGRATION vs. CONFIGURAL ENCODING

Even in the absence of visual information, as we will describe, people can remember their path through the environment, update their position with respect to environmental features, and choose novel paths to reach targeted locations. In some instances, such as blind walking along an indirect path to a previously viewed target, performance is quite accurate (see review by Loomis, Klatzky, Golledge, & Philbeck, 1999).

The remainder of this chapter focuses on a distinction between two kinds of navigation based on self-motion—-path integration and configural encoding. Path integration refers to updating one's position based on information about velocity or acceleration. Configural encoding is the construction of a representation of one's path of travel, from which one's position can be determined. Thus both of these mechanisms can be used to navigate; however, they differ conceptually in several ways, as outlined in Table 1.

Navigation by nonvisual path integration is conceived of as an essentially continuous process of updating. Idiothetic information conveys a navigator's movement through the world by means of velocity or acceleration signals. From these, the navigator computes, moment by moment, her location and orientation relative to a surrounding world. If asked to indicate a location in the environment, by report or by traveling to it, she can directly retrieve the required bearing and distance. Thus the traveler can quickly turn toward and ambulate to the desired target.

A particular version of path integration, called the homing-vector model, assumes further that the navigator maintains a minimal representation indicating the path of travel back to an origin; the history of the traveled path is discarded (Fujita, Loomis, Klatzky, & Golledge, 1990; Müller & Wehner, 1988).

Now consider the second navigation process, configural encoding. If one

TABLE 10.1
Features distinguishing path integration and configural encoding

Path integration	Configural encoding
Update location and orientation from velocity or acceleration signal; respond by readout	Form representation of travelled path; respond by computation on representation
Perceptual	Cognitive/imaginal
From moment to moment, update position relative to environmental location(s); no need to retain path	From segment to segment, encode path representation; no need to update position
Generally faster, more accurate response to location query	Generally slower, more error-prone response to location query
Errors can arise from perceiving environment, updating, or response execution	Errors can arise from configural encoding or response computation/execution
Low capacity demands during response computation; supports navigation to off-path landmarks; may not support reproduction	High capacity demands during response computation; may not support navigation to off-path landmarks; supports reproduction
Hypothesis: Promoted by perceptually based representation (e.g., prior vision, rich imagery); strong cues to movement (e.g., self-control of locomotion)	*Hypothesis:* Promoted by minimal access to anchor locations or reference frame; weak cues to movement (e.g., guidance by others)

thinks in terms of a perceptual-to-cognitive dimension to describe spatial processing, configural encoding is more cognitive than path integration, and relatively error prone. Sensory input concomitant with motion is used to encode a description of the path. The position and orientation of features of the environment, most notably the origin of travel, need not be updated from one moment to the next. Instead the navigator can maintain a representation of the path alone. In order to indicate the position of an environmental feature, its bearing and distance must be computed from the record of the path.

At this point, let us consider path integration in more detail. Path integration is a process by which an organism perceives cues to velocity or acceleration arising from movement, calibrates them relative to spatial displacement, and integrates the spatial changes so as to continuously update a representation of self-position and orientation. The cues are ideothetic in origin, that is, from kinesthetic or vestibular sources. Calibration of the cues with respect to space allows a representation of position and orientation to be updated and potentially remembered over a period of time. There is no requirement that the organism performing path integration retain a record of the path of travel; what is maintained at any moment is the location relative to a set of reference destinations (potentially, only the origin). The representation is set within an environmental frame of reference defined by those destinations, which need not be on the traveled path.

For a simplified model of path integration, consider a city-block traveler, who makes only right-angle turns to the left or right. The traveler receives a velocity signal, giving the linear or rotational spatial displacement for some ideothetic measurement unit (e.g., kinesthesis from a forward leg swing). Suppose the traveler starts at at the origin of a Cartesian coordinate system, facing along the y axis, or North. He travels for 3 units at a constant displacement per kinesthetic unit, arriving at a new position, (0, 3). To keep track of orientation as well as position, the traveler must have an additional coordinate for orientation, thus: (0, 3, North). The person then makes a rightward turn and travels for 4 units, arriving at (4, 3, East). The record of position in the coordinate system has been achieved without visual signals, given the velocity input and the binary information about direction of rotation.

The 90-degree turn situation is actually a restricted version of the more general case, where we allow the traveler the ability to make turns at any angle. Now, if the person is at (0, 3, North) and turns rightward some angle ø, some process must do the equivalent of decomposing the turn into its sine and cosine components, adjusting the x- and y-coordinates of the system accordingly, and replacing the orientation coordinate (North, in the above example) with the angle ø.

A traveler using configural processing does not represent his or her position in a coordinate system that is external to the path of travel, but rather, records the path of travel itself. Under this model, the city-block traveler who has walked 3 units, turned right, and then walked 4 units more would not have the coordinate representation (4, 3, East). Rather, she would have the representation (3, right, 4), indicating the lengths of linear segments and the directions of turns. A traveler walking a similar path but allowed turns other than right angles, would have a vector (3, ø, 4), where ø is the angle of the first turn, and so on. With configural encoding, the traveler maintains a list of path components, legs and turns, until computation of some trajectory is desired. The computation might be put off until the list length is substantial, or positional updating might occur as quickly as at the end of each new segment. Unlike path integration, however, positional updating by configural encoding is not done on an essentially continuous basis; it is delayed at least until the end of the current straight segment (leg) or turn.

To summarize, a person who is performing path integration knows from moment to moment where she is in space with respect to environmental locations and can read out a response; a person performing configural encoding knows from moment to moment what displacing segments he has executed and can compute a response by some more cognitive process. The path integrator may be able to reconstruct the path, although memory is not guaranteed. The configural encoder can compute where he is in space from the path description; however, the computation of spatial position and orientation is not necessarily done from moment to moment and may be substantially delayed.

Sources of error

When navigation is performed by means of path integration, errors can arise because the starting representation of the environment is inaccurate, because updating is fallible, or because, even knowing the target direction and location, the execution of the desired response is faulty. In particular, if subjects miscalibrate their movements, that is, show fallible updating, the effects differ according to whether the error applies to distances or angles. If angles are systematically rescaled, then the internal representation of the path's shape is changed. This will lead to both turn and distance error, if the desired response is executed perfectly. If the miscalibration is of leg length but not angle, then the shape of the path is maintained, but the path as a whole is rescaled.

When rescaling is the only source of internal error, observable errors may or may not occur, depending on how responses are regulated (Loomis et al., 1993). If the navigator uses path integration to regulate the response in the same way as the outbound path, then the response trajectory will have errors that perfectly compensate for the errors in outbound navigation. The navigator may think the target is only half the distance away it actually is, but he or she will also underestimate the return journey, so that the response will be only half as long as the navigator thinks it is. There will then be no visible errors.

Configural encoding requires that the traveler encode the segments of legs and turns in the outbound path, determine a desired response by some computational process, and then—as in path integration—execute the response. Errors in configural encoding can arise, then, because the path is misencoded, because the computation of the relationship to the environment is incorrect, or because the execution of the desired response is faulty.

As in the case of path integration, it is possible for configural encoding errors to be matched by misencoding of the response, so that the errors cancel. For example, if the subject follows two legs of a right triangle with values 3 and 4, the hypotenuse should have distance 5, but if the values are scaled to only half, the subject will represent it as a 1.5, 2 right triangle. His intention is to return to the origin by walking 2.5; however, the same misencoding of the return trajectory will lead to a response of 5.0, which is objectively correct although the subject thinks it is only 2.5. There will be no error.

However, our data suggest that error will be observed, for two reasons. The data suggest, first, that when a response is desired, it is computed and then executed by a process other than configural encoding, so that the encoding error is not canceled by a commensurate error in the response. Second, the data suggest that misencoding the path does not take the form of simple proportional rescaling. Consider, for example, that if there has been proportional error in estimating outbound distances but not turns, the response turns will be executed perfectly, but the distance error will have the same proportion as the miscalibration. From experimental data, it is easy to spot such pure rescaling errors. When the value of the response distance is regressed against the value of the correct distance, the slope of the regression will indicate the rescaling proportion, and the intercept will be zero. Typically, it is not. We will return to the importance of the nonzero intercept later.

One might think that the computation of the response is a particularly demanding aspect of navigation by configural encoding. If the navigator has encoded an extensive sequence of legs and turns, the inference process needed to compute a trajectory to a target location is trigonometrically very complex and demanding of memory. Computational errors may not be as high as one might expect, however. First, the configural updating model says that computation of a traveler's location may be delayed, but not that it *must* be delayed to the end of outbound travel. The traveler could update self-position after every segment, for example, to minimize memory demands. We describe later a model of the errors in the task of completing a triangle, which assumes no error whatever in computing the homeward response. Rather, the major source of error is found to be in encoding the path segments. For this reason the model is called the encoding-error model.

Information-processing demands of the two processes

As described earlier, path integration and configural encoding have different information-processing demands. Configural encoding is demanding of memory, since the path representation must be retained until a computation of the desired response is done. That representation might be subject to regularization or assimilation to a prototype. The response computation from configural encoding presumably requires more capacity than a simple read-out, as occurs during path integration. The differential demands of path integration and configural encoding during the processing of the outbound path are not known. In this section we describe some experiments that have used measures and manipulations related to information-processing characteristics of the two navigation processes.

Lindberg and Gärling (1981) directly addressed the capacity requirements for nonvisual (and visually guided) navigation, by having subjects learn a multisegment path while a concurrent task (counting backwards) was used to limit cognitive capacity. The results indicated that the concurrent task during outbound travel shifted subjects' processing from path integration to configural encoding. When there was no concurrent task, response latency was essentially independent of path complexity (number of segments), suggesting that the response was available immediately at the end of the path. Not only did the concurrent task increase errors in distance and angle estimation, it also caused response latency to increase with path complexity. Subjects appeared, then, to use one process (path integration) when concurrent demands were low and another when demands were high. Clearly the shift in processing indicates that path integration demanded central capacity—hardly surprising for the task of voluntarily encoding a complex path. The evidence for a shift to configural encoding, given high-capacity demands during outbound travel, suggests it might have used less capacity (in this experimental setting) than path integration during the outbound phase, but at a cost of greater capacity during computation of the homeward trajectory at the end of travel.

May and Klatzky (2000) compared the effects of two distractor activities during nonvisual navigation—articulatory suppression (repeating a phrase over and over) and counting backward. The distractor activity was introduced during a pause in the outbound path. (Locomotor interference tasks were also investigated but are not relevant to the current discussion.) When the navigation task was to replicate the length of a single-leg path, a period of counting yielded no higher error than one of rote verbalization. However, in a triangle-completion task, where the interpolated activity occurred during the second leg of the triangle, there was higher constant error after the counting distractor than after verbal suppression. One possible interpretation of these results is that the same process was used with the simple (one-leg) and more complex (triangular) paths, and interference became evident with greater complexity. Another interpretation is that two different processes were used—path integration with the single-leg path and configural encoding with the triangular one—and only configural encoding was interfered with by counting backwards.

Loomis et al. (1993) found that in a nonvisual path completion task, where subjects walked back to the origin of travel, the latency to initiate the response increased with path complexity, even without a concurrent task on the outbound path. The Loomis et al. data suggest that subjects used configural processing even when there were no competing capacity demands. Below we review a number of factors that might have promoted encoding of the path configuration in this case.

Another measure that can be used to differentiate between information-processing characteristics of the two navigation mechanisms is performance on replicating or reproducing a path. If subjects use path integration to monitor the location of the origin, but fail to store a representation of the outbound path, then they should not be able to reproduce it. In a study reported by Loomis et al. (1993), subjects were given unexpected trials in which they had to reproduce an outbound path rather than complete it (the more usual response). They performed quite well at remembering the path's gross configural properties (number of segments, crossovers, etc.). In the same study, the latency to initiate the completion response increased with path complexity, indicating configural processing was used to compute the direction and distance home on the trials where this was the required response. Thus both the completion and reproduction trials indicated that configural encoding was used to navigate.

Further experiments are needed to assess the information-processing characteristics of navigation mechanisms. What is needed is both control of which process is used (or at least, a means of inferring which is used, post hoc) and a variable that manipulates the information-processing demands. For example, adding a memory load at the time of the response (cf. during the execution of an outbound path) might be expected to affect performance more when configural encoding is used than when path integration is used. Another prediction is that people performing path integration should find it easier to navigate to off-path landmarks in their environment than people who have encoded the path configuration. However, the critical experiments to test these predictions are difficult to perform, since loading the task so that it taxes one process may lead to the other's being used exclusively. For example, if one wants to test people's ability to walk to off-path landmarks, one must teach them about the spatial environment in which the path is set, and this appears to promote the use of path integration and not configural encoding. We discuss the factors that motivate one process or another in the next sections.

WHICH PROCESS IS USED WHEN? A HYPOTHESIS

Extant data suggest that both path integration and configural encoding can be invoked by people attempting to navigate without vision. They are invoked, however, under different circumstances, and with different degrees of success. We suggest that navigation by path integration is promoted when there is a rich environmental representation at the outset of travel and strong cues to self-motion. Lacking a representation of informative environmental features, and with weaker cues to self-motion, a traveler is more likely to use configural encoding as a means of path integration.

Conditions that promote path integration

That path integration is promoted by a rich perceptual representation before travel is suggested by experiments in which people attempt to walk to a perceptually designated starting point. Loomis, Da Silva, Fujita, and Fukusima (1992) reviewed several studies in which people attempted to walk to a visually designated target over a range of up to approximately 25 meters. Performance was highly accurate when people viewed the target, then closed their eyes and walked directly to it. This suggests that they could keep a record of their distance from the target and update it while walking, as the path integration model proposes.

But, one might ask, why should walking to a visually previewed target, without vision, constitute path integration rather than configural encoding? After all, the configural-encoding model says that people encode a path and then compute a response and execute it. It might be argued that people use the visual preview to encode the configuration (i.e., length) of the target path, then execute a path of the computed length with little output error. An argument against such pre-computing of the response from visual preview comes from Fukusima, Loomis, and Da Silva (1997; see also Loomis et al., 1992), who showed that a person asked to walk on an oblique path past a visual target could continuously orient his or her arm toward it, indicating that the person represented the momentary changes in the target direction while walking. Yet another type of evidence comes from the finding that people can walk to a perceptually previewed target indirectly, on a path they could not plan. Philbeck, Loomis, and Beall (1997) had people view a target; then, rather than walk directly toward it, walk forward an unknown distance, after which they were signaled by the experimenter to turn and walk to the target. They performed as well with this indirect walking as with direct walking. Note that the foregoing argument about pre-computing the response path could not apply when the indirect condition was required, because subjects did not know where they would be asked to turn toward the target.

Moreover, Loomis, Klatzky, Philbeck, and Golledge (1998) found the same equivalence between direct and indirect walking when the target was signaled by an auditory cue. What is particularly important about this study is that in the auditory case, both the direct and indirect paths produced considerable error—people tended to underwalk to relatively distant targets and to overwalk to near ones. This error was made not only when they walked directly to the targets but also when they walked indirectly, indicating that the error arose in initial perception of the target location, not in updating its position over time.

As a whole, these results indicate that when a target location is cued by a strong perceptual signal, and people who are denied vision can initiate their response quickly, they can update their position relative to the target as they travel. This occurs under circumstances that preclude their pre-computing a path of travel based directly on the signal itself (i.e., the circumstances require updating spatial position). It is still possible that the task might be performed by configural encoding. For example, the subject might encode the response path as a configuration, determine the current end location of that configuration from time to time, and compare it to the location of the previewed target. However, this type of closed-loop process requires intermittent updating and comparison to the target location, and it does not explain how people could point continuously to the target as they walk.

The high level of accuracy with a visually previewed target has further implications. Since the sources of error under path integration are in initial representation of the environment, updating while navigating, and executing the desired response, it indicates that people can update their position and execute the response trajectory with little error. When the initial perceptual signal provides an accurate representation of target location, as occurs with vision but not with an auditory cue, then accurate updating and response execution produce a low level of systematic overall error.

Rieser and associates (e.g., Rieser & Frymire, 1995; Rieser, Frymire, & Berry, 1997; see Rieser, 1999) have reported a number of findings suggesting that even relatively complex environments and paths can still support path integration. In these studies, the subject walked a path of some number of segments (e.g., 1, 3, or 5) and then estimated the distance and/or direction of the origin or attempted to walk to it. Rieser and Frymire (1995) compared performance in this task under three conditions—when the subject (1) had no information about the environment, (2) imagined objects within surrounding space, or (3) remembered objects within the environment. Performance improved over these three conditions. Rieser (1999) suggested that with remembered or imagined environments, subjects could use an "environment-centered" representation, within which they updated their location and orientation even without optical input. Without such information, subjects operated within a "virtual ganzfeld" and used a "person-centered representation," that is, they updated in terms of body positions. The environment-centered updating appears to be equivalent to path integration. The person-centered updating is more ambiguous, because subjects could use kinesthesis from changing body positions either as input to path integration or to configural encoding. If path integration was used across all three conditions in Rieser and Frymire's experiment, the results suggest that the stronger the representation of environmental features, the better it was performed.

Another finding that points even more directly to nonvisual path integration (Rieser et al., 1997) comes from a situation where subjects visually previewed an environment with features distributed over several azimuths. They then traveled a path without vision and performed the task of pointing back to the origin. They performed better when the environment had nearby

questions). Working memory is therefore a form of short-term memory (Baddeley, 1986) but, interestingly, other short-term memory tasks show little effect of aging. Simple digit span, for example, declines only slightly with age, and the relatively good recall of the final few items in a list (the recency effect) is unaffected by aging. All of these results are illustrated and discussed in recent reviews of the area (Balota, Dolan, & Duchek, 2000; Craik & Jennings, 1992; Zacks et al., 2000).

The scientific problem is therefore to give a principled account of these strengths and weaknesses. Why is it that some forms of memory hold up well with advancing age whereas other forms apparently decline in efficiency? One obvious candidate for such a principled account is the memory systems viewpoint proposed by Endel Tulving and his colleagues (Tulving, 1983; Tulving & Schacter, 1990). There are five separate memory systems in Tulving's scheme; the perceptual representational system (PRS), working memory, procedural memory, semantic memory, and episodic memory. Is it simply the case that some of these systems are vulnerable to the effects of aging whereas others are not? This possibility works well for some systems but not so well for others. The findings that perceptual memory performance and procedural memory performance are little affected by age fits the idea that these systems are relatively unaffected by aging. In some ways semantic memory also appears to be immune to the effects of aging, in that general knowledge and vocabulary are well maintained in older adults (Salthouse, 1982). However, retrieving well-known *names* is one of the major difficulties reported by older people, and such names are presumably part of semantic memory. Working memory is a system that is quite sensitive to aging but, as described earlier, some "short-term memory" tasks such as digit span show little change with age. It seems therefore that *some* working memory tasks decline whereas other quite similar tasks do not, and this does not fit well with a memory systems account. Finally, aging produces variable effects on episodic memory tasks. Free recall, paired-associate learning, and context recall are all vulnerable to aging (Craik & Jennings, 1992) but recognition memory is not (Craik & McDowd, 1987). Again, it appears that some tasks within a system are affected by aging whereas others are not.

Another possibility is that it is not *memory systems* as such that are sensitive or invulnerable to the effects of aging, but rather that certain types of *processing operations* become more difficult with advancing age, regardless of the "system" they are in. I have previously suggested (Craik, 1983, 1986) that memory tasks vary in the amount of "self-initiated processing" they require. The basic idea is that successful retrieval necessarily involves specific mental operations that are partly induced by the task and the external context, and partly rely on boot-strapping operations generated by the rememberer. The two factors of "self-initiated processing" and "environmental support" are complementary—less environmental support means that more self-initiated processing must be deployed. As examples, recognition memory involves relatively good environmental support, given that the item itself is re-presented, whereas free recall is not well supported by outside cues, so more self-initiated processing is required. The further suggestion (Craik, 1983, 1986) was that whereas there are large individual differences in the ability to muster and deploy self-initiated processes efficiently and effectively at any age, older people may be particularly deficient in this respect, and this form of processing inefficiency may be linked to age-related impairments in "executive control" and "working memory" (Craik & Jennings, 1992; Jennings & Jacoby, 1993). These deficiencies in turn may be caused by age-related impairments in frontal lobe functioning (Craik, Morris, Morris, & Loewen, 1990; West, 1996). The general scheme is shown in Figure 1.

From this perspective, it need not be surprising that some tasks within one memory system hold up with age whereas others in the same system decline. It is the *type of processing* that is important, not the system. Thus episodic recall is impaired but episodic recognition holds up well with age, because the latter benefits from greater amounts of environmental support and therefore requires less self-initiated activity. I have also suggested (Craik & Bosman, 1992) that the relevant support for appropriate retrieval operations can come from well-learned schematic information—"schematic support"—and this may be the reason that general semantic knowledge remains available to older people but highly specific information, such as names, does not. In general, it appears that aging affects those tasks that require substantial amounts of novel processing, both at encoding and at retrieval, whereas tasks that are well supported either by past learning or by the external environment hold up well across the adult years.

One way of characterizing the age-related losses in self-initiated activity and in executive control is as a reduction in *processing resources* (e.g., Craik & Byrd, 1982). The idea is that attentional capacity (or "mental energy") declines with age, presumably as a consequence of biological changes, and this age-related loss results in impairments of encoding and retrieval processing. Possible candidates for this "reduction in processing resources" include disrupted blood flow allocation, inefficient glucose utilization by cortical neurons, or a reduction in the amount of cortex available to carry out appropriate mental activities.

One line of research that supports the processing resource hypothesis involves dual-task processing in young adults. The general finding is that when young adults are given a secondary task to perform while simultaneously attempting to encode or retrieve information in a memory task, their performance resembles that of older adults working under full attention conditions (Anderson, Craik, & Naveh-Benjamin, 1998; Craik, 1982; Jennings & Jacoby, 1993). As an illustration, Table 1 shows data from the free recall and cued recall experiments by Anderson et al. (1998). Participants

Age-related memory loss a function of:

a) PERSON unable to execute controlled processing (self-initiated activity; frontal inefficiency)

b) Task requires self-initiated processing

c) ENVIRONMENT fails to compensate (via cues, context)

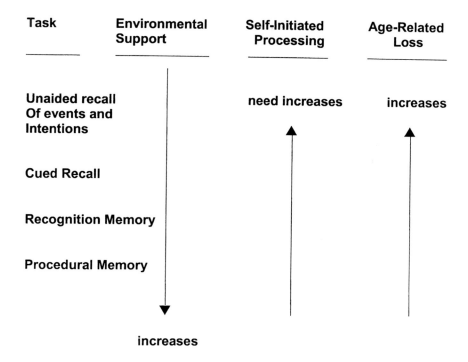

Task	Environmental Support	Self-Initiated Processing	Age-Related Loss
Unaided recall Of events and Intentions		need increases	increases
Cued Recall			
Recognition Memory			
Procedural Memory			

increases

Figure 1.   Scheme illustrating the relations among environmental support, self-initiated processing, and age-related memory loss.

encoded lists of unrelated words for later free recall, or word pairs for later cued recall, either under full attention conditions or while also performing a concurrent reaction time (RT) task. The data shown in Table 1 are the proportions recalled in the memory task, and RTs on the concurrent task, under conditions of full attention (i.e., the task performed on its own) or under divided attention (DA) conditions, when participants were instructed to give primary emphasis to the *other* task. That is, memory scores are shown for the

TABLE 11.1

Proportions recalled from two memory tasks (proportion correct) and reaction times (RT, in ms) from a secondary task as a function of age and attentional condition (data from Anderson et al., 1998).

Experimental condition	Memory		RT	
	Young	Old	Young	Old
Free recall				
Full attention	.82	.53	408	570
Divided attention[a]	.51	.28	530	815
Cued recall				
Full attention	.85	.49	404	510
Divided attention[a]	.50	.25	502	745

[a] Divided attention scores are for the conditions in which the *other* task was given major emphasis at the time of encoding.

condition in which attention was divided at encoding and performance on the concurrent RT task was emphasized; RT scores are shown for the condition in which attention was divided at encoding and performance on the memory task was emphasized. Under these conditions there is a striking similarity between the scores of young adults in the DA condition and older adults in the full attention condition, supporting the notion that when attentional resources are reduced, young adults' performance approximates that of older adults. In turn, this finding gives some credibility to the argument that attentional resources decrease in the course of normal aging. One further advantage of studying dual-task performance in young people as a way to simulate the effects of aging is that attention can be manipulated independently at encoding and retrieval. The results of a number of studies (Anderson et al., 1998; Craik et al., 1996; Naveh-Benjamin, Craik, Gavrilescu, & Anderson, 2000) have shown that DA at encoding has a much greater deleterious effect on memory than DA at retrieval, and this finding suggests that a substantial part of the age-related memory deficit is attributable to less effective encoding or initial learning, owing to a reduction in processing resources.

The similarity between the effects of aging and DA in young adults is also shown in several recent neuroimaging studies. It is now well established that effective encoding operations are associated with activation in the left prefrontal cortex (Kapur et al., 1994; Tulving, Kapur, Craik, Moscovitch, & Houle, 1994), and it might therefore be expected that impoverished encoding conditions would be marked by a reduction in cortical activation in this area of the brain. Such reductions have in fact been demonstrated, both in the case of older adults (Cabeza et al., 1997; Grady et al., 1995) and in the case of divided attention in young adults (Iidaka, Anderson, Kapur, Cabeza, &

Craik, 2000; Shallice et al., 1994). A study by Anderson and her colleagues (2000) has shown directly that DA in young participants results in much the same pattern of frontal activation as is found in older adults working under conditions of full attention. This similarity between the effects of DA and the effects of aging lends support to the argument that the changes in processing that accompany aging may be characterized as a loss of processing resources, and that this reduction in resources (especially at the time of encoding) is at least one major factor underlying age-related deficits in memory performance.

In summary, then, my position on why some kinds of memory performance decline with age has been that normal aging is accompanied by a reduction in processing resources (which may be thought of also as "attentional capacity" or "working memory capacity"), and that certain memory operations (e.g., encoding, conscious recollection of items and their contexts) require such resources to operate effectively. This viewpoint is supported by the similarity between the effects of aging and the effects of DA on young adults, and also by the results from neuroimaging studies. Finally, the detrimental effects of resource reduction can be offset by enhancing schematic and environmental support, notably at the time of retrieval.

CHANGES TO THIS POSITION

In previous articles (e.g., Anderson & Craik, 2000; Craik, 1986, 1994) I have tended to stress the encoding side of age-related memory deficits, but this may have been a mistake—or at least an unbalanced view. If older people have fewer attentional resources, and this in turn leads to inefficient encoding, then different ways of supporting or boosting the encoding process should result in a disproportionate benefit to older participants. Typically, however, this is not the case; the more usual finding is that enhanced encoding results in equivalent benefits to younger and older adults (Light, 1991). One dramatic example of such parallel effects is provided in a study by Rönnlund and his colleagues (Rönnlund, Nyberg, Bäckman, & Nilsson, 2002). Previous experiments have shown that memory for simple commands such as "point to the ceiling" and "pick up the book" can be increased by having the participant actually perform the actions; these are so-called "subject-performed tasks" or SPTs, compared with "verbal tasks" or VTs. If SPTs boost encoding, the present question is whether this manipulation will enhance performance more for older than for younger adults. The results of Rönnlund and colleagues (2002) are shown in Figure 2. The beneficial effect of SPTs is clearly equivalent for participants ranging in age from 35 to 80 years, and this result is in line with previous research (Nilsson & Craik, 1990).

A second illustration of the same point was provided by data collected several years ago by Jan Rabinowitz, Brian Ackerman, and myself and

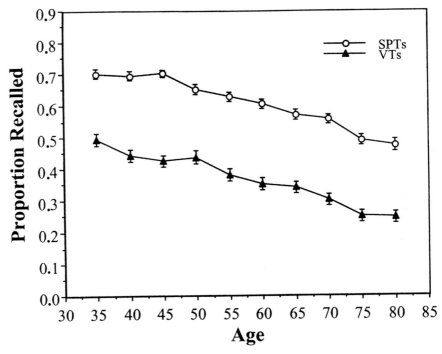

Figure 2. Proportions of phrases recalled by adults of different ages as a function of whether the phrases were presented as "subject-performed tasks" (SPTs) or "verbal tasks" (VTs) (after Rönnlund et al., 2001).

reported in a chapter by Craik and Byrd (1982). In this experiment, stimuli were presented either as words or as pictures of the objects represented by the words. After presentation of these lists there was a recall test for all items followed by a recognition test in which all the recognition stimuli were words, even when the items were presented initially as pictures. Table 2 shows first that recall was boosted by picture presentation relative to word presentation, but equally for younger and older participants (by 0.19 in both cases). Second, when the recognition test is considered, the age-related deficit is essentially eliminated in the condition in which picture presentation is paired with a recognition test. It therefore appears that the age-related memory deficit is not reduced by encoding manipulations alone, or indeed by retrieval manipulations alone (word encoding and recognition test), but only by improving *both* encoding and retrieval.

A further reservation concerns the type of processing that older adults achieve at the time of encoding. Given the well-established relation between deep, semantic processing and later memory (Craik & Tulving, 1975), it seemed attractive to postulate that the poorer memory performance of older

TABLE 11.2
Mean proportions recalled and recognized as a function of age and type of material
(Craik & Byrd, 1982)

Age group	Recall		Recognition	
	Words	*Pictures*	*Words*	*Pictures*
Young	.33	.52	.73	.84
Old	.17	.36	.63	.83

people is attributable to an age-related impairment in semantic processing (Craik, 1977; Craik & Simon, 1980; Eysenck, 1974). Recent work on the false memory paradigm (Roediger & McDermott, 1995) has cast some doubt on this suggestion, however. In this paradigm, word lists containing high semantic associates of a nonpresented critical word are presented for later recall or recognition, and the finding is that the critical word is recalled and recognized almost at the level of words that were actually presented. Apparently there is considerable semantic generalization to the representation of the critical word. If older adults exhibit impaired semantic processing they should be less vulnerable to such illusions of memory, but in fact several studies have now shown that they are at least as susceptible as young adults to this type of error (Balota et al., 1999; Benjamin, 2001; Kensinger & Schacter, 1999). One possible resolution of this discrepancy between previous suggestions and current data is that older people do not suffer from a *general* impairment of semantic processing but rather their semantic processing is less precise, less distinctive, and less episodically based (Craik & Simon, 1980). This notion is elaborated in a later section.

In addition, whereas Craik (1986, 1994) gave heavy emphasis to age-related inefficiencies of *encoding*, it now seems clear that age-related *retrieval* problems play at least as large a part in the overall picture (see also Burke & Light, 1981; Light, 1991). The evidence comes from a variety of sources. First, retrieval of proper names becomes increasingly difficult with advancing age, even names that are well known and were well encoded many years earlier. Second, experiments using the dual-task procedure have shown that retrieval processing is generally more "costly" than encoding processing in terms of the deleterious effects on the concurrent task (Craik et al., 1996; Johnston, Greenberg, Fisher, & Martin, 1970), and these costs are substantially higher in older than in younger adults (Anderson et al., 1998; Craik & McDowd, 1987), suggesting that retrieval is especially effortful for the older group. Third, the work from my own lab showing that environmental support is differentially helpful to older people, leading to a reduction in age-related memory deficits, is typically supported at *retrieval* (Craik, 1983; Craik, Byrd, & Swanson, 1987; Craik & McDowd, 1987). This result suggests again that unsupported retrieval processes are in fact vulnerable to the effects of aging. Finally, the recent work of Jacoby and his colleagues (e.g., Hay & Jacoby, 1999; Jennings & Jacoby, 1993, 1997) strongly implicates problems of conscious recollection in age-related memory difficulties.

In summary, retrieval deficits are clearly implicated in the problems that older people have in remembering. Of course this need not mean that encoding processes are free from problems; both sets of processes are likely to be affected by aging. The next section describes some initial work in my lab that points to a slightly different encoding problem that may also play some part in the overall picture.

ANOTHER TYPE OF ENCODING PROBLEM?

The levels of processing framework proposed by Craik and Lockhart (1972) suggests that memory performance can be understood largely in terms of the qualitative type of processing that the event underwent at the time of its initial encoding. Deeper (that is, more elaborate and meaningful) processing is associated with higher levels of subsequent memory, provided that the retrieval environment is compatible with the qualitative way in which the information was encoded (Craik, 1979; Tulving & Thomson, 1973). This notion suggests in turn that variables such as aging and divided attention, which are associated with poor memory performance, have their effect by reducing the depth or degree of elaboration achieved at the time of encoding. There is some evidence to support this suggestion (Naveh-Benjamin et al., 2000) but also some evidence implying that it is not the whole story.

This latter point emerges from pilot work conducted in my lab by Jill Kester, Aaron Benjamin, and myself. We argued that if the degree of semantic elaboration is equated between conditions of full and divided attention, subsequent memory should also be equivalent for the elaborated items. That is, divided attention would have its effect by reducing depth and elaboration of encoded items, but later memory would reflect the degree of elaboration actually achieved. However, Kester, Benjamin, and I carried out an experiment in which participants rated how meaningful pairs of presented words were to them. A long series of unrelated word pairs were presented, and participants attempted to form a meaningful relation between members of each pair and indicated their personal degree of meaningfulness on a subjective scale of 0–5, where 0 indicated no meaningful connection and 5 indicated a very meaningful connection. Two groups of participants performed this task, one group under full attention conditions and the other under divided attention conditions; in the latter condition participants saw the word pairs on a screen and simultaneously performed an auditory digit monitoring task. Following the first rating phase, participants were given an unexpected memory task (under full attention for both groups) in which the first word of each

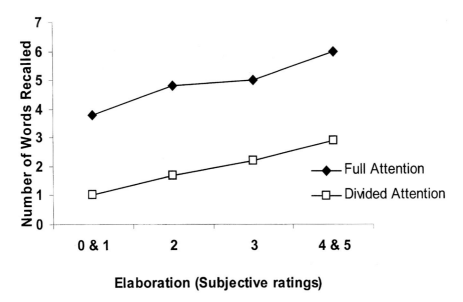

Figure 3.   Mean numbers of words recalled as a function of elaboration and attentional condition (adapted from Craik & Kester, 2000).

pair was presented as a cue for its paired second word. Our expectation was that memory performance would be better for the more meaningful pairs, and that equivalent ratings of meaningfulness would be associated with equivalent levels of cued recall.

The results are shown in Figure 3. Ratings are collapsed over 0 and 1, also over 4 and 5 to yield a reasonably large number of observations at each level of elaboration. The figure shows that memory performance does increase as the degree of meaningful elaboration increases but, surprisingly, the divided attention group's performance is approximately 25% lower at all levels of elaboration. That is, it appears that even when participants in the divided attention condition achieved the same degree of meaningful elaboration as participants working under full attention, later memory was impaired in the former group. Further details of this and related experiments are given in Craik and Kester (2000).

At first this result seems anomalous—especially in light of the levels of processing framework, which suggests that later memory is simply a function of the type of processing carried out during encoding. However, other results may also fit the same pattern of equivalent on-line processing leading to different levels of subsequent memory depending on the amount of processing resources available to carry out the initial on-line processing. For example, Charness (1981) has shown that older players of chess and bridge can perform as well as younger players, but that later memory for board positions or bridge hands is poorer for older players of equivalent strength to younger players. Again there appears to be an age-related dissociation between the type of processing needed to carry out the initial task and later memory for that event. It seems that some further process beyond the initial processes of perception and comprehension is necessary to support later memory, and that this further process is impaired in older people and in young adults working under conditions of divided attention. The nature of this extra step is quite unclear at present although, speculatively, it may fall under the general heading of consolidation processes, which are known to be impaired in cases of organic amnesia (e.g., Squire, 1987). Another (perhaps related) possibility is that aging, and perhaps divided attention, are associated with a decline in the efficiency of associative or "binding" processes, and that this reduced efficiency is reflected in lower levels of performance (Chalfonte & Johnson, 1996; Naveh-Benjamin, 2000).

FURTHER AGE-RELATED RETRIEVAL PROBLEMS

One way of linking the difficulty experienced by older adults in remembering names with their difficulty in the conscious recollection of episodes is by the suggestion that aging is accompanied by a decreasing ability to recall specific detail, regardless of whether the detail resides in episodic or semantic memory. A more radical suggestion is that semantic and episodic memory are *not* separate systems, as proposed by Tulving (1972, 1983) and others, but that individual episodes simply constitute the end points of a knowledge hierarchy, with commonalities among related groups of episodes forming progressively higher-order nodes, as illustrated in Figure 4. As an example, individual instances of meeting my friend Tom at the university form some of the lowest-level nodes, and meetings with Tom at the tennis club form further low-level nodes. Higher nodes represent "Tom-at-the-university" and "Tom-at-the-tennis-club," and a superordinate node will represent my general context-independent concept of Tom. The higher nodes may be termed "semantic memory" and the lower nodes "episodic memory" but, rather than view these types of memory as arising from different systems, the present suggestion is that they exist on a continuum of specificity running from individual instances, rich in specific contextual detail, to abstract context-free knowledge, which of course originated from the amalgamation of specific instances.

As a further suggestion, the distinction between items that an experimental participant "remembers" were on a previously presented list, as opposed to items that he or she merely "knows" were on the list (Gardiner & Richardson-Klavehn, 2000; Tulving, 1985), may also reflect access to information at different levels of the episodic-semantic hierarchy, with items given "know" judgments representing the higher level (Figure 4). After all, items

Hierarchical Model

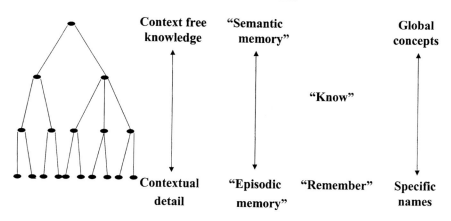

Figure 4.   Hierarchical representation of knowledge and memory (after Byrd, 1981).

that a participant "knows" were on a list are still "episodic"—the participant remembers that they occurred as part of a list in the experimental setting—they are simply not recollected with the same amount of episodic detail as items given "remember" judgments.

It is at least plausible that it is more effortful (i.e., requires more processing resources) to recollect contextual detail than to reactivate higher nodes in the knowledge hierarchy; for one thing, higher nodes have been activated on several previous occasions (because they represent the commonalities among several episodes) whereas individual instances are less likely to have been reactivated since they were laid down. In fact, higher nodes may always be activated in conjunction with lower nodes; the higher nodes will therefore receive more practice and so require fewer resources to activate them. If this is so, it follows that older adults, with fewer attentional resources at their disposal, will be less able to recollect episodic detail than context-free knowledge. It is clear that the distinction between general categorical knowledge and knowledge of specific names is not the same as the distinction between semantic and episodic knowledge, but these two slices through the knowledge base may both be organized hierarchically, and share the characteristic that the higher-order, general nodes are more accessible than the specific, terminal nodes. The idea that episodic memory is organized hierarchically was previously suggested by Estes (1982), although he did not link episodic and semantic memories together in one common system.

Is there further evidence that older adults have particular difficulty in recollecting specific detail? Two illustrations of the problem are first that older participants are differentially poorer at recalling details as opposed to

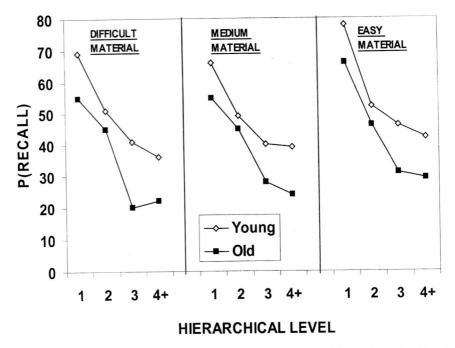

Figure 5. Recall of text passages as a function of age, type of material, and hierarchical level (Byrd, 1981). Reprinted with the permission of the publisher.

the general sense from a text passage. Figure 5 shows some data from a study by Mark Byrd (1981) in my lab. Byrd presented younger and older adults with text passages of three levels of difficulty and then analyzed recall according to the hierarchical level system developed by Kintsch (1974). The data yielded an interaction between age and level, with older individuals recalling relatively fewer propositional units at the lower hierarchical levels—those representing specific details in the original text. As a second example, Levine, Svoboda, Moscovitch, and Hay (2002) carried out a study of age-related differences in autobiographical memory, and found that the recollections of older participants contained more general information but fewer contextual details than the recollections of younger individuals.

A second type of retrieval difficulty may also pose greater problems for older people. In the studies carried out on the effects of divided attention on encoding and retrieval processes, my colleagues and I have consistently found that divided attention at the time of retrieval has surprisingly small effects on memory performance (Anderson et al., 1998; Craik et al., 1996; Naveh-Benjamin et al., 2000). If the effects of aging resemble those of divided attention, as I have argued, it follows that aging should *not* be associated with difficulties of retrieval, which is inconsistent with the evidence presented earlier. The key to resolving this paradox may follow from the results of a recent study by Fernandes and Moscovitch (2000). These researchers showed that when the secondary task in a dual-task paradigm was a perceptual-motor task (visual choice RT), it caused substantial interference with later recall of a word list when it was performed during the encoding phase, but caused very little interference during the retrieval phase of the word list. This result replicates the findings of Craik et al. (1996). However, when Fernandes and Moscovitch used a second *verbal* task as their concurrent task (e.g., classifying words as naturally occurring or man-made objects), they now found substantial divided attention effects at retrieval as well as at encoding. One way of talking about this interesting result is that participants in the dual-task condition at retrieval found it difficult to discriminate the wanted items (words from the memory list) from the similar items being processed in the concurrent task. There is a difficulty in keeping the two classes of words apart, whereas this difficulty does not arise when the concurrent task involves material that is easily distinguished, and so processed separately, from the material to be recalled.

The analogy to aging here is that older people may also suffer from a chronic difficulty in keeping processing streams separate. That is, they are more vulnerable to interference from concurrent distracting information or from irrelevant thoughts (Hasher & Zacks, 1988), perhaps because the under-lying cortical processes begin to overlap and interfere as people grow older (Kinsbourne, 1980). This type of age-related difficulty has been attributed to an impairment of inhibition processes (Hasher & Zacks, 1988; Zacks et al., 2000) connected to less efficient working memory operations and ultimately to the declining efficiency of the frontal lobes (Cabeza et al., 1997; Craik et al., 1990; Grady et al., 1995). It is often the case that a second source of information is liable to interfere with performance of the primary task and so must indeed be inhibited, but perhaps the more general case is one in which the efficient processor of information must distinguish various types of information and keep them separate. Older people may lack the necessary "resolving power" to distinguish wanted from irrelevant information in an effective manner, especially when the two streams of information are qualitatively similar. In turn, this inefficiency of processing makes it difficult for older people to process two streams of information simultaneously—they may concentrate on one stream and neglect the other (Broadbent & Heron, 1962)—and also makes it difficult to inhibit one source in order to deal effectively with material from the wanted source.

CONCLUSIONS

In previous articles (e.g., Craik, 1986, 1994) I have suggested that the memory difficulties experienced by older adults are largely attributable to problems of encoding. One major reason for taking this position was that other conditions which appear to mimic the effects of aging have much greater effects at encoding than at retrieval; such conditions include divided attention (e.g., Craik et al., 1996), the effects of alcohol (e.g., Birnbaum et al., 1978), and the effects of depressive drugs (e.g., Curran, 1991). The common factor among these various conditions is plausibly a reduction in processing resources, or perhaps a reduction in cognitive control (Jacoby, 1991). It now seems, however, that this theoretical stance was unnecessarily restricted, and that other factors also play a role.

At encoding, it now appears that there are two rather different sources of difficulty. One is embodied in my previous suggestion that older people encode new information less deeply and elaborately, owing fundamentally to an age-related reduction in processing resources or cognitive control. The second encoding difficulty follows from our observation that divided attention at encoding results in a reduction in memory performance even when degrees of elaboration are equated between full and divided attention. This second type of deficit may relate to problems of binding, of association, or perhaps of consolidation.

At retrieval, I have also discussed two major problems. One is the age-related difficulty involving processes of conscious recollection (e.g., Jennings & Jacoby, 1997) and it is this type of difficulty that may be relieved in older people by providing greater degrees of environmental and schematic support (Craik, 1983, 1986; Craik & Bosman, 1992). A second source of problems appears to be the difficulty that older people have in the recollection of specific detail—both episodic detail (context) and semantic detail (names). This difficulty may stem from age-related problems in the ability to "resolve" or discriminate between various sources of information.

In overview, there is no doubt that memory problems increase as people age, but the picture is not entirely negative. First, some types of memory and learning are relatively unaffected by the aging process—implicit memory, procedural memory, sensory memory, primary (short-term) memory, and general knowledge of facts and vocabulary are examples of this large class of abilities. Second, even the types of memory that *do* show age-related losses— such as episodic recall of events and their contexts, the episodic source of remembered facts, working memory, and prospective memory—are open to improvement by allocating more attentional resources to memory processes, and by making better use of environmental and schematic supports. Thus, whereas memory does decline with age, with greater attention to encoding and retrieval conditions we can ameliorate the deficit for others—and, with luck, for ourselves.

ACKNOWLEDGEMENTS

Preparation of this chapter was facilitated by grants from the Natural Sciences and Engineering Research Council of Canada and from the National Institute of Aging, USA. I am grateful to Aaron Benjamin, Ellen Bialystok, Alan Castel, and Jill Kester for very helpful comments on an earlier version, and to Jennie Sawula and Sharyn Kreuger for help in preparing the manuscript.

REFERENCES

Anderson, N.D., & Craik, F.I.M. (2000). Memory in the aging brain. In E. Tulving & F.I.M. Craik (Eds.), *The Oxford handbook of memory* (pp. 411–425). New York: Oxford University Press.

Anderson, N.D., Craik, F.I.M., & Naveh-Benjamin, M. (1998). The attentional demands of encoding and retrieval in younger and older adults: I. Evidence from divided attention costs. *Psychology and Aging, 13*, 405–423.

Anderson, N.D., Iidaka, T., Cabeza, R., Kapur, S., McIntosh, A.R., & Craik, F.I.M. (2000). The effects of divided attention on encoding- and retrieval-related brain activity: A PET study of younger and older adults. *Journal of Cognitive Neuroscience, 12*, 775–792.

Baddeley, A. (1986). *Working memory*. Oxford: Oxford University Press.

Balota, D.W., Cortese, M.J., Duchek, J.M., Adams, D., Roediger, H.L., III, McDermott, K.B., & Yenys, B.E. (1999). Veridical and false memories in healthy older adults and dementia of the Alzheimer's type. *Cognitive Neuropsychology, 16*, 361–384.

Balota, D.A., Dolan, P.O., & Duchek, J.M. (2000). Memory changes in healthy older adults. In E. Tulving & F.I.M. Craik (Eds.), *The Oxford handbook of memory* (pp. 395–409). New York: Oxford University Press.

Benjamin, A.S. (2001). On the dual effects of repetition on false recognition. *Journal of Experimental Psychology: Learning, Memory, and Cognition, 27*, 941–947.

Birnbaum, I.M., Parker, E.S. Hartley, J.T., & Noble, E.P. (1978). Alcohol and memory: Retrieval processes. *Journal of Verbal Learning and Verbal Behavior, 17*, 325–335.

Broadbent, D.E., & Heron, A. (1962). Effects of a subsidiary task on performance involving immediate memory in younger and older men. *British Journal of Psychology, 53*, 189–198.

Burke, D.M., & Light, L.L. (1981). Memory and aging: The role of retrieval processes. *Psychological Bulletin, 90*, 513–546.

Byrd, M. (1981). *Age differences in memory for prose passages*. Unpublished PhD thesis, University of Toronto, Canada.

Cabeza, R., Grady, C.L., Nyberg, L., McIntosh, A.R., Tulving, E., Kapur, S., Jennings, J.M., Houle, S., & Craik, F.I.M. (1997). Age-related differences in neural activity during memory encoding and retrieval: A positron emission tomography study. *Journal of Neuroscience, 17*, 391–400.

Chalfonte, B.L., & Johnson, M.K. (1996). Feature memory and binding in young and older adults. *Memory and Cognition, 214*, 403–416.

Charness, N. (1981). Aging and skilled problem solving. *Journal of Experimental Psychology: General, 110*, 21–38.

Craik, F.I.M. (1977). Age differences in human memory. In J.E. Birren & W. Schaie (Eds.), *Handbook of the psychology of aging* (pp. 324–420). New York: Van Nostrand Reinhold.

Craik, F.I.M. (1979). Levels of processing: Overview and closing comments. In L.S. Cermak & F.I.M. Craik (Eds.), *Levels of processing and human memory* (pp. 447–461). Hillsdale, NJ: Lawrence Erlbaum Associates Inc.

Craik, F.I.M. (1982). Selective changes in encoding as a function of reduced processing capacity. In F. Klix, J. Hoffmann, & E. van der Meer (Eds.), *Cognitive research in psychology* (pp. 152–161). Berlin: Deutscher Verlag der Wissenschaften.

Craik, F.I.M. (1983). On the transfer of information from temporary to permanent memory. *Philosophical Transactions of the Royal Society, Series B302*, 341–359.

Craik, F.I.M. (1986). A functional account of age differences in memory. In F. Klix & H. Hagendorf (Eds.), *Human memory and cognitive capabilities, mechanisms and performances* (pp. 409–422). Amsterdam: Elsevier.

Craik, F.I.M. (1994). Memory changes in normal aging. *Current Directions in Psychological Science, 3*, 155–158.

Craik, F.I.M., & Bosman, E.A. (1992). Age-related changes in memory and learning. In H. Bouma & J.A.M. Graafmans (Eds.), *Gerontechnology* (pp. 79–92). Amsterdam: IOS Press.

Craik, F.I.M., & Byrd, M. (1982). Aging and cognitive deficits: The role of attentional resources. In F.I.M. Craik & S.E. Trehub (Eds.), *Aging and cognitive processes* (pp. 191–211). New York: Plenum Press.

Craik, F.I.M., Byrd, M., & Swanson, J.M. (1987). Patterns of memory loss in three elderly samples. *Psychology and Aging, 2*, 79–86.

Craik, F.I.M., Govoni, R., Naveh-Benjamin, M., & Anderson, N.D. (1996). The effects of divided attention on encoding and retrieval processes in human memory. *Journal of Experimental Psychology: General, 125*, 159–180.

Craik, F.I.M., & Jennings, J.J. (1992). Human memory. In F.I.M. Craik & T.A. Salthouse (Eds.), *The Handbook of aging and cognition* (pp. 51–110). Hillsdale, NJ: Lawrence Erlbaum Associates Inc.

Craik, F.I.M., & Kester, J.D. (2000). Divided attention and memory: Impairment of processing or consolidation? In E. Tulving (Ed.), *Memory, consciousness, and the brain: The Tallinn Conference* (pp. 38–51). Philadelphia, PA: Psychology Press.

Craik, F.I.M., & Lockhart, R.S. (1972). Levels of processing: A framework for memory research. *Journal of Verbal Learning and Verbal Behavior, 11*, 671–684.

Craik, F.I.M., & McDowd, J.D. (1987). Age differences in recall and recognition. *Journal of Experimental Psychology: Learning, Memory, and Cognition, 13*, 474–479.

Craik, F.I.M., Morris, L.W., Morris, R.G., & Loewen, E.R. (1990). Relations between source amnesia and frontal lobe functioning in a normal elderly sample. *Psychology and Aging, 5*, 148–151.

Craik, F.I.M., & Simon, E. (1980). Age differences in memory. The roles of attention and depth of processing. In L. Poon, J.L. Fozard, L.S. Cermak, D. Arenberg, & L.W. Thompson (Eds.), *New directions in memory and aging* (pp. 95–112). Hillsdale, NJ: Lawrence Erlbaum Associates Inc.

Craik, F.I.M., & Tulving, E. (1975). Depth of processing and the retention of words in episodic memory. *Journal of Experimental Psychology: General, 104*, 268–294.

Curran, H.V. (1991). Benzodiazepines, memory and mood: A review. *Psychopharmacology, 105*, 1–8.

Estes, W.R. (1982). Multiple coding and processing stages: A review. In F. Klix, J. Hoffmann, & E. van der Meer (Eds.), *Cognitive research in psychology* (pp. 14–21). Berlin: Deutscher Verlag der Wissenschaften.

Eysenck, M.W. (1974). Age differences in incidental learning. *Developmental Psychology, 19*, 936–941.

Fernandes, M.A., & Moscovitch, M. (2000). Divided attention and memory: Evidence of substantial interference effects of retrieval and encoding. *Journal of Experimental Psychology: General, 129*, 155–176.

Gardiner, J.M., & Richardson-Klavehn, A. (2000). Remembering and knowing. In E. Tulving & F.I.M. Craik (Eds.), *The Oxford handbook of memory* (pp. 229–244). New York: Oxford University Press.

Grady, C.L., McIntosh, A.R., Horwitz, B., Maisog, J.M., Ungerleider, L.G., Mentis, M.J., Pietrini, P., Schapiro, M.B., & Haxby, J.V. (1995). Age-related reductions in human recognition memory due to impaired encoding. *Science, 269*, 218–221.

Hasher, L., & Zacks, R.T. (1988). Working memory, comprehension, and aging: A review and a new view. In G.H. Bower (Ed.), *The psychology of learning and motivation* (pp. 193–225). New York: Academic Press.

Hay, J.F., & Jacoby, L.L. (1999). Separating habit and recollection in young and older adults: Effects of elaborative processing and distinctiveness. *Psychology and Aging, 14*, 122–134.

Iidaka, T., Anderson, N.D., Kapur, S., Cabeza, R., & Craik, F.I.M. (2000). The effect of divided attention on encoding and retrieval in episodic memory revealed by positron emission tomography. *Journal of Cognitive Neuroscience, 12*, 267–280.

Jacoby, L.L. (1991). A process dissociation framework: Separating automatic from intentional uses of memory. *Journal of Memory and Language, 30*, 513–541.

Jennings, J.M., & Jacoby, L.L. (1993). Automatic versus intentional uses of memory: Aging, attention, and control. *Psychology and Aging, 8*, 283–293.

Jennings, J.M., & Jacoby, L.L. (1997). An opposition procedure for detecting age-related deficits in recollection: Telling effects of repetition. *Psychology and Aging, 12*, 352–361.

Johnston, W.A., Greenberg, S.N., Fisher, R.P., & Martin, D.W. (1970). Divided attention: A vehicle for monitoring memory processes. *Journal of Experimental Psychology, 83*, 164–171.

Kapur, S., Craik, F.I.M., Tulving, E., Wilson, A.A., Houle, S., & Brown, G.M. (1994). Neuroanatomical correlates of encoding in episodic memory: Levels of processing effect. *Proceedings of the National Academy of Sciences, USA, 91*, 2008–2011.

Kensinger, E.A., & Schacter, D.L. (1999). When true memories suppress false memories: Effects of aging. *Cognitive Neuropsychology, 16*, 399–415.

Kinsbourne, M. (1980). Attentional dysfunctions and the elderly: Theoretical models and research perspectives. In L.W. Poon, J.L. Fozard, L.S. Cermak, D. Arenberg, & L.W. Thompson (Eds.), *New directions in memory and aging* (pp. 113–129). Hillsdale, NJ: Lawrence Erlbaum Associates Inc.

Kintsch, W. (1974). *The representation of meaning in memory*. Hillsdale, NJ: Lawrence Erlbaum Associates Inc.

Levine, B., Svoboda, E., Moscovitch, M., & Hay, J.F. (2002). *Autobiographical memory in younger and older adults*. Manuscript submitted for publication.

Light, L.L. (1991). Memory and aging: Four hypotheses in search of data. *Annual Review of Psychology, 42*, 333–376.

Naveh-Benjamin, M. (2000). Adult age differences in memory performance: Tests of an associative deficit hypothesis. *Journal of Experimental Psychology: Learning, Memory, and Cognition, 26*, 1170–1187.

Naveh-Benjamin, M., Craik, F.I.M., Gavrilescu, D., & Anderson, N.D. (2000). Asymmetry between encoding and retrieval processes: Evidence from divided attention and a calibration analysis. *Memory and Cognition, 28*, 965–976.

Nilsson, L.-G., Bäckman, L., & Karlsson, T. (1989). Priming and cued recall in elderly, Alcohol-intoxicated and sleep-deprived subjects: A case of functionally similar memory deficits. *Psychological Medicine, 19*, 423–433.

Nilsson, L.-G., & Craik, F.I.M. (1989). Additive and interactive effects in memory for subject-performed tasks. *European Journal of Cognitive Psychology, 2*, 305–324.

Roediger, H.L., III, & McDermott, K.B. (1995). Creating false memories: Remembering words not presented in lists. *Journal of Experimental Psychology: Learning, Memory, and Cognition*, *21*, 803–814.

Rönnlund, M., Nyberg, L., Bäckman, L., & Nilsson. L.-G. (2002). *Recall of subject-performed tasks, verbal tasks, and cognitive activities across the adult life span: Parallel age-related deficits.* Manuscript submitted for publication.

Salthouse, T.A. (1982). *Adult cognition: An experimental psychology of human aging.* New York: Springer-Verlag.

Shallice, T., Fletcher, P., Frith, C.D., Grasby, P., Frackowiak, R.S. J., & Dolan, R.J. (1994). Brain regions associated with acquisition and retrieval of verbal episodic memory. *Nature, 368*, 633–635.

Squire, L.R. (1987). *Memory and brain.* New York: Oxford University Press.

Tulving, E. (1972). Episodic and semantic memory. In E. Tulving & W. Donaldson (Eds.). *Organization of memory* (pp. 382–404). New York: Academic Press.

Tulving, E. (1983). *Elements of episodic memory.* New York: Oxford University Press.

Tulving, E. (1985). How many memory systems are there? *American Psychologist, 40*, 385–398.

Tulving, E., Kapur, S., Craik, F.I.M., Moscovitch, M., & Houle, H. (1994). Hemispheric encoding/retrieval asymmetry in episodic memory: Positron emission findings. *Proceedings of the National Academy of Sciences, USA, 91*, 2016–2020.

Tulving, E., & Schacter, D.L. (1990). Priming and human memory systems. *Science, 247*, 301–306.

Tulving, E., Thomson, D.M. (1973). Encoding specificity and retrieval processes in episodic memory. *Psychological Review, 80*, 352–373.

West, R.L. (1996). An application of prefrontal cortex theory to cognitive aging. *Psychological Bulletin, 120*, 272–292.

Zacks, R.T., Hasher, L., & Li, K.Z.H. (2000). Human memory. In F.I.M. Craik & T.A. Salthouse (Eds.), *The handbook of aging and cognition* (2nd ed., pp. 293–357). Mahwah, NJ: Lawrence Erlbaum Associates Inc.

SECTION THREE

Psychological health

CHAPTER TWELVE

Multidimensional interactionism: Stress, anxiety, and coping

Norman S. Endler
York University, North York, Canada

INTRODUCTION

Interactionism

The first empirical studies on interactionism were conducted in the 1960s; however, the concept of interactionism dates back as far as Aristotle (384–322 BC; see Shute, 1973). Kantor (1924, 1926) was one of the first to postulate a person-situation interaction theory of behaviour. The main unit of study is the individual as he or she interacts with various types of situations. Later, Tolman (1935) and Lewin (1935) emphasized the importance of taking both the person and situation factors into account. The interaction of person and situation factors was also characteristic of Murray's (1938) need-press theory, in which the unit of analysis is the organism-environment interaction.

There are two types of interactionism: mechanistic (or structural) and dynamic (or process) interactionism (Endler, 1983). The mechanistic model of interaction is concerned with interactions of many factors, including persons, situations, or modes of response. The assumption of this model is that there is a linear and additive relationship (interaction) between person and situation factors (i.e., the independent variables) in determining behaviour (i.e., the dependent variable). Dynamic interactionism, on the other hand, is concerned with the reciprocal interaction between behaviour and both situation factors and person factors. This is an ongoing process that is multidirectional.

The *interactional model* of personality (Endler, 1997; Endler &

Magnusson, 1976; Magnusson & Endler, 1977) focuses on person by situation interactions in personality. "Behavior involves an indispensable, continuous interaction between individuals and the situations they encounter" (Endler & Magnusson, 1976, p. 958). In contrast to classical social learning theorists, cognitive processes play an important role in the interaction model of personality. Modern interactionist perspectives (Endler, 1997; Endler & Magnusson, 1976; Magnusson & Endler, 1977) parallel the framework recently delineated by Mischel and Shoda (1995) in that behaviour is conceptualized as an ongoing, dynamic, and multidirectional interaction between persons and situations. Their model of human behaviour, the Cognitive Affective Personality System (CAPS), is both cognitively and affectively based and emphasizes the situation and context (Shoda & Mischel, 2000).

Endler and Magnusson (1976) summarized interactional psychology in terms of four main features: "1. Actual behavior is a function of a continuous process or multidirectional interaction (feedback) between the individual and the situation that he or she encounters. 2. The individual is an intentional active agent in the interaction process. 3. On the person side of the interaction, cognitive factors are the essential determinants of behaviour, although emotional factors do play a role. 4. On the situation side, the psychological meaning of the situation for the individual is the important determining factor" (p. 968). More recently, Magnusson (1998) has discussed holistic interactionism that highlights the individual as the organizing principle. This approach takes into account cognitive research, biological aspects, developmental psychology, and longitudinal research. According to the holistic approach, to explain why individuals behave as they do, all elements of the person (i.e., perceptions, goals, biological factors) as well as elements of the situation must be taken into account.

Other models of personality

In addition to interactionism, there are at least three other models of personality.

Trait psychology

Historically, the field of personality has been primarily influenced by the *trait psychology model* (Endler & Magnusson, 1976). Although the various trait theorists (e.g., Allport, 1937; Cattell, 1950, 1957, 1965; Costa & McCrae, 1985; Eysenck, 1953, 1975, 1982) disagree as to the specific structure and content of traits, they do agree that (1) traits are dispositions; and (2) they account for behavioural consistency across a wide range of situations.

Psychodynamic

Like trait theories, psychodynamic theories also focus on person factors as determinants of behaviour. The elements of personality structure (the id, ego, and superego) conflict with one another, producing anxiety which the individual defends with various defense mechanisms.

Situationism

Situationism or social learning theory (Bandura, 1986), on the other hand, emphasizes the stimuli in the situation or the situation factors as the prime determinants of behaviour. Historically sociologists and social psychologists (Cooley, 1902; Cottrell, 1942a, b; Dewey & Humber, 1951; Lindesmith & Strauss, 1949; Mead, 1934) have emphasized the role of social learning in personality, but have not denied the presence of individual differences.

There has been much criticism of the situationism, trait, and psychodynamic models of personality. They neglect the cognitive variables and processes that affect the relationship between the person and the situation (Endler, 2000). More recent personality theories incorporate cognition to varying degrees (McCann & Endler, 2000). For example, since the mid 1980s social cognitive personality theorists (e.g., Bandura, 1986; Mischel & Shoda, 1995; Shoda & Mischel, 2000) have stressed the role of cognition as a mediator between the reinforcing characteristics of the situation and the person's development of new behaviours.

Methodology

There have been two broad approaches to interactionism: cross-sectional and longitudinal. Cross-sectional research tests interactions (e.g., anxiety) at one time period and determines the relationships among various person variables. Others have used a longitudinal research methodology. Before discussing cross-sectional research, we will consider one area of longitudinal interactionism research that has focused on criminality (Magnusson, 1986, 1992).

Longitudinal research

Magnusson's (1986, 1992) Örebro or "Individual Development and Adjustment" (IDA) research project investigated the way that "individual characteristics and environmental factors—individually and interacting with one another—govern a person's development from childhood to adulthood" (Magnusson, 1992, p. 119). One study in this research programme focused on the developmental background of antisocial behaviour in terms of criminal activity in adulthood among males. Data were collected for the 3rd-grade students during their school years and up through the 12th grade. A random sample of 13-year-old boys was taken from this data. The 13-year-old boys ($N = 296$) who showed no indications of problem behaviours at age 13 appeared significantly less frequently than expected in criminal records. The boys who at the age of 13 were categorized by only one indicator of behavioural problems did not appear significantly more in crime records as adults than boys who had no behavioural indicators. Only in the categories where boys displayed a multidimensional pattern of severe behavioural problems, was the number of boys listed in public records for crimes higher than the number that could be expected according to a random model. Endler (1993) suggests that these longitudinal findings are quite robust and impressive.

Cross-situational perspective

Interactionism argues that there is stability over time (longitudinal consistency), but there may not be cross-situational consistency. For example, Block's (1971, 1977, 1981) research has continually supported the existence of longitudinal consistency. Although Mischel and Peake (1982) have found little or no evidence for cross-situational consistency, they have found support for moderate temporal stability (longitudinal consistency). There may be other reasons for the high correlations of behaviour in longitudinal studies apart from actual stability. If everyone changes consistently over time, high correlations would be obtained. Another reason for high correlations could be that the situations people encounter and/or select are similar across the different time periods. Because people are "creatures of habit" they continually encounter situations that they find rewarding and avoid situations that they find punishing.

Nevertheless, interactionism also focuses on cross-situational inconsistencies. There is little evidence for cross-situational consistency for social and personality variables. However, for structural variables (e.g., intelligence, abilities, and cognitions) there is evidence for moderate cross-situational consistency (Endler, 1983, 1988). When situations are similar there is evidence for consistency; however, when situations are dissimilar there is little or no consistency. Prior to discussing cross-sectional research, we will define stress, anxiety, and coping, terms relevant for this research.

DEFINITION OF TERMS

Research in the areas of stress, anxiety, and coping has expanded over the past decade. A recent (December, 2000) look at PsycINFO showed 64,046 citations for stress, 61,718 citations for anxiety, and 26,525 citations for coping during the last century.

Stress

Stress, a term derived from the field of physics, refers to a mechanical force acting on a body; strain is the reaction to stress. Stress occurs when demands are placed on an individual which exceed his or her ability to adjust (Lazarus, 1976). Many life events (e.g., bereavement, personal injury, or illness) are stressful and can possibly make a person prone to illness.

Anxiety

Anxiety is an ambiguous construct because it has been conceptualized in many ways. Aubrey Lewis (1970) defined anxiety "as an emotional state, with the subjectively experienced quality of fear as a closely related emotion" (p. 77). Lewis points out that the emotion is unpleasant, negative, out of proportion to the threat, future directed, and involves both subjective aspects and manifest bodily disturbances.

State vs. Trait Anxiety

Cicero distinguished between *angor* and *anxietas*. Cattell and Scheier (1961), on the bases of *empirical* factor analyses of anxiety items, found two distinct anxiety factors: state and trait anxiety (Cattell, 1966). Spielberger (1966) suggested that *conceptual* clarity could be achieved by recognizing a distinction between trait anxiety, an individual's predisposition to respond, and state anxiety, a transitory emotion involving physiological arousal and consciously perceived feelings of apprehension, dread, and tension. Spielberger (1972) was the first to systematically investigate the relationships between state and trait anxiety in ego-threatening situations.

Endler's integration of state-trait anxiety and interactionism

The distinction between state and trait anxiety has achieved wide recognition since the mid 1960s (cf. Dreger, 1985; Endler, 1997; Endler & Edwards, 1985; Spielberger, 1985). However, conceptual confusions, controversies, and questions remain (Allen, 1985; Allen & Potkay, 1981; Endler, 1997). A renewed focus on an interaction model of personality (Endler, 1983, 1988, 1997; Endler & Magnusson, 1976) has been a consequence of re-evaluations of personality models and the state-trait distinction.

Coping

Coping is concerned with a person's typical manner of encountering a stressful situation and reacting to it (Endler & Parker, 1990, 1994; Folkman & Lazarus, 1985, 1988). Persons may have preferred coping styles, but situational demands may "override" and interact with their preferences. There are three basic coping styles: task-oriented coping, emotion-oriented coping, and avoidance-oriented coping (Endler & Parker, 1999; see Figure 1). Note that Avoidance-oriented coping further breaks down into social diversion and distraction-oriented coping.

Task-oriented coping is aimed at purposeful efforts to solve the problem; *emotion-oriented* coping is concerned with emotional reactions that are self-oriented; *avoidance-oriented* coping describes activities and cognitive changes aimed at avoiding the situation via *distraction* or *social diversion*. These constructs are assessed via the *Coping Inventory for Stressful Situations* (CISS; Endler & Parker, 1999).

There has been a proliferation of coping research over the past two or three decades and coping has become a main area of study in psychology (Somerfield & McCrae, 2000). Recently, the coping field has been criticized for the quality of this research (Lazarus, 1993, 1998), and the lack of integration of coping research with stress management and clinical intervention (Coyne & Racioppo, 2000). There has been criticism regarding the measures used in coping research as well as other methodological issues (Endler &

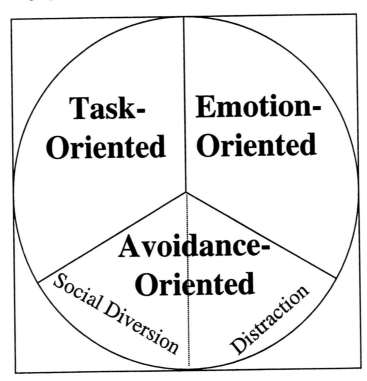

Figure 1.   Facets of coping.

Parker, 1994). Recently, Lazarus (2000) presented an optimistic view of stress and coping research, as the presence of longitudinal and in-depth designs have increased. Assessment techniques such as behavioural observation, in addition to self-report measures, are as important in coping research as they are in anxiety and other areas of personality research (Magnusson & Endler, 1977). Lazarus (2000) suggests that the synthesis of scientific studies is often lacking in the area of coping research. Taylor et al. (2000) present a synthesis of gender differences in coping research.

Gender differences in coping

Bateson (2000) presented an evolutionary perspective of gender differences in various areas. On coping with stress, she suggests that men respond to stress with aggression and women respond to stress with depression, corresponding to the evolutionary process, which has favoured aggressive men and docile women. Similarly Taylor et al. (2000) suggest that although flight or flight characterizes the physiological response to stress for both men and women, behaviourally, women are more likely to respond in a "tend and befriend" manner. Figure 2 illustrates this gender difference.

In the past, "fight or flight" was considered to be the coping pattern used by both men and women when confronted with stressful situations. Now it appears that women are more likely to seek social support or respond by nurturing others, a coping pattern labelled "tend and befriend" by Taylor et al. (2000). They analyzed the findings of hundreds of human and animal stress studies in arriving at their conclusions. This response is not only characteristic of human females, but also characteristic of females of other species.

MULTIDIMENSIONAL INTERACTION MODEL OF ANXIETY

The *Endler Multidimensional Anxiety Scales* (EMAS; Endler, Edwards, & Vitelli, 1991) assess state anxiety, trait anxiety, and the perception of the threatening situation. Whereas Spielberger (1972) conceptualizes both state and trait anxiety as unidimensional constructs, the EMAS assess state and trait anxiety as multidimensional constructs. The state measure (EMAS-State or A-State) assesses the cognitive worry (C-W) and autonomic-emotional (A-E) components of A-State, plus a total score. The EMAS-Perception (EMAS-P) assesses the *perception* of the stressful situation. The EMAS assesses trait anxiety in four situational domains: social evaluation, physical danger, ambiguous, and daily routines.

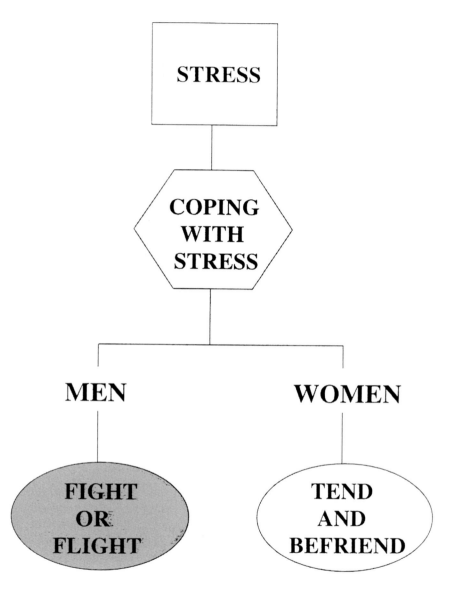

Figure 2. Gender differences in coping with stress (based on Taylor et al., 2000).

Expanding the multidimensionality of A-trait

Research is currently under way to expand the multidimensionality of the Trait scale to include other facets of trait anxiety. Figure 3 displays the original facets of trait anxiety, as well as the facets under current investigation. In their present form, the EMAS-Trait scales (Endler et al., 1991) measure only one component of interpersonal or social anxiety: *social evaluation anxiety*. Research on social anxiety, however, shows that *separation anxiety* and *self-disclosure anxiety* are also facets of the general construct of interpersonal anxiety (e.g., Doi & Thelen, 1993; Muris, Merckelback, Schmidt, & Tierney, 1999). Therefore, we propose that social anxiety is composed of at least a *triad* of trait anxiety dimensions: social evaluation, self-disclosure, and separation anxiety (Endler & Flett, 2002; Endler, Flett, Macrodimitris, Corace, & Kocovski, 2001a). Figure 4 illustrates this triad of trait social anxiety.

The DSM-IV (American Psychiatric Association, 1994) states that separation anxiety is rare in adults and does not specify criteria for diagnosis. However, it has been found that this disorder does occur in adults (Manicavasagar, Silove, & Curtis, 1997). Self-disclosure is the other area that we are currently researching. People are comfortable with varying levels of self-disclosure. A review of the literature has indicated that revealing secrets is generally advantageous; however, the situational context should be taken into

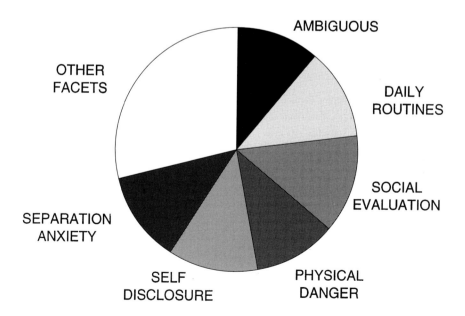

Figure 3. Multidimensional facets of trait anxiety (revised).

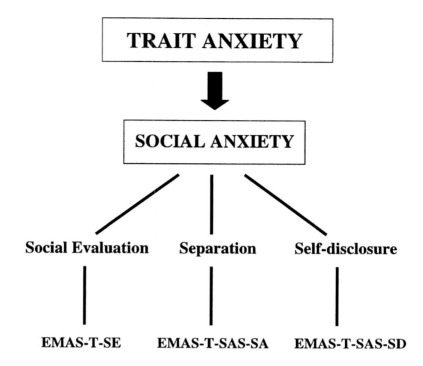

Figure 4. Social anxiety triad. EMAS = Endler Multidimensional Anxiety Scales; SAS = Social Anxiety Scales; T = Trait; SE = Social Evaluation; SA = Seperation Anxiety; SD = Self-Disclosure.

account before making that determination (Kelly & McKillop, 1996). Table 1 presents preliminary findings on the addition of the separation anxiety and self-disclosure subscales to the EMAS-Trait (called the EMAS- Social Anxiety Scales or SAS; Endler & Flett, 2002).

There were significant mean gender differences between all of the trait anxiety scales, with women scoring higher than men on most of the facets of trait anxiety (social evaluation, physical danger, and ambiguous trait anxiety). Of the new trait anxiety facets (EMAS-SAS), women scored higher than men on both separation anxiety and both of the self-disclosure trait anxiety scales (disclosure to family and disclosure to friends). Next, the means for the self-disclosure subscales show that both men and women had higher anxiety surrounding self-disclosure to a family member than self-disclosure to a close friend. The alpha levels for each of the subscales range from .83 for social evaluation to .94 for self-disclosure to a close friend for women. For men, the alpha levels for each of the subscales range from .85

TABLE 12.1

Descriptive statistics for EMAS-T and EMAS-T-SAS Scales for undergraduate sample (1999–2000)

Variable	Men (N = 251)			Women (N = 251)			
	Mean	SD	α	Mean	SD	α	t-test
EMAS-Trait							
Social evaluation	42.16	9.84	.86	48.85	9.61	.83	7.71***
Physical danger	52.63	9.64	.85	61.72	8.68	.85	11.10***
Ambiguous	40.43	9.42	.86	46.21	9.70	.88	6.78***
Daily routines	28.85	10.36	.89	25.55	8.18	.86	3.97***
EMAS-Trait-SAS							
Separation anxiety	47.98	11.04	.87	52.32	11.10	.89	4.39***
Self-Disclosure: Family	49.85	12.43	.91	55.90	11.51	.92	5.66***
Self-Disclosure: Close Friend	41.95	12.14	.90	45.74	12.87	.94	3.39***

EMAS = Endler Multidimensional Anxiety Scales, SAS = Social Anxiety Scales. Number of items for each scale = 15.

***$p < .001$.

for physical danger to .91 for self-disclosure to a family member. Finally, test–retest reliabilities (1 week time interval; $N=98$) ranged from .70 for self-disclosure to a family member to .80 for separation anxiety.

A principal components factor analysis with a varimax rotation was conducted, entering each of the social anxiety subscales: social evaluation of the original EMAS, the new separation anxiety scale, and the two self-disclosure scales. The scree plot showed the potential for a four-factor solution accounting for 47.18% of the variance. Factors 1 and 2 represented a combination of self-disclosure to a family member and self-disclosure to a friend; Factor 3 was separation anxiety; and Factor 4 was social evaluation. This gave a good indication that the two newly developed EMAS-T scales (Separation anxiety and self-disclosure—family or friend) are indeed measuring separate constructs.

Table 2 presents correlations among the social anxiety scales as well as state anxiety for men (above the diagonal) and for women (below the diagonal). Overall, relationships among the variables are similar for both men and women. As expected, most of the social anxiety variables demonstrated low to moderate correlations with each other, suggesting separate but related constructs.

To test the *validity* of the newly constructed EMAS-SAS-T separation anxiety scale, it was correlated with two other scales that measure similar constructs: the Homesickness Questionnaire and the Dundee Relocation Inventory (see Table 3). There was a moderate ($r=.38$) relationship between

TABLE 12.2

Intercorrelations among EMAS-T-SE, EMAS-T-SAS, and EMAS-State Scales for undergraduate sample—men above the diagonal ($N = 251$) women below the diagonal ($N = 251$)

Variable	1	2	3	4	5
1. EMAS-T-SE	—	.23***	.28***	.22***	.27***
2. EMAS-T-SAS-SA	−.06	—	.38***	.31***	.11
3. EMAS-T-SAS-SD-FA	.13*	.31***	—	.59***	.06
4. EMAS-T-SAS-SD-FR	.17**	.19**	.59***	—	.21***
5. EMAS-State	.15*	.22***	.18**	.15*	—

EMAS = Endler Multidimensional Anxiety Scales, T = Trait, SE = Social Evaluation, SAS = Social Anxiety Scales, SA = Separation Anxiety, SD = Self-disclosure, FA = Family, FR = Friend.

*$p < .05$; **$p < .01$; ***$p < .001$.

TABLE 12.3

Intercorrelations among EMAS-State, EMAS-T-SAS-Separation Anxiety, Homesickness Questionnaire, and the Dundee Relocation Inventory for undergraduate sample—men above the diagonal ($N = 251$), women below the diagonal ($N = 251$)

Variable	1	2	3	4
1. EMAS-State	—	.11	.43***	.56***
2. EMAS-T-SAS-SA	.22**	—	.22**	.22**
3. HQ	.30***	.38***	—	.61***
4. DRLI	.45***	.16*	.47***	—

EMAS = Endler Multidimensional Anxiety Scales, T = Trait, SAS = Social Anxiety Scales, SA = Separation Anxiety, HQ = Homesickness Questionnaire, DRLI = Dundee Relocation Inventory.

*$p < .05$; **$p < .01$; ***$p < .001$.

homesickness and separation anxiety for women and a lower correlation between homesickness and separation anxiety for men ($r=.22$). There was also a low relationship between separation anxiety and the Dundee Relocation Inventory for both men ($r=.22$) and women ($r=.16$). Both men and women showed higher relationships between state anxiety and the two validation measures than between state anxiety and trait separation anxiety. Overall, social or interpersonal anxiety appears to be comprised of: social evaluation, self-disclosure, and separation anxiety.

Endler's (1980, 1983, 1988, 1993, 1997) multidimensional interaction model of anxiety focuses on both the multidimensionality of anxiety and on interactions, and it also distinguishes between trait anxiety and state anxiety. There are several assumptions of the multidimensional interaction model of anxiety. The first basic assumption of the interaction model of anxiety is that both A-State and A-Trait are multidimensional. In addition, this model makes explicit predictions concerning person by situation interactions. Therefore, the second assumption of this model is that for a person (facet of A-Trait) by situation (stress condition) interaction to be effective in inducing A-State changes, it is necessary for the threatening situation to be *congruent* with the facet of A-Trait being investigated.

Testing the model

A number of laboratory and field studies (in real-life situations) have provided empirical support for the multidimensional interaction model of anxiety.

Physical danger

The first study examined the physical danger facet of trait anxiety, and parachute jumping from a plane as the physical danger situational stressor (Endler, Crooks & Parker, 1992).

A group of male military personnel were administered the EMAS-S and EMAS-T in a nonthreatening situation and the EMAS-S just prior to parachute jumping. They were also administered the EMAS-P just prior to the parachute jumping task, to assess if they perceived the task as a physical danger situation. The military personnel were then classified as high (top 40%) or low (bottom 40%) on physical danger.

A trials (neutral situation and stressful parachute jumping situation) by persons (Physical Danger A-Trait) analysis of variance was then performed on their A-State scores. There was a person by situation (P x S) interaction when situational physical danger threat was congruent with physical danger A-Trait. No interactions occurred when P and S variables were not congruent. A test of the interaction model of anxiety in a social evaluation situation, namely a competitive equestrian setting, follows.

Social evaluation

Adolescent girls were assessed during practice and then again in preparation for a competitive horse jumping situation—a social evaluation situation (Trotter & Endler, 1999). There was a significant Social Evaluation A-Trait by social evaluation stressor situation interaction. The results were analogous to the previous example on physical danger. That is, there was a person by situation (P × S) interaction when social evaluation situational threat was congruent with Social Evaluation A-Trait. No interactions occurred when P and S variables were not congruent.

Field studies have been conducted in such diverse settings as classroom examination situations, track and field and karate situations, actors performing on the stage, dental surgery situations, women undergoing a dilation and curettage (D and C) or a laparoscopy, psychotherapy settings, and bankers in management positions in stressful on-the-job situations (cf. Endler, 1983). Over 80% of these tests have provided support for the interaction model of anxiety (Endler, 1997). That is, differential hypotheses were confirmed in over 80% of the studies that have been conducted so far to test the interaction model of anxiety.

MULTIDIMENSIONAL INTERACTION MODEL OF STRESS, ANXIETY, AND COPING

In the early 1990s we extended our model to include a process-oriented interaction model of stress, anxiety, and *coping* (see Figure 5). During phase 1, on the left side of the figure, we start out with *person variables* (e.g., A-Trait, vulnerability, cognitive style, heredity, emotionality, activity, sociability). Person variables may be temperamental in nature, may interact with one another, and may interact with *situation variables* (e.g., life events, hassles, pain, disasters, crises, traumas, etc.). Situation variables also may interact with one another. The person by situation *interaction* leads to the perception of danger or threat (phase 2), which in turn can affect person and situation variables (phase 1) and lead to changes in A-State (phase 3), which in turn leads to *reactions* to the changes in A-state in phase 4 (e.g., coping responses, defences,

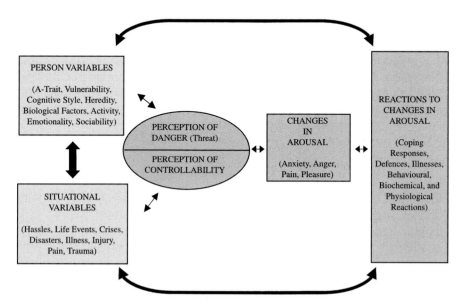

Figure 5.   Multidimensional interaction model of stress, anxiety, and coping.

illness, behavioural, biochemical, and physiological reactions), which in turn affects the person variables and stressful situations.

Coping and control

Adjustment is influenced by how much control we have over our lives. The most efficacious coping style in one situation is not necessarily the most efficacious in another situation. The amount of control one has is an important variable in determining coping style (Compas, Malcarne, & Fondacaro, 1988; Folkman, 1984; Forsythe & Compas, 1987; Vitaliano, 1990). The effects of experimental and perceived controllability on coping styles and coping efficacy have been assessed in laboratory studies (Endler, Macrodimitris, & Kocovski, 2000a; Endler, Speer, Johnson, & Flett, 2000b, 2001b).

   The basic task in these studies was a cognitive one, namely the solution of anagrams (a criterion for efficacy). We found that *high control* participants (both experimental and perceived) solved significantly more anagrams (were more efficacious) than *low control* participants. Furthermore, *high perceived control* participants were lower on state anxiety and situation-specific emotion-oriented coping than *low perceived control* participants, but higher on situation-specific task-oriented coping. With respect to the "goodness of fit" hypothesis, we found that task-oriented coping was most efficacious in perceived controllable situations, whereas emotion-oriented coping was best in situations perceived as uncontrollable. We have most recently extended this study to consist of two tasks: (1) a cognitive task—solving anagrams, and (2) an interpersonal story-telling task, and found similar results for these tasks (Endler et al., 2000b).

COPING WITH DISTRESS AND ILLNESS

Stress and illness are becoming more pervasive as our population ages. More and more of our resources will be needed for Health Psychology: the field of the future.

Coping with illness

In about 1990 we started developing a scale to assess coping with illness, the CHIP: *Coping with Health Injuries and Problems* (Endler & Parker, 2000; Endler, Parker, & Summerfeldt, 1998). After a fair amount of work: item preparation, data collection, data analyses, etc., we have developed four 8-item reliable and valid scales: distraction, palliative, instrumental, and emotional preoccupation. Figure 6 displays these four coping dimensions.

   Distraction coping includes responses such as thinking about things other than the health problem or engaging in activities that are unrelated to the

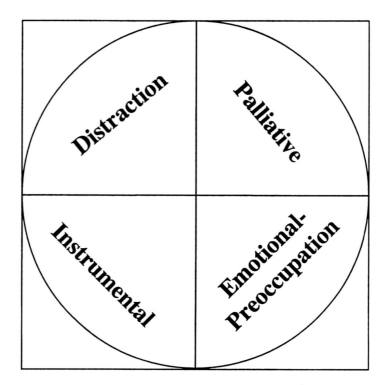

Figure 6.   Facets of coping with illness.

health problem. *Palliative* coping consists of responses aimed at alleviating the unpleasantness of the health problem. Examples include getting plenty of rest and making oneself comfortable. *Instrumental* coping consists of efforts aimed at solving the health problem such as obtaining health advice and adhering to the treatment regimen. *Emotional preoccupation* coping includes responses such as negative thoughts and preoccupation with the health problem. We have conducted a number of studies in the area of coping with health problems, but this chapter will only focus on four areas: (1) acute vs. chronic illness, (2) cancer patients, (3) diabetes patients, and (4) coronary heart disease (CHD) patients.

Acute vs. chronic illness

The criterion validity of the CHIP (Endler et al., 1998) was examined by comparing the coping behaviours of adults with chronic health problems and those with acute health problems. Four raters classified 390 general medical patients into "acute" and "chronic" health problem cases. For chronic illness/

injuries, the criteria were (1) it was unlikely that there would be a tangible "cure" for the patient's problem in the near future; and (2) the individual would have to confront the health problem for a considerable length of time (> 2 months). Chronic problems included diabetes, cancer, and arthritis; acute problems included respiratory infections, fractures or injuries, and short-term gastrointestinal problems. A total of 98 patients (44 men; 54 women) were classified as having an acute health problem; 109 (44 men; 65 women) as having a chronic health problem; 183 patients (76 men; 107 women) could not be classified (Kappa = .964).

Figure 7 presents the means for "acute" and "chronic" illness for men and women (men, women, chronic, acute for distraction, palliative, instrumental, and emotional preoccupation). As predicted, the patients in the chronic illness/injury group used more emotional preoccupation coping than the patients in the acute illness/injury group. The patients in the chronic group also reported more instrumental coping than those in the acute group. Furthermore, for palliative and instrumental coping there were gender by group interactions. For palliative coping, women were higher than men for acute illness; for chronic illness men were higher than women. For instrumental coping women were higher than men on acute illness; men were higher than women on chronic illness.

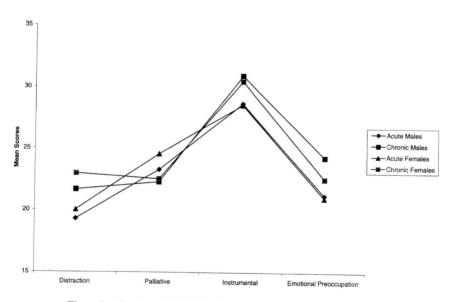

Figure 7.   Coping with Health, Injuries and Problems (CHIP) scales.

Cancer

Courbasson, Endler, and Cunningham (1998) investigated coping in cancer patients. Distraction (D) coping and instrumental coping (I) were *negatively* related to anxiety and depression. Emotional preoccupation (EP) was *positively* related to anxiety and depression. Palliative coping was unrelated to depression and anxiety. Thus, for cancer patients, distress is negatively related to distraction and instrumental coping and positively related to emotional preoccupation coping.

Type 2 diabetes

Macrodimitris and Endler (2001) investigated coping, perceived control, and adjustment in 115 adults with type 2 diabetes (65 women, 50 men, mean age 59.79, no gender differences). This sample of people with type 2 diabetes used primarily instrumental and distraction coping. Long-term blood glucose control, the "objective" control variable, was determined by the Haemoglobin A1c test (HbA_{1c}), a blood test that provides the person's average blood glucose levels over the last 2–3 months. They had high perceptions of control over their type 2 diabetes, and their average HbA_{1c} results were within the "good control" range ($M = 7.89\%$, which is within the 6.5–8.0% or good control range).

Palliative, emotional preoccupation, and rumination coping were each positively related to anxiety and depression. Instrumental coping was negatively related to depression. Perceived control was negatively related to depression and anxiety, and was the only variable found to be negatively related to HbA_{1c}. Thus, people with high perceived control had lower HbA_{1c} scores, showing that those who saw diabetes as controllable actually had better blood glucose control. In terms of relationships between the coping variables, emotional preoccupation and rumination were highly correlated ($r = .70$); distraction and palliative were moderately correlated ($r = .43$); palliative coping was moderately correlated with each of the emotion-oriented coping variables (rumination $r = .33$, emotional preoccupation $r = .40$); instrumental coping was correlated with palliative ($r = .33$) and distraction ($r = .30$) coping. Perceived control was negatively related to emotional preoccupation coping ($r = -.38$) and rumination coping ($r = -.33$). In general, the results showed that having high perceptions of control leads to better physical and psychological outcomes, including better actual blood glucose control, in people with type 2 diabetes.

Coronary heart disease and social support

Another essential ingredient for adjustment is social support. In a study conducted in Berlin, Germany, Schröder, Schwarzer, and Endler (1997) found that recovery of patients undergoing cardiac bypass surgery was facilitated by personal and social resources such as perceived self-efficacy (Bandura, 1997) and social support. Patients (302 men; 79 women) were surveyed once before (Time 1) and twice after surgery (5–10 days after; and $1\frac{1}{2}$ years later) regarding their quality of life. Their partners (spouses) were surveyed at Time 1. Patients' recovery from surgery and coping at Time 2, and their readjustment to normal life $1\frac{1}{2}$ years later (Time 3) "could be partly predicted by spouses' perceived self-efficacy and social support as measured at Time 1" (Schröder et al., 1997, p. 231). Furthermore, higher levels of social support lead to more optimistic ways of thinking (Corace, 2000).

The use of denial coping is associated with rapid recovery in the early phases of rehabilitation, but the long-term prognosis is hindered by poor treatment compliance and failure to make lifestyle changes in patients who continue to deny the severity of their condition. Thus, a minimizing coping strategy (denial) may be adaptive in the short-term, but accepting the disease is more adaptive long-term (Agren et al., 1993; Havik & Maeland, 1988; Levine et al., 1987).

FUTURE DIRECTIONS FOR ANXIETY AND FOR INTERACTIONISM

It is important to assess anxiety and other constructs using various measurement techniques. Beyond self-report measures, one can use behavioural and physiological measures and ratings by others. Magnusson (1999) suggests a *qualitative* approach, in addition to the *quantitative* approach that is most often the case in personality research. To explicate psychological processes, both research methodologies may be necessary. Finally, future research in this field should also focus on longitudinal, genetic, cross-cultural, and clinical studies.

SUMMARY AND CONCLUSIONS

Stress, anxiety, and coping all involve complex processes and all interact with one another. All three constructs have both theoretical and practical implications. Not only must we examine the interaction *between* person factors, but we should also assess the interaction *within* the categories of person variables and of situation variables. An amplification of the basic interaction models appears in Figure 8.

Note that this "between" and "within" person by situation interaction model focuses on subcategories within each basic construct (Endler, 1993).

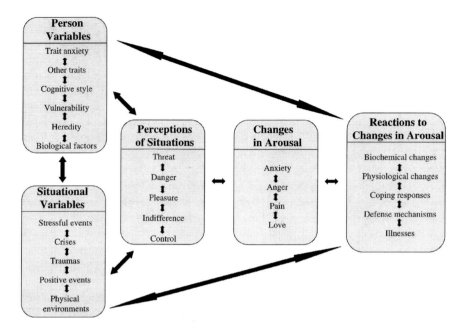

Figure 8. Interaction model: Between and within persons, situations, and reactions.

The squares refer to "between" variables (e.g., persons and situations) and the subcategories within the squares refer to "within" variables (e.g., cognitive styles, traits, biological variables). The left side of the figure refers to person and situation variables, the next phase to perception of situation variables, followed by changes in arousal, and finally, the right side refers to reactions to changes in arousal. Each phase has subcategories that interact with one another dynamically. For example, in the reactions to changes in the arousal phase, the within variables include biochemical and physiological changes, coping responses, defence mechanisms, and illnesses. All phases mutually influence and interact with one another.

The multidimensional interaction model of stress, anxiety, and coping, and experiments designed to test this model, were presented. These laboratory and applied studies contribute theoretical, empirical, and practical knowledge about stress, anxiety, and coping and about their interactions.

ACKNOWLEDGEMENTS

A modified version of this chapter was presented as a State-of-the-Art Invited Lecture at the XXVII International Congress of Psychology, Stockholm, Sweden, July 23–28, 2000. The author would especially like to thank Professor David Magnusson for his very kind and gracious introduction at the lecture. It is over a quarter of a century since my family and I spent a sabbatical in Stockholm. David and I had a very fruitful collaboration which resulted in two books, two *Psychological Bulletin* articles, a number of other papers, and an international conference on Interactionism—resulting in the book *Personality at the crossroads*. The collaboration of Professor David Magnusson and myself, I believe, resulted in the initiation of modern interactionism, as a viable personality model. Therefore, I was especially delighted to have presented this invited lecture in Stockholm.

The preparation of this paper was partially supported by Research Grant No 410–94–1473 from the Social Sciences and Humanities Research Council of Canada (SSHRC). The author also wishes to thank Nancy L. Kocovski for her comments, editorial assistance, and preparation of some of the figures, and Kimberly M. Corace for her comments.

REFERENCES

Agren, B., Ryden, O., Johnsson, P., & Nilsson-Ehle, P. (1993). Rehabilitation after coronary bypass surgery: Coping strategies predict metabolic improvement and return to work. *Scandinavian Journal of Rehabilitation Medicine, 25*, 83–95.

Allen, B.P. (1985). The adjective generation technique (AGT) and the trait-anxiety, state-anxiety distinction. *The Southern Psychologist, 2*(4), 49–58.

Allen, B.P., & Potkay, C.R. (1981). On the arbitrary distinction between states and traits. *Journal of Personality and Social Psychology, 41*(5), 916–928.

Allport, G.W. (1937). *Personality: A psychological interpretation.* New York: Holt.

American Psychiatric Association (1994). *Diagnostic and statistical manual of mental disorders – 4th ed. (DSM-IV).* Washington: Author.

Bandura, A. (1986). *Psychological modelling: Conflicting theories.* New York: Aldine-Atherton.

Bandura, A. (1997). *Self-efficacy: The exercise of control.* New York: W.H. Freeman and Co.

Bateson, M.C. (2000). *Full circles, overlapping lives.* New York: Random House.

Bernstein, L. (1949). *Second symphony, "The age of anxiety".* New York.

Block, J. (1971). *Lives through time.* Berkeley, CA: Bancroft Books.

Block, J. (1977). Advancing the psychology or personality: Paradigmatic shift or improving the quality of research. In D. Magnusson and N.S. Endler (Eds.), *Personality at the crossroads: Current issues in interactional psychology* (pp. 37–65). Hillsdale, NJ: Lawrence Erlbaum Associates Inc.

Block, J. (1981). Some enduring and consequential structure of personality. In A.I. Rabin, J. Arnoff, A.M. Barclay, & R.A. Zucker (Eds.), *Further explorations in personality* (pp. 27–43). New York: John Wiley and Sons.

Cannon, W.B. (1932). *The wisdom of body.* New York: Norton.

Cattell, R.B. (1950). *Personality: A systematic theoretical and factual study.* New York: McGraw-Hill.

Cattell, R. B. (1957). *Personality and motivation structure and measurement.* Yonkers-on-Hudson, NY: World Book Co.

Cattell, R.B. (1965). *The scientific analysis of personality.* Chicago: Aldine.

Cattell, R.B. (1966). *Handbook of multivariate experimental psychology.* Chicago: Rand McNally.

Cattell, R.B., & Scheier, I.H. (1961). *The meaning and measurement of neuroticism and anxiety.* New York: Ronald Press.

Compas, B.E., Malcarne, V.L., & Fondacaro, K.M. (1988). Coping with stressful events in older children and young adolescents. *Journal of Consulting and Clinical Psychology, 56*, 405–411.

Conway, V.J., & Terry, D.J. (1992). Appraised controllability as a moderator of the effectiveness of different coping strategies: A test of the goodness of fit hypothesis. *Australian Journal of Psychology*, *44*, 1–7.

Cooley, C.H. (1902). *Human nature and the social order*. New York: Scribner's.

Corace, K.M (2000). *Predicting cardiac patients' quality of life from coping, optimism, and perceived social support*. Unpublished Master's thesis, York University, Toronto, Canada.

Costa, P.T., & McCrae, R.B. (1985). Hypochondriasis, neuroticism, and aging: When are somatic complaints unfounded? *American Psychologist*, *40*(1), 19–28.

Cottrell, L.S. Jr. (1942a). The analysis of situational fields. *American Sociological Review*, *7*, 370–382.

Cottrell, L.S. Jr. (1942b). The adjustment of the individual to his age and sex roles. *American Sociological Review*, *7*, 618–625.

Courbasson, C.M.A., Endler, N.S., & Cunningham, A.J. (1998). *Coping, control and distress in women with cancer*. Manuscript in preparation.

Coyne, J.C., & Racioppo, M.W. (2000). Never the twain shall meet? Closing the gap between coping research and clinical intervention research. *American Psychologist*, *55*, 655–664.

Dewey, R., & Humber, W.J. (1951). *The development of human behavior*. New York: Macmillan.

Dobkin, P.L., Da Costa, D., Dritsa, M., Fortin, P.R., Senecal, J., Goulet, J.R., Choquette, D., Esdaile, J.M., Beaulieu, A., Cividino, A., Edworthy, S., Barr, S., Ensworth, S., Gladman, D., Smith, D., Zummer, M., Rich, E., & Clarke, A.E. (1999). Quality of life in SLE during active and inactive disease states: Differential contributors to mental and physical health [Abstract]. *Psychosomatic Medicine*, *61*, 102.

Doi, S.C., & Thelen, M.H. (1993). The fear of intimacy scale: Replication and extension. *Psychological Assessment*, *5*(3), 377–383.

Dreger, R.M. (1985). Real and random P-technique analyses of the State-Trait Anxiety Inventory and their relation to R-technique analyses. *The Southern Psychologist*, *2*, 17–28.

Endler, N.S. (1980). Person-situation interaction and anxiety. In I.L. Kutash & L.B. Schlesinger (Eds.), *Handbook on stress and anxiety: Contemporary knowledge, theory and treatment* (pp. 241–266). San Francisco, CA: Jossey Bass.

Endler, N.S. (1983). Interactionism: A personality model, but not yet a theory. In M.M. Page (Ed.), *Nebraska Symposium on Motivation 1982: Personality—current theory and research* (pp. 155–200). Lincoln, NE: University of Nebraska Press.

Endler, N.S. (1988). Hassles, health and happiness. In M.P. Janisse (Ed.), *Individual differences, stress, and health psychology* (pp. 24–56). New York: Springer-Verlag.

Endler, N.S. (1993). Personality: An interactional perspective. In P.J. Hettema & I.J. Deary (Eds.), *Foundations of personality* (pp. 251–268). Dordecht, The Netherlands: Kluwer Academic.

Endler, N.S. (1997). Stress, anxiety and coping: The multidimensional interaction model. *Canadian Psychology*, *38*, 136–153.

Endler, N.S. (1999). *Interactionism: Anxiety, coping, efficacy and stress (ACES)*. Paper presented at the Clinical Recognition Award Day, Department of Psychology, Dalhousie University, Halifax, Nova Scotia, April 9.

Endler, N.S. (2000). The interface between personality and cognition. *European Journal of Personality*, *14*, 377–389.

Endler, N.S., Crooks, D.S., & Parker, J.D.A. (1992). The interaction model of anxiety: An empirical test in a parachute jumping situation. *Anxiety, Stress, and Coping*, *5*, 301–311.

Endler, N.S., & Edwards, J.M. (1985). Evaluation of the state-trait distinction within an interaction model of personality. *The Southern Psychologist*, *2*, 63–71.

Endler, N.S., Edwards, J.M., & Vitelli, R. (1991). *Endler Multidimensional Anxiety Scales (EMAS): Manual*. Los Angeles, CA: Western Psychological Services.

Endler, N.S., & Flett, G.L. (2002). *Endler Multidimensional Anxiety Scales—Social Anxiety Scales: Manual*. Los Angeles, CA: Western Psychological Services.

Endler, N.S., Flett, G.L., Macrodimitris, S.D., Corace, K.M., & Kocovski, N.L. (2001a). *Separation, self-disclosure, and social-evaluation anxiety as interpersonal facets of trait anxiety*. Manuscript submitted for publication.

Endler, N.S., Macrodimitris, S.D., & Kocovski, N.L. (2000a). Control in cognitive and interpersonal tasks: Is it good for you? *Personality and Individual Differences, 29*, 951–962.

Endler, N.S. & Magnusson, D. (1976). Personality and person by situation interactions. In N.S. Endler & D. Magnusson (Eds.), *Interactional psychology and personality* (pp. 1–25). Washington, DC: Hemisphere.

Endler, N.S., & Parker, J.D.A. (1990). Multidimensional assessment of coping: A critical evaluation. *Journal of Personality and Social Psychology, 58*, 844–854.

Endler, N.S., & Parker, J.D.A. (1994). Assessment of multidimensional coping: Task, emotion and avoidance strategies. *Psychological Assessment, 6*, 50–60.

Endler, N.S., & Parker, J.D.A. (1999). *The Coping Inventory for Stressful Situations (CISS): Manual* (2nd ed.). Toronto: Multi-Health Systems.

Endler, N.S., & Parker, J.D.A. (2000). *Coping with Health Injuries and Problems Scale (CHIP): Manual*. Toronto: Multi-Health Systems.

Endler, N.S., Parker, J.D.A., & Summerfeldt, L.J. (1998). Coping with health problems: Developing a reliable and valid multidimensional measure. *Psychological Assessment, 10*, 195–205.

Endler, N.S., Speer, R.L., Johnson, J.M., & Flett, G.L. (2000b). Controllability, coping, efficacy, and distress. *European Journal of Personality, 14*, 245–264.

Endler, N.S., Speer, R.L., Johnson, J.M., & Flett, G.L. (2001b). General self-efficacy and control in relation to anxiety and cognitive performance. *Current Psychology: Developmental · Learning · Personality · Social, 20*, 36–52.

Eysenck, H.J. (1953). *The structure of human personality*. New York: Methuen.

Eysenck, H.J. (1975). The structure of social attitudes. *British Journal of Social and Clinical Psychology, 14*(4), 323–331.

Eysenck, H.J. (1982). *Personality, genetics and behaviour*. New York: Praeger.

Flett, G.L., Endler, N.S., & Fairlie, P. (1999). The threat of Quebec's separation from Canada. *Journal of Personality and Social Psychology, 76*, 143–150.

Folkman, S. (1984). Personal control and stress and coping processes: A theoretical analysis. *Journal of Personality and Social Psychology, 46*, 839–852.

Folkman, S., & Lazarus, R.S. (1985). If it changes it must be a process: A study of emotion and coping during three stages of a college examination. *Journal of Personality and Social Psychology, 48*, 150–170.

Folkman, S., & Lazarus, R.S. (1988). *Manual for the Ways of Coping Questionnaire*. Palo Alto, CA: Consulting Psychologists Press.

Forsythe, C.J., & Compas, B.E. (1987). Interaction of cognitive appraisals of stressful events and coping: Testing the goodness of fit hypothesis. *Cognitive Therapy and Research, 11*, 473–485.

Freud, S. (1924). *A general introduction to psychoanalysis*. New York: Washington Square Press.

Goldberg, D., Williams, P., & The Institute of Psychiatry. (1991). *The General Health Questionnaire manual*. Windsor, UK: NFER/Nelson.

Havik, O.E., & Maeland, J.G. (1988). Verbal denial and outcome in myocardial infarction patients. *Journal of Psychosomatic Research, 32*(2), 145–157.

Kantor, J.R. (1926). *Principles of psychology, Vol. 1*. Bloomington: Principia Press.

Kantor, J.R. (1926). *Principles of psychology, Vol. 2*. Bloomington: Principia Press.

Kelly, A.E., & McKillop, K.J. (1996). Consequences of revealing personal secrets. *Psychological Bulletin, 120*, 450–465.

Lazarus, R.S. (1976). *Patterns of adjustment* (3rd ed.). New York: McGraw-Hill.

Lazarus, R.S. (1993). Coping theory and research: Past, present, and future. *Psychosomatic Medicine, 55*, 234–247.

Lazarus, R.S. (1998). *Fifty years of the research and theory of R.S. Lazarus: An analysis of historical and perennial issues.* Mahwah, NJ: Lawrence Erlbaum Associates Inc.

Lazarus, R.S. (2000). Toward better research on stress and coping. *American Psychologist, 55*, 665–673.

Levine, J., Warrenberg, S., Kerns, R., Schwartz, G.E., Delaney, R., Fontana, A., Gradman, A., Smith, S., Allen, S., & Cascione, R. (1987). The role of denial in recovery from coronary heart disease. *Psychosomatic Medicine, 49*, 109–117.

Lewin, K. (1935). *A dynamic theory of personality: Selected papers.* New York: McGraw-Hill.

Lewis, A. (1970). The ambiguous word "anxiety". *International Journal of Psychiatry, 9*, 62–79.

Lindesmith, A.R., & Strauss, A.L. (1949). *Social psychology.* Fort Worth, TX: Dryden Press.

Macrodimitris, S.D., & Endler, N.S. (2001). Coping, control and adjustment in type 2 diabetes. *Health Psychology, 20*, 208–216.

Magnusson, D. (1986). Antisocial conduct of boys and autonomic activity/reactivity. *Reports from the Department of Psychology*, University of Stockholm, No. 544.

Magnusson, D. (1992). Back to the phenomena: Theory, methods and statistics in psychological research. *European Journal of Personality, 6*, 1–14.

Magnusson, D. (1998). The logic and implications of a person-oriented approach. In R.B. Cairns, L.R. Bergman, & J. Kagan (Eds.), *Methods and models for studying the individual* (pp. 33–64). Thousand Oaks, CA: Sage.

Magnusson, D. (1999). Holistic interactionism: A perspective for research on personality development. In L.A. Pervin & O.P. John (Eds.), *Handbook of personality: Theory and research* (pp. 219–247). New York: Guilford Press.

Magnusson, D., & Endler, N.S. (1977). Interactional psychology: Present status and future prospects. In D. Magnusson & N.S. Endler (Eds.), *Personality at the crossroads: Current issues in interactional psychology* (pp. 3–31). Hillsdale, NJ: Lawrence Erlbaum Associates Inc.

Manicavasagar, V., Silove, D., & Curtis, J. (1997). Separation anxiety in adulthood: A phenomenological investigation. *Comprehensive Psychiatry, 38*, 274–282.

May, R. (1950). *The meaning of anxiety.* New York: W.W. Norton.

McCann, D., & Endler, N.S. (2000). Editorial: Personality and cognition. *European Journal of Personality, 14*, 371–375.

McNair, D.M., Lorr, M., & Droppelman, F.L. (1981). *Profile of Mood States manual.* San Diego, CA: Educational & Industrial Testing Service.

Mead, G.H. (1934). *Mind, self and society.* Chicago: University of Chicago Press.

Mischel, W., & Peake, P.K. (1982). Beyond déjà vu in the search for cross-situational consistency. *Psychological Review, 89*, 730–755.

Mischel, W., & Shoda, Y. (1995). A cognitive-affective system theory of personality: Reconceptualizing situations, dispositions, dynamics, and invariance in personality structure. *Psychological Review, 102*, 246–268.

Muris, P., Merckelbach, H., Schmidt, H., & Tierney, S. (1999). Disgust sensitivity, trait anxiety and anxiety disorders symptoms in normal children. *Behaviour Research and Therapy, 37*(10), 953–961.

Murray, H.A. (1938). *Explorations in personality.* New York: Oxford University Press.

Nolen-Hoeksema, S., Morrow, J., & Frederickson, B.L. (1993). Response styles and the duration of episodes of depressed mood. *Journal of Abnormal Psychology, 102*, 20–28.

Sawyer-Radloff, L. (1977). The CES-D Scale: A self-report depression scale for research in the general population. *Applied Psychological Measurement, 1*, 385–401.

Scheier, M.F., Carver, C.S., & Bridges, M.W. (1994). Distinguishing optimism from neuroticism (and trait anxiety, self-mastery, and self-esteem): A re-evaluation of the Life Orientation Test. *Journal of Personality and Social-Psychology, 67*, 1063–1078.

Schröder, K.E.E., Schwarzer, R., & Endler, N.S. (1997). Predicting cardiac patients' quality of life from the characteristics of their spouses. *Journal of Health Psychology, 2,* 231–244.

Shacham, S. (1983). A shortened version of the Profile of Mood States. *Journal of Personality Assessment, 47,* 305–306.

Shoda, Y., & Mischel, W. (2000). Reconciling contextualism with the core assumptions of personality psychology. *European Journal of Personality, 14,* 407–428.

Shute, C. (1973). Aristotle's interactionism and its transformations by some 20th century writers. *The Psychological Record, 23,* 283–293.

Somerfield, M.R., & McCrae, R.R. (2000). Stress and coping research: Methodological challenges, theoretical advances, and clinical applications. *American Psychologist, 55,* 620–625.

Spielberger, C.D. (1966). The effects of anxiety on complex learning and academic achievement. In C.D. Spielberger (Ed.), *Anxiety and behaviour* (pp. 361–398). New York: Academic Press.

Spielberger, C.D. (1972). Current trends in theory and research on anxiety. In C.D. Spielberger (Ed.), *Anxiety: Current trends in theory and research, Vol. 1* (pp. 3–19). New York: Academic Press.

Spielberger, C.D. (1985). *Anxiety, cognition and affect: A state-trait perspective.* Hillsdale, NJ: Lawrence Erlbaum Associates Inc.

Taylor, S.E., Klein, L.C., Lewis, B.P., Gruenewald, T.L., Gurung, R.A.R., & Updegraff, J.A. (2000). Biobehavioral responses to stress in females: Tend-and-befriend, not fight-or-flight. *Psychological Review, 107,* 411–429.

Tolman, E.C. (1935). Psychology versus immediate experience. *Philosophy of Science, 2,* 356–380.

Trotter, M., & Endler, N.S. (1999). An empirical test of the interaction model of anxiety in a competitive equestrian setting. *Personality and Individual Differences, 27,* 861–875.

Vitaliano, P.P. (1990). Appraised changeability of a stressor as a modifier of the relationship between coping and depression: A test of the hypothesis of fit. *Journal of Personality and Social Psychology, 59,* 582–592.

Ware, J.E., Jr, Snow, K.K., Kosinski, M., et al. (1993). *SF-36 Health Survey: Manual and interpretation guide.* Boston, MA: The Health Institute, New England Medical Center.

CHAPTER THIRTEEN

Ancient humans in the newborn millennium: Stress and gender perspectives

Marianne Frankenhaeuser
University of Stockholm, Sweden

RAPID SOCIAL CHANGE

It is our good fortune to live in a time when environments can be moulded to suit people. The demands and pressures facing people in the industrialized world today are largely human-made. This means that they are not as unchangeable as were those confronting our ancestors.

But our age has its own problems, many of them psychological and social in nature. And we need not be starved, or cold, or physically exhausted for stress to occur (Cannon, 1932; Frankenhaeuser, 1979; Mason, 1975; Selye, 1956). Our life is quite different from the small face-to-face groups that characterized millions of years during which our ancestors were evolving into the present species. The dramatic technology-driven changes have rapidly brought about the erosion of traditional institutions and guidelines for behavior. All this leaves us in great perplexity: What to believe, how to be useful, what is worthwhile, how to ensure attachments, how to make the environment reasonably predictable. These are great dilemmas, created by the rapid transformation of the environment.

People develop in interaction with their surroundings. Each of us is born with a wide range of potentialities, and which of these we develop depends upon the nature of the influences to which we are exposed. In short, we become only one of the many individuals that we are capable of becoming.

Among external influences that shape us in adult life, the work we do is probably the most powerful one. And job content and job design depend increasingly on how technology is applied. Technology, depending upon how it is used, can make people grow, just as it can make people shrink. As yet, we have only begun to exploit the enormous opportunities to adapt jobs to people's needs, their abilities, and their constraints. Technology continues to be applied in ways that frustrate basic psychological and social needs, such as the need to understand, to predict, and to control what goes on in the surroundings. This is why stress has become a major issue of our time, in spite of the fact that, today, life conditions in the rich part of the world are physically less strenuous and less taxing than the conditions experienced by any previous generation.

THE EVOLUTIONARY PERSPECTIVE

The mismatch between the ancient humans and the modern environment should be viewed in an evolutionary perspective. We are so firmly anchored in the present that it is difficult to comprehend how new our world really is in evolutionary terms (Hamburg, Elliot, & Parron, 1982). There is nothing in the history of humankind to prepare us for coping with the high-technology environment that we have so rapidly created for ourselves. Our ancestors adapted gradually to an environment which changed very slowly, and it was the slowness of the change that made adaptation possible. With the industrial revolution, the rate of change began to increase drastically, and in the electronic era the rate keeps accelerating.

In striking contrast, the human brain and body have remained essentially the same over several thousands of years. Thus, we have been faced with two seemingly incompatible phenomena: the accelerating pace of social evolution and the slowness of genetic evolution. Recently, a spectacular scenario has been added: the possibility of manipulating human genes. As yet, we cannot even imagine the consequences of transforming the ancient humans by genetic manipulation.

KEY ROLES OF PSYCHOLOGY IN
STRESS RESEARCH

Psychology has at least two key roles in dealing with problems of stress and maladjustment. One involves changing unhealthy behavior patterns, the other changing the environments that promote unhealthy behavior. Changing behavior may involve education, training, counselling, behavior therapy, or psychotherapy. Such procedures fit well into traditional clinical-psychological and medical thinking. The other approach, changing the structure of the environment, may involve altering the conditions under which people work and function, the tasks they perform, and the rewards they obtain. Approaches involving changes at the structural and systems level are much more complex than are changes at the individual level. Nevertheless, psychological stress research is beginning to have an impact on the systems level, too. This is true, in particular, of work environments. Here stress research does not serve merely to provide warning signals of excessive human strain and impending burnout. It plays a more constructive role by providing knowledge that can be used for redesigning jobs and modifying ways in which society is organized (Frankenhaeuser, 1991).

UNDERLOAD AND OVERLOAD

In order to adapt work to suit people we have to take into account the brain's need for an adequate degree of stimulation from the external world. Brain research and behavioral research have taught us under which conditions people perform well and when performance breaks down (Frankenhaeuser & Gardell, 1976). When the total load of impressions from the outside world falls below a critical level, disturbances occur in brain function and behavior. We tend to become inattentive and bored, and to loose initiative. Under the opposite condition, when the stimulus flow exceeds a certain level, brain function is likewise disturbed. We lose our ability to integrate messages, thought processes become fragmented, and judgment is impaired. We suffer from information overload. This inverted-U relationship between stimulus level and brain function is a fundamental biological principle with wide application.

The crucial point is that large groups of people spend their lives outside the optimal zone of mental stimulation that would provide opportunities for them to develop their full potential. Their abilities are constantly either underutilized or overtaxed. In Sweden, known for its advanced work reform programs, recent statistics show that every third woman and every fourth man has a job that is understimulating and does not allow them to develop their potential by learning new things (Frankenhaeuser, 1991; Lundberg, Mård-berg, & Frankenhaeuser, 1994; Statistics Sweden, 1992). This is a waste of human talent.

THE EFFORT–DISTRESS MODEL

With the development of biochemical techniques that permit determining exceedingly small amounts of hormones in blood, urine, and saliva, neuroen-docrine responses have come to play an increasingly important role in stress research (Euler & Lishajko, 1961).

In my research group we have focused on two major elements of mental stress and their neuroendocrine correlates. One is effort, the other distress. Our results show that effort and distress are selectively related to two neuroendocrine systems. Effort activates the sympathetic-adrenal medullary system (the fight-flight system) with the release of the catecholamines, adrenaline and noradrenaline. Distress activates the pituitary-adrenal cortical system with the release of cortisol. In short: catecholamines are our effort hormones, while cortisol is our distress hormone.

In situations where we experience both effort and distress (which is in fact typical of stress in everyday life) both catecholamine and cortisol secretion increase. These are situations where we go on pushing hard, although we may start feeling uncomfortable and questioning our self-confidence. If, however, distress gets overwhelming, we eventually give up, feeling helpless and depressed. Such an overwhelming distress can be caused by losing one's job, by serious illness, economic crisis, or bereavement. With all effort gone, the catecholamines decrease and the cortisol-producing system takes command. Under such conditions our immune defense is down, and our cardiovascular system is at risk (Frankenhaeuser, 1986; McEwen, 1998).

In sharp contrast, we may experience effort but no distress. Effort without distress is a joyous happy state. It makes us alert, confident of mastering the challenges facing us. We are functioning at the peak of our ability, our talents being neither underused nor overtaxed. In such situations catecholamines are high, while the cortisol system is put to rest.

Who are the lucky ones experiencing happy stress? We find them among artists, craftsmen, researchers, entrepreneurs. In short, those who have a high degree of control over their work. This, in summary, is the effort-distress model, that has inspired a great deal of research in our group (Frankenhaeuser, 1983).

One of the ambitions of today's psychobiological research is to improve the recording techniques by which bodily responses can be monitored, even in natural settings, without interfering with people's everyday activities (Williams et al., 1997). Such techniques help us to find out what makes the blood pressure rise, the heart beat faster, the muscles tense up. These are important pieces of information which, together with stress-hormone assays, help in identifying aversive aspects of the environment. Moreover, they aid in identifying factors that protect people against harmful stress. In other words, when searching the environment for harmful and protective factors, we can use the people themselves as "measuring rods". Hence, research at the intersection of psychology and neurobiology may open new possibilities for prevention and intervention. In our research group we have found urinary measurements of stress hormones particularly useful for assessing stress levels under a variety of conditions (Frankenhaeuser et al., 1989).

COMBINING LABORATORY AND FIELD STUDIES

An important feature of our research strategy is the combination of laboratory and field studies. In laboratory studies, specific problems are extracted from natural settings and brought into the laboratory for systematic examination. The field studies take laboratory-based experimental techniques into natural settings and apply them to persons engaged in their everyday activities. Let me illustrate this by one example from our real-life studies (Singer, Lundberg, & Frankenhaeuser, 1978).

We wanted to study the stress involved in daily commuting by train between one's home and work place. How much did the length of the trip add to the stress versus the crowdedness of the train? We compared different groups of passengers upon their arrival at the Stockholm Central station. Stress was assessed by self-reports and by urinary stress hormones. Collecting urine samples under standardized conditions at a train station was no easy task. We managed, however, to convince the Swedish Railway Company of the importance of our study. They responded generously by putting a private toilet at our disposal. This was a toilet ordinarily reserved for royalties arriving at the station. This arrangement made it possible for us to obtain the urine samples with the same care as under experimental conditions. The results showed that the duration of the trip did not add much to the stress, provided one could choose one's own seat and company in a not yet crowded train.

In the early 1970s my late colleague, Dr Bertil Gardell, social and organizational psychologist, and my research group initiated a joint research program. The idea to integrate theory and methods from organizational psychology and psychobiology proved fruitful. In a study of assembly-line workers, we were able to demonstrate how neuroendocrine measurements could be used in pinpointing aversive factors in the work process such as short repetitive work cycles, lack of control over pace, and inability to communicate with other workers (Frankenhaeuser & Gardell, 1976). All of these were reflected in increased physiological arousal.

The physiological measures turned out to be powerful tools. They reinforced the workers' verbal reports of stress, dissatisfaction, and psychosomatic symptoms. They provided a novel input into work reform programs by increasing the awareness of psychosocial factors. It was exciting to witness how much weight these physiological measures carried when presented, not only to corporate health care departments, but also to unions and management. Their potential importance as early warnings of long-term health risks was so obvious.

CONTROL—A KEY TO COPING

I have already emphasized the role of personal control as a key to coping with the demands and pressures facing us (Frankenhaeuser, 1979; Karasek, 1979). Being in control and having influence over one's surroundings adds enormously to our ability to tolerate stress. However, we must recognize some new features related to new complexities in daily life. Today, exercizing personal control requires more effort on part of the individual. Control has become more taxing, involving more self-discipline than ever before. One reason is the changing patterns of working life. Having a permanent, regular 9–5 job is becoming more and more unusual. Instead, people engage in projects. Moving in and out of new projects is stimulating and enriching. But it also means that life has less of a given structure, and fewer rules and regulations. It is up to us as individual beings to set the rules, to draw the boundaries and limits. This new freedom exacts a price in terms of stress.

THE ISSUE OF UNWINDING

A mechanism by which personal control might exert its positive influence on health outcomes has to do with the ability to unwind after stressful encounters (Frankenhaeuser et al., 1989). While we are immersed in work, the body's "stress machinery" tends to stay in full gear. This can be seen as the price we pay for good achievement. But when the work is over, how quickly do we unwind? Our research shows that the rate of unwinding depends on the type of task and the type of person.

As to differences between people, we have found that "rapid unwinders" tend to be mentally better balanced and more efficient in achievement situations than slow unwinders. It is also significant that the time for unwinding varies predictably with the individual's state of general wellbeing. Thus, a study by Johansson (1976) showed that, when rested and in good shape after a vacation period, a group of white-collar workers were able to unwind more quickly than before the vacation period. In contrast, excessive overtime in a group of engineers at Ericsson was shown by Rissler (1979) to be accompanied by slow unwinding, not only during the period of overtime but for weeks or even months after.

DOES WOMEN'S STRESS DIFFER FROM MEN'S?

A couple of decades ago, when gender roles were more rigid than today, women and men tended to respond differently to achievement demands. The old fight-flight pattern involving catecholamine increase was more readily elicited in men (Frankenhaeuser, 1983).

As attitudes and values of women and men have become more similar, they also respond similarly in terms of stress hormones. Professional women have taken over the men's response pattern and tend to respond to achievement demands even more strongly than men. This is the new trend. It indicates that women in managerial positions are overadapting to the organizational structures and value systems shaped by men. Today's women leaders tend to be dynamic, forceful, and hard-driving. They love their job, but pay a price in terms of stress (Ekvall, Frankenhaeuser, & Parr, 1994; Frankenhaeuser, 1991).

During the time that stress research was focused on men, the workplace was seen as the primary stressor. The home was viewed as the place where one recovers from stress at work (Wortman, Biernat, & Lang, 1991). However, if we are to come to grips with the sources of stress in both women and men, we have to take into account their total work load: the sum of paid and unpaid work.

The most obvious obstacle for unwinding in the evening is "the second job" that a large section of the employees take up when they return home: demands related to family, children, and household duties. This is largely the women's job. It is therefore not surprising that women tend to unwind more slowly in the evenings after work. While men's arousal level tends to drop after 5 pm, women's arousal continues to increase (Frankenhaeuser, 1996).

WORK–FAMILY CONFLICT

Women's involvement in their occupation has not decreased their involvement in home and family. Their average total workload exceeds that of men at all occupational levels (Kahn, 1991). On average, women carry the main responsibility for 14 out of 17 daily duties at home. When interviewed, a woman executive at Volvo expressed what many women were feeling by the words: "I wish I could split in two!" (Frankenhaeuser et al., 1989; Lundberg & Frankenhaeuser, 1999).

On average, stress reaches its peak between ages 30 and 40. That is the point in life when demands from the family coincide with a critical phase in career development. After 40 the conflict lessens, and life is experienced as more controllable (Frankenhaeuser, 1988). Women above 40 are, in fact, the greatest unexploited resource in large parts of the world.

THE WORK–LEISURE RELATIONSHIP

The issue of unwinding after a day's work is crucial for the wider issue of the work-leisure relationship. The prevailing view until a few decades ago was that one could compensate for a dull, boring job by stimulating activities in one's free time. We now know that it is not so. There is a "spill-over" from the job experience to leisure.

A specific aspect of this spill-over from job to leisure is that people holding stimulating jobs might be more likely to engage in physical activity and other health behaviors. In traditional corporate health-promotion programs the focus is on teaching the individual employees healthy lifestyles. One conclusion from stress research is that improving psychosocial work conditions may, in fact, be the most effective means of motivating people to engage in health behaviors in their free time. In other words: investing in job content and work organization may enhance the employees personal effort to improve their lifestyle. This, in turn, may reduce the risk for severe stress and burnout.

STRESS AND BURNOUT

Stress and burnout are, of course, closely related. However, the two concepts refer to two different aspects of mental strain. Stress is often acute. It can strike suddenly and may disappear quickly. Burnout is the result of accumulated long-term stress (Maslach, 1982). It is a process that takes time to develop, and time to get rid of. At risk for burnout are those who engage themselves deeply in a task, but are prevented from achieving their goal. Being forced to give up after a long-term involvement may kill self-confidence and motivation. Common reasons for having to give up are, for example, unforeseen organizational changes, severe economic crises, or relational conflicts.

We can all agree that in the short-term, high speed is almost always a blessing. But in the longer-term stress accumulates unless time is allowed for unwinding and recovery. And it is the accumulation of stress over long periods that constitutes a threat to physical and mental health. In many work situations health risks can be reduced by inserting adequate rest pauses. Thus, for example, Lundberg et al. (1999) showed in a recent electromyographic study of supermarket cashiers that 1-hour rest pauses during the workday counteracted muscular tension and, hence, reduced the risk for muscular disorder.

One can speculate that constant environmental demands to maximize speed may lead to a loss of ability for slowness. This may not seem a serious loss, but it is a fact that some kinds of cognitive processes require slowness. For example, Charles Darwin is said to have been a slow thinker. And so was Albert Einstein. However, today there is not much opportunity for slow thinking and reflection. Overload is the hallmark of our stress culture.

OVERLOAD—THE HALLMARK OF OUR STRESS CULTURE

We are all victims of the acceleration syndrome, ruled by the tyranny of speed. By the acceleration syndrome I mean that ever-larger groups of people spend a lot of time and effort striving to gain time. And the time we gain, we use trying to gain even more time. In this way the tempo of life is speeded up in a never-ending accelerative process.

The computer has set new norms for how long things should take. In the old times, the tempo and pace of life were determined by the human nervous system. This meant a slower pace than that set by the computer. Therefore, people today seem to be constantly short of breath, experiencing a fear of not keeping up, of lagging behind. This mentality demands instant activity, instant information, instant communication, instant "everything" (including, of course, instant food).

The seductive feature of electronic communication is its incredible speed. The number of communications and contacts can be enormously increased by electronic means. This, however, does not ensure time for building deep relationships and attachments. Everyting in life cannot be speeded up without quality suffering. Building emotional relationships requires time. It is inherent in the process and cannot be speeded up. Any relationship demanding empathy and confidence takes time to build. Psychotherapy is but one example.

THE PLACELESS ELECTRONIC CULTURE

A remarkable aspect of electronic communication is that it makes us independent of place. It does not make much difference whether we are close or far geographically. Both work and relations have acquired a placeless quality. In our culture, focus is entirely on time—place does not matter as it used to (Forberg & Möller, 1999).

The wish for rapid communication has affected our everyday lifestyle. A survey conducted at Stanford University showed that sending e-mail twice an hour, instead of walking over to the colleague, leads to a considerable weight gain per year. Faxing from the computer, instead of walking to the fax machine, decreases physical activity by several kilometers a year. As evermore of our daily activities are conducted from our cellular phones, the need to move about may become even less.

We should ask ourselves whether the demands for rapidity and speediness will affect our image of the ideal human being. Will our future ideal be a person who is endlessly flexible and smart, adapting easily to market demands, changing swiftly from one belief to another? Or will the obsession with speed that we experience today be replaced by other values, such as empathy, tolerance, and gentleness?

PLEA FOR DIALOGUE

Looking back at psychology over the past decades has strengthened my conviction that human motives, abilities, and constraints provide guidelines for adapting environments to people. To make effective use of such knowledge, we need to increase the dialogue between the scientific community and the worlds of politics, health care, social establishments, and working life. As long as the gaps between these worlds are not bridged, a wealth of knowledge and ideas on both sides will remain unutilized.

The dialogue between the worlds of science and societal institutions takes time to develop. There are no short-cuts for a productive exchange of ideas and competencies between researchers and their speaking partners in practical life. Insofar as researchers become partners in this process, it will reduce the risk that research findings remain isolated fragments, which will not even touch base with the problems that stimulated the research in the first place.

This is to say that technical development, human resources, and values are intimately linked. Just as there are limits to how much change human beings can comfortably tolerate in their lives, there are limits to how much change a society and an organization can successfully accommodate in a given time period. Above a certain level, both productivity and quality are likely to suffer as events outpace the people who are supposed to be in control of the development.

Stated in the language of psychology and psychobiology, the central lesson is that human beings have a need—deeply rooted in their nervous system—to comprehend and to control what goes on in their surroundings, and to predict how changes are likely to affect their future.

REFERENCES

Cannon, W.B. (1932). *The wisdom of the body*. New York: W.W. Norton.

Ekvall, G., Frankenhaeuser, M., & Parr, D. (1994). *Leadership style and leadership stress. A study of male and female clinic managers in public dental health care*. Stockholm: FA Institute for Research on Business and Work Life Issues, Report No. 4.

Euler, U.S. von, & Lishajko, F. (1961). Improved technique for the fluorimetric estimation of catecholamines. *Acta Physiologica Scandinavica, 51*, 348–355.

Forberg, K.H., & Möller, B. (1999). *Demanding information*. Bachelor Thesis, Lund University, Department for Informatics.

Frankenhaeuser, M. (1979). Psychoneuroendocrine approaches to the study of emotion as related to stress and coping. In H.E. Howe & R.A. Dienstbier (Eds.), *Nebraska Symposium on Motivation 1978* (pp. 123–161). Lincoln, NE: University of Nebraska Press.

Frankenhaeuser, M. (1983). The sympathetic-adrenal and pituitary-adrenal response to challenge: Comparison between the sexes. In T.M. Dembroski, T.H. Schmidt & C. Blumchen (Eds.), *Biobehavioral bases of coronary heart disease* (pp. 91–105). New York: Karger.

Frankenhaeuser, M. (1986). A psychobiological framework for research on human stress and

These labels and definitions have since been revised, primarily because of criticism directed at their denigrating, stigmatizing nature (see Figure 4). However, the focus here is on their scientific status and on whether the definitions can be operationalized as three separate constructs. Measures exist which purport to assess disability (Bowling, 1997), but it is not clear that they are distinguishable from measures claiming to assess handicap such as the London Handicap Scale (Harwood, Rogers, Dickenson, & Ebrahim, 1994). When expert judges were asked to use the WHO ICIDH (1980) definitions to classify questionnaire items from the UK version of the Sickness Impact Profile (SIP) (Bergner, Bobbitt, & Pollard, 1981; Patrick & Peach, 1989), they found the task difficult (Johnston & Pollard, in press). Thus the definitions in Table 1 are not easy to implement.

For items where there was satisfactory agreement between judges about the allocation to disability or handicap, it was possible to assess the empirical separation of the constructs. Using confirmatory factor analysis and the judges' classification of UK SIP items, evidence of separate constructs was found in stroke patients assessed at 1 month and 6 months after discharge from hospital (Johnston & Pollard, 1997). Further, these analyses allowed investigation of the distinction between these constructs and an additional consequence of stroke, the emotional impact. On both occasions, it was possible to separate disability from handicap, and both of these from emotional state as assessed by the HADS (Zigmond & Snaith, 1983). Table 2 shows the stroke data at the two points in time.

However, when the same analyses were performed with data from myocardial infarction patients, it was not possible to get clear separation of disability and handicap constructs on each of the three occasions it was investigated (Johnston & Pollard, in press). Thus, disability may be distinguishable from handicap for some clinical groups, but not for all clinical conditions. Where the constructs are not distinct, then a more general construct of "behavioural limitations", combining disability and handicap, may be more suitable. This has implications for modelling the process and explanatory mechanisms in disability. For example, where disability and handicap are not separate constructs, it is inappropriate to posit that

TABLE 14.2

Confirmatory Factor Analyses of stroke data testing separation of disability (D), handicap (H), and emotional state (E): Evidence of fit for model with these three factors

	χ^2	p	NFI	NNFI	CFI
1 month	19.1	.32	.86	.97	.98
6 months	17.8	.40	.91	.99	1.00

Fit is indicated by nonsignificant χ^2 and fit indices greater than .90. NFI = normed fit index; NNFI = non-normed fit index; CFI = comparative fit index (Bentler & Bonett, 1980).

handicap is the result of disability, as the WHO ICIDH (1980) model proposes.

MODELS OF MEASUREMENT

Self-report methods

The methods used to measure disability are most commonly self-report measures such as the SIP (see Bowling, 1997). For example, scales may use items such as:

> *I only walk with a physical aid* (mobility)
> *I need assistance to wash myself* (self-care)

The selection of items is clearly critical to the content validity of the scales and the earlier analyses demonstrate that it is possible to examine the construct validity of scale items statistically. However, the methods of scoring and scaling items cannot be chosen simply on the basis of their statistical and psychometric convenience since they additionally reflect an underlying model of the process of disability.

A variety of models of scaling have been used to investigate disability, including Thurstone, Guttman, item response theory models, and simple summation models. In Thurstone scaling, it is assumed that one point or one specific item on the scale truly reflects the status of the individual. Using an appropriate methodology, items are given values to reflect the severity of the disability involved. For example, on the UK SIP, the item *"I walk more slowly"* carries a value of 39, whereas the item *"I do not walk at all"* has a value of 126. In true Thurstone scaling, the individual would select the item that most closely described their state and the score for this item would be their scale score[1]. By contrast, in Guttman scaling, items have a cumulative relationship and failure on an item implies that the individual is unable to perform any of the more difficult items. For example, Table 3 shows a Guttman scale of limitations in a community sample of women. The individual's score indicates not only the total number of items they are unable to perform, but also *which* items they cannot perform.

Simple summation models, which add up the number of items the person cannot do but where the scale does not have Guttman status, imply that disabilities do not have systematic relationships with each other. High scores do not necessarily have different items checked from low scores, but may only

---

[1] In fact, the SIP and its variations, including the UK SIP, while allocating scores to items using Thurstone methods, does not adopt true Thurstone scaling, but instead uses a weighted sum technique. The mismatch between the item development and scoring is one source of problems in SIP scoring and scaling (Pollard & Johnston, 2001).

TABLE 14.3
Guttman scaling of behavioural limitations in women in the community (Williams, Johnston, Willis, & Bennett, 1976)

Item	No. of items disabled
Cannot do all own washing clothes, cleaning, shopping	1
Does not use transport accompanied	2
Does not walk out of doors unaccompanied	3
Cannot do all own cooking	4
Cannot wash without help	5
Cannot dress without help	6
Cannot undress without help	7
Cannot use w.c. or commode without help	8
Cannot sit and stand without help	9
Does not get out of bed	10
Cannot eat without personal help	11

indicate the checking of more items of similar kind and severity. In weighted summed scores, some items carry more weight, but, unlike the Guttman scaling model, there is still no implication in the model of measurement that highly weighted items will be more commonly checked by those with high scores. Measurement based on item response theory carries a different set of assumptions, for example that different items may be sensitive at different levels of disability and that items will vary in the size of the range of sensitivity; so that some items may be as sensitive to differences in level of disability amongst those with severe and those with mild disabilities, whereas others may be highly sensitive over a very narrow range.

Each of these scaling models portrays a different underlying model of disability. Thurstone scaling implies distinct patterns of disabilities characterizing each level of severity. The Guttman approach suggests that the acquisition or recovery process follows a predictably ordered sequence and that a scale score indicates the individual's position on this sequence. Summation implies that all disabilities are equivalent and that there is no order or pattern in the acquisition of, or recovery from, disability. By contrast, item response theory scaling suggests that change in disability level may be achieved by gradual change or by acute shifts, and that both processes may be occurring simultaneously.

Typically, scaling methods are chosen with little reference to these underlying models of the disability process. Yet, different models may be applicable in different situations or for different conditions. For example, Guttman scaling may be appropriate for conditions with a gradual accumulation of disorder as in osteoarthritis, summation methods may apply in a condition such as multiple sclerosis, which can affect different functions unpredictably, and item response theory may detect a recovery process where rehabilitation affects rapid progress on some functions while gradual recovery occurs on others.

Other methods

The use of self-report methods implies that the individual can recall and report the behaviours characterized as disability without bias and clearly this is not the case. For example, one might expect more limitations to be reported in individuals showing high negative affectivity (Watson & Pennebaker, 1989). A similar problem arises with self-report in other areas of psychological measurement, but there are additional possible confounds in this area. In particular, we have noted the possible confound with mental representations of the condition. In our investigations of the responses of patients with chronic illness, factor analytic studies of general disability and perceived control measures showed these constructs were distinguishable (Bonetti, 2001). Nevertheless, it is possible that these distinctions will not be made by respondents with other conditions, or using more specific measures. For example, some items on disability scales are quite similar to those on self-efficacy scales and it may be extremely difficult to differentiate a particular disability item such as "*can you walk unaided?*" from a self-efficacy item, "*how confident are you that you can walk unaided?*".

There are alternative methods that may help to overcome the validity problems. Self-report can be improved by the use of diary methods to overcome problems of recall, and behavioural observational methods can address issues of observer bias. A major problem with observational methods is that they are restricted to times and places where the observer is present and therefore the full picture outside the clinic, laboratory, or observation situation is not assessed. A more extensive record of behaviour free from self-report bias can be obtained by using automatic monitoring to measure actual activity levels. Figure 2 illustrates monitoring of daily activities; periods when the individual is walking slowly, walking faster, or not walking can be clearly distinguished and totals obtained for specified periods.

Summary

There are significant problems with current models of measurement of disability. First, even when the same construct definition is applied, it is difficult to reach agreement on the distinction between disability and handicap and further work needs to be done on refining these constructs. Where a distinction cannot be made, we suggest the term "behavioural limitation." Second, even with a satisfactory definition, there are problems in selecting an appropriate measurement model. Measurement methods imply different underlying processes and the links between theory, definition, and

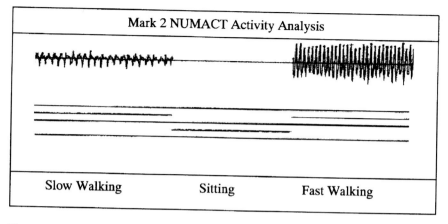

Figure 2.   Automatic recording of activity. The record shows an initial period of slow walking steps, followed by a period of sitting, followed by a period of faster walking.

measurement models have not been made explicit in this field. It may be that different clinical conditions require different measurement models. Third, the methods of collecting data are subject to various sources of confounding, so that apparent patterns may emerge which reflect processes other than disability, such as negative affectivity or self-efficacy. This is an important problem for this field and one that may require the use of multiple methods including not only self-report but additionally observational and automatic measurement of the actual behaviours.

These problems may be addressed by further investigation of methods of data collection, item selection, scoring, and scaling. However, progress will also depend on better theoretical modelling of disability per se.

MODELS OF EXPLANATION

Several models are appropriate for explaining the consequences of disability. A mental health model would address the impact of disability on emotional disorder, a life events models would consider disablement along with other events, and stress and coping models would view disability as an ongoing stressor or as depletion of coping resources.

Nonetheless, the focus here is not on models of consequences, but on models explaining disability per se. Medical models explain disability in terms of the underlying disease. Psychological models explain disability in terms of cognitive and emotional processes.

Medical model

The dominant medical model is the WHO ICIDH (1980) model or some variant on it (see Ebrahim, 1999; Johnson & Wolinsky, 1993; Nagi, 1991; Wilson & Cleary, 1995). The ICIDH model postulates that disability is a result of impairment and that handicap is a result of impairment or disability (see Figure 3). This model has been seen as a descriptive, clinical model, but it makes clear predictions and can be evaluated as a scientific model.

Since it is possible to distinguish disability and handicap in stroke patients, the ICIDH model was tested with these patients, using path analyses. There was support for the model in that there was a path from disability at 1 month to handicap at 6 months, but not from handicap at 1 month to disability at 6 months. However, there was neither support for the path from impairment, assessed neurologically while the patient was in hospital, to disability, nor from impairment to handicap at 1 month (Johnston & Pollard, in press). Thus the model performed poorly in explaining disability.

In the revised ICIDH model (ICIDH-2: WHO, 1998), the updated disability construct of activity (limitations) is not only influenced by impairment as before, but additionally by participation (formerly handicap), and contextual factors (environmental and personal). Figure 4 illustrates. The possibility of an explanatory model of disability that combines both medical and psychological factors is clear.

Disability has been associated with, or predicted by, a vast number of psychological variables including anxiety, depression, negative affectivity, optimism, illness representations, self-efficacy, coping, health value, outcome expectancy, social support, social identity, satisfaction with care, pain, and neuropsychological deficits. One might simply insert some combination of these psychological variables into the ICIDH-2 model, just as we have previously proposed the introduction of perceived control into the ICIDH model (Johnston, 1996). This proposal was based on our findings that perceived

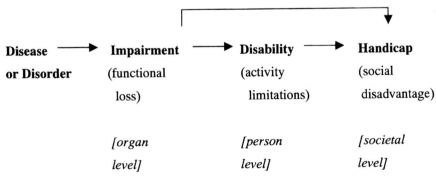

Figure 3. Biomedical model: ICIDH model (WHO, 1980). Reprinted with permission from WHO.

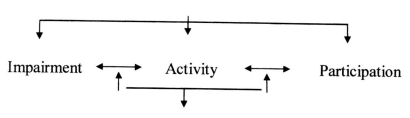

Health Condition (disorder/disease)

Impairment   Activity   Participation

Contextual Factors

A. Environmental

B. Personal

Activity
Nature and extent of functioning at the level of the person. Activity limitation (formerly disability) is the limitation in the performance of the activity that derives totally from the person. Limitations can be in duration and quality.

Impairment
Loss/abnormality of body structure or of physiological or psychological function.

Participation
Nature and extent of a person's involvement in life situations in relationship to impairment, activities, health conditions, and contextual factors.

Health condition
Any alteration or attribute of health status which may lead to distress, interference with daily activities, or contact with health services: e.g., disease (acute or chronic), disorder, injury, trauma, pregnancy, ageing, stress, congenital anomaly, or genetic predisposition.

Contextual factors
This is the complete background to the person's life and living, *Environmental factors* are composed of components of the natural environment (weather or terrain), the human-made environment (tools, furnishing, the built-environment, social attitudes, customs, rules, institutions, and other individuals). *Personal factors* are composed of features of the person that are not parts of a health condition or disablement, including age, race, gender, education, personality, character style, experiences, aptitudes, other health conditions, fitness, lifestyle, habits, upbringing, social background, profession, and past and current experiences.

Figure 4.   ICIDH-2 model (WHO, 1998). Reprinted with permission from WHO.

control predicts disability levels (Johnston, Morrison, MacWalter, & Partridge, 1999; Orbell, Johnston, Rowley, Espley, & Davey, 1998; Partridge & Johnston, 1989) and that changes in perceived control are associated with changes in disability (Fisher & Johnston, 1996; Frank, Johnston, Morrison, Pollard, & MacWalter, in press). However, this approach integrates a psychological construct into the medical model without reference to the context of the psychological theory in which the construct is embedded. An alternative approach is to insert the medical construct of impairment into psychological models predicting behaviour, since the latter can encompass the constructs of disability and activity limitations.

Psychological models

If one re-examines the ICIDH-2 medical model in Figure 4, activity appears determined by health condition, impairment, and participation. Psychological variables function as contextual factors moderating the effect of these variables on activity. However, psychological theories have an entirely different emphasis. They would propose that behaviour or activity is determined by motivational states and that impairments might modify these effects (see Figure 5). The critical difference between medical and psychological models is in the role of motivational variables, such as intentions and beliefs about performing the behaviour. The psychological model proposes that motivational variables are necessary for the behaviour (see Figure 5a) whereas motivation is not essential in the medical model (see Figure 5b). Given the vast amount of evidence to the contrary, it seems reasonable to posit that Figure 5a gives a more valid representation of the phenomena.

Examples of relevant psychological models are models that address the individual's perceptions of the disease or disorder, or their beliefs about the behaviours assessed as disability. We have examined Leventhal's Self-Regulation model (Brownlee, Leventhal, & Leventhal, 2000), postulating that disability might be seen as a consequence of the individual's mental representations of their condition (Johnston et al., 1999). Impairment was proposed to be part of the individual's perceptual experience, influencing their mental representations of their condition, including their perceptions of its controllability. If the individual then adopted coping procedures to address these representations, this might affect health outcomes including disability or activity outcomes.

Other models that might be applied to disability are those which address mental representations of the behaviour, especially perceived control over the performance of the behaviour (Johnston, 1996). For example, Bandura's Social Cognitive model (Bandura, 1997) postulates that self-efficacy and outcome expectancy with regard to the behaviour will influence the likelihood of its performance; or the Theory of Planned Behaviour (TPB; Azjen, 1991)

(a) Impairment modifying the effect of motivation on activity limitations

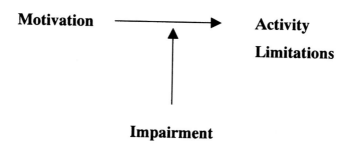

(b) Motivation modifying the effect of impairment on activity limitations

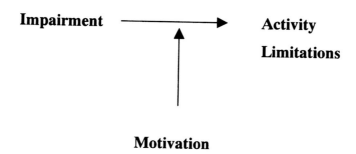

Figure 5. Motivation (a) or impairment (b) as determinants and effect modifiers.

proposes that attitudes to the behaviour, subjective norm, and perceived behavioural control predict behavioural intention, which in turn determines behaviour. The medical model could be integrated with these models by proposing that impairment affects beliefs about the behaviour, e.g., reducing self-efficacy beliefs or influencing one's attitudes toward performing the behaviour. Figure 6 suggests how the medical model might be integrated with the TPB, although additional variables may be required to overcome the recognized intention-behaviour gap in the TPB (Johnston, 1996).

This integrated model makes important predictions. It suggests that reducing impairments may not have maximal effect on reducing activity limitations unless it affects beliefs about the performance of the behaviour. It also suggests that reductions in disability may be achieved without reversing disorder or curing disease and without reducing impairment. These predictions are consistent with evidence from experimental studies in which activity limitations are reduced without changing impairment (Fisher & Johnston, 1996). Similarly there is evidence that intervention programmes enhance activities without amending disease or impairment by focusing on beliefs, e.g., in individuals with arthritis, MI, or chronic pain (Ewart, Taylor, Reese, & Debusk, 1984; Lorig, Chastain, Ung, Shoor, and Holman, 1989; Williams et al., 1993). In a controlled trial with patients following MI, a cardiac rehabilitation and counselling intervention designed to enhance control beliefs resulted in

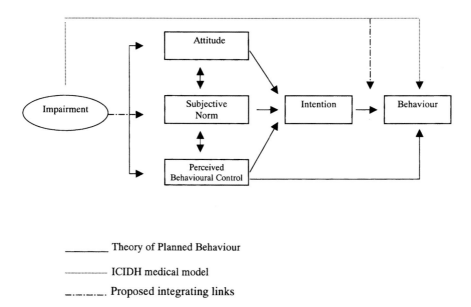

_____ Theory of Planned Behaviour

.... ICIDH medical model

_.._.._. Proposed integrating links

Figure 6.   Integrating the WHO ICIDH model and the Theory of Planned Behaviour (adapted from WHO, 1980, 1998; and Ajzen, 1991).

changed beliefs about the condition and in greater activity levels, and this latter effect persisted 1 year later (Johnston et al., 1999). We are currently conducting a trial of an intervention designed to enhance perceived control in stroke patients, examining whether it has an effect on disability outcomes following preliminary evidence that it can effect mood (Morrison, Johnston, MacWalter, & Pollard, 1998).

CONCLUSION

Disability is a common phenomenon, but there are continuing problems with its definition and measurement. A number of different models of measurement have been used, each with a different implicit model of the underlying process. To date, there has been little attempt to reconcile the models of measurement with the explanatory models used in this field.

Disability has mainly been investigated as a disease-based construct rather than as a behavioural construct. The recent revision of the ICIDH model has moved the focus to activity but continues to propose that impairment is a key determinant of these behaviours. We are suggesting that impairment is more appropriately postulated as a modifier of the effects of psychological variables such as motivation and intention on the performance of activity. An effective model will integrate psychological and medical models rather than simply insert psychological variables into a medical model. There are a number of options for the psychological model that might be used, but our data suggest that a model with a perceived control construct is necessary. We have explored models that postulate perceived control over the illness and others postulating perceived control over behaviours such as those assessed as disability. In both cases, the model allows one to predict that changing psychological states can reduce disability and this is consistent with the evidence from interventions.

ACKNOWLEDGEMENTS

We are grateful to Sara Joice, Val Morrison, Rachael Powell, and Ron MacWalter for their contributions to the work discussed here.

REFERENCES

Ajzen, I. (1991). The Theory of Planned Behaviour. *Organizational Behaviour and Human Decision Processes, 50*, 179–211.

Bandura, A. (1997). *Self-efficacy: The exercise of control.* New York: Freeman.

Bentler, P.M., & Bonett, D.G. (1980). Significance tests and goodness of fit in the analysis of covariance structures. *Psychological Bulletin, 88*, 588–606.

Bergner, M., Bobbitt, R.A., & Pollard, W.A. (1981). The Sickness Impact Profile: Development and final revision of a health status measure. *Medical Care, 19*, 787–806.

Bonetti, D. (2001). Dimensions of perceived control: A factor analysis of three measures and an examination of their relation to activity level and mood in a student and cross-cultural patient sample. *Psychology and Health, 16*(6), 655–674.

Bowling, A. (1997). *Research methods in health: Investigating health and health services.* Buckingham, UK: Open University Press.

Brownlee, S., Leventhal, H., & Leventhal, E.A. (2000). Regulation, Self-regulation, and construction of the self in the maintenance of physical health. In. M. Boekaerts, P.R. Pintrick, & M. Zeidner (Eds.), *Handbook of self-regulation.* San Diego, CA: Academic Press.

Ebrahim, S. (1999). Disability in older people: A mass problem requiring mass solutions. *The Lancet, 353*, 1990–1992.

Ewart, C.K., Taylor, C.B., Reese, L.B, & Debusk, R.F. (1984). Effects of early postmyocardial infarction exercise testing on self-perception and subsequent physical activity. *American Journal of Cardiology, 41*, 1076–1080.

Fisher, K., & Johnston, M. (1996). Experimental manipulation of perceived control and its effect on disability. *Psychology and Health, 11*, 657.

Frank, G., Johnston, M., Morrison, V., Pollard, B., & MacWalter, R. (in press). Perceived control and recovery from functional limitations: Preliminary evaluation of a workbook based intervention for discharged stroke patients. *British Journal of Health Psychology.*

Harwood, R.H., Rogers, A., Dickenson, E., & Ebrahim, S. (1994). Measuring handicap: The London Handicap Scale: A new outcome measure for chronic disease. *Qual Health Care, 3*, 11–16.

Johnson, R.J., & Wolinsky, F.D. (1993). The structure of health among older adults: Disease, disability, functional limitation, and perceived health. *Journal of Health and Social Behaviour, 44*, 105–124.

Johnston, M. (1996). Models of disability. *The Psychologist, May*, 205–210.

Johnston, M., & Bonetti, D. (2001). Disability: Psychological and social aspects. In N.J. Smelser & P.B. Baltes (Eds.), *International Encyclopaedia of the Social and Behavioural Sciences* (pp. 3704–3710). Oxford: Elsevier.

Johnston, M., Morrison, V., MacWalter, R.S., & Partridge, C.J. (1999). Perceived control, coping and recovery from disability following stroke. *Psychology and Health, 14*, 181–192.

Johnston, M., & Pollard, B. (1997). Measuring emotional, disability, handicap and quality of life outcomes of chronic disease. *Report to the NHS Executive R&D Programme for People with Physical and Complex Disabilities*, School of Psychology: University of St Andrews.

Johnston, M., & Pollard, B. (in press). Consequences of disease: Testing the WHO ICIDH model. *Social Science and Medicine.*

Lorig, K., Chastain, R., Ung, E., Shoor, S., & Holman, H.R. (1989). Development and evaluation of a scale to measure the perceived self-efficacy of people with arthritis. *Arthritis and Rheumatism, 32*, 7–44.

Martin, J., Meltzer, H., & Elliot, D. (1988). *The prevalence of disability among adults.* London: HMSO.

Melzer, D., McWilliams, B., Brayne, C., Johnson, T., & Bond, J. (1999). Profile of disability in elderly people: Estimates from a longitudinal population study. *British Medical Journal, 318*, 1108–1111.

Morrison, V., Johnston, M., MacWalter, R., & Pollard, B. (1998). Improving emotional outcomes following acute stroke: A preliminary evaluation of a work-book based intervention. *Scottish Medical Journal, 43*, 52–53.

Nagi, S.Z. (1991). Disability concepts revisited: Implications for prevention. In A. Pope & A. Tarlow (Eds.), *Disability in America: Toward a national agenda for prevention* (pp. 309–326). Washington, DC: National Academy Press.

Orbell, S., Johnston, M., Rowley, D., Espley, A., & Davey, P. (1998). Cognitive representations of illness and functional and affective adjustment following surgery for osteoarthritis. *Social Science and Medicine, 47*, 93–102.

Partridge, C., & Johnston, M. (1989). Perceived control of recovery from physical disability: Measurement and prediction. *British Journal of Clinical Psychology, 28*, 53–59.

Patrick, D.L., & Peach, H. (1989). *Disablement in the community*. Oxford: Oxford University Press.

Pollard, B., & Johnston, M. (2001). Problems with the Sickness Impact Profile: A theoretically based analysis and a proposal for a new method of implementation and scoring. *Social Science and Medicine, 52*, 921–934.

Watson, D., & Pennebaker, J.W. (1989). Health complaints, stress, and distress: Exploring the central role of negative affectivity. *Psychological Review, 96*, 234–254.

WHO (1980). *The international classification of impairments, disabilities and handicaps*. Geneva: World Health Organization.

WHO (1998). *The international classification of impairments, activities and participation: A manual of the dimensions of disablement and health*. www.who.int/msa/mnh/ems/icidh/introduction.htm

Williams, A.C.deC., Nicholas, M.K., Richardson, P.H., Pither, C.E., Justins, D.M., Chamberlain, J.H., Harding, V.R., Ralphs, J.A., Dieudonne, I., Featherstone, J.D., Hodgson, D.R., Ridout, K.L., & Shannon, E.M. (1993). Evaluation of a cognitive behavioural programme for rehabilitating patients with chronic pain. *British Journal of General Practice, 43*, 513–518.

Williams, R.G., Johnston, M., Willis, L., & Bennett, A. (1976). Disability: A model and a measurement technique. *British Journal of Preventative and Social Medicine, 30*, 71–78.

Wilson, I.B., & Cleary, P.D. (1995). Linking variables with health-related quality of life. *JAMA, 273*, 59–65.

Zigmond, A.S., & Snaith, R.P. (1983). The Hospital Anxiety and Depression Scale. *Acta Psychiatrica Scandinavica, 67*, 361–370.

CHAPTER FIFTEEN

Psychology and the risk for cardiovascular disorder: A developmental perspective

Liisa Keltikangas-Järvinen
University of Helsinki, Finland

Coronary artery disease (CAD), which gradually progresses leading to coronary heart disease, i.e. sudden death, myocardial infarction, and angina pectoris, is still the leading cause of illness and death in Western industrialized countries. During the last decades there has been a decrease of mortality, but not of morbidity. In addition, this disease has decreased in Western countries, but increased in the Eastern ones, so that total mortality remains high.

A pathologic process, responsible for (CAD) is atherosclerosis. Progression of atherosclerosis is a slow process beginning in early childhood (Raitakari, 1999). Various risk factors accelerate the development of atherosclerosis, the most important ones being dyslipidemia, hypertension, cigarette smoking, and a family history of CAD (Kwiterowich, 1993).

The childhood origins of CAD risk factors are well documented. The large prospective epidemiological studies, such as the Bogalusa Heart Study (Berenson, Srinivasan, & Bao, 1997), the Cardiovascular Risk in Young Finns Study (Porkka & Viikari, 1994), and the Muscatine Study (Mahoney, Lauer, Lee, & Clarke, 1991), have shown that levels of serum lipids and lipoproteins, hypertension, and body fat are likely to track even from early childhood. In addition to the tracking of single parameters, the coexistence and accumulation of different risk factors is also evident. The clustering and tracking are particularly apparent in families with CAD history, which refers to the inheritance of disease proneness (Kwiterowich, 1993).

Although the inherited, even genetic disposition to CAD is documented, the endpoint, which is coronary heart disease (CHD), is, however, seen as a lifestyle disease. In fact, lifestyle factors are suggested to explain up to 50% of the development of CHD. Health behavior like smoking, alcohol consumption, physical inactivity, and dietary habits are traditionally listed as lifestyle factors. In addition, certain behavioral and personality characteristics are also seen as "lifestyle" factors, Type A behavior and hostility being the most widely studied ones. The "list" of behavioral risk factors is not indisputable, as conflicting findings exist for each behavioral factor.

The most recent systematic review of the epidemiological literature of prospective cohort studies has been published by Hemingway and Marmot (1999) covering articles between 1966–97, and identifying four psychosocial or behavioral factors, which have been most rigorously tested and which meet the quality standard. They are: Type A behavior/hostility, depression, psychosocial work characteristics, and social support. So, in spite of conflictual findings, focusing on the early development of these characteristics is justified as far as childhood or adolescent origins of behavioral or personality risk factors of CHD are concerned.

From these risk factors, Type A has received the most attention, because it was the first behavioral risk variable of CHD, and was already discovered in the 1950s by Friedman and Rosenman (1959). Type A behavior is a well-known concept: by definition an action-emotion complex that consists of behavioral dispositions, certain speech and motor stylistics, and emotional responses. Hostility is comprised of cognition, affect, and behavior. The cognitive component consists of negative beliefs about others, like cynicism, mistrust, and paranoia. The affective component varies from irritation and anger to aggression that often occurs in response to provocation. Hostile behavior is reflected in a multitude of aggressive behaviors that may manifest verbally or physically, and directly and indirectly. Among the most typical forms are hateful insults, opposition, argumentativeness and sarcasm. Depression in the prospective studies, in turn, varies from depressive mood to clinical depression, and social support mostly refers to perceived social support rather than social network or the frequency of social relationships.

From the perspective of the development of these risk factors, the basic questions are as follows: (1) When and how are Type A behavior, hostility, depression, and social support manifested, and what is their degree of stability? (2) Do these factors contribute to the progress of atherosclerosis already in childhood? (3) What are their developmental origins or precursors? (4) Are there other childhood behavioral risk factors which might increase the adulthood disease proneness, but which are not yet recognized?

The first question is: When and how these behavioral risk factors are manifested, and what is their stability? Generally speaking, these features have been identified as early as it has been possible to assess them. They are behavioral characteristics that appear earlier than attitudes, which have been assessed as early as the subjects have become able to describe themselves. Type A behavior has been identified among 3-year-old children in the classical study by Lundberg (1983), and hostility among 10-year-old children by Matthews (e.g. Woodall & Matthews, 1993). Self-reports on depressive mood and a lack of social support have been documented in preadolescence.

Concerning stability, only Type A behavior has been followed over different developmental periods from childhood to adolescence or even longer. It has been shown that Type A behavior is highly stable from childhood to adolescence (Keltikangas-Järvinen, 1990), and moderately stable from adolescence to adulthood (Keltikangas-Järvinen, 1989). Hostility is also shown to be rather stable (Woodall & Matthews, 1993), and depressive mood has expressed the greatest variance.

The second question was whether childhood Type A behavior, hostility, depression, and social support themselves are morbid; in other words, do they increase the proneness to disease in adulthood. To answer this question there is no solid evidence available as yet, because the longest prospective studies starting in early childhood, i.e. the Bogalusa Heart Study and the Cardiovascular Risk in Young Finns Study, both have a follow-up of 20 years. This is not long enough to predict mortality. So, the early contribution of Type A behavior, hostility, depression, and social support to the pathogenesis of CAD must be evaluated by comparing these factors with the known somatic factors, but here we must not forget the fact that correlations of risk factors in healthy children are not the same as mortality in adulthood.

In order to throw light on the second and third questions, i.e. the role of behavioral risk factors in the childhood progress of atherosclerosis and the developmental roots of these factors, a set of findings from the Cardiovascular Risk in Young Finns Study will be presented. This is a prospective, epidemiological study with a population-based sample of 3600 subjects, comprising six age cohorts. As of now, the subjects have been followed for 20 years, from childhood to early adulthood and middle-age (Åkerblom et al., 1991).

In addition to a population-based sample and a long follow-up, the multifactorial approach, connecting epidemiological study to experimental laboratory studies, is a special benefit of this study. Medical and behavioral parameters, as well as experimentally produced physiological responses, are all assessed and followed in the same subjects, which increases the reliability of the findings.

In the Cardiovascular Risk in Young Finns Study we found that in adolescents, the impatience-aggression factor correlated with a high level of serum lipids (Keltikangas-Järvinen & Räikkönen, 1989a), and in adolescent boys, an increase of Type A behavior predicted an increase of a level of serum cholesterols and BMI (Keltikangas-Järvinen & Räikkönen, 1989b). Further, in adolescent boys Type A behavior predicted the level of metabolic

> - **A prospective epidemiological study**
> - **3596 participants (randomly selected**
>   **population based sample)**
> - **Age at baseline: cohorts: 3-6-9-12-15-18 yrs**
> - **Baseline in 1980; 5 follow-up stages**

Figure 1.   Design of the Cardiovascular Risk in Young Finns Study.

syndrome both cross-sectionally and over a period of 3 years, from adolescence to early adulthood (Ravaja, Keltikangas-Järvinen, & Keskivaara, 1996). Hostility did not correlate with the major somatic risk factors of CHD, but, however, was likely to explain smoking and drinking behavior (Räikkönen & Keltikangas-Järvinen, 1991). In adolescent boys, changes in social support were inversely associated with changes in WHR (an indicator of chronic stress) over the 3-year follow-up period (Ravaja, Keltikangas-Järvinen, & Viikari, 1998).

Summarizing, there were significant relationships and clusterings of somatic and behavioral risk factors already in adolescence, even in childhood, but the number of negative findings was also remarkable. At least, the findings do not suggest any intervention or prevention programs among children and adolescents. It is, of course, always good to decrease hostility and increase social support and to make the world a little bit better, but the significance of this activity for the development of atherosclerosis remains unknown.

From the point of view of prevention, it might be more relevant to study the childhood roots of adulthood behavioral risk factors, which was the third question of this paper. It has been mentioned before that the stability of Type A behavior and hostility is high, so that Type A children are likely to grow up as Type A adults. Childhood Type A behavior is, however, likely to explain 5–15% of the variance of adulthood Type A behavior, so that there is a lot of space for other predictors, too.

The developmental roots of adult Type A behavior have been widely studied in the Cardiovascular Risk in Young Finns Study. Environmental characteristics that were expected to be of relevance were mothers' child-rearing practices, parental life satisfaction (or dissatisfaction), parental Type A behavior, and the socioeconomic situation of the family. Children's characteristics to be assessed in this epidemiological study were Type A behavior and temperament, comprising activity, emotionality, and sociability. Activity focused on motor hyperactivity, emotionality on anger-proneness, while sociability referred to cooperativeness.

Parental life satisfaction was used as an index of emotional family atmosphere. It consisted of three dimensions from both the mothers and the fathers. The dimensions were the father's and mother's satisfaction with his or her role as a spouse and as a parent, and satisfaction with his or her work.

In the baseline of the Cardiovascular Risk in Young Finns Study, 20 years ago, these variables were chosen as general risk factors for childhood development. Later on, the literature has demonstrated that these environmental factors do not only represent a general risk, but are relevant also for the development of Type A, hostility, and depression. Literature has shown that mother's dissatisfaction with her motherhood is associated with negative mood and depression in adolescents (King, Radpour, Segal, & Naylor, 1995). In addition, both hostile (Matthews, Woodall. Kenyon, & Jacob, 1996) and Type A persons (Matthews & Woodall, 1988) have described a lack of cohesion and emotional distance as characteristic of their chilhood families.

Parental child-rearing practice is one of the most widely used variables to assess the quality of parent–child relationship. In the Cardiovascular Risk in Young Finns study we used Schaefer's (1959) concept of hostile child-rearing practices, to be evaluated by the mothers. This concept consists of three dimensions. The first is the mother's intolerance of a child's normal activity. A mother sees the child as hyperactive and restless, requiring a lot of care, and likely to be a burden that prevents a mother's self-fulfilment.

The second is unacceptance and emotional rejection. The child is not emotionally close to the mother, and the mother herself feels that she is not emotionally significant for her child. The third is a high control and strict disciplinary style that the mother uses in order to compensate for her helplessness in child-rearing. These three dimensions comprised a general negative attitude towards a child that was labelled as hostile child-rearing practice. This concept was already developed in 1959, and since then has been shown to correlate with or predict a wide scope of different behavioral and personality problems, including delinquency, social maladjustment, and depression, for instance (e.g., Katainen, 1999). Again, later on this variable has been shown to be of relevance in this particular context also, although this was not established 20 years ago when the Cardiovascular Risk in Young Finns study started. Type A parents have been observed to be pushy and ambitious. They set high demands for their children but do not give them support (Matthews, 1977).

Individuals with high hostility have reported retrospectively less acceptance, more rigid control, and emotional rejection from their parents during their childhood (Houston & Vavak, 1991). It has been asked whether this perception is true or a bias caused by their own hostility. Our prospective study may now answer that question. In addition, Matthews and her co-workers (1996) have shown that a family environment characterized as non-supportive, unaccepting, and conflictual correlates with the development of hostility in adolescent boys.

Concerning depression, the research has repeatedly shown that a lack of parental acceptance and emotional closeness easily leads to later depression (Ge, Lorenz, Conger, Elder, & Simons, 1994) and, finally, the first perception of social support is a child's perception of parental acceptance and support (Sarason, Pierce, Bannerman, & Sarason, 1993).

Regarding other characteristics which were assessed in our study, parental Type A behavior as such is a type of child-rearing practice. Concerning the child's characteristics, childhood Type A behavior is, of course, a key concept. Temperament, in turn, has been shown to have a strong moderating effect. A child's early temperament is in many ways related to maternal practices. It also plays a role in interaction, which then determines how successful a mother feels herself as a mother.

The design of our study on the development of behavioral risk factors is as follows: parental characteristics as well as children's temperament were assessed twice during childhood, that is at the baseline and at the first follow-up, 3 years later. These characteristics were used to predict Type A behavior in adolescence, 6 years later, social support in an early adulthood, 12 years later, and hostility and depression in adulthood, 17 years later.

CHILDHOOD ENVIRONMENT PREDICTING ADULTHOOD RISK FACTORS

Summarizing the main findings (see Figure 3) of the Cardiovascular Risk in Young Finns Study, Type A behavior in boys was predicted by their own childhood Type A behavior, and a mother's high job-involvement and a high satisfaction with her work, but a dissatisfaction with her role as a mother, as well as her hostile child-rearing practices and a low education. For girls, there was only one significant predictor, which was the mother's dissatisfaction with her maternal role.

Several childhood factors predicted adulthood hostility (see Figure 4). We found that childrens' impatience-aggression, which is shown to be a pathogenic component of Type A behavior (Keltikangas-Järvinen, & Räikkönen, 1989a), parental job-involvement and role dissatisfaction, maternal hostile child-rearing practices, as well as a low family socioeconomic situation, predicted boys' self-rated hostility 17 years later. Only one correlation was found for girls. It was their own childhood Type A behavior, that is, impatience-aggression (Keltikangas-Järvinen, 2000).

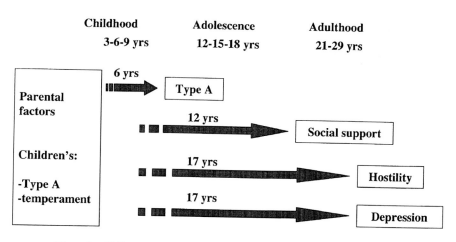

Figure 2. Follow-up periods for the development of behavioral risk factors.

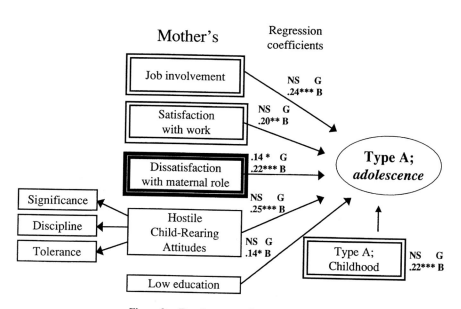

Figure 3. Development of Type A behavior.

341

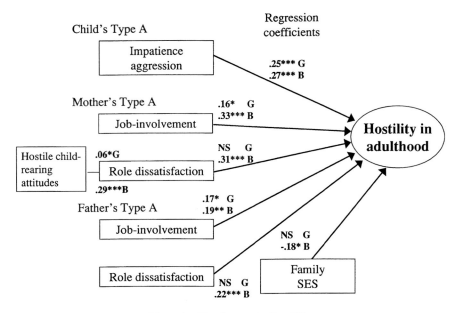

Figure 4. Development of hostility.

Regarding depression, maternal dissatisfaction in girls, and dissatisfaction and hostile child-rearing practices in boys, predicted later depression (see Figure 5; Katainen, Räikkönen, Keskivaara, & Keltikangas-Järvinen, 1999).

Childhood predictors of perceived social support are shown in Figures 6 and 7. The main information is that a lack of social support in young women was predicted by parental role dissastisfaction in early childhood, for both mothers and fathers. However, mothers' child-rearing practices were not important. Here, mothers' job-involvement predicted a high level of perceived social support. These findings conflict with previous ones, where high job-involvement was related to a negative endpoint. In boys, however, mothers' hostile child-rearing practices were the most significant predictors of the lack of social support, whereas parental life satisfaction was not important (Räikkönen, Katainen, Keskivaara, & Keltikangas-Järvinen, 2000)

To conclude: first, the mothers' hostile child-rearing practices or attitudes were the most important predictors for later manifestation of behavioral CHD risk factors. In boys, they contributed to the development of all risk factors, and to Type A behavior and depression in girls. In addition, mothers' job-involvement and dissatisfaction with motherhood played a role, although not so systematically as hostile practices. This agrees with previous findings. Hostile child-rearing attitudes have been shown to correlate with hostility in

Regression coefficients

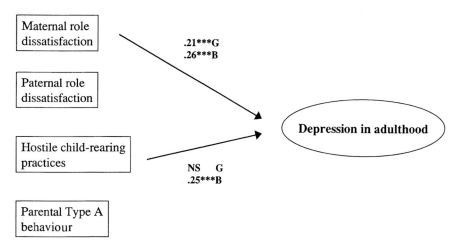

Figure 5. Development of depression.

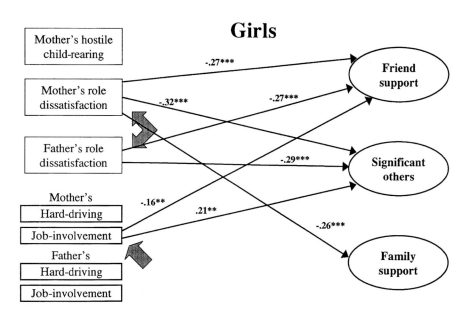

Figure 6. Development of social support in girls.

343

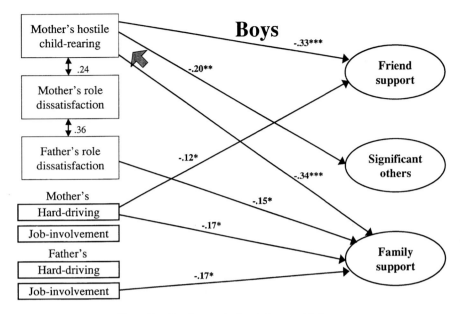

Figure 7.   Development of social support in boys.

adolescents (Houston & Vavak, 1991; Matthews et al., 1996), and the studies consistently suggest that depression is associated with a lack of parental care, nurture, or support, with parental exercise of authority and control, criticism, and disapproval (King et al., 1995).

Hostile child-rearing practices in the form of rejection and unacceptance can be suggested to have their influence on the development of both depression and hostility. Depression is contributed through self-definition (Blatt & Homann, 1992), and hostility through environmental interpretations. Parental unacceptance and emotional rejection are likely to promote negative self-concept in a child as well as self-criticism, which are both likely to contribute to the progress of depression.

Hostile biases of social interpretations have been claimed as an important characteristic of hostile persons, which hypothesis we have recently experimentally supported. We found (Keltikangas-Järvinen, Puttonen, & Ravaja, 2000) that during a public speech, which was used as a test of social stress, hostile persons were likely to see an audience as negative and unsupportive towards them whereas nonhostile persons saw the same audience as neutral. The basis of this bias might lay in a mother's hostility, which may serve as an external cue that an environment is generally hostile. This perception, in turn, might promote a hostile attribution bias in children's social information processing and social problem solving. This interpretation is consistent with Pettit, Dodge, and Brown (1988), who have demonstrated that mothers' hostility and harshness of discipline promoted a hostile attribution bias in children's social problem solving.

The second notion was the boys' higher vulnerability. They were more sensitive to negative environment, lack of acceptance, and emotional distance than girls. That is, these environmental characteristics were more evidently correlated with later behavioral risk factors among boys than among girls. This agrees with some previous findings which suggest that boys are more likely to react to their mother's negativity and marital dissatisfaction with increasing difficulty than are girls (Whitehead, 1979; Woodall & Matthews, 1993).

The last finding was the high family cohesion, in other words agreement between mothers and fathers with regard to the characteristics to be studied here, that is parental Type A behavior and satisfaction with different life roles. The importance of including both mothers and fathers in the developmental studies has been emphasized because the father does not replicate the child's relationship with the mother, but the mother and the father are primary sources of different socialization. The present results, however, justify speaking about family atmosphere on the basis on the mother's characteristics, because the within and between correlations were so high. In our study the risk-related characteristics of the mother, that is, job-involvement and dissatisfaction with her role as a spouse and mother, correlated with each other as well as with the corresponding features of the father. That means that Type A people are likely to get married to each other, or are likely to become similar during their marriage, and if the mother is job-involved and dissatisfied with her spouse and family life, the father is too, or very soon becomes so. In Finland, at least the families are this boring.

It is worth emphasizing that the environmental effect revealed gender differences but was independent of age. That is, it did not make a difference whether the starting point was a 3-, 6-, or 9-year cohort, the same effects remained. So, the child-rearing practices and role satisfaction were likely to be a mother's characteristics and not highly dependent on changes in the child, although an interaction also existed.

GENERAL OR SPECIFIC RISK ENVIRONMENT?

In spite of the association between the risk-prone environment to be identified by our study and the behavioral risk factors of CHD, this environment is likely to be a general risk environment with several psychological, social, and somatic endpoints, as the existing literature shows. In addition, there are correlations between adult Type A behavior, hostility, and social support; the correlations are not so high that the overlapping of these concepts would explain their similar developmental paths, but this developmental similarity additionally supports the claim to a general risk environment.

Thus, it could be asked, what is typical for the risk for cardiac disorders? Have we found something which is not good for the child's development, but which is not new and has been found several times before. From the present point of view, it is not of primary importance to demonstrate that a certain environment might promote Type A or hostile behavior but rather to show that a particular environment is likely to turn into the somatic endpoint of atherosclerosis. In this context we might speak of childhood stress. In terms of the present findings, the parental attitudes and practices, that is, job-involved Type A parents with hostile child-rearing practices and dissatisfaction with their parental roles, are likely to create a stressful environment with a lack of support. It is worth remembering that the last environmental adulthood risk factor to be identified by the review of Hemingway and Marmot (1999) was titled "job-characteristics". That refers to work with high demands and low control. The childhood environment to be found here is equivalent to this stressful adulthood work environment. The pushy Type A parents set their children high demands, and high external control, so that their self-control is lacking. In addition, the parents take away their support and acceptance.

It is, however, a well-known fact that a variation in environmental stressors alone is insufficient to explain the distribution of stress-related disease, and individuals vary widely in how they respond to the environment, both emotionally and physiologically. Individual differences in psychobiological responsiveness to stress are, in turn, associated with increased susceptibility to illness. Thus, it might be the individual characteristics of the child which explain the child's personal adjustment to the demands of an environment, and especially the somatic reactions that result from a nonadjustment.

An inherited temperament is the very concept for this purpose, as well as the concept of "goodness of fit", which refers to the adaptive and maladaptive interaction between a child's inherited temperament and environmental demands. There are several definitions for the concept of temperament, the most relevant in this context being that temperament refers to individual differences in reactivity and self-regulation, and is assumed to have a constitutional basis (see, for instance, Bates and Wachs, 1995). In other words, temperament is a child's individual response to environmental stress, both behavioral and physiological. Temperament has its origins in brain functions, and different temperament dimensions are related to different inherited physiological and neuroendocrine dispositions. Thus, individual differences in temperament explain the great individual differences in physiological stress reactions, and help us understand why similar daily hassles and environmental demands produce such different stress reactions in different persons and, particularly, why these reactions have such different somatic endpoints in different persons.

In the literature on childhood development, less attention has been paid to individual differences because the main focus has been in identifying the general developmental lines. In addition, childhood has been seen as a happy time, and has not commonly been spoken of in terms of stress.

Actually, the Swedish Longitudinal Study was one of the first to link childhood temperament to adult Type A behavior (McEvoy et al., 1998). In accordance with that, we found (Räikkönen & Keltikangas-Järvinen, 1992) that childhood hyperactivity predicted adulthood Type A behavior. In the Cardiovascular Risk in Young Finns Study we also found that early temperament, more specifically hyperactivity and impatience, predicted the levels of Apolipoproteins A-l and B both cross-sectionally and over the 3-year follow-up period (Räikkönen, Keltikangas-Järvinen, & Solakivi, 1990), whereas motor activity in childhood and mental vitality in adolescence were correlated with Apolipoprotein E phenotypes (Keltikangas-Järvinen, Räikkönen, & Lehtimäki, 1993). Finally, hyperactivity and negative emotionality predicted a high level of insulin resistance syndrome, again both cross-sectionally and over the follow-up period of 3 years (Ravaja & Keltikangas-Järvinen, 1995).

To summarize, early temperament predicted later manifestation of Type A behavior. Temperamental dimensions in childhood were also correlated with or predicted different somatic risk factors of CHD or clusters of them and, most importantly, correlations between temperament and CHD risk factors were stronger than correlations between childhood Type A behavior or hostility and CHD risk. Furthermore, the genetic basis of hostility, for instance, has been seen to consist of low sociability and high activity, which are temperamental factors. This might suggest that a possible genetic contribution to the development of Type A behavior and hostility goes through an inherited temperament.

The last question of the present paper was whether there are other relevant childhood risk factors that have not yet been identified. Temperament would be an answer. Individual temperament, especially its physiological concomitants, would explain why a general risk environment is likely to lead particularly to CAD risk in some children. That is, why some children are more likely to respond to environmental stress with disease-prone physiological reactivity.

Thus, the last point would be highlighting the question of how the child's temperament interacts with the environmental risk factors identified here. The findings are, again, derived from the Cardiovascular Risk in Young Finns Study. Mothers' perceptions of their daughters as having difficult childhood temperament, that is, high activity, anger-proneness, and low sociability, accounted for a significant proportion of the variance in the girls' self-rated hostile attitudes 12 years later (Figure 8). Perceived difficultness of the daughter appeared to promote more negative attitudes in the mother, but neither maternal attitudes nor the daughter–mother interaction predicted

Hostility (Girls)

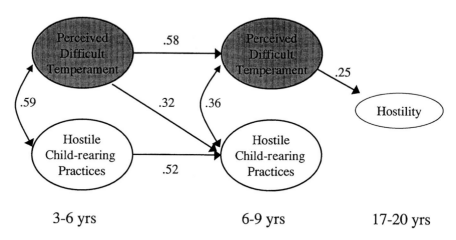

Figure 8. Temperament and hostility in girls.

girls' self-rated hostile attitudes; the effect was found only for the childhood temperament.

In contrast, mothers' hostile child-rearing attitudes accounted for a significant proportion of the variance of boys' self-rated hostile attitudes 12 years later, whereas perceived difficult temperament played no significant role for boys as a predictor of adolescents' and young adults' self-rated hostility (Figure 9).

Concerning depression, the main finding for both girls and boys was that perceived child difficultness promoted hostile child-rearing practices in the mothers, and these practices, in turn, affected depression (Figures 10 and 11). So, an influence went through child-rearing practices. There was one gender-related difference: in boys, but not in girls, mothers' dissatisfaction and the perception of a child's difficult temperament were correlated. In addition, mothers' dissatisfaction with her role as a mother had a direct effect on girls' later depression.

Regarding social support, mothers' hostile child-rearing practices and role dissatisfaction affected lack of social support, although the temperament had a moderating effect in girls. In boys, mothers' hostile practices and temperament had independent effects (see Figure 12).

Generally, temperament was likely to have a direct effect in girls whereas boys were more vulnerable to the mothers' general negativity. It is, however, worth noting that maternal evaluation on a child's difficult temperament may

Hostility (Boys)

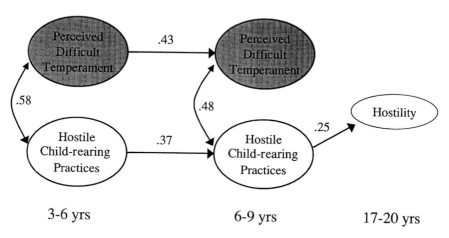

Figure 9.   Temperament and hostility in boys.

Depression (Girls)

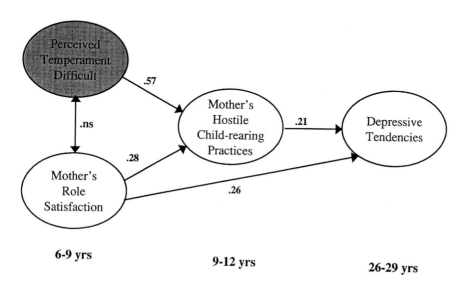

Figure 10.   Temperament and depression in girls.

Depression (Boys)

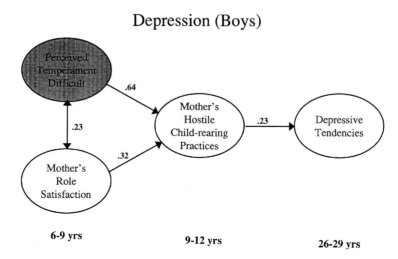

Figure 11. Temperament and depression in boys.

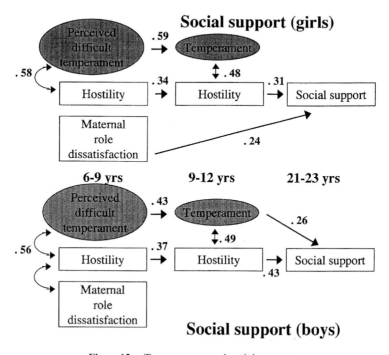

Figure 12. Temperament and social support.

reflect a hostile mother rather than a child who is temperamentally pre-disposed to hostility, so that the differences between boys and girls must be taken with caution.

LOOKING TO THE FUTURE

Including temperament with the risk factors of CAD would give the pos-sibility of throwing light on individual stress proneness, perhaps partially inherited, and to answer the questions why life is not fair, as the same environment is a challenge to one child, and a disease risk to another.

REFERENCES

Åkerblom, H.K., Uhari, M., Pesonen, E., Dahl, M., Kaprio, E.A., Nuutinen, E.M., Pietikäinen, M., Salo, M.K., Aromaa, A., Kannas, L., Keltikangas-Järvinen, L., Kuusela, V., Räsänen L., Rönnemaa, T., Knip, M., Telama, R., Välimäki, I., Pyörälä, K., & Viikari, J. (1991). Cardiovascular risk in young Finns. *Annals of Medicine*, *23*, 35–39.

Bates, J.E. & Wachs, T.D. (1995). *Temperament. Individual differences at the interface of biology and behavior.* Washington, DC: American Psychological Association.

Berenson, G.S., Srinivasan, S.R., & Bao, W. (1997). Precursors of cardiovascular risk in young adults from a biracial (black-white) population: The Bogalusa Heart Study. *Annals of the New York Academy of Sciences*, *817*, 189–198.

Blatt, S.J., & Homann, E. (1992). Parent–child interaction in the etiology of dependent and self-critical depression. *Clinical Psychology Review*, *12*, 47–91.

Friedman, M., & Rosenman, R.H. (1959). Association of specific overt behavior pattern with blood and cardiovascular findings. *Journal of American Medical Association*, *169*, 1286–1296.

Ge, X., Lorenz, F.O., Conger, R.D., Elder, G.H., & Simons, R.L. (1994). Trajectories of stressful life events and depressive symptoms during adolescence. *Developmental Psychology*, *30*, 467–483.

Hemingway, H., & Marmot, M. (1999). Psychosocial factors in the aetiology and prognosis of coronary heart disease: A systematic review of prospective cohorts studies. *British Medical Journal*, *29*, 1460–1467.

Houston, B.K., & Vavak, C.R. (1991). Cynical hostility: Developmental factors, psychosocial correlates, and health behaviors. *Health Psychology*, *10*, 9–17.

Katainen, S. (1999). *Temperament and development: A longitudinal study of temperament–mothering interaction and the development of temperament, depressive tendencies and hostility.* Unpublished doctoral dissertation, University of Helsinki, Finland.

Katainen, S., Räikkönen, K., Keskivaara, P., & Keltikangas-Järvinen, L. (1999). Maternal child-rearing attitudes and role satisfaction and children's temperament as antecedents of ado-lescent depressive tendencies: a follow-up study of 6- to 15-year-olds. *Journal of Youth and Adolescence*, *28*, 139–163.

Keltikangas-Järvinen, L. (1989). Stability of Type A behavior during adolescence, young adult-hood and adulthood. *Journal of Behavioral Medicine*, *12*, 387–396.

Keltikangas-Järvinen, L. (1990). Continuity of Type A behavior during childhood, preadolescence and adolescence. *Journal of Youth and Adolescence*, *19*, 221–232.

Keltikangas-Järvinen, L. (2000). *Childhood predictors of adulthood hostility.* Manuscript submit-ted for publication.

Keltikangas-Järvinen, L., Puttonen, S., & Ravaja, N. (2000). Stress, personality and the metabolic syndrome. In *Re Berzelius Symposium on Social Causation of Disease—Biological Mechan-isms*, symposium by the Swedish Society of Medicine, Stockholm, Sweden, May.

Keltikangas-Järvinen, L., & Räikkönen, K. (1989a). Pathogenic and protective factors of Type A behavior. *Journal of Psychosomatic Research, 33*, 591–602.

Keltikangas-Järvinen, L. & Räikkönen, K. (1989b). Developmental trends in Type A behavior as predictors for the development of somatic CHD risk factors. *Psychotherapy and Psychosomatics, 51*, 210–215.

Keltikangas-Järvinen, L., Räikkönen, K., & Lehtimäki, T. (1993). Dependence between Apolipoprotein E phenotypes and temperament in children, adolescents and young adults. *Psychosomatic Medicine, 55*, 155–163.

King, C.A., Radpour, L., Segal, H.G., & Naylor, M.W. (1995). Parents' marital functioning and adolescent psychopathology. *Journal of Consulting and Clinical Psychology, 63*, 749–753.

Kwiterowich, P.O. (1993). Prevention of coronary disease starting in childhood: What risk factors should be identified and treated? *Coronary Artery Disease, 4*, 611–630.

Lundberg, U. (1983). Note on Type A behavior and cardiovascular responses to challenge in 3–6-year-old children. *Journal of Psychosomatic Research, 27*, 39–42.

Mahoney, L.T., Lauer, R.M., Lee, J., & Clarke, W.R. (1991). Factors affecting tracking of coronary heart disease risk factors in children. The Muscatine Study. *Annals of the New York Academy of Sciences, 623*, 120–132.

Matthews, K.A. (1977). Caregiver–child interactions and the Type A coronary-prone behavior pattern. *Child Development, 48*, 1752–1756.

Matthews, K.A., & Woodall, K.L. (1988). Childhood origins of overt Type A behaviors and cardiovascular reactivity to behavioral stressors. *Annals of Behavioral Medicine, 10*, 71–77.

Matthews, K.A., Woodall, K.L., Kenyon, K., & Jacob, T. (1996). Negative family environment as a predictor of boy's future status on measures of hostile attitudes, interview behavior, and anger expression. *Health Psychology, 15*, 30–37.

McEvoy, B., Lambert, W.W., Karlberg, P., Karlberg, J., Klagenberg–Larsson, I., & Klagenberg, G. (1988). Early affective antecedents of adult Type A behavior. *Journal of Personality and Social Psychology, 54*, 108–115.

Pettit, G.S., Dodge, K.A., & Brown, M.M. (1988). Early familiy experiences, social problem solving patterns, and children's social competence. *Child Development, 59*, 107–120.

Porkka, K.V.K., & Viikari, J.S.A. (1994). Should children or young adults be screened for serum lipid levels to prevent adult coronary heart disease? Experience from the Cardiovascular Risk in Young Finns study. *Journal of Internal Medicine, 236*, 115–123.

Räikkönen, K., Katainen, S., Keskivaara, P., & Keltikangas-Järvinen, L. (2000). Temperament, mothering and hostility attitudes: A 12-year longitudinal study. *Personality and Social Psychology Bulletin, 25*, 3–12.

Räikkönen, K., & Keltikangas-Järvinen, L. (1991). Hostility and its association with behaviorally induced and somatic coronary risk indicators in Finnish adolescents and young adults. *Social Science and Medicine, 33*, 1171–1178.

Räikkönen, K., & Keltikangas-Järvinen, L. (1992). Childhood hyperactivity and the mother–child relationship as predictors of risk Type A behavior in adolescence—a six-year follow-up. *Personality and Individual Differences, 13*, 321–327.

Räikkönen, K., Keltikangas-Järvinen, L., & Solakivi, T. (1990). Behavioral coronary risk indicators and apolipoproteins A-1 and B in young children: Cross-sectional and predictive associations. *Preventive Medicine, 19*, 656–666.

Raitakari, O.T. (1999). Imaging of subclinical atherosclerosis in children and young adults. *Annals of Medicine, 31*, 33–40.

Ravaja, N., & Keltikangas-Järvinen, L. (1995). Temperament and metabolic syndrome precursors in children: A three-year follow-up. *Preventive Medicine, 24*, 518–527.

Ravaja, N., Keltikangas-Järvinen, L., & Keskivaara, P. (1996). Type A factors as predictors of changes in the metabolic syndrome precursors in adolescents and young adults—a three-year follow-up study. *Health Psychology, 15*, 18–29.

Ravaja, N., Keltikangas-Järvinen, L., & Viikari, J. (1998). Perceived social support and abdominal fat distribution in adolescents and young adults: A structural equation analysis of prospective data. *Appetite, 31*, 21–35.

Sarason, B.R., Pierce, G.R., Bannerman, A., & Sarason, I.G. (1993). Investigating the antecedents of perceived social support. Parents views of and behavior toward their children. *Journal of Personality and Social Psychology, 65*, 1071–1085.

Schaefer, E.S. (1959). A circumplex for maternal behavior. *Journal of Abnormal Social Psychology, 59*, 226–335.

Whitehead, L. (1997). Sex differences in children's responses, to family stress: A re-evaluation. *Journal of Child Psychology and Psychiatry, 20*, 247–254.

Woodall, K.L., & Matthews, K.A. (1993). Changes in and stability of hostile characteristics: Results from a 4-year longitudinal study of children. *Journal of Personality and Social Psychology, 64*, 491–499.

SECTION FOUR

Interaction between cognitive and emotional processes

CHAPTER SIXTEEN

Prefrontal cortex and amygdala contributions to emotion and affective style

Richard J. Davidson
University of Wisconsin, Madison, USA

For most of the last century, the domains of personality and emotion were mainly the province of literature and philosophy. The social sciences and psychiatry began to address these phenomena in the latter half of the 20th century with mixed success. The categories that are widely used in the study of both personality and emotion are those that first emerged in the earliest eras of scholarship in these arenas. Traditional personality theory and the descriptive nosology of psychiatry were important influences on the development of these constructs.

In the past 10 years, a remarkable change has occurred in our conceptualization of these topics and in our ability to study them in intact human beings. The change represents the emergence of new areas of interdisciplinary research that represent the melding of basic neuroscience with the psychological study of individual differences and emotion. Termed affective neuroscience (Davidson, 1995; Panksepp, 1998), this new interdisciplinary area is having major impact on our conception of personality, emotion and disorders of emotion. This article will consider some of these promising new trends and illustrate some of the key changes in how we conceptualize these topics that these new developments are suggesting.

THE ROLE OF THE NEUROSCIENCES IN THE STUDY OF PERSONALITY AND EMOTION

Prior to the advent of neuroimaging to study human brain function, most of the neuroscientific research on emotion was confined to the study of animals, mostly rodents, in whom lesions were made in various subcortical nuclei and the behavioral consequences of these lesions were measured. This work has had and continues to have enormous impact and has been of great import-ance to the development of more sophisticated models of brain function and emotion in humans (Panksepp, 1998). Most of this work is performed in rodents, which have a relatively small cerebral cortex. In humans, it is undoubtedly the case that the cortex plays a very important role in emotion (Rolls, 1999), and it was not until studies in nonhuman primates, as well as in humans, that the role of various cortical territories in emotion was widely appreciated.

Human research has highlighted the role of various territories of the pre-frontal cortex (PFC) in particular that are crucial to different aspects of emotion (Davidson & Irwin, 1999). The PFC is especially important to emo-tion regulation and individual differences in affective style, as will be described later. Emotion regulation refers to processes that enhance, sup-press, or maintain an emotional response whereas affective style refers to consistent individual differences in basic parameters of emotional reactivity and emotion regulation. Many of the regulatory processes implemented in the PFC operate relatively automatically and are thus opaque to direct self-report and only get represented indirectly in self-report measures. For this reason, the neuroscientific work on affective style and emotion regulation has uncovered certain components of emotion, emotion regulation, and indi-vidual differences that could not have been discovered through self-report methods. Moreover, the identification of the mechanisms of emotional reactivity provide a more direct path to understanding how both genetic and experiential factors may operate synergistically on a final common pathway to shape personality and emotion.

THE CENTRAL CIRCUITRY OF EMOTION

The prefrontal cortex

Though approaching the topic from very different perspectives, a growing body of literature is converging on the idea that there exist two fundamental systems underlying approach and withdrawal-related emotion and motiv-ation, or positive and negative affect (Cacioppo & Gardner, 1999; Davidson & Irwin, 1999; Gray, 1994; Lang, Bradley, & Cuthbert, 1990; Schneirla, 1959). The precise description of these systems differs somewhat across investiga-tors, as does the anatomical circuitry that is featured, but the essential elements are quite similar in each of these different proposals. The approach system has been described by Davidson and Irwin as facilitating appetitive behavior and generating particular types of positive affect that are approach-related, such as the emotion occurring as an organism moves closer toward a desired goal. The withdrawal system, on the other hand, facilitates the withdrawal of an organism from sources of aversive stimulation and/or organizes appropriate responses to cues of threat. This system also generates withdrawal-related negative emotions such as disgust and fear. A variety of evidence indicates that these systems are implemented in partially separable circuits and it is to this evidence that we now turn. Our focus will be on two key components of this circuitry—the prefrontal cortex (PFC) and the amygdala. For more extensive discussion of this entire circuitry including other regions not considered here, see Davidson and Irwin (1999).

A large corpus of data at both the animal and human levels implicate various sectors of the PFC in emotion. The PFC is not a homogeneous zone of tissue but rather, has been differentiated on the basis of both cytoarchitectonic as well as functional considerations. The three subdivisions of the primate PFC that have been consistently distinguished include the dorsolateral, ventromedial, and orbitofrontal sectors. In addition, there appear to be important functional differences between the left and right sides within each of these sectors.

The case for the differential importance of left and right PFC sectors for emotional processing was first made systematically in a series of studies on patients with unilateral cortical damage (Gainotti, 1972; Robinson, Starr, & Price, 1984; Sackeim et al., 1982). Each of these studies compared the mood of patients with unilateral left- or right-sided brain damage and found a greater incidence of depressive symptoms following left-sided damage. In most cases, the damage was fairly gross, probably included more than one sector of PFC, and often included other brain regions as well. The general interpretation that has been placed upon these studies is that depressive symptoms are increased following left-sided anterior PFC damage because this brain territory participates in a certain way that underlies certain forms of positive affect. When damaged, it leads to deficits in the capacity to experience positive affect, a hallmark feature of depression (Watson et al., 1995). Though most of the extant lesion data are consistent with this general picture (see Robinson & Downhill, 1995, for a review), some inconsistencies have also appeared (e.g., Gainotti, Caltagirone, & Zoccolotti, 1993; House et al., 1990). Davidson (1993) has reviewed these studies in detail and has addressed a number of critical methodological and conceptual concerns in this literature. The most important of these issues is that according to the diathesis-stress model of anterior activation asymmetry proposed by Davidson and colleagues (e.g., Davidson, 1995, 1998a; Henriques & Davidson, 1991), individual differences in anterior activation asymmetry, whether lesion-induced or functional, represent a diathesis. As such, they alter the probability that specific forms of emotional reactions will occur in response to the requisite environmental challenge. In the absence of such a challenge, the pattern of asymmetric activation will simply reflect a propensity but will not necessarily culminate in differences in mood or symptoms. In a recent study with the largest sample size to date ($N = 193$) for a study of mood sequelae in patients with unilateral lesions, P.L.P. Morris et al. (1996) found that among stroke patients, it was only in those with small-sized lesions that the relation between left-PFC damage and depressive symptoms was observed. It is likely that larger lesions intrude on other brain territories and mask the association between left-PFC damage and depression.

A growing corpus of evidence in normal intact humans is consistent with the findings derived from the lesion evidence. Davidson and his colleagues have reported that induced positive and negative affective states shift the asymmetry in prefrontal brain electrical activity in lawful ways. For example, film-induced negative affect increases relative right-sided prefrontal and anterior temporal activation (Davidson, Ekman, Saron, Senulis, & Friesen, 1990) whereas induced positive affect elicits an opposite pattern of asymmetric activation. Similar findings have been obtained by others (e.g., Ahern & Schwartz, 1985; Jones & Fox, 1992; Tucker, Stenslie, Roth, & Shearer, 1981). In addition, we will review in the next section a body of evidence that supports the conclusion that individuals who vary in their baseline levels of asymmetric activation in these brain regions differ in their dispositional affective style. Using an extended picture presentation paradigm designed to evoke longer-duration changes in mood, (Sutton, Davidson, Donzella, Irwin, & Dottl, 1997), we measured regional glucose metabolism with positron emission tomography (PET) to ascertain whether similar patterns of anterior asymmetry would be present using this very different and more precise method to assess regional brain activity (Sutton et al., 1997). During the production of negative affect, we observed right-sided increases in metabolic rate in anterior orbital, inferior frontal, middle, and superior frontal gyri, while the production of positive affect was associated with a pattern of predominantly left-sided metabolic increases in the pre- and post-central gyri. Using PET to measure regional cerebral blood flow, Hugdahl (1998) and his colleagues (Hugdahl et al., 1995) reported a widespread zone of increased blood flow in the right PFC including the orbitofrontal and dorsolateral cortices and inferior and superior cortices during the extinction phase after learning had occurred compared with the habituation phase, prior to the presentation of the experimental contingencies.

Other investigators have used clinical groups to induce a stronger form of negative affect in the laboratory than is possible with normal controls. One common strategy for evoking anxiety among anxious patients in the laboratory is to present them with specific types of stimuli that are known to provoke their anxiety (e.g., pictures of spiders for spider phobics; making a public speech for social phobics). Davidson, Marshall, Tomarken, and Henriques (2000b), in a study using brain electrical activity measures, have recently found that when social phobics anticipate making a public speech, they show large increases in right-sided anterior activation. Pooling across data from three separate anxiety-disordered groups, Rauch, Savage, Alpert, Fischman, and Jenike (1997) found two regions of the PFC that were consistently activated across groups: the right inferior PFC and right medial orbital PFC.

The ventromedial PFC has been implicated in the anticipation of future positive and negative affective consequences. Bechara and his colleagues (Bechara, Damasio, Damasio, & Anderson, 1994) have reported that patients with bilateral lesions of the ventromedial PFC have difficulty anticipating future positive or negative consequences, although immediately available rewards and punishments do influence their behavior. Such patients show decreased levels of electrodermal activity in anticipation of a risky choice compared with controls, while controls exhibit such autonomic change before they explicitly know that it is a risky choice (Bechara, Damasio, Damasio, & Lee, 1999; Bechara, Damasio, Tranel, & Damasio, 1997; Bechara, Tranel, Damasio, & Damasio, 1996).

The findings from the lesion method when effects of small unilateral lesions are examined and from neuroimaging studies in normal subjects and patients with anxiety disorders converge on the conclusion that increases in right-sided activation in various sectors of the PFC is associated with increased negative affect. Less evidence is available for the domain of positive affect, in part because positive affect is much harder to elicit in the laboratory and because of the negativity bias (see Cacioppo & Gardner, 1999; Taylor, 1991). This latter phenomenon refers to the general tendency of organisms to react more strongly to negative compared with positive stimuli, perhaps as a consequence of evolutionary pressures to avoid harm. The findings from Bechara et al. on the effects of ventromedial PFC lesions on the anticipation of future positive *and* negative affective consequences are based upon studies of patients with bilateral lesions. It will be of great interest in the future to examine patients with unilateral ventromedial lesions to ascertain whether valence-dependent asymmetric effects are present for this sector of PFC as well.

Systematic studies designed to disentangle the specific role played by various sectors of the PFC in emotion are lacking. Many theoretical accounts of emotion assign it an important role in guiding action and organizing behavior toward the acquisition of motivationally significant goals (e.g., Frijda, 1994; Levenson, 1994). This process requires that the organism should have some means of representing affect in the absence of immediately present rewards and punishments and other affective incentives. Such a process may be likened to a form of affective working memory. It is likely that the PFC plays a key role in this process (see Watanabe, 1996). Damage to certain sectors of the PFC impairs an individual's capacity to anticipate future affective outcomes and consequently results in an inability to guide behavior in an adaptive fashion. Such damage is not likely to disrupt an individual's responding to immediate cues for reward and punishment, only the anticipation before and sustainment after an affective cue is presented. This proposal can be tested using current neuroimaging methods (e.g., fMRI) but has not yet been rigorously evaluated. With regard to the different functional roles of the dorsolateral and ventromedial sectors of the PFC, Davidson and Irwin (1999) suggested, on the basis of considering both human and animal studies, that the latter sector is most likely to be involved in the representation of elementary positive and negative affective states in the absence of immediately present incentives, whereas the former sector is most directly involved in the representation of goal states toward which these more elementary positive and negative states are directed.

The amygdala

A large corpus of research at the animal—mostly rodent—level has established the importance of the amygdala for emotional processes (Aggleton, 1993; Cahill & McGaugh, 1998; LeDoux, 1996). Since many reviews of the animal literature have appeared recently, a detailed description of these studies will not be presented here. LeDoux and his colleagues have marshaled a large corpus of compelling evidence to suggest that the amygdala is necessary for the establishment of conditioned fear. Whether the amygdala is necessary for the expression of that fear following learning and whether the amygdala is the actual locus of where the learned information is stored is still a matter of some controversy (see Cahill, Weinberger, Roozendaal, & McGaugh, 1999; Fanselow & LeDoux, 1999). Also not resolved is the extent to which the amygdala participates in all learning of stimulus-incentive associations, both negative and positive, and whether there are functional differences between the left and right amygdala (Davidson & Irwin, 1999). The classic view of amygdala damage in nonhuman primates resulting in major affective disturbances as expressed in the Kluver-Bucy syndrome where the animal exhibits abnormal approach, hyperorality and sexuality, and little fear, is now thought to be a function of damage elsewhere in the medial temporal lobe. When very selective excitotoxic lesions of the amygdala are made that preserve fibers of passage, nothing resembling the Kluver-Bucy syndrome is observed (Kalin, Shelton, Kelley, & Davidson, 2001; Meunier et al., 1999). The upshot of this diverse array of findings is to suggest a more limited role for the amygdala in certain forms of emotional learning, though the human data imply a more heterogeneous contribution.

Although the number of patients with discrete lesions of the amygdala is small, they have provided unique information on the role of this structure in emotional processing. A number of studies have now reported specific impairments in the recognition of facial expressions of fear in patients with restricted amygdala damage (Adolphs, Damasio, Tranel, & Damasio, 1995, 1996; Broks et al., 1998; Calder et al., 1996). Recognition of facial signs of other emotions was found to be intact. In a study that required subjects to make judgments of trustworthiness and approachability of unfamiliar adults from facial photographs, patients with bilateral amygdala damage judged the unfamiliar individuals to be more approachable and trustworthy than did control subjects (Adolphs, Tranel, & Damasio, 1998). Recognition of vocalic signs of fear and anger was found to be impaired in a patient with bilateral amygdala damage (Scott et al., 1997), suggesting that this deficit is not restricted to facial expressions. Other researchers (Bechara et al., 1995) have demonstrated that aversive autonomic conditioning is impaired in a patient with amygdala damage despite the fact that the patient showed normal declarative knowledge of the conditioning contingencies. Collectively, these findings from patients with selective bilateral destruction of the amygdala suggest specific impairments on tasks that tap aspects of negative emotion processing. Most of the studies have focused on the perceptual side, where the data clearly show the amygdala to be important for the recognition of cues of threat or danger. The conditioning data also indicate that the amygdala may be necessary for acquiring new implicit autonomic learning of stimulus-punishment contingencies. In one of the few studies to examine the role of the amygdala in the expression of already learned emotional responses, Angrilli and colleagues (1996) reported on a patient with a benign tumor of the right amygdala in an emotion-modulated startle study. Among control subjects, they observed the well-known effect of startle potentiation during the presentation of aversive stimuli. In the patient with right amygdala damage, no startle potentiation was observed in response to aversive versus neutral stimuli. These findings suggest that the amygdala might be necessary for the expression of already learned negative affect.

Since 1995, a growing number of studies using PET and fMRI to investigate the role of the amygdala in emotional processes have begun to appear. Many studies have reported activation of the amygdala detected with either PET or fMRI when anxiety-disordered patients have been exposed to their specific anxiety-provoking stimuli compared with control stimuli (e.g., Breiter et al., 1996a; Rauch et al., 1996). When social phobics were exposed to neutral faces, they showed activation of the amygdala comparable to what was observed in both the phobics and controls in response to aversive compared with neutral odors (Birbaumer, et al., 1998). Consistent with the human lesion data, a number of studies have now reported activation of the amygdala in response to facial expressions of fear compared with neutral, happy, or disgust control faces (Breiter et al., 1996b; J.S. Morris et al., 1996;

Phillips, et al., 1997; Whalen et al., 1998). In the Breiter et al. (1996b) fMRI study, they observed rapid habituation of the amygdala response, which may provide an important clue to the time-limited function of the amygdala in the stream of affective information processing. In a recent study, Whalen and his colleagues (1998) observed activation of the amygdala in response to masked fear faces that were not consciously perceived. Unpleasant compared with neutral and pleasant pictures have also been found to activate the amygdala (Irwin et al., 1996; Lane et al., 1997). Finally, a number of studies have reported activation of the amygdala during early phases of aversive conditioning (Buchel, Morris, Dolan, & Friston, 1998; LaBar, Gatenby, Gore, LeDoux, & Phelps, 1998; Morris, Ohman, & Dolan, 1998). Amygdala activation in response to several other experimental procedures for inducing negative affect has been reported, including unsolvable anagrams of the sort used to induce learned helplessness (Schneider et al., 1996), aversive olfactory cues (Zald & Pardo, 1997), and aversive gustatory stimuli (Zald, Lee, Fluegel, & Pardo, 1998). Other data on individual differences in amygdala activation and their relation to affective style will be treated in the next section. The issues of whether the amygdala responds preferentially to aversive versus appetitive stimuli, is functionally asymmetric, and is required for both the initial learning and subsequent expression of negative emotional associations are considered in detail elsewhere (Davidson & Irwin, 1999).

AFFECTIVE STYLE

Davidson (1992, 1998a) has used the term affective style to refer to the broad range of individual differences in different subcomponents of affective reactivity and dispositional mood. This is a very global term and it is imperative to specify with more precision which particular system one is measuring affective reactivity in and which subcomponent of reactivity is being targeted for study. For example, one could measure affective reactivity in different response systems by using startle magnitude, MR signal change in the amygdala, or ratings on a self-report scale as the measure. Each of these obviously reflects activity in very different systems and activation in these systems will not necessarily cohere. What is meant by subcomponent of reactivity has been articulated in detail in Davidson (1998a) and includes the following parameters: tonic level, threshold to respond, peak or amplitude of response, rise time to peak of response, and recovery time (see Figure 1). These are not necessarily meant to reflect an exhaustive list of subcomponents; they are merely offered as examples. Each of these subcomponents can potentially be studied in different response systems, leading to many parameters of affective style. We know virtually nothing about the psychometric characteristics of measures of these different parameters, except for self-report measures (for two recent efforts examining different subcomponents of affective style in two

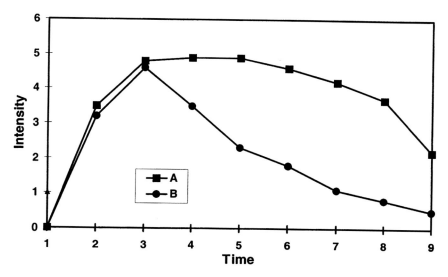

Figure 1.   Hypothetical timecourses of two individuals in response to an emotionally arousing stimulus. Both individuals show comparable initial reactivity but differ in the recovery. Individual A shows a prolonged recovery while individual B recovers more rapidly.

different physiological response systems, see Tomarken, Davidson, Wheeler, & Kinney, 1992; Larson, Ruffalo, Nietert, & Davidson, 2000), though this information is crucial if we are to develop rigorous measures of these constructs. In this section, we review data on the contributions of individual differences in prefrontal and amygdala function to affective style.

In two decades of previous research, we have performed a large number of studies designed to examine the role of activation asymmetries in prefrontal cortex and other anterior cortical zones in aspects of affective style. This work has been reviewed recently (Davidson, 1995; 1998a) and only highlights will be presented here. Using measures of scalp-recorded brain electrical activity, we found that indices of activation asymmetry based upon power spectral measures were stable over time and exhibited excellent internal consistency reliability (Tomarken, Davidson, Wheeler, & Doss, 1992) thus fulfilling a number of important psychometric criteria for an index of a trait-like construct. In a series of studies, we found that there are large individual differences in the magnitude and direction of baseline asymmetric activation in brain electrical activity measures obtained from prefrontal scalp regions in both infants (Davidson & Rickman, 1999) and adults (Davidson & Tomarken, 1989). In 10-month-old infants we found that those with greater relative right-sided prefrontal activation in prefrontal scalp regions were more likely to cry in response to a brief period of maternal separation compared with their left-activated counterparts (Davidson & Fox, 1989). In toddlers and young children, we have observed that those individuals with greater relative right-sided prefrontal activation show more behavioral inhibition and wariness measured through laboratory-based behavioral observation (Davidson & Rickman, 1999). In adults, we have found that individual differences in such measures predict dispositional mood (Tomarken et al., 1992a), self-report measures of behavioral activation and inhibition (Sutton & Davidson, 1997), repressive defensiveness (Tomarken & Davidson, 1994), reactivity to positive and negative emotion elicitors (Tomarken, Davidson, Wheeler, & Doss, 1990; Wheeler, Davidson, & Tomarken, 1993), baseline immune function (Kang et al., 1991), and reactivity of the immune system to emotional challenge (Davidson, Coe, Dolski, & Donzella, 1999). In recent work (Larson, Sutton, & Davidson, 1998) we found that individual differences in electrophysiological measures of prefrontal asymmetry predicted the magnitude of recovery following a negative affective stimulus. These data suggest that the prefrontal cortex may play a role in regulating the timecourse of emotional responding and/or in the active inhibition of negative affect. We will return to these issues later in the article.

We have also found that individual differences in these brain electrical measures of anterior asymmetry are associated with mood and anxiety disorders. In particular, we have found that depressed subjects and individuals who are currently euthymic but have a history of past depression exhibit less left prefrontal activation compared with never-depressed controls (Henriques & Davidson, 1990, 1991). We have also found that when social phobics anticipate making a public speech, they show large increases in right-sided prefrontal activation though they do not differ from controls at baseline (Davidson et al., 2000b).

In a series of studies with Kalin (Davidson, Kalin, & Shelton, 1992, 1993; Kalin, Larson, Shelton, & Davidson, 1998), we have demonstrated that similar activation asymmetries can be measured in rhesus monkeys and that they predict similar types of behavior and biology to those we observe in humans. In the most recent effort of this kind, we (Kalin et al., 1998) found that animals with greater relative right-sided prefrontal activation exhibit higher basal levels of the stress hormone cortisol. Similar data have recently been reported in humans (Buss, Dolski, Malmstadt, Davidson, & Goldsmith, 1997).

A number of our original EEG observations have now been independently replicated by others (Ahern & Schwartz, 1985; Allen, Iacono, Depue, & Arbisi, 1993; Dawson, Klinger, Panagiotides, Hill, & Spieker, 1992; Fox, 1991; Jacobs & Snyder, 1996; Harmon-Jones & Allen, 1997; Wiedemann et al., 1999), though a few studies have appeared reporting only partial replications of aspects of our original findings (Hagemann, Naumann, Becker, Maier, & Bartussek, 1998; Reid, Duke, & Allen, 1998). Davidson (1998b) has called attention to a number of crucial methodological and conceptual issues in these replication attempts and suggests that the difficulties in replication are mostly a function of significant methodological limitations. Moreover, few studies using neuroimaging to address the role of prefrontal asymmetries in affective processes have appeared. As noted by Davidson and Irwin (1999), only a very small handful of studies using PET or fMRI have conducted the proper statistical comparison to uncover asymmetry effects in their data. They comment on the complexity of performing these analyses. Since the structural anatomy is not symmetrical, particularly for cortical tissue, it is very difficult to extract homologous regions for asymmetry analyses. The size of the regions may differ on the two sides of the brain, the anatomical homologue may not be in exactly the same location in each hemisphere, and the shape of the cortical territory on each side of the brain is often different. These facts present formidable methodological obstacles when using neuroimaging to make inferences about patterns of asymmetric activation.

The data from the Larson et al. (1998) study indicated that individuals with greater relative left-sided prefrontal activation at baseline have greater recovery of startle potentiation following the offset of a negative stimulus. Moreover, the measure of asymmetric prefrontal activation accounted for more variance in the magnitude of startle post-negative-stimulus offset (i.e., startle recovery) than it did during the stimulus. These findings imply that individual differences in prefrontal activation asymmetry may play a role in regulating the time course of emotional responding and that those individuals with more left-sided prefrontal activation may recover more quickly from negative affect or stress than their right-activated counterparts.

A clue to the mechanism that may underlie this consequence of left prefrontal activation is provided by a study from LeDoux's laboratory, where they found that rats with lesions of the medial prefrontal cortex show dramatically slower extinction of a learned aversive response compared with sham operated controls (Morgan, Romanski, & LeDoux, 1993). These findings imply that there is a descending pathway between the medial PFC and the amygdala (Amaral, Price, Pitänen, & Carmichael, 1992) that is inhibitory and thus represents an active component of extinction. In the absence of this normal inhibitory input, the amygdala remains unchecked and continues to remain activated. Whether this inhibitory input from the medial PFC is an important component of the prominent habituation observed in the amygdala remains to be clarified. Davidson (1998a) has suggested that in humans and possibly other primates, the major inhibitory influence on the amygdala may derive from the left prefrontal cortex. Consistent with this idea, recent PET findings suggest that in normal human subjects, glucose metabolism in the left medial and lateral prefrontal cortex is reciprocally coupled to metabolic activity in the amygdala, such that those subjects with increased left prefrontal metabolic rate have decreased metabolic rate in the amygdala (Abercrombie et al., 1996). We propose that this mechanism may be responsible for the dampening of negative affect and the shortening of its timecourse in those individuals who appear to be more resilient. Such an affective style may also facilitate the maintenance of approach-related positive affect.

The two key features of the circuitry underlying positive and negative affect highlighted herein are the prefrontal cortex and the amygdala. In the previous section, we detailed studies on the basic function of the amygdala in affective behavior. Here we ask the question about individual differences in amygdala function and its relation to affective style. Although most research on the amygdala has emphasized its phasic function, there is a tonic level of activation in the amygdala that can be assessed with PET measures of regional glucose metabolism. Using MRI-based coregistration, we can draw regions-of-interest around the amygdala on an MR scan coregistered to the PET image and extract metabolic activity in such small regions without using any spatial filtering of the PET image. This provides high resolution than could ordinarily be achieved using conventional cross-subject aggregation methods that require spatial smoothing of the images (see Schaefer et al., 2000). Using such procedures, we have found that individual differences in metabolic activity in the right amygdala, in particular, predicts dispositional negative affect on the Positive and Negative Affect Schedule (PANAS; Watson, Clark, & Tellegen, 1988) in a group of depressed patients (see Figure 2) (Abercrombie et al., 1998). Using the same measure of negative affect, we (Irwin et al., 1998) have also found MR signal change in the amygdala in

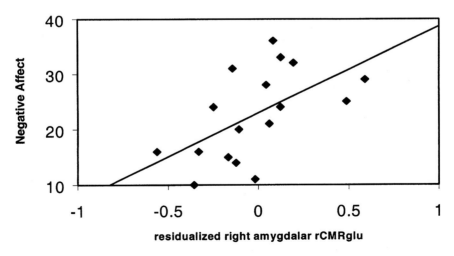

Figure 2. Scatter plot of the relation between metabolic rate in the right amygdala and dispositional negative affect. Metabolic rate in the amygdala was obtained by coregistering MRI and PET images and then drawing regions-of-interest (ROIs) on the MRIs around the amygdala. These ROIs were then automatically transferred to the PET images and glucose metabolic rate for these regions was determined. From Abercrombie et al. (1998).

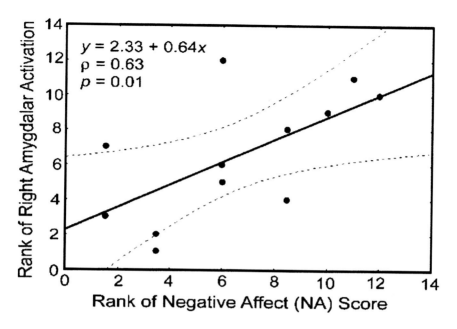

$y = 2.33 + 0.64x$
$\rho = 0.63$
$p = .01$

Figure 3. Scatter plot of the relation between MR signal change in the right amygdala in response to unpleasant versus neutral pictures assessed with functional MRI and dispositional negative affect assessed with the Positive and Negative Affect Schedule. From Irwin et al. (1998). Reprinted with the permission of the publisher.

response to negative versus neutral stimuli accounts for a substantial amount of variance in PANAS trait negative affect scores ($r = .63$; see Figure 3). Other researchers have found that individual differences in right amygdala glucose metabolic rate in response to emotional films predicts the recall of negative emotional films assessed 3 weeks following the PET procedure. Those individuals with higher levels of glucose metabolism in the right amygdala recalled more of the negative film clips (Cahill et al., 1996). Other investigators using both PET (Furmark, Fischer, Wik, Larsson, & Fredrikson, 1997) and fMRI (LaBar et al., 1998) reported that those subjects with greater activation in the amygdala during classical aversive conditioning showed greater evidence of electrodermal conditioning. Ketter et al. (1996), using the anesthetic procaine as a pharmacological challenge, reported that those individuals who had a dysphoric response to the drug had significantly greater activation of the amygdala compared with subjects exhibiting a euphoric response. Moreover, amygdala blood flow correlated positively with fear and negatively with euphoria on self-report measures of emotional intensity.

Some of the data reviewed on relations between amygdala activation and dispositional negative affect appear, at least on the surface, to be inconsistent with the animal and human neuroimaging data, implying that the amygdala is important only in the initial learning of stimulus-threat associations (Buchel et al., 1998; LaBar et al., 1998) but not in the expression of pre-existing temperamental variation, such as behavioral inhibition. For example, in our own data using PET-derived measures of glucose metabolism in the amygdala (Abercrombie et al., 1998), we found that subjects with greater metabolic rate in the right amygdala report higher levels of dispositional negative affect as assessed by the PANAS. A similar association was found using the identical affect measure with fMRI, where subjects showing larger MR signal increases in the amygdala in response to negative versus neutral pictures reported higher levels of dispositional negative affect. The PANAS requires subjects to rate a series of single-word adjectives on a 1–5-point scale to indicate the extent to which that emotion is present during their daily life. Thus, in these experiments, it appears that activation levels in the amygdala are associated with the expression of a pre-existing affective style. We believe the key to resolving this apparent inconsistency among these findings lies in a more in-depth understanding of the strategies people use to respond to questionnaires like the PANAS. When subjects are asked to make global inferences about the affective dispositions that are extended in time, they are not veridical integrators of the momentary affective states that unfolded over the period in question. Rather, as a number of commentators have forcefully argued, they exhibit systematic heuristic biases that reflect the information that is accessible at the time (Kahneman, 1999; Schwartz & Strack, 1999). In particular, in a series of elegant studies, Kahneman (1999) has demonstrated that individuals tend to adopt what he refers to as the "peak-end" rule for forming these retrospective affective evaluations. Thus, although an individual might be asked to rate how "nervous" he was during the past month, he is likely to weigh excessively information about the peak episode of nervousness during this period, as well as his level of nervousness very recently. The peak intensity of the emotion in question may be especially related to amygdala activation, since it is likely to represent a response to a particularly threatening or novel episode. Such complexities in measuring subjective aspects of emotion underscores the need to develop more objective measures that do not depend upon self-report and that can better capture the time-course of emotional responding or what Davidson (1998a) has referred to as affective chronometry.

The fact that there exist reliable individual differences in baseline metabolic rate in the amygdala also requires comment in light of the earlier discussion about the amygdala's role in phasic affective processes. There is clearly intrinsic neural activity in the amygdala, even during sleep (Maquet et al., 1996). As a number of studies have now shown, baseline nontask ("resting") levels of activation in the amygdala are associated with dispositional negative affect (Abercrombie et al., 1998) and depression (Drevets et al., 1992).

Whether these baseline differences in amygdala activation reflect activation in response to the PET environment or whether such differences predict the magnitude of task-induced activation in the amygdala in response to emotion elicitors are questions that must be addressed in future research. We believe that when PET is used to measure baseline differences in amygdala activation, at least for the right amygdala, it probably reflects an important influence of the experimental situation itself. This claim is made on the basis of the fact that our recent evidence (Schaefer et al., 2000), using MR-coregistration to extract glucose metabolic rate in several subcortical regions, revealed that test–retest reliability over a 6-month period is excellent for all subcortical regions we examined (hippocampus, caudate, thalamus, left amygdala) except for the right amygdala. These findings are consistent with the idea that situational influences are important in modulating activation in the right amygdala.

IMPLICATIONS AND CONCLUSIONS

The concepts and findings reviewed in this article underscore the utility of the modern melding between neuroscience and studies of personality and emotion. Certain aspects of automatic emotional processes, such as the automatic regulation of the timecourse of emotional responding, are opaque to consciousness and therefore will not be directly revealed in self-reports. The study of the underlying brain mechanisms associated with basic parameters of affective style and emotion regulation will provide us with new and better methods to parse the domains of emotion and personality.

A critical issue not addressed here concerns the distal causes of the individual differences in affective style that have been featured. As I have detailed extensively elsewhere (Davidson, Jackson, & Kalin, 2000a), the fact of biological differences among individuals says nothing about the origins of those differences. A large corpus of neuroscience research over the past decade has underscored the importance of experiential determinants of the structure and function of the circuitry that has been featured here. Social influences on brain structure, activation patterns, neurogenesis, and even gene expression have all been demonstrated (see Davidson et al., 2000a, for review). Although heritable influences surely occur, environmental influences, particularly when they occur repetitively over time, can be extremely powerful and produce lasting changes in the brain. The fact that such experiential influences occur provides an impetus for the development of neurally inspired training programs to transform dysfunctional affective styles into ones that may be more adaptive (see Davidson, Putnam, & Larson, 2000c). This is only a promissory note at the present time and requires much additional study and validation.

ACKNOWLEDGEMENTS

The research from the Laboratory for Affective Neuroscience and the Wisconsin Center for Affective Science reported in this article was supported by NIMH grants MH43454, MH40747 and P50-MH52354, by Research Scientist Award K05-MH00875 and by a grant from the Research Network on Mind-Body Interaction of the John D. and Catherine T. MacArthur Foundation to RJD. I wish to thank the members of the Laboratory for Affective Neuroscience and the members of the Wisconsin Center for Affective Science for their sustained contributions to this research program. Parts of this article were adapted from Davidson (2001).

REFERENCES

Abercrombie, H.C., Schaefer, S.M., Larson, C.L., Oakes, T.R., Holden, J.E., Perlman, S.B., Krahn, D.D., Benca, R.M., & Davidson, R.J. (1998). Metabolic rate in the right amygdala predicts negative affect in depressed patients. *NeuroReport, 9*, 3301–3307.

Abercrombie, H.C., Schaefer, S.M., Larson, C.L., Ward, R.T., Holden, J.E., Turski, P.A., Perlman, S.B., & Davidson, R.J. (1996). Medial prefrontal and amygdalar glucose metabolism in depressed and control subjects: An FDG-PET study [Abstract]. *Psychophysiology, 33*, S17.

Adolphs, R., Damasio, H., Tranel, D., & Damasio, A.R. (1995). Fear and the human amygdala. *Journal of Neuroscience, 15*, 5879–5891.

Adolphs, R., Damasio, H., Tranel, D., & Damasio, A.R. (1996). Cortical systems for the recognition of emotion in facial expressions. *Jounal of Neuroscience, 16*, 7678–7687.

Adolphs, R., Tranel, D., & Damasio, A.R. (1998). The human amygdala in social judgement. *Nature, 393*, 470–473.

Aggleton, J.P. (1993). The contribution of the amygdala to normal and abnormal emotional states. *Trends in Neuroscience, 16*, 328–333.

Ahern, G.L., & Schwartz, G.E. (1985). Differential lateralization for positive and negative emotion in the human brain: EEG spectral analysis. *Neuropsychologia, 23*, 745–755.

Allen, J.J., Iacono, W.G., Depue, R.A., & Arbisi, P. (1993). Regional electroencephalographic asymmetries in bipolar seasonal affective disorder before and after exposure to bright light. *Biological Psychiatry, 33*, 642–646.

Amaral, D.G., Price, J.L., Pitkänen, A., & Carmichael, T. (1992). Anatomical organization of the primate amygdala complex. In J.P. Aggleton (Ed.), *The amygdala* (pp. 1–66). New York: Wiley-Liss.

Angrilli, A., Mauri, A., Palomba, D., Flor, H., Birbaumer, N., Sartori, G., & Di Paola, F. (1996). Startle reflex and emotion modulation impairment after a right amygdala lesion. *Brain, 119*, 1991–2000.

Bechara, A., Damasio, A.R., Damasio, H., & Anderson, S.W. (1994). Insensitivity to future consequences following damage to human prefrontal cortex. *Cognition, 50*, 7–15.

Bechara, A., Damasio, H., Damasio, A.R., & Lee, G.P. (1999). Different contributions of the human amygdala and ventromedial prefrontal cortex to decision-making. *Journal of Neuroscience, 19*, 5473–5481.

Bechara, A., Damasio, H., Tranel, D., & Damasio, A.R. (1997). Deciding advantageously before knowing the advantageous strategy. *Science, 275*, 1293–1295.

Bechara, A., Tranel, D., Damasio, H., Adolphs, R., Rockland, C., & Damasio, A.R. (1995). Double dissociation of conditioning and declarative knowledge relative to the amygdala and hippocampus in humans. *Science, 269*, 1115–1118.

Bechara, A., Tranel, D., Damasio, H., & Damasio, A.R. (1996). Failure to respond autonomically to anticipated future outcomes following damage to prefrontal cortex. *Cerebral Cortex*, *6*, 215–225.

Birbaumer, N., Grodd, W., Diedrich, O., Klose, U., Erb, E., Lotze, M., Schneider, F., Weiss, U., & Flor, H. (1998). fMRI reveals amygdala activation to human faces in social phobics. *NeuroReport*, *9*, 1223–1226.

Breiter, H.C., Etcoff, N.L., Whalen, P.J., Kennedy, W.A., Rauch, S.L., Buckner, R.L., Strauss, M.M., Hyman, S.E., & Rosen, B.R. (1996b). Response and habituation of the human amygdala during visual processing of facial expression. *Neuron*, *17*, 875–887.

Breiter, H.C., Rauch, S.L., Kwong, K.K., Baker, J.R., Weisskoff, R.M., Kennedy, D.N., Kendrick, A.D., Davis, T.L., Jiang, A., Cohen, M.S., Stern, C.E., Belliveau, J.W., Baer, L., O'Sullivan, R.L., Savage, C.R., Jenike, M.A., & Rosen, B.R. (1996a). Functional magnetic resonance imaging of symptom provocation in obsessive-compulsive disorder. *Archives of General Psychiatry*, *53*, 595–606.

Broks, P., Young, A.W., Maratos, E.J., Coffey, P.J., Calder, A.J., Isaac, C.L., Mayes, A.R., Hodges, J.R., Montaldi, D., Cezayirli, E., Roberts, N., & Hadley, D. (1998). Face processing impairments after encephalitis: Amygdala damage and recognition of fear. *Neuropsychologia*, *36*, 59–70.

Buchel, C., Morris, J., Dolan, R.J., & Friston, K.J. (1998). Brain systems mediating aversive conditioning: An event-related fMRI study. *Neuron*, *20*, 947–957.

Buss, K., Dolski, I., Malmstadt, J., Davidson, R.J., & Goldsmith, H.H. (1997). EEG asymmetry, salivary cortisol, and affect expression: An infant twin study [Abstract]. *Psychophysiology*, *34*, S25.

Cacioppo, J.T., & Gardner, W.L. (1999). Emotion. *Annual Review of Psychology*, *50*, 191–214.

Cahill, L., Haier, R.J., Fallon, J., Alkire, M.T., Tang, C., Keator, D., Wu, J., & McGaugh, J.L. (1996). Amygdala activity at encoding correlated with long-term, free recall of emotional information. *Proceedings of the National Academy of Sciences, USA*, *93*, 8016–8021.

Cahill, L., & McGaugh, J.L. (1998). Mechanisms of emotional arousal and lasting declarative memory. *Trends in Neurosciences*, *21*, 294–299.

Cahill, L., Weinberger, N.M., Roozendaal, B., & McGaugh, J.L. (1999). Is the amygdala a locus of "conditioned fear"? Some questions and caveats. *Neuron*, *23*, 227–228.

Calder, A.J., Young, A.W., Rowland, D., Perrett, D.I., Hodges, J.R., & Etcoff, N.L. (1996). Facial emotion recognition after bilateral amygdala damage: Differentially severe impairment of fear. *Cognitive Neuropsychology*, *13*, 699–745.

Davidson, R.J. (1992). Emotion and affective style: Hemispheric substrates. *Psychological Science*, *3*, 39–43.

Davidson, R.J. (1993). Cerebral asymmetry and emotion: Conceptual and methodological conundrums. *Cognition and Emotion*, *7*, 115–138.

Davidson, R.J. (1995). Cerebral asymmetry, emotion and affective style. In R.J. Davidson & K. Hugdahl (Eds.), *Brain asymmetry* (pp. 361–387). Cambridge, MA: MIT Press.

Davidson, R.J. (1998a). Affective style and affective disorders: Perspectives from affective neuroscience. *Cognition and Emotion*, *12*, 307–320.

Davidson, R.J. (1998b). Anterior electrophysiological asymmetries, emotion and depression: Conceptual and metholological conundrums. *Psychophysiology*, *35*, 607–614.

Davidson, R.J. (2001). The neural circuitry of emotion and affective style: Prefrontal cortex and amygdala contributions. *Social Science Information*, *40*, 11–37.

Davidson, R.J., Coe, C.C., Dolski, I., & Donzella, B. (1999). Individual differences in prefrontal activation asymmetry predict natural killer cell activity at rest and in response to challenge. *Brain, Behavior, and Immunity*, *13*, 93–108.

Davidson, R.J., Ekman, P., Saron, C., Senulis, J., & Friesen, W.V. (1990). Approach/withdrawal and cerebral asymmetry: Emotional expression and brain physiology. *Journal of Personality and Social Psychology, 58,* 330–341.

Davidson, R.J., & Fox, N.A. (1989). Frontal brain asymmetry predicts infants' response to maternal separation. *Journal of Abnormal Psychology, 98,* 127–131.

Davidson, R.J., & Irwin, W. (1999). The functional neuroanatomy of emotion and affective style. *Trends in Cognitive Sciences, 3,* 11–21.

Davidson, R.J., Jackson, D.C., & Kalin, N.H. (2000a). Emotion, plasticity, context and regulation. *Psychological Bulletin, 126,* 890–906.

Davidson, R.J., Kalin, N.H., & Shelton, S.E. (1992). Lateralized effects of diazepam on frontal brain electrical asymmetries in rhesus monkeys. *Biological Psychiatry, 32,* 438–451.

Davidson, R.J., Kalin, N.H., & Shelton, S.E. (1993). Lateralized response to diazepam predicts temperamental style in rhesus monkeys. *Behavioral Neuroscience, 107,* 1106–1110.

Davidson, R.J., Marshall, J.R., Tomarken, A.J., & Henriques, J.B. (2000b). While a phobic waits: Regional brain electrical and autonomic activity in social phobics during anticipation of public speaking. *Biological Psychiatry, 47,* 85–95.

Davidson, R.J., Putnam, K.M., & Larson, C.L. (2000c). Dysfunction in the neural circuitry of emotion regulation—a possible prelude to violence. *Science, 289,* 591–594.

Davidson, R.J., & Rickman, M.D. (1999). Behavioral inhibition and the emotional circuitry of the brain: Stability and plasticity during the early childhood years. In L.A. Schmidt & J. Schulkin (Eds.), *Extreme fear, shyness, and social phobia: Origins, biological mechanisms, and clinical outcomes* (pp. 67–87). New York: Oxford University Press.

Davidson, R.J., & Tomarken, A.J. (1989). Laterality and emotion: An electrophysiological approach. In F. Boller & J. Grafman (Eds.), *Handbook of neuropsychology Vol 3* (pp. 419–441). Amsterdam: Elsevier.

Dawson, G., Klinger, L.G., Panagiotides, H., Hill, D., & Spieker, S. (1992). Frontal lobe activity and affective behavior of infants of mothers with depressive symptoms. *Child Development, 63,* 725–737.

Drevets, W.C., Videen, T.O., Price, J.L., Preskorn, S.H., Carmichael, S.T., & Raichle, M.E. (1992). A functional anatomical study of unipolar depression. *The Journal of Neuroscience, 12,* 3628–3641.

Fanselow, M.S., & LeDoux, J.E. (1999). Why we think plasticity underlying Pavlovian fear conditioning occurs in the basolateral amygdala. *Neuron, 23,* 229–232.

Fox, N.A. (1991). If it's not left, it's right Electroencephalograph asymmetry and the development of emotion. *American Psychologist, 46,* 863–872.

Frijda, N.H. (1994). Emotions are functional, most of the time. In P. Ekman & R.J. Davidson (Eds.), *The nature of emotion: Fundamental questions* (pp. 112–122). New York: Oxford University Press.

Furmark, T., Fischer, H., Wik, G., Larsson, M., & Fredrikson, M. (1997). The amygdala and individual differences in human fear conditioning. *NeuroReport, 8,* 3957–3960.

Gainotti, G. (1972). Emotional behavior and hemispheric side of lesion. *Cortex, 8,* 41–55.

Gainotti, G., Caltagirone, C., & Zoccolotti, P. (1993). Left/right and cortical/subcortical dichotomies in the neuropsychological study of human emotions. *Cognition and Emotion, 7,* 71–93.

Gray, J.A. (1994). Three fundamental emotion systems. In P. Ekman & R.J. Davidson (Eds.), *The nature of emotion: fundamental questions* (pp. 243–247). New York: Oxford University Press.

Hagemann, D., Naumann, E., Becker, G., Maier, S., & Bartussek, D. (1998). Frontal brain asymmetry and affective style: A conceptual replication. *Psychophysiology, 35,* 372–388.

Harmon-Jones, E., & Allen, J.J.B. (1997). Behavioral activation sensitivity and resting frontal EEG asymmetry: Covariation of putative indicators related to risk for mood disorders. *Journal of Abnormal Psychology, 106,* 159–163.

Henriques, J.B., & Davidson, R.J. (1990). Regional brain electrical asymmetries discriminate between previously depressed subjects and healthy controls. *Journal of Abnormal Psychology*, *99*, 22–31.

Henriques, J.B., & Davidson, R.J. (1991). Left frontal hypoactivation in depression. *Journal of Abnormal Psychology*, *100*, 535–545.

House, A., Dennis, M., Mogridge, L., Hawton, K., & Karlow, C. (1990). Life events and difficulties preceding stroke. *Journal of Neurology, Neurosurgery, and Psychiatry*, *53*, 1024–1028.

Hugdahl, K. (1998). Cortical control of human classical conditioning: Autonomic and positron emission tomography data. *Psychophysiology*, *35*, 170–178.

Hugdahl, K., Berardi, A., Thompson, W.L., Kosslyn, S.M., Macy, R., Baker, D.P., Alpert, N.M., & LeDoux, J.E. (1995). Brain mechanisms in human classical conditioning: A PET blood flow study. *NeuroReport*, *6*, 1723–1728.

Irwin, W., Davidson, R.J., Lowe, M.J., Mock, B.J., Sorenson, J.A., & Turski, P.A. (1996). Human amygdala activation detected with echo-planar functional magnetic resonance imaging. *NeuroReport*, *7*, 1765–1769.

Irwin, W., Mock, B.J., Sutton, S.K., Anderle, M.J., Kalin, N.H., Sorenson, J.A., Turski, P.A., & Davidson, R.J. (1998). Ratings of affective stimulus characteristics and measures of affective reactivity predict MR signal change in the human amygdala [Abstract]. *Neuroimage*, *7*, S908.

Jacobs, G.D., & Snyder, D. (1996). Frontal brain asymmetry predicts affective style in men. *Behavioral Neuroscience*, *110*, 36.

Jones, N.A., & Fox, N.A. (1992). Electroencephalogram asymmetry during emotionally evocative films and its relation to positive and negative affectivity. *Brain and Cognition*, *20*, 280–299.

Kahneman, D. (1999). Objective happiness. In E. Kahneman, E. Diener, & N. Schwartz (Eds.), *Well-being: The foundations of hedonic psychology* (pp. 3–25). New York: Russell Sage Foundation.

Kalin, N.H., Larson, C.L., Shelton, S.E., & Davidson, R.J. (1998). Asymmetric frontal brain activity, cortisol, and behavior associated with fearful temperament in Rhesus monkeys. *Behavioral Neuroscience*, *112*, 286–292.

Kalin, N.H., Shelton, S.E., Kelley, A.E., & Davidson, R.J. (2001). The primate amygdala mediates acute fear but not the behavioral and physiological components of anxious temperament. *Journal of Neuroscience*, *21*, 2067–2074.

Kang, D.H., Davidson, R.J., Coe, C.L., Wheeler, R.W., Tomarken, A.J., & Ershler, W.B. (1991). Frontal brain asymmetry and immune function. *Behavioral Neuroscience*, *105*, 860–869.

Ketter, T.A., Andreason, P.J., George, M.S., Lee, C., Gill, D.S., Parekh, P.I., Willis, M.W., Herscovitch, P., & Post, R.M. (1996). Anterior paralimbic mediation of procaine-induced emotional and psychosensory experiences. *Archives of General Psychiatry*, *53*, 59–69.

LaBar, K.S., Gatenby, J.C., Gore, J.C., LeDoux, J.E., & Phelps, E.A. (1998). Human amygdala activation during conditioned fear acquisition and extinction: a mixed-trial fMRI study. *Neuron*, *20*, 937–945.

Lane, R.D., Reiman, E.M., Bradley, M.M., Lang, P.J., Ahern, G.L., & Davidson, R.J. (1997). Neuroanatomical correlates of pleasant and unpleasant emotion. *Neuropsychologia*, *35*, 1437–1444.

Lang, P.J., Bradley, M.M., & Cuthbert, B.N. (1990). Emotion, attention and the startle reflex. *Psychological Review*, *97*, 377–398.

Larson, C.L., Ruffalo, D., Nietert, J., & Davidson, R.J. (2000). Temporal stability of the emotion-modulated startle response. *Psychophysiology*, *37*, 92–101.

Larson, C.L., Sutton, S.K., & Davidson, R.J. (1998). Affective style, frontal EEG asymmetry and the time course of the emotion-modulated startle [Abstract]. *Psychophysiology*, *35*, S52.

LeDoux, J.E. (1996). *The emotional brain: The mysterious underpinnings of emotional life.* New York: Simon & Schuster.

Levenson, R.W. (1994). Human emotion: A functional view. In P. Ekman & R.J. Davidson (Eds.), *The nature of emotion: Fundamental questions* (pp. 123–126). New York: Oxford University Press.

Maquet, P., Peters, J., Aerts, J., Delfiore, G., Degueldre, C., Luxen, A., & Franck, G. (1996). Functional neuroanatomy of human rapid-eye-movement sleep and dreaming. *Nature, 383,* 163–166.

Meunier, M., Bachevalier, J., Murray. E.A., Malkova, L., & Mishkin, M. (1999). Effects of aspiration versus neurotoxic lesions of the amygdala on emotional responses in monkeys. *European Journal of Neuroscience, 11,* 4403–4418.

Morgan, M.A., Romanski, L., & LeDoux, J.E. (1993). Extinction of emotional learning: Contribution of medial prefrontal cortex. *Neuroscience Letters, 163,* 109–113.

Morris, J.S., Frith, C.D., Perrett, D.I., Rowland, D., Young, A.W., Calder, A.J., & Dolan, R.J. (1996). A differential neural response in the human amygdala to fearful and happy facial expressions. *Nature, 383,* 812–815.

Morris, J.S., Ohman, A., & Dolan, R.J. (1998). Modulation of amygdala activity by masking of aversively conditioned visual stimuli. *Neuroimage, 7,* S52.

Morris, P.L.P., Robinson, R.G., de Carvalho, M.L., Albert, P., Wells, J.C., Samuels, J.F., Eden-Fetzer, D., & Price, T.R. (1996). Lesion characteristics and depressed mood in the stroke data bank study. *Journal of Neuropsychiatry and Clinical Neurosciences, 8,* 153–159.

Panksepp, J. (1998). *Affective neuroscience.* New York: Oxford University Press.

Phillips, M.L., Young, A.W., Senior, C., Brammer, M., Andrew, C., Calder, A.J., Bullmore, E.T., Perrett, D.I., Rowland, D., Williams, S.C.R., Gray, J.A., & David, A.S. (1997). A specific neural substrate for perceiving facial expressions of disgust. *Nature, 389,* 495–498.

Rauch, S.L., Savage, C.R., Alpert, N.M., Fischman, A.J., & Jenike, M.A. (1997). The functional neuroanatomy of anxiety: A study of three disorders using positron emission tomography and symptom provocation. *Biological Psychiatry, 42,* 446–452.

Rauch, S.L., Van der Kolk, B.A., Fisler, R.E., Alpert, N.M., Orr, S.P., Savage, C.R., Fischman, A.J., Jenike, M.A., & Pitman, R.K. (1996). A symptom provocation study of posttraumatic stress disorder using positron emission tomography and script-driven imagery. *Archives of General Psychiatry, 53,* 380–387.

Reid, S.A., Duke, L.M., & Allen, J.J.B. (1998). Resting frontal electroencephalographic asymmetry in depression: What are the mediating factors? *Psychophysiology, 35,* 389–404.

Robinson, R.G., & Downhill, J.E. (1995). Lateralization of psychopathology in response to focal brain injury. In R.J. Davidson & K. Hugdahl (Eds.), *Brain asymmetry* (pp. 693–711). Cambridge, MA: MIT Press.

Robinson, R.G., Starr, L.B., & Price, T.R. (1984). A two year longitudinal study of mood disorders following stroke: Prevalence and duration at six months follow-up. *British Journal of Psychiatry, 144,* 256–262.

Rolls, E.T. (1999). *The brain and emotion.* New York: Oxford University Press.

Sackeim, H.A., Weiman, A.L., Gur, R.C., Greenberg, M., Hungerbuhler, J.P., & Geschwind, N. (1982). Pathological laughter and crying: Functional brain asymmetry in the expression of positive and negative emotions. *Archives of Neurology, 39,* 210–218.

Schaefer, S.M., Abercrombie, H.C., Lindgren, K.A., Larson, C.L., Ward, R.T., Oakes, T.R., Holden, J.E., Perlman, S.B., Turski, P.A., & Davidson, R.J. (2000). Six-month test-retest reliability of MRI-defined PET measures of regional cerebral glucose metabolic rate in selected subcortical structures. *Human Brain Mapping, 10,* 1–9.

Schneider, F., Gur, R.E., Alavi, A., Seligman, M.E.P., Mozley, L.H., Smith, R.J., Mozley, P.D., & Gur, R.C. (1996). Cerebral blood flow changes in limbic regions induced by unsolvable anagram tasks. *American Journal of Psychiatry, 153,* 206–212.

Schneirla, T.C. (1959). An evolutionary and developmental theory of biphasic processes under-lying approach and withdrawal. In M. R. Jones (Ed.), *Nebraska Symposium on motivation* (pp. 1–42). Lincoln, NA: University of Nebraska Press.

Schwartz, N., & Strack, F. (1999). Reports of subjective well-being: Judgmental processes and their methodological implications. In D. Kahneman, E. Diener, & N. Schwartz (Eds.), *Well-being: The foundations of hedonic psychology* (pp. 61–84). New York: Russell Sage Foundation.

Scott, S.K., Young, A.W., Calder, A.J., Hellawell, D.J., Aggleton, J.P., & Johnson, M. (1997). Impaired auditory recognition of fear and anger following bilateral amygdala lesions. *Nature, 385*, 254–257.

Sutton, S.K., & Davidson, R.J. (1997). Prefrontal brain asymmetry: A biological substrate of the behavioral approach and inhibition systems. *Psychological Science, 8*, 204–210.

Sutton, S.K., Davidson, R.J., Donzella, B., Irwin, W., & Dottl, D.A. (1997). Manipulating affect-ive state using extended picture presentation. *Psychophysiology, 34*, 217–226.

Sutton, S.K., Ward, R.T., Larson, C.L., Holden, J.E., Perlman, S.B., & Davidson, R.J. (1997). Asymmetry in prefrontal glucose metabolism during appetitive and aversive emotional states: An FDG-PET study. *Psychophysiology, 34*, S89.

Taylor, S.E. (1991). Asymmetrical effects of positive and negative events: The mobilization-minimization hypothesis. *Psychological Bulletin, 110*, 67–85.

Tomarken, A.J., & Davidson, R.J. (1994). Frontal brain activation in repressors and non-repressors. *Journal of Abnormal Psychology, 103*, 339–349.

Tomarken, A.J., Davidson, R.J., Wheeler, R.E., & Doss, R.C. (1992a). Individual differences in anterior brain asymmetry and fundamental dimensions of emotion. *Journal of Personality and Social Psychology, 62*, 676–687.

Tomarken, A.J., Davidson, R.J., Wheeler, R.E., & Kinney, L. (1992b). Psychometric properties of resting anterior EEG asymmetry: Temporal stability and internal consistency. *Psychophysiology, 29*, 576–592.

Tucker, D.M., Stenslie, C.E., Roth, R.S., & Shearer, S.L. (1981). Right frontal lobe activation and right hemisphere performance. *Archives of General Psychiatry, 39*, 169–174.

Watanabe, M. (1996). Reward expectancy in primate prefrontal neurons. *Nature, 382*, 629–632.

Watson, D., Clark, L.A., & Tellegen, A. (1988). Development and validation of brief measures of positive and negative affect: The PANAS scales. *Journal of Personality and Social Psy-chology, 54*, 1063–1070.

Watson, D., Clark, L.A., Weber, K., Assenheimer, J.S., Strauss, M.E., & McCormick, C.M. (1995). Testing a tripartite model: I. Evaluating the convergent and discriminant validity of anxiety and depression symptom scales. *Journal of Abnormal Psychology, 104*, 3–14.

Whalen, P.J., Rauch, S.L., Etcoff, N.L., McInerney, S.C., Lee, M.B., & Jenike, M.A. (1998). Masked presentations of emotional facial expressions modulate amygdala activity without explicit knowledge. *The Journal of Neuroscience, 18*, 411–418.

Wheeler, R.E., Davidson, R.J., & Tomarken, A.J. (1993). Frontal brain asymmetry and emotional reactivity: A biological substrate of affective style. *Psychophysiology, 30*, 82–89.

Wiedemann, G., Pauli, P., Dengler, W., Lutzenberger, W., Birbaumer, N., & Buchkremer, G. (1999). Frontal brain asymmetry as a biological substrate of emotions in patients with panic disorders. *Archives of General Psychiatry, 56*, 78–84.

Zald, D.H., & Pardo, J.V. (1997). Emotion, olfaction, and the human amygdala: Amygdala activation during aversive olfactory stimulation. *Proceedings of the National Academy of Sciences, USA, 94*, 4119–4124.

Zald, D.H., Lee, J.T., Fluegel, K.W., & Pardo, J.V. (1998). Aversive gustatory stimulation activates limbic circuits in humans. *Brain, 121*, 1143–1154.

CHAPTER SEVENTEEN

Fear and anxiety: Animal models and human cognitive psychophysiology

Peter J. Lang
University of Florida, Gainesville, FL, USA

Michael Davis
Emory University, Atlanta, GA, USA

Arne Öhman
Karolinska Institutet, Stockholm, Sweden

Cognitive scientists increasingly view mental contents as associative networks of information units. These knowledge structures subsist in memory and may be activated by input that contacts representational units within the structure. Thus, for example, the word cat, or an outline drawing of a cat, prompts memory retrieval of a series of declarative associations, i.e., such cat facts as: has fur, whiskers, and a tail; makes a good pet, but can scratch—all this, along with an apparently three-dimensional cat picture in the mind's eye. Cat cues can also activate episodic memories, such as the time you were watching TV and the cat jumped into your lap and spilled the coffee. Computational neuroscientists view the underlying representations and the connecting networks as fundamentally neural—perhaps, aggregates of Hebbian cell assemblies in the cerebral cortices.

Of particular pertinence here is the fact that some memorial information has a special "qualia." That is, some stimuli and the associations they evoke prompt a state of emotional arousal: the phobic is filled with terror seeing—even just remembering—the snake coiled to strike. His palms sweat and muscles tense. An athlete may feel great joy when recalling a race he won. His heart beats rapidly and his face is flushed with pleasure. Cognitive scientists have not, however, generally considered emotional factors as fundamental to

This chapter first appeared in the *Journal of Affective Disorders*, *61*, Lang, Davis, & Öhman (2001). 'Fear and anxiety: animal models and human cognitive psychophysiology.' pp. 137–159. Copyright (2001), reprinted with permission from Elsevier Science.

the mind's work and, until very recently, few basic models of cognition even considered affective variables. Such concepts as emotional modulation are rarely included in computational models of learning and retention, despite its well-known importance in human memory. It is an aim of this paper, however, to explicate what is special about emotional information processing in the brain—particularly, the neural foundations that underlie the experience and expression of fear.

We will begin with a description of fundamental neural circuits that prompt a defensive posture in mammals. It will be shown that these circuits are activated in rodents by fear conditioning and sensitization, and that their activation primes other emotional behaviors. Furthermore, recent experiments demonstrate that when similar fear induction paradigms are used with human subjects, comparable autonomic reactivity and somatic reflex modulation are found. We will consider neural structures that appear to be differentially active in explicitly fearful situations, compared to contexts that prompt more generalized anxiety. Parallels in the responses of normal human subjects and patients are illustrated, as humans respond emotionally to symbolic stimuli and memory imagery. Finally, again emphasizing links between the animal and human data, we focus on attentional factors in emotional processing: The automaticity of fear reactions, reactivity to minimal cues, and evidence that the physiological responses in fear may be independent of slower, language based appraisal processes.

MOTIVATION AND EMOTION

How is the associative network of an emotion different from other knowledge structures in the brain? The answer proposed here is that the neural networks underlying emotion include direct connections to the brain's primary motivational systems. These systems are neural circuits that were laid down early in our evolutionary history, in primitive cortex, sub-cortex and mid-brain, and mediate behaviors basic to the survival of individuals and species. These motivational circuits are activated by unconditioned appetitive and aversive stimuli. They determine the general mobilization of the organism, the deployment of reflexive approach and withdrawal behaviors, and mediate the formation of conditioned associations based on primary reinforcement.

Human emotions are, of course, highly varied in their expression. However, many investigators have argued (e.g., Konorski, 1967) that emotion's motivational organization has a simpler, biphasic structure. Pleasant emotions are associated with an appetitive system—the basic neural mediation of approach, hunger, sexual, and nurturant behavior; unpleasant emotions are driven by a defensive system, primarily associated with withdrawal, escape from pain, and defensive aggression. It is this latter system that is presumed to be active in human fear and anxiety.

THE NEUROPHYSIOLOGY OF FEAR

What we know about the brain's defense circuitry comes primarily from neuroscience research with animals, using relatively simple experimental procedures in which nociceptive events (e.g., electric shock) are paired with previously innocuous lights and tones. Using various neurosurgical, pharmacological, and electrophysiological tools, the chain of probable neural activation has been traced in the brain, starting from the input end in the sensory system—proceeding through the necessary connecting structures—to the autonomic and motor output effectors.

These studies have repeatedly implicated a small, almond-shaped structure located deep within the temporal lobe—the amygdala—to be at the center of a defense system involved in both the expression and acquisition of conditioned fear (Davis, 1992; Gloor, 1960; Gray, 1989; Kapp and Pascoe, 1986; Kapp, Pascoe, & Bixler, 1984; LeDoux, 1987; Sarter and Markowitsch, 1985). The amygdala receives highly processed sensory information from all modalities through its lateral and basolateral nuclei. In turn, these nuclei project to the central nucleus of the amygdala, which then projects to a variety of hypothalamic sites, the central gray, and brainstem target areas that directly mediate specific signs of fear and anxiety (cf. Davis, 1992). Electrical stimulation of the amygdala elicits many of the behaviors used to define a state of fear, with selected target areas of the amygdala producing specific effects (Figure 1).

These autonomic and somatic patterns have great variety; however, they can be functionally organized into two broad output classes: (1) defensive immobility (i.e., "freezing," "fear bradycardia," and hyper-attentiveness, e.g., Campbell, Wood, & McBride, 1997; Kapp, Whalen, Supple, & Pascoe, 1992)

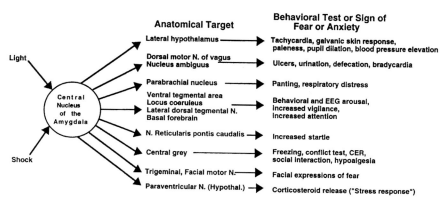

Figure 1. Schematic diagram showing direct connection between the central nucleus of the amygdala and a variety of hypothalamic and brainstem target areas that may be involved in different animal tests of fear and anxiety. Projections to the basal forebrain that may be involved in attention also are shown.

in which the organism is passive but "primed" to respond actively to further stimulation); (2) defensive action (i.e., variations in fight/flight which are more or less direct responses to nociception or imminent attack). These outputs may be stages in the normal, mammalian defense reaction, with an attentional set dominant when threat is more remote, but giving way to action with greater imminence of an aversive event (see Blanchard and Blanchard, 1989; Fanselow, 1994; Lang, Bradley, & Cuthbert, 1997).

It is probable, furthermore, that as representations of simple lights and tones can, through aversive association come to activate neural defense circuits in animals, more complex networks of information that characterize human cognition also come to activate the same defense system. Thus, at the level of human recall and recognition, the property of an emotion memory network that differentiates it from other knowledge structures is that the emotion network has a strong connection to this primitive motivational circuitry—appetitive or defensive (Lang, 1994). Fear states, whether driven by external threat or internal association, are defined by defense system activation and its reflexive autonomic and somatic output.

THE STARTLE REFLEX AND EMOTIONAL PRIMING

From an evolutionary perspective, human emotions such as fear are usefully considered to be dispositions to action. That is, they may have evolved from preparatory states evoked by threat cues, in which survival depended on delay or inhibition of overt behavior. In this sense, they derive from the first stage of defense that is associated with vigilance and immobility, when the organism is automatically mobilized, primed to respond, but not yet active. A measurable feature of this fear state is an exaggerated startle reflex to any suddenly imposed stimulus. It is an example of what cognitive psychologists call "priming". That is, a prior stimulus or state raises the activation level of an associated S-R event, for example, as the prime "bread" prompts a faster reaction time response to the word "butter", or as a depressed person's associations are persistently affectively negative. In the present instance, the induced defense state of the organism primes an independently instigated reflex, but one connected to the defense system. As will be described later, considerable progress has been made in understanding the neurophysiology of startle priming. This methodology has, furthermore, proved to be a powerful tool in the study of emotion.

The fear-potentiated startle effect

When the startle reflex of a rodent is elicited by a loud sound 3–4 s after a light has been turned on, there is no systematic change in the amplitude of the startle reflex. However, if the day before, or even a month before, the light came on 3–4 s before an electric shock, the sound-induced startle will sub-sequently be potentiated, i.e., during the 3–4 s after the light comes on the animal now shows an exaggerated startle reaction. This fear-potentiated startle effect (first described by Brown, Kalish, & Farber, 1951) only occurs following prior light-shock pairings and not when lights and shocks have been presented in an unpaired or random relationship (Davis & Astrachan, 1978), indicating its dependence on prior Pavlovian fear conditioning. If the conditioned stimulus is presented repeatedly, without further light-shock pairings, it no longer increases startle (Falls, Miserendino, & Davis, 1992), indicative of extinction of prior fear conditioning. Apparently, the signal light produces a state of fear which increases reflexive behavior, because drugs like diazepam or buspirone, which reduce fear in humans, block the increase in startle in the presence of the conditioned light stimulus, but do not alter startle systematically in the absence of the light signal when appropriate doses are used (see Davis, Falls, Campeau, & Kim, 1993, for a review).

One of the advantages of using the startle response to study fear is that different conditioned and unconditioned anxiogenic phenomena can be measured by modification of a simple reflex which has a non-zero baseline. The non-zero baseline is important because potentially it allows one to separate the effects of a treatment on the hypothetical state of interest (e.g., fear) from the effects of the treatment on the response that is used to measure that hypothetical state. For example, although freezing is a sensitive measure of fear, it is only measurable during a state of fear. Thus, if some treatment blocks freezing one might conclude that it blocks fear. However, that treatment might simply make animals incapable of holding still, without actually affecting the broader neurobehavioral complex that constitutes fear. The startle measure, however, is not so easily compromised. The reflex is not a specific component of the fear state, but rather a response to a probe event that is primed when the state is present. Thus, the basic reflex can readily be evoked in the absence of fear, and its susceptibility to modulation, can be independently verified with other procedures that do not involve fear (e.g., the pre-pulse methodology).

The other advantage of using a reflex is that it can be elicited by a stimulus that is controlled by the experimenter so that different response levels can be produced. If some treatment reduces or increases the reflex response, the experimenter can increase or decrease the loudness of the startle stimulus to produce a response level in the treatment condition equivalent to that in the control condition, allowing assessment of fear or anxiety at equivalent parts of the measurement scale. Finally, and most importantly, because reflexes generally have short latencies, it is possible to determine the neural pathway that mediates the reflex which can then serve as a starting point to determine the neural pathway involved in fear or anxiety.

The primary acoustic startle pathway

The extraordinary short latency of the rat's acoustic startle reflex (e.g., 8 ms measured electromyographically in the hindleg), indicates that it is mediated by a simple neural pathway. In 1982, Davis and colleagues (Davis, Gendelman, Tischler, & Gendelman, 1982) proposed that acoustic startle was mediated by four synapses; three in the brainstem (the ventral cochlear nucleus; an area just medial and ventral to the ventral nucleus of the lateral lemniscus, and the nucleus reticularis pontis caudalis) and one synapse onto motoneurons in the spinal cord. Electrolytic lesions of these nuclei eliminated aeonstic startle and single pulse electrical stimulation of these nuclei elicited startle-like responses with a progressively shorter latency as the electrode was moved farther down the startle pathway.

Subsequent research has supported this conception, with a further simplification of the auditory pathway. The cochlear root neurons receive direct input from the spiral ganglion cells in the cochlea, making them the first acoustic neurons in the central nervous system. Their axons proceed to deep layers of the superior colliculus, but pass close to the lateral lemniscus. It previously appeared that there was a necessary synapse at the lemniscus; it is now clear, however, that axon collaterals of the root neurons terminate directly in the nucleus reticularis pontis caudalis (Lingenhohl & Friauf, 1994; Lopez et al., 1993), on the reflex-critical cells that project to motoneurons in the spinal cord (Lingenhohl & Friauf, 1994). Furthermore, bilateral, chemically induced lesions of the cochlear root neurons essentially eliminate acoustic startle in rats, and there is an excellent correlation between the number of root neurons destroyed and the decrease in startle (Lee et al., 1996).

In summary, although there is some disagreement (Frankland et al., 1995), the acoustic startle pathway appears to be simpler than had originally been thought, consisting of only three synapses onto (1) cochlear root neurons; (2) neurons in the nucleus reticularis pontis caudalis; and (3) motoneurons in the facial motor nucleus (pinna reflex) or spinal cord.

The role of the amygdala in fear-potentiated startle

As previously noted, during exposure to a previously conditioned fear stimulus, an abrupt acoustic stimulus will prompt a potentiated startle response. This suggests that the startle circuit must, at some point, connect with the organism's fear/defense system. Furthermore, the amygdala appears to be this system's focal neural structure, modulating both input and output, and as such it is a logical focus for neurophysiological study of fear's effects on the startle reflex.

Lesions of the central nucleus of the amygdala block the expression of fear-potentiated startle using either a visual (Hitchcock & Davis, 1986) or auditory conditioned stimulus (Campeau & Davis, 1995; Hitchcock & Davis, 1987). Blockade of glutamate receptors in the central nucleus of the amygdala via local infusion of a non-NMDA (N-methyl-D-aspartate) glutamate receptor antagonist has a similar effect (Kim et al., 1993). Thus, the central nucleus clearly serves a key mediational role in reflex potentiation.

Other amygdaloid nuclei are also important, relaying sensory information to the central nucleus. For example, selective destruction of cell bodies via local infusion of neurotoxic doses of NMDA into the lateral and basolateral nuclei caused a complete blockade of fear-potentiated startle when the lesions were made either before or after training with either light (Sananes & Davis, 1992) or auditory conditioned stimuli (Campeau & Davis, 1995). These results are consistent with other work that indicates that the lateral nucleus of the amygdala provides a critical link for relaying auditory information involved in fear conditioning to the amygdala (LeDoux et al., 1990).

Both conditioned fear and sensitization of startle by footshocks appear to ultimately modulate startle at the level of the nucleus reticularis pontis caudalis (Berg & Davis, 1985; Boulis & Davis, 1989; Krase et al., 1994). The central nucleus of the amygdala projects directly to the nucleus reticularis pontis caudalis (Rosen et al., 1991) and electrolytic lesions along this path block the expression of fear-potentiated startle (Hitchcock & Davis, 1991). It earlier appeared that this direct path alone mediated both fear potentiated startle and footshock sensitization of startle (Hitchcock et al., 1989; Hitchcock & Davis, 1991). However, the presence of obligatory synapses at points along this pathway could not be ruled out (Hitchcock & Davis, 1991). More recent data suggests the presence of a synapse between the amygdala and central gray, because fiber-sparing chemical lesions of the central gray have been shown to block both fear phenomena (Franklin & Yeomans, 1995; Fendt et al., 1996).

Startle modulation in human emotion

The animal data clearly link potentiated startle to the same neural structures involved in the general mediation of other fear/defense responses. Furthermore, these same structures and connections exists in the human brain, and appear to have parallel functions (e.g., see Aggleton, 1992a,b). Several years ago, Vrana, Spence, and Lang (1988; see also Lang, Bradley, & Cuthbert, 1990) proposed that the elaborate cognitive networks representing affective experience were connected to these more basic motivational circuits. It was further suggested that startle reflex priming could be used as a test of this assumption. In this view, aversive attentive states—even those occasioned by higher-order mediators such as picture or film stimuli, text, or memory imagery—should prime startle potentiation. Sudden acoustic startle probes could be presented while subjects watched unpleasant or frightening stimuli. Larger startle reflexes would be expected during the viewing of these negative images than during neutral or pleasant stimuli. In the case of positive percepts, furthermore, given the frequent reciprocal engagement of defense and appetitive systems, probe reflex inhibition could be anticipated.

Probing emotional perception

In studies with human beings, rapid eye closure is one of the most reliable components of the behavioral cascade that constitutes the startle reflex. The latency (occurring within 30–50 ms of stimulus onset) and magnitude of the blink can be measured by monitoring the orbicularis oculi muscle, using electrodes placed just beneath the lower lid. The acoustic stimulus used to evoke the blink is relatively modest—typically a 50-ms burst of white noise at around 95 dB which, while prompting a clear blink response, rarely interferes with ongoing foreground tasks. Several studies have confirmed reliable potentiation of the blink response in humans—associated with sensitization by electric shock or with shock conditioning of specific stimuli—that parallels the modulatory patterns of the whole body startle response in rats (Greenwald, Bradley, Cuthbert, & Lang, 1998; Grillon and Davis, 1997; Hamm, Greenwald, Bradley, & Lang, 1993).

The hypothesis that representations of unpleasant events (i.e., reduced cues that activate emotion, but not directly associated with imminent danger or pain) would also modulate the reflexive startle response was first tested using projected photographic stimuli. We have since developed a library of these picture stimuli, covering the whole range of emotional reactions, normatively rated for affective valence and arousal (The International Affective Picture System: IAPS; Center for the Study of Emotion and Attention, 1998). In most experiments, the pictures are organized into three affective classes—unpleasant (e.g., poisonous snakes, aimed guns, pictures of violent death), pleasant (e.g., happy babies, appetizing food, erotica), and neutral (e.g., people doing routine tasks, neutral faces, common household objects)— and differences between the picture types are tested.

As mentioned earlier, picture viewing is an observational, intake task in which—like a "freezing" rat (or an attentive predator)—subjects are generally immobile, with sensory processors engaged. When startle probes are administered in this context, results have consistently conformed to the motivational priming hypothesis: A significant linear trend is reliably observed over judged picture valence, with the largest startle blink responses occurring during unpleasant pictures, moderate responses to neutral pictures, and the smallest during pleasant pictures (e.g., Bradley, Cuthbert, & Lang, 1996; Vrana et al., 1988). These opposite valence effects—relative inhibition to pleasant stimuli and potentiation to unpleasant stimuli—are more pronounced when emotional stimuli are judged to be highly "arousing" (Cuthbert, Bradley, & Lang, 1996).

These emotional–perceptual effects appear to be ubiquitous. Balaban (1995) found affective modulation of startle probe responses during picture viewing (of smiling, neutral, and angry faces) in 5-month-old infants. Jansen and Frijda (1994), using evocative video film clips (fearful and erotic), and Hamm, Stark, and Vaitl (1990), using LAPS pictures, have obtained this affect–startle effect in European subjects. Spence and Lang (1990) have shown a startle affect modulation when subjects read emotional texts on a computer screen. Furthermore, affective modulation is not confined to visual percepts: When the foreground stimuli are emotionally evocative sound clips (e.g., sounds of love-making; babies crying; bombs bursting), using a visual light-flash as the startle probe, the same affect–reflex effect is obtained as for pictures (Bradley, Zack, & Lang, 1994).

As might be anticipated, phobic subjects (Figure 2) show greater than normal startle potentiation when they view pictures of the phobic object (Hamm, Cuthbert, Globisch, & Vaitl, 1997; Sabatinelli, Bradley, Cuthbert, & Lang, et al., 1996). In contrast, incarcerated psychopaths—particularly those characterized by manipulativeness and lack of remorse—fail to show normal probe potentiation when viewing unpleasant picture stimuli (Patrick et al., 1993; Patrick, Cuthbert, & Lang, 1994) (interestingly, the affective reports of these psychopathic subjects are no different from normals).

The psychophysiology of emotion

Sensory, representational input (pictures, sounds, text) can directly activate emotional networks in the brain that mediate a broad range of physiological and behavioral events. Thus, the same picture stimuli that modulate startle also directly prompt a host of measurable affect-driven responses. These measures include evaluative judgments, viewing behavior, and physiological changes (i.e., changes in the facial musculature, skin conductance, heart rate, and cortical event-related potentials recorded from the scalp surface). All are valuable measures of emotional expression. Their specific pattern (e.g., whether heart rate accelerates or decelerates) varies with context and task. The underlying organization of these data, however, is dictated by the motivational systems that control our emotional destiny. Table 1 presents the results of a factor analysis of the responses of normal subjects watching emotional pictures. It will be noted that the data group themselves into two factors, affective valence and arousal. That is, individual responses either define the engagement of the specific motive system (appetitive or defensive) or reflect the vigor and intensity of that engagement.

Modulation of the probe startle reflex similarly reflects defensive activation. It differs importantly from the measures considered above in that it is

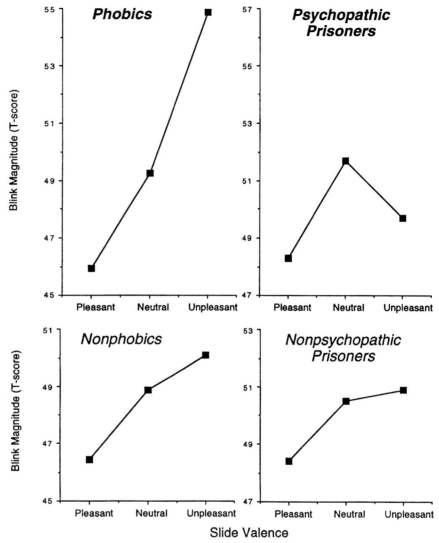

Figure 2. Phobic college students show significantly larger probe startle responses when viewing "unpleasant" stimuli (pictures of snakes) than do nonphobic students (Sabatinelli et al., 1996). The reduced probe response to "pleasant" stimuli (erotic pictures) was similar in both groups. College students ($N = 16$) were defined as phobic if they had high scores (scored at or above the 95th percentile for their gender) on the Snake Fear Questionnaire (Klorman, Hastings, Weerts, Melamed, & Lang, 1974). They are compared with a sample of college students whose Snake Fear Questionnaire scores were below this criterion ($N = 48$). Psychopathic prisoners show significantly smaller probe startle responses when viewing "unpleasant stimuli" (e.g., pictures of mutilated bodies, attacking animals or people, etc.) than nonpsychopathic prisoners (Patrick, Bradley, & Lang, 1993). Both Prisoner groups showed a reduced probe response (relative to neutral) while viewing "pleasant" stimuli (e.g., pictures of sports, food, erotica, etc.). Prisoners were defined as psychopathic ($N = 16$) if they had high scores (PCL-R score = 30) on Hare's Psychopathy Checklist (Hare et al., 1990). The scores of the nonpsychopathic group ($N = 34$) fell below this criterion.

TABLE 17.1
Factor analyses of measures of emotional picture processing
sorted loadings of dependent measures on principal
components (Lang, Greenwold, Bradley, & Hamm, 1993)

Measure	Factor 1 (valence)	Factor 2 (arousal)
Valence ratings	0.86	−0.00
Corrugator muscle	−0.85	0.19
Heart rate	0.79	−0.14
Zygomatic muscle	0.58	0.29
Arousal ratings	0.15	0.83
Interest ratings	0.45	0.77
Viewing time	−0.27	0.76
Skin conductance	−0.37	0.74

not a direct response to the primary stimulus. It is a reaction to a secondary probe that is administered after an emotional reaction is already ongoing. It shows the emotional state priming of a defensive response, and is functionally equivalent to the mood priming of negative associations to neutral stimuli in depressed individuals. Startle modulation provides strong evidence that the old motivational circuits are active, and indicates their directional orientation, i.e., reflex augmentation after aversive stimulation and relative diminution following appetitive input. The reflex modulation also measures intensity of motivational arousal. That is, startle potentiation is greatest during viewing of the most intense aversive stimuli; conversely, the reflex is smallest (maximally inhibited) when viewing the most arousing pleasant stimuli (Cuthbert, Bradley, & Lang, 1996).

FEAR AND ANXIETY: CUE-SPECIFIC VERSUS GENERALIZED DISTRESS

Clinicians have traditionally made a distinction between fear and anxiety, and several theoretical models have been proposed to discriminate between these states. Although not all views converge, fear is generally held to be a reaction to an explicit threatening stimulus, with escape or avoidance the outcome of increased cue proximity. Anxiety is usually considered a more general state of distress, more long lasting, prompted by less explicit or more generalized cues, involving physiological arousal but often without organized functional behavior. The Pavlovian conditioning and sensitization paradigms that potentiate startle appear to prompt the cue-specific fear state. Recently, startle modulation has been examined in two other animal research paradigms that evoke a broader state of aversion, suggestive of generalized anxiety.

Unconditioned startle enhancement

It has been repeatedly observed that bright light produces anxiety-like responses in the rat (see Walsh & Cummins, 1976, for a review; Crawley, 1981; File, 1980). Recently, Walker and Davis (1997a) found that untrained animals exposed to a bright light for an extended period (5–20 min) show an increase in the startle reflex, similar to conditioned potentiation. This effect was decreased by anxiolytic drugs like buspirone (Walker & Davis, 1997a) and chlordiazepoxide (Walker & Davis, unpublished observations), suggesting that the startle enhancement was due to light's anxiogenic property. The phenomenon is clearly unconditioned and, at least in the rat, does not extinguish within or across several test sessions (Walker & Davis, 1997a).

Intraventricular administration of the peptide, corticotropin releasing hormone (CRH) produces general activation and a variety of behavioral and neuroendocrine effects similar to those seen during fear and anxiety. Furthermore, intraventricular administration of the CRH antagonist α-helical CRH9-41 blocks the behavioral and neuroendocrine effects of natural stressors or conditioned fear (Dunn & Berridge, 1990). Swerdlow, Geyer, Vale, and Koob (1986) reported that intraventricular administration of CRH increased the acoustic startle reflex and that this effect could be blocked by the benzodiazepine chlordiazepoxide, suggesting that the excitatory effect of CRH on startle reflects the hormone's anxiogenic effect. This work has been confirmed and extended by Davis and colleagues, showing that intraventricular infusion of CRH (0.1–1.0 5 g) produced a pronounced, dose-dependent enhancement of the acoustic startle reflex in rats (Liang et al., 1992b) that lasts for several hours. This effect still occurs after adrenalectomy, indicating that it is not dependent on the release of corticosterone from the adrenal glands (Lee, Schulkin, & Davis, 1994). Thus, startle enhanced by corticotropin-releasing hormone, like light-enhanced startle, appears to be an example of a long-lasting, unconditioned anxiety.

The anatomy of anxiety

It was presumed initially that these startle phenomena were like fear-conditioning effects, attributable to amygdala activation. Subsequent research has indicated, however, that the story is more complex and that a different, though closely associated, neural structure plays a primary role. The bed nucleus of the stria terminalis is considered to be part of the so-called extended amygdala, because it is highly similar to the central nucleus of the amygdala in terms of its transmitter content, cell morphology, and efferent connections (cf. Alheid, deOlmos, & Beltramino, 1995). However, lesions of the bed nucleus of the stria terminalis fail to block either fear-potentiated startle (Hitchcock & Davis, 1991) or conditioned freezing using an explicit cue (LeDoux, Iwata, Cicchetti, & Reis, 1988), suggesting that it may not be involved in explicit cue conditioning. On the other hand, several studies indicate that the bed nucleus of the stria terminalis might be involved in elevations of startle that are more long-lasting than explicit cue conditioning. For example, lesions of the bed nucleus blocked long-term sensitization of the startle reflex (Gewirtz, McNish, & Davis, 1998) or the excitatory effect of the peptide corticotropin releasing hormone on startle (Lee & Davis, 1997).

The hypothesis of bed nucleus involvement in more sustained startle enhancement was pursued, using infusion of the glutamate antagonist NBQX to render inactive selected nuclei in the brain. Following local application of this compound, animals with inactivation of either the basolateral nucleus of the amygdala or the bed nucleus of the stria terminalis showed a significant decrease in light-enhanced startle. Surprisingly, however, infusion of the glutamate antagonist into the central nucleus of the amygdala had no effect (Figure 3).

In a further test of this view, the rats used in the light-enhanced startle experiment were trained and tested for fear-potentiated startle after infusion of NBQX into either the amygdala or bed nucleus of the stria terminalis. Figure 4 shows that consistent with previous results, infusion of the glutamate antagonist into the central nucleus of the amygdala completely blocked

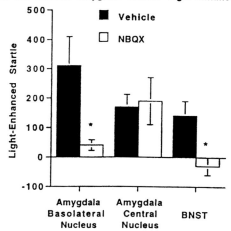

Figure 3. Mean change in startle amplitude from the dark phase to the light phase (light-enhanced startle) after infusion of the glutamate antagonist NBQX or its vehicle into either the basolateral nucleus of the amygdala, the central nucleus of the amygdala, or the lateral bed nucleus of the stria terminalis (adapted from Walker & Davis, 1997b. Copyright 1997 by the Society of Neuroscience).

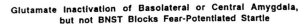

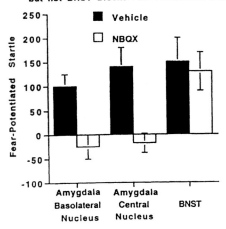

Glutamate Inactivation of Basolateral or Central Amygdala,
but not BNST Blocks Fear-Potentiated Startle

Figure 4. Mean change in startle amplitude on the light-noise versus the noise alone trails (fear-potentiated startle) after infusion of the glutamate antagonist NBQX or its vehicle into either the basolateral nucleus of the amygdala, or the lateral bed nucleus of the stria terminalis (adapted from Walker & Davis, 1997b. Copyright 1997 by the Society of Neuroscience).

the expression of fear-potentiated startle. Basolateral amygdala infusion produced this same result. In contrast, inactivation of the bed nucleus of the stria terminalis had no effect on fear-potentiated startle. These data show a double dissociation between inactivation of the central nucleus of the amygdala versus the bed nucleus of the stria terminalis in the mediation of fear-potentiated versus light-enhanced startle. Thus, if light-enhanced startle is an animal model of anxiety, its functional anatomy is clearly different from cue-specific conditioned fear.

Because CRH-enhanced startle has certain similarities to light-enhanced startle, it was hypothesized that this effect would also be dependent on the bed nucleus of the stria terminalis, and not the central nucleus of the amygdala. To test this, the same nuclei were lesioned, and intraventricular cannulas were implanted to infuse the corticotropin releasing hormone. Two weeks later the animals were tested for startle before and after hormone infusion. Remarkably, chemical lesions of the amygdala failed to block hormone-enhanced startle. On the other hand, lesions of the bed nucleus of the stria terminalis completely prevented this effect (Lee & Davis, 1997). Furthermore, it was found in other animals that infusion of low doses of CRH directly into the bed nucleus produced a rapid and large increase in startle amplitude, whereas earlier work had failed to see this following local infusion of the hormone into the amygdala (Liang et al., 1992a). Finally, infusing a hormone antagonist directly into the bed nucleus of the stria terminalis blocked the excitatory effect of the hormone given intraventricularly. This did not occur when the antagonist was infused into the amygdala. These data indicate that the bed nucleus of the stria terminalis, and not the amygdala, is the primary receptor site mediating the corticotropin releasing hormone's startle enhancing effect.

In summary, the bed nucleus of the stria terminalis may be a system that responds to signals more akin to anxiety than fear, whereas the central nucleus of the amygdala is clearly involved in fear and perhaps less so in anxiety (Figure 5). Both these structures have very similar efferent connections to various hypothalamic and brainstem target areas known to be involved in specific signs and symptoms of fear and anxiety (cf. Davis, 1992). Both receive highly processed sensory information from the basolateral nucleus of the amygdala and hence are in a position to respond to emotionally significant stimuli.

Corticotropin-releasing hormone is known to be released during periods of stress or anxiety. Some of this may come from neurons in the central

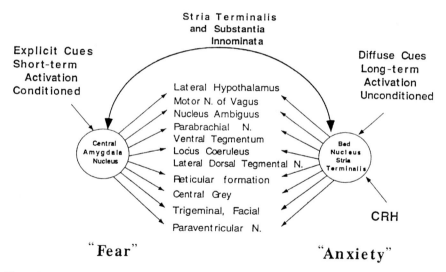

Figure 5. Hypothetical schematic suggesting that the central nucleus of the amygdala and the bed nucleus of the stria terminalis may be differentially involved in fear versus anxiety, respectively. Both brain areas have highly similar hypothalamic and brainstem targets known to be involved in specific signs and symptoms of fear and anxiety. However, the stress peptide CRH appears to act on receptors in the bed nucleus of the stria terminalis rather than the amygdala, at least in terms of an increase in the startle reflex. Furthermore, the bed nucleus of the stria terminalis seems to be involved in the anxiogenic effects of a very bright light presented for a long period of time but not when that very same light has previously been paired with a shock. Just the opposite is the case for the central nucleus of the amygdala, which is critical for fear conditioning using explicit cues such as light or tone paired with aversive stimulation (i.e., conditioned fear) (adapted from Davis, Walker, & Lee, 1997, with permission from the New York Academy of Sciences).

nucleus of the amygdala which contains the hormone, and which project to and act on receptors in the bed nucleus of the stria terminalis (Sakanaka, Shibasaki, & Lederis, 1986). Thus, phasic activation of the amygdala by certain stressors could lead to long-term activation of the bed nucleus of the stria terminalis via corticotropin-releasing hormone. Potential clinical implications of this neurophysiological distinction between sustained (anxiety) and phasic (fear) activation have led to further investigation of the functional similarities and differences between these two parts of the extended amygdala.[1]

Clinical anxiety and the startle response

When nocturnal species are exposed to light, they characteristically show avoidance and other signs of stress; conversely, diurnal species such as human beings appear to be stressed by darkness. When the lights go off, many people feel more anxious, especially if they were afraid of the dark when they were young. Recently, it has been shown that humans show a significant increase of startle amplitude when they are alone in the dark (Grillon, Pellowski, Merikangas, & Davis, 1997). Furthermore, in patients with combat-related post-traumatic stress disorder (PTSD), startle is increased in the dark to a greater degree than that seen in combat-experienced controls (Grillon, Morgan, Davis, & Southwick, 1998). Some patients reported that the

---

[1] Researchers have also implicated the hippocampus in animal studies of anxiety. There are, however, conflicting views concerning both its function and pertinence based on results that vary with the experimental paradigm and dependent measures employed. McNaughton and Gray (2000) hold the strongest view, arguing that the hippocampus is the central structure in a complex Behavioral Inhibition System (BIS) that is the basic mediator of clinical anxiety. Their theory is founded on the general observation that anxiolytic drugs have effects on animals that are similar to those occasioned by hippocampal lesions, i.e., behavioral inhibition is reduced, while arousal and attention (vigilance) are often incremented. Other researchers assign a narrower role to the hippocampus: LeDoux (1996), for example, has suggested that the particular importance of the hippocampus (and its cortical connections) is to maintain "conscious" fear-related memories in humans. In animal studies, both Kim and Fanselow (1992) and Phillips and LeDoux (1992) found that lesions of the hippocampus disrupt anxiety-like reactions in the context of *potential* danger (i.e., "freezing" behavior was less in lesioned than in control animals replaced in cages where they had previously received shock training trials). On the other hand, hippocampal lesions did not block the response to a specific fear cue (i.e., "freezing" when the conditioned stimulus is presented). These data are often interpreted to mean that hippocampal lesions disrupt the animal's ability to form the complex, polymodal associations that are needed to functionally represent a context. More recently, however, McNish, Gewirtz, and Davis (1997) found that, despite dorsal hippocampal lesions, startle reflexes were potentiated when probes were presented in the training cage. Thus, with startle as a measure of defense motivation, rather than "freezing", there was no disturbance of context conditioning. These latter authors suggest that the previously observed lesion-based disruption of "freezing" indicates that the hippocampus plays a primary role in the inhibition of movement, but not in disrupting contextual anxiety itself (see p. 7).

darkness prompts combat memories, such as being back at their guardpost in Vietnam and anxious about being hit by an incoming mortar. These thoughts might serve as specific fear cues. The effect could also have resulted, however, from a greater anxious apprehension in patients, prompted by the novel and stressful context of psychophysiological testing (Grillon et al., 1998). Darkness would accentuate the effect, in this sense analogous to the sustained startle enhancement found in rats taken from their home cages and exposed to light.

A recent experiment assessed startle in a group of 95 anxiety patients (subgroups of simple and social phobia, PTSD, and panic) and 22 normal controls (Cuthbert, Drobes, Patrick, & Lang, 1994). Acoustic startle probes were presented during both fear and neutral memory imagery, and during inter-trial rest periods. Most subjects showed larger startle responses to probes presented during fear than neutral imagery, but this difference was not consistently larger for patients than controls. In terms of absolute reflex magnitude; however, diagnoses that scored higher on questionnaire measures of anxiety and depression (i.e., panic and PTSD) had significantly larger base reflex reactions than controls, or than diagnoses with lower depression or anxiety questionnaire scores (i.e., simple and social phobia). This effect was clearly apparent only at the initial assessment session.

Much work needs to be done to clarify interpretation of these phenomena. These results suggest, however, that a general startle sensitivity may characterize patients with high "negative affect," a temperamental disposition associated with persistent anxiety and depression (e.g., see Watson, Clark, & Tellegen, 1988). In a further exploration of this hypothesis, the modulating effect of a comorbid mood disorder (DSM-IV diagnosis) on startle magnitude was evaluated. As can be seen in Figure 6, patients who were also depressed showed significantly larger base startle reflexes than those without this comorbidity. Although this is a general phenomenon across diagnoses, it is worth noting that the incidence of mood disorder is significantly higher in PTSD and panic than in the other diagnoses.

In summary, these data suggest that startle enhancement occurs in clinical populations independent of a specific, conditioned fear cue, analogous to the phenomenon in animal subjects. It was further proposed that patients with a disposition to negative affect may be particularly vigilant and apprehensive when confronting novel or unusual circumstances. Assuming the same mechanism in humans as in animals, the bed nucleus of the stria terminalis, rather than the central nucleus of the amygdala, may be the active mediator of enhanced startle as well as other autonomic and somatic responses that are associated with the clinical phenomenon of sustained anxious apprehension.

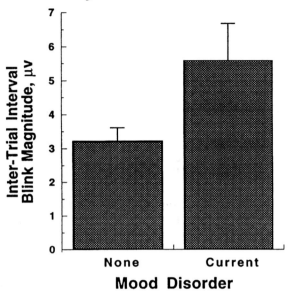

Figure 6.   A significant difference in blink reflex magnitude (during rest trials) between anxiety research subjects with no current comorbid mood disorder and subjects satisfying DSM-IV criteria for a current mood disorder, $F(1,114) = 4.17$, $p < .05$ (see Lang, Bradley, & Cuthbert, 1998b).

ATTENTION TO THREAT

Animal behavior researchers (e.g., Blanchard & Blanchard, 1989) note that defensive behaviors increase systematically with a reduction in distance from a predator or other dangerous or potentially painful stimulus. Thus, given the availability of an escape route, proximity is associated with an increased probability of active flight. In the absence of an escape option or when the threat stimulus is distant or not clearly discriminable, an animal such as the rat "freezes while oriented toward the predator" (p. S5). The Blanchards note further that increases in "the amplitude of the startle response to sudden stimuli accompany decreasing defensive distance" (p. S5).

   Using the concepts introduced by Timberlake (1993) and Timberlake and Lucas Gary (1989), Fanselow (1991, 1994) has made a parallel analysis of fear behavior, describing three behavioral stages, increasingly proximal to a predator: pre-encounter defense, pre-emptive behavior that occurs in a foraging area where predators were previously encountered; post-encounter defense, responses prompted by the detection of a distant predator;

circa-strike defense, behaviors such as defensive attack that occur in the region of physical contact or its close imminence. Behaviorally, there is a shift from nonspecific threat vigilance at pre-encounter, to post-encounter freezing and orienting to a specific predator or predator cue, to the circa-strike stage when the organism is beyond vigilance and engaged in vigorous defensive action.

Fanselow conceives these stages as organized by the amygdala, interacting with the dorsolateral and ventral central gray. Significantly, much of the behavior controlled by these systems is in the service of orienting and attention. Kapp et al. (1992) have also signaled the initial attentional nature of defense, and its dependence on subcortical neural circuits: "the central nucleus of the amygdala and associated structures contribute to the rapid acquisition of an increased level of nonspecific attention or arousal, as manifested in a variety of rapidly acquired CRs (e.g., bradycardia, EEG desynchronization, pupillary dilation) which emerge during Pavlovian conditioning" (pp. 229–230). Other indices of orienting could be added to this list, such as increased sweat gland activity, respiration changes, eye tracking.

Lang et al. (1997) recently proposed an adaptation of the predator stage model for explicating human psychophysiolgical reactions to unpleasant and threatening stimuli. They suggest that the human laboratory participant, responding to stimuli presented by the experimenter, is functioning at a response stage analogous to post-encounter, i.e., like the freezing rat, he is immobile, vigilant, with easy escape blocked (in this case by instructions and social compliance). For the animal subject, increasing proximity to an aversive stimulus (greater nociceptive imminence) prompts an increase in general activation or arousal. This same effect is generated in the human psychophysiological laboratory as stimuli become more threatening or aversive. As illustrated in Figure 7, the increased vigilance in the post-encounter period is characterized by a progressive augmentation of physiological indices of attention—greater skin conductance, increased heart rate deceleration and, when arousal is still relatively low, inhibition of the probe startle reflex.

The arousal abscissa of Figure 7 also constitutes a dimension of greater probability of motor action that modulates the startle response. Thus, as a close encounter becomes more imminent, the direction of the probe response reverses. In place of motor inhibition, the startle reflex now shows a potentiation that progressively increases in magnitude as probes occur more proximal to actual, overt defensive action. Startle potentiation begins in the context of "freezing" and vigilance and could be viewed as a premature triggering of defensive action. With a further increment in threat the heart rate response also reverses the direction of change from orienting to defense (Graham, 1979; Sokolov, 1963)—from a vigilance-related fear bradycardia to action mobilization and cardiac acceleration.

These phenomena have been demonstrated repeatedly in the context of

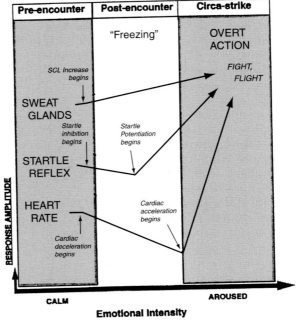

Figure 7. A schematic presentation of the defense response cascade generated by increasingly arousing aversive stimuli. The arousal or intensity dimension (monotonically covarying with skin conductance increase) is viewed here as analogous to the dimension of predator imminence in studies of animal fear. Stimuli presented in the post-encounter period occasion an initial, partial inhibition of startle probe reflexes, "freezing", immobility, "fear bradycardia", and a focused attentive set. The probability of an overt defensive action increases with predatory imminence (or aversive stimulus arousal). This motor disposition is reflected by an increase in potentiated startle to probe stimuli. Heart rate acceleration and a general sympathetic dominance of the autonomic system are characteristic of the circa-strike period, just prior to overt fight or flight. See Lang et al. (1997) for a fuller description of this model. Reprinted with permission from Lawrence Erlbaum Associates Inc.

aversive picture viewing. Thus, mildly unpleasant pictures prompt startle inhibition when compared to neutral stimuli; but with increasing picture aversiveness probe responses are increasingly potentiated (e.g., Cuthbert et al., 1996). For normal subjects, unpleasant pictures rarely prompt heart rate acceleration; rather, heart rate deceleration increments with ratings of greater intensity of reported unpleasant affect. Consistent with a high threat state (approaching circa-strike), however, when phobic subjects view pictures of their phobic object, heart rate clearly accelerates and probe reflexes show greater than normal potentiation (Hamm et al., 1997).

Detecting threat stimuli

The conception outlined here suggests that deployment of defensive behaviors (type and intensity) is modulated by degree of threat—the imminence of danger—which is defined in the wild by distance between predator and prey. Detection of the predator is clearly the key event in the process: It initiates the post-encounter stage—with abrupt focusing of attention and a more stimulus-specific pattern of action mobilization. Early initiation of this stage can be critical to survival (Öhman, 1997). Predators act swiftly and natural selection has favored those giving few anticipatory cues to potential prey. As a counter-measure in this evolutionary arms race, prey animals have been shaped to detect threat quickly (Dawkins & Krebs, 1979) through "built-in" affordances or through Pavlovian conditioning of subtle anticipatory cues that come to activate defense (Hollis, 1982). Given commonalities in the architecture of mammalian motive systems, it is reasonable to presume that vestiges of such an "early warning system" would be found in humans. That is, humans could be expected to react quickly to signs of danger, even if cues are brief or reduced in clarity. Data relevant to this evolutionary view were recently provided by Globisch, Hamm, Esteves, and Öhman (1999). They found that when pictures of snakes or spiders were exposed as briefly as 150 ms, phobic subjects produced the same enhanced skin conductance responses, heart rate acceleration, and blood pressure increase found with longer presentations (Figure 8). Furthermore, startle reflex potentiation was found when probes were presented as early as 300 ms after onset of phobia-relevant pictures.

In theorizing about the memorial organization of specific phobia, Lang (1985) suggested that its network structure was characterized by high associative strength among its elements, facilitating rapid activation—with autonomic and somatic output—even by very "degraded stimulus matches." Thus, "fear production will often occur under what appear to be minimal, external instigating conditions" (p. 159). Seligman (1971) (see also Öhman, Dimberg, & Öst, 1985) proposed, furthermore, that human beings (like many animals) might be biologically "prepared" to associate fear easily to potentially dangerous stimuli that have provided recurrent survival threats throughout mammalian evolution (e.g., snakes, closed spaces). In this case, part of the network might be "hard wired", further expediting defensive responding.

The defense system that we have described is part of the brain's ancient survival heritage. It originally evolved to serve the needs of simpler organisms, long before the primate line gained enough neocortex to support language or complex rational thought. It is clear that this fear motivational circuitry can be activated in humans by language prompts and imaginal representations (e.g., Lang, 1985) that depend on evolutionarily younger cortical

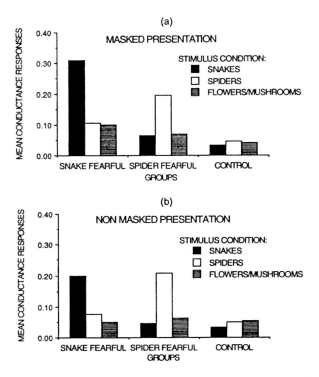

Figure 8. Skin conductance responses to backwardly masked (a) and nonmasked (b) presentations of pictures of snakes, spiders, flowers, and mushrooms in snake fearful, spider fearful, and control subjects. From Öhman and Soares (1994); © 1994 The American Psychological Association, reprinted with permission.

structures. On the other hand, given this fear circuit's direct connections to primary sensory systems, it is also reasonable to suppose that it can be accessed *without* the participation of the brain's language-processing centers. Interestingly, LeDoux (1990, 1996), in research with rodents, reported that simple stimuli (lights or tones), associated with nociceptive events and thus conditioned to be fearful, retain their fear-inducing potency despite severance of connections between the defense circuit and sensory cortex. Under these conditions, only the primitive sensory thalamus remains to resolve the stimulus and provide input to the amygdala. LeDoux hypothesized, furthermore, that this thalamic route could be a fast path for some more complex fear stimuli (e.g., potentially dangerous snakes), bypassing the slow multi-synaptic pathway via the cortex, in order to prompt early responding to threats. An important implication of this model is that some fear stimuli (e.g., historically dangerous animals or events) might activate defense reactions with unusual rapidity. Moreover, these fear responses might occur without activating language-processing centers in the cortex—in effect, without "conscious" recognition of the stimulus[2].

Preattentive processing

The hypothesis that fear activation does not require a reportable perception of the fear-eliciting stimulus has been examined using a test paradigm based on backward masking. In this method a target stimulus is presented very briefly and immediately followed by a second, masking stimulus that interrupts its processing (which would normally continue after offset). With short target-mask intervals (say, less than 50 ms), subjects often have great difficulty reporting anything about the content of the first stimulus.

This method has been used in the efforts of cognitive psychologists to tease apart nonconscious *automatic* mechanisms of stimulus analysis from conscious appraisal (*controlled* processing) of the stimulus, with the boundary between the two types of processing defined by above-chance recognition performance in a forced-choice task (e.g., Marcel, 1983; see Öhman, in press, for discussion). The extent to which the target stimulus is reliably reported depends on the interval between the onsets of the target and the masking stimulus—called the stimulus-onset-asynchrony (SOA). Even though the mask may completely block the target stimulus from awareness, it can be demonstrated that the target content still influences the person's behavior (see Bornstein & Pittman, 1992, for reviews). Marcel (1983), for example, showed that reaction times to identify the color of stimulus "patches" were modulated by preceding color-words, even when the words were impossible to recognize because of backward masking.

Esteves and Öhman (1993) and Öhman and Soares (1993, 1994) adapted the backward masking technique for use with pictorial emotional stimuli. As masks for common phobic objects, such as pictures of snakes and spiders, Öhman and Soares used pictures of similar objects that were cut in pieces and then randomly reassembled and re-photographed so that no central object could be discerned. Esteves and Öhman examined the effectiveness of facial pictures with a neutral emotional expression as masks for facial pictures portraying affects of anger or happiness.

Using a forced-choice procedure with a long series of stimulus pairs with varying SOAs, subjects were required to guess the nature of the first, target stimulus, and then to state their confidence in the guess. The results showed

---

[2] It is obvious that most information processing, cortical and subcortical, occurs outside our awareness, e.g., we are not "conscious" of the motor program that directs our tennis swing nor of the many computations that organize the simplest visual percept. Thus, the general hypothesis that fear activation might occur without our being able to report the stimulus does not depend on severing connections to the cortex, nor on the mediating circuit including only subcortical structures.

that the subjects required a SOA of about 100 ms between targets and masks for confident correct recognition of the target stimulus, and there were no differences between the stimulus categories. When the SOA was 30 ms or less, the subjects both performed and felt as if they were guessing. These results were stable whether or not the subjects were randomly selected nonfearful university students or classified as highly fearful or nonfearful on the basis of questionnaire data.

Phobic responses to masked stimuli

Using the backward masking technique, Öhman and Soares (1994) tested the hypothesis that phobic fear can be preattentively activated, i.e., activated without reported recognition of the stimulus. Subjects selected to be highly fearful of either snakes or spiders (but not of both), as well as nonfearful controls, were exposed to a stimulus series in which target pictures showing snakes, spiders, flowers, and mushrooms were masked by an immediately following, nonrecognizable picture (cut and randomly reassembled), with an SOA of 30 ms. In a second series, targets were presented without masks. Skin conductance responses were recorded as an index of fear arousal. Subjects subsequently viewed an extra series, rating the pictures for pleasantness, arousal, and their feeling of being in control.

Masking had only a minimal effect on skin conductance responding. The subjects who were afraid of snakes showed elevated skin conductance responding to snakes compared to spiders and neutral stimuli, the spider fearful subjects showed elevated responses to spiders, and the nonfearful subjects did not differentiate between the categories, regardless of masking condition. Thus, response recruitment apparently occurred before the stimulus content could be identified. Interestingly, the affective ratings paralleled the physiological findings: The fearful subjects reported feeling more unpleasant, more aroused, and less in control when exposed to the masked feared pictures than to any other pictures, whereas the nonfearful control subjects did not differentiate between the stimulus categories. Thus, some affective cues were apparently available to the cognitive system even though "conscious" content recognition was absent. This could mean that there are different processors for content and affect, or possibly, that preattentively activated bodily response guided the ratings.

These results strongly suggest that nonconscious, preattentive processing of a phobic stimulus is sufficient to recruit at least part of the phobic response. When the stimulus information is eventually registered in consciousness (i.e., detailed content is reportable), this occurs against a background of rising physiological activation that could contribute to the appraisal of the stimulus as an emotional event. As noted earlier, the reflexive, autonomic components of this reaction indicate activation of the amygdala and the rest of the brain's defense system through Pavlovian conditioning (e.g., Davis, 1992; LeDoux, 1996). Previous conditioning work with human subjects (e.g., Cook, Hodes, & Lang, 1986; Öhman, 1993; Öhman & Dimberg, 1978; see reviews by Dimberg & Öhman, 1996) suggests further that such conditioning would be especially successful with stimuli that most commonly evoke fear in natural settings (e.g., snakes, spiders, angry faces).

Preattentive processing in human conditioning

An effective masking interval (< 30 ms) has been used in several studies examining conditioned skin conductance responses to masked presentation of fear relevant stimuli (snakes, spiders, angry faces), following conditioning training to nonmasked stimuli. Öhman and Soares (1993) conditioned human subjects to pictures of snakes or spiders by pairing them with an electric shock unconditioned stimulus, and then presented the stimuli masked during extinction. They reported enhanced responding to masked shock-associated stimuli (CS +) compared to masked non-shocked stimuli (CS −) when they were fear-relevant (snake or spider) but not when they were fear-irrelevant (flower or mushroom). Esteves, Dimberg, and Öhman (1994a) and Parra, Esteves, Flykt, and Öhman (1997) reported a series of further experiments in which the fear-relevant stimuli were angry faces and the fear-irrelevant stimuli happy faces. After conditioning to nonmasked stimuli in a differential conditioning paradigm in which angry faces served as CS + and the happy faces as CS − , or vice versa, the emotional faces were presented masked by neutral faces during extinction. Again, the conditioned responses to the fear-relevant angry faces survived backwards masking, whereas responses conditioned to the fear-irrelevant happy faces did not.

The skin conductance data reported by Esteves et al. (1994a) and Parra et al. (1997) were replicated by Wong, Shevrin, and Williams (1994). They used negatively and positively evaluated schematic faces as CSs and included measurement of slow cortical potentials as an additional measure. Similarly to the studies from Öhman's laboratory, they found reliable differential skin conductance responses between masked presentations of the CS + and the CS − during extinction. Furthermore, the electrocortical data showed a distinct slow negative potential after CS + onset that increased over the conditioning interval. This differential cortical waveform, which has been related to expectancy of a second, motivationally relevant, stimulus (see, e.g., Simons, Öhman, & Lang, 1979) suggests that some cortical coding occurred even though the stimuli were masked.

The data show clearly that if unmasked stimuli are aversively conditioned, and these stimuli are then masked for presentation at extinction, autonomic response differentiation will persist. Another set of experiments has addressed the question: If stimuli are masked at the outset, can differential autonomic conditioning be achieved? And further, does such conditioning depend on fear content? Both these questions appear to receive affirmative answers. Öhman and Soares (1998) reported reliable conditioning to masked pictures of snakes and spiders, but not to masked flowers and mushrooms, in subsequent nonmasked test-trials, even though CS recognition could be excluded on the basis of simultaneously collected recognition data. Esteves, Parra, Dimberg, and Öhman (1994b) used happy or angry face stimuli as CSs and neutral stimuli as masks during acquisition training. Again, the results showed that conscious perception (verbal coding) of a facial CS was not necessary for conditioning, provided that the CS was a threatening angry display. With a nonthreatening happy display, such conditioning effects were not observed.

Overall, these data show that fear stimuli can evoke part of fear's physiology even with "degraded input". Furthermore, the autonomic effects can occur in the absence of clear semantic appraisal. Consistent with the evolutionary analysis, this result suggests that activation of language centers in the left cortical hemisphere was minimal or absent, and that the mediating brain mechanism could be the same subcortical circuit delineated in animal research. The fact that the masking data on human aversive conditioning were clearcut only for fear-relevant stimuli, such as angry faces and fearsome animals (snakes and spiders), is consistent with the evolutionary preparedness hypothesis (Öhman et al., 1985; Seligman, 1971)—a view echoed more recently by LeDoux (1996): "perhaps neurons in the amygdala that process prepared stimuli have some prewired but normally impotent connections to other cells that control emotional responses. The trauma might only have to mildly massage these pathways rather than create from scratch novel synaptic assemblages between the input and output neurons of the amygdala" (p. 254).

Brain mechanisms in human conditioning

There is increasing evidence that human conditioned skin conductance responses are mediated through the amygdala. Bechara et al. (1995) reported that two patients with bilateral lesions of the amygdala failed to acquire conditioned conductance responses, despite the fact that they were aware of the CS-US contingency. On the other hand, trained patients with bilateral hippocampal damage were unable to verbalize the conditioning contingency but did acquire conditioned electrodermal responses. LaBar, LeDoux, Spencer, and Phelps (1995) studied 22 patients with unilateral surgical removal of the amygdala. They found impaired skin conductance conditioning in patients, as compared to normal controls, although the patients were generally aware of the contingency and showed normal conductance responses to the noise unconditioned stimulus.

Furmark, Fischer, Wik, Larsson, and Fredrikson (1997) conditioned pictures of snakes or spiders using electric shock as the unconditioned stimulus, scanning coincident regional blood flow in the brain with positron emission tomography (PET). They reported a strong correlation between skin conductance responses to pictures and conditioned regional cerebral bloodflow in the right amygdala. A critical role for the amygdala in the perception of emotional facial expression, particularly fearful faces, is also suggested both from neuropsychological (Adolphs, Tranel, Damasio, & Damasio, 1995) and PET data (Morris, Frith, Perrett, & Rowland, 1996; Whalen et al., 1998).

To test directly whether the amygdala mediates conductance responses to masked face stimuli, Morris, Öhman, and Dolan (1998) conditioned subjects to one of two angry faces by having it followed by an aversive noise. During an extinction series, regional blood flow in the brain was measured by PET. Stimuli were presented either unmasked, or masked by a neutral face. In agreement with the hypothesis, comparison of cerebral blood flow between previously shocked and nonshocked angry faces showed that the effect of conditioning specifically pertained to activation of the amygdala. Curiously, the masking factor interacted with brain laterality: the conditioned masked angry face activated the right amygdala; the unmasked conditioned face activated the left amygdala. This effect is as yet unreplicated, but it is striking that the nonmasked stimuli activated the left, verbal hemisphere, whereas the effect of masked CSs were specific to the right hemisphere.

In concert, the neuropsychological and PET data present a good case that the amygdala is critically involved in human aversive conditioning, as would be expected from the animal literature. Furthermore, the data are consistent with LeDoux's notion of a thalamic fastpath for fear information, although a role for cortical areas has not necessarily been ruled out. For example, the masking experiments all use repeated presentation of threat stimuli. Such repetition might consolidate a subliminal cue image in sensory cortex, rendering the short, masked exposure less critical for any individual trial. Such stimulus information could be consolidated at the level of the temporal lobe or hippocampus, which provide input to the amygdala. This is likely when there is general defense system engagement in a context of electric shock sensitization and threat. In the view of Kapp et al. (1992), once the amygdala is activated with its projections to basal forebrain, brainstem, and dorsal medulla, it provides "optimal conditions for sensory processing by lowering detection thresholds for environmental stimuli . . . " (p. 230). Similarly, despite the absence of verbal reports indicating conscious recognition of the stimuli, it is not clear that sensory cortex is not involved. Amaral, Price, Pitkanen, and Carmichael (1992) note that the amygdala receives substantial input from the visual related cortices of the temporal and occipital lobes, and that the amygdala, in turn, projects back to sensory cortex. In an experiment using functional magnetic resonance imaging (fMRI), Lang et al. (1998a,b,c) (see also the PET study of Lane et al., 1997) recently showed that arousing unpleasant pictures generated more extensive activation than neutral pictures in occipital sensory cortex—a finding consistent with re-entrant processing from the amygdala. Whatever the mechanism, however, the findings for masked phobic stimuli provide dramatic evidence that the evocation of autonomic components of the fear reaction do not depend on semantic analysis or conscious appraisal, encouraging the view that the animal model is an appropriate guide to the understanding of human fear and anxiety.

SUMMARY AND CONCLUSIONS

The aim of this paper has been to present an integration of neuroscience and cognitive science conceptions of fear and anxiety. It was proposed that negative human emotions are founded on motivational circuits in the brain that evolved to facilitate survival in a dangerous environment. Research with animals has shown that the nuclei of the amygdala, and the structures to which it directly projects, form a general defense motivation system, mediating autonomic and somatic reflexes that characterize distress responses in both animals and man. Using the startle reflex as an exploratory tool, important differences were uncovered in the anatomy of cue-specific fear and more generalized anxiety—in the former case implicating the central nucleus of the amygdala, and in the latter, the bed nucleus of the stria terminalis. Parallel phenomena were signaled in human psychophysiology which merit further intensive investigation.

The fear context studied most in both animals and human subjects is a state of heightened attention, characterized by either a temporal and/or spatial orientation to a specific threat cue, or a nonspecific state of vigilance in a context of ill-defined threat. In animals, the first function of the amygdala and other defense motive structures is to facilitate orienting and lower detection thresholds; with close proximity to threat, the system prompts active fight/flight. Evidence was presented that the emotional patterns evoked in humans—by unpleasant/fearful memorial, imagined, or media stimuli—are similar to the early, attention-oriented defense reactions found in animal subjects. Neurological findings and neuroimaging studies of emotional perception suggest that the same defense motivation circuit is activated in man as in other mammals. Research using masked stimuli has further strengthened the case that the primitive defense system plays a significant role in attention. When perceptual processing is limited to milliseconds, and subjects are unable to clearly report the content of the stimulus, autonomic arousal still occurs that is specific to conditioned fearful or threatening images. It has been determined that this autonomic detection occurs when previously conditioned stimuli are masked at extinction, and also when masking limits perceptual processing during initial fear conditioning. Furthermore, these effects are clearest when the conditioned inputs are so-called "prepared" stimuli—snakes, spiders, threatening facial expressions—that may have an intrinsic evolutionary foundation. Finally, these data emphasize that fear reactions can be activated in an automated way and, as in animal subjects, they are not dependent on language processing or conscious appraisal.

In summary, the paper has described a neuro-anatomical model of defense behavior in animals and shown its application in studies of human emotion. This research is currently under rapid development in several laboratories. These efforts focus on further specification of the subcortical circuits, on pursuing applications of the model to human psychopathology, and in defining connections (and possible disconnections) between the defense circuit and the more elaborate information networks of the human cerebral cortices.

ACKNOWLEDGEMENTS

Michael Davis's participation was supported by NIMH Grant MH-57250, MH-47840, Research Scientist Development Award MH-00004, a grant from the Air Force Office of Scientific Research, and the State of Connecticut. Peter Lang's participation was supported in part by National Institute of Mental Health grants MH37757, MH43975, and P50-MH52384 (NIMH Center for the Study of Emotion and Attention (CSEA), University of Florida, Gainseville, FL). The participation of Arne Öhman was supported by a grant from the Swedish Council for Research in the Humanities and Social Sciences. Thanks to Jack Maser and Greg Miller for their helpful comments on the initial draft of this manuscript.

REFERENCES

Adolphs, R., Tranel, D., Damasio, H., & Damasio, A.R. (1995). Fear and the human amygdala. *Journal of Neuroscience, 15*, 5879–5891.

Aggleton, J.P. (1992a). In J.P. Aggleton (Ed.), *The amygdala: Neurobiological aspects of emotion, memory, and mental dysfunction.* New York: John Wiley.

Aggleton, J.P. (1992b). The functional effects of amygdala lesions in humans: A comparison with findings from monkeys. In J.P. Aggleton (Ed.), *The amygdala: Neurobiological aspects of emotion, memory, and mental dysfunction* (pp. 485–503). New York: John Wiley.

Alheid, G., deOlmos, J.S., & Beltramino, C.A. (1995). Amygdala and extended amygdala. In G.T. Paxinos (Ed.), *The rat nervous system*; (2nd Edn.; pp. 495–578). New York: Academic Press.

Amaral, D.G., Price, J.L., Pitkanen, A., & Carmichael, S.T. (1992). Anatomical organization of the primate amygdaloid complex. In J.P. Aggleton (Ed.), *The amygdala: Neurobiological aspects of emotion, memory, and mental dysfunction* (pp. 1–66). New York, John Wiley.

Balaban, M.T. (1995). Affective influences on startle in 5-month-old infants: Reactions to facial expressions of emotion. *Child Development, 66*, 28–36.

Bechara, A., Tranel, D., Damasio, H., Adolphs, R., Rockland, C., & Damasio, A.R. (1995). Double dissociation of conditioning and declarative knowledge relative to the amygdala and hippocampus in humans. *Science, 269*, 1115–1118.

Berg, W.K., & Davis, M. (1985). Associative learning modifies startle reflexes at the lateral lemniscus. *Behavioral Neuroscience, 99*, 191–199.

Blanchard, R.J., & Blanchard, D.C. (1989). Attack and defense in rodents as ethoexperimental models for the study of emotion. *Progress in Neuro-Psychopharmacology and Biological Psychiatry, 13*, 3–14.

Bornstein, R.F., & Pittman, T.S. (1992). *Perception without awareness*. New York: Guilford Press.

Boulis, N., & Davis, M. (1989). Footshock-induced sensitization of electrically elicited startle reflexes. *Behavioural Neuroscience, 103*, 504–508.

Bradley, M.M., Cuthbert, B.N., & Lang, P.J. (1996). Picture media and emotion: Effects of a sustained affective context. *Psychophysiology, 33*, 662–670.

Bradley, M.M., Zack, J., & Lang, P.J. (1994). Cries, screams, and shouts of joy: Affective responses to environmental sounds. *Psychophysiology, 31*, S29 [Abstract].

Brown, J.S., Kalish, H.I., & Farber, I.E. (1951). Conditional fear as revealed by magnitude of startle response to an auditory stimulus. *Journal of Experimental Psychology, 41*, 317–328.

Campbell, B.A., Wood, G., & McBride, T. (1997). Origins of orienting and defense responses: an evolutionary perspective. In P.J. Lang, R.F. Simons, &, M.T. Balaban (Eds.), Attention and orienting: Sensory and motivational processes pp. 41–67. Hillsdale, NJ: Lawrence Erlbaum Associates Inc.

Campeau, S., & Davis, M. (1995). Involvement of the central nucleus and basolateral complex of the amygdala in fear conditioning measured with fear-potentiated startle in rats trained concurrently with auditory and visual conditioned stimuli. *Journal of Neuroscience, 15*, 2301–2311.

Center for the Study of Emotion and Attention (CSEA-NIMH). (1998). *The international affective picture system* [IAPS: photographic slides]. Gainsville, FL: University of Florida.

Cook, E.W. III, Hodes, R.L., & Lang, P.J. (1986). Preparedness and phobia: Effects of stimulus content on human visceral conditioning. *Journal of Abnormal Psychology, 95*, 280–286.

Crawley, J.N. (1981). Neuropharmacologic specificity of a simple animal model for the behavioral actions of benzodiazepines. *Pharmacology, Biochemistry, and Behavior, 15*, 695–699.

Cuthbert, B.N., Bradley, M.M., & Lang, P.J. (1996). Probing picture perception: Activation and emotion. *Psychophysiology, 33*, 103–111.

Cuthbert, B.N., Drobes, D.J., Patrick, C.J., & Lang, P.J. (1994). Autonomic and startle responding during affective imagery among anxious patients. *Psychophysiology, 31*, S37.

Davis, M. (1992). The role of the amygdala in conditioned fear. In J. Aggleton (Ed.), The amygdala: Neurobiological aspects of emotion, memory and mental dysfunction (pp. 255–305). New York: John Wiley.

Davis, M., & Astrachan, D.I. (1978). Conditioned fear and startle magnitude: Effects of different footshock or backshock intensities used in training. *Journal of Experimental Psychology: Animal Behavior Process, 4*, 95–103.

Davis, M., Falls, W.A., Campeau, S., & Kim, M. (1993). Fear-potentiated startle: A neural and pharmacological analysis. *Behavioral Brain Research, 58*, 175–198.

Davis, M., Gendelman, D.S., Tischler, M.D., & Gendelman, P.M. (1982). A primary acoustic startle circuit: Lesion and stimulation studies. *Journal of Neuroscience, 6*, 791–805.

Davis, M., Walker, D.L., & Lee, Y. (1997). Roles of the amygdala and bed nucleus of the stria terminalis in fear and anxiety measured with the acoustic startle reflex: Possible relevance to PTSD. *Annals of the New York Academy of Sciences, Psychobiology of Post-traumatic Stress Disorder, Vol. 821* (pp. 305–331). New York: The New York Academy of Sciences.

Dawkins, R., & Krebs, J.R. (1979). Arms races between and within species. *Proceedings of the Royal Society of London, B 205*, 489–511.

Dimberg, U., & Öhman, A. (1996). Behold the wrath: Psycho-physiological responses to facial stimuli. *Motivation Emotion, 20,* 149–182.

Dunn, A.J., & Berridge, C.W. (1990). Physiological and behavioral responses to corticotropin-releasing factor administration: Is CRF a mediator of anxiety or stress responses? *Brain Research Review, 15,* 71–100.

Esteves, F., Dimberg, U., & Öhman, A. (1994a). Automatically elicited fear: Conditioned skin conductance responses to masked facial expressions. *Cognition Emotion, 8,* 393–413.

Esteves, F., & Öhman, A. (1993). Masking the face: Recognition of emotional facial expressions as a functions of the parameters of backward masking. *Scandivanian Journal of Psychology, 34,* 1–18.

Esteves, F., Parra, C., Dimberg, U., & Öhman, A. (1994b). Nonconscious associative learning: Pavlovian conditioning of skin conductance responses to masked fear-relevant facial stimuli. *Psychophysiology, 31,* 375–385.

Falls, W.A., Miserendino, M.J.D., & Davis, M. (1992). Extinction of ear-potentiated startle: Blockade by infusion of an NMDA antagonist into the amygdala. *Journal of Neuroscience, 12,* 854–863.

Fanselow, M.S. (1991). The midbrain periaqueductal gray as a coordinator of action in response to fear and anxiety. In A. Depaulis & R. Brandler (Eds.), *The midbrain periaqueductal gray matter* (pp. 151–173). New York: Plenum Press.

Fanselow, M.S. (1994). Neural organization of the defensive behavior system responsible for fear. *Psychonomic Bulletin Review, 1,* 429–438.

File, S.E. (1980). The use of social interaction as a method for detecting anxiolytic activity of chlordiazepoxide-like drugs. *Journal of Neuroscientific Methods, 2,* 219–238.

Fendt, M., Koch, M., & Schnitzler, H.-U. (1996). Lesions of the central grayblock conditioned fear as measured with the potentiated startle paradigm. *Behavioral Brain Research, 74,* 127–134.

Frankland, P.W, Scott, B.W. & Yeomans, J.S. (1995). Axons and synapses mediating electrically evoked startle: Collision tests and latency analysis. *Brain Research, 670,* 97–111.

Franklin, P.W., & Yeomans, J.S. (1995). Fear-potentiated startle and electrically evoked startle mediated by synapses in rostrolateral midbrain. *Behavioral Neuroscience, 109,* 669–680.

Furmark, T., Fischer, H., Wik, G., Larsson, M., & Fredrikson, M. (1997). The amygdala and individual differences in human fear conditioning. *NeuroReport, 8,* 3957–3960.

Gewirtz, J.C., McNish, K.A., & Davis, M. (1998). Lesions of the bed nucleus of the stria terminalis block sensitization of the acoustic startle reflex produced by repeated stress, but not fear-potentiated startle. *Progress in Neuro-Psychopharmacology and Biological Psychiatry, 22,* 625–648.

Globisch, J., Hamm, A.O., Esteves, F., & Öhman, A. (1999). Fear appears fast: Temporal course of startle reflex potentiation in animal fearful subjects. *Psychophysiology, 36,* 1–10.

Gloor, P. (1960). Amygdala. In J. Field (Ed.), *Handbook of physiology: Sect. I. Neurophysiology* (pp. 1395–1420). Washington, DC: American Physiological Society.

Graham, F.K. (1979). Distinguishing among orienting, defense, and startle reflexes. In H.D. Kimmel, E.H. Van Olst, & J.F. Orlebeke (Eds.), *The orienting reflex in humans* (pp. 137–167). Hillsdale, NJ: Lawrence Erlbaum Associates Inc.

Gray, T.S. (1989). Autonomic neuropeptide connections of the amygdala. In Y. Tache, J.E. Morley, M.R. Brown (Eds.), *Neuropeptides and stress* (pp. 92–106). New York: Springer.

Greenwald, M.K., Bradley, M.M., Cuthbert, B.N., & Lang, P.J. (1998). Sensitization of the startle reflex in humans following aversive electric shock exposure. *Behavioral Neuroscience, 112,* 1069–1079.

Grillon, C., & Davis, M. (1997). Fear-potentiated startle conditioning in humans: Effects of explicit and contextual cue conditioning following paired versus unpaired training. *Psychophysiology, 34,* 451–458.

Grillon, C., Morgan, C.A., Davis, M., & Southwick, S.M. (1998). Effects of darkness on acoustic startle in Vietnam veterans with PTSD. *American Journal of Psychiatry*, *155*, 812–817.

Grillon, C., Pellowski, M., Merikangas, K.R., & Davis, M. (1997). Darkness facilitates the acoustic startle reflex in humans. *Biological Psychiatry*, *42*, 461–471.

Hamm, A.O., Cuthbert, B.N., Globisch, J., & Vaitl, D. (1997). Fear and startle reflex: Blink modulation and autonomic response patterns in animal and mutilation fearful subjects. *Psychophysiology*, *34*, 97–107.

Hamm, A.O., Greenwald, M.K., Bradley, M.M., & Lang, P.J. (1993). Emotional learning, hedonic change, and the startle probe. *Journal of Abnormal Psychology*, *102* , 453–465.

Hamm, A.O., Stark, R., & Vaitl, D. (1990). Classical fear conditioning and the startle probe reflex. *Psychophysiology*, *27*, S37 [Abstract].

Hare, R.D., Harpur, T.J., Hakstian, A.R., Forth, A.E., Hart, S.D., & Newman, J.P. (1990). The Revised Psychopathy Checklist: Reliability and factor structure. *Psychological Assessment, A Journal of Consulting and Clinical Psychology*, *2*, 338–341.

Hitchcock, J.M., & Davis, M. (1986). Lesions of the amygdala, but not of the cerebellum or red nucleus, block conditioned fear as measured with the potentiated startle paradigm. *Behavioral Neuroscience*, *100*, 11–22.

Hitchcock, J.M., & Davis, M. (1987). Fear-potentiated startle using an auditory conditioned stimulus: Effect of lesions of the amygdala. *Physiological Behavior*, *39*, 403–408.

Hitchcock, J.M., & Davis, M. (1991). The efferent pathway of the amygdala involved in conditioned fear as measured with the fear-potentiated startle paradigm. *Behavioral Neuroscience*, *105*, 826–842.

Hitchcock, J.M., Sananes, C.B., & Davis, M. (1989). Sensitization of the startle reflex by footshock: Blockade by lesions of the central nucleus of the amygdala or its efferent pathway to the brainstem. *Behavioral Neuroscience*, *103*, 509–518.

Hollis, K.L. (1982). Pavlovian conditioning of signal-centered action patterns and autonomic behavior: A biological analysis of function. In J.S. Rosenblatt, R.A. Hinde, C. Beer, & M.C. Busnell (Eds.), *Advances in the study of behavior, Vol. 12*. New York: Academic Press.

Jansen, D.M., & Frijda, N. (1994). Modulation of acoustic startle response by film-induced fear and sexual arousal. *Psychophysiology*, *31*, 565–571.

Kapp, B.S., & Pascoe, J.P. (1986). Correlation aspects of learning and memory: Vertebrate model systems. In J.L. Martinez, & R.P. Kesner (Eds.), *Learning and memory: A biological view* (pp. 399–440). New York: Academic Press.

Kapp, B.S., Pascoe, J.P., & Bixler, M.A. (1984). The amygdala: A neuroanatomical systems approach to its contribution to aversive conditioning. In N. Butters, & L.S. Squire (Eds.), *The neuropsychology of memory* (pp. 473–488). New York: Guilford Press.

Kapp, B.S., Whalen, P.J., Supple, W.F., & Pascoe, J.P. (1992). Amygdaloid contributions to conditioned arousal and sensory information processing. In J.P. Aggleton (Ed.), *The amygdala: Neurobiological aspects of emotion, memory, and mental dysfunction* (pp. 229–254). New York: Wiley-Liss.

Kim, M., Campeau, S., Falls, W.A., & Davis, M. (1993). Infusion of the non-NMDA receptor antagonist CNQX into the amygdala blocks the expression off ear-potentiated startle. *Behavioral Neural Biology*, *59*, 5–8.

Kim, J.J., & Fanselow, M.S. (1992). Modality-specific retrograde amnesia of fear. *Science*, *256*, 675–677.

Klorman, R., Hastings, J.E., Weerts, T.C., Melamed, B.G., & Lang, P.J. (1974). Psychometric description of some specific fear questionnaires. *Behavior Therapy*, *5*, 401–409.

Konorski, J. (1967). *Integrative activity of the brain: An interdisciplinary approach*. Chicago: University of Chicago Press.

Krase, W., Koch, M., & Schnitzler, H.U. (1994). Substance P is involved in the sensitization of the acoustic startle response by footshock in rats. *Behavioral Brain Research*, *63*, 81–88.

LaBar, K.S., LeDoux, J.E., Spencer, D., & Phelps, E. (1995). Impaired fear conditioning follow-ing unilateral temporal lobectomy in humans. *Journal of Neuroscience, 15,* 6846–6855.

Lane, R.D., Reiman, E.M., Bradley, M.M., Lang, P.J., Ahern, G.L., Davidson, R.J., & Schwartz, G.E. (1997). Activation of thalamus and medial prefrontal cortex during emotion. *Neuro-psychologia, 35,* 1437–1444.

Lang, P.J. (1985). The cognitive psychophysiology of emotion: Fear and anxiety. In A.H. Tuma & J.D. Maser (Eds.), *Anxiety and the anxiety disorders* (pp. 131–170). Hillsdale, NJ: Lawrence Erlbaum Associates Inc. Reprinted in *Psychotherapeutisch Pasport, 3,* 3–62.

Lang, P.J. (1994). The motivational organization of emotion: Affect-reflex connections. In S.VanGoozen, N.E. Van de Poll, & J.A. Sergeant (Eds.), *Emotions: Essays on emotion theory* (pp. 61–93). Hillsdale, NJ: Lawrence Erlbaum Associates Inc.

Lang, P.J., Bradley, M.M., & Cuthbert, B.N. (1990). Emotion, attention, and the startle reflex. *Psychological Review, 97,* 377–398.

Lang, P.J., Bradley, M.M., & Cuthbert, B.N. (1997). Motivated attention: Affect, activation and action. In P.J. Lang, R.F. Simons, & M.F. Balaban (Eds.), *Attention and orienting: Sensory and motivational processes* (pp. 97–135). Hillside, NJ: Lawrence Erlbaum Associates Inc.

Lang, P.J., Bradley, M.M., & Cuthbert, B.N. (1998a). *International Affective Picture System* (IAPS): *Technical manual and affective ratings.* Gainesville, FL: The Center for Research in Psychophysiology, University of Florida.

Lang, P.J., Bradley, M.M., & Cuthbert, B.N. (1998b). Emotion, motivation, and anxiety: Brain mechanisms and psychophysiology. *Biological Psychiatry, 44,* 1248–1263.

Lang, P.J., Bradley, M.M., Fitzsimmons, J.R., Cuthbert, B.N., Scott, J.D., Moulder, B., & Nangia, V. (1998c). Emotional arousal and activation of the visual cortex: An fMRI analysis. *Psycho-physiology, 35,* 1–13.

Lang, P.J., Greenwald, M.K., Bradley, M.M., & Hamm, A.O. (1993). Looking at pictures: Affective, facial, visceral, and behavioral reactions. *Psychophysiology, 30,* 261–273.

LeDoux, J.E. (1987). Emotion. In F. Plum (Ed.), *Higher functions of the brain. Handbook of Physiology, Sec. 1, Neurophysiology, Vol. 5* (pp. 416–459). Bethseda, MD: American Psycho-logical Society.

LeDoux, J.E. (1990). Information flow from sensation to emotion plasticity in the neural compu-tation of stimulus values. In M. Gabriel, & J. Moore (Eds.), *Learning and computational neuroscience: Foundations of adaptive networks* (pp. 3–52). Cambridge, MA: Bradford Books/MIT Press.

LeDoux, J.E. (1996). *The emotional brain.* New York: Simon & Schuster.

LeDoux, J.E., Cicchetti, P., Xagoraris, A., & Romanski, L.M. (1990). The lateral amygdaloid nucleus, sensory interface of the amygdala in fear conditioning. *Journal of Neuroscience, 10,* 1062–1069.

LeDoux, J.E., Iwata, J., Cicchetti, P., & Reis, D.J. (1988). Different projections of the central amygdaloid nucleus mediate autonomic and behavioral correlates of conditioned fear. *Jour-nal of Neuroscience, 8,* 2517–2529.

Lee, Y., & Davis, M. (1997). Role of the hippocampus, bed nucleus of the stria terminalis and amygdala in the excitatory effect of corticotropin releasing (CRH) hormone on the acoustic startle reflex. *Journal of Neuroscience, 17,* 6434–6446.

Lee, Y., Lopez, D.E., Meloni, E.G., & Davis, M. (1996). A primary acoustic startle circuit: obligatory role of cochlear root neurons and the nucleus reticularis pontis caudalis. *Journal of Neuroscience, 16,* 3775–3789.

Lee, Y., Schulkin, J., & Davis, M. (1994). Effect of corticosterone on the enhancement of the acoustic startle reflex by corticotropin releasing factor (CRF). *Brain Research, 666,* 93–98.

Liang, K.C., Melia, K.R., Campeau, S., Falls, W.A., Miserendino, M.J.D., & Davis, M. (1992a). Lesions of the central nucleus of the amygdala, but not of the paraventricular nucleus of the hypothalamus, block the excitatory effects of corticotropin releasing factor on the acoustic startle reflex. *Journal of Neuroscience, 12,* 2313–2320.

Liang, K.C., Melia, K.R., Miserendino, M.J.D., Falls, W.A., Campeau, S., & Davis, M. (1992b). Corticotropin-releasing factor: Long-lasting facilitation of the acoustic startle reflex. *Journal of Neuroscience, 12*, 2303–2312.

Lingenhohl, K., & Friauf, E. (1994). Giant neurons in the rat reticular formation: A sensorimotor interface in the elementary acoustic startle circuit? *Journal of Neuroscience, 14*, 1176–1194.

Lopez, D.E., Merchan, M.A., Bajo, VM., & Saldana, E. (1993). The cochlear root neurons in the rat, mouse and gerbil. In M.A. Merchan (Ed.), The mammalian cochlear nuclei: Organization and function (pp. 291–301). New York: Plenum Press.

Marcel, A. (1983). Conscious and unconscious perception: An approach to the relations between phenomenal experience and perceptual processes. *Cognitive Psychology, 15*, 238–300.

McNaughton, N., & Gray, J.A. (2000). Anxiolytic action on the behavioural inhibition system implies multiple types of arousal contribute to anxiety. *Journal of Affective Disorders, 61*, 161–176.

McNish, K.A., Gewirtz, J.C., & Davis, M. (1997). Evidence of contextual fear after lesions of the hippocampus: A disruption of freezing but not fear-potentiated startle. *Journal of Neuroscience, 17*, 9353–9360.

Morris, J.S., Frith, C.D., Perrett, D.I., & Rowland, D. (1996). A differential neural response in the human amygdala to fearful and happy facial expression. *Nature, 383*, 812–815.

Morris, J., Öhman, A., & Dolan, R. (1998). Conscious and unconscious emotional learning in the human amygdala. *Nature, 393*, 467–470.

Öhman, A. (1993). Stimulus prepotency and fear learning: Data and theory. In N. Birbaumer, & A. Öhman (Eds.), *The structure of emotion: Psychophysiological, cognitive, and clinical aspects* (pp. 218–239). Washington, DC: Hogrefe & Huber.

Öhman, A. (1997). As fast as the blink of an eye: Evolutionary preparedness for preattentive processing of threat. In P.J. Lang, R.F. Simons, & M.T. Balaban (Eds.), *Attention and orienting: Sensory and motivational processes* (pp. 165–184). Hillsdale, NJ: Lawrence Erlbaum Associates Inc.

Öhman, A. (in press). Distinguishing unconscious from conscious emotional processes: Methodological considerations and theoretical implications. In T. Dalgleish & M. Power (Eds.), *Handbook of cognition and emotion*. Chichester, UK: John Wiley.

Öhman, A., & Dimberg, U. (1978). Facial expressions as conditioned stimuli for electrodermal responses: A case of "preparedness"? *Journal of Personality and Social Psychology, 36*, 1251–1258.

Öhman, A., Dimberg, U., & Öst, L.-G. (1985). Animal and social phobias: Biological constraints on learned fear responses. In S. Reiss & R.R. Bootzin (Eds.), *Theoretical issues in behavior therapy* (pp. 123–175). New York: Academic Press.

Öhman, A., & Soares, J.J.F. (1993). On the automatic nature of phobic fear: Conditioned electrodermal responses to masked fear-relevant stimuli. *Journal of Abnormal Psychology, 102*, 121–132.

Öhman, A., & Soares, J.J.F. (1994). "Unconscious anxiety": Phobic responses to masked stimuli. *Journal of Abnormal Psychology, 103*, 231–240.

Öhman, A., & Soares, J.J.F. (1998). Emotional conditioning to masked stimuli: Expectancies for aversive outcomes following nonrecognized fear-relevant stimuli. *Journal of Experimental Psychology: General, 127*, 69–82.

Parra, C., Esteves, F., Flykt, A., & Öhman, A. (1997). Pavlovian conditioning to social stimuli: Backward masking and the dissociation of implicit and explicit cognitive processes. *European Psychology, 2*, 106–117.

Patrick, C.J., Bradley, M.M., & Lang, P.J. (1993). Emotion in the criminal psychopath: Startle reflex modulation. *Journal of Abnormal Psychology, 102*, 82–92.

Patrick, C.J., Cuthbert, B.N., & Lang, P.J. (1994). Emotion in the criminal psychopath: Fear image processing. *Journal of Abnormal Psychology, 103*, 523–534.

Phillips, R.G., & LeDoux, J.E. (1992). Differential contribution of amygdala and hippocampus to cued and contextual fear conditioning. *Behavioral Neuroscience, 106*, 274–285.

Rosen, J.B., Hitchcock, J.M., Sananes, C.B., Miserendino, M.J.D., & Davis, M. (1991). A direct projection from the central nucleus of the amygdala to the acoustic startle pathway: Anterograde and retrograde tracing studies. *Behavioral Neuroscience, 105*, 817–825.

Sabatinelli, D., Bradley, M.M., Cuthbert, B.N., & Lang, P.J. (1996). Wait and see: Aversion and activation in anticipation and perception. *Psychophysiology, 33*, S72.

Sakanaka, M., Shibasaki, T., & Lederis, K. (1986). Distribution and efferent projections of corticotropin-releasing factor-like immunoreactivity in the rat amygdaloid complex. *Brain Research, 382*, 213–238.

Sananes, C.B., & Davis, M. (1992). N-Methyl-D-aspartate lesions of the lateral and basolateral nuclei of the amygdala block fear-potentiated startle and shock sensitization of startle. *Behavioral Neuroscience, 106*, 72–80.

Sarter, M., & Markowitsch, H.J. (1985). Involvement of the amygdala in learning and memory: A critical review, with emphasis on anatomical relations. *Behavioral Neuroscience, 99*, 342–380.

Seligman, M.E.P. (1971). Phobias and preparedness. *Behavioral Therapy, 2*, 307–321.

Simons, R.F., Öhman, A., & Lang, P.J. (1979). Anticipation and response set: Cortical, cardiac, and electrodermal correlates. *Psychophysiology, 16*, 222–233.

Sokolov, E.N. (1963). *Perception and the conditioned reflex*. Pergamon, Oxford.

Spence, E., & Lang, P.J. (1990). Reading affective text: The startle probe response. *Psychophysiology, 27*, S65.

Swerdlow, N.R., Geyer, M.A., Vale, W.W., & Koob, G.F. (1986). Corticotropin-releasing factor potentiates acoustic startle in rats: Blockade by chlordiazepoxide. *Psychopharmacology, 88*, 147–152.

Timberlake, W. (1993). Behavior systems and reinforcement: An integrative approach. *Journal of Experimental Analysis of Behavior, 60*, 105–128.

Timberlake, W., & Lucas Gary, A. (1989). Behavior systems and learning: From misbehavior to general principles. In S.B. Klein & R.R. Mowrer (Eds.), *Contemporary learning theories: Instrumental conditioning theory and the impact of biological constraints on learning* (pp. 237–275). Hillsdale, NJ: Lawrence Erlbaum Associates Inc.

Vrana, S.R., Spence, E.L., & Lang, P.J. (1988). The startle probe response: A new measure of emotion? *Journal of Abnormal Psychology, 97*, 487–491.

Walker, D.L., & Davis, M. (1997a). Anxiogenic effects of high illumination levels assessed with the acoustic startle paradigm. *Biological Psychiatry, 42*, 461–471.

Walker, D.L., & Davis, M. (1997b). Double dissociation between the involvement of the bed nucleus of the stria terminalis and the central nucleus of the amygdala in light-enhanced versus fear-potentiated startle. *Journal of Neuroscience, 17*, 9375–9938.

Walsh, R.N., & Cummins, R.A. (1976). The open-field test: A critical review. *Psychological Bulletin, 83*, 482–504.

Watson, D., Clark, L.A., & Tellegen, A. (1988). Development and validation of brief measures of positive and negative affect: the PANAS scales. *Journal of Personality and Social Psychology, 54*, 1063–1070.

Whalen, P.J., Rauch, S.L., Etcoff, N.L., McInerney, S.C., Lee, M.B., & Jenike, M.A. (1998). Masked presentations of emotional facial expressions modulate amygdala activity without explicit knowledge. *Journal of Neuroscience, 18*, 411–418.

Wong, P.S., Shevrin, H., & Williams, W.J. (1994). Conscious and nonconscious processes: An ERP index of an anticipatory response in a conditioning paradigm using visually masked stimuli. *Psychophysiology, 31*, 87–101.

CHAPTER EIGHTEEN

Cardiac defense and emotion: Psychophysiological and clinical implications

Jaime Vila
University of Granada, Spain

GENERAL BACKGROUND

The topic of this chapter is a basic research one related to the field of cardiac psychophysiology. But I wish to emphasize in the context of this basic research some critical issues that affect the relationships between basic and applied psychology. In particular, I would like to question why many psychologists, especially those who deal with people's problems and try to help them with psychological treatments and interventions, pay so little attention to current basic research on the psychological processes involved in the disorders they are trying to treat. Surprisingly, this gap between basic and applied psychology is even evident in many psychologists who call themselves behaviorally or cognitively oriented. This movement by behavior and cognitive therapists away from current experimental research, both in animals and humans, on psychological processes relevant to the therapeutic programs they are trying to implement, means a clear breakdown of the original commitment of behavior therapy, in the 1950s and 60s, to establish a solid bridge between experimental psychology and applied psychology. But the gap is also evident in the work of many psychologists dedicated to basic experimental research. Indeed, experimental psychology seems to have contributed very little, especially in the last few decades, to the understanding of clinical problems related to emotion and stress.

A critical analysis of current clinical psychology shows that in spite of the numerous contributions of the behavioral and cognitive approaches to the

413

development of more effective treatments, clinical psychology continues to be a cocktail of different theoretical orientations, schools, and paradigms. It is evident that behaviorism, the dominant paradigm in experimental psychology during the first half of the 20th century, did not finish off the preceding dominant paradigm: psychoanalysis. As it is also evident that cognitive psychology, the dominant paradigm during the second half of the 20th century, has not finished off either psychoanalysis or behaviorism. Current psychology is still a mixture of multiple theoretical paradigms that are difficult to reconcile with each other.

A possible explanation of the relative failure of experimental psychology to become the driving motor for clinical applications, as was intended in the 1950s and 60s, is the fact that emotions and affects—which are central features of almost all clinical problems—have been left out of the main areas of interest of the two paradigms which have dominated the field of experimental psychology in the last century: behaviorism and cognitive psychology.

Although it is a simplification, an analysis of the two metaphors of human behavior proposed by behaviorism and cognitive psychology illustrates this point. The behavioristic metaphor is the *sensorimotor machine*, an apparatus with sensory organs to receive the external stimuli and with skeletal muscles to produce the external responses, but with no heart and no brain. The sensorimotor metaphor is, in essence, a machine that behaves but does not feel or think. On the other hand, the cognitive metaphor is the *electronic computer*, an apparatus with a brain to process information but with few skeletal muscles and no heart.

These two metaphors are fundamentally wrong. Neither the sensorimotor machine nor the electronic computer have any similarity with a real living organism. A real living organism is a biological system with muscles, with heart and with brain, a system that needs blood, sweat, and tears to function effectively. This qualitative aspect of behavior. which is intrinsic to the concept of emotion, has been unfortunately absent in both behaviorism and cognitive psychology.

The scientific study of human behavior is certainly enriched when it is done in close relationship with the biological body that sustains behavior. This is the specific field of psychophysiology, a field which has experienced a tremendous boost in the last years thanks to the development of new technologies for the functional and noninvasive recording of the brain, heart, and muscles. The psychophysiological techniques are like windows into the living body that allow us to visualize what happens in the brain, the heart, and the muscles when we think, feel, and behave. The research I am going to summarize now aims to be an illustration of the potential contribution of the psychophysiological approach to reducing the gap between basic and applied psychology.

DEFENSE RESPONSE AND STRESS

The origin of the concepts of defense and stress is linked to the idea that organisms react physiologically to the presence of danger or threat. This reactivity has a protective function since it provides the logistic and instrumental basis for adaptive behaviors such as fight or flight. However, if maintained for long periods, this protective or defensive reactivity may become a health risk, compromising the normal functioning of the organs involved. For many scientists, excessive physiological reactivity is the main mechanism linking stress to illness.

The historical antecedents of these concepts are rooted in the work of Ivan Pavlov and Walter Cannon. At the beginning of the 20th century, Pavlov and other Russian reflexologists used the term *defense reflex* to refer to protective physiological responses elicited by noxious stimulation, such as hand withdrawal to an electric shock, eyeblink to a puff of air, or vomit to bad food. A few years later, Cannon used the term defense to refer to the *fight or flight response*, a sympathetically mediated cardiovascular response to emergency situations aimed at providing energy supply to the body to facilitate adaptive behaviors such as attack or escape. By the middle of the last century and following Cannon's ideas, Hans Selye had introduced the concept of *stress* and used the term *alarm response* to refer to the first stage of the physiological response to stressful situations.

Subsequent research on the defense response has been extensive throughout the 20th century. Two major psychophysiological approaches, both emphasizing the cardiovascular components, can be identified: the cognitive approach and the motivational approach. The ***cognitive approach***, built on Pavlov's distinction between orienting and defense, assumes that cardiac changes to environmental stimuli reflect attentional and perceptual mechanisms aimed at facilitating or inhibiting the processing of the stimuli. The orienting response (a deceleration of the heart rate to moderate or novel stimulation) facilitates attention and perception of the stimuli, whereas the defense response (an acceleration of the heart rate to intense or aversive stimulation) reduces attention and perception as a form of protection against the stimuli. In this context, the orienting-defense distinction proposed by Eugene Sokolov (1963) and Frances Graham (1979) is equivalent to the intake-rejection distinction proposed by John and Beatrice Lacey (Lacey & Lacey, 1970, 1974).

The ***motivational approach***, built on Cannon's ideas on the fight and flight response, assumes that cardiac changes in response to environmental demands reflect metabolic mechanisms aimed at providing the necessary energy to the body to support behavioral adjustments (Obrist, 1981). If the appropriate behavior is to be passive and quiet, then the cardiac response will be a heart-rate deceleration. If the appropriate behavior is to be active, either physically or psychologically, then the cardiac response will be a heart-rate acceleration. To study cardiac defense, this approach has mainly used tasks that involve emotionally or cognitively challenging situations such as pressing a key as fast as possible to avoid shocks, or doing complex arithmetic tasks. The term *mental stress* was introduced in this context to refer to tasks that require *mental effort* instead of *physical effort* (Steptoe & Vögele, 1991).

The cognitive and motivational approaches to cardiac defense have been difficult to reconcile in the past. However, in recent years new data have been accumulated on defense responses, both in animals and humans, and on the neurophysiological brain circuits controlling such responses, which not only facilitate integration of the classic approaches but also have potential implications for the concept of stress and stress-related illnesses.

THE CARDIAC DEFENSE RESPONSE: EMPIRICAL FINDINGS

The classic model of cardiac defense assumes the following characteristics:

1. The response is a heart-rate acceleration peaking at 3–6 s after stimulus onset.
2. The eliciting stimulus can be of any sensory modality but must be of high intensity (> 95 dB), long duration (> 500 ms), and long rise time (> 24 ms), to differentiate it from cardiac startle, which also requires high intensity but shorter duration and shorter rise time.
3. The response shows slow habituation with repeated stimulation.
4. Its physiological mediation is exclusively sympathetic.
5. Its functional significance is a decrease in sensory processing as a form of protection against the stimulus.

The data I am going to present now are a summary of the research conducted by different people at the University of Granada using, as a basic paradigm, the presentation of an intense noise under different physical and psychological conditions while recording heart rate together with other somatic and autonomic variables.

Description of the response

Figure 1 represents, in the bottom row, the beat-by-beat heart-rate response of one subject to three presentations of an intense noise (109 dB of 500 ms duration and instantaneous rise time) with an interstimulus interval of 95 s and an adaptation period prior to the first noise of 10 mins. The top row represents the respiration and the middle row the blood pulse amplitude recorded from the finger. In the bottom row we can clearly see the presence of a

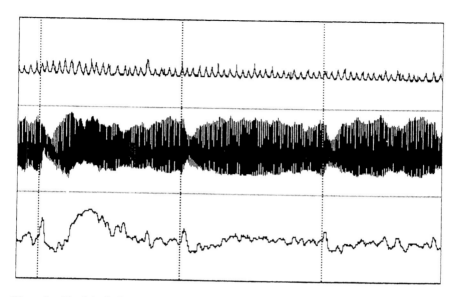

Figure 1. Physiological recording of respiration (top), blood pulse amplitude (middle), and heart rate (bottom) in one subject during three presentations of an intense noise (vertical lines) with an inter-stimulus interval of 95 s. The heart-rate response to the first presentation of the noise is referred to as the cardiac defense response. After Vila, J. (1996) *Una introducción a la psicofisiología clínica*. Madrid: Pirámide.

complex heart-rate response to the first noise with two large accelerative components, one of short and the other of long latency. The fast habituation of the second accelerative component is also evident in this representation.

Figure 2 plots the average heart-rate response to the first presentation of the stimulus expressed in terms of second-by-second HR changes with respect to baseline (top figure) and a simplified description of the same response based on 10 points corresponding to the medians of 10 progressively longer intervals (bottom figure): two of 3 s, two of 5 s, three of 7 s, and three of 13 s.

From these data, it is clear that the response within 80 s after stimulus onset is not a heart-rate acceleration, but rather a complex pattern with two accelerative and two decelerative components in alternating order.

Stimulus parameters

Four stimulus parameters have been systematically studied: sensory modality (auditory, visual, and electrocutaneous), intensity, duration, and rise time (Ramírez, 1999; Sánchez, 2000; Vila & Fernández, 1989; Vila, Fernández, & Godoy, 1992; Vila, Sánchez, Ramírez, & Fernández, 1997).

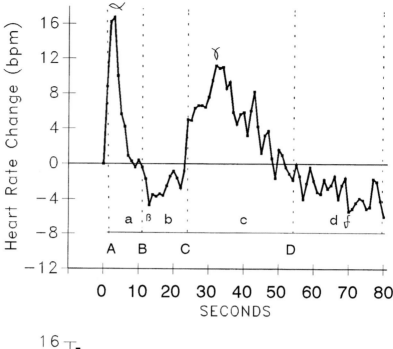

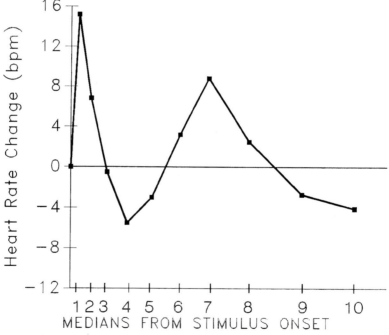

Figure 2. Average second-by-second heart-rate response of 15 subjects to the first presentation of the intense noise (top) and the same data expressed in terms of the medians of 10 intervals (bottom). Adapted from Vila, J., Fernández, M.C., & Godoy, J. (1992), *Journal of Psychophysiology*, 6, 140–154.

Sensory modality

A comparison of three sensory modalities (auditory, visual, and electrocutaneous). matched in intensity, shows that only the auditory and electrocutaneous modalities elicited the cardiac defense response (see Figure 3). The visual modality did not.

Intensity

Intensity is not the unique factor eliciting the response. At high intensity (109 dB) the accelerative components are larger. At moderate intensity (79 dB) the accelerative components are smaller but the full pattern is still present (Figure 3).

Duration

The duration of the stimulus (white noise of 105 dB and instantaneous rise time) does affect the amplitude of the first and second accelerative components of the cardiac response (see Figure 4): the first acceleration increases linearly as a function of duration (from 50 ms to 500 ms), whereas the second acceleration was present only in the two longest duration conditions (500 ms and 1000 ms).

Rise time

The rise time of the stimulus (white noise of 105 dB and 1000 ms duration manipulated at five different rise times: 0, 24, 48, 96, and 240 ms) does not affect at all the amplitude of any of the cardiac components (see Figure 5).

The above data refer exclusively to the first presentation of the stimulus. In all four studies, repetition of the auditory stimulus with an inter-stimulus interval of about 120s resulted in rapid habituation of the last three components of the response. The first acceleration also showed habituation but the habituation trend was less pronounced.

Individual differences

Using the basic procedure (unexpected noise of 100–109 dB, 500 ms duration and instantaneous rise time) marked individual differences have been observed in the form of the response. Two major groups of subjects can be identified: a group showing the whole pattern of the response with a clear second acceleration (called accelerators) and a group not showing the second acceleration (called decelerators). These differences have been related to some psychobiological factors (like temperament, menstrual cycle, or alcoholism) but the most consistent result refers to sexual differences: men consistently show a smaller first acceleration and a larger second acceleration than do women (see Figure 6) (Fernández & Vila, 1989c; Vila et al., 1992).

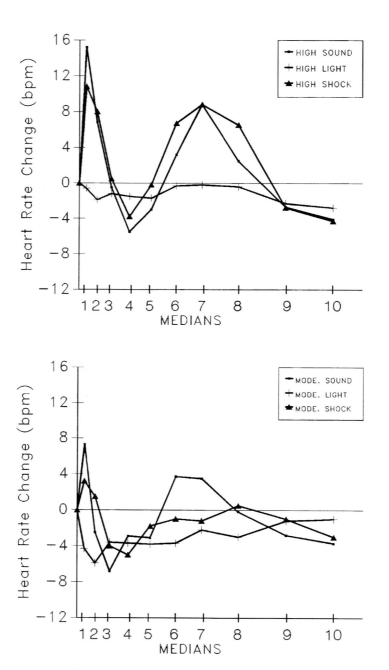

Figure 3. Cardiac Defense Response as a function of sensory modality (auditory, visual and electrocutaneous) and of stimulus intensity (left figure: high intensity; right figure: moderate intensity). Adapted from Vila, J., Fernández, M.C., & Godoy, J. (1992), *Journal of Psychophysiology*, 6, 140–154.

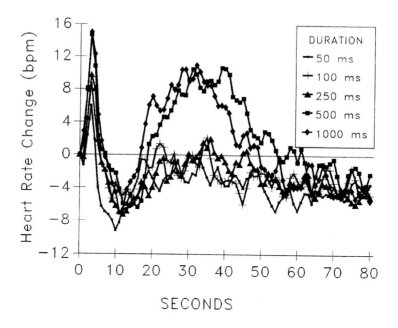

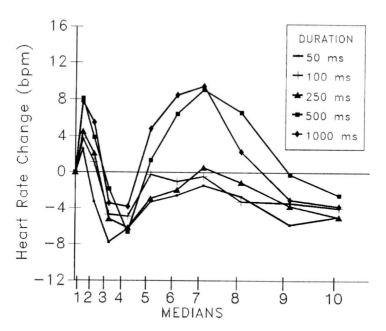

Figure 4. Cardiac Defense Response as a function of stimulus duration. The same data are represented as second-by-second changes (top) and as medians of 10 intervals (bottom).

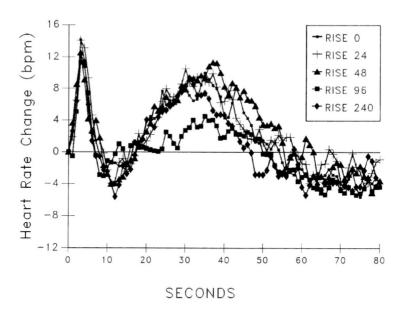

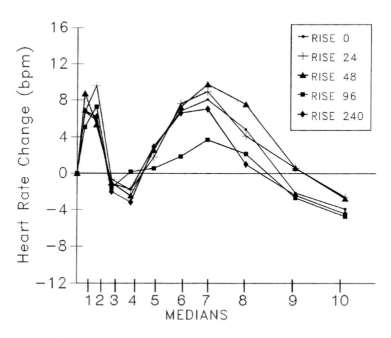

Figure 5. Cardiac Defense Response as a function of stimulus rise time. The same data are represented as second-by-second changes (top) and as medians of 10 intervals (bottom).

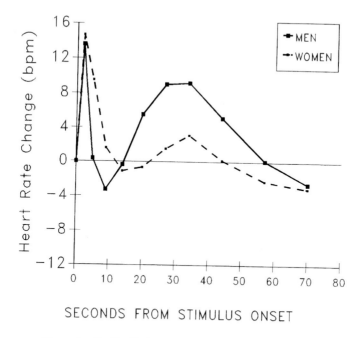

Figure 6.   Cardiac Defense Response as a function of gender.

Physiological mechanisms

We have used two indirect indices of sympathetic mediation—Pulse Transit Time and Stroke Volume—and two of parasympathetic mediation—Respiratory Sinus Arrhythmia and the Baroreceptor Reflex—to examine the autonomic mechanisms underlying the cardiac defense response (Fernández & Vila, 1989a; Reyes, Godoy, & Vila, 1993; Reyes, Vila, & García, 1994; Vila, 1995).

Pulse Transit Time (PTT)—the time between the peak of the R-wave of the electrocardiogram and the peak of the pulse wave in the finger or in any other peripheral location—has been considered an indirect measure of ventricular contractility and, therefore, an index of beta-adrenergic influences on the heart. A shortening of the time is interpreted as an increase in sympathetic activation. Figure 7 shows the cardiac defense response (top)—expressed in terms of cardiac period, the reciprocal of the heart rate (HR)—and the simultaneous recording of PTT (middle). An initial decrease in sympathetic activation is followed by a sustained increase that reaches its maximum amplitude coinciding with the peak of the second acceleration. When both variables are represented together (in z-scores) it is clear that the only coincidences occur during the second acceleration and second

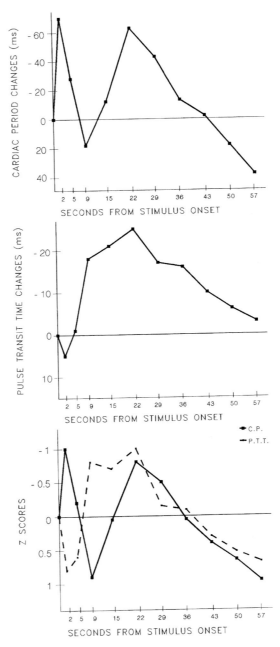

Figure 7. Simultaneous recording of Cardiac Period (top) and Pulse Transit Time (middle) during the evocation of the defense response; z-scores are given in the bottom graph. Adapted from Fernández, M.C., & Vila, J. (1989), *Biological Psychology*, 28, 123–133.

deceleration (bottom figure). During the first acceleration and first deceleration HR and PTT move in opposite directions suggesting a nonsympathetic mediation of these early components.

The data on Stroke Volume measured through impedance cardiography—another index of ventricular contractibility—show identical results (Figure 8). In addition, in this study we found that the pattern of sympathetic activation disappeared under pharmacological blockade, confirming the sympathetic origin of the last two components of the response.

Respiratory Sinus Arrhythmia (RSA)—the cyclical changes in heart rate coinciding with each respiratory cycle—has been proposed as a noninvasive index of vagal control because the arrhythmia is exclusively due to vagal inhibition during inspiration. The greater the amplitude of the arrhythmia between inspiration and expiration the greater the vagal control on the heart rate. Analysis of the RSA during the evocation of the cardiac defense response shows a clear reduction of vagal control coinciding with the first acceleration followed by a great increase coinciding with the first deceleration, a new decrease during the second acceleration and a final increase during the second deceleration (see Figure 9). The RSA changes move in opposite directions to the heart rate changes, suggesting a clear involvement of parasympathetic control during the defense response.

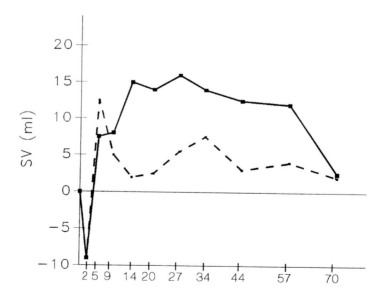

Figure 8.   Stroke Volume recording during the evocation of the defense response before (continuous line) and after (broken line) beta-adrenergic blockade. Adapted from Reyes del Paso, G., Godoy, J., and Vila, J. (1992), *Biological Psychology, 35,* 17–35.

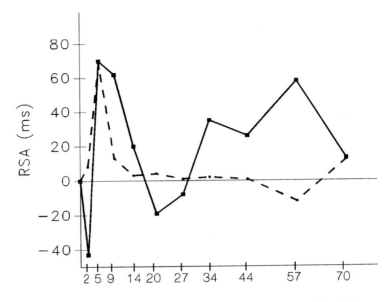

Figure 9. Respiratory Sinus Arrhythmia recording during the evocation of the defense response (continuous line: subjects who did evoke the second acceleration; broken line: subjects who did not evoke the second acceleration). Adapted from Reyes del Paso, G., Godoy, J., and Vila, J. (1992), *Biological Psychology*, *35*, 17–35.

Finally, the simultaneous recording of heart rate and blood pressure also suggests the implication of the Baroceptor Reflex (baroreflex) in the elicitation of the response. The baroreflex is a homeostatic mechanism, mediated exclusively by the vagus, and is manifested by increases in blood pressure that are followed by decreases in heart rate, or vice versa. As can be seen in Figure 10, the heart rate and the systolic blood pressure move in opposite directions during the evocation of the defense response (the top and middle figure). In the group not showing the second acceleration (bottom figure), the baroreflex seems to be inhibited.

In general, these results suggest a clear vagal dominance during the first acceleration and first deceleration and a clear sympathetic-vagal reciprocal interaction, with sympathetic dominance, during the second acceleration and second deceleration.

Psychological significance

I will focus now on the psychological significance of cardiac defense. Two major psychological factors have been studied: attentional and emotional.

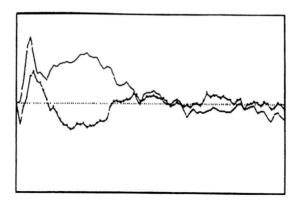

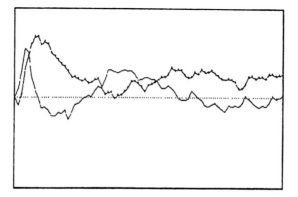

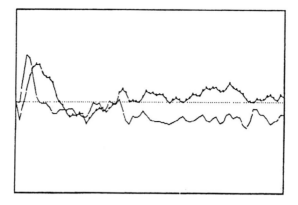

Figure 10. Simultaneous recording of heart rate and systolic blood pressure for subjects who did show the second acceleration (top and middle graph) and subjects who did not show the second acceleration (bottom graph).

Attentional factors

According to the classic model, cardiac defense should be accompanied by a decrease in sensory processing as a form of attentional rejection of the stimulus. Accordingly, cardiac defense should correlate positively with indices of sensory rejection (internal attention) and negatively with indices of sensory intake (external attention), using Lacey's terminology.

Several studies have been conducted to test this hypothesis and the results consistently confirm the opposite prediction: a clear positive relationship of cardiac defense with attentional processes of sensory intake (increase in external attention). In one of these studies we superimposed the evocation of the defense response on a secondary task in which we manipulated the direction of the attentional mechanism: external versus internal. Subjects had either to press a telegraph key tracking an external light that was on and off every half second during the period in which the cardiac response was evoked (external attention) or to press the same telegraph key in coincidence not with the light but with the perception of their heartbeats (internal attention). Figure 11 shows the results of this study (Vila, Pérez, Fernández, Pegalajar, & Sánchez, 1997). There is a clear potentiation of the second accelerative component of the response when subjects were performing the externally directed attention task (intake). This modulatory effect of external attention on cardiac defense is also consistent with a significant relationship found in a previous study between the presence of the second accelerative component and greater cardiac reactivity in tasks of simple reaction time (intake), but not with respect to tasks of mental arithmetic (rejection) (Fernández & Vila, 1989b).

Subsequent studies have tried to answer the question of whether this potentiation was dependent on the *direction* of attention during the task or on the *extent* of attention as represented by workload and demand, as suggested by Turpin (1986). Figure 12 shows the results of a study in which we manipulated cognitive demand by introducing a different internally directed task—Sternberg's *memory search task* at two levels of task difficulty (easy being to memorize only two letters; and difficult being to memorize seven letters)—in addition to the control group and the tracking group of the previous study (Pérez, Fernández, Vila, & Turpin, 2000). Results again show potentiation of cardiac defense only in the tracking (external attention) task. A final study also manipulated the direction of attention (external versus internal) by comparing two parallel cognitive tasks: Sternberg's *memory search task* (internal) versus Sternberg's *visual search task* (external). In the memory task, subjects had to recognize a letter as belonging or not belonging to a previously memorized set of letters. In the visual task, subjects had to detect a letter within a currently presented set of letters. In addition, two levels of task difficulty and two levels of task-defense response contingency

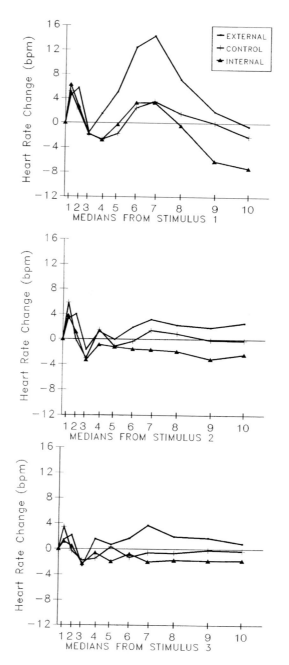

Figure 11. Modulation of cardiac defense by external attention (light tracking) versus internal attention (heart-beat tracking), plus control, along three stimulus presentations (top, middle, and bottom graphs). After Vila, J., Pérez, M.N., Fernández, M.C., Pegalajar, J., & Sánchez, M. (1997), *Psychophysiology, 34*, 482–487.

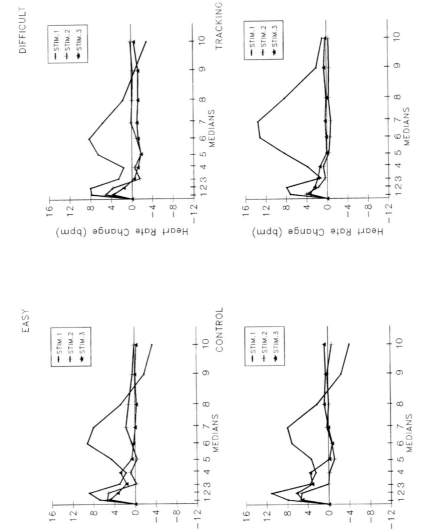

Figure 12. Modulation of cardiac defense by external attention (light tracking) versus internal attention (Sternberg's memory search task at two levels of difficulty: easy and difficult), plus control, along three stimulus presentations. After Pérez, M.N., Fernández, M.C., Vila, J., & Turpin, G. (2000), *Psychophysiology, 37, 275–282.*

were manipulated. Results (Ramírez, Pérez, Sánchez, & Vila, 1999) again show a potentiation of the second accelerative component of the response in the visual condition (external attention). There was also a main effect of contingency whereas task difficulty did not affect the response at all (Figure 13).

Emotional factors

As regards emotional modulation, we have used different procedures to study the response under different emotional states (García León, 1997; Sánchez, 2000). In our latest studies we have closely followed Peter Lang's paradigm of emotional modulation of the eye blink startle response during the presentation of affective pictures. The IAPS (*International Affective Picture System*) is an instrument to study emotion in laboratory conditions developed by the group of Lang at the University of Florida. It consists of a large set of pictures evaluated in two major emotional dimensions: Valence (pleasant-unpleasant) and Arousal (relaxing-activating). The startle response is a motor response elicited by abrupt and brief intense stimuli such as a white noise of 100 dB, of 50 ms duration and instantaneous rise time. The first component of startle is an eye blink that can be measured recording the electromyogram of the orbicularis oculi. One of the major results obtained, using Lang's paradigm of superposing acoustic probes to picture viewing, is the potentiation of the eye-blink response when subjects are viewing unpleasant pictures and the inhibition of the response when subjects are viewing pleasant pictures.

Lang (1995) and Lang, Bradley, and Cuthbert (1997) have elaborated a theoretical model to explain this phenomenon: the *motivational priming theory*. According to this model, defensive reflexes, such as startle, are potentiated when there is congruence between the emotional state of the subject—negative—and the motivational system underlying the reflex—aversive. By contrast, inhibition is expected to happen if there is incongruence between the emotional state—positive—and the motivational system underlying the reflex—aversive.

In our studies (Sánchez, 2000), we have examined the effect of viewing unpleasant and phobic pictures on both cardiac defense and eye-blink startle. In the first study, we used three pleasant, three neutral, and three unpleasant pictures selected from the Spanish IAPS (Moltó et al., 1999). The order of presentation was balance using a *latin square* design. Results not only show a clear potentiation of cardiac defense to the first noise when subjects were viewing the unpleasant picture but also a profound modification of the pattern of the response: the first deceleration disappeared and the two accelerations got closer together (see Figure 14). This effect was only observed in the first trial, whereas the results concerning eye-blink magnitude replicated similar findings by Lang and coworkers.

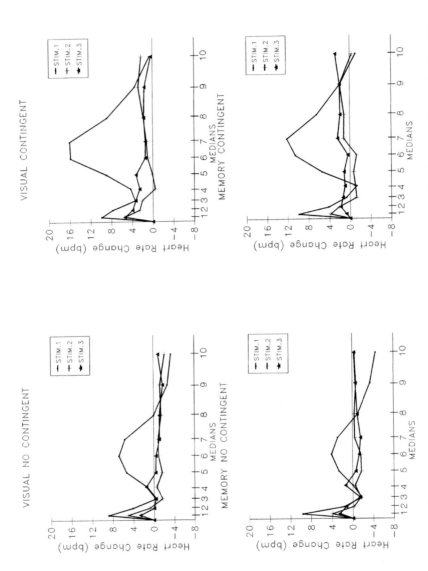

Figure 13. Modulation of cardiac defense as a function of external attention (Sternberg's visual search task) versus internal attention (Sternberg's memory search task), and of noise-task contingency versus no-contingency, along three stimulus presentations.

432

FIRST STIMULUS

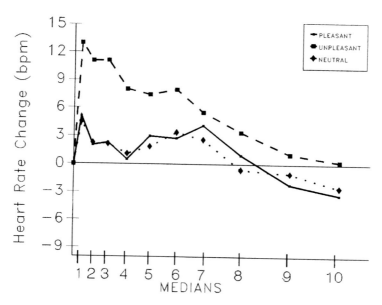

Figure 14. Emotional modulation of cardiac defense by simultaneously viewing unpleasant, neutral, and pleasant pictures.

A final study examined the effect on cardiac defense and eye-blink startle of viewing phobic and nonphobic pictures. We expected an even greater potentiation of cardiac defense under these conditions. Three groups of subjects were examined: (a) a group of 20 animal phobic but not blood phobic subjects; (b) a group of 20 blood phobic but not animal phobic subjects; and (c) a group of 20 subjects with no fear of animals or blood. All subjects had only two defense acoustic trials: one while viewing a picture of the animal and the other while viewing the picture of blood in counterbalanced order. Results again showed a clear potentiation of the accelerative components of the response when phobic subjects were viewing their phobic object as compared to their nonphobic object or to both in nonphobic subjects (Figure 15). Also evident in this graph is the topographic change of the form of the cardiac response. As regards eye-blink startle, our results again replicate those of Lang and colleagues.

In general, these results strongly support the implication of both attentional and emotional factors in the elicitation of the cardiac defense response in line with Lang's theory of motivational priming.

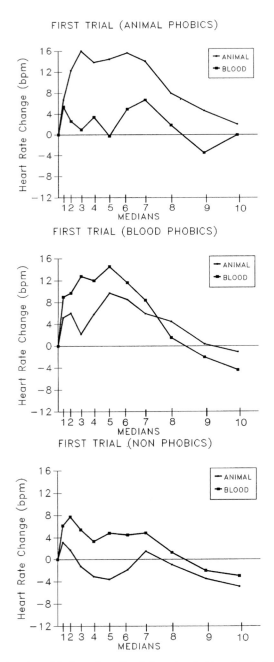

Figure 15. Emotional modulation of cardiac defense in phobic subjects (animal versus blood phobia) by simultaneously viewing phobic versus nonphobic pictures. Top graph: animal phobic subjects; middle graph: blood phobic subjects; bottom graph: nonphobic subjects.

434

CONCEPTUAL AND CLINICAL IMPLICATIONS

The data I have summarized on the cardiac defense response support a description and interpretation of cardiac defense that is different from the classic model of heart-rate acceleration, exclusive sympathetic mediation, and either cognitive or motivational significance. Cardiac defense is characterized by a complex sequence of heart-rate changes with both accelerative and decelerative components, with both parasympathetic and sympathetic influences, and with both attentional and emotional significance. The implications of this new conceptualization are various.

Natural defense

The new data on defense emphasize the dynamic character of the defense response—obvious in natural settings—and the simultaneous involvement of different physiological and psychological mechanisms. In natural settings, such as the imminence of a predator, the defense reaction is not a unique response that could be conceptualized as cognitive versus motivational, or vice versa. Rather, the defense reaction follows a dynamic sequential process with initial phases in which aversively motivated attentional factors predominate, aimed at detection and analysis of the potential danger, and if the process continues, later phases in which aversively motivated protective actions predominate, aimed at active defense such as fight or flight. Depending on the spatial and temporal proximity of the predator, different components of the defense reaction may take place successively (Lang et al., 1997).

The brain's defense system

The structural foundation of the defense reactions is in the brain's aversive motive system. Neuroscientists have traced the chain of neural activation in the brain, starting from the sensory input, proceeding through the subcortical and cortical connecting structures, and finishing in the autonomic and motor effectors (Davis, 1996; LeDoux, 1996). A critical structure in this circuit is the *amygdala*, a subcortical center that receives inputs from the sensory *thalamus* and various cortical structures. Downstream from the amygdala, the defense circuit branches into different structures, controlling separate forms of defense. This hierarchical organization, together with the learned plasticity in the anatomy and functioning of the brain's structures, provides considerable variety in the pattern of defensive output. Depending on the situational context and on the weight of the local pathways within the circuit, the aversively motivated responses can be escape or avoidance, aggressive behavior, hormonal and autonomic responses, or the augmentation of protective reflexes (Lang, 1995).

The stress concept and stress-related illnesses

The traditional approach to cardiac defense did not emphasize the dynamic character of the defense response—obvious in natural settings, as mentioned before—nor the simultaneous involvement of different psychological processes—attentional and motivational. The new approach matches better with the prevalent model of stress in health-related disciplines: the cognitive-transactional model (Lazarus & Folkman, 1984). The continuous dynamic interaction between the situation and the person, leading to activation or deactivation of the stress response, is the main feature of the transactional model. In addition, the new approach to defense can help to better define the specific nature of stress, differentiating it from other related concepts such as anxiety, fear, or arousal. Based on the new approach, stress can be defined as *the sustained activation of the brain's defense motivational system* (Vila, 2001 press). A state of maintained activation of this system implies a variety of specific defense responses being continuously elicited, including neural and humoral responses that correlate with poor physical and mental health: sustained increases in heart rate and blood pressure, and sustained decreases in respiratory sinus arrhythmia and cardiac variability.

The scientific study of human behavior

I would like to finish this chapter by summarizing in a few sentences some implications that this recent body of research on emotions and the defense system also have for the scientific study of human behavior in general.

Evolutionary perspective

Human behavior cannot be completely understood without an evolutionary perspective. Emotions play a fundamental role in the adaptation of the organisms to their environment. Emotions help to organize our world as good or bad, as positive or negative, facilitating adaptive behaviors of approach or avoidance.

Emotional brain

The basic mechanisms that control emotions and stress are in the brain. But in this case it is not the cognitive brain, that part of the brain developed in the latest stages of evolution—the neocortex. It is the *emotional brain*, that part of the brain located in subcortical and deep cortical structures, like the *amygdala* or the *bed nucleus of stria terminalis*, that humans share with other animals lower in the phylogenetic scale.

Unconscious mechanisms

The basic mechanisms controlling emotions are not conscious. But they are not unconscious in the Freudian sense of being repressed processes. The causes of emotional unconsciousness are the existence of different brain circuits for emotional learning (unconscious) and for emotional memory (conscious). The first one depends on a direct and automatic circuit involving the thalamus and the amygdala without passing through the neocortex. The second one depends on indirect circuits involving various cortical structures (LeDoux, 1996).

Cognitive brain

In normal conditions both neural circuits work interactively and there are numerous connections between the emotional and the cognitive brain. The interconnections explain why some emotional reactions can be activated or inhibited by cognitive actions such as the anticipation of a danger or the re-evaluation of the situation.

Heart and muscles: Emotion and motivation

Both the emotional brain and the cognitive brain need the rest of the body for their own functioning. The implication of the whole body is fundamental to our understanding of human behavior. It is essential to understand the distinction between motivation, emotion, and cognition. The concept of *motivation* always *implies movement towards some goal* (muscles = the motor system). The concept of *emotion* also implies movement, but *movement from within the body towards the surface* (blood, sweat, and tears = the autonomic system).

Pathology

The adaptive functioning of the organism can be disrupted through any of the elements involved: the emotional brain, the cognitive brain, the muscles, and the heart. Neither the negative emotions nor the stress are pathological per se. But they constitute a perfect condition for pathology to develop if the defensive motivational system (the basis of negative emotions and stress) remains activated for prolonged periods.

Therapy and education

There are efficient procedures to help people to control their stress and pathological emotions. Nevertheless, the important question is not whether we have effective techniques but whether we know the mechanisms of their effectiveness. The magnitude and generality of the emotional problems we all suffer point to the inadequacy not only of our existing treatment techniques but also of our educational and social systems as a whole. And the only way of improving our techniques is to improve our scientific knowledge of the mechanisms underlying the techniques. Clinical psychology must recover its optimism about the value of basic science. The only way of doing so is by working actively to establish solid bridges between experimental and clinical psychology, between basic and applied research.

ACKNOWLEDGEMENTS

The investigations reported in this chapter were supported by grants from the Spanish Ministry of Education (projects CICYT PB93/1096 and PB/0841) and from La Junta de Andalucia (Research Group HUM 388).

REFERENCES

Davis, M. (1996). Differential roles of the amygdala and bed nucleus of the stria terminalis in conditioned fear and startle enhanced by corticotropin-releasing hormone. In T. Ono, B.L. McNaughton, S. Molotchnikoff, E.T. Rolls, & H. Nishijo (Eds.), *Perception, memory and emotion: Frontiers in neuroscience* (pp. 525–546). Oxford: Elsevier.

Fernández, M.C., & Vila, J. (1989a). Sympathetic-parasympathetic mediation of the cardiac defense response in humans. *Biological Psychology, 28*, 123–133.

Fernández, M.C., & Vila, J. (1989b). Cognitive versus motivational significance of the cardiac response to intense auditory stimulation. *International Journal of Psychophysiology, 8*, 49–59.

Fernández, M.C., & Vila, J. (1989c). La respuesta cardíaca de defensa en humanos (II): Diferencias sexuales e individuales. *Boletín de Psicología, 24*, 7–29.

García León, A. (1997). *Efectos de la hostilidad/ira sobre la reactividad cardiovascular en paradigmas tónicos y fásicos (La respuesta cardiaca de defensa)*. PhD thesis, University of Granada.

Graham, F.K. (1979). Distinguishing among orienting, defense and startle reflexes. In H.D. Kimmel, E.H. van Olst, & F.J. Orlebeke (Eds.), *The orienting reflex in humans* (pp. 137–167). Hillsdale, NJ: Lawrence Erlbaum Associates Inc.

Lacey, B.C., & Lacey, J.I. (1974). Studies of heart rate and other bodily processes in sensoriomotor behavior. In P.A. Obrist, A.H. Black, J. Brener, & L.V. DiCara (Eds.), *Cardiovascular psychophysiology: Current issues in response mechanisms, biofeedback and methodology* (pp. 538–564). Chicago: Aldine.

Lacey, J.I., & Lacey, B.C. (1970). Some autonomic-central nervous system interrelationships. In P. Black (Ed.), *Physiological correlates of emotion* (pp. 205–227). New York: Academic Press.

Lang, P.J. (1995). The emotion probe: Studies of motivation and attention. *American Psychologist, 50*, 372–385.

Lang, P.J., Bradley, M.M., & Cuthbert, B.N. (1997). Motivated attention: Affect, activation, and action. In P.J. Lang, R.F. Simons, & M.T. Balaban (Eds.), *Attention and orienting* (pp. 97–135). Hillsdale, NJ: Lawrence Erlbaum Associates Inc.

Lazarus, R.S., & Folkman, S. (1984). *Stress, appraisal and coping*. New York: Springer.

LeDoux, J.E. (1996). *The emotional brain*. New York: Pergamon Press.

Moltó, J., Montañés, S., Poy, R., Segarra, P., Pastor, M.C., Tormo, M.P., Ramírez, I., Hernández, M.A., Sánchez, M., Fernández, M.C., & Vila, J. (1999). Un nuevo método para el estudio

quite widely in the extent to which they show positive biases. People who are depressed, or are prone to becoming depressed, often show a less marked positive bias in memory, particularly for self-related events or trait adjectives. In the studies cited earlier the memory bias favoring recall of positive information related to oneself was eroded in depressed individuals or even completely abolished. Importantly, recovery from depression is accompanied by a return to a normal positive memory bias, but induction of negative mood reinstates the more negative pattern in previously depressed people (Teasdale & Dent, 1987). Findings of this kind weaken explanations invoking relatively stable structures in memory such as a "self-schema" and suggest instead that memory effects in vulnerable individuals are variable, and depend on contextual factors, including retrieval strategies and current mood.

Some recent studies have tested the idea that the apparent recovery of positive bias in previously depressed people depends on the use of active control strategies. For example, Wenzlaff and Bates (1998) used a scrambled sentence task, in which people had to construct five-word sentences from a set of six words presented in random order (e.g., equal am I inferior others to). It is fairly obvious to most people that sentences with either negative or more positive meanings can be constructed from these words, so perhaps it is not too surprising that depressed individuals constructed more negative sentences (e.g., I am inferior to others) from the words than did a nondepressed group. In fact, previously depressed people were quite similar in their performance on this task to nondepressed people, who did not report having been depressed in the past. More interesting was how these previously depressed people performed when they had to construct sentences while simultaneously holding in mind a set of digits. With this mental load, the previously depressed people now resembled the currently depressed group in producing more negative sentences. In contrast, the never-depressed group remained just as positively biased in the sentences they produced, despite a mental load. It appears as if those who have recovered from a period of depression are making an effort to perceive or present themselves in a positive manner. When their processing resources are reduced by having to maintain a mental load, a relatively negative bias is revealed. These results suggest that people vulnerable to negative emotional states can bring related processing biases under control, but that such efforts make demands on limited cognitive resources.

BIASES IN THE INTERPRETATION OF EMOTIONAL INFORMATION

Many everyday stimuli or events can be interpreted as having different emotional connotations. For example, in an ambiguous situation such as an interview, the interviewer's smile in response to your answer to their question may be interpreted as either approval or derision. For most people there appears to be a slight optimistic bias, so as to favor interpretations consistent with a positive self-view (the rose-colored glasses effect). In contrast, people who are anxious or depressed seem to be biased in a relatively negative direction. Thus highly anxious people are more likely than others to perceive the more threatening meaning of ambiguous words (Richards & French, 1992) or more complex material such as sentences or text (Eysenck, Mogg, May, Richards, & Mathews, 1991; Hirsch & Mathews, 1997, 2000).

In the study by Eysenck et al. (1991), for example, anxious patients and control groups listened to a series of ambiguous sentences (such as "Every one laughed at Sandy's speech"). When later tested with recognition items that represented either positive or negative interpretations of these sentences, controls tended to reject threatening interpretations and endorsed mainly those items that had been disambiguated in a positive direction. In contrast, anxious patients endorsed as many threatening as positive items, suggesting that the normal positive interpretative bias had been reversed. Consistent with the findings with memory bias, however, a group of patients who had recovered from an anxiety state showed the same positive bias as nonanxious controls.

Richards and French (1992) presented high and low trait anxious students with homographs having both threatening and nonthreatening meanings (e.g., stroke) followed by words or nonwords about which they were to make lexical decisions. High anxious students were relatively faster to endorse words that were associated with the threatening meaning (e.g., disease rather than caress). Again, this implies that threatening interpretations are more accessible in anxious than nonanxious individuals. However, Hirsch and Mathews (2000) found evidence that socially phobic patients failed to make either threatening or positive on-line inferences while reading texts describing ambiguous situations. In contrast, nonanxious groups consistently drew positive inferences about the same descriptions, as indicated by faster lexical decisions for matching words. The main conclusion from this last evidence is that social phobia seems to be associated with a reduced capacity for making the on-line positive inferences that seem to occur in most people. Positive inferences may be useful in protecting against social anxiety and loss of self-esteem, so that this loss may make it difficult for social phobics to make use of any corrective positive information.

BIASES IN ATTENTION TO EMOTIONAL INFORMATION

Two main methods have been used to study attentional biases, interference, and spatial probe tasks. In interference tasks, such as the emotional Stroop, participants must respond to a target attribute (e.g., naming the colour of a word) in the presence of emotionally distracting attributes (e.g., threatening word content). Under some circumstances, negative or threatening words will slow color-naming more than neutral words, although this effect is more reliable in anxious patients, or nonclinically anxious individuals under stress, and when the word content matches the individuals concerns (see Williams, Mathews, & MacLeod, 1996, for a review).

In spatial probe tasks, a target may appear in one of two (or more) locations, which have previously been occupied by emotional or neutral distracters. Attention to the distracter is then inferred from the speed with which the target is identified. If the target is identified faster when it is in the location previously occupied by a threatening (rather than a neutral) distracter, it is inferred that attention had been allocated to the former. Again, anxious patients are more likely to show evidence of attention to threat than are nonanxious control groups (Mathews & MacLeod, 1994).

Although the distracting stimuli have commonly been words varying in valence, several recent studies have shown that similar effects are obtained with faces varying in emotional expression (e.g., Mogg & Bradley, 1999), and pictures varying in threatening content. For example, using the IAPS pictures, we have found that students selected for their high trait-anxiety scores were relatively faster than were their low anxious counterparts to detect targets replacing the more threatening of a simultaneously presented pair of pictures (Yiend & Mathews, 2001). Low anxious students were significantly slower to detect targets in the location of threatening pictures, suggesting that they were avoiding them. In other studies, only one picture was presented in one of two possible locations, and the target followed either in the same location as the picture, or in the other (noncued) location. Anxiety-related differences for responses following threatening pictures occurred only for targets in the noncued location. Highly anxious individuals did not differ from others when targets were in the same location as threatening pictures, but they were specifically slowed when target was in a different location, necessitating an attentional shift. From this result we concluded that anxious individuals have greater difficulty in disengaging their attention from threatening cues, and that this may underlie the findings from both spatial probe and interference tasks.

ARE ATTENTIONAL BIASES AUTOMATIC?

Attentional biases are often thought of as automatic, because they can occur without intention or awareness (McNally, 1995). If so, then it is not obvious how, or even if, they can be modified, as implied by my title. In this section I want to examine the evidence that has been used to support the claim of automaticity, and—to anticipate—I will conclude that attentional biases are an example of what Bargh (1989) has called "conditional automaticity." That is, they have some properties often associated with automatic processes, such as occurring without conscious intent, but other properties suggesting that they are more like controlled processes, that can be modified under the right conditions.

So what is the evidence for automaticity? The strongest evidence is that attentional biases can be observed even when the emotional stimuli are masked, and cannot be reported. Some of the most compelling evidence that masked stimuli are in fact detected nonconsciously is that pictures of feared animals (e.g., spiders or snakes) cause skin conductance responses in phobic subjects (Öhman & Soares, 1994, 1998). These pictures were displayed very briefly, and then obscured by a random pattern mask, such that subjects could not report their content at better than chance levels. Similar responses have recently been reported with masked words related to the fears of phobic individuals (Van den Hout, De Jong, & Kindt, 2000).

Consistent with this psychophysiological evidence, Stroop interference effects can still be observed when threatening words are presented for a few milliseconds and then masked. For example, Mogg, Bradley, Williams, and Mathews (1993) reported that anxious, but not depressed, patients were slower to color name masked threatening words than they were to color name masked neutral or positive words. Very similar results have recently been reported by Lundh, Wikstrom, Westerklund, and Ost (1999) with panic disorder patients. Interference from masked words has been reported in high trait anxious students, but only when under examination stress (MacLeod & Rutherford, 1992) or when preceded by unmasked exposure to the same word (Fox, 1996). Effects of masked words have also been reported using spatial probe tasks (e.g., Bradley, Mogg, & Lee, 1997; Mathews, Ridgeway, & Williamson, 1996). Overall, there seems little doubt that attentional effects can be observed without the people involved being able to report on when the relevant threatening stimuli were present. It is difficult to avoid the conclusion that attentional bias effects do not depend on awareness or specific intentional responses.

The fact that attentional biases may not depend on awareness does not imply that they are invariant, however. On the contrary, a great deal of evidence shows that attentional bias alters with context and emotional vulnerability. In one study using the spatial probe task we found that under normal nonstressful conditions, students neither attended nor avoided attending words related to performance failures (MacLeod & Mathews, 1988). When tested just prior to an examination, however, high trait anxious students had become vigilant for these words, as indicated by their faster detection times for probes in their vicinity. Low trait anxious students, in contrast, became if anything more avoidant of the same words. Thus, despite both groups becoming more anxious as the examination approached, only those who reported habitually feeling anxious attended more to relevant threatening cues.

Another example of variability in bias is the effect of treatment on anxious patients. After successful treatment, the interfering effects of threatening words disappear (Mathews, Mogg, Kentish, & Eysenck, 1995). The same elimination of attentional bias is seen even if when threatening words are masked (Mogg, Bradley, Millar, & White, 1995). The latter study found that amount of change in the masked Stroop was related to extent of reduction in intrusive worries, suggesting that nonconscious interference depends on current state factors as well as more enduring vulnerability. Interestingly, however, nonconscious interference in anxious patients does not vary according to the exact match between the material presented and the specific concerns of that individual, as it does when the same material is presented within awareness. Thus Mogg et al. (1993) found that anxious patients were slowed equally by masked words related to depression as by those related more to anxious concerns. This implies that the level of analysis possible prior to consciousness may be fairly crude, perhaps no more specific than that a negatively valenced stimulus may have been present. In any event, this evidence clearly shows that attentional bias, like biases in memory and interpretation, varies according to state and context factors, and is far from automatic in the sense of being invariant.

HOW DOES ATTENTIONAL BIAS DEVELOP?

The conclusion that emotional processing biases are variable raises the question of how it is that biases develop and change over time. Previous findings of differences between anxiety patients and control groups has left open the issue of how such differences arise. One problem in interpreting the results obtained in experimental studies of attentional bias using already familiar cues (like words or angry faces), is that we have no knowledge of any prior learning experiences with these cues. Perhaps everyone attends cues that have been associated with aversive experiences, and anxious people may simply have had more frequent recent aversive experiences or life events associated with these cues. It seems obvious, for example, that after a life event involving someone dying of cancer, the emotional meaning of the word cancer will have changed and be more likely to capture attention.

Alternatively, we could suppose that exactly the same negative events might result in greater associative learning in anxiety-prone people, so that the same cues seem more threatening. A third possibility, however, is that even with the same degree of learning and perceived threat, negative cues are still more likely to capture attention in anxiety-prone people than in others. Some experiments carried out by Fulcher, Mathews, Mackintosh, and Law (2001) appear to support this third possibility.

These experiments tested if novel stimuli could cause attentional interference after they have acquired a new emotional meaning. Pictures of emotionally neutral scenes were randomly paired with either positive, neutral, or negative images, in groups with either high or low negative emotionality scores (Neuroticism). After these learning trials, negative-paired pictures were disliked more than those paired with positive images. However, there were no differences between the groups in either liking for the pictures, or memory for which image they had been paired with. Differences emerged, however, in an attentional task when to-be-detected targets were superimposed on the pictures. High neuroticism individuals were slower (i.e., showed more interference) when targets appeared with negative-paired pictures, while low neuroticism individuals showed more interference due to positive-paired pictures. Thus despite failing to find any differences in learned evaluations of previously neutral pictures, interference differences associated with neuroticism were found in an attentional search task. Anxiety-prone individuals seem more likely to have their attention captured by threatening cues, even when prior learning has been equated.

Although these experiments were concerned with the effects of learning on attention, it is also possible that selective attention has effects on learning. If new cues associated with threat capture more attentional resources in anxiety-prone individuals, it seems likely that this enhanced attention could then serve to maintain or even strengthen the learned association. Consequently, the range of cues associated with threat may spread more easily and extensively in people who are prone to develop anxiety problems.

ESTABLISHING THE CAUSAL NATURE OF EMOTIONAL PROCESSING BIAS

The fact that processing biases are associated with anxiety or depressive states has led many researchers to speculate about the causal relationship between them. For example, it has been suggested that stressful events elicit different processing styles in people having high versus low levels of trait anxiety (e.g., Mathews & Mackintosh, 1998; Mogg & Bradley, 1998; Williams, Watts, MacLeod, & Mathews, 1997). In some (high trait) individuals, stressful events may elicit a "vigilant" processing mode, in which attention is readily captured by related threatening cues. If this is so, then these individuals will in effect be exposed to a stream of information about possible dangers, leading to increased anxiety. In less vulnerable people, however, the same event may be insufficient to produce vigilance and thus they will be less prone to anxiety. It is clear that any such *causal* account must remain entirely speculative, however, if for no other reason than that all the relevant evidence is correlational in nature. Evidence often cited for the causal hypothesis includes findings that emotional processing bias differentiates between anxious patients and controls, that differences disappear with effective treatment, that stressful events can induce differential bias in high and low trait individuals, and that bias measures can predict later distress (Mathews & MacLeod, 1994). However, none of this evidence rules out alternative noncausal explanations, in which both emotional vulnerability and processing biases are the incidental products of another process, as yet unidentified. The only decisive method of testing the hypothesis that processing bias *causes* vulnerability to anxiety is thus to manipulate bias directly.

CAN BIASES BE BROUGHT UNDER CONTROL?

The results discussed so far demonstrate that emotional processing biases are certainly not constant—they can be induced (in vulnerable people) by stress, reduced or eliminated by treatment, and attached to novel stimuli by learning. Clearly, then, emotional processing biases cannot be said to be automatic in the strong sense of the term (e.g., invariable and uncontrollable). Nonetheless, since they are sometimes elicited by stimuli that cannot be reported, it seems that at least some biases may be deployed without awareness or deliberate intent, despite any efforts to suppress them (cf. Wenzlaff & Bates, 1998).

There are many instances, however, where apparently automated behavior can be brought under executive control when required. For example, after a great deal of practice we can drive a car, and respond appropriately to relevant signals, without paying any conscious attention to these cues, and often without being able to report them afterwards. Similarly, emotional processing biases may be brought under control by practice in encoding different meanings, despite the individual concerned being unaware of the processes involved.

In a recent series of experiments, we have shown that emotional processing biases can be induced experimentally in volunteers (Mathews & Mackintosh, 2000). In these experiments, participants read about and imagined themselves in social situations (training descriptions) that ended in an emotionally positive or negative outcome, depending on group assignment. Thus, one such description ended with the sentence *"Getting ready to go, you think that the new people you will meet will find you boring (friendly)."* Thereafter, they read new test descriptions that remained ambiguous in emotional outcome and finally, gave recognition ratings for disambiguated versions of the final sentence. For example, one ambiguous test description about giving a speech ended with the sentence *"As you speak, you notice some people in the audience start to laugh"*. Sample recognition items included *"As you speak, people in the audience laugh appreciatively"* and *"As you speak, people in the audience find your efforts laughable"*.

Across several experiments that involved variations in the number and wording of the training descriptions, recognition ratings for the disambiguated test descriptions consistently confirmed that subsequent emotional interpretations were influenced in a direction congruent with the training received. Those who had been exposed to positive outcomes resembled the nonanxious controls tested by Eysenck et al. (1991), and made more positive interpretations of new ambiguous events, while those exposed to negative outcomes behaved more like anxious patients. Furthermore, this effect remained equally strong when an interval intervened between reading the ambiguous descriptions and making recognition judgements. Apparently, if an emotional event is interpreted in a biased fashion, that event will be stored in memory as it was interpreted at the time.

BIASES CAUSE ANXIETY WHEN USED TO PROCESS EMOTIONALLY SIGNIFICANT EVENTS

In the experiments described here, whether the induction of bias also pro-duced changes in anxiety depended critically on whether or not participants actively generated valenced interpretations for themselves. In experiments involving active generation, participants completed a word fragment at the end of each training description that resolved its emotional meaning, and answered a "comprehension" question that forced them to elaborate further on that emotional resolution. For example, one description ended ". . . . the new people you meet find you b-ring" (= boring), followed by "Will you be disliked by your new acquaintances?" (correct answer = Yes). After such active generation the group trained to make negative interpretations reported increases in anxiety while the positive trained group tended to report decreases. By contrast, in control conditions in which participants read exactly the same emotional material, but completed neutral words and questions, no changes in anxiety occurred. Despite this striking difference, both active generation and passive exposure conditions induced identical interpretation biases, as measured using their responses on the recognition test.

The results of these experiments suggest two important conclusions. First, interpretation bias can be temporarily induced in unselected volunteers by giving them practice in accessing positive or negative meanings of ambiguous events. Thus, emotional processing biases are indeed controllable, although it may not be obvious to the people concerned that such control is possible. In these experiments, for example, participants were questioned about their recognition responses and none credited their prior exposure to valenced descriptions as having had any influence, even when asked directly. Although some thought that their mood might have had some effect, the results clearly showed that an interpretation bias could be induced quite independently of whether mood was changed or not. The second conclusion suggested by the data is that mood change occurred if, and only if, the induced bias was actively deployed in generating personally relevant interpretations. Mood change itself appeared to be unnecessary for the induction of interpretation bias, but deployment of bias was apparently critical in producing mood change.

CAN ATTENTIONAL BIASES BE CONTROLLED?

Experiments carried out by MacLeod and colleagues (e.g., MacLeod, Rutherford, Campbell, Ebsworthy, & Holker, in press) have provided even more convincing evidence of control over attentional bias. The method used was based on the earlier finding that anxious patients detected targets in the prior location of threatening words faster than those in the prior location of neutral words, unlike controls (MacLeod, Mathews, & Tata, 1986). In the adapted version, two words, one with a threatening meaning and one neutral, were displayed for 500 ms, followed by a target to be identified (one or two dots) appearing in the prior location of one or other of these words. These targets always appeared in the location of threatening words, or in that of neutral words, depending on random group assignment. A smaller number of test trials, involving new words and in which targets appeared in either location with equal frequency, were interleaved over the second half of training. In these test trials there was a highly significant interaction of group with type of word probed, such that participants trained to attend to threat word locations were significantly slowed when targets unexpectedly appeared in the location of neutral words. Importantly, therefore, training induced a general set to attend to new threatening words (or otherwise), rather than just those that had been attended previously.

In other experiments, groups trained to attend to or avoid threat were exposed to a mildly stressful experience before and after training. The stress task consisted of attempting to solve 30 difficult anagrams under timed conditions while being videotaped. Dysphoric mood state (a composite of anxiety and depression) did not differ across groups either before or immediately after training. However, mood assessed after the post-training stress task showed increases in those trained to attend to threatening words, and decreases in those trained to avoid them. This reduced anxiety response to stress was correlated ($r = .34$, $p < .01$) with an index of the decrease in speed to detect targets in the location of threat words. In other words, training to avoid attending to threatening words seemed to temporarily decrease emotional vulnerability to stress, and the extent of this decrease was modestly but significantly related to the size of attentional changes.

In the final phase of this research, experiments were designed to investigate the impact of several thousand training trials extended across 8–10 sessions, prior to a real-life examination stress. In one condition, target probes consistently appeared in the prior location of nonthreatening words, thus discouraging attention to threatening information. In the other (control) condition, targets appeared equally often in both locations. Test trials before and after training involved new word pairs presented for only 16 ms before being masked. Analysis of these test trials showed that the groups did not differ in attention to masked words in pre-training test trials, but that the "avoid threat" training group had become relatively less attentive to threatening words by the end of training. Furthermore, measures of trait anxiety scores from pre- to post-training showed significant reductions only in the group trained to avoid threat words.

Again, these results suggest a number of important conclusions. First, attentional deployment tasks used previously to assess biases occurring naturally in anxious patients can be adapted to induce similar biases in the laboratory. Second, after extended training, effects can be seen for stimuli that have been masked to restrict awareness, suggesting that conscious monitoring becomes unnecessary to maintain the induced bias. Third, and perhaps most important, the results show that induced attentional bias influences response to stress, at least in the short term, providing convincing evidence of a causal relationship between bias and emotional vulnerability.

CONCLUSIONS

As I have tried to show in this review, we have now learned quite a lot about the nature of emotional processing bias. Emotional bias seems to be an example of what Bargh (1989) has termed "conditional automaticity". Like automatic processes, emotional biases can operate outside awareness and without intention. We are unaware of our positive bias when making inferences, and anxious individuals can be unaware of stimuli that disrupt their attention. However, unlike automatic processes, biases are variable and dependent on context. Furthermore, biases can be changed by treatment or training procedures, showing that they can indeed be brought under control.

The training research described here is important in showing that biases can have a causal role in producing negative mood states. These studies show that biases can be "latent", in the sense of being primed, but have no effect on mood until they are actively deployed to process significant events. Onset of emotional problems may thus depend both on the presence of a prior tendency to process events in a biased way, and on the nature and frequency of events that are encountered and serve to elicit biased processing. The findings reviewed also support the view that the crucial difference between normal negative mood and clinical emotional disorders may be precisely the extent of cognitive control that is possible. As the tendency for negative information to capture processing priority increases under stress or mental load, efforts at control will eventually fail, because they depend on limited cognitive resources. This failure may represent the onset of an emotional disorder, just as recovery may depend on the reimposition of effective control.

The last 20 years have thus seen substantial progress in establishing the existence of biases in memory, attention, and interpretation. Now it may be time to refocus some of our research questions, taking account of what has been learned so far. We need now to focus on issues of change and causation—how biases can most effectively be changed, and with what consequences. As well as resolving critical causal questions, this research promises to answer questions relevant to the treatment and prevention of emotional disorders.

REFERENCES

Bargh, J.A. (1989). Conditional automaticity: Varieties of automatic influence in social perception and cognition. In J.S. Uleman & J.A. Bargh (Eds.), *Unintended Thought*. New York: Guilford Press.

Bower, G.H. (1981). Mood and memory. *American Psychologist, 36*, 129–148.

Bradley, B., & Mathews, A. (1988). Memory bias in recovered clinical depressives. *Cognition and Emotion, 2*, 235–246.

Bradley, B., Mogg, K., & Lee, S.C. (1997). Attentional biases for negative information in induced and naturally occurring dysphoria. *Behaviour Research and Therapy, 35*, 911–927.

Dykman, B.M., Abramson, L.Y., Alloy, L.B., & Hartlage, S. (1989). Processing of ambiguous and unambiguous feedback by depressed and nondepressed students. *Journal of Personality and Social Psychology, 56*, 431–445.

Eysenck, M.W., Mogg, K., May, J., Richards, A., & Mathews, A.M. (1991). Bias in interpretation of ambiguous sentences related to threat in anxiety. *Journal of Abnormal Psychology, 100*, 144–150.

Fox, E. (1996). Selective processing of threatening words in anxiety: The role of awareness. *Cognition & Emotion, 10*, 449–480.

Fulcher, E.P., Mathews, A., Mackintosh, B., & Law, S. (2001). Evaluative learning and the allocation of attention to emotional stimuli. *Cognitive Therapy and Research, 25*, 261–280.

Hirsch, C.R., & Mathews, A. (1997). Interpretive inferences when reading about emotional events. *Behaviour Research and Therapy, 35*, 1123–1132.

Hirsch, C.R., & Mathews, A. (2000). Impaired positive inferential bias in social phobia. *Journal of Abnormal Psychology, 109*, 705–712.

Lundh, L.G., Wikstrom, J., Westerlund, J., & Ost, L.G. (1999). Preattentive bias for emotional information in panic disorder with agoraphobia. *Journal of Abnormal Psychology, 108*, 222–232.

MacLeod, C., & Mathews, A. (1988). Anxiety and the allocation of attention to threat. *Quarterly Journal of Experimental Psychology, 40*, 653–670.

MacLeod, C., Mathews, A., & Tata, C. (1986). Attentional bias in emotional disorders. *Journal of Abnormal Psychology, 95*, 15–20.

MacLeod, C., & Rutherford, E.M. (1992). Anxiety and the selective processing of emotional information: Mediating roles of awareness, trait and state variables, and personal relevance of stimulus materials. *Behaviour Research and Therapy, 30*, 479–491.

MacLeod, C., Rutherford, E.M., Campbell, L., Ebsworthy, G., & Holker, L. (in press). Selective attention and emotional vulnerability: Assessing the causal basis of their association through the experimental induction of attentional bias. *Journal of Abnormal Psychology.*

Mathews, A., & Mackintosh, B. (1998). A cognitive model of selective processing in anxiety. *Cognitive Therapy and Research, 22*, 539–560.

Mathews, A., & Mackintosh, B. (2000). Induced emotional interpretation bias and anxiety. *Journal of Abnormal Psychology, 109*, 602–615.

Mathews, A., & MacLeod, C. (1994). Cognitive approaches to emotion and emotional disorders. *Annual Review of Psychology, 45*, 25–50.

Mathews, A., Mogg, K., Kentish, J., & Eysenck, M. (1995). Effect of psychological treatment on cognitive bias in generalised anxiety disorder. *Behaviour Research and Therapy, 33*, 293–303.

Mathews, A., Ridgeway, V., & Williamson, D. (1996). Evidence for attention to threatening stimuli in depression. *Behaviour Research and Therapy, 34*, 695–705.

McNally, R.J. (1995). Automaticity and the anxiety disorders. *Behaviour Research and Therapy, 33*, 747–754.

Mogg, K., & Bradley, B.P. (1998). A cognitive-motivational analysis of anxiety. *Behaviour Research and Therapy, 36*, 809–848.

Mogg, K., & Bradley, B.P. (1999). Orienting to threatening facial expressions presented under conditions of restricted awareness. *Cognition and Emotion, 13*, 713–740.

Mogg, K., Bradley, B.P., Millar, N., & White, J. (1995). A follow-up study of cognitive bias in generalised anxiety disorder. *Behaviour Research and Therapy, 33*, 927–935.

Mogg, K., Bradley, B.P., Williams, R., & Mathews, A. (1993). Subliminal processing of emotional information in anxiety and depression. *Journal of Abnormal Psychology, 102*, 1–8.

Öhman, A., & Soares, J.J.F. (1994). Unconscious anxiety: Phobic responses to masked stimuli. *Journal of Abnormal Psychology, 103*, 231–240.

Öhman, A., & Soares, J.J.F. (1998). Emotional conditioning to masked stimuli: Expectancies for aversive outcomes following nonrecognized fear-relevant stimuli. *Journal of Experimental Psychology: General, 127*, 69–82

Richards, A., & French, C.C. (1992). An anxiety-related bias in semantic activation when processing threat/neutral homographs. *Quarterly Journal of Experimental Psychology, 45*, 503–525.

Rolls, E.T. (1999). *The brain and emotion*. New York: Oxford University Press.

Taylor, S.E., & Brown, J.D. (1988). Illusion and wellbeing: A social psychological perspective on mental health. *Psychological Bulletin, 103*, 193–210.

Teasdale, J.D. & Dent, J. (1987). Cognitive vulnerability to depression: An investigation of two hypotheses. *British Journal of Clinical Psychology, 26*, 113–126.

Van den Hout, M.A. De Jong, P., & Kindt, M. (2000). Masked fear words produce increased SCRs: An anomaly for Öhman's theory of pre-attentive processing in anxiety. *Psychophysiology, 37*, 283–288.

Wenzlaff, R.M., & Bates, D.E. (1998). Unmasking a cognitive vulnerability to depression: How lapses in mental control reveal depressive thinking. *Journal of Personality and Social Psychology, 75*, 1559–1571.

Williams, J.M.G., Mathews, A., & MacLeod, C. (1996). The emotional Stroop task and psychopathology. *Psychological Bulletin, 120*, 3–24.

Williams, J.M.G., Watts, F., MacLeod, C., & Mathews, A. (1997). *Cognitive psychology and emotional disorders*, London: John Wiley.

Yiend, J., & Mathews, A. (2001). Anxiety and attention to threatening pictures. *Quarterly Journal of Experimental Psychology, 54*, 665–681.

CHAPTER TWENTY

Feeling and thinking: The influence of affect on social cognition and behavior

Joseph P. Forgas
University of New South Wales, Sydney, Australia

INTRODUCTION

How does temporary mood influence the way people think and behave in social situations? Although most people are intuitively aware that feelings can have a profound influence on their thoughts, judgments and behaviors, we do not yet fully understand how and why these influences occur. This paper presents an integrative review of past and present ideas about the role of affect in social behavior, and offers a theoretical explanation of these effects based on the multi-process Affect Infusion Model (AIM; Forgas, 1995a). A series of programmatic experiments looking at affective influences on social thinking, judgments, and behaviors carried out in our laboratory will also be described. It will be argued that the different information-processing strategies people adopt in different situations play a key role in promoting, inhibiting, or even reversing affective influences on cognition and behavior. Indeed, the evidence to be reviewed here will suggest that it is the very complexity and indeterminacy of many social situations that promotes affective influences on interpersonal behaviors. The principle appears to be that the more complex and ambiguous a social situation, the more likely it is that people will need to engage in open, elaborate, and constructive thinking, drawing on their own memory-based ideas in order to produce an appropriate response. A number of theories as well as empirical studies now predict that such open, elaborate processing strategies are especially likely to be influenced by affective states (Fiedler, 1991; Forgas, 1995a).

EARLY THEORIZING ABOUT THE ROLE OF AFFECT
IN SOCIAL BEHAVIOR

Since the dawn of civilization, understanding the delicate relationship between affect and cognition, feeling and thinking, has been one of the recurrent puzzles that occupied artists, writers, and philosophers. The basic idea that affect may overwhelm and subvert rational processes has been echoed in many social and psychological theories throughout the ages. For example, the psychoanalytic view of affect suggested that managing affective states required considerable psychological resources. However, important advances in social cognition, neuroanatomy, and psychophysiology during the last decade led to the recognition that affect is not necessarily a disruptive influence on social thinking and behavior (Adolphs & Damasio, 2001; Ito & Cacioppo, 2001). For example, research with brain-damaged patients showed that individuals who suffer lesions that interfere with affective reactions but leave cognitive capacities intact tend to make disastrous social decisions and their social relationships suffer accordingly, even though their intellectual problem-solving ability may be unimpaired (Damasio, 1994).

Recent affect-cognition research also emphasizes the close interdependence between feeling and thinking in human social life (Forgas, 2000a; Zajonc, 2000). Much of the present discussion will focus on the role of moods in interpersonal behavior. Moods, unlike emotions, are relatively low-intensity, diffuse, and enduring affective states that have no salient cause and little cognitive content (such as feeling good or feeling bad, being in a happy or sad mood). Paradoxically, because moods tend to be less subject to conscious monitoring and control, and often elude awareness, their effects on social thinking, judgments, and behavior tend to be potentially more insidious, enduring, and subtle.

Psychodynamic explanations

Freud's psychodynamic theory played a key role in highlighting the important, if often latent, influence of affect on interpersonal behavior. According to this view, affective impulses are largely located within the id, and in seeking expression, they exert "pressure" against the countervailing forces of rational, controlled ego mechanisms. These ideas rapidly permeated popular thinking about affect. In a typical early study Feshbach and Singer (1957) tested the psychoanalytic prediction that attempts to suppress affect should generate greater "pressure" for affect infusion into unrelated judgments or behaviors. They found that fearful subjects were in fact more likely to "perceive another person as fearful and anxious" (p. 286), and this effect was especially strong when subjects were trying to suppress their fear, because "suppression of fear facilitates the tendency to project fear onto another social object" (p. 286). However, such psychoanalytic explanations soon declined in popularity, because of the absence of any direct evidence for the psychodynamic mechanisms postulated, and the devastating epistemological criticisms leveled at psychoanalysis as fundamentally unscientific by philosophers such as Karl Popper and others.

Associationist explanations

Although radical behaviorism contributed little to our understanding of affective phenomena, the Watsonian principle (Watson & Rayner, 1920) that affect may influence unrelated thoughts and judgments through conditioned associations was eventually applied to complex social situations by Byrne and Clore (1970; Clore & Byrne, 1974). According to this view, experiencing aversive or pleasant environments (the unconditioned stimuli) can produce an affective reaction (the unconditioned response) that can become associated with an otherwise neutral target (such a person first met in that environment). Thus, Griffitt (1970) found that people who felt bad after exposure to excessive heat and humidity made more negative judgments of a newly encountered person, indicating that "evaluative responses are . . . determined by the positive or negative properties of the total stimulus situation" (p. 240). Other experiments by Gouaux (1971) used a similar paradigm and found that prior exposure to happy or depressing films influenced liking for another person, as if attraction was "a positive function of the subject's affective state" (p. 40). It is interesting that whereas mood congruence in the 1960s and 1970s was largely explained in terms of "blind" conditioning principles, contemporary studies focus on the cognitive, information-processing mechanisms that link feelings and thinking (Berkowitz, Jaffee, Jo, & Troccoli, 2000; Clore, Schwarz, & Conway, 1994). Ultimately, neither psychoanalytic nor conditioning theories could account for the apparent situation- and context-specificity of affect infusion. Recent social cognitive theories focus on the information-processing mechanisms responsible for mediating affective influences on thinking and action.

SOCIAL COGNITIVE THEORIES

By the early 1980s, affect was once again to occupy center stage in psychological theorizing (Bower, 1981; Zajonc, 1980). However, it soon transpired that affective influences on cognition are most likely to occur in circumstances that facilitate open, constructive processing and thus promote the incidental use of affectively primed information (Bower & Forgas, 2001; Eich & Macauley, 2000; Fiedler, 1991; Forgas, 1995a). "Constructive" processing may be defined as involving the active elaboration and transformation of the available stimulus information, requiring the activation and use of previous knowledge structures, and resulting in the creation of new knowledge from the combination of stored information and new stimulus details. It now appears that affective influences on social cognition and behavior are largely dependent on what kind of information-processing strategies people employ to deal with a particular task, as also argued in the Affect Infusion Model (Forgas, 1995a).

Two theories that explain affective influences on social judgments and behavior have received empirical support. The *affect-as-information* model (Schwarz & Clore, 1988) argues that people may directly use their affect as information when inferring a response to social situations. The alternative *affect priming theory* predicts that affect should influence social thinking and behavior through selectively priming affect-related constructs, facilitating their use when planning and executing social behaviors (Bower, 1981; Bower & Forgas, 2001).

The "affect as information" approach

According to this view, when "computing a judgment . . . individuals may . . . ask themselves: 'How do I feel about it?', and, in doing so, they may mistake feelings due to a pre-existing state as a reaction to the target" (Schwarz, 1990, p. 529). Thus, affective influences occur because of an inferential error. For example, when people have just seen happy or sad films and are then asked to respond to unexpected questions in a street survey, there is a significant pattern of affect congruence in their reactions (Forgas & Moylan, 1987). Similarly, off-the-cuff responses to an unexpected telephone survey may show similar effects (Schwarz & Clore, 1988), as respondents may simply rely on their mood to infer a positive or negative response. However, most strategic interpersonal behaviors involve more extensive processing, and are unlikely to be influenced in such a simple way by misattributed affect. A complementary theory, the affect priming model, can explain how affect infusion occurs when more elaborate processing strategies are used.

The affect priming explanation

According to the affect priming model (Bower, 1981), affect is an integral aspect of cognitive representations about the social world. Affect thus automatically primes related ideas and memories, facilitating their use in tasks that require constructive thinking. Numerous studies support these predictions (Baron, 1993; Bower, 1981; Clark & Isen, 1982; Forgas & Bower, 1987; Isen, 1984, 1987; Sedikides, 1992, 1995). Current research suggests that affect infusion into strategic behaviors and judgments is most likely when actors face complex and demanding social situations that require the use of open, constructive processing strategies that facilitate the incidental use of affectively primed information (Fiedler, 1991, 2000; Forgas, 1995a; 1999a,b; Sedikides, 1995). Theories such as the Affect Infusion Model (AIM; Forgas, 1995a) specifically argue that the nature and extent of affective influences on social behavior should critically depend on the kind of information-processing strategies people employ.

Affective influences on information-processing strategies

Affect may not only influence the content of thinking and behavior, but also the *process* of cognition, that is, *how* people think about and evaluate social information (Bless, 2000; Clark & Isen, 1982; Fiedler, 2000; Fiedler & Forgas, 1988). Early research suggested that positive affect produces less effortful and more superficial processing strategies; in contrast, negative affect seemed to trigger a more effortful, analytic, and vigilant processing style (Clark & Isen, 1982; Isen, 1984, 1987; Schwarz, 1990). More recent work showed, however, that people in a positive mood are more likely to adopt creative, open, constructive, and inclusive thinking styles, use broader categories, show greater cognitive and behavioral flexibility, and perform well on secondary tasks (Bless, 2000; Fiedler, 2000; Isen, 1987). Based on such evidence, Fiedler and Bless (in press) argued that the processing consequences of affect can best be understood in terms of a fundamental dichotomy between *accommodation* and *assimilation*, a distinction originally discussed by Piaget. Accommodation involves focusing on the demands of the external world. Assimilation is a complementary process where the individual relies on well-established internal schemas and routines to respond to a situation. Thus, positive affect should promote a more assimilative, schema-based, top-down processing style, whereas negative affect produces a more accommodative, bottom-up, and externally-focused processing strategy (Bless, 2000; Fiedler, 2000; Higgins, 2001). These processing consequences of affect do have significant implications for how people plan and execute various social tasks, as the research to be reviewed here will suggest.

THE AFFECT INFUSION MODEL (AIM)

The Affect Infusion Model was developed as an integrative theory that can explain both the presence and the absence of affective influences on social thinking and behavior in various circumstances. The model maintained that social actors rely not just on one, but on a variety of processing approaches available to them when dealing with social situations. The multi-process Affect Infusion Model incorporates the affect priming principle, but specifically predicts that this mechanism should only lead to mood congruence when constructive, substantive processing is used. The model also predicts that mood congruity is relatively easily eliminated in circumstances when a response can be based on reproducing prior reactions, or when motivational goals come to dominate responding (Berkowitz et al., 2000; Fiedler, 1991; Forgas, 1990, 1991). Thus, the AIM (Forgas, 1995a) predicts that affect infusion should only occur in circumstances that promote an open, constructive processing style, and also specifies the kind of task-, person-, and situation-characteristics that produce such a processing style (Fiedler, 1991; Forgas, 1992b, 1995b).

The model identifies four alternative processing strategies people may use in responding to a social situation: *direct access, motivated, heuristic*, and *substantive* processing. These four strategies differ in terms of two basic dimensions: the degree of *effort* exerted in seeking a solution, and the degree of *openness* and constructiveness of the information search strategy. The combination of these two processing dimensions, quantity (effort), and quality (openness/constructiveness), produces four distinct processing styles: *direct access processing* (low effort, closed, not constructive), *motivated processing* (high effort, closed, not constructive), *heuristic processing* (low effort, open, constructive), and *substantive processing* (high effort, open, constructive) (Fiedler, 2001). According to the AIM, affect infusion is most likely when a constructive processing strategy is used, such as substantive or heuristic processing. In contrast, affect should not influence the outcome of closed, merely reconstructive tasks involving motivated or direct access processing (see also Fiedler, 1991, 2001).

The *direct access strategy* involves the direct retrieval of a pre-existing response, and is most likely when the task is highly familiar and when no strong cognitive, affective, situational, or motivational cues call for more elaborate processing. The *motivated processing strategy* involves highly selective and targeted thinking that is dominated by a particular motivational objective. This strategy also precludes open information search, and should be impervious to affect infusion (Clark & Isen, 1982). In fact, motivated processing may also produce a reversal of affect infusion effects, for example, when the goal is affect control (Berkowitz et al., 2000; Erber & Erber, 2001; Forgas, 1991; Forgas & Fiedler, 1996).

The two other processing styles, *heuristic* and *substantive* processing, do require a degree of constructive and open-ended information search, and thus facilitate affect infusion. *Heuristic processing* is most likely when the task is simple, familiar, of little personal relevance, cognitive capacity is limited, and there are no motivational or situational pressures for more detailed processing. Heuristic processing can lead to affect infusion as long as people adopt the "how do I feel about it" heuristic to produce a response (Clore et al., 1994; Schwarz & Clore, 1988). *Substantive processing* requires individuals to select, encode, and interpret novel information and relate this information to their pre-existing memory-based knowledge in order to produce a response. Substantive processing is promoted when the task is unusual, demanding, complex, or personally relevant, there are no direct access responses available, there are no clear motivational goals to guide processing, and there are adequate time and other processing resources available. Substantive processing is an inherently open and constructive strategy, allowing affect to prime access to, and facilitate the use of, related thoughts, ideas, memories, and interpretations. The AIM makes the interesting and counter-intuitive prediction that affect infusion should be greater when more extensive processing is required to deal with more complex, demanding, or novel tasks. This nonobvious pattern has now been confirmed in several experiments (Forgas, 1992b; 1993; 1995b; 1998a,b; Forgas & Bower, 1987; Sedikides, 1995).

The advantages of a multi-process approach

The AIM is fundamentally a contextual theory of affective influences on social behavior. The model asserts that personal and situational factors combine to recruit one of four distinct kinds of processing strategies that moderate the kind of influence that affective states can have on behavior. The AIM also incorporates the mood-congruence mechanisms proposed by affect-priming and affect-as-information theories, and specifies the circumstances under which they are most likely to be used. The AIM was formulated in such a way that its empirical predictions can be clearly tested. The definition of four distinct processing strategies as moderators opens up whole new avenues of research where analyzing the information-processing strategies of social actors becomes a key aspect of understanding affective influences on their behaviors. The implications of this model have now been tested in a number of experiments, as the next section will summarize.

THE EMPIRICAL EVIDENCE

Skilled social behavior necessarily requires constructive inferential thinking (Heider, 1958). One of the key predictions of the AIM is that affect infusion should be significantly dependent on the processing strategies used. The more people need to draw on their pre-existing, memory-based ideas and interpretations to produce a response, the more likely that affectively primed information will influence the outcome.

This prediction has been tested in a number of experiments where the complexity of the social situation was manipulated to create more or less demand for an open and substantive processing style. For example, if one observes usual or unusual people in a public setting such as a restaurant or a cafe, a well-matched couple is much more "typical" and should require less elaborate and constructive processing than do couples where the partners are obviously mismatched in terms of features such as age or physical attractiveness. Several recent experiments tested this prediction (Forgas, 1993, 1995b). In a controlled replication of the restaurant scenario, participants feeling happy or sad after viewing standard mood induction films were presented with images of well-matched or badly matched couples. Their judgments showed significant mood congruence as happy participants formed more positive impressions of the couples than did sad participants. However, when the couples were atypical and badly matched, mood had a much greater effect on judgments than for couples who were typical and well matched (Forgas, 1993, 1995b). In fact, the size of mood effects on judgments was strongest when the couples were most mismatched, intermediate when they were partly matched, and smallest when they were well matched (Forgas, 1995b).

Similar results were also obtained when we asked participants to respond to people who varied in terms of their prototypicality (Forgas, 1992a). An analysis of processing latency and recall memory data confirmed that forming impressions about more unusual and atypical persons took longer, and there was correspondingly greater affect infusion into these more constructive responses. Surprisingly, the same kinds of effects can also be obtained when people respond to highly realistic social information, such as making judgments about their own intimate relationships (Forgas, 1994). In a counterintuitive pattern, mood effects were consistently greater when more extensive, constructive processing was required to deal with more complex and serious rather than simple, everyday interpersonal issues. Jointly, these series of experiments provide strong evidence for the process sensitivity of affect infusion into cognition and interpersonal behaviors. Similar effects may also influence the way people interpret real-life social behaviors, as the next section will suggest.

Affect and the interpretation of social behaviors

As making sense of ambiguous observed behaviors by definition requires some degree of substantive processing, there should also be affect infusion into behavior interpretation. This hypothesis was tested (Forgas, Bower, & Krantz, 1984) by asking happy or sad participants to monitor and rate their own and their partner's behaviors on a videotape recording their social interactions on a previous occasion. As predicted, happy people "saw" significantly more positive, skilled and fewer negative, unskilled behaviors both in themselves and in their partners than did sad subjects. Objective observers who received no mood manipulation displayed no such monitoring biases. In terms of the AIM, these effects occur because affect priming subtly influences the kinds of interpretations, constructs, and associations that become available as people evaluate intrinsically complex and indeterminate social behaviors in the course of substantive, inferential processing. The same smile that is seen as "friendly" in a good mood may be judged as "awkward" when the observer is in a negative mood; discussing the weather could be seen as "poised" in a good mood but "boring" when in a bad mood, and so on.

Later experiments found that these effects also extend to the way people evaluate themselves. People in a negative mood made more critical, self-deprecatory interpretations of their own behaviors, but those in a positive mood selectively looked for and found lenient and optimistic explanations for identical outcomes (Forgas, Bower, & Moylan, 1990). Rather surprisingly, such mood-induced distortions can also influence reactions to highly familiar, intimate events involving close partners (Forgas, 1994). When partners in long-term intimate relationships were asked to evaluate their own and their partner's behaviors in more or less serious interpersonal conflicts, positive mood produced lenient, self-serving explanations. These mood effects were even stronger when the events judged were more complex and serious and thus required more constructive processing.

Affect can also influence the kind of information-processing strategies people adopt. We recently found, for example, that the kind of vigilant, systematic attention to external stimulus details recruited by negative moods tends to reduce or even eliminate such common judgmental mistakes as the fundamental attribution error (FAE; Forgas, 1998c). As positive affect often produces a more schematic, top-down, and heuristic processing style (Bless, 2000), the schematic perception of a "unit relation" between the actor and the act leading to the FAE appears to be promoted by positive affect, and reduced by negative affect. This pattern was also confirmed in unobtrusive field studies. People who had just seen happy or sad films made judgments about the writers of popular and unpopular essays in an ostensible "street survey". Positive affect again increased and negative affect decreased the FAE. Happy judges mistakenly assumed that the views advocated in a coerced essay were in fact the writer's own, but sad judges realized that the essays were coerced and discounted their relevance. Subsequent mediational analyses (Forgas, 1998c, Exp. 3) confirmed that these attributional biases were due to affect-induced differences in *processing* strategies: sad judges also thought longer about their responses than did happy judges.

Affective influences on processing strategies also influence eyewitness accounts of observed social events. In a recent investigation (Forgas, 2000b) participants witnessed complex social events such as a wedding or a robbery on a videotape. Some time later, they were exposed to a mood induction, and then received questions about the incident that either included, or did not include, "planted" misleading details. After a further interval, participants' recognition memory for the incidents was tested. Temporary positive mood at the time when the misleading information was presented significantly increased, and negative mood decreased the mistaken incorporation of planted information into eyewitness memories. These effects were replicated in a field study, where students observed a staged incident during a lecture (Forgas, 2000b). About a week later, they were induced to feel good or bad through watching videotapes, and were then exposed to questions about the incident that included or did not include planted incorrect information. Once again, those feeling good while hearing the planted information were more likely later to incorporate "planted" details heard during the questioning with actually witnessed details. In contrast, negative affect reduced the incidence of such mistakes. These results, together with the evidence for mood effects on inferential mistakes such as the FAE, confirm that mild, transient affective states can have a marked influence on the way people process, interpret, and remember observed social behaviors. Does affect also impact on actual interactive behaviors? This possibility was explored in several recent studies.

AFFECTIVE INFLUENCES ON SPONTANEOUS INTERACTION

As long as an open, constructive strategy is used, positive affect should prime positive information and produce more confident, assertive, optimistic and cooperative "approach" behaviors, whereas negative affect should prime negative memories and produce more avoidant, defensive, or unfriendly behaviors. This prediction was evaluated in a simple experiment we carried out in collaboration with Anoushka Gunawardene (Forgas & Gunawardene, 2000). Female undergraduates were first induced into a positive or negative mood by watching happy or sad videotapes as part of an "unrelated" study. Next, they participated in an interview about student life with a confederate, and their behavior was recorded by a hidden video camera. These videotapes were subsequently observed and rated by trained judges who were blind to the manipulation. Results indicated a significant pattern of mood-congruence: happy participants displayed more smiles, communicated more, disclosed more personal information about themselves, and generally behaved in a more poised, skilled, and rewarding manner. Sad participants were generally rated by observers as significantly less friendly, confident, relaxed, comfortable, active, interested, and competent than were happy participants (Figure 1).

AFFECTIVE INFLUENCES ON REQUESTING

Making a request is a difficult and complex interpersonal task. Requesting involves uncertainty, and requesters must try to maximize the likelihood of compliance (by being direct), yet avoid the danger of giving offence (by not being *too* direct). In terms of the AIM, happy people should adopt a more confident, direct requesting style, as a result of the greater availability and use of positively valenced thoughts and associations in their minds (Forgas, 1998b, 1999a,b). Further, in terms of the AIM these mood effects should be

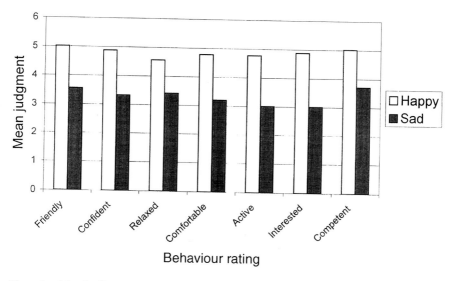

Figure 1. Mood effects on spontaneous interpersonal behaviors in a real-life interaction. Observers rate the behavior of those induced into a positive mood after watching a happy film as more friendly, confident, relaxed, comfortable, active, interested, and competent (data based on Forgas & Gunawardene, 2000).

greater when the request situation is more complex and difficult, and requires more substantive processing. This prediction was tested in several experiments. In one study, mood was induced by asking participants to recall and think about happy or sad autobiographical episodes (Forgas, 1999a, Exp. 1). Next, participants were asked to identify more or less polite request forms they would prefer to use in an easy, routine and a difficult, embarrassing request situation. Happy participants generally preferred more direct, impolite requests, whereas sad persons preferred more cautious, indirect, and polite requests. Further, mood effects on requesting were much stronger when the request situation was demanding and difficult, and required more extensive, substantive processing (Figure 2).

In a follow-up experiment, participants formulated their own open-ended requests, which were subsequently rated for politeness and elaboration by trained judges (Forgas, 1999a, Exp. 2). Positive mood again produced more direct, impolite and less elaborate requests than did negative mood, and these mood effects were greater when the request situation was difficult and problematic. Further studies also showed (Forgas, 1999b, Exp. 1) that affective influences on request preferences seem greatest when people consider using direct, impolite and unconventional requests that most clearly violate cultural conventions, and thus recruited the most substantive, elaborate, processing strategies.

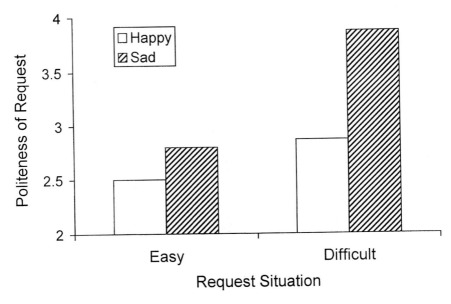

Figure 2. The effects of good and bad mood on the politeness of requests. Happy mood produced more direct and less polite requests, and sad mood produced a preference for less direct and more polite requests. These mood effects were significantly greater when the request situation was difficult and demanding, and thus required more substantive processing strategies (after Forgas, 1999a).

Overall, these results show that affect infusion into requesting is increased or reduced depending on just how much open, constructive processing is required to deal with a more or less difficult interpersonal task. These mood effects also occur in real-life interactions. In an unobtrusive experiment (Forgas, 1999b, Expt. 2), affect was induced by asking participants to view happy or sad films. Next, in an apparently impromptu development, the experimenter casually asked participants to get a file from a neighboring office. Their words in requesting the file were recorded by a concealed tape recorder.

Negative mood resulted in significantly more polite, elaborate, and more hedging requests than did positive mood (Figure 3). Those in a negative mood were also more hesitant, and delayed making their requests for significantly longer. An analysis of recall memory for the exact words they used—an index of elaborate processing—showed that recall accuracy was positively related to the degree of affect infusion, as predicted by the AIM.

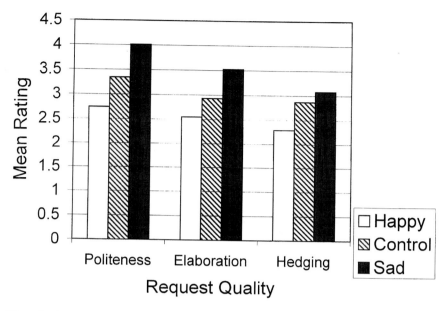

Figure 3.   Mood effects on the level of politeness, elaboration, and hedging in naturally produced requests: positive mood produces less polite, less elaborate, and less hedging requests in a naturalistic situation (data based on Forgas, 1999b).

AFFECTIVE INFLUENCES ON RESPONDING TO UNEXPECTED SOCIAL SITUATIONS

Frequently we must respond almost instantaneously to a new social situation. When such events involve uncertainty and require constructive processing, responses should also be subject to affect infusion effects. This prediction was evaluated in a series of recent field experiments (Forgas, 1998b), where we assessed how people respond to being unexpectedly approached by another person in a public place such as a university library. Affect was induced by leaving folders containing pictures (or text) designed to induce positive or negative mood on unoccupied library desks. Students entering the library were surreptitiously observed as they exposed themselves to the mood induction. A few minutes later, they were approached by another student (in fact, a confederate) who made an unexpected polite or impolite request for several sheets of paper needed to complete an essay. Their responses were noted.

A short time after this incident a second confederate approached the participants and explained that the situation was in fact staged, and asked them to complete a brief questionnaire assessing their perception and evaluation of the request and the requester, and their recall of the request. Students who received the negative mood induction were significantly more likely to report a critical, negative evaluation of the request and the requester and were less likely to comply than were positive mood participants. In a particularly interesting result, mood and the politeness of the requester had an interactive effect on responses: mood effects were markedly greater when responding to an impolite and unconventional rather than a polite request. An analysis of later recall memory for the incident confirmed the more substantive processing (and better recall) of impolite requests. Conventional, polite requests, on the other hand, were processed less substantively, were recalled less well, and responses were less influenced by mood. These results confirm that affect infusion into responding to unexpected situations is also significantly moderated by the processing strategy people employ.

AFFECTIVE INFLUENCES ON BARGAINING AND NEGOTIATION

If affect infusion is a function of substantive, elaborate processing, we might expect affective states to play a particularly important role in elaborately planned interpersonal encounters such as bargaining and negotiating encounters (Forgas, 1998a). In these studies, mood was induced by giving participants positive, negative, or neutral feedback about their performance on a verbal test. Next, they engaged in highly realistic interpersonal and intergroup negotiation in what they believed was a separate experiment. The question we were interested in was how temporary moods might influence people's goals, plans, and, ultimately, their behaviors in this interaction.

Results showed that happy participants were more confident about the encounter, formed higher expectations about their success, and also planned and used more optimistic, cooperative, and integrative strategies than did control or negative mood participants (Figure 4). Surprisingly, these mood effects on bargaining behavior actually produced significantly better outcomes for happy participants than for those who were feeling bad. These findings clearly suggest that even slight changes in affective state due to an unrelated prior event influenced the goals that people set for themselves, the action plans they formulated, and the way they ultimately behaved and succeeded in strategic interpersonal encounters.

The role of individual difference variables

In these studies we also found that high Machiavellians and those high in need for approval were less influenced by mood in formulating their plans and behaviors than were low scorers on these measures. Theoretically, as implied by the AIM, affect infusion should be constrained for individuals who habitually approach interpersonal tasks such as bargaining from a highly motivated perspective. It is almost as if high Machiavellians and those high in need

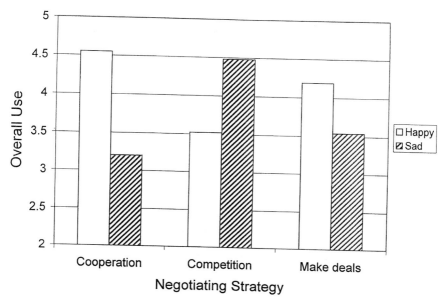

Figure 4. The effects of mood on bargaining and negotiation strategies: positive mood increases cooperation and the willingness to make deals, and negative mood increases competitive strategies both in interpersonal and in intergroup negotiation (after Forgas, 1998a).

for approval had their minds made up about what to do even before they started, thus limiting the extent of open processing and incidental affect infusion. There is growing evidence that individual differences related to information-processing styles play an important role in mediating affective influences on social cognition and behavior. For example, we also found that people who score low on traits such as Openness to Feelings seem less likely to be influenced by affect in how they respond to social information than are high scorers (Ciarrochi & Forgas, 2000). Trait anxiety can also moderate affect infusion (Ciarocchi & Forgas, 1999). Low anxious people respond in a mood-congruent, negative manner to an out-group when experiencing aversive mood. However, high trait anxious individuals displayed an opposite pattern, consistent with their greater sensitivity to aversive affect, and reliance on motivated processing designed to eliminate negativity.

AFFECTIVE INFLUENCES ON PERSUASIVE COMMUNICATION

Amateur persuaders—and that means all of us—must produce their persuasive strategies on-line, and be sensitive to the situation and any feedback they receive. As we have seen, affect can significantly influence information-processing strategies. People in a negative mood often pay greater attention to the demands of the situation (Bless, 2000; Fiedler, 2000; Forgas, 1998a,b). Thus, negative affect may also have a beneficial influence on some social influence strategies such as the production of persuasive messages. Despite much research on affective influences on how people *respond* to persuasion (Petty, DeSteno, & Rucker, 2001) there has been little work on how affect influences the *production* of persuasive messages. This question was investigated in several recent unpublished experiments (Forgas, Ciarrochi, & Moylan, 2000a). In the first study, student participants were induced into positive or negative mood by watching short videotapes. After the mood induction, they were asked to produce persuasive arguments either for, or against (1) the proposition that student fees should be increased, and (2) Aboriginal land rights in Australia (most students were against fees, and for land rights). Each participant argued the popular position on one issue and the unpopular position on the other, in a 2 × 2 design, with mood and issue popularity as the independent variables. The arguments produced were rated by two judges blind to the manipulations in terms of their overall quality, persuasiveness, and valence (positivity-negativity). As quality and persuasiveness were strongly correlated ($r = .78$), these two scales were combined. Mood significantly influenced argument quality: those in a negative mood produced significantly higher-quality and more persuasive arguments than did happy persuaders. Issue popularity had no main or interactive effects on argument quality, indicating that mood influenced argument quality *irrespective* of the issues argued. An analysis of argument valence showed a trend towards a mood-congruent pattern, as happy persons produced more positive, and sad persons produced more negative, arguments. A second experiment confirmed these findings. This time, happy and sad participants were asked to argue either for or against Australia becoming a republic, and for or against the right-wing One Nation party. Results showed that sad mood resulted in arguments that were of higher quality and more persuasive than by happy persons, with an intermediate performance by the neutral group (Figure 5). This result is consistent with negative mood promoting a processing style that is more attuned to the requirements of a particular situation.

However, happy participants produced more arguments overall than did sad participants. This result is interesting because it contradicts some earlier suggestions that the processing benefits of negative mood are simply due to more effortful thinking. It seems that affective influences on argument quality were not simply caused by more or less effort being extended. Rather, they occurred because of the more or less top-down, internally driven or bottom-up, situationally oriented processing styles promoted by feeling good or feeling bad (Bless, 2000; Fiedler, 2000). The next, third study replicated these effects, using a different, autobiographical mood induction method.

In Experiment 4 persuasive arguments were produced while interacting

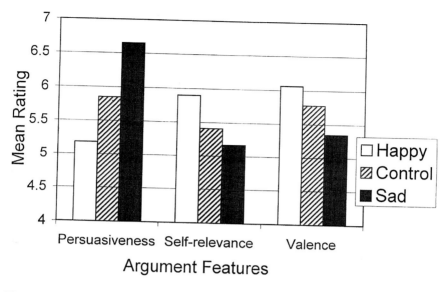

Figure 5. Affective influences on the production of persuasive messages: people in negative mood produce more persuasive and higher-quality messages, but positive mood increases the rated originality and creativity of persuasive messages. There is also a tendency for people to rely on more mood-congruent arguments when formulating persuasive communication (after Forgas, Ciarrochi, & Moylan, 2000b).

with a "partner" through a computer keyboard as if exchanging e-mails. In fact, the computer was preprogrammed to "respond" indicating increasing agreement or disagreement. Motivation to be persuasive was also manipulated, by offering some participants a significant reward (the chance to win highly desired movie passes). The task was to persuade another student to volunteer for an unpleasant experiment, an adaptation of the well-known forced-compliance persuasion procedure used in cognitive dissonance research (Festinger, 1957). Responses by the "partner" communicated increasingly positive, accepting ("I am somewhat persuaded . . . ", "I like what you are saying . . . ", . . . "I agree to do the study"), or increasingly negative and rejecting reactions to the persuasive messages ("I somewhat disagree . . . ", "I don't like what you are saying . . . ", "I don't want to do the study"). Participants readily accepted the genuineness of the procedure.

Two raters rated each argument for quality, complexity, persuasiveness, originality, and valence. As ratings of argument quality and originality were correlated, an analysis of covariance was carried out. There was a significant mood main effect, as the negative mood group generated significantly higher quality arguments than the neutral group, who in turn did better than the positive group. In an interesting pattern, this mood effect was further qualified by a significant interaction with the reward condition. Mood had a greater effect on argument quality in the low reward condition than the high reward condition. This finding is consistent with the Affect Infusion Model, and shows that the provision of a reward reduced the size of mood effects on argument quality by imposing a strong motivational influence on how the task was approached. These experiments provide convergent evidence that even slight changes in mood can produce profound differences in the quality and effectiveness of persuasive arguments. Similar results were obtained both in hypothetical situations and in realistic interactions, with a variety of attitude topics, using a range of different mood induction procedures and irrespective of the popularity and social desirability of the position argued. These results make sense in terms of our theoretical predictions, and suggest that negative affect promotes a more externally focused and bottom-up information-processing style that was previously also found to lead to the reduction of some attribution errors and the reduction of eye-witness memory distortions (Forgas, 1998c). This kind of processing also produces discernible behavioral effects, leading to more persuasive interpersonal strategies.

SOME EXTENSIONS AND APPLICATIONS

The research reviewed so far shows that affective states have a marked informational and processing influence on the way people perform strategic interpersonal behaviors. In this section we will consider some of the possible extensions and applications of this research to some related areas of inquiry. As positive affect often promotes a schematic, top-down information-processing strategy (Bless, 2000), it also facilitates reliance on group *stereotypes* as long as there are no other demands for more elaborate processing. Once activated, stereotyped knowledge may guide responses such as the allocation of rewards to members of ingroups and outgroups (Forgas & Fiedler, 1996). Negative affect can also function as a warning signal, indicating the need for a motivated reassessment of potentially prejudiced responses. We found that this "alerting" effect of negative mood is particularly strong for individuals who are habitually anxious and score high on trait anxiety (Ciarrochi & Forgas, 1999).

Affect also plays an important role in mediating the *attitude-behavior link*, as several recent reviews indicate (Harmon-Jones, 2001; McGuire & McGuire, 2001; Petty et al., 2001). For example, as cognitive dissonance involves feelings of arousal and negative affect, affective states can influence the presence and extent of dissonance reduction strategies (Harmon-Jones, 2001). Several studies suggest that positive affect decreases, and negative affect increases dissonance reduction even if the source of affect is unrelated. And conversely, once consonance is restored, affective state also tends to improve (Harmon-Jones, 2001).

Affect also has an additional important influence on social behavior: positive mood may serve as a *resource* that allows people to overcome defensiveness and deal more effectively with potentially threatening situations (Trope, Ferguson, & Ragunanthan, 2001). People in a positive mood are more likely to expose themselves to threatening but diagnostic information from others. This mood-as-a-resource hypothesis may well also extend to behavioral effects. The evidence given earlier, demonstrating the superior bargaining performance by people in a good mood, certainly supports such a hypothesis (Forgas, 1998a). People in positive mood also process in greater detail and remember negatively valenced arguments about health risks better (Trope et al., 2001).

The role of affect in *health-related behaviors* is receiving growing attention (Salovey, Detweiler, Steward, & Bedell, 2001). Positive or negative affective states may promote healthy or unhealthy attitudes and behaviors, and may ultimately also influence physical wellbeing. Numerous studies found a clear correlation between good moods and positive health outcomes. For example, sick students who were suffering from cold or flu reported nearly twice as many aches and pains when feeling sad than those made to feel happy—even though there were no differences between the two groups before the mood induction (Salovey et al., 2001). It is not really surprising that ill-health should be associated with negative moods. The more interesting possibility is that induced mood may have a causal influence on health symptoms. Individuals who experience negative moods report more and more severe physical symptoms, and report more negative attitudes and less confidence in their ability to manage their health. Optimism, for example, can have a direct effect not only on health-related behaviors, but also on immune system functioning (Salovey et al., 2001). Recent studies confirm that affective states can also have a significant influence on many organizational behaviors such as personnel selection, appraisal, consumer reactions, and bargaining strategies (Ciarrochi & Forgas, 2000; Forgas, 1998a). Different information-processing strategies seem to play a critical role in moderating these effects (Forgas & George, in press).

The management of everyday moods

The research reviewed here also implies that substantive processing and motivated processing may function as two countervailing cognitive strategies that jointly constitute a dynamic, self-correcting mood management system (Ciarrochi, Forgas & Mayer, in press). Substantive processing facilitates affect infusion and the maintenance and accentuation of the prevailing affective state; once affect intensity reaches a threshold level, motivated processing may be triggered producing affect-incongruent responses, leading to an attenuation of the affective state. Such an automatic switch from affect infusion to affect control was illustrated in a suggestive study by Sedikides (1994), and was further developed in the mood-management model developed by Forgas (2001; Forgas, Ciarrochi, & Moylan, 2000b). This model predicts that mood should initially lead to affect-infusion until a threshold level of negativity is reached, at which point people should automatically switch to motivated mood control and mood-incongruent responses (Figure 6). Several recent studies evaluated this hypothesis (Forgas & Ciarrochi, in press), and found that when responses are monitored over time, initial mood congruence spontaneously gives way to mood incongruent responses, especially in negative moods. In later experiments, we found that participants who score high on self-esteem are more effective in managing their moods in this way.

The existence of a homeostatic mood-management mechanism involving the spontaneous alternation between substantive processing (affect infusion) and motivated processing (affect control; Figure 6) suggests that in normal subjects at least, extreme mood effects on thinking and judgments are likely to be relatively short-lived and spontaneously reversed. Indeed, many experimental studies suggest that laboratory mood induction typically does not last very long. These mood management strategies are likely to influence not only cognitive responses, but also behavioral choices in complex situations.

SUMMARY AND CONCLUSIONS

This paper argued that mild everyday affective states do have a significant influence on the way people perceive and interpret social behaviors, and the way they plan and execute strategic interactions. Different information-processing strategies seem to play a key role in explaining these effects. Multi-process theories such as the Affect Infusion Model (Forgas, 1995a) offer a simple and parsimonious explanation of when and how affect infusion into social behaviors occurs. Several experiments found that more extensive, substantive processing enhances mood congruity effects, consistent with the predictions of the AIM (Forgas, 1992b; 1994; 1995b). The paper also reviewed a number of empirical studies demonstrating how such principles can be translated into behavioral research, and how affective states impact on both simple and complex interpersonal behaviors.

These experiments show that affect can influence behavior monitoring and interpretation, as well as the actual performance of interpersonal behaviors, such as the formulation of and responses to requests; the planning and execution of strategic negotiations; and the production of persuasive arguments. In contrast, affect infusion is reduced or absent whenever a social cognitive task could be performed using a simple, well-rehearsed direct access strategy, or a highly motivated strategy. In these conditions, there is little need and little opportunity for incidentally primed mood-congruent information to infuse

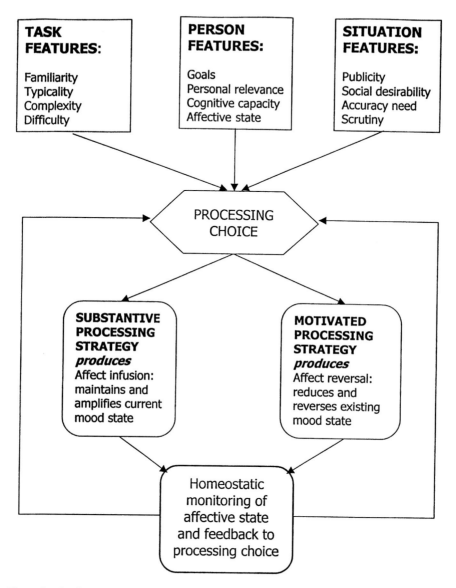

Figure 6. Outline of the mood management hypothesis; task, person, and situation features jointly influence the kind of information-processing strategy adopted to deal with a social task. Substantive processing produces affect infusion and mood congruity, whereas motivated processing produces affect control. Social actors automatically switch between these two processing strategies helping them to maintain a balanced affective state. Thus, substantive processing and motivated processing operate in an interactive fashion, jointly constituting a homeostatic mood management system.

information processing (Fiedler, 1991; Forgas, 1995a). Several of the field experiments also showed that affect infusion occurs not only in the laboratory, but also in many real-life situations. These findings have many applied implications. Affect is likely to have a significant influence on relationship behaviors, group behaviors, organizational decisions, consumer preferences, and health-related behaviors. The tendency to alternate between substantive and motivated processing strategies, producing affect infusion and affect control respectively, could also be considered as part of an ongoing homeostatic strategy of self-regulatory mood management (Forgas, 2001; Forgas et al., 2000b).

Other studies showed that affective states have an important and asymmetrical processing effect on cognition. It seems that positive mood increases and negative mood decreases judgmental errors in how interpersonal behavior is monitored and explained, such as the fundamental attribution error (Forgas, 1998c), and the accuracy of eyewitness accounts (Forgas, 2000b).

In summary, this paper argued that different information-processing strategies play a key role in explaining how affect influences social cognition and interpersonal behavior. The Affect Infusion Model in particular offers a parsimonious integrative account of the conditions likely to facilitate or inhibit affect infusion processes. Much of the evidence reviewed here suggests that affect infusion is most likely in conditions requiring constructive, substantive processing. Other processing strategies such as direct access or motivated processing result in the absence, or even reversal, of affect infusion. Obviously a great deal more research is needed before we can fully understand the multiple influences that affect has on interpersonal behavior. Hopefully, this summary will help to stimulate further interest in this fascinating and important area of inquiry.

ACKNOWLEDGEMENTS

This work was supported by a Special Investigator award from the Australian Research Council, and the Research Prize by the Alexandor von Humboldt Foundation. The contribution of Joseph Ciarrochi, Stephanie Moylan, Patrick Vargas, and Joan Webb to this project is gratefully acknowledged.

REFERENCES

Adolphs, R., & Damasio, A. (2001). The interaction of affect and cognition: A neurobiological perspective. In J.P. Forgas (Ed.), *The handbook of affect and social cognition*. Mahwah, NJ: Lawrence Erlbaum Associates Inc.

Baron, R.A. (1993). Affect and organizational behavior: When and why feeling good (or bad) matters. In J.K. Murnighan (Ed.), *Social psychology in organizations: Advances in theory and research* (pp. 63–88). Englewood Cliffs, NJ: Prentice-Hall.

Berkowitz, L., Jaffee, S., Jo, E., & Troccoli, B.T. (2000). On the correction of feeling-induced judgmental biases. In J.P. Forgas (Ed.), *Feeling and thinking: The role of affect in social cognition* (pp. 131–152). New York: Cambridge University Press.

Bless, H. (2000). The interplay of affect and cognition: The mediating role of general knowledge structures. In J.P. Forgas (Ed.), *Feeling and thinking: The role of affect in social cognition* (pp. 201–222). New York: Cambridge University Press.

Bower, G.H. (1981). Mood and memory. *American Psychologist, 36*, 129–148.

Bower, G.H., & Forgas, J.P. (2001). Mood and social memory. In J.P. Forgas (Ed.), *The handbook of affect and social cognition*. Mahwah, NJ: Lawrence Erlbaum Associates Inc.

Byrne, D., & Clore, G.L. (1970). A reinforcement model of evaluation responses. *Personality: An International Journal, 1*, 103–128.

Ciarrochi, J.V., & Forgas, J.P. (1999). On being tense yet tolerant: The paradoxical effects of trait anxiety and aversive mood on intergroup judgments. *Group Dynamics: Theory, Research and Practice. 3*, 227–238.

Ciarrochi, J.V., & Forgas, J.P. (2000). The pleasure of possessions: Affect and consumer judgments. *European Journal of Social Psychology, 30*, 631–649.

Ciarrochi, J.V., Forgas, J.P., & Mayer, J. (Eds.). (in press). *Emotional intelligence: A scientific approach*. Philadelphia, PA: Psychology Press.

Clark, M.S., & Isen, A.M. (1982). Towards understanding the relationship between feeling states and social behavior. In A.H. Hastorf & A.M. Isen (Eds.), *Cognitive social psychology* (pp. 73–108). New York: Elsevier/North-Holland.

Clore, G.L., & Byrne, D. (1974). The reinforcement affect model of attraction. In T.L. Huston (Ed.), *Foundations of interpersonal attraction* (pp. 143–170). New York: Academic Press.

Clore, G.L., Schwarz, N., & Conway, M. (1994). Affective causes and consequences of social information processing. In R.S. Wyer & T.K. Srull (Eds.), *Handbook of social cognition* (2nd ed.). Hillsdale, NJ: Lawrence Erlbaum Associates Inc.

Damasio, A.R. (1994). *Descartes' error*. New York: Grosste/Putnam.

Eich, E., & Macauley, D. (2000). Fundamental factors in mood-dependent memory. In J.P. Forgas (Ed.). *Feeling and thinking: the role of affect in social cognition* (pp. 109–130). New York: Cambridge University Press.

Erber, M.W., & Erber, R. (2001). The role of motivated social cognition in the regulation of affective states. In J.P. Forgas (Ed.), *The handbook of affect and social cognition*. Mahwah, NJ: Lawrence Erlbaum Associates Inc.

Feshbach, S., & Singer, R.D. (1957). The effects of fear arousal and suppression of fear upon social perception. *Journal of Abnormal and Social Psychology, 55*, 283–288.

Festinger, L. (1957). *A theory of cognitive dissonance*. Palo Alto, CA: Stanford University Press.

Fiedler, K. (1991). On the task, the measures and the mood in research on affect and social cognition. In J.P. Forgas (Ed.), *Emotion and social judgments* (pp. 83–104). Oxford: Pergamon Press.

Fiedler, K. (2000). Towards an integrative account of affect and cognition phenomena using the BIAS computer algorithm. In J.P. Forgas (Ed.), *Feeling and thinking: The role of affect in social cognition*. New York: Cambridge University Press.

Fiedler, K. (2001). Affective influences on social information-processing. In J.P. Forgas (Ed.), *The handbook of affect and social cognition*. Mahwah, NJ: Lawrence Erlbaum Associates Inc.

Fiedler, K., & Bless, H. (in press). The formation of beliefs in the interface of affective and cognitive processes. In N. Frijda, A. Manstead, & S. Bem (Eds.), *The influence of emotions on beliefs*. New York: Cambridge University Press.

Fiedler, K., & Forgas, J.P. (Eds.). (1988). *Affect, cognition, and social behavior: New evidence and integrative attempts* (pp. 44–62). Toronto: Hogrefe.

Forgas, J.P. (1990). Affective influences on individual and group judgments. *European Journal of Social Psychology*, *20*, 441–453.

Forgas, J.P. (1991). Mood effects on partner choice: Role of affect in social decisions. *Journal of Personality and Social Psychology*, *61*, 708–720.

Forgas, J.P. (1992a). Affect in social judgments and decisions: A multi-process model. In M. Zanna (Ed.), *Advances in experimental social psychology, Vol. 25* (pp. 227–275). New York: Academic Press.

Forgas, J.P. (1992b). On bad mood and peculiar people: Affect and person typicality in impression formation. *Journal of Personality and Social Psychology*, *62*, 863–875.

Forgas, J.P. (1993). On making sense of odd couples: Mood effects on the perception of mismatched relationships. *Personality and Social Psychology Bulletin*, *19*, 59–71.

Forgas, J.P. (1994). Sad and guilty? Affective influences on the explanation of conflict episodes. *Journal of Personality and Social Psychology*, *66*, 56–68.

Forgas, J.P. (1995a). Mood and judgment: The affect infusion model (AIM). *Psychological Bulletin*, *117*, 39–66.

Forgas, J.P. (1995b). Strange couples: Mood effects on judgments and memory about prototypical and atypical targets. *Personality and Social Psychology Bulletin*, *21*, 747–765.

Forgas, J.P. (1998a). On feeling good and getting your way: Mood effects on negotiation strategies and outcomes. *Journal of Personality and Social Psychology*, *74*, 565–577.

Forgas, J.P. (1998b). Asking nicely? Mood effects on responding to more or less polite requests. *Personality and Social Psychology Bulletin*, *24*, 173–185.

Forgas, J.P. (1998c). Happy and mistaken? Mood effects on the fundamental attribution error. *Journal of Personality and Social Psychology*, *75*, 318–331.

Forgas, J.P. (1999a). On feeling good and being rude: Affective influences on language use and request formulations. *Journal of Personality and Social Psychology*, *76*, 928–939.

Forgas, J.P. (1999b). Feeling and speaking: Mood effects on verbal communication strategies. *Personality and Social Psychology Bulletin*, *25*, 850–863.

Forgas, J.P. (Ed.) (2000a). *Feeling and thinking: The role of affect in social cognition*. New York: Cambridge University Press.

Forgas, J.P. (2000b). *The effects of mood on the accuracy of eyewitness reports of observed social events*. Unpublished manuscript, University of New South Wales, Sydney, Australia.

Forgas, J.P. (Ed.). (2001). *The handbook of affect and social cognition*. Mahwah, NJ: Lawrence Erlbaum Associates Inc.

Forgas, J.P., & Bower, G.H. (1987). Mood effects on person perception judgements. *Journal of Personality and Social Psychology*, *53*, 53–60.

Forgas, J.P., Bower, G.H., & Krantz, S. (1984). The influence of mood on perceptions of social interactions. *Journal of Experimental Social Psychology*, *20*, 497–513.

Forgas, J.P., Bower, G.H., & Moylan, S.J. (1990). Praise or blame? Affective influences on attributions for achievement. *Journal of Personality and Social Psychology*, *59*, 809–818.

Forgas, J.P., & Ciarrochi, J.V. (in press). On managing moods: Evidence for the role of homeostatic cognitive strategies in affect regulation. *Personality and Social Psychology Bulletin.*

Forgas, J.P., Ciarrochi, J.V., & Moylan, S.J. (2000a). *Affective influences on the production of persuasive messages*. Unpublished manuscript, University of New South Wales, Sydney, Australia.

Forgas, J.P., Ciarrochi, J.V., & Moylan, S. J. (2000b). Subjective experience and mood regulation: The role of information-processing strategies. In H. Bless & J.P. Forgas (Eds.), *The message within: The role of subjective experience in social cognition*. Philadelphia, PA: Psychology Press.

Forgas, J.P., & Fiedler, K. (1996). Us and them: Mood effects on intergroup discrimination. *Journal of Personality and Social Psychology*, *70*, 36–52.

Forgas, J.P., & George, J.M. (in press). Affective influences on judgment, decision making, and behavior in organizations: An information-processing perspective. In *Organizational Behavior and Human Decision Processes* (Special Issue Ed., H. Weiss).

Forgas, J.P., & Gunawardene, A. (2000). *Affective influences on spontaneous interpersonal behaviors.* Unpublished manuscript, University of New South Wales, Sydney, Australia.

Forgas, J.P., & Moylan, S.J. (1987). After the movies: The effects of transient mood states on social judgments. *Personality and Social Psychology Bulletin, 13,* 478–489.

Gouaux, C. (1971). Induced affective states and interpersonal attraction. *Journal of Personality and Social Psychology, 20,* 37–43.

Griffitt, W. (1970). Environmental effects on interpersonal behavior: Ambient effective temperature and attraction. *Journal of Personality and Social Psychology, 15,* 240–244.

Harmon-Jones, E. (2001). The role of affect in cognitive dissonance processes. In J.P. Forgas (Ed.). *The handbook of affect and social cognition.* Mahwah, NJ: Lawrence Erlbaum Associates Inc.

Heider, F. (1958). *The psychology of interpersonal relations.* New York: John Wiley.

Higgins, E.T. (2001). Promotion and prevention experiences: Relating emotions to non-emotional motivational states. In J.P. Forgas (Ed.), *The handbook of affect and social cognition.* Mahwah, NJ: Lawrence Erlbaum Associates Inc.

Isen, A.M. (1984). Towards understanding the role of affect in cognition. In R. S. Wyer & T. K. Srull (Eds.), *Handbook of social cognition, Vol. 3* (pp. 179–236). Hillsdale, NJ: Lawrence Erlbaum Associates Inc.

Isen, A.M. (1987). Positive affect, cognitive processes and social behaviour. In L. Berkowitz (Ed.), *Advances in experimental social psychology, Vol. 20* (pp. 203–253). New York: Academic Press.

Ito, T., & Cacioppo, J. (2001). Affect and attitudes: A social neuroscience approach. In J.P. Forgas (Ed.), *The handbook of affect and social cognition.* Mahwah, NJ: Lawrence Erlbaum and Associates Inc.

McGuire, W.J., & McGuire, C.V. (2001). Dimensions of the social mind: Size, asymmetries, congruence, and sex differences in thought systems focused on self or other persons. In J.P. Forgas, K.R. Williams, & L. Wheeler (Eds.), *The social mind: Cognitive and motivational aspects of interpersonal behavior.* New York: Cambridge University Press.

Petty, R.E., DeSteno, D., & Rucker, D. (2001). The role of affect in attitude change. In J.P. Forgas (Ed.), *The handbook of affect and social cognition.* Mahwah, NJ: Lawrence Erlbaum Associates Inc.

Salovey, P., Detweiler, J.B., Steward, W.T., & Bedell, B.T. (2001). Affect and health-relevant cognition. In J.P. Forgas (Ed.), *The handbook of affect and social cognition.* Mahwah, NJ: Lawrence Erlbaum Associates Inc.

Schwarz, N. (1990). Feelings as information: Informational and motivational functions of affective states. In E.T. Higgins & R. Sorrentino (Eds.), *Handbook of motivation and cognition: Foundations of social behaviour, Vol. 2* (pp. 527–561). New York: Guilford Press.

Schwarz, N., & Clore, G.L. (1988). How do I feel about it? The informative function of affective states. In K. Fiedler & J.P. Forgas (Eds.), *Affect, cognition, and social behavior* (pp. 44–62). Toronto: Hogrefe.

Sedikides, C. (1992). Changes in the valence of self as a function of mood. *Review of Personality and Social Psychology, 14,* 271–311.

Sedikides, C. (1994). Incongruent effects of sad mood on self-conception valence: It's a matter of time. *European Journal of Social Psychology, 24,* 161–172.

Sedikides, C. (1995). Central and peripheral self-conceptions are differentially influenced by mood: Tests of the differential sensitivity hypothesis. *Journal of Personality and Social Psychology, 69,* 759–777.

Trope, Y. Ferguson, M., & Raghunanthan, R. (2001). Mood as a resource in processing self-revalant information. In J.P. Forgas (Ed.). *The handbook of affect and social cognition.* Mahwah, NJ: Lawrence Erlbaum Associates Inc.

Watson, J.B., & Rayner, R. (1920). Conditioned emotional reactions. *Journal of Experimental Psychology, 3*, 1–14.

Zajonc, R.B. (1980). Feeling and thinking: Preferences need no inferences. *American Psychologist, 35*, 151–175.

Zajonc, R.B. (2000). Feeling and thinking: Closing the debate over the independence of affect. In J.P. Forgas (Ed.), *Feeling and thinking: The role of affect in social cognition.* New York: Cambridge University Press.

SECTION FIVE

Higher cognitive processes

VISIONS OF RATIONALITY

These two examples illustrate two different visions of rationality. In Figure 3, I have labeled them *demons* and *bounded rationality*. Demons are popular in the social, cognitive, and behavioral sciences. There are two species of demons: those that exhibit *unbounded rationality* and those that *optimize under constraints*.

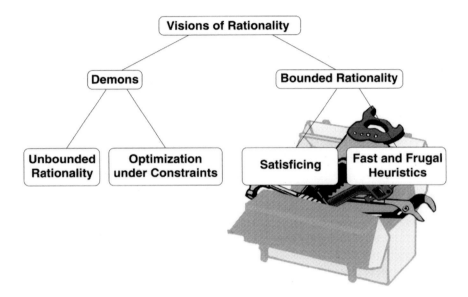

Figure 3.   Visions of rationality. The label "demons" stands for models of human, animal, and artificial intelligence which assume that the agent has complete knowledge (or a complete "mental representation") of its environment, and uses optimization calculations (i.e., to compute a maximum or minimum of a function) to make decisions based on this knowledge. Omniscience and optimization are the key ideas of unbounded rationality, whereas models of optimization under constraints relax some of these strong assumptions by building in constraints such as limited time and information costs. However, the more constraints are built in, the more complex the optimization calculations tend to become, which can prevent both psychological plausibility and mathematical tractability. Models of bounded rationality, in contrast, dispense with optimization as the process of decision making—although, in the right environment, they can lead to optimal or good-enough outcomes. Note that optimization does not guarantee optimal outcomes; for instance, some of the simplifying assumptions on which optimization in the messy real world needs to be built, may be false.

---

the point where the ball lands. I do not think so. The gaze heuristic can also provide the information for when to stop trying. For instance, when the player realizes that he cannot run fast enough to keep the angle of gaze constant (or within a certain range), then he knows he will not catch the ball and stops running—without computing the point where the ball actually lands.

Unbounded rationality

Unbounded rationality is about decision strategies that ignore the fact that humans (and other animals) have limited time, knowledge, and computational capacities. In this framework, the question is: If individuals were omniscient and had all eternity at their disposal, how would they behave? Maximizing expected utility, Bayesian models and *Homo economicus* are examples of unbounded rationality frameworks. *Homo economicus*, for instance, chooses an action from a set of alternatives by first determining all possible consequences of each action, then computing the probabilities and utilities of these consequences, then calculating the expected utilities of each action, and finally choosing the action that maximizes the expected utility. Psychological theories have incorporated the same ideal. For instance, expectation-value theories of motivation assume that, of the many courses of action, the one chosen has the highest subjective expected value (see Heckhausen, 1991). Theories of causal attribution assume that a cause is attributed to an event in the same way that a statistician of the Fisherian school (Kelley & Michaela, 1980) or a Bayesian statistician (e.g., Ajzen, 1977) would test a causal hypothesis. In general, unbounded rationality assumes some form of omniscience and optimization. Omniscience is epitomized in the assumption that, in order to make appropriate decisions, an individual must have a complete representation of its environment (as in good old-fashioned AI and in optimal foraging theories). Optimization means that using this information, the maximum or minimum of a function (such as expected utility) is calculated. Thus, optimization is a process, not an outcome.

Unbounded rationality recreates humans in the image of God, or in a secularized version thereof—Laplace's superintelligence. The weakness of unbounded rationality is that it does not describe the way real people think—not even philosophers, as the following anecdote illustrates. A philosopher from Columbia was struggling to decide whether to accept an offer from a rival university or to stay where he was. His colleague took him aside and said: "Just maximize your expected utility—you always write about doing this." Exasperated, the philosopher responded: "Come on, this is serious."

Optimization under constraints

In 1961, the economist George Stigler made the image of *Homo economicus* more realistic. He introduced the fact that humans are not omniscient and therefore need to *search* for information—which costs time and money. However, Stigler chose to retain the ideal of optimization and assumed that search is stopped when the costs of further search exceed its benefits; in other words, an optimal stopping point is calculated. This vision of rationality is known as *optimization under constraints* (such as time). Few psychological theories have included search (a noteworthy exception is Anderson, 1990). Similarly, few experiments allow participants to search for information. Most of them lay all the relevant information out in front of the participant, and thereby exclude search, either in memory or in the outside world. For instance, experiments on classification (see Berretty, Todd, & Martignon, 1999), reasoning, and judgment and decision making (see Gigerenzer, 1996) typically use artificial or hypothetical content, which makes search for information irrelevant. Note that elimination of search in experiments and the postulate of optimization go hand in hand. If search for information, in memory or in the outside world, were allowed, this would increase the two to four dimensions on which artificial stimuli are typically allowed to vary to a much larger and potentially infinite number, which can quickly turn optimization computationally intractable.

Even devoted proponents of optimization under constraints have pointed out that the resulting models generally become more demanding than models of unbounded rationality, both mathematically and psychologically. In optimization under constraints, humans are recreated in the image of econometricians, one step above the gods.

In contrast, Herbert Simon (e.g., 1956, 1992), the father of "bounded rationality" argued that a theory of rationality has to be faithful to the actual cognitive capacities of humans—to their limitations in knowledge, attention, memory, and so on. To Simon's dismay, his term *limitations* has often been interpreted as being synonymous with "constraints for optimization," and the term "bounded rationality" confused with optimization. In a personal conversation, he once remarked with a mixture of humor and anger that he had considered suing authors who misused his concept of bounded rationality to construct even more complicated and unrealistic models of the human mind.

Bounded rationality: The adaptive toolbox

The metaphor of the *adaptive toolbox* can help to avoid the misapprehension that making rationality more realistic just means making optimization more complex. The adaptive toolbox of a species contains a number of heuristics, not one general optimization calculus. Some are inherited, others learned or designed. The gaze heuristic and the medical decision tree are tools in the box. Like hammers and wrenches, they are designed for specific classes of problems; there is no general-purpose tool. The gaze heuristic, for instance, only works for a limited class of problems that involve the interception of moving objects, such as when an animal pursues potential prey. The heuristic also works for avoiding collisions. For instance, if you learn to fly an airplane, you will be taught a version of this heuristic: When another plane is approaching, look at a scratch in your windshield and see whether the other plane moves relative to that scratch. If it does not, dive away quickly.

There are various kinds of tools in the adaptive toolbox. One kind, Simon's *satisficing*, involves search and an aspiration level that stops search. For instance, when searching for a house, satisficers search until they find the first house that meets their aspiration level, stop search, and go for it. I will talk today about a second kind: fast and frugal heuristics (Gigerenzer et al., 1999). The difference is this: Satisficing involves search across alternatives, such as houses and potential spouses, assuming that the criteria are given (the aspiration level). Fast and frugal heuristics, in contrast, search for criteria or cues, assuming that the alternatives are given. For instance, classifying heart attack patients into high- and low-risk categories is such a situation: The alternatives are given (high or low risk), and one has to search for cues that indicate to which of the alternative categories a patient belongs. Asking at most three yes-no questions is a fast and frugal heuristic: fast, because it does not involve much computation, and frugal, because it only searches for some of the information.

The adaptive toolbox is, in two respects, a Darwinian metaphor for decision making. First, evolution does not follow a grand plan, but results in a patchwork of solutions for specific problems. The same goes for the toolbox: Its heuristics are domain specific, not general. Second, the heuristics in the adaptive toolbox are not good or bad, rational or irrational, per se, only relative to an environment, just as adaptations are context-bound. I explain this concept of ecological rationality later. In these two restrictions lies their potential: Heuristics can perform astonishingly well when used in a suitable environment. The rationality of the adaptive toolbox is not logical, but rather ecological.

How can one identify and experimentally study fast and frugal heuristics? I first use the most frugal heuristic my research group at the Max Planck Institute has studied for illustration: The *recognition heuristic*, which is an instance of a class of heuristics I call *ignorance-based decision making*. It only can be applied if you are sufficiently ignorant, for example, are unable even to recognize relevant names.

IGNORANCE-BASED DECISION MAKING

The recognition heuristic

Which city, San Diego or San Antonio, has more inhabitants? Daniel G. Goldstein and I posed this question to undergraduates at the University of Chicago. Sixty-two per cent of them got the answer right (San Diego). Then we asked German students. They not only knew very little about San Diego, many of them had not even heard of San Antonio. What percentage of the

Germans got the answer right? 100%. How can this be? The answer is that the German students used the recognition heuristic: If one city is recognized and the other is not, then infer that the recognized city has the higher value. Note that the American students could *not* use the recognition heuristic because they had heard of both cities (Goldstein & Gigerenzer, 1999, 2002).

Now consider sports. Ayton and Önkal (1997) asked British and Turkish students to predict the results of all 32 English FA Cup third-round soccer matches. The Turkish students knew very little about English soccer and had not heard of many of the teams. In 95% of the cases where one team was recognized (familiar to some degree) but the other was not, they bet that the team whose name they had heard of would win. Their predictions were almost as good as those of the experienced British students. As before, the recognition heuristic turned partial ignorance into reasonable inferences.

When the task is to predict which of two objects has a higher value on some criterion (e.g., which team will win), the recognition heuristic can be simply stated:

> If one of two objects is recognized and the other is not, then infer that the recognized object has the higher value.

Note that the recognition heuristic can *only* be applied when one of the two objects is not recognized, that is, under partial ignorance. In a domain where recognition correlates negatively with the criterion, "higher" needs to be replaced with "lower" in the definition.

Ecological rationality

Like all heuristics in the adaptive toolbox, the recognition heuristic is not foolproof. It works in certain situations, but would be useless in others. Its rationality depends on the environment, a term which I use as a shorthand for the *structure* of the environment, as it is known to an agent. This notion of *ecological rationality* differs from the notion of rationality as internal coherence, in which rationality is defined by internal laws of judgment, such as transitivity, that do not relate to specific structures of environments. *The recognition heuristic is ecologically rational when ignorance is systematic rather than random: when lack of recognition is correlated with the criterion.* This correlation, the recognition validity a, can be determined empirically.

How accurate is the recognition heuristic? Equation 1 specifies the proportion of correct predictions c that the recognition heuristic will make, such as in predicting the outcomes of a series of sports games or multiple-choice tests with N objects (e.g., teams or cities).

$$c = 2\left(\frac{n}{N}\right)\left(\frac{N-n}{N-1}\right)a + \left(\frac{N-n}{N}\right)\left(\frac{N-n-1}{N-1}\right)\tfrac{1}{2} + \left(\frac{n}{N}\right)\left(\frac{n-1}{N-1}\right)\beta \qquad (1)$$

All four variables, a, β, N, and n are empirically measurable; no parameter fitting is involved. A person's recognition validity a and her knowledge validity β are easily measured: The recognition validity is the proportion of correct choices among all pairs in which one alternative is recognized and the other is not; the knowledge validity is the same proportion when both alternatives are recognized. The right side of the equation breaks into three parts: the leftmost term equals the proportion of correct inferences made by the recognition heuristic; the middle term equals the proportion of correct inferences resulting from guessing; the rightmost term equals the proportion of correct inferences made when knowledge beyond mere recognition can be used. Thus, the three terms cover the three possible states: one, none, or both objects are recognized. Inspecting this equation, we see that if the number of objects recognized, n, is 0, then all questions will lead to guesses and the proportion correct will be .5. If $n = N$, then the two leftmost terms become zero and the proportion correct will be β. We can also see that the recognition heuristic will come into play most when the participant is operating under "half ignorance," that is, when half of the objects are recognized ($n = N - n$), because this condition maximizes the number of pairs $n(N - n)$ in which one object is recognized and the other is not.

Less-is-more-effect

A little mathematics reveals that the recognition heuristic can lead to a counterintuitive phenomenon: the *less-is-more effect*. The less-is-more effect occurs when less knowledge leads to more accurate predictions. This happens when a person's recognition validity a is larger than her knowledge validity β:

A less-is-more effect occurs when $a > \beta$.

Figure 4 shows an example of a less-is-more effect: With increasing knowledge, performance increases up to a certain point and then drops, as the recognition heuristic can be used less and less often. That's mathematics, you may say, but can the effect be observed in the real world? Can it be that there are situations in which more knowledge can hurt? If you know significantly *more* about one domain than another, can it be that you will systematically perform *worse*? Equation 1 specifies the conditions under which one can produce a less-is-more effect experimentally. For instance, Daniel Goldstein and I gave University of Chicago students the names of the 22 largest American cities and asked them, for each of the resulting 231 pairs of cities, which one has the larger population. Then the American students were asked to do

A Less-Is-More Effect (α = .8; β = .6)

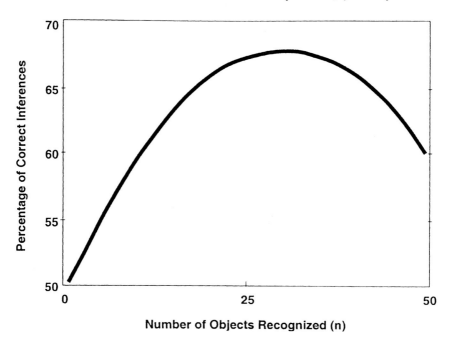

Number of Objects Recognized (n)

Figure 4. Illustration of a less-is-more effect. The recognition validity is .8, that is, among all pairs of objects where one is recognized by a person and the other is not, the recognized object scores higher on a criterion in 80% of the cases—e.g., wins the game. The knowledge validity is .6, that is, among all pairs of objects where both are recognized by a person, the person makes 60% correct predictions. When a person has not heard of any of the objects (n = 0), performance is at chance level; when the number of objects known increases, performance increases. But from some point, which can be computed by Equation 1, performance counterintuitively decreases with increasing knowledge.

the same with the largest German cities, about which they knew very little. To their own surprise, more answers were accurate for German cities than for American cities—less is more (Goldstein & Gigerenzer, 1999).

Recognition dominates contradicting information

The use of this simple heuristic can lead to other surprising behavioral results. For instance, the recognition heuristic is a strategy that several species employ for food choice. Wild Norway rats rely on recognition when choosing between two foods: They prefer the one they recognize from having tasted it, or from having smelled it on the breath of a fellow rat. This heuristic is followed even if the fellow rat is sick at the time (Galef, McQuoid, & Whiskin,

1990). That is, recognition dominates illness information. In technical terms, the recognition heuristic is noncompensatory. What is the empirical evidence for the heuristics in humans? In various experiments, typically some 90% of the participants rely on this heuristic in appropriate situations, that is, where recognition is correlated with the criterion (Goldstein & Gigerenzer, 1999). The noncompensation phenomenon that has been reported for rats—they choose the recognized object (e.g., the food smelled on the breath of a fellow rat) despite negative information (the fellow rat is sick)—has also been observed in experiments with humans. The proportion of people who followed the recognition heuristic remained unchanged when they received information that indicated that the recognized city would not be the larger—for instance, that it has no soccer team in the major league (Goldstein & Gigerenzer, 1999). Recognition dominated contradictory information.

Brand name recognition

Naturally, if organisms and institutions rely on recognition, from animal foraging and kin recognition to the hiring of star professors, there are also others who exploit this heuristic. Advertising is a case in point. Firms such as Benetton do not waste time describing their product; they just try to increase brand name recognition. Oliviero Toscani, the designer of the Benetton ads, pointed out that already in 1994 the ads had pushed Benetton beyond Chanel into the top-five best-known brand names worldwide (Toscani, 1997), and Benetton's sales increased by a factor of 10. For instance, the Benetton advertisement campaign featuring pictures of prison inmates sentenced to death would otherwise make little sense. The recognition heuristic offers a rationale for the Benetton strategy. Consumer behavior relies on name recognition, and this fact can be exploited by firms who increase their name recognition rather than the quality of their products.

Brand name recognition is also relevant to investing on the stock market. If you read the Wall Street Journal, you know that experts are often outperformed by randomly selected stocks. Can the recognition heuristic do better than both? To answer this question, one needs sufficiently ignorant people. In a large study, we interviewed several hundred pedestrians in downtown Chicago and downtown Munich, and created portfolios from the stocks that 90% of them recognized. In the period investigated, the eight portfolios of US and German stocks chosen by the recognition heuristic outperformed the randomly picked stocks and less recognized stocks, and, in six out of eight cases, also outperformed major mutual funds and the market as a whole (Borges, Goldstein, Ortmann, & Gigerenzer, 1999).

To conclude: The recognition heuristic is one of the fast and frugal heuristics in the adaptive toolbox. It feeds on an adaptation, the capacity to recognize—face, smell, and name recognition. Face recognition, for instance is so complex that there is, as yet, no artificial system that can perform as well as a 3-year-old child. The recognition heuristic itself, however, is very simple; it can be written in one line of a computer program. The heuristic can exploit ignorance, that is, lack of recognition, and is ecologically rational when recognition is correlated with what needs to be predicted. Ecological rationality defines the domains in which the heuristic works, and those in which it does not.

ONE-REASON DECISION MAKING

Take The Best

A second heuristic I discuss is Take The Best (Gigerenzer & Goldstein, 1996, 1999). It belongs to the class of *one-reason decision making*, and has the same sequential structure as the heart attack decision tree. However, the way in which the order of cues is generated is much simpler. The task of Take The Best is to infer, or to predict, which of two objects or alternatives scores higher on a criterion. The recognition heuristic can be the initial step of Take The Best, which illustrates the *nesting* of heuristics in the adaptive toolbox:

Step 0. If applicable, use the recognition heuristic; that is, if only one object is recognized, predict that it has the higher value on the criterion. If both are recognized go on to Step 1.

Step 1. Ordered search: Choose the cue with the highest validity that has not yet been tried for this choice task. Look up the cue values of the two objects.

Step 2. Stopping rule: If one object has a positive cue value ("1") and the other does not (i.e., either "0" or unknown value) then stop search and go on to Step 3. Otherwise go back to Step 1 and search for another cue. If no further cue is found, then guess.

Step 3. Decision rule: Predict that the object with the positive cue value has the higher value on the criterion.

Take The Best is fast (it does not involve much calculation) and frugal (it searches for only part of the information, that is, cues). The ordering of the cues can be learned by a simple but robust criterion that ignores dependencies between cues (Gigerenzer & Goldstein, 1999), or it may be genetically coded, as in mate choice in various animal species (e.g., Dugatkin, 1996).

There is evidence that the Take The Best heuristic is in the toolbox of several species. Female guppies, for instance, choose males on the basis of both physical and social cues, such as bright orange color, large body size, and whether they have observed the male in question mating with another female (Dugatkin, 1996). These cues seem to be organized in a dominance order, as in Figure 5, with the orange-color cue dominating the social cue. If a female has a choice between two males, one of them much more orange than

Take The Best
(One-Reason Decision Making)

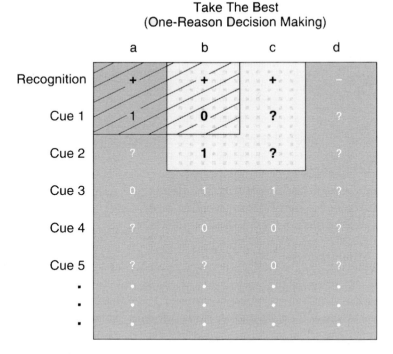

Figure 5. Illustration of Take The Best. Objects *a*, *b*, and *c* are recognized (+), *d* is not (−). Cue values are binary (0 or 1); missing knowledge is shown by a question mark. For instance, to compare *a* to *b*, Take The Best looks up the values in the lined space and concludes *a* > *b*. To compare *b* to *c*, search is limited to the dotted space and the conclusion is *b* > *c*. The other cue values are not looked up and so are shown within the diagram as shrouded in the fog of memory.

the other, she will choose the more orange one. If the males, however, are close in orangeness, she prefers the one she has seen mating with another female. Mate choice in guppies illustrates limited search, simple stopping rules, and one-reason decision making. Humans also tend to use this heuristic. Bröder (2000) reported that when the search for information is costly, about 65% of the participants' choices were consistent with Take The Best, compared to fewer than 10% with a linear rule (for similar results see Rieskamp & Hoffrage, 1999).

Accuracy and frugality

But how accurate is this heuristic? After all, it does not follow the prescriptions of rational choice theory: it does not look up most of the information, does not calculate an optimal order of cues, does not calculate an optimal stopping point, and relies on one-reason decision making. To answer this question, Czerlinski, Gigerenzer, and Goldstein (1999) tested its predictive accuracy in 20 different situations with varying numbers of cues and varying difficulties of the problem. These situations included: predicting homelessness rates in American cities based on 6 cues including rent control and temperature; predicting dropout rates in Chicago public high schools based on 18 cues such as average SAT scores and the percentage of low-income students; predicting the mortality rates in US cities based on 15 cues including pollution levels and the percentage of non-whites; predicting professors' salaries based on 5 cues such as gender and rank; predicting the number of eggs of female Arctic charr based on 3 cues including each fish's weight and age; and predicting obesity at age 18 from 10 cues measured from age 2 on such as leg circumference and strength. The task for Take The Best was always to predict which of two objects had the higher value on the criterion.

As with the heart-attack decision tree described earlier, the cues were treated as yes/no alternatives, and all cue values and objects were known (i.e., no "?" values), which excludes the recognition heuristic. Figure 6 illustrates one of these 20 tests: predicting which of two American cities had a higher homelessness rate based on six powerful cues. For instance, the best predictor for homelessness was rent control—if there is rent control, homelessness rates tend to be high. In the case of Los Angeles and Chicago, Take The Best stopped search after the first cue, because Los Angeles has rent control and Chicago does not. Take The Best infers that Los Angeles had the higher homelessness rate, which happens to be correct. When comparing Los Angeles and New York, search is extended until the last cue, and the inference is made that Los Angeles had a higher rate, which again is correct. When comparing Chicago and New York, however, Take The Best made an error.

Take The Best is certainly fast and frugal, but is it any good? How close does its predictive accuracy come to that of multiple regression, a linear strategy that uses all predictors, weights them, and combines them? How close does it come to a simpler linear strategy, which also uses all predictors but uses unit weights, that is, +1 or −1, instead of computing the optimal regression weights? We tested the performance of these strategies on 50 American cities and the six predictors shown in Figure 6, using cross-validation, that is, the strategies learned their parameters on half of the data (learning sample), and were tested on the other half (test sample). The surprising result was that Take The Best was more accurate in predicting homelessness than multiple regression and the unit-weight strategy.

Figure 7 shows that this result holds across all 20 problems. The *x*-axis shows the frugality of each strategy, that is, the number of cues looked up, and the *y*-axis shows its predictive accuracy. Take The Best was more frugal than the linear strategies: It searched on average only through 2.4 cues, whereas the linear strategies used all cues, which were on average 7.7. Figure 7

	Los Angeles	Chicago	New York	New Orleans
Rent control	1	0	1	0
Vacancy rate	1	0	1	0
Temperature	1	0	1	1
Unemployment	1	1	1	1
Poverty	1	1	1	1
Public housing	1	1	0	0

Figure 6.   Predicting which of two American cities has a higher homelessness rate with Take The Best (without recognition and missing data). All cues and 4 out of 50 cities are pictured.

also shows a trade-off region, spanned by the performance of multiple regression. The idea of the trade-off is that if a strategy is more frugal than regression, it has to pay some price in accuracy. Therefore, a more frugal strategy should lie within that region, as indeed one other heuristic, the Minimalist, does. The Minimalist differs from Take The Best only in Step 1: it searches for cues randomly instead of according to an order estimated from the learning set. Take The Best, by contrast, performed outside of the trade-off region. Compared to the two linear strategies, it was both more frugal and more accurate.

Note also that the simple linear strategy (which uses unit weights rather than regression weights) also did slightly better than multiple regression, showing the robustness reported earlier by Dawes and Corrigan (1974). This confirms the counterintuitive findings that the choice of weights, except for their signs, does not matter much. The demonstration that Take The Best outperformed both of these linear strategies is new. This result is stable across various changes in the way the strategies are tested (Czerlinski et al., 1999; Gigerenzer & Goldstein, 1996).

Performance Across 20 Data Sets

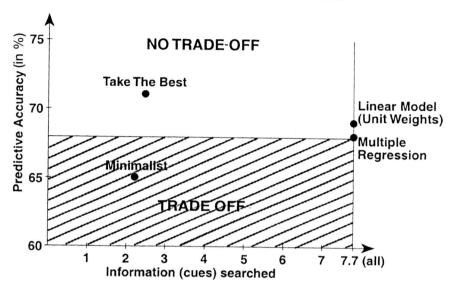

Figure 7. Average accuracy and frugality of Take The Best in predicting a total of 20 criteria, including homelessness, compared to two linear strategies (Czerlinski et al., 1999).

Ecological rationality

How can one reason be better than many? There are two answers. One is the concept of ecological rationality—that is, the match of a heuristic with the structure of an environment. Figure 8 (left) shows one structure that Take The Best can exploit (there are others; see Martignon & Hoffrage, 1999); Figure 8 (right) shows one that it cannot. Recall that Take The Best is a noncompensatory strategy: It relies on one cue, and even if all others point in the opposite direction, they cannot compensate. Figure 8 shows examples for noncompensatory and compensatory structures. For instance, binary cues with weights that decrease exponentially, such as $\frac{1}{2}, \frac{1}{4}, \frac{1}{8}$, and so on, are noncompensatory—the sum of all cue weights to the right of a cue can never be larger than its own weight. When the environment has the same noncompensatory structure as Take The Best, one can prove mathematically that no linear model, including multiple regression, can outperform the faster and more frugal Take The Best (Martignon & Hoffrage, 1999).

The research program on ecological rationality is in the spirit of the earlier ecological programs of Egon Brunswik and J.J. Gibson. Both were studying the structure of environments, although with different tools: Brunswik was looking for the correlational texture of environments and Gibson for

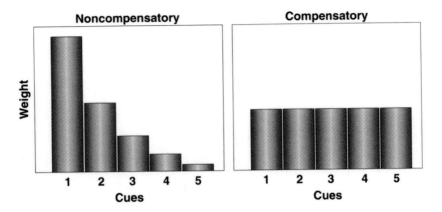

Figure 8. Ecological rationality of Take The Best. One of the structures of environments that Take The Best can exploit is cues with noncompensatory weights, as shown on the left side (Martignon & Hoffrage, 1999).

invariants in the ambient light. Both were behaviorists: They hesitated to model mental strategies, that is, they did not want to open the "black box." Here the program of ecological validity differs: It studies not just environmental structure, but the degree of match between the heuristics in the adaptive toolbox and the structure of environments (Gigerenzer & Todd, 1999). The black box is a toolbox.

Robustness

The second answer to the question "How can one reason be better than many?" is robustness. A strategy is robust to the degree it can be used in new situations. In a situation where there is uncertainty—and there is, for instance, a lot of uncertainty in predicting homelessness—only part of the information one can obtain today will be of predictive value for the future. For instance, if one records the temperature of each day in this year in Chicago, one can find a mathematical equation with sufficiently complex exponential terms that represents the jagged temperature curve almost perfectly. However, this equation may not be the best predictor of next year's temperature; a simpler curve that ignores much of this year's measurements may do better. In other words, only part of the information available in one situation generalizes to another. To make good decisions or predictions under uncertainty, one *has* to ignore much of the information available, and the art is to find *that* part that generalizes. Since Take The Best relies only on the best cue on which the two objects differ, its chances of ignoring less robust information are good.

Note that ecological rationality and robustness are two independent concepts that both explain when simple heuristics work and when they do not. Figure 8 (left) illustrates an environmental structure that Take The Best can exploit, that is, where its use is ecologically rational. This structure makes Take The Best *as* accurate as any linear strategy of whatever complexity. But this noncompensatory structure does not yet explain how Take The Best can actually be *more* accurate than multiple linear regression (for structures that lead to this result see Martignon & Hoffrage, 1999). This result follows when we consider that the results in Figure 7 are about how well the strategies predict new data, rather than fit old data. When making predictions about noisy environments, simpler strategies (e.g., with less free parameters) tend to be more robust than more complex ones. The details of this relationship are given in Geman, Bienenstock, and Doursat (1992) and Forster and Sober (1994). Thus, the example in Figure 8 illustrates when a simple heuristic can be as accurate as any linear strategy (ecological rationality), and the concept of robustness, which enters when predictions need to be made in noisy environments, explains the additional edge that the heuristic has over strategies that use more knowledge and computational power.

WHY MODELS WITH THE BEST FIT ARE NOT NECESSARILY THE BEST

Assume you have several competing models, and you want to determine the one that most likely describes the "true" strategy an individual uses. You have a body of data and find that one model fits the data significantly better than the others. You conclude that the empirical evidence supports this model and propose it as the likely actual decision strategy. Isn't this how science works? Not exactly. There are two ways to select a model: to choose the model with the best fit, or the most robust one. Data fitting measures how well a model can fit *given* data; the generalizability to new data is not evaluated. Robustness refers to a situation where a model estimates its parameters from a learning sample, but is tested on a *new* sample, such as in Figure 7. Surprisingly, most research programs in the behavioral and social sciences never proceed beyond data fitting, and take a good fit as evidence of the validity of the model tested (Roberts & Pashler, 2000). The same strategy can be observed in animal research, such as when the data on avoidance learning in goldfish is explained by a theory with three equations and six adjustable parameters (Zhuikov, Couvillon, & Bitterman, 1994). However, a good fit by itself is not a good reason to choose between competing models. Why is this?

First, mathematical models with a sufficiently large number of adjustable parameters always lead to an excellent fit—*here, a good fit is a mathematical truism, not an empirical validation of a model.* If a model is too powerful (such as a neural network model with numerous hidden units and adjustable parameters), it can fit almost any data, even those generated by contradicting underlying processes. These models are largely immune to being falsified. Success in fitting comes at the price of *overfitting*, that is, fitting noise and idiosyncratic parts of the data that do not generalize to new situations. In contrast, fast and frugal heuristics such as the recognition heuristic, Take The Best, and the Minimalist have no adjustable parameters; all concepts such as the recognition validity and the cue validities are empirically measurable. As a consequence, predictions such as in Equation 1 can be proven wrong. In statistical terminology, models of heuristics show "bias" whereas models with numerous adjustable parameters show "variance" (Geman et al., 1992).

Second, from a Darwinian point of view, the program of identifying behavioral strategies by means of data fitting neglects the function of strategies. For an organism, the best strategy (e.g., foraging, mate search) is not the one that best fits past data in the individual's history, or in the evolutionary history of a species. A better strategy is one that predicts future data. In an uncertain world, these two strategies are *not* the same. (In a certain world they would be the same.) To be useful for new situations, a strategy needs to be robust, that is, not to overfit—but the strategy with the best fit is often the one that overfits most. For instance, in data fitting, multiple regression had the best fit across the 20 problems mentioned before, but in predictive accuracy it took the highest loss and was outperformed by simpler and more robust strategies (see Figure 7). Multiple regression overfitted the data.

CAN COGNITIVE LIMITATIONS BE ADAPTIVE?

Thus, from an evolutionary point of view, heuristics need to generalize to new situations, not to fit memories of past experiences. This argument leads to an—admittedly speculative—answer to the question: Why did humans and other animals not evolve "perfect" cognitive functions, such as perfect memory, attention span, and computational skills? In principle, these abilities might have evolved, as the occasional person with an astonishing memory or computational powers indicates. The answer is that in uncertain environments, precise monitoring and recording of past data is neither necessary nor desirable, because perfect data fitting can be counterproductive. A robust strategy must *ignore* part of the available information. This can be achieved by limited information search, forgetting, or other tools that prevent omniscience. The more uncertain an environment is, the more information that needs to be ignored. The art is to ignore the right information, that is, to pay attention to the proper, powerful cues and forget the rest. Thus, so-called limited information-processing capacities can actually be adaptive, not merely a sign of shoddy mental software.

Ecological rationality and robustness are key research tools of a Darwinian approach to decision making. Ecological rationality differs from logical rationality. It defines the reasonableness of a heuristic by its fit to an environmental structure, not by its fit to laws of logic and internal coherence, such as transitivity and additivity of probabilities. However, a glance through today's journals and textbooks on thinking, intelligence, judgment, and decision making reveals that the structure of environments is not part of the investigation (for an exception see Anderson, 1990). For instance, if an individual ignores relevant cues, ignores the dependencies between cues, and does not even integrate the few cues it knows, it is treated in this literature as an illustration of human irrationality. These fallacies are usually attributed to "limited information-processing capacities," "confirmation biases," and other deficient mental software (see the extensive literature on so-called cognitive illusions, e.g., Piattelli-Palmerini, 1994). Individuals who use Take The Best commit all these three "sins." However, as Figure 7 shows, their decisions can actually be more frugal and more accurate than strategies that look rational by traditional standards. A rethinking of rationality is needed—the ecological way.

THE BUILDING BLOCKS OF THE ADAPTIVE TOOLBOX

Recombining building blocks

The building blocks of the heuristics in the adaptive toolbox include rules for search, stopping search, and decision making. By recombining different building blocks, the adaptive toolbox can create new heuristics. For instance, in a situation in which Take The Best cannot be used because an individual does not have the knowledge to order the cues according to their validity, a less demanding search rule can be used instead that searches for cues in random order or simply tries the cue first that stopped search the last time. This simplification of the search rule results in the Minimalist (see Figure 7) and Take The Last heuristic, respectively (Gigerenzer & Goldstein, 1999). The adaptive toolbox, therefore, has a large number of heuristics at its disposal built from a smaller number of building blocks.

In this chapter, I have described only a few of the heuristics in the adaptive toolbox, and I have focused on heuristics for choice, such as Take The Best. Similar building blocks underlie heuristics for categorization, such as Categorization By Elimination (Berretty et al., 1999) and estimation, such as

QickEst (Hertwig, Hoffrage & Martignon, 1999). Simple heuristics for various important adaptive problems have been identified recently, such as how humans infer intentions from movements (Blythe, Todd, & Miller, 1999), how honey bees choose a location for a new hive (Seeley, 2001), and how to find a mate without optimization (Miller & Todd, 1999). For an overview of what we know about the adaptive toolbox see Gigerenzer et al. (1999) and Gigerenzer and Selten (2001).

Nesting of heuristics

New heuristics can be created not only by recombining building blocks, but also by nesting heuristics. For instance, the recognition heuristic can function as the initial step for Take The Best (Figure 5). The recognition heuristic draws on recognition memory, whereas Take The Best uses recall memory. Recognition memory seems to develop earlier than recall memory, both onto-genetically and evolutionarily, and the nesting of heuristics can be seen as analogous to the addition of a new adaptation on top of an existing one. In other words, a heuristic can become a building block of another heuristic.

Emotions and social norms

In the examples given in this chapter, the building blocks of heuristics were cognitive, such as recognition and ordered search. However, emotions can also function as building blocks for guiding and stopping search. For instance, falling in love can be a powerful stopping rule that ends search for a partner and strengthens commitment to the loved one. Similarly, feelings of parental love, triggered by one's infant's presence or smile, can be seen as commitment tools, which *prevent* cost-benefit computations with respect to proximal goals, so that the question of whether to endure all the sleepless nights and other challenges associated with baby care never arise. For important adaptive tasks, emotion can be more efficient than cognition (Gigerenzer & Todd, 1999; Tooby & Cosmides, 1990). For instance, the stopping rule in satisficing—stop search after the first person is found who meets or exceeds an aspiration level—does not generate the commitment to a partner that love can. When a new and slightly more attractive partner comes along, nothing prevents the satisficer from leaving the partner on the spot. Emotions, like motivations, are substantially domain-specific and are part of the heuristics in the adaptive toolbox. Social norms can also function as tools for bounded rationality, freeing individuals from making a large number of potential decisions. Building blocks and heuristics can be learned in a social manner, through imitation, word of mouth, or cultural heritage—a topic dealt with in Gigerenzer and Selten (2001).

BEYOND DEMONS

In this paper, I introduced the main concepts for the study of the adaptive toolbox: ecological rationality, frugality, robustness, and the building blocks of heuristics—simple rules for search, stopping, and decision. The underlying vision of rationality is that of domain-specific heuristics that do not involve optimization and are ecologically rational when used in a proper environment.

The perspective of the adaptive toolbox conflicts with several attractive ideals. It conflicts with Laplace's superintelligence and Leibniz's dream of a universal calculus and its modern offspring. For instance, if you open a contemporary textbook on human reasoning and decision making, you will notice the predominance of mental logic, probability theory, and the maximization of expected utility—all attempts at attaining the dream of a universal calculus of reason. Heuristics play little role, and if they do, it is mainly in the form of vague words that supposedly "explain" errors in logic and probability theory (see Gigerenzer, 1996). The emphasis on simplicity and transparency conflicts with the preference of many cognitive scientists who are in love with complex mathematical models: The more mathematically sophisticated and nontransparent a model is, the better. For instance, what happens in a neural network is nontransparent, whereas simple heuristics are transparent (Regier, 1996). Finally, simplicity and robustness can conflict with legal values. A doctor who classifies heart-attack patients without having measured all variables runs the risk of being sued. Legal systems, like bureaucracies, often run on the defensive vision that more is always better.

The surprising performance of the heuristics—such as the less-is-more effect and the absence of a trade-off between frugality and accuracy—may give us pause and cause us to rethink the notion of bounded rationality. For many, boundaries come from within the human mind—limited capacities for memory, attention, and other constraints *within* which evolution had to work. However, a Darwinian view would emphasize that the selective forces impinging on our cognitive evolution came largely from outside our minds, from interaction with our physical and social world (Todd, 2001). The notion of ecological rationality provides a framework for understanding the match between heuristics and environment. Simple heuristics are not the shoddy software of a limited mind. Rather, they *enable* adaptive behavior.

Rational choice theory—the idea that sound decisions are reached by optimization, with or without constraints—has been criticized as *descriptively* inadequate, but maintained as the only *normative* standard. The research program of studying the adaptive toolbox goes one step further: It analyzes how sound decisions can actually be made without omniscience, optimization, or a general logical calculus. Psychological theories need less Aristotle and more Darwin.

REFERENCES

Ajzen, I. (1977). Intuitive theories of events and the effects of base-rate information on predictions. *Journal of Personality and Social Psychology*, *35*, 303–314.

Anderson, J.R. (1990). *The adaptive character of thought*. Hillsdale, NJ: Lawrence Erlbaum Associates Inc.

Ayton, P., & Önkal, D. (1997). *Forecasting football fixtures: Confidence and judged proportion correct*. Unpublished manuscript.

Berretty, P.M., Todd, P.M., & Martignon, L. (1999). Categorization by elimination: Using few cues to choose. In G. Gigerenzer, P.M. Todd, & the ABC Research Group, *Simple heuristics that make us smart* (pp. 235–257). New York: Oxford University Press.

Blythe, P.W., Todd P.M., & Miller, G.J. (1999). How motion reveals intention: Categorizing social interactions. In G. Gigerenzer, P.M. Todd, & the ABC Research Group, *Simple heuristics that make us smart* (pp. 257–286). New York: Oxford University Press.

Borges, B., Goldstein, D.G., Ortmann, A., & Gigerenzer, G. (1999). Can ignorance beat the stock market? In G. Gigerenzer, P.M. Todd, & the ABC Research Group, *Simple heuristics that make us smart* (pp. 59–72). New York: Oxford University Press.

Breiman, L., Friedman, J.H., Olshen, R.A., & Stone, C.J. (1993). *Classification and regression trees*. New York: Chapman & Hall.

Bröder, A. (2000). Assessing the empirical validity of the "Take The Best" heuristic as a model of human probabilistic inference. *Journal of Experimental Psychology: Learning, Memory, and Cognition*, *26*, 1332–1346.

Czerlinski, J., Gigerenzer, G., & Goldstein, D.G. (1999). How good are simple heuristics? In G. Gigerenzer, P.M Todd, & the ABC Research Group, *Simple heuristics that make us smart* (pp. 97–118). New York: Oxford University Press.

Dawes, R.M., & Corrigan, B. (1974). Linear models in decision making. *Psychological Bulletin*, *81*, 95–106.

Dugatkin, L.A. (1996). Interface between culturally based preferences and genetic preferences: Female mate choice in Poecilia reticulata. *Proceedings of the National Academy of Sciences*, *93*, 2770–2773.

Forster, M., & Sober, E. (1994). How to tell when simpler, more unified, or less ad hoc theories will provide more accurate predictions. *British Journal of Philosophical Science*, *45*, 1–35.

Galef, B.G., Jr, McQuoid, L.M., & Whiskin, E.E. (1990). Further evidence that Norway rats do not socially transmit learned aversions to toxic baits. *Animal Learning and Behavior*, *18*, 199–205.

Geman, S.E., Bienenstock, E., & Doursat, R. (1992). Neural networks and the bias/variance dilemma. *Neural Computation*, *4*, 1–58.

Gigerenzer, G. (1996). On narrow norms and vague heuristics: A rebuttal to Kahneman and Tversky (1996). *Psychological Review*, *103*, 592–596.

Gigerenzer, G., & Goldstein, D.G. (1996). Reasoning the fast and frugal way: Models of bounded rationality. *Psychological Review*, *103*, 650–669.

Gigerenzer, G., & Goldstein, D.G. (1999). Betting on one good reason: The Take The Best heuristic. In G. Gigerenzer, P.M. Todd, & the ABC Research Group, *Simple heuristics that make us smart* (pp. 75–96). New York: Oxford University Press.

Gigerenzer, G., & Selten, R. (Eds.) (2001). *Bounded rationality: The adaptive toolbox*. Cambridge, MA: MIT Press.

Gigerenzer, G., & Todd, P.M. (1999). Fast and frugal heuristics: The adaptive toolbox. In G. Gigerenzer, P.M. Todd, & the ABC Research Group, *Simple heuristics that make us smart* (pp. 3–34). New York: Oxford University Press.

Gigerenzer, G., Todd, P.M., & the ABC Research Group. (1999). *Simple heuristics that make us smart*. New York: Oxford University Press.

Goldstein, D.G., & Gigerenzer, G. (1999). The recognition heuristic: How ignorance makes us smart. In G. Gigerenzer, P.M. Todd, & the ABC Research Group, *Simple heuristics that make us smart* (pp. 37–58). New York: Oxford University Press.

Goldstein, D.G., & Gigerenzer, G. (2002). Models of ecological rationality: The recognition heuristic. *Psychological Review, 109* (No. 1).

Heckhausen, H. (1991). *Motivation and action* (Translated by Peter K. Leppmann). Berlin: Springer-Verlag.

Hertwig, R., Hoffrage, U., & Martignon, L. (1999). Quick estimation: Letting the environment do the work. In G. Gigerenzer, P.M. Todd, & the ABC Research Group, *Simple heuristics that make us smart* (pp. 209–234). New York: Oxford University Press.

Kelley, H.H., & Michaela, I.L. (1980). Attribution theory and research. *Annual Review of Psychology, 31*, 457–501.

Martignon, L., & Hoffrage, U. (1999). Why does one-reason decision making work? A case study in ecological rationality. In G. Gigerenzer, P.M. Todd, & the ABC Research Group, *Simple heuristics that make us smart* (pp. 119–140). New York: Oxford University Press.

McLeod, P., & Dienes, Z. (1996). Do fielders know where to go to catch the ball or only how to get there? *Journal of Experimental Psychology: Human Perception and Performance, 22*, 531–543.

Piattelli-Palmarini, M. (1994). *Inevitable illusions: How mistakes of reason rule our minds.* New York: Wiley.

Regier, T. (1996). *The human semantic potential. Spatial language and constrained connectionism.* Cambridge, MA: MIT Press.

Rieskamp, J., & Hoffrage, U. (1999). When do people use simple heuristics and how can we tell? In G. Gigerenzer, P.M. Todd, & the ABC Research Group, *Simple heuristics that make us smart* (pp. 141–168). New York: Oxford University Press.

Roberts, S., & Pashler, H. (2000). How persuasive is a good fit? A comment on theory testing. *Psychological Review, 107*, 358–367.

Seeley, T.D. (2001). Decision making in superorganisms: How collective wisdom arises from the poorly informed masses. In G. Gigerenzer & R. Selten (Eds.), *Bounded rationality: The adaptive toolbox* (pp. 249–261). Cambridge, MA: MIT Press.

Simon, H.A. (1956). Rational choice and the structure of environments. *Psychological Review, 63*, 129–138.

Simon, H.A. (1992). *Economics, bounded rationality, and the cognitive revolution.* Aldershot, UK: Elgar.

Stigler, G.J. (1961). The economics of information. *Journal of Political Economy, 69*, 213–225.

Todd, P. (2001). Fast and frugal heuristics for environmentally bounded minds. In G. Gigerenzer & R. Selten (Eds.), *Bounded rationality: The adaptive toolbox.* Cambridge, MA: MIT Press.

Todd, P.M., & Miller, G.F. (1999). From pride and prejudice to persuasion. In G. Gigerenzer, P.M. Todd, & the ABC Research Group, *Simple heuristics that make us smart* (pp. 287–308). New York: Oxford University Press.

Tooby, J., & Cosmides, L. (1990). The past explains the present: Emotional adaptations and the structure of ancestral environments. *Ethology and Sociobiology, 11*, 375–424.

Toscani, O. (1997). *Die Werbung ist ein lächelndes Aas.* Frankfurt: Fischer.

Zhiukov, A.Y., Couvillon, P.A., & Bitterman, M.E. (1994). Quantitative two-process analysis of avoidance conditioning in goldfish. *Journal of Experimental Psychology: Animal Behavior Processes, 20*, 32–43.

CHAPTER TWENTY-TWO

Literacy effects on language and cognition

José Morais
Université Libre de Bruxelles, Belgium

Régine Kolinsky
Université Libre de Bruxelles and FNRS, Belgium

INTRODUCTION

The aim of the present chapter is to draw a brief review of the main empirical evidence, which is available either in the literature or as results from authors' recent work, about the effects of literacy on language and cognition. Concerning language, the evidence is reviewed separately for metalinguistic and linguistic abilities. Brain differences are also evoked. Concerning cognition, we examine, in this order, visual processes, memory, semantic knowledge, reasoning, and executive processes. Finally, we draw the theoretical implications of the reviewed findings.

In the psychological literature, the concept of *literacy* has received two quite different definitions. Some distinctions regarding other concepts are also worth making.

For a number of scholars, mainly cognitive psychologists who subscribe to a modular view of mind, literacy is the ability to read and write. For others, mainly the "social-construction" oriented psychologists, literacy is the whole corpus of knowledge and strategies that is acquired through the constant exercise of those abilities.

We adopt the first meaning for three reasons. First, it is not clear how one could distinguish, within the individual's knowledge database, the part acquired through reading and writing from the part acquired by other means. Second, contrary to whole knowledge, the ability to read and write can be both defined operationally and estimated quantitatively. Third—this is the more important reason for the present purpose—one wants to describe not whole knowledge, which is eminently variable from an individual to another, but how the ability to read and write and the exercise of this ability can change principles of knowledge organization and acquisition.

Literacy is highly associated with *education*. However, the two notions are distinct. Earlier, we defined literacy as the ability to read and write. Now, we define education as the whole corpus of knowledge acquired not exclusively, but for a large part, through the exercise of literacy.

Literacy is also associated with *schooling*. Indeed, they both contribute to the formation of the educated mind. Schooling incorporates many other experiences besides literacy. According to Coppens, Parente, and Lecours (1998, p. 184), "literacy is virtually impossible to separate from schooling". However, although both factors are indistinguishable most of the time, it is possible, as it will be seen below, to find populations in which literacy and schooling are dissociated.

Even before any data is examined, it is certain that literacy must have effects on the human mind. The advantages of a graphic representation over spoken language are, of course, those of a supplementary code. In this particular case, the supplementary code is one of huge potentialities. These include the possibility of much less time- and space-constrained processing, since the taker-up of information can in principle recover the stimulus when and where it is necessary.

Besides, the development of literacy abilities leads to the implementation of a system presenting important modular characteristics such as fast and mandatory processing. Highly specific areas develop in the brain differentially for components of this processing. For example, it was found, using electrodes placed at the surface of the striate and prestriate cortex, that some neurons respond to letters but not to digits (Allison, McCarthy, Nobre, Puce, & Belger, 1994). Indeed, letters tend to co-occur in texts and skilled readers have processed millions and millions of letters. In the same vein, there are areas responding to words and to legal sequences of letters, i.e., to pseudo-words, but not to illegal sequences of consonant strings (e.g., Cohen et al., 2000; Petersen, Fox, Snyder, & Raichle, 1990).

Obviously, the processing system specifically devoted to literacy activities is not isolated from all the other systems involved in language and cognition. There are connections with the spoken language and semantic systems as well as, presumably, with pictorial representations, reasoning, problem solving, control, and executive systems. The acquisition of literacy might in principle influence all these functions through these connections. Thus, it seems justified to undertake a widespread investigation of the possible effects of literacy.

The isolation of the specific effects of literacy can be done empirically by comparing illiterate adults to "ex-illiterate" adults, in other words people who never attended school in childhood but became literate later on in special classes. Differences in performance or behavior exhibited by these two populations provide an indication of the specific effects of literacy. By contrast, whenever both illiterate and ex-illiterate adults perform or behave similarly but display differences in comparison with literate, schooled adults, these differences would reveal schooling, or education, effects.

To our knowledge, Sylvia Scribner and Michael Cole (1981) have carried out the only large-scale investigation of literacy effects. They studied Vai people from Liberia with the initial purpose of using the same comparative design that we have outlined earlier. Given unavoidable confounding with other variables, they then used multiple regression analyses. There were other outstanding studies aimed at examining literacy effects, in particular Alexander Luria's investigation in Central Asia (Luria, 1976). However, as Scribner and Cole pointed out, those studies confounded literacy with other variables, namely—depending on the study—age, schooling, and professional variables.

The literacy effects observed by Scribner and Cole (1981) are relative to the particular case of a syllabary, in which, with the exception of 7 vowels and a nasal, all the symbols (more than 200) represent individual syllables. In the present chapter, we are concerned with another particular case of literacy, *alphabetic literacy*.

The alphabet is a code that represents language roughly at the level of units called phonemes. Acquiring alphabetic literacy requires a greater analytic effort than acquiring syllabic literacy and therefore one could expect alphabetic literacy to elicit larger effects on both language and cognition.

THE EFFECTS OF LITERACY ON LANGUAGE

In the present review of the effects of literacy on language, we distinguish between "knowing language" and "believing about language", in other words between *linguistic* and *metalinguistic* abilities, respectively.

The distinction between linguistic and metalinguistic abilities is actually a distinction between two *levels* of representation and processing: unconscious or unintentional, the former; conscious or intentional, the latter. For example, illiterate adults are able to discriminate between minimal pairs (Adrian, Alegria, & Morais, 1995; Scliar-Cabral, Morais, Nepomuceno, & Kolinsky, 1997) but are unable to manipulate phonemes intentionally (Morais, Bertelson, Cary, & Alegria, 1986; Morais, Cary, Alegria, & Bertelson, 1979). These results are not contradictory if one considers that phonological decoding is a perceptual unconscious process whereas phonological manipulation is a postperceptual conscious process.

Since the main data relative to literacy effects on language were first obtained for the postperceptual level, metalinguistic abilities are considered here before linguistic abilities.

Metalinguistic abilities

Today it is widely accepted that the ability to read and write plays a critical role in the emergence and development of at least some metalinguistic abilities, namely in the phonological domain.

Studies of children have generally shown a dramatic increase in performance on tasks supposed to reflect *phoneme awareness*, from kindergarten to first grade. As Shankweiler and Liberman (1976) pointed out, the dramatic progress in intentional phonemic segmentation observed between ages 5 and 6 years might stem either from the fact that reading instruction typically begins between these ages or from cognitive growth not specifically dependent on training.

Clear-cut evidence on this issue was obtained by comparing illiterate and ex-illiterate adults in Portugal (Morais et al., 1979). The task was either to delete the initial consonant of a short verbal item or to add one at the onset. Illiterates were unable to do either of these tasks, whereas ex-illiterates obtained a high performance level. Nearly half of the illiterate participants did not make a single correct response while nearly half of the ex-illiterate participants succeeded in every trial. These results show that the awareness of phonemes does not develop spontaneously. Learning to read and write allows phoneme awareness to develop.

In a similar vein, Lukatela, Carello, Shankweiler, and Liberman (1995), testing adult unschooled speakers of Serbo-Croatian, found a very clear association between letter knowledge and performance on phoneme deletion. All the subjects (7) who had poor letter recognition ability (less than 50% correct identifications) scored 0% in phoneme deletion, and all the subjects (also 7) who identified all the letters scored between 70 and 100% correct in the same deletion test. It should be noted that in Serbo-Croatian the grapheme-phoneme correspondences are highly transparent.

Using the same kind of procedure as Morais et al. (1979), Read, Zhang, Nie, and Ding (1986) compared alphabetized and nonalphabetized but literate Chinese readers. The performance displayed by the nonalphabetized but literate Chinese adults was similar to that of the Portuguese illiterates, whereas the results obtained by the alphabetized Chinese adults were similar to those of the Portuguese ex-illiterates. From this finding one can conclude that what entails phoneme awareness is not literacy in general but literacy in a writing system that, at some level, represents phonemes.

Morais et al. (1986) showed, moreover, that the illiterates' inability to analyze language is not general, since many of them performed reasonably well in a task involving the deletion of the initial syllable. *Conscious access to syllables* does not depend crucially on alphabetic literacy.

As shown in the same study, many illiterates can also appreciate *rhyme*. Bertelson, De Gelder, Tfouni, and Morais (1989) replicated this finding, which, moreover, was supported quite dramatically by the observations made on illiterate poets (Cary, Morais, & Bertelson, 1989; Morais, 1991; Morais, 1994). Interestingly, in spite of their astonishing ability to produce rhymes in poems, the illiterate poets remained as poor as the other illiterates in consonant deletion. It seems, therefore, that rhyme may be appreciated and produced, even with a degree of accuracy allowing it not to be confounded with mere assonance, on the basis of *unsegmented* phonological representations.

In the same vein, Kolinsky, Cary, and Morais (1987) found that many illiterates were able to say which of two object names, evoked by the presentation of corresponding pictures, *sounds longer*. Still more impressively, some of them were able to resist semantic interference when the longer name referred to a smaller object (for example, when "butterfly" was paired with "cat").

In conclusion, it seems that what alphabetic literacy specifically promotes, as regards phonological aspects, is awareness of phonemes. However, the acquisition of literacy may also help some people to manipulate syllables and appreciate rhyme, as suggested by the fact that, on the average, the ex-illiterate group scored higher than the illiterate group (e.g., Morais et al., 1986).

It ought to be emphasized that, contrary to the basic linguistic abilities, which can only develop in childhood, the awareness of phonemes may be elicited by learning to read in adulthood, as the results of the ex-illiterate people clearly show. In addition, a phoneme deletion training experiment yielded a significant improvement in the performance of illiterate participants (Morais, Content, Bertelson, Cary, & Kolinsky, 1988), similar to the one obtained by preliterate children (Content, Kolinsky, Morais, & Bertelson, 1986). This provides a clear demonstration that there is no critical period for the acquisition of phoneme awareness and literacy.

We consider now whether or not literacy stimulates the emergence of conscious knowledge of the *word* unit. The results obtained depended on task. In illiterates, the command to repeat, one word at a time, an orally presented sentence elicits a segmentation into main syntactic constituents (e.g., "the car / stands / in front of the door"; Cary, 1988). Cary and Verhaeghe (1991) reported that illiterates only produced 4% word segmentations whereas ex-illiterates produced 48% and literate participants 86%. However, in the repetition of the last "bit" of an interrupted sentence, illiterates scored 72% word responses (Cary & Verhaeghe, 1991). In the subsequently presented segmentation task, the same illiterates still produced 80% Subject—Verb—Complement segmentations. Thus, although illiterates are usually biased to process meaning, they may consciously access the word unit.

Linguistic abilities

We consider now possible effects of literacy on linguistic abilities.

Illiterates and ex-illiterates have not been compared for *syntactic abilities*. Karanth, Kudva, and Vijayan (1995) reported so-called literacy effects, but in their study unschooled illiterates were compared with schooled literate people so that the effects obtained could be due to schooling. In addition, the groups' socioeconomic status was not controlled.

Lexical knowledge presumably increases with both literacy activity and schooling. Reading activities would account for about half of the 3000 new words that a schoolchild acquires each year (Nagy, Anderson, & Herman, 1987). One may, however, presume that ex-illiterates who have acquired the ability to read but read infrequently, which implies indeed a rather low level of reading ability, do not have a much larger mental lexicon than illiterates.

The remainder of this section is concerned more specifically with the *phonological abilities* involved in the perception of speech sounds and the recognition of spoken words.

The recognition of spoken language includes the unconscious and mandatory operation of perceptual mechanisms that are biologically determined and require critical experiences in early childhood. They should, in principle, be unaffected by alphabetic literacy. Indeed, the idea that literacy-dependent knowledge does not influence perceptual processes is a plausible one. When the child begins to acquire literacy, his/her basic processes of speech perception have been established long ago and their reorganization under the influence of a still growing, necessarily imperfect and unstable, body of orthographic knowledge would introduce undesirable sources of error in the speech system.

As a matter of fact, four types of phenomena, all related to the extraction of *phonetic information*, were found to be literacy-independent. These phenomena are the following:

1. The *categorical identification* of consonant stimuli spanning an acoustic continuum that differs in terms of voicing or place of articulation.
2. The *McGurk effect*, due to the influence that the visual information about the movements of the speaker's mouth has on the perception of speech, so that, in an incongruent situation, an auditory /ga/ together with a visual /ba/ may lead to the perception of /da/.
3. The *feature blending* error observed in dichotic listening: combining the place value of the stimulus delivered to one ear with the voicing value of the stimulus delivered to the other ear.
4. The *speech unit migration* error, also observed in dichotic listening: reporting a word illusion that, given certain control conditions, can only result from the fact that a unit (e.g., a phoneme) of one stimulus

takes the place of the corresponding unit in the other stimulus. The migration error provides evidence of perceptual segmentation into the involved units.

For all these four phenomena, illiterates behaved like literate participants (Castro, 1993; Kolinsky & Morais, 1996; Morais, Castro, Scliar-Cabral, Kolinsky, & Content, 1987; Morais & Kolinsky, 1994; Morais & Mousty, 1992).

The speech unit migration illusion is less well known than the other phenomena and so deserves additional specification. In this experimental paradigm, a consonant migration effect is obtained when, for example, discriminating between the presence and the absence of the Portuguese target word /biʃu/ in a pair of pseudowords is more difficult when the pair is /kiʃu-bɔvʌ/ than when it is /kiʃu-dɔvʌ/ (detailed description of the technique and of its rationale can be found in Kolinsky, Morais, & Cluytens, 1995, and in Kolinsky & Morais, 1996). Among the units and features examined for the Portuguese language, the initial consonant yielded the strongest migration illusion (Kolinsky & Morais, 1993). For the present purpose, the important point is that this effect was displayed not only by literate participants but also by illiterate adults. This finding was obtained both in Portugal and Brazil (Morais & Kolinsky, 1994). Consistently, preliterate Portuguese children showed the same pattern of performance as the illiterates (Castro, Vicente, Morais, Kolinsky, & Cluytens, 1995). This means that, at least for the Portuguese language, consonants have psychological reality at the perceptual level of processing, and that their role in speech perception can be demonstrated in a population that is unable to represent them consciously (Liberman, Shankweiler, Fisher, & Carter, 1974; Morais et al., 1979, 1986).

In sum, while conscious representations of phonemes are acquired under the influence of learning alphabetic literacy, unconscious perceptual representations of units that correspond to our concept of phoneme develop prior to the onset of literacy.

Literacy-dependent knowledge might nevertheless influence the recognition of spoken language at late stages of processing. According to the stage-processing model of spoken word recognition (Kolinsky, 1998; Morais & Kolinsky, 1994; Morais, Kolinsky, Ventura, & Cluytens, 1997; Ventura, Kolinsky, Brito-Mendes, & Morais, 2001), spoken word recognition involves two broad stages, perceptual and postperceptual. Whereas at the first stage, operations of segmentation of the acoustic information into perceptual units are modular in the Fodor's (1983) sense of modularity, at the second stage the perceptual output is re-elaborated by attentional processes before conscious recognition of the word is reached.

Contrary to highly interactive models of spoken word recognition (e.g., McClelland & Elman, 1986), this kind of partially autonomous and partially interactive model may quite easily incorporate the assumption that phonological representations are independent from literacy-related knowledge at the perceptual stage but modulated by it at a postperceptual stage.

Evidence for literacy effects on spoken word recognition is suggested, for instance, by the comparison of illiterate and literate Portuguese listeners as regards the so-called phonological fusion effect. The phonological fusion effect (e.g., hearing "black" when presented dichotically with "back"–"lack") gives evidence of intrasyllabic perceptual analysis. Illiterate as well as literate people display it similarly when the spelling of the potential fusion of, e.g., "pena" and "lena", is consistent with the spelling of the corresponding word (PLENA). However, when there is inconsistency, for example, when /par/–/lar/ would yield the word /plar/, which is spelled PELAR, the illusion is strongly reduced in the literate participants. This suggests that the recombination process, subsequent to segmentation, is inhibited, or that its outcome is corrected, by spelling knowledge (Castro & Morais, unpublished data reported by Morais & Kolinsky, 1995).

Besides, there is evidence for a literacy effect on the use of attentional processes in word recognition. In a dichotic word recognition experiment (Morais et al., 1987), we calculated the proportion of errors on one segment only, for instance on the initial consonant (segmental errors), and the proportion of errors on at least both segments of a syllable (global errors). The results showed that the proportion of segmental errors was higher in literate than in illiterate people, whereas the proportion of global errors showed the opposite trend. This effect may reflect the availability in literate people, who are aware of phonemes, of an attentional mechanism focusing on the phonemic structure of speech. That this mechanism is at least in part strategic was demonstrated by a further experiment with university students in which the pattern of errors was more "segmental" when the listeners were instructed to pay attention to the phonemes than when they were not (Castro, 1993; Morais, Castro, & Kolinsky, 1991).

To sum up, it appears that alphabetic literacy does not affect early phonetic processing, but that it may have an effect on later processing, either by allowing orthographic knowledge to influence the integration of phonemic sequences or by contributing to the deployment of a phonemic attentional strategy.

Brain differences for language

Whether or not there are brain differences between literate and illiterate people has been matter of debate for a long time. This issue was first examined as regards hemispheric specialization for language. Several authors considered the hypothesis that illiterates display less left-hemisphere specialization for language than literate people. In spite of some discrepant results, it seems clear today that this hypothesis is wrong. The number of cases with aphasic symptoms due to left-hemisphere lesions is similar in literate and illiterate patients (Damasio, Castro-Caldas, Grosso, & Ferro, 1976). Moreover, in the dichotic listening situation, when one calculates an index of laterality that takes differences in overall performance into account, the right-ear superiority for verbal material is similar in literate and illiterate people (Castro & Morais, 1987).

Obviously, as indicated in the Introduction, specific areas in the brain subtend the processing of written language. It may also be the case that some neural pathways are more developed in literate than in illiterate people because these pathways, for instance the fibers of some parts of the corpus callosum, play a role in literacy activities (Castro-Caldas et al., 1999).

A distinct question is whether or not brain areas not directly involved in reading and writing differ between these groups.

Recently, Castro-Caldas, Petersson, Reis, Stone-Elander, and Ingvar (1998), using PET imagery, investigated brain differences between literate and illiterate people for speech repetition. While there was no brain activation difference between literate and illiterate people during word repetition, the two groups did not activate the same neural structures during pseudoword repetition. The two groups also differed from each other in pseudoword repetition performance. We suggest that, in the repetition task, literate people use an attentional strategy based on segmental phonological representations. Illiterate people could not develop this strategy, because they are not aware of phoneme segments. They could repeat words correctly because they were helped by the availability of the corresponding phonological forms in the mental lexicon. This interpretation accounts well for the fact that Petersson, Reis, Askelöf, Castro-Caldas, and Ingvar (2000), reanalyzing the brain data, found that network interactions were different during word and pseudoword repetition only in the illiterate group.

It is important to note also that the literacy effect on repetition may require more than just the knowledge of orthography. In fact, we had found that ex-illiterates are not better than illiterates on pseudoword repetition (cf. Morais & Mousty, 1992). Thus, it seems that only a literacy experience typical of schooled people can support the development of such a segmental strategy. Indeed, the absence of a difference between illiterates and ex-illiterates may be related to the ex-illiterates having reached an insufficient level of literacy.

LITERACY EFFECTS ON COGNITION

Effects on visual cognition

For visual cognition, as for language, we must distinguish between on the one hand, early perceptual processes leading to object recognition, and on the other hand, postperceptual processes involved in the conscious, intentional analysis of the perceptual representation (cf. Kolinsky & Morais, 1999). As regards early perceptual processes, one of the phenomena used to study the extraction of features from the visual stimulus is the occurrence of illusory conjunctions under masking and distraction conditions. Kolinsky (1989) found a clear increase of feature extraction between 5 and 7 years of age. However, comparing illiterate and literate adults, we (Kolinsky, Morais, & Verhaeghe, 1994) found no difference at all.

For conscious postperceptual analytic processes, differences between literate and illiterate people have been reported in the literature (for example, Luria, 1976). There is now evidence that such differences are not associated with literacy but actually to schooling level, since ex-illiterates do not generally perform above illiterates. For example, in part verification or detection of three more or less dispersed segments within a figure, unschooled adults obtained much poorer scores than second graders, but there was no significant difference between illiterates and ex-illiterates (e.g., Kolinsky, Morais, & Brito Mendes, 1990; Kolinsky, Morais, Content, & Cary, 1987).

Curiously, ex-illiterates displayed better mirror-image discrimination skills than illiterates (Verhaeghe & Kolinsky, 1992). This literacy effect might be related to the fact that our writing system includes mirror-image letters like "b" vs. "d". Readers of a written system that does not incorporate mirror-image signs (the Tamil syllabary) are as poor as illiterates in discriminating mirror-images (Danziger & Pederson, 1999). However, other activities (e.g., lace-making) drawing the observer's attention to the left-right orientation of the stimuli may promote mirror image discrimination as well (Verhaeghe & Kolinsky, 1992). Thus, one can conclude that no genuine, specific effect of literacy is observed in visual cognition.

Luria's (1976, p. 22) claim, according to which "neither the processing of elementary visual information nor the analysis of visual objects conforms to the traditional laws of psychology", thus seems unmotivated. On the one hand, unschooled literates and ex-illiterates do not differ from more educated people at the level of perceptual, nonexplicit processes of feature extraction. On the other hand, only schooling and not literacy per se affects conscious analysis in visual cognition.

Literacy effects on memory

We examine next the possibility of literacy effects on memory, especially short-term memory.

Illiterates displayed a rhyme effect in the immediate ordered recall of a series of pictures, thus showing that they spontaneously use phonological codes (Morais et al., 1986). In this task, the memory span of both illiterates and ex-illiterates was far smaller than the span obtained by the literate adults. In recent work carried out in Brazil (Morais, Da Silva, Dos Passos, Grimm-

Cabral, & Kolinsky, unpublished data), our group confirmed this schooling effect in a digit span task and found in addition a small but significant difference between illiterates and ex-illiterates. This literacy effect may actually be due to the fact that ex-illiterates had also received instruction on arithmetic operations.

The poor digit and word spans of unschooled people is not due to output constraints like, for example, the interference that might result, in each trial, from the production of an item on the production of other items. Indeed, in a probed recall situation, in which the participants were asked to produce only one item, the one following a probe in the series, the spans of the unschooled people remained very small.

Ex-illiterate people with a few months of literacy instruction presented, as is usually the case in literate people, a larger span for words than for pseudo-words. This suggests that people with a very rudimentary level of literacy instruction can use lexical specifications of the item phonological structure, i.e. long-term representations, and not only phonological short-term memory, to supplement recall. However, they lacked the length effect (contrasting monosyllabic and trisyllabic items) that was displayed in our study by a group of fourth-grade children. Poorer performance for longer items compared to shorter ones can be due to the burden that the former items provoke on verbal encoding and rehearsal and/or on the mapping of phonological representations onto output plans (cf. Henry, Turner, Smith, & Leather, 2000). It thus seems that, by enhancing one or both of these two capacities, the activities involved in schooling contribute to make item length a relevant variable.

Interestingly, we found an interaction between the nature of the material used in the span task and schooling. The superiority of the schooled people over the unschooled was greater in the digit span task than in the Corsi's blocks task, thus greater with verbal than with visuospatial material. A further experiment using Corsi's blocks showed that the unschooled participants could greatly benefit from well-structured tapping sequences compared to ill-structured ones.

Finally, it is worth noting that Scribner and Cole (1981) compared illiterates to Qur'anic literate people for recall of studied lists of words. When there was no order constraint on recall, there was no literacy effect. However, for ordered recall, the literate participants, presumably influenced by the incremental method of learning the Qur'an, performed better than the illiterates.

Briefly, empirical evidence points to a strong effect of schooling on performance in memory tasks. As regards the possibility of a specific effect of literacy, the only positive data collected up to now are in all likelihood related to particular conditions of literacy acquisition (simultaneous instruction on arithmetic operations and incremental text learning). Anyway, further research on this issue would be useful both to investigate more systematically possible literacy effects and to highlight the differences in memory abilities at encoding, retention, and retrieval stages, between schooled and unschooled people.

Literacy effects on semantic knowledge and organization

In his study of illiterate and unschooled populations in Central Asia, Luria (1976) devoted much attention to classification abilities. His assumption was that these people "would be unable to group objects—or even to pick out their abstract features—according to abstract semantic categories" (p. 18). Luria found that the way in which the illiterate unschooled individuals grouped drawings of objects "hinged on concrete, situational thinking rather than abstract operations" (p. 77). According to his observations, they remained unconvinced by "every attempt to suggest the possibility of categorical grouping" (p. 77). They do not use words "to codify objects in conceptual schemes but to establish the practical interrelationship of those objects" (p. 99). Thus, to this author, concrete thinking and the lack of categorical classification result from illiteracy and rudimentary types of activity.

As noted earlier, Luria (1976) did not distinguish clearly between literacy and schooling. Scribner and Cole (1981), studying the Vai people, and looking for literacy effects independent of those of schooling, found results that "discourage conclusions about a strong influence of literacy on categorization and abstraction" (p. 124).

There is, however, a preliminary and more important issue. This concerns Luria's (1976) conclusion that illiterate unschooled people lack taxonomic knowledge. This conclusion seems questionable if one takes into account the fact that the categorization capacity appears very early in development. Three-year-olds already understand the logic of class inclusion, for example that "car" and "bike" belong to the superordinate "vehicle" (Markman, 1984). Four-year-olds are able to match figures in terms of taxonomic category. Presented with fish, car, and boat, they put the last two together, in spite of the fact that fishes and boats are found in water (Rosch, Mervis, Gray, Johnson, & Boyes-Braem, 1976). By the same age, children can very efficiently use, as cues in recall tasks, schematic (zoo-elephant) and superordinate (animal-elephant) relations between cue and target (Blewitt & Toppino, 1991). In 5-year-olds, categorical relationships led to more false recognitions of a probe in a sentence than the part-whole relationship (Mansfield, 1977). Furthermore, these children were more affected when the probe was a superordinate than when it was a subordinate. This directional effect argues against the interpretation that young children simply learned category names as synonyms (e.g., "Lassy", "dog", and "animal" as alternative names). Finally, Radeau (1983) observed an auditory semantic priming effect in 6-year-olds when primes and targets were taxonomically related (coordinate: "arm-leg", or superordinate: "fruit-apple"). All these findings seem to reflect the taxonomic organization of semantic memory in preliterate children.

These developmental data and Luria's (1976) observations on illiterate unschooled people appear to be discrepant. This discrepancy can be accounted for in two ways. One possibility is that adults who are not stimulated to think categorically lose this knowledge. The other possibility is that they keep taxonomic knowledge but develop a strong preference for practical schemes.

In recent unpublished work carried out in Brazil in collaboration with Scliar-Cabral and Monteiro, we used a classification test requiring the participants to match a target with either a taxonomically related or an unrelated item. Illiterates made about as many taxonomic choices (93% and 82% for images and words, respectively) as poorly literate people did. The latter participants were adults who had completed only four school grades in childhood.

In another test, participants were presented with 12 drawings taken from four categories and were required to group them. Illiterates grouped the items correctly. Moreover, most of their verbal justifications were of a taxonomic kind. However, there was an increase with educational level of the responses consisting of near superordinates.

When asked to provide a superordinate term for three items, the illiterate group provided the nearest superordinate in almost half of the trials. The proportion of these responses was not significantly different from the one given by the adults who had completed 4 years in school. However, the comparison with the more educated groups shows a clear schooling effect.

Interestingly, when asked to choose between a taxonomic and a functional relationship, both illiterate and poorly literate participants chose the taxonomic relationship less frequently than the more educated people. Even when the choice was taxonomic, they sometimes offered a functional justification. For example, the "bus" and the "kettle" were matched "because when people travel they like to drink coffee, it's so tasty". In the same vein, the "ring" and the "scissors" were matched "because, if I don't cut my fingernails with scissors, I can't put the ring on and won't be pretty". These justifications are consistent with Luria's (1976) observations. Thus, categorical thinking is strongly stimulated by schooling.

Finally, in fluency tests, the illiterates produced, on the average, 12.9 words per semantic category (animals, furniture, vehicles, etc.) in 2 minutes and the poorly literate adults 11.9. Highly educated people produced 23.9. Previous studies by Reis and Castro-Caldas (1997) and by Ratcliff et al. (1998), in Portugal and India, respectively, also reported that illiterate unschooled adults were inferior to literate schooled ones. More interesting, however, is the analysis of the sequence of responses. In our study, we calculated the ratio of subcategory repetitions (Bousfield, 1953) and the mean size of consistent subcategory groupings (Troyer, Moscovitch, & Winocur, 1997). These measures, indicating taxonomic clustering, were similar in all the literacy groups tested. Thus, illiterates display both categorical knowledge and a hierarchical organization of categories. On the contrary, the number of subcategories present in the participants' responses increased with the degree of education. Obviously, content knowledge is influenced both by the experience of literacy (since much information is acquired through reading) and by schooling. For example, knowledge about biological categories, as revealed by the entries of the Oxford English Dictionary, increased from the 16th to the 19th centuries but then greatly declined (Wolff, Medin, & Pankratz, 1999).

It is also interesting to note that, in free recall tasks, when item categories are explicitly indicated to the participants or simply suggested by having them sort the items into piles, illiterates rely on category organization (Cole, Gay, Glick, & Sharp, 1971; Scribner, 1974).

To sum up, illiterate people possess hierarchically organized taxonomic knowledge. However, both illiterate and ex-illiterate people prefer, in most situations, to establish relations on the basis of their own life experience and of some functional attributes of the objects. Thus, schooling rather than literacy stimulates categorical thinking as well as, obviously, the acquisition of content knowledge.

Literacy effects on reasoning

Both Goody (1968) and Luria (1976) considered literacy to be a precondition for syllogism. For example, Luria (1976) reported that illiterates could not perceive the logical relation between the parts of the syllogism. However, according to Scribner and Cole (1981), logic problems demonstrated the strongest effects of schooling, and neither Vai nor Arabic literacy had an effect on number of correct responses or on theoretical justifications. Coherently with Scribner and Cole's view, in Brazil, Tfouni (1988) noticed that 5 out of the 16 illiterates that she interviewed could understand and explain syllogisms after displaying the behavior described by Luria. For example, one illiterate participant was presented with the following syllogism: "These people only visit their friends on Sundays. Today they are visiting their friends. What day is today?" He first responded: "I like to go and visit on Saturday night; then, the day after, I can sleep until late in the morning." At this point, the examiner read the syllogism again, and the participant said: "Only on Sundays? Well, we are Sunday. Given what you said, I should answer Sunday".

A clear case of schooling influence concerns the "intelligence" tests, including the Raven Progressive Matrices (Coloured Progressive Matrices and Standard Progressive Matrices, Raven, 1963, 1969). The dramatic effect we observed, however, seems to stem from differences in educational level rather than from literacy. As a matter of fact, differences between illiterates and ex-illiterates were not obtained in this test (Cary, 1988; Verhaeghe, 1999). For example, in comparison with Raven, Court, and Raven's (1990) norms for 7-year-old European and American children, both illiterates and ex-illiterates performed at the percentile 50, and below that percentile when compared to adults of similar average age.

Huge schooling effects had already been reported in studies on poorly educated adults (e.g., Raven, 1973; Verhaegen, 1956). In addition, in the last decades, there has been an increase of performance on the Raven Progressive Matrices (e.g., Flynn, 1987; Neisser, 1998; Raven, 2000). For example, there has been an increase of 21 IQ points between 1952 and 1982 in the Netherlands, where all young males had to run it as part of a military induction requirement (Flynn, 1987). This increase may be partly related to an increase in the mean number of schooling years, which probably includes an increasing familiarization with ordered matrices.

However, the sources of the unschooled people's inferiority in intelligence tests may be multiple. In some versions of the test it is necessary not only to extract abstract relations from a series of meaningless figures but also, as Neisser (1998, p. 10) writes, to perform "a special form of visual analysis (. . .): each entry must be dissected into the simple line segments of which it is composed before the process of abstraction can operate". As we have seen earlier, this kind of cognitive, explicit visual analysis is itself strongly influenced by schooling (cf. Kolinsky et al., 1987, 1990). The visual complexity of the task seems to affect illiterates and unschooled, ex-illiterates in the same way, showing once again that visual cognition is influenced by schooling but not by literacy.

Interestingly, on the items of the Colored Progressive Matrices that involve more specifically analogical reasoning, there was no difference between illiterates and ex-illiterates either. Actually, both groups obtained virtually null scores on these problems, and, as illustrated by their spontaneous comments, were very reluctant to solve them. For example, one of the ex-illiterate participants seemed much more worried by aesthetic than by logical criteria in the choice of his response. Although not influenced by literacy, abstract analogical reasoning on geometrical figures does not seem to be part of the unschooled mind's universe.

Hypothetico-deductive reasoning in unschooled people was investigated recently in Brazil (Morais, Mengarda, Grimm-Cabral, & Kolinsky, 2001). We tested illiterates, semiliterate adults (who succeeded in school until the 4th or 5th grade) and university academics on Wason's (1966) selection task. This is a reasoning task that involves a conditional rule that is conventionally expressed as "if P then Q". Evaluation of the truth or falsity of the rule must logically focus upon the conjunction of P and *not-Q*, since only this conjunction can falsify the rule. Wason's task invites participants to specify which of four possible cases need to be investigated in order to establish the truth or falsity of such a rule. In our study, the participants were shown four cards. On the visible face were, for example, Pelé (a famous Brazilian soccer player), Gustavo Kuerten ("Guga", a famous Brazilian tennis player), a soccer ball, and a tennis racquet. They were told that, when the visible face showed a famous player, on the invisible face there was a piece of sports equipment, and vice-versa. They were required to point the cards that needed to be turned over to check the following statement "If there is Pelé on one side of the card, then there is a soccer ball on the other side of the card". The university people performed far better than the illiterates, on the average. However, the most interesting result is the fact that the best performers, with 9 entirely correct choices in 10 trials, were one illiterate and one academic. The successful illiterate responded quickly in all the correct trials, picking systematically the less obvious *not-Q* card before the *P* one (in the example, the cards showing the tennis racquet and Pelé, respectively). However, when, at the end, he was asked to justify his choices, he was unable to provide any verbal explanation. It thus seems that correct hypothetico-deductive reasoning may be observed in a minority of illiterate people, even if there is no explicit verbal access to the underlying mental operations. Current investigations are examining whether more illiterates may succeed on the Wason task when more pragmatic schema (e.g., conditional permission rules) are used, as has been shown with young—although already schooled—children (e.g., Frydman, Light, & Alegria, 1999).

Literacy effects on executive processes

Executive processes seem to separate into at least three different functions: shifting back and forth between multiple tasks, operations, or mental sets; updating and monitoring of representations; and deliberate inhibiting of dominant or prepotent responses (see, e.g., Miyake, Friedman, Emerson, Witzki, & Howerter, 2000).

A prototypical inhibition task is the Stroop task, in which one needs to inhibit the tendency to produce a more dominant or automatic response (in the classical Stroop test, to name the color word, cf. Stroop, 1935). In recent work run in Brazil (Kolinsky, Da Silva & Morais, 2001) we used a digit Stroop test, given that most illiterates can identify digit symbols. The task was to report the number of symbols appearing on a computer screen rather than their numerical value (e.g., to answer "3" to the stimulus "2 2 2"). Literate participants were significantly faster than illiterate and ex-illiterate ones, but the size of the interference effect observed in the incongruent condition and of the facilitation observed in the congruent condition did not vary between the groups.

However, the ability to inhibit irrelevant information and to selectively attend to one dimension of the stimulus, although not affected by literacy, seems to depend on schooling level. Using Garner's (1974) paradigm of visual speeded classification, Kolinsky (1988) and Verhaeghe (1999) found that Portuguese unschooled adults (both illiterates and ex-illiterates) have some difficulty at selectively attending to, e.g., the form dimension when color is varied orthogonally.

The California Card Sorting Test involves shifting between various alternative classification criteria. In an adaptation of this task, in which six cards could be classified according to two semantic and three perceptual criteria, Brazilian illiterates and ex-illiterates could shift from one type of dimension to the other and performed similarly (Kolinsky et al., 2001). When compared with a literate group there was a schooling effect, with literate people finding more criteria, but the lack of interaction between group and criterion indicates that the relative tendency to focus on perceptual or semantic criteria was universal.

The function of updating and monitoring representations is closely linked to the notion of working memory. As a matter of fact, some tasks require appropriately revising the items held in working to keep track of which information is old and no longer relevant, and replacing it by newer, more relevant information (e.g., Jonides & Smith, 1997; Miyake et al., 2000; Morris & Jones, 1990). This is the case, for example, in the running digit span task, which requires recalling the last *n* digits of a sequence that was stopped at an unpredictable position. The effect of schooling was again observed in this task, but the effect of literacy was not significant (Kolinsky et al., 2001). This suggests that illiterates are not specifically poorer than ex-illiterates for the executive component of working memory.

Planning ability was more specifically evaluated with the Tower of London test (cf. Shallice, 1982), although this test (also called in some versions the "Tower of Hanoi") also involves an important inhibition component (see, e.g., Miyake et al., 2000). In the Tower of London test, a starting configuration of a three-dimensional puzzle, consisting of three differently colored disks positioned on three pegs of varying size, has to be reconfigured into a goal state in the fewest moves possible. The main constraint is that participants can only move one disk at a time. Thus, a sequence of moves must be planned, monitored, and possibly revised, and in some trials, an incorrect move suggested by a local resemblance with the goal state has to be inhibited. The results showed no significant difference between illiterate and ex-illiterate participants in either number of movements or time of execution. Both groups tended to present more movements than literates, and took less time before initiating their response than literates, in particular for complex items. Careful planning thus seems to be a more common strategy in schooled than in unschooled people, although it is far from clear whether all educated people use such a strategy (e.g., see discussion in Miyake et al., 2000). In any case, literacy per se does not seem to favor it.

It is interesting to note that the Tower of London test involves both visuospatial working memory and executive components of working memory (either general or specific to the visuospatial system). For example, concurrent articulation has a beneficial effect on performance whereas pattern tapping has a detrimental one (Philipps, Wynn, Gilhooly, Della Sala, & Logie, 1999). The illiterates' behavior in the Tower of London test is consistent with the fact mentioned earlier, that illiterates (actually the same subjects) are relatively good, although inferior to the literate group, in the Corsi task. It also appears that the small inferiority displayed by the illiterates in the Corsi task should not be attributed to an executive functioning impairment.

CONCLUSIONS

Trying to summarize the findings presented here on language, visual cognition, memory, semantic knowledge, reasoning and executive processes, it seems justified to say that the effects of literacy are rather circumscribed. At this point in our inquiry, it appears that the acquisition of alphabetic literacy influences metaphonological development, being responsible for the establishment of phoneme awareness, and that it stimulates some spoken language processing strategies, but nothing else, as can be observed in Table 1.

We are thus much closer to denying literacy per se a role in the development of the human mind structure than to making literacy responsible for the emergence of a new kind of mind. Literacy significantly changes neither the pre-existent modular systems involved in speech and visual perception nor the basic nonmodular cognitive processes that are involved in attending to and categorizing information in abstract ways, selecting and inhibiting information, planning actions, etc.

Scribner and Cole (1981) wrote: "If we were to regard only general consequences as worthy of serious attention, we would have to dismiss literacy activities among the Vai as being of little psychological interest" (p. 234). Having noted this, Scribner and Cole proposed that the practices of literacy rather than literacy skills per se might have great cognitive consequences, the most apparent being what they called "verbal explanation". The findings reviewed here support this idea. Schooling and the practice of literacy of which it is part seem to have more dramatic cognitive effects than literacy per se, especially on the development of both knowledge bases and higher-level strategic processes of explicit analysis of information.

TABLE 22.1
An overview of the cognitive effects of literacy

Language
Early perceptual processes—NO
Recognition strategies—YES
Word and pseudoword repetition—NO (but influence of schooling)
Phoneme awareness—YES (huge effect)
Other metaphonological abilities—NO (for some individuals)
Lexical growth—YES (also influenced by schooling)
Notion of word—YES (but task-dependent)
Syntactic abilities:—? (effect may be due to schooling)

Visual cognition
Early perceptual processes—NO
Recognition of incomplete/superimposed/local versus global figures—NO (but schooling effects in some cases)
Fragment detection—NO (huge effect of schooling)
Dimensional classification—NO (effect of schooling)
Mirror-image discrimination—YES (but literacy is not necessary)
Mental rotation—NO

Memory
Phonological coding in short-term memory—YES and *NO* (available, but less precise)
Orthographic or symbolic coding in short-term memory—YES (obvious)
Visuospatial working memory—NO (but possible schooling effect)
Phonological loop—YES (poor rehearsal, but this may be due to schooling)
Recall of studied lists of words—NO (but possible effect on ordered recall)

Semantic knowledge and abilities
Categorical (taxonomic) knowledge—NO
Hierarchical organization of categories—NO
Categorical thinking—NO (but increase due to schooling)
Content knowledge—YES (additional influence of schooling)

Reasoning
Syllogisms—? (effect may be due to schooling)
Raven's Progressive Matrixes—NO (effect due to schooling)
Analogical reasoning—NO (effect due to schooling)
Conditional hypothesis testing—? (effect may be due to schooling)

Executive functions
Selective attention—NO (but a schooling effect for visual dimensions)
Flexibility in dimensional shifting—NO
Inhibitory processes—NO
Planning actions to reach a goal—NO (but schooling effect)
Executive component of working memory—NO

ACKNOWLEDGEMENTS

Preparation of this paper was supported by the National Fund for Scientific Research (FNRS, convention 1.5.119.99). The second author is a Research Associate of the FNRS.

REFERENCES

Adrián, J.A., Alegria, J., & Morais, J. (1995). Metaphonological abilities of Spanish illiterate adults. *International Journal of Psychology*, *30*, 329–353.

Allison, T., McCarthy, G., Nobre, A., Puce, A., & Belger, A. (1994). Human extrastriate visual cortex and the perception of faces, words, numbers, and colors. *Cerebral Cortex*, *4*, 544–554.

Bertelson, P., De Gelder, B., Tfouni, L.V., & Morais, J. (1989). Metaphonological abilities of adult illiterates: New evidence of heterogeneity. *European Journal of Cognitive Psychology*, *1*, 239–250.

Blewitt, P., & Toppino, T.C. (1991). The development of taxonomic structure in lexical memory. *Journal of Experimental Child Psychology*, *51*, 296–319.

Bousfield, W.A. (1953). The occurrence of clustering in recall of randomly arranged associates. *Journal of General Psychology*, *49*, 229–240.

Cary, L. (1988). *A análise explícita das unidades da fala nos adultos não alfabetizados*. Unpublished Doctoral dissertation, University of Lisbon.

Cary, L., Morais, J., & Bertelson, P. (1989). A consciência fonológica dos poetas analfabetos. *Anais do Simpósio Latino-Americano de Psicologia do Desenvolvimento* (pp. 160–166). Recife, Brazil: Ed. Universitária da EFPE.

Cary, L., & Verhaeghe, A. (1991). Efeito da prática da linguagem ou da alfabetização no conhecimento das fronteiras formais das unidades lexicais: Comparação de dois tipos de tarefas. *Actas das 1as Jornadas de Estudo dos Processos Cognitivos* (pp. 33–49).

Castro, S.L. (1993). *Alfabetização e percepção da fala*. Porto, Portugal: Instituto Nacional de Investigação Científica.

Castro, S.L., & Morais, J. (1987). Ear differences in illiterates. *Neuropsychologia*, *25*, 409–417.

Castro, S.L., Vicente, S., Morais, J., Kolinsky, R., & Cluytens, M. (1995). Segmental representation of Portuguese in 5- and 6-year olds: Evidence from dichotic listening. In I. Hub Faria & J. Freitas (Eds.), *Studies on the acquisition of Portuguese. Proceedings of the First Lisbon Meeting on Child Language* (pp. 1–16). Lisboa, Portugal: Colibri.

Castro-Caldas, A., Miranda, P., Carmo, I., Reis, A., Leote, F., Ribeiro, C., & Ducla-Soares, E. (1999). Influence of learning to read and write on the morphology of the corpus callosum. *European Journal of Neurology*, *6*, 23–28.

Castro-Caldas, A., Petersson, K.M., Reis, A., Stone-Elander, S., & Ingvar, M. (1998). The illiterate brain. Learning to read and write during childhood influences the functional organization of the adult brain. *Brain*, *121*, 1053–1063.

Cohen, L., Dehaene, S., Naccache, L., Lehéricy, L. Dehaene-Lamberts, G., Hénaff, M.-A., & Michel, F. (2000). The visual word form area. Spatial and temporal characterization of an initial stage of reading in normal subjects and posterior split-brain patients. *Brain*, *123*, 291–307.

Cole, M., Gay, J., Glick, J.A., & Sharp, D.W. (1971). *The cultural context of learning and thinking*. New York: Basic Books.

Content, A., Kolinsky, R., Morais, J. & Bertelson, P. (1986). Phonetic segmentation in prereaders: Effect of corrective information. *Journal of Experimental Child Psychology*, *42*, 49–72.

Coppens, P., Parente, M.A.M.P., & Lecours, A.R. (1998). Aphasia in illiterate individuals. In

P. Coppens, Y. Lebrun, & A. Basso (Eds.), *Aphasia in atypical populations* (pp. 175–202). Mahwah, NJ: Lawrence Erlbaum Associates Inc.

Damasio, A.R., Castro-Caldas, A., Grosso, J.T., & Ferro, J.M. (1976). Letter to the Editor. *Archives of Neurology, 33,* 300–301.

Danziger, E., & Pederson, E. (1999). Through the looking-glass: Literacy, writing systems and mirror-image discrimination. *Written Language and Literacy, 1,* 153–164.

Flynn, J.R. (1987). Massive IQ gains in 14 nations: What IQ tests really measure. *Psychological Bulletin, 101,* 171–191.

Fodor, J.A. (1983). *The modularity of mind.* Cambridge, MA: MIT Press.

Frydman, O., Light, P., & Alegria, J. (1999). Pragmatic determinants of children's responses to the Wason selection task. *Psychologia, 42,* 59–68.

Garner, W.R. (1974). *The processing of information and structure.* Potomac, NJ: Lawrence Erlbaum Associates Inc.

Goody, J. (1968). *Literacy in traditional societies.* Cambridge: Cambridge University Press.

Henry, L.A., Turner, J.E., Smith, P.T., & Leather, C. (2000). Modality effects and the development of the word length effect in children. *Memory, 8,* 1–17.

Jonides, J., & Smith, E.E. (1997). The architecture of working memory. In M.D. Rugg (Ed.), *Cognitive neuroscience* (pp. 243–276). Cambridge, MA: MIT Press.

Karanth, P., Kudva, A., & Vijayan, A. (1995). Literacy and linguistic awareness. In B. de Gelder & J. Morais (Eds.), *Speech and reading. A comparative approach* (pp. 303–316). Hove, UK: Psychology Press.

Kolinsky, R. (1988). *La séparabilité des propriétés dans la perception des formes.* Unpublished Doctoral dissertation, Université Libre de Bruxelles.

Kolinsky, R. (1989). The development of separability in visual perception. *Cognition, 33,* 243–284.

Kolinsky, R. (1998). Spoken word recognition: A stage-processing approach to language differences. *The European Journal of Cognitive Psychology, 10,* 1–40.

Kolinsky, R., Cary, L., & Morais, J. (1987). Awareness of words as phonological entities: The role of literacy. *Applied Psycholinguistics, 8,* 223–232.

Kolinsky, R., Da Silva, F., & Morais, J. (2001). *Executive functions in unschooled adults.* Manuscript in preparation.

Kolinsky, R., & Morais, J. (1993). Intermediate representations in spoken word recognition: A cross-linguistic study of word illusions. *Proceedings of the 3rd European Conference on speech communication and technology, Eurospeech '93* (pp. 731–734). Berlin, Germany.

Kolinsky, R., & Morais, J. (1996). Migrations in speech recognition, *Language and Cognitive Processes* (Special Issue: A Guide to Spoken Word Recognition Paradigms), *11,* 611–619.

Kolinsky, R., & Morais, J. (1999). We all are Rembrandt experts—or how task dissociations in school learning effects support the discontinuity hypothesis. *Behavioral & Brain Sciences, 22,* 381–382.

Kolinsky, R., Morais, J., & Brito Mendes, C. (1990). Embeddedness effects on part verification in children and unschooled adults. *Psychologica Belgica, 30,* 49–64.

Kolinsky, R., Morais, J., & Cluytens, M. (1995). Intermediate representations in spoken word recognition: Evidence from word illusions. *Journal of Memory and Language, 34,* 19–40.

Kolinsky, R., Morais, J., Content, A., & Cary, L. (1987). Finding parts within figures: A developmental study. *Perception, 16,* 399–407.

Kolinsky, R., Morais, J., & Verhaeghe, A. (1994). Visual separability: A study on unschooled adults. *Perception, 23,* 471–486.

Liberman, I.Y., Shankweiler, D., Fisher, F.W., & Carter, B. (1974). Explicit syllable and phoneme segmentation in the young child. *Journal of Experimental Child Psychology, 18,* 201–212.

Lukatela, K., Carello, C., Shankweiler, D., & Liberman, I.Y. (1995). Phonological awareness in illiterates: Observations from Serbo-Croatian. *Applied Psycholinguistics, 16,* 463–487.

Luria, A.R. (1976). *Cognitive development. Its cultural and social foundations.* Cambridge, MA: Harvard University Press.

Mansfield, A.F. (1977). Semantic organization in the young child: Evidence for the development of semantic feature systems. *Journal of Experimental Child Psychology, 23,* 57–77.

Markman, E.M. (1984). The acquisition and hierarchical organization of categories by children. In M. Sophian (Ed.), *Origins of cognitive skills.* Hillsdale, NJ: Lawrence Erlbaum Associates Inc.

McClelland, J.L., & Elman, J.L. (1986). The TRACE model of speech perception. *Cognitive Psychology, 18,* 1–86.

Miyake, A., Friedman, N.P., Emerson, M.J., Witzki, A., Howerter, A., & Wager, T.D. (2000). The unity and diversity of executive functions and their contributions to complex "frontal lobe" tasks: A latent variable analysis. *Cognitive Psychology, 41,* 49–100.

Morais, J. (1991). Constraints on the development of phonemic awareness. In S.A. Brady & D.P. Shankweiler (Eds.), *Phonological processes in literacy. A tribute to Isabelle Y. Liberman* (pp. 5–27). Hillsdale, NJ: Lawrence Erlbaum Associates Inc.

Morais, J. (1994). *L'art de lire.* Paris: Odile Jacob.

Morais, J., Bertelson, P., Cary, L., & Alegria, J. (1986). Literacy training and speech analysis. *Cognition, 24,* 45–64.

Morais, J., Cary, L., Alegria, J., & Bertelson, P. (1979). Does awareness of speech as a sequence of phones arise spontaneously? *Cognition, 7,* 323–331.

Morais, J., Castro, S.L., & Kolinsky, R. (1991). La reconnaissance des mots chez les adultes illettrés. In R. Kolinsky, J. Morais, & J. Segui (Eds.), *La reconnaissance des mots dans les différentes modalités sensorielles. Etudes de psycholinguistique cognitive* (pp. 59–80). Paris: Presses Universitaires de France.

Morais, J., Castro, S.L., Scliar-Cabral, L., Kolinsky, R., & Content, A. (1987). The effects of literacy on the recognition of dichotic words. *Quarterly Journal of Experimental Psychology, 39A,* 451–465.

Morais, J., Content, A., Bertelson, P., Cary, L., & Kolinsky, R. (1988). Is there a critical period for the acquisition of segmental analysis? *Cognitive Neuropsychology, 5,* 347–352.

Morais, J., & Kolinsky, R. (1994). Perception and awareness in phonological processing: The case of the phoneme. *Cognition, 50,* 287–297.

Morais, J., & Kolinsky, R. (1995). The consequences of phonemic awareness. In B. de Gelder & J. Morais (Eds.), *Speech and reading: Comparative approaches* (pp. 317–337). Hove, UK: Psychology Press.

Morais, J., Kolinsky, R., Ventura, P., & Cluytens, M. (1997). Levels of processing in the phonological segmentation of speech. In G.T. Altmann (Ed.) *Cognitive models of speech processing. Psycholinguistic and computational perspectives on the lexicon* (pp. 871–875). Hove, UK: Psychology Press.

Morais, J., Mengarda, E., Grimm-Cabral, L., & Kolinsky, R. (2001). *Testing conditional hypotheses in unschooled adults.* Manuscript in preparation.

Morais, J., & Mousty, P. (1992). The causes of phonemic awareness. In J. Alegria, D. Holender, J. Junça de Morais, & M. Radeau (Eds.), *Analytic approaches to human cognition* (pp. 193–211). Amsterdam: Elsevier.

Morris, N., & Jones, D.M. (1990). Memory updating in working memory: The role of the central executive. *British Journal of Psychology, 81,* 111–121.

Nagy, W.E., Anderson, R.C., & Herman, P.A. (1987). Learning word meanings from context during normal reading. *American Educational Research Journal, 24,* 237–270.

Neisser, U. (1998). Introduction: Rising test scores and what they mean. In U. Neisser (Ed.), *The rising curve. Long-term gains in IQ and related measures.* Washington, DC: American Psychological Association.

Petersen, S.E., Fox, P.T., Snyder, A.Z., & Raichle, M.E. (1990). Activation of extrastriate and frontal cortical areas by visual words and word-like stimuli. *Science, 249,* 1041–1043.

Petersson, K.M., Reis, A., Askelöf, S., Castro-Caldas, A., & Ingvar, M. (2000). Language processing modulated by literacy: A network analysis of verbal repetition in literate and illiterate subjects. *Journal of Cognitive Neuroscience, 12,* 1–19.

Philipps, L.H., Wynn, V., Gilhooly, K.J., Della Sala, S., & Logie, R.H. (1999). The role of memory in the Tower of London task. *Memory, 7,* 209–231.

Radeau, M. (1983). Semantic priming between spoken words in adults and children. *Canadian Journal of Psychology, 37,* 547–556.

Ratcliff, G., Ganguli, M., Chandra, V., Sharma, S., Belle, S., Seaberg, E., & Pandav, R. (1998). Effects of literacy and education on measures of word fluency. *Brain and Language, 61,* 115–122.

Raven, J.C. (1963). *Raven's Progressive Matrices,* London: Lewis.

Raven, J.C. (1969). *Coloured Progressive Matrices,* London: Lewis.

Raven, J.C. (1973). *Standard Progressive Matrices, PM47, Manual.* Paris: CERP.

Raven, J. (2000). The Raven's Progressive Matrices: Changes and stability over culture and time. *Cognitive Psychology, 41,* 1–48.

Raven, J.C., Court, J.H., & Raven, J. (1990). *Manual for Raven's Progressive Matrices and vocabulary scales,* Oxford: Oxford Psychologist Press.

Read, C., Zhang, Y., Nie, H., & Ding, B. (1986). The ability to manipulate speech sounds depends on knowing alphabetic writing. *Cognition, 24,* 31–44.

Reis, A., & Castro-Caldas, A. (1997). Illiteracy. A bias for cognitive development. *Journal of the International Neuropsychological Society, 3,* 444–450.

Rosch, E., Mervis, C., Gray, W., Johnson, D., & Boyes-Braem, P. (1976). Basic objects in natural categories. *Cognitive Psychology, 8,* 382–439.

Scliar-Cabral, L., Morais, J., Nepomuceno, L., & Kolinsky, R. (1997). The awareness of phonemes: So close-so far away. *International Journal of Psycholinguistics, 13,* 211–240.

Scribner, S. (1974). Developmental aspects of categorized recall in a West African society. *Cognitive Psychology, 6,* 475–494.

Scribner, S., & Cole, M. (1981). *The psychology of literacy.* Cambridge, MA: Harvard University Press.

Shallice, T. (1982). Specific impairments in planning. *Philosophical Transactions of the Royal Society London (Biology), 298,* 199–209.

Shankweiler, D., & Liberman, I.Y. (1976). Exploring the relations between reading and speech. In R.M. Knights & D.J. Bakker (Eds.), *Neuropsychology of learning disorders: Theoretical approaches.* Baltimore, MD: University Park Press.

Stroop, J.R. (1935). Studies of interference in serial verbal reactions. *Journal of Experimental Psychology, 18,* 643–662.

Tfouni, L.V. (1988) *Adultos não alfabetizados: o avesso do avesso.* Campinas, Brazil: Pontes.

Troyer, A.K., Moscovitch, M., & Winocur, G. (1997). Clustering and switching as two components of verbal fluency: Evidence from younger and older healthy adults. *Neuropsychology, 11,* 138–146.

Ventura, P., Kolinsky, R., Brito-Mendes, C., & Morais, J. (2001). Mental representations of the syllable internal structure are influenced by orthography. *Language and Cognitive Processes, 16,* 393–418.

Verhaegen, P. (1956). Utilité actuelle des tests pour l'étude psychologique des autochtones congolais. *Revue de Psychologie Appliquée, 6,* 139–151.

Verhaeghe, A. (1999). *L'influence de la scolarisation et de l'alphabétisation sur les capacités de traitement visuel.* Unpublished Doctoral dissertation, University of Lisbon.

Verhaeghe, A., & Kolinsky, R. (1992). Discriminação entre figuras orientadas em espelho em função do modo de apresentação em adultos escolarizados e adultos iletrados. *Proceedings of the I Jornadas de Estudo dos Processos Cognitivos da Sociedade Portuguesa de Psicologia* (pp. 51–67). Lisbon: Astoria.

Wason, P. (1966). Reasoning. In B. Foss (Ed.), *New horizons in psychology*. Harmondsworth, UK: Penguin Books.

Wolff, P., Medin, D.L., & Pankratz, C. (1999). Evolution and devolution of folkbiological knowledge. *Cognition, 73*, 177–204.

CHAPTER TWENTY-THREE

Representational and communicative aspects as two facets of contemporary psycholinguistics

Ida Kurcz
Polish Academy of Sciences and Warsaw School of Advanced Social Psychology, Poland

This chapter could also be entitled: cognitivism versus pragmatism in contemporary psycholinguistics, or simply the main controversies in this discipline as I see them. I have chosen the title *Representational and communicative aspects as two facets of contemporary psycholinguistics* because I treat these two notions—representation and communication—as the fundamental notions for any approach to language studied within this domain. Human language—a system of signs and rules governing their organization—serves as a medium of representation of the external world in human minds as well as a medium of communication among people. The two central themes for psycholinguistic research which have been proposed, linguistic competence (Chomsky, 1965) and communicative competence (Hymes, 1972), I see related to these functions. Let us look briefly at how these two basic functions of natural language have been understood over the 50 years of the history of psycholinguistics. By natural language is meant the system which has evolved through biological evolution.

HISTORICAL BACKGROUND OF STUDIES OF THE TWO LANGUAGE FUNCTIONS: REPRESENTATIONAL AND COMMUNICATIVE

We can distinguish four main periods in the development of contemporary psycholinguistics which itself was brought into existence at an interdisciplinary symposium at Cornell University (USA) in 1951. Its aim was to study, by

531

use of psychological methods, the reality of diverse models of language functioning in the human mind, i.e., how people acquire, produce, and understand language. The four periods are characterized by the following focal issues or focal notions dominating in the given period:

I.   (the 50s) language as a code;
II. (the 60s and partly 70s) language as a grammar;
III. (the 70s and 80s) language as discourse;
IV. (the 90s) language as a Universal Grammar.

The first two designations I have borrowed from the French psycholinguist Jean Caron (1983). Language designated as a code was characteristic of the first period when the mathematical theory of information and communication served as the principal model for psycholinguistic research.

Language designated as a grammar is connected strictly with Noam Chomsky's theory of generative and transformational grammar, which revolutionized not only linguistic but psycholinguistic research as well. This term—linguistic competence as the tacit knowledge of an idealized speaker about how to understand and produce sentences in a given language—has since gained wide currency as the leading model in both general and developmental psycholinguistics. The actual use of language, or linguistic performance, due to its errors and other limitations, was treated as an imperfect source for speculation about the ideal model. Furthermore, other than strictly linguistic factors could be responsible for linguistic performance.

Language as discourse, a new period of psycholinguistic research in the 1970s, started with the recognition of those other factors, and the notion of communicative competence was introduced. This competence allows not only for understanding and producing sentences but also how to do so taking into account the receiver's competencies and the actual social situation. The basic unit of this competence is not the sentence but the utterance and the underlying speech act, which specifies the speaker's intention. Two adjacent utterances might suffice to form a discourse. I am using this last term to refer to the whole period. The flourishing advances in this period of new methods of discourse analysis and the widespread use of the term has clearly reflected this change in thinking toward communicative aspects of language.

Further elaboration of new models of generative grammar led to the introduction of the notion of Universal Grammar (UG) in the 1980s. In the course of development of evolutionary psychology, with its focus on the emergence of language as a milestone in human phylogenesis (the evolution of Homo Sapiens), UG has become the focal issue in the contemporary period. This does not mean that discourse has ceased to be also a current line of research: it has simply ceased to be the dominant one.

In the following sections I present the specificity of both fundamental functions in their relation to human language and I shall then try to explain how I understand their role in its origin and acquisition.

THE SPECIFIC FEATURES OF THE REPRESENTATIONAL AND COMMUNICATIVE FUNCTIONS OF HUMAN LANGUAGE

The presentation of the four periods in the development of psycholinguistics has shown, I hope, how the accent on a given function has shifted from one period to another. The starting point was the communicative function, the next the representative, then again communicative, and the final one I wish to describe as dualistic. But first, let us look at each function separately.

The specificity of the representational function

Every natural communicative system in the entire animal kingdom, apart from its communicative aspects, has to serve a representational function in the sense of reference to something outside the system. What is specific for the representational aspects of human language?

Different authors, like Karl Bühler, John Lyons, or Michael A.K. Halliday, used various terms to describe this function—symbolic, descriptive, referential, ideational, etc. Roman Jakobson (1960), at the time when a model of language as a code dominated psycholinguistic research, discerned several representational, or referential, functions of the linguistic message. They are attached to different parts of the model:

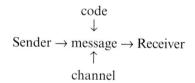

$$\begin{array}{c} \text{code} \\ \downarrow \\ \text{Sender} \rightarrow \text{message} \rightarrow \text{Receiver} \\ \uparrow \\ \text{channel} \end{array}$$

The main representational function of a message refers to the reality outside the whole model. But it may refer to different parts of the model, for instance, the sender of the message, in which case it is called emotional or expressive. It may concern the receiver, the function then being instrumental, pragmatic, conative (in the sense of evoking a given reaction). It may take into account the channel—"do you hear me?"—or the code itself—"do you understand me?"—or the message itself, what Jakobson called the poetic or esthetic function. Thus even in the clearly communicative model of language use its representational functions are fully present.

But what is really crucial for the specificity of the representational function of natural language is the duality of patterning, or two levels of representation, by this system. On one level, the meaningless elements, the so-called phonemes (vowels and consonants) are combined by rules of phonology to form meaningful words (or better, morphemes—the smallest meaningful elements of language). On the second level, these meaningful elements are combined by rules of syntax to form other meaningful compositions, that is, sentences whose meanings are not just the sum of meanings of their composite words.

The other natural communication systems dispose of only some equivalents of the first patterning system—all sorts of signs with their associated meanings (like different calls of vervet monkeys signifying distinct kinds of danger: eagle, snake, or leopard). Only human language, as Chomsky claims after Humboldt, can make infinite use of finite means. And from the three language components—phonology, semantics, and syntax—only the last is responsible for this unique achievement. For these reasons, syntax (or Universal Grammar) was treated by Chomsky and other generativists (with the exception of Ray Jackendoff, 1997) as the only generative component of linguistic competence or I-language (internal, intentional).

Given that syntax is decisive for the functioning of linguistic competence, is it at all possible to use language without syntax? The answer is Yes. It will be a sort of protolanguage, the supposed candidate for the prelinguistic forms in phylogenesis and ontogenesis of human language. Derek Bickerton (1990), the well-known researcher in the domain of protolanguages, distinguishes four different forms still in existence for Homo sapiens and one, under special conditions, for his nearest cousin—the chimpanzee.

What does a protolanguage look like? We can imagine it as a form of mental lexicon without syntax operating on the lexical entries. It is simply the first level of symbol patterning. Its existing forms are the following:

1. pidgin (but not creole where syntax is in full use);
2. language of the child under 2 years of age;
3. language of the child not exposed to any human language until puberty (the famous case of Genie);
4. language spoken in very disturbed conditions;
5. American Sign Language (ASL) used by chimps.

ASL comprises a full human language, yet what chimps who are taught this form of language reveal is a complete lack of grammar in their "utterances".

Let us treat the last three cases as special and not of concern here. The first two will serve as the arguments in our later discussion on the role of the two language functions in phylo- and ontogenesis.

The specificity of the communicative function

First, some marginal remarks on terminology. I use the term "communicative" only in the sense of communication between people or eventually with oneself (alter ego in internal speech). But the term is also used in a different sense by philosophers of language (Carruthers & Boucher, 1998). They distinguish two approaches to the study of the relations between language and cognition—one, the so-called "cognitive," when thought is equated with language, and the other "communicative," when there is no equivalence between these two systems, which only "intercommunicate" in the human mind.

The communicative function of language is given priority by such authors as Jerome Bruner, Herbert Clark, and Michael Tomasello. They stress the role of shared attention between mother and child during language acquisition as well as between two adult speakers.

What is important in these approaches is the assumption that human communication is based on the mutual sharing of beliefs about the world, about the mind (the so-called theory of mind, TOM; Baron-Cohen, 1999) and how to communicate effectively with one another. The latter example of shared knowledge is well captured by Paul Grice's (1975) maxims: of quantity (make your contribution as informative as is required), of quality (do not say what you believe to be false), of relation (be relevant), and of manner (avoid obscurity and ambiguity). This is not simply wishful thinking about how we ought to behave, but describes how we actually behave in most everyday communicative situations. Only when people deviate from these maxims is this really noticed and becomes a problem to be solved. Normally, things go smoothly.

To become a transactive self who is able to use the narrative mode of thought is, in Bruner's (1986) opinion, a distinctive prerequisite of humanity. The foundations for human use of language are, in Clark's (1996) view, joint action and common ground. And for Tomasello (1999), the only prerequisite for the evolution of language in hominids was a feature absent in chimpanzees—the ability to decentrate, take the perspective of others, and understand their intentions. I will call this ability social cognition.

What is characteristic of the main theoretical approaches to the study of human uniqueness in the use of language is that they either stress the emergence of grammar as the turning point in language evolution or the emergence of a theory of mind, the ability to understand others, that is, the ability for social cognition. According to the view presented here, both features are equally important as prerequisites for the descent of human language and for its ascent in the young child.

THE DESCENT OF HUMAN LANGUAGE

Let us first look at the representative function of language for which the emergence of syntax, that is, of Universal Grammar (UG), is considered the decisive and specific factor.

First, some newly established facts about hominid evolution, which began less than 6 million years ago when Australopithecus started his bipedal life in the very hard and dangerous environment of the south-eastern African savannas. The main feature of this evolution was a significant growth of the hominid brain reaching, in Homo sapiens, the highest encephalization quotient (and especially the neocortex ratio) among the primates. While no further brain growth tendency has been observed with the emergence of Homo sapiens, the encephalization quotient is still regarded as an important prerequisite for the Homo sapiens entry on the scene, when many branches of the hominid evolutionary tree had already died off with only a few still existing (Homo erectus, Homo neanderthalensis). The date of this entry is still a matter of discussion, with the tendency to shorten this period even to 45,000 years ago (Corballis, 1999). Other estimates do not cross the border of 200,000 years.

Around 45,000 years ago the intensive cultural evolution of Homo sapiens started a steady development as compared with the more than 2-million year existence of Homo erectus with almost no change in their use of tools. This cultural evolution is often linked with the emergence of full language, that is, language with syntax as defined earlier. Language created humans, not the other way around. The argument goes like this—language, being itself a product of biological evolution (or, as some prefer to maintain— Gould, Chomsky—a byproduct of it) is the main factor in cultural evolution.

Let us see what was really crucial for the biological evolution of syntax. There are several hypotheses, most of them based on the prior existence of protolanguage in hominid development. One, gradualistic, presupposes the gradual development and enrichment of protolanguage ending through the process of natural selection with the emergence of syntax (Pinker, 1994; Pinker & Bloom, 1990). The other, catastrophic, sees the emergence of syntax as a result of sudden genetic mutation (Bickerton, 1990). According to Derek Bickerton (1990, 1995; but not Bickerton, 2000; see later), protolanguage was useful at the first stage of representation, common to humans and animals, but with syntax the second stage of representation became possible, allowing for abstraction and all sorts of displacement.

One can now see—I think—a quite new step in this evolutionary way of thinking about the emergence of syntax. In an article in *Nature* (March 2000), Martin A. Nowak, J.B. Plotkin, and V.A.A. Jansen presented a mathematical model for the evolutionary dynamics leading to the transition from a nonsyntactic to a syntactic form of language. Their model is based on the reproductive ratio of signals (or words) in protolanguage. The emergence of syntax will only be favored by natural selection when the number of these signals exceeds a threshold value (which, according to their calculations, comes to around 400 elements). This means that the protolanguage consisting of fewer than 400 signals (each signal S_{ij} denoting one event E_{ij}) is even preferred to the language with syntax which requires the decomposition of S_{ij} in relation to different aspects $_i$ and $_j$ of E. Let us imagine that an event E_{ij} is composed of an action (A_j) of hunting where the object (O_i) is an antelope. The whole event is signaled in protolanguage by S_{ij}. There are also other signals denoting eating the antelope or hunting a bison, eating the bison, and so on. But when the critical threshold of events to be signaled has been exceeded, the decomposition of S_{ij} into N_i and V_j has to become the preferred option.

$$S_{ij}$$
$$\downarrow$$
$$E_{ij} = O_i + A_j$$
$$\downarrow \quad \downarrow$$
$$N_i \quad V_j$$

Verbs (V) denoting different actions: hunting, eating, etc; nouns (N) denoting different objects: antelopes, bisons, etc.

A nonsyntactic language or protolanguage has signals that refer to events. A syntactic language has signals or words (verbs and nouns) for objects and actions and rules for combining these words. The mathematical analysis developed by Nowak et al. can be adapted to more complicated situations. I merely want to show the idea underlying their reasoning.

I am not concerned here with the form of protolanguage realization. Probably for a long time it was realized in manual fashion. According to Philip Lieberman (1973), the appropriate development of the vocal tract for producing speech sounds, among all hominids, was only reached by Homo sapiens. But since the neural/brain localization is just the same for human vocal speech and for sign language used by deaf people (which is probably a later readaptation), this question does not change the whole reasoning.

So if we accept that the proof for the evolution of syntactic language has been obtained and that using syntax constitutes the crucial feature of the representational function of human language, does this suffice for using language for communicative purposes? While many authors really stop here in their reasoning about the biological bases of human language, several others who even ignore the role of syntax seek other biologically evolved features for the specificity of human communication. As I have already mentioned, this specificity consists of the ability of decentration, of understanding the other person's perspective, of having a theory of mind, i.e., of social cognition.

Again, there are several hypotheses concerning the evolutionary prerequisites for these social linguistic abilities. Derek Bickerton, in his dialogue with William H. Calvin about *Lingua ex machina* (2000), sees the source of syntactic rules that map the predicate to argument(s) relations in reciprocal altruism as opposed to kin altruism, both being the well-known mechanisms of Dawkins' selfish gene. But a specific prerequisite should by definition be unique to humans, so the proof ought to be forthcoming that it is not shared with other primates. But there are some doubts about that.

Such a proof is offered by Michael Tomasello (1999, pp. 16–17) in his decentration thesis when he compares the cognitive and social abilities of chimpanzees with those of humans. Both are social beings. Among their common cognitive abilities are the following:

1. In perceiving and understanding the physical world:
    an episodic memory (what, where, when);
    a perceptual object constancy;
    an ability to categorize based on perceptual similarity;
    an insight into problem solving;
    an ability to manipulate small numbers of things in working memory.
2. In perceiving and understanding the social world:
    an ability to identify particular members in a group;
    to make direct relations with other members based on kinship, friendship, and dominance;
    to understand third-party relationships;
    to cooperate in problem-solving situations;
    to learn from observation;
    to foresee the behavior of others on the bases of their movement directions and emotional states; and
    to use strategies to out-compete others for valued resources.

So what really differs in the social cognition of these two species? Tomasello's findings, based on his intensive comparative studies of infant and chimp behaviors, are that, in contrast to humans, nonhuman primates *do not* (1999, p. 21):

point to objects or places for others;
offer anything to others;
hold things to show them to others;
intentionally teach others new behaviors.

Some authors (Gòmez, 1998) maintain that great apes are capable of ostensive behavior—showing things to others—but probably they do this only for instrumental reasons. They want others to do something for them, it is not for the benefit of others.

Tomasello's conclusion is that all these behaviors, which are precisely typical of humans, comprise the sufficient biological endowment for using language. There is no reason to look for other evolutionary factors responsible for this phenomenon.

There are several other theories with a similar conclusion. Particularly representative here are the authors of social mind theories like Andrew Whiten (1999) and Simon Baron-Cohen (1999).

In my view, syntax and social cognition, representation, and communication could even develop independently, each responsible for the unique characteristics of human language. I will try to explain this view in the next part of this chapter.

THE ASCENT OF HUMAN LANGUAGE

The very well-known arguments in developmental psycholinguistics coming from generative theories state that children are innately equipped with a common human possession—the language faculty or language organ. They go through fixed stages with a rapid transition from one to the next, starting from prelinguistic babbling through one word, two words, and finally attaining the full grammar stage at the age of about 3 years. At these peak periods of language growth, the child is acquiring words at a rate of about one word per hour and the child's tacit knowledge of language grammar vastly surpasses what his/her experience has provided. In Chomsky's own words: "Language acquisition seems much like the growth of organs generally; it is something that happens to a child, not what the child does." (2000, p. 7).

But children acquire with equal ease any language spoken on the Earth independently of their diversity and complexity. So the theories of language should satisfy not only the descriptive adequacy (how well they account for the properties of the given language) but also explanatory adequacy, i.e., "a theory of language must show how each particular language can be derived from a uniform initial state under the 'boundary conditions' set by experience" (Chomsky, 2000, p. 7). This initial state is what a child is equipped with, recently called Universal Grammar (UG).

Many proposals of generative grammars as theories of linguistic competence have been elaborated during the last 40 years and many of them have been discarded, especially in the most recent approaches called the minimalist program (Chomsky, 1995) or the internalist linguistic theory (Chomsky, 2000). What remains is the Principles and Parameters theory (Chomsky, 1981) as the basic approach to the study of UG. The principles are universal and the parameters their specific realizations by particular languages. In this approach the rules of grammar (like transformational rules for passive or relative clauses) are decomposed into general principles which interact to yield the properties of linguistic expressions. Thus UG consists of a fixed network (principles) that is connected to a sort of switch box (Chomsky's expression); the switches are the options to be determined by experience with a particular language.

The nature of these universal principles is still a matter of discussion among the prominent authors in this domain like Chomsky (1995, 2000), Lasnik (2000), Pinker (1999), and Jackendoff (1997). I will not enter here into the details of this discussion; I will simply treat this general approach as the one accentuating the specificity of language competence taken as a biological organ. This approach is not concerned with any cognitive or social prerequisites for that competence.

Nevertheless, there are many previously mentioned authors like Bruner and Tomasello who accentuate the role of social cognitive factors in language acquisition. Tomasello (1999) stresses that there is a culmination in the understanding of others as intentional agents at precisely 9 months of age, prior even to the one-word stage (12 months), and offers a simulation explanation of this 9-month revolution.

The understanding of others rests on a special kind of knowledge different from that which we use to understand inanimate objects. It is based on the analogy to self. According to Tomasello, when human infants attempt to understand others they use their own experiences especially with regard to self-agency. In his simulation model—others are like me—the child sees the difference between animate and inanimate objects which are much less like me. The understanding of others, so well documented in the observation of infants between 9 and 12 months of age, is a result of a uniquely human biological adaptation which also offers to the child the possibility of a new understanding of his/her own intentional actions. There are some connections between this approach and the so-called "theory theory" (a protoscientific theorizing) approach by Alison Gopnik and Andrew Meltzoff (1997), who propose that this infant attitude—others are like me—starts even from birth. I mentioned earlier other theorists of mind theories. The child's attitude provides him or her with the prerequisites to communicate with others using linguistic means. Language gives the opportunities, especially for cultural development.

There are also opponents to any nativist approach in developmental psycholinguistics who emphasize much more the role of experience and who treat linguistic competence as a special case of a more general cognitive competence for information processing (Slobin, Bates, McWhinney). But the arguments for an independent development of linguistic and intellectual skills (language is acquired by children with very low IQ, or who are severely mentally retarded) are for me strong enough to accept the nativist perspective of language as a specific organ.

CONCLUSIONS

Coming now to conclusions, I would like to stress that both approaches to language acquisition are for me quite consistent. The child enters into his or her interactions with the external world biologically equipped with the ability to understand others and then uses another biologically evolved ability to acquire language. Children start with protolanguge going through one- and two-word stages, then enter very smoothly into a full grammar stage (a sort of replication of phylogenetic evolution). Although the followers of generative approaches stress the link of the linguistic organ to other systems of mind, especially the cognitive and intentional, they do not occupy themselves with where these intentions come from.

The proponents of specific decentration abilities of the young child, i.e., of intuitive sociocognitive knowledge, treat this knowledge as the sufficient prerequisite for language. The crucial argument for their thesis are autistic children, the only humans who lack this social knowledge, who do not understand other people's intentions, and whose language is not well developed. But there are autistic children with quite well-developed linguistic skills, so the argument goes the other way around. There are human beings who acquire language without any theory of mind.

The main arguments for keeping both biological endowments in the theory of language acquisition and of language use come from the pathological cases. I do not refer to aphasiological studies, since the loss of language in these cases is due to external factors operating later in life. I mean pathological cases where genetic causes seem to enter into play. We observe the independent impairment of only one of the two skills under consideration. The genetically transmitted grammatical impairment studied by Myrna Gopnik in one family is one of the examples of a linguistic deficit alone. Children with SLI (Specific Language Impairment) also suffer only from linguistic deficit. On the other hand, children with the Williams syndrome, with language fully developed but general intelligence very low, can serve as evidence for the independence of linguistic and intellectual abilities. And those cases of autistic children, and especially of schizophrenics with social intelligence impairment but linguistic abilities intact, might be also treated as an example of their independent functioning. The normal use of language involves both linguistic functions, representational and communicative, but the existing evidence speaks for their independent sources and independent impairment.

The emergence of syntax based on social cognition started a new period of human evolution, the so-called cultural evolution as opposed to the biological one. The cultural evolution, which involves new ways of social life, influences the particular forms of a given language and bootstraps language acquisition in particular children.

ACKNOWLEDGEMENTS

Parts of this chapter have been taken from 'Language-Cognition-Communication', which appeared in *Psychology of Language and Communication*, 5(1), 5–16, 2001. Reproduced with the permission of Matrix S.C., Poland.

REFERENCES

Baron-Cohen, S. (1999). The evolution of the theory of mind. In M.C. Corballis & S.E.G. Lea (Eds.), *The descent of mind. Psychological perspective on hominid evolution*. Oxford: Oxford University Press.

Bates, E., & MacWhinney, B. (1982). Functionalist approaches to grammar. In E. Wanner & L.R. Gleitman (Eds.), *Language acquisition: The state of the art*. Cambridge: Cambridge University Press.

Bickerton, D. (1990). *Language and species*. Chicago: University of Chicago Press.

Bickerton, D. (1995). *Language and human behavior*. Seattle, WA: University of Washington Press.

Bruner, J.S. (1986). *Actual minds, possible worlds*. Cambridge, MA: Harvard University Press.

Bühler, K. (1934). *Sprachtheorie*. Jena, Germany: Fisher.

Calvin, W.H., & Bickerton, D. (2000). *Lingua ex machina*. Cambridge, MA: MIT Press.

Caron, J. (1989). *Précis de psycholinguistique*. Paris: PUF.

Carruthers, P., & Boucher, J. (1998). *Language and thought. Interdisciplinary themes*. Cambridge: Cambridge University Press.

Chomsky, N. (1965). *Aspects of the theory of syntax*. Cambridge, MA: MIT Press.

Chomsky, N. (1981). Principles and parameters in syntactic theory. In N. Hornstein & D. Lightfoot (Eds.), *Explanations in linguistics*. London: Longman.

Chomsky, N. (1995). *The minimalist program*. Cambridge, MA: MIT Press.

Chomsky, N. (2000). *New horizons in the study of language and mind*. Cambridge: Cambridge University Press.

Clark, H. (1996). *Using language*. Cambridge, UK: Cambridge University Press.

Corballis, M.C. (1999). Phylogeny from apes to humans. In M.C. Corballis & S.E.G. Lea (Eds.), *The descent of mind. Psychological perspectives*. Oxford: Oxford University Press.

Gòmez, J.-C. (1998). Some thoughts about the evolution of LADs: With special reference to TOM and SAM. In P. Carruthers & J. Boucher (Eds.), *Language and thought. Interdisciplinary themes*. Cambridge: Cambridge University Press.

Gopnik, A., & Meltzoff, A.N. (1997). *Words, thoughts, and theories*. Cambridge, MA: MIT Press.

Gopnik, M. (1990). Feature-blind grammar and dysphasia. *Nature*, *275*, 344–346.

Grice, P. (1975). Logic and conversation, In P. Cole & J. Morgan (Eds.), *Speech acts, syntax, and semantics*. New York: Academic Press.

Halliday, M.A.K. (1970). Language structure and language function, In J. Lyons (Ed.), *New horizons in linguistics*. Harmondsworth, UK: Penguin.

Hymes, D. (1972). On communicative competence. In J.B. Pride & J. Holmes (Eds.), *Sociolinguistics*. Harmondsworth, UK: Penguin.

Jackendoff, R. (1997). *The architecture of the language faculty*. Cambridge, MA: MIT Press.

Jakobson, R. (1960). Linguistics and poetics. In T. Sebeock (Ed.), *Style in language*. New York: Wiley.

Lasnik, H. (2000). *Syntactic structures revisited*. Cambridge MA: MIT Press.

Lyons, J. (1977). *Semantics*. Cambridge: Cambridge University Press.

Nowak, M.A., Plotkin, J.B., & Jansen, V.A.A. (2000). The evolution of syntactic communication. *Nature, 404*, 495–498.

Pinker, S. (1994). *The language instinct*. New York: Harper Collins.

Pinker, S. (1999). *Words and rules*. New York: Basic Books.

Pinker, S., & Bloom, P. (1990). Natural languages and natural selection. *Behavioral and Brain Sciences, 13*, 707–726.

Slobin, D. (1997). The origins of grammaticalizable notions: Beyond the individual mind. In D. Slobin (Ed.), *The cross-linguistic study of language acquisition*. Mahwah, NJ: Lawrence Erlbaum Associates Inc.

Tomasello, M. (1999). *The cultural origins of human cognition*. Cambridge, MA: Harvard University Press.

Whiten, A. (1999). The evolution of deep social mind in humans. In M.C. Corballis & S.E.G. Lea (Eds.), *The descent of mind. Psychological perspective on hominid evolution*. Oxford: Oxford University Press.

CHAPTER TWENTY-FOUR

Aviation psychology

Christopher D. Wickens
University of Illinois, Savoy, USA

Aviation psychology (Johnston, McDonald, & Fuller, 1994) may be defined as the applications of psychology, both its principles and theory, to understanding and analyzing the tasks of pilots, air traffic controllers, and aviation maintenance personnel. It may be distinguished from aviation human factors (Garland, Wise, & Hopkin, 1994; Orlady & Orlady, 1999; Wiener & Nagel, 1989) in that the latter accommodates aviation psychology as well as both the nonpsychological aspects of pilot capabilities (e.g., body dimensions, physiology), and the issues of employing both psychological and nonpsychological principles in the design and evaluation of aviation systems. The focus of the current writing is on the more restricted characteristics of aviation psychology.

THE PSYCHOLOGICAL CHALLENGES OF AVIATION

The challenge to the aviation psychologist is imposed by a number of features; many of which equally challenge the aircraft pilot. One such feature is the *complexity* of the aircraft system dynamics as shown in Figure 1. Unlike the automobile, which travels in two dimensions, the aircraft is typically represented as a six degrees-of-freedom system which, as shown in the figure, has three degrees of rotation (pitch, roll, and yaw), and three degrees of translation. The latter are generally normalized along the direction of flight, thereby allowing these to be defined as vertical, lateral, and longitudinal. As shown in the figure, the pilot typically exercises control (either directly on the yoke and

545

throttle, or mediated through automation) to influence the aircraft's values on these six parameters. Such control is typically exercised by rolling the aircraft to the left or right, by pitching it downward or upward, and by either accelerating it or decelerating it along the flight path.

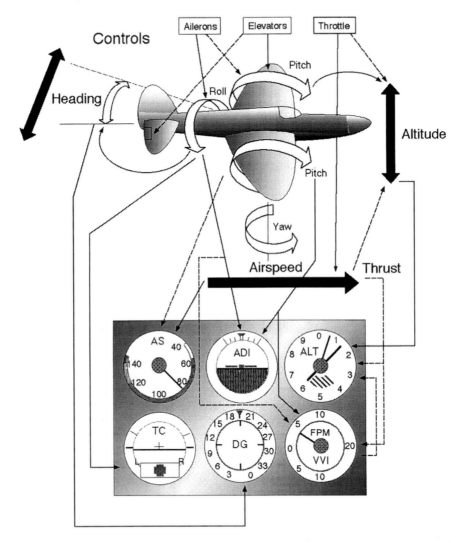

Figure 1.   Schematic representation of the degrees of freedom of aircraft movement, influenced by controls (top) and perceived in the displays of the instrument panel (bottom). The thin arrows indicate influences between axes, controls, or displays. After Wickens, C.D. (1999). Cognitive factors in aviation. In F.T. Durso, R.S. Nickerson, R.W. Schvaneveldt, S.T. Dumais, D.S. Lindsay, & M.T.H. Chi (Eds.), *Handbook of applied cognition* (pp. 274–282). Copyright 1999. © John Wiley & Sons Ltd. Reproduced with permission.

There are two additional features that add to the complexity of this six-axis control task. First, there is often a *lag* between when the pilot exercises the controls, and when the plane responds. The lag is greater with larger aircraft, but is also greater on some axes than others. For example, it takes longer for the aircraft to translate laterally along a flight path, than it does to roll to the left or the right. A considerable amount of research has revealed that controlling systems with lags imposes heavy mental demands, associated with prediction and anticipation (Van Breda, 1999; Wickens, Gempler, & Morphew, 2000a; Wickens & Hollands, 2000). Second, these dynamics are characterized by *cross coupling*. That is, changes on one of the six axes may partially influence changes on the others. For example, slowing the aircraft may lead to a loss of altitude, and banking the aircraft to the left or right will lead to a pitch downward, a corresponding loss of altitude, and a possible increase in speed.

The skilled pilot, then, must develop an accurate *mental model* of these aircraft dynamics (Bellenkes, Wickens, & Kramer, 1997; Carbonnell, Ward, & Senders, 1968), which can be employed to anticipate the future state of the aircraft, and the consequences of all inputs that are applied to the controls.

Another feature of the pilot's task defines the *goals* of flight and, hence, both the tasks that pilots perform and their relative prioritization. Pilots may be characterized as having four "meta-tasks" that may be prioritized in the order: (1) *aviate*, (2) *navigate*, (3) *communicate*, (4) *systems management*. (Sometimes there are added mission requirements such as search and rescue, or combat attack, which may lie at any level of this hierarchy.) The highest-priority task of aviating is carried out by adjusting the controls, to keep adequate airflow parallel to the surface of the wings, in order to generate *lift*, and thereby keep the aircraft from stalling (falling out of the sky). It is obvious why this task is of highest priority. Without lift the plane will not fly.

The second level task of navigation can be described as *translating* the aircraft along its three axes, in order to *reach* particular XYZ coordinates of the airspace, often at particular times, and to *avoid* other points or volumes of space, occupied by hazardous weather, terrain, or other aircraft. The first of these two subtasks in navigation, flight path tracking, presents a challenge because of the complexity of flight path dynamics, as we have already noted. The second, hazard avoidance, becomes challenging because of the probabilistic or uncertain nature of many of these hazards. Indeed, only the position of the terrain is known with relative certainty; but future behavior of both weather and other traffic is inherently uncertain and ambiguous.

The third-level task is *communication*. Most such communication takes place either between the crew members on the flight deck (i.e., pilot and co-pilot), or between the pilot and the air traffic controller. Most of it is by voice and, of course, voice communication always remains vulnerable to confusion, forgetting, and ambiguity (Morrow, Lee, & Rodvold, 1993).

The fourth level in the task hierarchy is occupied by the task of systems management. This is typically considered less important, because its requirements are generally imposed less frequently than those of aviating, navigating, and communicating. It involves a great deal of *monitoring* to insure that such variables as remaining fuel, engine temperature, or oil pressure are within acceptable bounds.

The pilot must delicately balance the visual sampling, cognitive activity, and motor activity associated with all four of these meta-tasks, in an elaborate and complex time-sharing strategy described by the term "cockpit task management" (Chou, Madhavan, & Funk, 1996; Funk, 1991; Wickens, 2002). Such management must be graded so that, whereas it is dangerous for a lower-priority task to be allowed to "pre-empt" a higher-priority one (the pilot engaged in systems management should not stall the aircraft, nor direct it into the path of another one), neither should that pilot abandon lower-priority tasks altogether, but only monitor their status less frequently. Furthermore, prioritization must be dynamic, so that at any time the pilot is prepared to elevate a lower-priority task to a higher level. For example, in cases of an engine fire, system management must take priority over navigation. Or when navigating to avoid a mid-air collision, the pilot may temporarily set aside concerns for stalling (aviating), if the aircraft is high above the earth.

A final feature of aviation is, of course, the high-risk environment in which the aircraft operates. Failures to perform any of the subtasks, particularly those of aviating and navigating, can easily lead to accidents and fatalities. However, "flying safely" (or, for an air traffic controller, directing aircraft safely) is not a simple objective. In addition to the complexity described earlier, all pilots must trade-off the goals of safety with those of "mission success" or productivity. Clearly the safest aircraft is one that does not take off at all! But then the mission cannot be accomplished. At the other extreme, it would be absurd to take off into the teeth of a thunderstorm, and hence in this case the mission objective should be sacrificed in the interests of safety. But between these circumstances there is a wide and complex range of options that pilots and controllers must balance in an uncertain world: Exactly how bad does the forecast weather need to be before a mission is cancelled, or before a route is changed which will delay mission completion? Across all aircraft, the premiums on mission completion vary tremendously, accommodating the range from a pleasure flight in a general aviation aircraft, to a routine passenger transport flight, to a life-saving helicopter rescue mission, or a critical military combat mission.

THE SUBDISCIPLINES OF AVIATION PSYCHOLOGY

In a sense the domain of aviation psychology is as wide as the domain of applied psychology itself. The main part of this chapter will only focus on a more restricted set of two issues that challenge the psychology of information processing as it pertains to the pilot in the airspace of the next century. However, before we address these two critical issues—of flight deck automation and saturated airspace capacity—it is important to briefly describe the broader range of subdisciplines of psychology, that have spawned well-developed theory and research within the field of aviation psychology.

The psychology of *communications* is highly relevant for understanding both the strengths and vulnerabilities of voice communication between pilots and air traffic controllers and between pilots within the flight deck. What kinds of errors in understanding occur (Morrow et al., 1993)? How can these be mitigated by adherence to communications protocols and procedures, or by using advanced technology of voice recognition and synthesis? Closely related to communications is the psychology of *crew resource management* or CRM (Wiener, Kanki, & Helmreich, 1993), which examines the relevance of a host of issues in social psychology to the performance of aviation teams. These teams are most frequently those formed on the flight deck (i.e., pilot and co-pilot), but may include those of other composition, such as pilot-controller teams, controller-controller teams, or pilot-flight attendant teams. CRM issues include how pilot personality and training can influence the communications pattern within the team, the trust between team members, and their ability to carry out coordinated flight-related tasks effectively.

Closely related to CRM is the study of pilot judgment and *aeronautical decision making* (Orasanu, 1993). This domain applies all aspects of the psychology of decision making to understanding and modeling how aviation personnel make the sorts of risky decisions that balance productivity against safety. What sources of information do they consult? How accurate is their inference of the current state of affairs, and how do they weigh the risks in choosing one course of action over another; for example, continuing with a landing approach in bad weather, or diverting to an alternative airport?

The psychology of *learning* is applied to the issues of pilot (and controller) training. What is the most effective use of different training devices, such as high-fidelity flight simulators, or low-cost PC simulators, in teaching pilots skills that will transfer to the aircraft (*International Journal of Aviation Psychology*, 1998)? How can skills in effective decision making and CRM be taught? These sorts of issues dominate research on pilot training. The issue of pilot training is closely intertwined with that of *pilot selection*, just as, in psychological theory, the issues of learning and abilities are closely related. Research questions in pilot selection address the sorts of abilities and skills that can be measured in the laboratory, which might predict those who will become more proficient pilots or controllers through their training.

Aviation psychology also has many ties to *organizational psychology*, when researchers address the characteristics of aviation organizations (i.e., different airlines, different ATC facilities) that may enhance or reduce morale, and when researchers consider the influence of such morale differences on safe behavior.

Finally, extensive research has been carried out on the pilot as an *information processing system*. What unique aspects of perception, cognition, attention, action selection, and feedback processing characterize the pilot's task, as portrayed in Figure 1, and how is this information processing system affected by the stresses imposed by flying, and assisted by the developments in aviation automation? Because this approach provides the structure for the two issues that we discuss in depth, the following section will discuss the pilot as an information processing system in more detail.

THE PILOT AS AN INFORMATION PROCESSOR

Figure 2 represents the pilot as an information processing system, capturing many of the elements in similar models presented elsewhere (e.g., Wickens & Hollands, 2000). For example, a pilot employing selective attention will deploy the senses to acquire a restricted amount of information, filtering much of the rest. Such information, when interpreted by reference to prior experience represented in long-term memory, is *perceived* (classified and understood). Perception may lead to immediate selection and execution of an action, as when a pilot perceives the aircraft to be off course to the left, and immediately *selects* and *executes* a rightward correction. Alternatively, the information perceived may be retained for some longer period of time without generating an action. Such retention can take place in the resource-demanding and fragile "workspace" of *working memory* (rehearsing an ATC instruction until it is executed), or may be given a more permanent representation in long-term memory (a critical incident, once perceived, is remembered after the flight is completed, or an aircraft approaching from the rear, once noted, may be recalled again within a minute or two, to assess if it remains a threat).

Within this traditional information processing model, three additional features can be highlighted. First, it is important to note that although the model presents an apparent ordering from attention (on the left) to action and response execution (on the right), the presence of the feedback loop indicates that activity may be initiated at any point within the model, as its consequences flow clockwise around the closed loop. For example, an action like checking a map may be initiated because a pilot spontaneously remembers that it needs to be done (an initiation from long-term memory). Or a

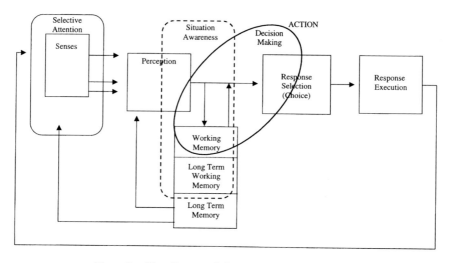

Figure 2.   The pilot as an information processing system.

control action that is carried out incorrectly may produce unexpected consequences that must be sensed, attended, and further processed for correction. In fact, the study of manual (flight) control depends critically upon understanding the continuous *closed loop* properties of the feedback system presented in Figure 2 (Wickens, 1986).

Our second feature is contained within the dotted box of Figure 2, representing those processing elements most critically important to the construct of *situation awareness* and situation assessment (Endsley & Garland, 2000). This construct, gaining great importance within the aviation community characterizes the awareness of a wide range of *dynamic* and changing elements within the pilot or air traffic controller's domain: evolving weather, traffic, changing automation levels, and changing responsibility for doing tasks. Not all of these changes are relevant for the pilot's immediate actions. But a well-prepared pilot should be aware of a wider range of such changes, should unexpected circumstances require a sudden response. The effectiveness of such situation awareness depends both upon accurately deploying selective attention, and possessing an accurate mental model of airspace and aircraft structure and procedures, into which attended information can be readily incorporated. Breakdowns in situation awareness have been directly associated with many tragic accidents in aviation, such as the crash at Cali Columbia, in which pilots were poorly aware of the relative location of nearby mountains, and of the aircraft navigational commands that had been issued by their automated flight management system (Strauch, 1997), a system we will discuss in detail later.

For the third feature, we highlight within the oval in Figure 2 those processes most critically involved in the study of pilot decision making or pilot judgment, a domain alluded to earlier. Not only does this domain include the choice of an action itself (the *product* of decision making), but, in all but the most impulsive decisions, it must involve careful assessment or awareness of the situation about which the decision is to be made, thereby assuring that the action chosen will be appropriate for the conditions existing in the world at that moment.

Although much of flying is "routine" and relatively automatic, there are many circumstances in which the processing operations outlined in Figure 2 are quite demanding in their call for attentional resources: for example, when flying in heavy traffic, low to the ground, in high turbulence, or encountering conditions with considerable uncertainty. Because of its particular limitations, demands upon working memory (Baddeley, 1986) are often a source of considerable workload for the pilot and controller. In addition to their resource demands, many of these operations in the flight environment are not carried out with the speed with which they are observed in more controlled laboratory studies of reaction time. Yet the dynamic properties of the airspace often impose heavy time constraints, leading to circumstances in which the time *required* to perform an operation may be dangerously close to the time *available* to do so safely. An example of such a situation is the pilot's required decision about whether or not to reject a takeoff, should a cockpit abnormality be observed as the aircraft nears takeoff speed on the runway (Inagaki, 1999). As revealed by half a century of psychological research, as the time available to process information is decreased, the accuracy of such processing may degrade, leading to errors in the choice and execution of action (Hick, 1952). In flight, of course, such errors can have disastrous consequences.

In the following pages, we discuss the implications of these limitations of resource demand and processing speed and accuracy as they impact two of the most important issues that will confront the field of aviation psychology over the next several years. First, we ask about the strengths and weaknesses of using computer automation to replace or augment pilot and controller performance, discussing two automated systems within the framework of an information processing taxonomy of automation. Second, we consider the psychological implications of solutions proposed to address one of the most pressing problems in future aviation: the tremendous overcrowding and "gridlock" that is present in the skies across Europe and much of North America. Although these two issues are but a small portion of the larger set to which aviation psychology is relevant, they provide important examples of the field.

AUTOMATION: THE HUMAN PERFORMANCE CONSEQUENCES

Given the limits on time, accuracy, and resource demands imposed by many of the mental operations in flight, designers have long worked to compensate for these by replacing or augmenting human performance with computer-based automation (Billings, 1996; Boehm-Davis et al., 1983; Wiener & Curry, 1980; Wiener & Nagel, 1989). In general, such trends in aviation have offered a mixed blessing. On the one hand, there is little doubt that much computer automation has increased the efficiency of flight. For example, the complex autopilots in the flight management system, which we describe in detail later, have allowed aircraft to fly routes that are more fuel- and time-efficient. So called "autoland" systems have enabled pilots to land at airports in poor visibility, in a way that would be impossible when relying upon the pilot's eyes, thereby greatly increasing the capacity at poor-weather airports in Europe and North America. On the other hand, whether or not automation has improved safety is problematic. Many automated alerting systems, such as those alerting the pilot as to an impending collision with another aircraft (the Traffic Alert and Collision Avoidance System or TCAS) or with the ground (Ground Proximity Warning System or GPWS) have provided valuable supports for the pilot's situation awareness. But other automation devices, by their very increase in productivity, have placed aircraft in more vulnerable situations (e.g., operating low to the ground, in bad weather), where the consequences of automation or human failures become much more severe. Safety consequences of automation then depend very heavily upon the *reliability* of the automation to function correctly, or to function as intended by the designer, and as expected by the pilot.

We deal with the issues related to automation reliability in some detail later. However, it is first important to consider what automation *does* for the pilot or controller, within the context of the information processing model presented in Figure 2, using a taxonomy of automation systems developed by Parasuraman, Sheridan, and Wickens (2000), and presented in Figure 3. According to this model, computer-based automation may be seen to assist (or replace) human performance in many of the operations analogous to those represented in Figure 2. Furthermore, at each stage of automation in Figure 3, the computer can be conceptualized in terms of its *level* of automation or the amount of cognitive "work" carried out by computers and machines to replace, or augment, human cognition.

At stage 1, the computer acts as a filter, to replace or assist the selective attention functions of the human operator, assessing and then displaying what is relevant to the task, and filtering that which the computer deems to be irrelevant (or less relevant). At a high level, the automation may act as an "aggressive" filter, entirely "hiding" *raw data* that is considered irrelevant.

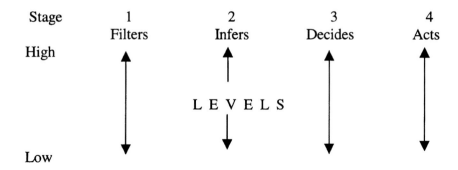

Figure 3. Four stages of automation, each of which can be implemented at a range of levels. Adapted from Parasuraman, R., Sheridan, T.B., & Wickens, C.D. (2000). A model for types and levels of human interaction with automation. *IEEE Transactions on Systems, Man, and Cybernetics: Part A: Systems and Humans, 30,* 286–297.

For example, intelligent computer automation, known as the Enhanced Ground Proximity Warning System (Phillips, 1997), will choose to display to a pilot only those terrain elements inferred to lie in the aircraft's immediate future path, filtering from view all others. Lower-level automation may guide the pilot or controller to information sources considered more important, for example, by highlighting them, but retain a visible display of those considered of lesser importance (e.g., presenting these in the "background" or lowlighted; Wickens, Kroft, & Yeh, 2000b). An air traffic controller's display that highlights or "flashes" a pair of aircraft projected to collide in the future, provides such an example. Such a device, known as the User Request Evaluation Tool, or URET (Wickens, Mavor, Parasuraman, & McGee, 1998), does not hide other aircraft from the controller's view, but only displays them with less psychological intensity or salience, compared to the pair deemed most important. It should be noted that most auditory warning signals also operate as lower-level stage 1 automation systems, typically guiding the user's attention to the visual display of a parameter or situation, identified as being of concern by the computer.

At stage 2 automation, the computer integrates data to draw some inference as to the current state of affairs—a "situation assessment"—as represented in Figure 2. For example, an intelligent diagnostic aid may integrate readings from a number of warning indicators to diagnose the likely identity of a midflight engine failure (Hicks & De Brito, 1998; Mosier, Skitka, Heers, & Burdick, 1998). Computer-based weather forecasts provide support for analogous cognitive functioning. Even a simple *predictor display* (Wickens et al., 2000a) performs such an inference by evaluating the aircraft's current trajectory and the autopilot's scheduled intentions, in order to project where the aircraft will be a few minutes into the future.

As with stage 1, so stage 2 automation can also be described by "levels" in terms of the amount of cognitive work done by the automation. However, since there are several different kinds of information processing necessary to reach an inference of an existing situation, this scale of levels may be considered to be an ordinal one. That is, the greater the number of different operations performed by the computer in integrating the raw data, the fewer that remain to be performed by the human, and the higher is the level of stage 2 automation. One form of such cognitive work is the display integration of information to produce emergent features that directly map onto inferred states (Wickens & Andre, 1990). A second form is the extent to which an automation assessment tool provides the user with only the most likely state of the world (higher automation), or provides the user with several plausible states (lower automation), requiring the user to engage in additional cognitive activity to diagnose which of the remaining states is true.

It is important to note the interdependence between stage 1 and stage 2 automation. That is, if only the most relevant data are highlighted at stage 1, it will lead operators to believe or trust in the hypotheses supported by those data, rather than other data that are not highlighted. Correspondingly, if stage 2 automation guides the user to consider a particular hypothesis or state of the world as most likely, this will lead the user to attend more to those data (at stage 1) that are consistent with the "chosen" hypothesis, in a cycle sometimes referred to as the "confirmation bias" (Klayman & Ha, 1987; Wickens & Hollands, 2000). For example, Mosier et al. (1998) found that pilots who had been guided to diagnose a particular failure type by an intelligent diagnostic system were only likely to recall seeing cues consistent with that failure type, even fabricating memory for such consistent cues after the fact, although they had not been present at the time of the failure.

At stage 3, automation uses the inferred state of the world to recommend or *decide* upon a course of action, considering as well the values (positive and negative) associated with different potential outcomes, should the inference turn out to be correct. At this stage, higher levels of automation are considered to be those that offer the user more constraints and fewer choices as to the "best" action to take, thereby reducing the complexity of the choice (Sheridan & Verplank, 1978). For example, a low level may offer a large number of recommended options. A higher level may offer only two. A still higher level may recommend only one, but allow the pilot to choose any other. Higher still is a system that informs the pilot as to the decision that *will be implemented* (at stage 4), but will allow the pilot to override that implementation (Olsen & Sarter, 2001). An example of an aircraft automation system at an intermediate (recommend one option) level is the TCAS system, which, detecting a pending collision with another aircraft, provides the pilot with an explicit command of one action to take (e.g., "climb climb climb"), but will not prevent the pilot from taking a different action.

Finally, stage 4 automation is that which actually *executes* the action manually for the pilot. The best example here is the autopilot, which will influence the wing and tail configuration in such a way as to replace the pilot's lower-level actions exerted on the ailerons and elevators, through the yoke, as shown in Figure 1. In this case, the amount of physical and computational work done by the automation defines the level of stage 4 automation. Within the framework of Figure 1, an autopilot that controls attitude (pitch and bank) is at a lower level than one that controls heading, which, in turn, is at a lower level than one that controls the aircraft's position in 3D space.

Given such a taxonomy, the designer may wish guidance as to the appropriate level of automation to be chosen at each stage. It turns out that the answer to this question depends, in good part, upon the reliability of the automation to perform its tasks as intended. In high-risk systems, Parasuraman et al. (2000) have argued that there are greater costs to unreliable automation if it is imposed at later stages of processing (3 and 4) than at earlier stages (2 and particularly 1). That is, for example, if automation incorrectly guides the user's attention to sources of information (unreliable stage 1), or incorrectly infers a given state of the world (unreliable stage 2), these consequences are less severe than if automation incorrectly recommends an option to be chosen (unreliable stage 3) or executes an action that was inappropriate (unreliable stage 4).

As one example of experimental evidence supporting this recommendation, Sarter and Schroeder (2000) compared two different systems for informing pilots about icing conditions on their aircraft. One system *diagnosed* the nature of the icing problem (stage 2), and the other *recommended* corrective actions to take on the aircraft (stage 3) in order to maintain flight stability. When both systems were accurate, there were advantages for the decision-recommendation automation. However, when the automation guidance was unreliable, the stage 3 recommendation-automation imposed more serious human performance problems, as pilots addressed the incorrect recommendation, than did the diagnosis automation, as pilots processed the incorrect diagnosis.

The guidance offered by Parasuraman et al. (2000) that higher levels of automation, in high-risk, uncertain systems, should be pursued at earlier, rather than later stages, was derived from a 3-year study identifying the potential human factors effects of introducing automation into the North American air traffic control system (Wickens, Mavor, & McGee, 1997; Wickens et al., 1998). We return to this issue at the end of the chapter. However, before we do so, we shall take a close look two of the more important automation systems in the modern pilot's repertoire, both of which illustrate clearly many of the psychological benefits and costs of automation: The *intelligent diagnostic systems*, which illustrates stage 1 and 2 automation and different levels of stage 3 automation, and the *flight management system*, or FMS, which illustrates stages 3 and 4 automation.

AUTOMATION OF INFERENCE: INTELLIGENT DIAGNOSTICS

The analysis of automation levels offered by Parasuraman et al. (2000), as described earlier, suggested that the higher levels of automation at the later stages could invite more serious problems when the automation is imperfect. Intelligent diagnostic systems for assisting pilots in assessing engine malfunctions are designed fundamentally to support stage 1 (information sampling) and stage 2 (inference) processes. These systems are extremely valuable aids for pilots for at least four reasons: first, because the complexity of many of those failures is high, and hence the cognitive complexity of unaided diagnosis may also be quite high. Second, because aircraft propulsion and guidance systems *are* highly reliable, there is a low expectancy for system failure and, hence, pilots encounter considerable delay in making an unaided diagnosis. Third, the aircraft may be operating in environments where added cognitive delays are simply unacceptable. Fourth, the very conditions of trying to diagnose an engine failure, in a life-threatening circumstance, can impose a stress which compromises the very cognitive processes necessary for effective problem solving (Svenson & Maule, 1993).

It is for these four reasons that major aircraft manufacturers have endorsed such intelligent diagnostic tools. However, an important analysis of the differences between such tools, across three versions of large transport aircraft, the Airbus A340, the Boeing 747-400, and the McDonald MD11 (Hicks & De Brito, 1998), reveals substantially different philosophies among them, concerning the stages and levels of automation that are incorporated, using the framework of Figure 3 (Hicks & De Brito, 1998). Although all three naturally include high levels of stage 1 automation (*selecting* relevant pieces of raw data—warning symptoms—to incorporate in their diagnosis), and all three offer a stage 2 diagnosis of the inferred failure state, it is in the following stages (3 and 4) that their philosophies differ. The 747-400 simply offers a diagnosis, with no further information. In contrast, the A340, following its diagnosis, presents a recommended *checklist* of remedial actions. This can be considered as an intermediate level of stage 3 automation; that is, the checklist can be disregarded if the pilot chooses to do so, but its visible presence signals a good deal of automation confidence that its inference is correct. Finally, the MD11 goes to a still higher level of stage 3 and 4 automation, by actually carrying out some of the actions, consistent with the inferred failure state, unless these are overridden by the pilot.

Although no systematic comparisons or experimental evaluations of these three systems have been carried out with pilots in the loop, it is an important exercise to consider the possible difference in pilot response among the three, should the automation in fact make an incorrect inference as to the nature of the failure, given the possibility of this situation, and given the known tendencies of pilots to trust automation diagnostics and follow their implicit or explicit guidance even when that guidance is incorrect (Mosier et al., 1998).

AUTOMATION OF ACTION SELECTION AND EXECUTION: THE FLIGHT MANAGEMENT SYSTEM

The flight management system or FMS, as it is commonly referred to, is a collection of autopilots, combined with an intelligent logic, that can accomplish the goal of navigating the aircraft to varying points and along varying trajectories in 3D space (Sarter & Woods, 1992, 1994, 1995, 1997; Sherry & Polson, 1999). That is, it is automation which makes navigational decisions about course and vertical flight changes (stage 3) and executes those decisions (stage 4) for the pilot. The FMS actually consists of a number of components, distributed throughout the flight deck, as shown in Figure 4. The pilot can program the FMS through a flight management computer, housed in a control-display unit (CDU) that is typically positioned between the seats. This may be accomplished before a route is flown (i.e., on the ground). Then the FMS will fly the aircraft along various 3D trajectories by setting various *modes* of operation: for example, climbing at a particular rate (feet per minute) or angle with the ground, reaching particular waypoints over the ground at particular times, and adjusting particular speeds. Because the 3D trajectories must be accomplished and coordinated in time, this is sometimes referred to as "4D navigation."

The pilot may intervene with this automation at any time, either by reprogramming through the CDU, or by setting in particular *target values* to a device called a mode control panel mounted at the top of the instrument panel just below the windshield. The pilot may also view what the automation is doing, or is about to do, as this is represented spatially on a 2D electronic map, the navigation display, and represented symbolically, through a set of three small windows, known as the flight mode annunciators, positioned at the top of the primary flight displays.

Although the FMS can be programmed to fly extremely efficient routes, both selecting (stage 3 automation) and executing (stage 4) control of heading, location, and altitude, past experience has identified a number of human factor problems for the pilot (e.g., Sarter & Woods, 1994, 1997). Primarily these problems concern inaccuracies of the mental model and mental picture that the pilot has of the airplane when the aircraft is controlled through the FMS, rather than being directly hand flown as shown in the representation in Figure 1. In this regard, we might describe the mental model as knowledge characterizing *what* the aircraft is doing at any moment in time, *why* it is

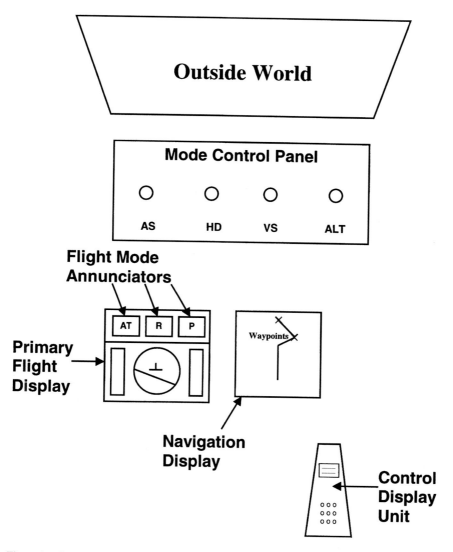

Figure 4. Components of the Flight Management System. (AS = airspeed, HD = heading, VS = vertical speed, ALT = altitude, AT = auto throttle, R = roll, P = pitch.)

doing so, as well as including a set of expectancies regarding the reliability of the automation system.

One source of the problem associated with the mental model of the FMS is simply inherent in its overwhelming complexity. The FMS has many *modes* (five different ways of changing altitude, for example), and these modes can be combined in many different ways. Furthermore, the logic within the FMS allows the plane to transition from one mode to another (a stage 3 decision) without any direct action from the pilot at the time of the transition. This may involve both activating certain modes (e.g., a speed control mode, once a certain target altitude is reached), or in some cases deactivating a mode. Thus, it is harder for the pilot to keep track of the changing modes (and resulting state of the aircraft), than would be the case if she were directly controlling the aircraft with the yoke and throttle, in spite of the higher workload required for such direct control.

Even assuming that a pilot fully understands all of the complexity of the modes (provided in a document that typically runs to several hundreds of pages), a second difficulty lies in the feedback or display to the pilot of what the FMS is doing at any given time (i.e., information necessary to update the mental picture or situation awareness of the automation). This difficulty results in part from the spatial separation of the necessary information across the cockpit (Figure 4), which needs to be integrated in the mind (a violation of the proximity compatibility principle; Wickens & Andre, 1990). It also results from the fact that most of the information about the aircraft's *vertical* flight behavior is contained in symbolic displays, not spatial displays like the electronic map that so compatibly represents lateral behavior. Such symbolic representation of vertical behavior is found in text on the pages of the flight management computer, visible in the CDU, and in alphanumeric mode abbreviations visible within the FMA windows. Thus, there is a violation of display compatibility in representing the inherently spatial information regarding vertical flight.

So, given the incompleteness of the mental model, caused by high complexity and poor feedback, it is possible to identify at least four consequences to pilot cognition and behavior, influencing the safety of the system as a whole.

Poor monitoring

As we have discussed in the context of Figure 2, effective situation awareness is heavily supported by the effective deployment of selective attention: looking at the right place at the right time in order to access evolving and changing information. Furthermore, it is also the case that effective monitoring must be guided by a good "mental model" that generates expectancies of where (which displays) and when events are likely to occur (Bellenkes et al., 1997; Carbonnell et al., 1968; Senders, 1964). However, in the case of the FMS, the high level of complexity and insufficient understanding of this complexity has left many pilots without the fully developed mental model to guide sampling appropriately. In particular, the research of Sarter and Woods (1994, 1995, 1997; Sarter, 2000) has revealed the extent to which the flight mode annunciators are not part of the pilot's regular scan pattern, because changes which occur there are often overlooked. More recently, Mumaw et al.

(2000) have found that many pilots do not scan these frequently, and even if they do, significant changes within them, quite relevant to the functioning of the automation, are apparently not detected.

Poor situation awareness

Effective monitoring is necessary, but not sufficient, to guarantee an accurate awareness or "mental picture" of the current state of a dynamic system. Indeed, it was a breakdown in situation awareness of the FMS-automated aircraft at Cali Columbia that caused pilots to allow their automation system to fly the aircraft into a mountain ridge (Strauch, 1998). Challenges to situation awareness are imposed by the very complexity of the automation, which leads to a deficient mental model of its operation. Such challenges are amplified by the inadequacy of the displays in portraying the vertical behavior of the aircraft, and what the automation is doing (or is about to do) with regard to vertical flight. As noted earlier, unlike the electronic map of lateral behavior, these vertical displays are neither integrated nor presented in the analog/pictorial mode that is compatible with the spatial understanding of the aircraft's behavior.

Situation awareness of automation state is also challenged by a psychological phenomenon referred to as the *generation effect* (Hopkin, 1994; Slamecka & Graf, 1978). The generation effect describes the extent to which one's memory of an event is better if that event were generated by one's own actions, rather than by the actions of another agent. In this case the relevant "memory" is the current and future state of the aircraft and its autopilots, and of course the "other agent" is the FMS itself, which often initiates changes in state and mode on its own, without direct intervention by the pilot at the time of the state change (Sarter & Woods, 1997).

Collectively, then, the incomplete mental model, the absence of intuitive displays, and the absence of direct control of many state changes, can leave the pilot with a poor awareness of the current and projected state of the aircraft (awareness of its state, and its trajectory relative to hazards), an awareness that becomes crucial should abnormal circumstances unexpectedly develop.

Poor skill for manual reversion

Should unexpected circumstances develop, circumstances with which the automation is not, for example, designed to cope, it may well be necessary for the pilot to intervene and assume control manually. Thus it is highly critical that the pilot's manual skills remain finely tuned, particularly because the circumstances in which automation may be unable to cope might be those that impose extremely difficult information processing challenges. However, it is also the case that the more automation is used, the less pilots or controllers will have an opportunity to *practice* those very tasks otherwise done by the automation; and without practice, the skills on many of these tasks will degrade, particularly those tasks involving procedures (as compared to the more overlearned psychomotor skills).

Poor calibration of reliability

Aviation automation systems are designed to be highly reliable, so that the sorts of abnormal circumstances discussed earlier represent extremely unlikely events. But they are not impossible, as witnessed by their contributing causes in many accidents (Hughes & Dornheim, 1995). However, the very reliability of their general operations means that most pilots will *not* have experienced their failure, leading to a possible overtrust of and overreliance on the automation (Mosier et al., 1998; Parasuraman & Riley, 1997; Skitka, Mosier, Burdick, & Rosenblatt, 2000). Placing excessive trust in the automation can lead to a state of *complacency*, in which symptoms of the health of its operation are monitored less than they should be (Parasuraman, Molloy, & Singh, 1993), and so those symptoms are less well detected on the infrequent occasions when they are observed. One of the very ironies of automation (Bainbridge, 1983) is that the more reliable the automation becomes, the less monitoring there will be for its imperfections, and the more vulnerable will be the operator when those imperfections are revealed.

OOTLUF: The syndrome and the cures

Collectively the four negative consequences of human's interacting with automation (here the FMS, which were outlined earlier), can be described by the syndrome of "Out Of The Loop Unfamiliarity" or OOTLUF (Wickens & Hollands, 2000). Automation will be poorly monitored, both because of its complexity and because of complacency, and situation awareness of the evolving state will be degraded. Hence, if a "failure" occurs (or a situation occurs with which automation cannot cope), its detection will be delayed, and the intervention based upon the mental picture of the evolving state will be delayed (or more likely to be in error). Furthermore, the intervention will be less practised and less skillful than it might be with an operator whose reliance on automation was less extensive.

It should, of course, be noted that the FMS described earlier is far from the only automation system in aviation (or other areas of technology) that encounters some of human-interaction deficiencies described. Furthermore, developers of the FMS, as well as those airplane manufacturers who incorporate the FMS into their aircraft, are aware of many of these problems, and are engaged in implementing various "cures." Two cures in particular, related to displays and to training, are self-evident given the problems described. Thus, considerable recent effort has gone into developing vertical flight displays (Gray et al., 2000) that depict, in spatially integrated form, the relation between programming commands in the FMS and planned and actual vertical flight path. At the same time, training can proceed along one of two tracks: training pilots as to the logic underlying the FMS operations (what its modes do and why; Irving, Polson, & Irving, 1994), and training as to the sorts of imperfect operations which automation can experience. Indeed, there appears to be evidence that training which provides experience with and feedback of such imperfections can improve the pilots' allocation of attention in monitoring system state to a level that may be considered the "optimal" (Wickens, 2000).

THE FUTURE OF AIR TRAFFIC MANAGEMENT: THE CAPACITY PROBLEM

A considerable amount has been written about how the current (and projected) state of much of aviation over North America is in gridlock (*Aviation Week and Space Technology*, 2000), with the projected increase in demands for travel only anticipated to make the problem more severe. There appear, at present, to be two somewhat different system-wide solutions that can be adopted to tackle this problem (Wickens et al., 1998). One focuses heavily upon developments in air traffic control and air traffic management, proposing, in particular, to introduce new sensor technology (global positioning system to replace or augment radar), and new automation in order to assist the controller with stage 1, 2, and 3 automation. The other focuses more heavily upon a concept referred to as *free flight*, whereby pilots take on many of the responsibilities that have been traditionally assumed by controllers, assuring the separation of their own aircraft from other traffic, and also assuming considerable responsibility for a flexible route planning that is not available in much of today's airspace. A careful analysis of both of these solutions reveals them to be laden with issues of direct relevance to the aviation psychologist. We describe the issues related to ATC automation first, briefly, before focusing in more depth upon the critical psychological issues imposed by the concept of free flight, and we then illustrate these by research in our own laboratory.

Air traffic control automation

Higher levels of ATC automation will enable computers to estimate, more precisely than is currently possible, the future trajectory of all aircraft, to estimate which aircraft are likely to be in conflict (stage 2 automation) and to recommend to the controllers the appropriate instructions, solutions, and schedules in order to expedite the safe flow of air traffic (stage 3) (Wickens et al., 1998). Indeed, such automation tools already exist within some air traffic control facilities (Harwood, Sanford, & Lee, 1998).

One concern for such a solution is that, unless care is taken, it could be implemented without concern for the sort of OOTLUF problems, described earlier, resulting if the automation is imperfect.

A second concern expressed by Wickens et al. (1998) pertains to what high levels of ATC automation would do to the ability to recover from a system failure. This concern is predicated on the notion that the very product of successful automation would be likely to increase the density of the air-space, a likely consequence of increasing its efficiency (i.e., more planes travelling, smaller separation en route). Under such circumstances, if a system failure were to occur, there would be substantially less time *available* for the controller to respond (i.e., because of the closer spacing), although the time *required* to respond appropriately could be increased, as argued earlier. Note that a "failure" here could be defined as any abnormality in the system: a failure of radar, of communications, of one of the automation tools, or the failure of one of the aircraft to comply with ATC instructions.

FREE FLIGHT IMPLICATIONS

The concept of free flight is more defined along a continuum than as an absolute state: it is an evolution *toward* greater authority for flight path choice in the cockpit and *away from* the constraints of air traffic control; but there are several different ways in which this shift in authority from ground to air can evolve; for example, in fewer, versus more, restricted regions in the air space; with less, versus more, opportunity for ATC to intervene and countermand pilot route selections, etc. While there are clear reasons for pilots and airline management to seek the greater authority availed by free flight in terms of flight efficiency, there are a number of explicit human factors and psychological safety concerns associated with the concept. We classify these concerns in two categories: concerns in the cockpit for the pilot, and concerns in the ATC environment for the controller.

Pilot concerns with free flight

In order for a free flight environment to operate, pilots must be equipped with an effective cockpit display of traffic information (CDTI; Figure 5), as well as a set of procedures for cooperative conflict avoidance. The safety concerns here are threefold, related to workload, information conflict in decision making, and conflict negotiations.

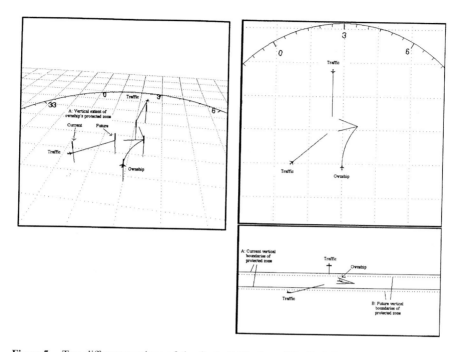

Figure 5. Two different versions of the Cockpit Display of Traffic Information (CDTI). Left: 3D display which imposes some cost of ambiguity as to where the traffic is in 3D space. Right: 2D coplanar display which requires visual scanning between the map view and the profile view. (After Merwin, Wickens, & O'Brien, 1998.)

First, it should be noted that the workload associated with traffic avoidance maneuver decisions is not trivial (Wickens et al., 2000a). After all, in many respects free flight asks the pilots to assume some of the duties of an air traffic controller, whose workload can be very high indeed (Hopkin, 1994; Wickens et al., 1997). Such workload may be partitioned into the *visual workload* display processing, bringing the pilot head down in the cockpit (which can present a major concern in general aviation flight), and the *cognitive workload*, associated with flight path planning, or maneuver decisions. Recently we have carried out an evaluation of free flight in which pilots flew a high-fidelity simulator with a CDTI (Figure 5 right), using it to avoid traffic conflicts, while visual scanning across the cockpit was assessed. We found that the visual workload associated with the CDTI processing can occupy up to 25% of a single pilot's attention, leaving a greatly reduced amount of time available to scan the outside world (Wickens, Helleberg, & Xu, in press).

Second, although it can be argued that cognitive workload can be reduced by intelligent automation guidance to the pilot regarding the appropriate maneuver to avoid conflict, in the same manner that the stage 3 automation used in the TCAS provides strong guidance on immediate traffic avoidance maneuvering ("climb climb"), such reduction brings its own problems. Indeed, the extent to which the CDTI should provide active automated guidance (stage 3 automation), in addition to accurate status and prediction (stage 2 automation), is not yet well resolved. But implementation of any guidance system must consider the pilot's ability to resolve at least three, possibly conflicting, sources of information regarding the appropriate maneuver (climb, descend, turn, speed or slow) in free flight: (1) the pilot's own predisposed conflict avoidance stereotypes or "habits" (which may be influenced by training); (2) stage 3 automation guidance offered by an intelligent CDTI conflict maneuver advisor: lessons learned from TCAS resolution advisories have revealed that such guidance is not always followed by pilots (Steenblik, 1996); and (3) the projected behavior of the conflicting aircraft.

How these three sources of information for the maneuver decision are integrated, and resolved if they conflict, represents a major challenge for decision analysis. Such conflicts represent very real possibilities. With respect to (1) (habits), we have found, for example, that pilot tendencies (stereotypes) are not necessarily consistent with formal rules that pilots may have been taught in their training Federal Air Regulations (Wickens et al., in press). For example, the formal rules dictate maneuvering laterally, whereas pilots show a preference to maneuver vertically. With regard to (2), analysis of stage 2 and stage 3 automation reveals that conflict resolution guidance based upon predicted behavior of the other aircraft (e.g., "climb because the other plane is about to descend") may be imperfect. Such imperfection is inherent in the probabilistic nature of any form of prediction involving human behavior (in this case the behavior of the other pilot; Wickens et al., 2000a). With regard to (3), research in our lab (Merwin et al., 1998) and others (Ellis, McGreevy, & Hitchcock, 1987) has revealed the extent to which the display format of the CDTI itself can influence the maneuver that is chosen. For example, 3D displays such as that shown in Figure 5 (left) tend to "invite" more spontaneous vertical maneuvering than 2D electronic maps. However, if the latter are accompanied by a plan view vertical "profile" display, such as that shown in Figure 5 (right), then more vertical maneuvering is invited (and chosen by the pilot) than with either the single map or the 3D map in which the vertical dimension is somewhat ambiguously represented.

The difficulties in resolving these potentially conflicting channels of information and guidance in formulating the decision of how to maneuver in free flight would not present serious problems if the hazards to be avoided were fixed in space. However, when the hazard is another aircraft, piloted by another human who is also possibly trying to resolve conflicting sources of decision information, then the dynamics of interpersonal relations (cooperation, competition, or simply lack of shared knowledge of intent) add another layer of psychological complexity to the analysis of free flight. It is easy to envision circumstances, in a busy airspace, in which the pilots' ability to resolve discrepant sources of information could not be accomplished in adequate time to avert a crisis.

The problem of negotiations brings us to the third level of pilot concerns: how does the time pressure imposed by an evolving conflict situation influence the quality of negotiations? Here some of the psychological research on conflict negotiations under time pressure is relevant (Carnevale, O'Connor, & McCusker, 1993). Research has shown that at least two different attributes of a conflict influence the ease of its resolution under time pressure: the extent to which the conflict is simple or complex, and the extent to which the participants are cooperative or competitive. Both simple conflicts and cooperative participants lead to more effective resolution under the time pressure characteristic of free flight conflict negotiations. However, resolution of complex and competitive conflicts is *not* found to improve with increasing time pressure. Furthermore it is a moot point whether pilots are entirely cooperative rather than competitive (who, for example, should "give way" and maneuver, when two aircraft of similar sizes are in conflict), and whether free flight conflict problems are "simple" or "complex." (Certainly complexity will be increased if three or more aircraft are affected by a maneuver.) A great deal more research is required to determine the extent to which the results on conflict negotiations under time pressure apply to pilot-pilot conflict avoidance negotiations.

Air traffic controller concerns

Four concerns with the concept of free flight can be identified from the air traffic controller's perspective. The first two, related to OOTLUF and to airspace density, mimic concerns expressed for air traffic control automation as already discussed. The third and fourth, related to airspace complexity and authority ambiguity, are added concerns. These four are discussed as follows.

First, just as the shift in decision-making authority from human controller to computer is found to produce concerns of OOTLUF, so a similar shift of authority from controller to pilot will be likely to produce those same concerns from the controller's perspective. Furthermore, it is possible that these problems might be exacerbated in free flight, relative to ground-based automation, because in the free flight case, a formal shift in authority and responsibility has occurred, whereas in the ground-based automation case, authority remains with the controller on the ground, while automation acts as an "assistant" to the controller. Indeed, evidence for controller OOTLUF has been observed in free flight simulations carried out by Endsley, Mogford, and Stein (1997), and by Galster, Duley, Masalonis, and Parasuraman (1999).

Second, just as automation is intended to increase the capacity of the airspace, and such an increase may well increase the density as well, so free flight, with the same goal, may achieve the same result. With a denser airspace, the challenges of failure recovery, in which a controller would need to intervene, will be the same as those described in the context of ATC automation concerns: more time required; less time available.

The third ATC concern is more unique to the free flight solution, and this relates to the fact that, under free flight, the *complexity* of the airspace will increase (Smith et al., 1998; Wyndemere, 1996). Such an increase is inherent in the very nature of free flight, allowing pilots to choose their own routes, rather than adhering to predefined air routes. As a consequence of this departure from the orderly flow, the controller no longer has a structured familiar airspace to monitor. Whereas "danger points" can currently be specified at predefined crossing or converging air routes under the current ATC system, and hence serve as focal points for controller attention, under free flight these would be distributed nearly uniformly across the display, to the detriment of effective monitoring, and at the cost of increasing workload (Wyndemere, 1996). In short, controller monitoring would be less able to capitalize on the perceptual expertise of the skilled controller to guide attention.

The fourth controller-centered concern relates to the third pilot-related concern discussed earlier, and this relates to the *ambiguity of authority* between ground and air. In this regard, even strong advocates of the free flight concept acknowledge that at some point controllers will need to assume authority, whether this assumption occurs upon entering the area around airports, at a final approach fix, or under the circumstances of an unresolvable (by the pilots) conflict. As noted earlier, problems of OOTLUF (exacerbated by airspace complexity) may be substantial just after authority is assumed by the controller. But prior to this point, there can be regions (or episodes) in which the residence of authority between pilot and controller is *ambiguous*, according to one of two different patterns: (1) both agents assume that they *have* authority, or, more seriously (2) both assume that the *other* maintains authority, a dangerous state which psychologists describe as one of *diffusion of responsibility* (O'Hare & Roscoe, 1990).

CONCLUSION REGARDING SOLUTIONS TO THE AIRSPACE CAPACITY PROBLEM

Table 1 provides a summary "tally sheet" of the human factor concerns identified with both of the two proposed solutions to the efficiency problems with current air traffic management. As should be evident from the table, the number of human-centered problems projected to be associated with a free flight solution are considerably more numerous than those projected for higher levels of automation of the current ATC system. It is for this reason

TABLE 24.1
Human factor concerns for both proposed solutions to efficiency
problems in air traffic management

| Problem locus | Authority | |
	ATC (Automation)	Pilot (Free flight)
ATC	OOTLUF	OOTLUF
	Failure recovery & airspace density	Failure recovery & airspace density
		Airspace complexity
		Authority ambiguity
Pilot		Increased workload
		Conflicting information
		Conflict resolution under time pressure

that our panel (Wickens et al., 1998) provided a strong recommendation to the Federal Aviation Administration that ground-based automation be the appropriate near-term solution to pursue, and that pursuit of the more pilot-autonomous versions of free flight only be undertaken following substantial additional research on the psychological issues of workload, decision, and negotiations discussed here.

CONCLUSION

In conclusion, the disciplines of psychology have tremendous relevance for the study of aviation safety, as illustrated in the previous pages by an in-depth look at two key issues. These are just a small sampling of relevant issues. But they serve to illustrate not only the potential relevance of psychological research, but also the challenge to psychological theory to address issues of the complexity of air safety.

REFERENCES

Aviation Week and Space Technology (2000). September 18, *153*, #12, 46–67.

Baddeley, A.D. (1986). *Working memory*. Oxford: Oxford University Press.

Bainbridge, L. (1983). Ironies of automation. *Automatica*, 19, 775–779.

Bellenkes, A.H., Wickens, C.D., & Kramer, A.F. (1997). Visual scanning and pilot expertise: The role of attentional flexibility and mental model development. *Aviation, Space, and Environmental Medicine*, 68, 569–579.

Billings, C. (1996). *Toward a human centered approach to automation*. Englewood Cliffs, NJ: Lawrence Erlbaum Associates Inc.

Boehm-Davis, D., Curry, R.E., Weiner, E.L., & Harrison, R.L. (1983). Human factors of flight deck automation. Report on a NASA-industry workshop. *Ergonomics*, 26, 953–961.

Carbonnell, J.R., Ward, J.L., & Senders, J.W. (1968). A queuing model of visual sampling: Experimental validation. *IEEE Transactions on Man-Machine Systems*, MMS-9, 82–87.

Carnevale, P.J., O'Connor, K.M., & McCusker, C. (1993). Time pressure in negotiation and mediation. In O. Svenson & A.J. Maule (Eds.), *Time pressure and stress in human judgment and decision making* (pp. 117–131). New York: Plenum Press.

Chou, C., Madhavan, D., & Funk, K. (1996). Studies of cockpit task management errors. *International Journal of Aviation Psychology*, *6*, 307–320.

Ellis, S.R., McGreevy, M.W., & Hitchcock, R.J. (1987). Perspective traffic display format and airline pilot traffic avoidance. *Human Factors, 29*, 371–382.

Endsley, M.R., & Garland, D.J. (2000). *Situation awareness analysis and measurement*. Mahwah, NJ: Lawrence Erlbaum Associates Inc.

Endsley, M.R., Mogford, R., & Stein, E. (1997). *Effect of free flight on controller performance, workload, and situation awareness* (Technical Report). Atlantic City, NJ: FAA Technical Center.

Funk, K. (1991). Cockpit task management: Preliminary definitions, normative theory, error taxonomy, and design recommendations. *The International Journal of Aviation Psychology*, *1*, 271–286.

Galster, S.M., Duley, J.A., Masalonis, A.J., & Parasuraman, R. (1999). Effects of aircraft self-separation on controller conflict detection performance and workload in mature free flight. In M.W. Scerbo & M. Mouloua (Eds.), *Automation technology and human performance: Current research and trends* (pp. 96–101). Mahwah, NJ: Lawrence Erlbaum Associates Inc.

Garland, D.J., Wise, J.A., & Hopkin, V.D. (Eds.) (1999). *Handbook of aviation human factors*. Mahwah, NJ: Lawrence Erlbaum Associates Inc.

Grey, W.M., Thurman, D.A., Palmer, M.T., & Mitchell, C.M. (2000). The Vprof tutor: Teaching MD-II vertical profile navigation using GT-ITACS. *IEA 2000/HFES2000 Congress Proceedings*. Santa Monica: Human Factors Society

Harwood, K., Sanford, B.D., & Lee, K.K. (1998). Developing ATC automation in the field: It pays to get your hands dirty. *The Air Traffic Control Quarterly*.

Hick, W.E. (1952). On the rate of gain of information. *Quarterly Journal of Experimental Psychology, 4*, 11–26.

Hicks, M., & De Brito, G. (1998). Civil aircraft warning systems: Who's calling the shots? In G. Boy, C. Graeber, & J.M. Robert (Eds.), *International Conference on Human Computer Interaction in Aeronautics* (HCI-Aero'98) (pp. 205–212). Montreal, Canada, Ecole Polytechnique de Montreal, 27–29 May.

Hopkin, D.V. (1994). Human performance implications of air traffic control automation. In M. Mouloua & R. Parasuraman (Eds.), *Proceedings of the First Automation Technology and Human Performance Conference: Human performance in automated systems: Current research and trends* (pp. 314–319). Hillsdale, NJ: Lawrence Erlbaum Associates Inc.

Hughes, D., & Dornheim, M.A. (1995). Accidents direct focus on cockpit automation. *Aviation Week & Space Technology*, Jan 30, 52–54.

Inagaki, T. (1999). Situation-adaptive autonomy: Trading control of authority in human-machine systems (pp. 154–158). In M.W. Scerbo & M. Mouloua (Eds.), *Automation technology and human performance: Current research and trends*. Mahwah, NJ: Lawrence Erlbaum Associates Inc.

International Journal of Aviation Psychology. (1998). Special issue #3: Simulation and training.

Irving, S., Polson, P., & Irving, J.E. (1994). A GOMS analysis of the advanced automated cockpit. *CHI-94 Conference Proceedings*. New York: Association of Computing Machinery.

Johnson, W.W., & Battiste, V. (1999). A cockpit display designed to enable limited flight deck separation responsibility (Paper 1999–01–5567). *Proceedings of the 1999 World Aviation Conference*. Warrendale, PA: Society of Automotive Engineers.

Johnston, N., McDonald, N., & Fuller, R. (Eds.) (1997). *Aviation psychology in practice*. Brookfield, VT: Ashgate Publishing.

Kirwan, B., & Ainsworth, L.K. (1992). *A guide to task analysis*. London: Taylor & Francis.

Klayman, J., & Ha, Y.W. (1987). Confirmation, disconfirmation, and information in hypothesis testing. *Journal of Experimental Psychology: Human Learning and Memory*, 00211–228.

Kochan, J.A., Jensen, R.S., Chubb, G.P., & Hunter, D.R. (1997). *A new approach to aeronautical decision-making: The expertise method.* (DOT/FAA/AM-97/6). Washington, DC: Office of Aviation Medicine, Federal Aviation Administration.

Merwin, D.H., Wickens, C.D., & O'Brien, J.V. (1998). Display format-induced biases in air traffic avoidance behavior. *Proceedings of the World Aviation Congress* (98WAC-71). Warrendale, PA: Society of Automotive Engineers.

Morphew, E.M., & Wickens, C.D. (1998). Pilot performance and workload using traffic displays to support free flight. *Proceedings of the 42nd Annual Meeting of the Human Factors & Ergonomics Society.* Santa Monica, CA: Human Factors Society.

Morrow, D., Lee, A., & Rodvold, M. (1993). Analysis of problems in routine controller-pilot communication. *The International Journal of Aviation Psychology, 3*, 285–302.

Mosier, K.L., Skitka, L.J., Heers, S., & Burdick, M. (1998). Automation bias: Decision making and performance in high-tech cockpits. *The International Journal of Aviation Psychology, 8*, 47–63.

Mumaw, R., Sarter, N., Wickens, C.D., Kimball, S., Marsh, R., Nikolic, M., & Xu, W. (2000). *Analysis of automation monitoring skills and strategies on modern "glass" cockpit aircraft* (Final NASA Technical Report). Seattle, WA: Boeing Commercial Airplane Co.

O'Hare, D., & Roscoe, S.N. (1990). *Flightdeck performance: The human factor.* Ames, IA: Iowa State University Press.

Olson, W.A., & Sarter, N.B. (2001) Management by consent in human–machine systems: When and why it breaks down. *Human Factors, 43*(2), 255–256.

Orasanu, J.M. (1993). Decision-making in the cockpit. In E.L. Wiener, B.G. Kanki, & R.L. Helmreich (Eds.), *Cockpit resource management* (pp. 137–73). San Diego, CA: Academic Press.

Orlady, H., & Orlady, L. (1999). *Human factors in multicrew flight operations.* Brookfield, VT: Ashgate.

Parasuraman, R., Molloy, R., & Singh, I.L. (1993). Performance consequences of automation-induced complacency. *International Journal of Aviation Psychology, 3*, 1–23.

Parasuraman, R., & Riley, V. (1997). Humans and automation: Use, misuse, disuse, abuse. *Human Factors, 39*, 230–253.

Parasuraman, R., Sheridan, T.B., & Wickens, C.D. (2000). A model for types and levels of human interaction with automation. *IEEE Transactions on Systems, Man, and Cybernetics: Part A: Systems and Humans, 30*, 286–297.

Phillips, E.H. (1997). FAA man mandate enhanced GPWS. *Aviation Week and Space Technology, April 21*, 22–23.

Sarter, N.B. (2000). The need for multisensory interfaces in support of effective attention allocation in highly dynamic event-driven domains: The case of cockpit automation. *The International Journal of Aviation Psychology, 10*, 231–245.

Sarter, N.B., & Schroeder, B. (2000). Supporting decision-making and action selection under time pressure and uncertainty: The case of in-flight icing. Submitted for presentation at the *39th AIAA Aerospace Sciences Meeting*, Reno, NV, January 2001.

Sarter, N.B., & Woods, D.D. (1992). Pilot interaction with cockpit automation: Operational experiences with the flight management system. *The International Journal of Aviation Psychology, 2*, 303–321.

Sarter, N.B., & Woods, D.D. (1994). Pilot interaction with cockpit automation II: An experimental study of pilots' model and awareness of the flight management system. *The International Journal of Aviation Psychology, 4*, 1–28.

Sarter, N.B., & Woods, D.D. (1995). How in the world did we ever get into that mode? Mode error and awareness in supervisory control. *Human Factors, 37*, 5–19.

Sarter, N.B., & Woods, D.D. (1997). Team play with a powerful and independent agent: Operational experiences and automation surprises on the Airbus A-320. *Human Factors and Ergonomics, 39*, 553–569.

Senders, J.W. (1964). The human operator as a monitor and controller of multidegree of freedom systems. *IEEE Transactions on Human Factors in Electronics, HFE-5*, 2–6.

Sheridan, T.B., & Verplank, W.L. (1978). *Human and computer control of undersea teleoperators* (Technical Report). Cambridge, MA: MIT Man-Machine Systems Laboratory.

Sherry, L., & Polson, P.G. (1999). Shared models of flight management system vertical guidance. *The International Journal of Aviation Psychology, 9*, 139–154.

Skitka, L.J., Mosier, K.L., Burdick, M., & Rosenblatt, B. (2000). Automation bias and error: Are crews better than individuals? *The International Journal of Aviation Psychology, 10*, 84–97.

Slamecka, N.J., & Graf, P. (1978). The generation effect: Delineation of a phenomena. *Journal of Experimental Psychology: Human Learning and Memory, 4*, 592–604.

Smith, P.J., Woods, D., McCoy, C.E., Billings, C., Sarter, N., Denning, R., & Dekker, S. (1998). Using forecasts of future incidents to evaluate future ATM system designs. *Air Traffic Control Quarterly, 6*, 71–86.

Steenblik, J.W. (1996). Pilot's comply with only half of TCAS RA's. *Airline Pilot, September*, 5.

Strauch, B. (1997). Automation and decision making: Lessons learned from the Cali accident. *Proceedings of the 41st Annual Meeting of the Human Factors and Ergonomics Society* (pp. 195–199). Santa Monica, CA: Human Factors & Ergonomics Society.

Svenson, O., & Maule, A.J. (Eds.) (1993). *Time pressure and stress in human judgment and decision making*. New York: Plenum Press.

Van Breda, L. (1999). *Anticipatory behavior in supervisory control*. Delft, The Netherlands: Delft University Press.

Wickens, C.D. (1986). The effects of control dynamics on performance. In K.R. Boff, L. Kaufman, & J.P. Thomas (Eds.), *Handbook of perception and performance Vol. II* (pp. 39–1/39–60). New York: John Wiley.

Wickens, C.D. (1992). *Engineering psychology and human performance* (2nd ed.). New York: Harper Collins.

Wickens, C.D. (1999). Cognitive factors in aviation. In F.T. Durso, R.S. Nickerson, R.W. Schvaneveldt, S.T. Dumais, D.S. Lindsay, & M.T.H. Chi (Eds.), *Handbook of applied cognition* (pp. 274–282). Chichester: John Wiley.

Wickens, C.D. (2000). *Imperfect and unreliable automation and its implications for attention allocation, information access and situation awareness*. University of Illinois Institute of Aviation Final Technical Report (ARL-00-10/NASA-00-2). Savoy, IL: Aviation Research Lab.

Wickens, C.D. (2002). Aviation displays. In P. Tsang & M. Vidulich (Eds.), *Principles and practice of aviation psychology*. Mahwah, NJ: Lawrence Erlbaum Associates Inc.

Wickens, C.D. & Andre, A.D. (1990). Proximity compatibility and information display: Effects of color, space, and objectness of information integration. *Human Factors, 32*, 61–77.

Wickens, C.D., Gempler, K., & Morphew, M.E. (2000a). Workload and reliability of predictor displays in aircraft traffic avoidance. *Transportation Human Factors Journal, 2*, 99–126.

Wickens, C.D., Helleberg, J., & Xu, X. (in press). Pilot maneuver choice and workload in free flight. *Human Factors*.

Wickens, C.D., & Hollands, J. (2000). *Engineering psychology and human performance* (3rd ed.). Upper Saddle River, NJ: Prentice-Hall.

Wickens, C.D., Kroft, P., & Yeh, M. (2000b). Database overlay in electronic map design: Testing a computational model. *Proceedings of the IEA 2000/HFES 2000 Congress* (pp. 3–451/3–454). Santa Monica, CA: Human Factors & Ergonomics Society.

Wickens, C.D., Mavor, A.S., & McGee, J.P. (Eds.) (1997). *Flight to the future: Human factors in air traffic control*. Washington, DC: National Academy Press.

Wickens, C.D., Mavor, A.S., Parasuraman, R., & McGee, J.P. (Eds.) (1998). *The future of air traffic control: Human operators and automation*. Washington, DC: National Academy Press.

Wiener, E.L. & Curry, R.E. (1980). Flight deck automation: Promises and problems. *Ergonomics, 23*, 995–1011.

Wiener, E.L., Kanki, B.G., & Helmreich, R.L. (Eds.) (1993). *Cockpit resource management*. San Diego, CA: Academic Press.

Wiener, E.L., & Nagel, D.C. (Eds.) (1989). *Human factors in aviation*. San Diego, CA: Academic Press.

Wyndemere (1996). *An evaluation of air traffic control complexity* (Final Report, Contract Number NAS 2-14284). Boulder, CO: Wyndemere, Inc.

Author index

Subject index